JOB #: 141144

Author Name: Lafargue

Title of Book: Tao and Method

ISBN: 9780791416020 / 079141602x

Publisher: SUNY Press

Trim Size: 6 x 9

Bulk in mm: 28

Tao and Method

SUNY Series in Chinese Philosophy and Culture
David L. Hall and Roger T. Ames, editors

Tao and Method

A Reasoned Approach to the Tao Te Ching

Michael LaFargue

State University of New York Press

Excerpts from *Ancient China in Transition,* by Cho-yun Hsu, are reprinted with permission of the publishers, Stanford University Press. © 1965 by the Board of Trustees of the Leland Stanford Junior University.

The excerpt on page 244 from THE FIRST TIME EVER I SAW YOUR FACE, by Ewan MacColl, is reprinted by permission of STORMKING MUSIC INC., © Copyright 1962 (renewed) by STORMKING MUSIC INC. All Rights Reserved.

Published by
State University of New York Press, Albany

© 1994   Michael LaFargue

For information, address State University of New York Press, State University Plaza, Albany, N.Y. 12246

Production by Dana Foote
Marketing by Dana E. Yanulavich

Library of Congress Cataloging-in-Publication Data
LaFargue, Michael.
    Tao and method : a reasoned approach to the Tao Te Ching /
Michael LaFargue
        p.   cm. — (SUNY series in Chinese philosophy and culture)
    Includes bibliographical references and index.
    ISBN 0–7914–1601–1 (alk. paper)
    1. Lao-tzu. Tao te ching. 2. Philosophy, Chinese — To 221 B.C.
3. China — Intellectual life — To 221 B.C. I. Lao-tzu. Tao te
ching. English. 1994. II. Title. III. Series.
BL1900.L35L32   1994
299'.51482 — dc20   93–50081
                                                                CIP

10 9 8 7 6 5 4 3 2 1

*This Book is Dedicated
to Dieter Georgi*

Contents

Part IV: Translation, Commentary, and Topical Glossary

Acknowledgments

I would like first of all to thank Dieter Georgi, to whom this book is dedicated. At a crucial time, he restored my confidence that rational and historical scholarship is worthwhile and relevant. I learned in his seminars the way of integrating historical research, close textual exegesis, and attention to fundamental philosophical issues that I try to develop further and put into practice in this book.

I owe a special debt to Russell Kirkland for his early encouragement and advice in this project. I worked out my ideas on the relation of social history to hermeneutics in conversation with Dick Horsley. Cho-Yun Hsu gave me valuable advice and encouragement regarding the historical essays in Part Two of this book. I thank David Hall and Roger Ames, the editors of this series, and Bill Eastman, director of SUNY Press, for their continued encouragement and support. And I would like to thank my wife, Hilda Dorgan, for her advice on many points and for putting up with the disruption in our lives while I worked on this manuscript.

Finally, thanks to all the students who over the years stimulated my thought about the *Tao Te Ching* with their comments and questions.

Introduction

This book has two goals. One is to reconstruct the meaning of a Taoist classic, the *Tao Te Ching*, as it was understood by its original authors and audience in ancient China. The other goal is to contribute to the development of religious hermeneutics—the theory and practice of interpreting religions and religious texts generally. Part One of this book addresses these methodological problems in hermeneutics at a theoretical level, and proposes some general principles that underlie the present interpretation of the *Tao Te Ching*. Parts Two and Three implement these general principles and work them out in further detail, in the course of addressing the specific methodological issues important to reconstructing the original meaning of the *Tao Te Ching*. My attempts to address these issues include a critical reformulation of some fundamental suppositions in the philosophy of religion, presented in Chapter 11. Part Four consists of a translation and detailed commentary on the *Tao Te Ching* itself.

Methodologically, one of my aims has been to revive and develop further the kind of hermeneutics that began to develop in the nineteenth and early twentieth centuries, particularly the attempts in this period to integrate close textual exegesis with attention to historical and sociocultural context, and with questioning inquiry into the most fundamental philosophical issues raised by the study of religious writings from distant cultures. I think it is unfortunate that the most recent developments in hermeneutic theory have tended to sever the connection between these three facets of interpretation, and have led to abandoning the project of recovering the original meaning of classic texts. What I hope to show is that the valid insights that generally motivate skeptical "postmodern" hermeneutics can lead instead to more sophisticated methods of recovering the thought of classic works and engaging seriously with it.

As to the plan of the book: Part One (Chapters 1 and 2) deals with hermeneutic theory. Chapter 1 situates the present hermeneutics in the context of the history of the interpretation of texts, and of philosophical theories concerning the status of meaning. Chapter 2 details the dependencies of the present hermeneutics on existential phenomenology, on semiotic theory, and on American philosophical Pragmatism.

Part Two (Chapters 3 through 5) is a study of the social milieu in which I believe the *Tao Te Ching* arose, the subculture of a certain group of idealistic men in ancient China, called *shih*, who hoped to reform political life through the influence they wielded as managers, administrators, and advisers at all levels of public life. If I am correct, a grasp of the social situation of *shih*, and the concerns and ambitions that shaped their response to it, is ultimately essential to empathically entering into the worldview of the *Tao Te Ching*'s author, and understanding their words as they themselves understood them. Chapter 3 outlines the general relation of *shih* to the cultural and political world of ancient China, relying mainly on the researches of the social historian Cho-Yun Hsu. Chapters 4 and 5 supplement Hsu's work with a more detailed look at the *Mencius*, a book roughly contemporary with the *Tao Te Ching*, whose stories about the Confucian *shih*-teacher Mencius give us detailed information about the social position and the concerns and ambitions of idealistic *shih* of this period. I argue that the *Tao Te Ching* and the *Mencius* reflect the same general political culture,[1] and that there are many formal similarities in the structure of their thought, despite many obvious differences in the content of their teaching.

Part Three (Chapters 6 through 12) addresses the main methodological issues important in the interpretation of the *Tao Te Ching* proper. Discussions here focus on the relation between verbal form, concrete context, and substantive thought. Chapters 6 and 7 develop and apply a model for analyzing the semantic structure of the proverb-like aphorisms that make up a good deal of the *Tao Te Ching*. Chapters 8 through 10 deal with those sayings commonly regarded as "metaphysical." I argue that their original life setting was not metaphysical speculation but the practice of self-cultivation, and show the kind of interpretation that this leads to. Chapter 11 sets the resultant interpretation of the transcendent Tao in the context of a reformulated philosophy of religion, continuing some discussions of this aspect of religious hermeneutics begun in Part One. It concludes with some suggestions about the relevance of the *Tao Te Ching* to the modern world.

Chapter 12 presents detailed arguments for my thesis about the composition of the eighty-one "chapters" that make up the *Tao Te Ching*. I argue that these chapters are made up primarily of sayings that once circulated as oral tradition in a particular school of ancient Chinese *shih*. But these sayings have now been deliberately and artfully arranged in sayings collages, so that understanding them requires understanding the connections between sayings implied by the way they are juxtaposed to each other.

Part Four consists of a translation of the Chinese text of the *Tao Te Ching*, a detailed commentary on each chapter, and a Topical Glossary containing brief essays on topics that recur in the *Tao Te Ching* or in the commentary. For the reader interested in more commentary on particular individual passages, I have provided an index of passages, which will direct her to all the discussions relevant to any given passage contained in Parts Two and Three.

This book is arranged as a series of systematic discussions of each major topic important to any attempt to recover the *Tao Te Ching*'s original meaning. This means that my argument about how to interpret this book does not proceed in linear fashion, but is presented in a series of interlocking essays. For example, the discussion of *shih* in Part Two is only relevant to my central topic if the *Tao Te Ching* is indeed the product of men belonging to this class, but I only present a summary of my arguments for this thesis at the very end of Part Two, referring to details only treated in Part Three. Chapters 6 through 10 rely in many places on arguments about the composition of the *Tao Te Ching* that are only presented in Chapter 12.

Finally, my emphasis on critical rational method might imply for many readers some claim to certainty and finality in the resultant interpretation of the *Tao Te Ching* I offer here. No such claim is intended. I am, in general, happy about the hermeneutic theory I try to develop and practice here. Concerning details, I am aware that a great deal more research could be done to shed light on the *Tao Te Ching* (e.g., more research on the position of *shih* and on the ancient meanings of many words used in the *Tao Te Ching*, and more comparisons to other contemporary works like the *Hsün Tzu*, etc.). And in the end all historical interpretation, like all historical research, is a matter of making educated guesses. I think that in the case of some great works like the *Tao Te Ching*, methodically making the best guesses we can on the best available evidence is worth all the effort we can put into it.

Part I

Hermeneutics

Introduction

Part One is an extended essay on general hermeneutics the theoretical underpinning of interpretive method. While the hermeneutic approach I adopt in this study draws on many traditional and recent ideas on this subject, it is in many respects an original attempt[1] to work out some key unresolved problems in this field, and on many points goes against currently prevailing hermeneutic theory and practice.

The two chapters in Part One explain, among other things, why I would like this work to be judged, not by whether one finds my interpretation of the *Tao Te Ching* agreeable or inspiring, but by whether one thinks it probably approximates the original meaning of this text. These chapters explain how many of the insights underlying "postmodern" hermeneutics can be integrated into an interpretive approach centered on the now old fashioned goal of recovering the original meaning of texts. They explain what I think is inadequate about strictly "philosophical" approaches to the Chinese classics, and why I think attention to concrete sociohistorical and experiential contexts is essential to grasping the substantive thought in these texts. And they explain how the suggested meanings of suggestive texts like the *Tao Te Ching* can be said to be definite—even though these meanings cannot be made explicit in any straightforward paraphrase—and how we might go about recovering and grasping these definite suggested meanings.

Interpretation and Meaning: Two Histories

Hermeneutics

The discipline of hermeneutics has its historical origin in the interpretation of texts that had in various cultures attained the status of "scriptures," "classics," or "canonical texts." The early and paradigm case of such texts are those writings that arose in the "axial period"[1] (c. 800 B.C. to 600 A.D.): the Upanishads, the Buddhist Pali Canon, the Bible, the Qur'an, the Greek Classics, and the Confucian and Taoist works from pre-Han China. The following is a very simplified and generalized history of the treatment of such texts, situating the approach I will take to the *Tao Te Ching* in the context of this history.[2]

At the beginning stands a person or a group who feel "carried away" with enthusiasm for a certain vision of the world, and who express this vision in verbal form. The vision itself is extraordinary, has an extraordinary greatness, but the human processes through which the vision first arises and is adopted are not fundamentally different from those processes through which world-views in general arise and are accepted. The human group in which this vision arose were substantially "people like us" relying on experiences of reality with which we can in principle empathically identify, given enough information and imaginative effort.

Next comes "canonization." The book becomes known outside the community of its origin. Others, in other communities and then in other eras, feel a greatness in it. Since they are out of touch with the original context and experiences out of which the book arose, substantial parts of the text become vague and ambiguous to them, and they fail to understand, or they misunderstand, large parts of it. But because of the book's aura of greatness, they fill in these gaps in ways that further enhance the book's status. That is, they read messages into the book which are actually more appropriate and inspirational for their own age than would have been the case had they stuck completely to the vision of the original community in all its particulars. The book gains in this way a "scriptural," "canonical," "classical" status. And the reading habits described above give rise to a certain genre, "scripture interpretation."[3] This genre is governed by an unquestioned presupposition that the text is a repository of authoritative norms for the culture. But this presupposition operates in a special way. That is, it does not lead to impartial empirical research to discover the text's original meaning, and to then taking this meaning as authoritative. Rather, the presupposition that to understand the meaning of the text *is* to discover something authoritative for us leads interpreters to take advantage of apparent ambiguities in the text to read into it whatever norms they take to be authoritative.[4] Interpreters do not of course regard themselves as reading these norms into the text. They experience the study of canonical texts as a process by which one *discovers* norms that are there in the text. In the best case, this impression reflects the fact that, psychologically, scriptural interpretation is an essentially divinatory process. The grand but mysterious language, the authoritative aura surrounding the text, and a sense of continuity with a long tradition of interpretation stimulate the interpreter's mind to rise to a higher level and grasp normative ideals in a more and more ideal form. What is "there" is the genuine ideal goodness[5] of these norms.

This habit of reading gradually generates the idea that the canonical text contains some inexhaustible hidden core of universal truths; each divergent interpretation represents a partial grasp of this hidden core. And this picture of the book's nature is projected back into stories of its origin. Such an extraordinary book cannot have arisen in the way books normally arise. It must have arisen, at the least, in the mind of a giant among men, a mind not bound down to the particularities of mundane life in a specific concrete community, a mind which pierced the clouds to achieve a direct, not-to-be-duplicated grasp of timeless and transcendent truths. The fact that the mental act of grasping these truths cannot be duplicated gives the truths themselves an authority beyond question.

Enter, in the late eighteenth and nineteenth centuries in the West, the modern study of history and culture,[6] governed by two key ideas. First, there is the idea that all great writings of the past are essentially human products, generated in a way not fundamentally different from the way our own ideas and writing are generated. The ideas in them did not fall from the transcendent sky, nor do they present to us timelessly authoritative doctrines to be blindly accepted. The ideas arose out of some human experiences, and to understand them is to reconnect them to their experiential roots, to empathically and vicariously relive the human experiences which gave rise to them.[7] The second basic idea of historical and cultural study is that to understand peoples of another era or another culture we must overcome the tendency to see them within the framework of our own culture, or within some "universal" framework, and try to enter empathically into another entire cultural framework.[8] This study has heightened immeasurably our appreciation of the particularity and the otherness of people of other cultures and of our own historical past, and correspondingly heightened our appreciation of the great imaginative effort and discipline that is needed if we are to understand these others in their otherness. A printed text becomes ambiguous when removed from its original context. Rather than taking advantage of this ambiguity to read modern meanings into classical texts, historical and cultural study tries systematically to reconnect them with their original contexts, and hence to reconstruct the meaning that the text had for its original authors and audience.

This historical hermeneutics is a hermeneutics focused on reconstructing original meanings: For historical hermeneutics an interpretation is a "good interpretation" insofar as the interpreter's understanding of the text approximates that of the original author and audience. This criterion for a good interpretation is fundamentally different from the criterion implicit in traditional scriptural hermeneutics. For scriptural hermeneutics, an interpretation is a "good interpretation" insofar as the reading it gives is meaningful for a modern audience.

The most recent development in the history of hermeneutics is the rejection of nineteenth-century historical hermeneutics and a return to an approach that either adopts, or is parasitic upon,[9] the basic aims and assumptions of traditional scriptural interpretation. This turn is represented in the writings of the most influential recent hermeneutic theorists, Hans-Georg Gadamer, Paul Ricoeur, and Jacques Derrida.[10] It is largely due to their influence that the word *hermeneutics* today has come to mean for many people the rejection of any attempt to reconstruct historical meanings, and a focus on giving readings the interpreter regards as most appropriate and meaningful for her modern audience. The most frequently cited reason for this turn against historical hermeneutics is the fact that we can never achieve an understanding of people culturally distant from ourselves that is completely accurate and completely certain.[11] Some advocates of historical hermeneutics did in fact hope for such accuracy and certainty, but the impossibility of accuracy and certainty in reaching a goal does not render all attempts to approximate the goal futile or self-contradictory. Most goals that are worth achieving perfectly and with certainty are also worth achieving partially and with some degree of probability. (Why else do we continue to value such imperfect disciplines as meteorology, economics, and diagnostic medicine?) There are other and more serious weaknesses in nineteenth-century historical hermeneutic theory, having to do primarily with the foundationalist ambitions of the theorists, and with their subjectivization of meaning (see p. 19). I hope to show in Chapter 2 that these weaknesses can be remedied in a way that makes historical hermeneutics a viable project.

If these weaknesses can be remedied, then there is nothing illogical or immoral in either the historical or the scriptural approach to interpretation. My choice of the historical approach is due to the fact that it facilitates a critical confrontation with classical texts, a confrontation that is open to rational public discussion. Several features of the scriptural approach place obstacles in the way of such critical confrontation.

Historical hermeneutics makes possible a rationally negotiated critical confrontation in two ways. First, historical hermeneutics can help us critically evaluate traditional ideas by tracing these ideas to the originating experiences that gave rise to them. The real value of writings like the *Tao Te Ching* that stand at the beginning of a tradition is precisely that the authors of such texts can*not* rely on "traditional authority" to carry the ideas they present. Composed before the ideas have gained established authority, these texts must evoke the human experiential[12] bases on which the ideas first became persuasive. These bases represent the best claim these ideas have to represent something authoritative. Reconnecting the ideas to their originating experiences is thus a precondition for a critical evaluation of their claims to authority. Understanding the experiential basis of a tradition is thus like understanding the experiments, data, and logic on which a scientific theory rests. It gives us critical leverage by which we can form some rational estimate of the ideas or theories themselves.

More specifically—and this will be crucial in the present interpretation of the *Tao Te Ching*—such understanding allows us to determine *under what interpretation* the ideas presented to us in such classic texts have some claim to our respect. This is what

German theorists call *Sachkritik*, a critical understanding of the text with reference to *die Sach*, "the thing," the reality of which the text speaks.[13] Here, however, *Sachkritik* has a particularist, experiential, historical basis, rather than a basis in timeless truths. This is the precise opposite of "scriptural" interpretation (including Gadamer's updated version), which *starts* with an uncritical belief[14] in the authority of classic texts, and which then takes it as its task to sustain this authority by producing plausibly authoritative or inspirational contemporary readings.

The second way that historical hermeneutics facilitates a critical confrontation with classical texts is that it makes possible a fully explicit, rational, public discussion concerning the contemporary relevance[15] of any given classic. Advances in historical and cultural studies on the one hand, and rapid and fundamental changes in the modern world on the other, render implausible the traditional assumption that we can and should try to live by ideals identical to those of our distant ancestors. Some critical sifting of traditions is an obvious necessity. The critical assessment of the modern relevance of any given classical text is made more complex and problematic, however, by the fact that any discussion of such relevance will necessarily involve some particular evaluative analysis of modernity itself. But the correctness of any given assessment of modernity is itself a problematic and hotly contested issue, quite apart from any relation to classic texts. Different American subcultures exist with radically different views about modernity.

In this context, rational and public discussion of the modern relevance of a classic text requires that we conceive of this as involving two separate projects.[16] One project consists in trying to recover the original meaning of the text. The other project consists in a critical assessment as to whether and how the message of the text is relevant to us today. Of course, these need not be separated into two chronologically separate steps. But they are *logically* separate projects, with different epistemologies. What counts as a good reason to say, "X is probably the meaning the *Tao Te Ching* had for its original authors and audience," is completely different from what counts as a good reason to say, "X is something we ought to take as a guide for our lives today." The fact that commentators in premodern times did not make this distinction is what limits the usefulness of traditional commentaries for modern historical hermeneutics. This does not imply that traditional commentators were unintelligent. They were simply not engaged in the same project as the modern historical interpreter.

If we conceive of these two projects separately, we can conduct rational and public discussion of both questions, in which the issues are made explicit and considerations truly relevant to any given issue can be put on the table and evaluated as such. For example, (1) in this case we can recognize that certain philological and historiographical skills give special weight to the opinions some people form about original meanings, but that these same skills are largely irrelevant in discussions about the character of modernity and hence of the contemporary relevance of the text. (2) We can also see that reconstructing original contexts already gives us important *negative* clues about modern relevance, by making clear important differences between ancient and modern social environments (e.g., paternalist vs. democratic governments, ethnocentrism, attitudes toward social and sexual inequalities, etc.). These make it necessary to reject certain elements woven into the fabric of ancient texts. (3) We can make explicit and open for critical discussion the different assessments of modernity that cause different subcultures today to evaluate classical texts in fundamentally different ways. Different subcultures might then be encouraged to discuss directly the fundamental differences that divide them, instead of making the classics a battleground in which competing groups struggle for control, turning "interpretation" into ideological warfare pursued by indirect means.[17]

The basically scriptural approach to hermeneutics advocated by recent theorists is incompatible with these two facets of the critical confrontation with classic texts made possible by historical hermeneutics. On the first count, the recovery of the originating experiences that gave rise to a given classical text requires a systematic and *in principle unrestricted* attempt to understand the historical other as other. We can never, of course, actually achieve a perfect and certain understanding of the culturally distant other as other. To say that our attempt should be *in principle* unrestricted is only to say that whenever we detect some way in which our interpretation is governed by cultural suppositions at odds with those of the text's author, we should regard this as a mistake and try to correct it. By contrast, scriptural interpretation guarantees that, no matter what, *some* particular cultural suppositions of ours will retain an important place in the framework within which the text is to be interpreted.[18] It guarantees this in advance and in principle. If we regard certain of our suppositions as important enough (e.g., our commitment to some cause, philosophy, or faith) it will never be a mistake to let these suppositions decisively influence our interpretation, even if these suppositions are at odds with those of the text's author. This will be, first, a restriction on our attempts to fully appreciate the originating experiences underlying the text, in all their concreteness and particularity, and to understand the text in the light of these experiences. Such an understanding, I will argue, is crucial to a critical assessment of the text's claim to authority. Secondly, since the text is being interpreted basically *within* a framework constituted by certain assumptions dear to the interpreter, these assumptions will automatically escape any possible challenge by the text. This is an artificial restriction on the critical confrontation between the classic text and the modern reader. The interpreter will never be required to explicitly defend her most favored personal assumptions against a challenge from the text.

On the second count, from a rational point of view traditional scriptural interpretation was always implicitly based on circular logic. Values and suppositions held quite independently of the text largely determine the nature of what interpreters "find" in the text. In scripture interpretation, the suppositions one goes in with largely determine the message one comes out with. But then one turns around and declares that these suppositions are especially authoritative because they are "based on" something discovered in this authoritative text. Though often done very creatively and for good causes, from a rational point of view this process always has the character of something achieved with smoke and mirrors. In the worst case, "interpretation" becomes a rhetorical trick by which one takes advantage of verbal ambiguity to attach one's own ideas to the words of an authoritative text, claiming that, because the same words are used, one's ideas are also clothed with the authority traditionally accorded to the text.

Ultimately the most important thing we can gain from the study of ancient classics is some guidance and inspiration for our own lives. And this ultimately demands a "fusion of horizons," a blending of our concerns, assumptions, and values with those of ancient thinkers. But this blending should be called what it is: syncretism. Masking this syncretism under the guise of "discovering the timeless core" of the text clouds rational discussion both of ancient thought and of our own modern problems.

Scripture interpretation as a social practice grew up in traditional authoritarian cultures. It was a device by which a scholarly elite guild determined the contents of a unitary high culture normative for the entire society. The implicit assumption that interpretation determines authoritative norms still governs much scholarly debate today, even though the non-scholarly public who share this assumption has shrunk drastically. It is difficult to transform this institution into an academic discipline in the context of an egalitarian, pluralist democracy committed to deciding public norms through rational public discussion. This context demands that one make a distinction between the evidence, arguments, and skills relevant to recovering original meanings, on the one hand, and the evidence and arguments relevant to assessing the contemporary relevance of these meanings.

These criticisms apply to interpretive scholarship as an academic discipline. There are other social contexts in which an essentially "scriptural" mode of interpretation still serves important purposes (e.g., scriptural interpretation as a mode of consciousness raising among the Christian poor in Latin America, or the reinterpretation of classical Buddhist ideas in the service of autonomous rural development programs in Sri Lanka[19]). Further, the above remarks are not directed against certain genres—for example, "Meditations on" or "Reflections on" classical writings—forms of "interpretation" different from "interpretive scholarship" as envisioned here. My only objection to these latter works is that their authors often make a show of special philological or historical expertise, as though these give special authority to their personal meditations. If such expertise is not seriously pressed into the service of historical hermeneutics, it becomes a mere status badge, a signal to other members of the scholarly elite that the author is one of them, and that therefore her personal meditations deserve special weight that would not be accorded to the meditations of the uneducated. This is simply ungrounded elitism.

Finally, these remarks are not directed against the project of studying "the interpretation of scriptures" as a discipline in its own right.[20] I would only say that the study of the way medieval Chinese Taoists understood the *Tao Te Ching*, for example, belongs to the study of medieval Chinese culture, an inquiry completely different from inquiry into the meaning of the *Tao Te Ching* in its original context.

The Ontology of Meaning: A History and a Proposal

The project of recovering original meaning is generally associated with philosophical foundationalism and/or with an identifi-

cation of textual meaning with "the author's intention." It is usually assumed that the rejection of foundationalism and "the
author's intention" renders incoherent the very idea of original
meaning. This is the fundamental position underlying "postmodern," "deconstructionist" approaches to interpretation.[21] The present hermeneutics accepts the postfoundational philosophical
suppositions underlying these latter approaches, but uses these as
a basis for better defining what "the original meaning" consists in,
and as a guide to its recovery. The crucial issue here is the ontology of meaning—not primarily the meaning of texts, but meaning
as it appears in what German philosophers call the *Lebenswelt*,[22]
the world as it appears in ordinary experience prior to conscious
critical reflection. Again I can best present the view taken in the
present study by situating it in the context of a historical narrative concerning the status of meaning.

Previous to the sixteenth century, there reigned a naive trust
in ordinary experience and a naive ethnocentrism. For ordinary
experience, meaning appears to be "out there" in the world. People attending a wedding ceremony do not experience certain
physical actions of the participants as "bare facts," to which are
then added some "meanings." They experience the physical
actions themselves as meaningful actions; their meaning appears
to be as objective and external as the color of the clothes, the
location of the parties, the sound of their speech, the slowness or
quickness of their motions. If a stranger happens by who comes
from a different culture, where marriage ceremonies look completely different, she of course would not perceive these meanings. But this does not generally shake people's confidence that
the meanings are out there. Most people are naively ethnocentric;
they assume that the meanings they perceive the actions to have
are objectively real, and that there is something defective about
the stranger's perception. She is like a blind person, who doesn't
know what's going on because she doesn't see what's really there.

Enter two developments decisive for a change in modern consciousness. (1) The development of the modern physical sciences
cast radical doubt on a naive trust in ordinary experience to tell us
what the world is really like. (2) A growing awareness of cultural
diversity undermined naive ethnocentrism. Both these developments render problematic the status of meanings. The methodolo-
gy of the physical sciences, with its emphasis on objectivity and
atomistic analysis, precludes the discovery of meanings in the
world. The awareness that different cultures attribute very differ-

ent meanings to the same phenomena contributes to the sense that meanings are not really out there in the world.

The growth and spectacular success of the physical sciences (1) by their rigorous methods gave rise to radically new and vastly higher standards concerning what objectivity and certainty in knowledge consists in, and (2) by many of their counterintuitive results undermined in a fundamental way people's naive trust in ordinary experience to tell them what the world is like.[23] This determined the ambitions of most early modern philosophers.[24] Borrowing what they took to be the fundamental features of scientific thought, they conceived of philosophical thought as a preemptive attack on mistakes. Rather than being a method of correcting individual mistakes about the *Lebenswelt* when they occur, reason would now aim to establish a body of knowledge that would entirely replace the *Lebenswelt*. This would be a body of knowledge guaranteed from the beginning to be a representation of reality that was entirely free of mistakes, because it consisted of conclusions deduced by rigorous logic from absolutely certain foundations. This describes the ambitions of what is now called "foundationalist" thought.[25] In foundationalist thought, epistemology became preoccupied with absolute certainty, and epistemology in turn determined ontology; what could not be known with certainty was implicitly excluded from the realm of the objectively real. Foundationalist epistemology thus had the indirect but important effect of limiting the kind of *categories* in which valid thought could take place. Not just any concepts one might derive from ordinary experience of the *Lebenswelt* will do, but only those categories susceptible of verification by objective foundations and rigorous logic.

Foundationalist thought recognized only two categories[26] of objective truth that could serve as certain foundations for knowledge: objective data gathered by exact observations like those in the physical sciences, and necessary truths, which include the truths of logic, and include also for Kantians the allegedly universal structure which the human mind imposes on reality in all acts of cognition. One important consequence was that goodness and rightness, as aspects of human experience, could have no claim to separate ontological status, but had to be ontologically reduced to something else.[27] Being morally wrong had to be reduced to being mistaken about some objective facts or some necessary truths, or to being logically inconsistent. (Objective facts seemed to many to be ruled out, however: The nature of "facts" had been narrowed to what could be scientifically verified. The factual world was thus stripped of all the human meanings it has in ordinary experience, including meanings having to do with good and bad. It is this stripping the world of human meaning that gave rise to the "fact/value" problem, the problem that values seem to have no basis in the world of facts.)

The foundationalist ambitions of modern philosophy were intrinsically bound up with the role that philosophy played in personal and political ambitions of modern philosophers. Philosophical reason is what makes an individual "auto-nomous," self-ruled, giving him or her independence and critical leverage over against tradition and religious and civil authorities, whose standards many philosophers felt to be alien. But philosophers also aspired to a leadership role in the modern world. They hoped that philosophical reason would provide universal and unifying norms for a disunited Europe, taking over the role of now fragmented medieval Christendom as the arbiter of high culture and the foundation for political authority.[28] Some philosophers relaxed the rigor of "scientific" thought, but a great deal of philosophical literature is still governed by the assumption that philosophy centers on a debate about the one correct set of categories through which we can grasp the truth about the world.

One result of foundationalism especially important for hermeneutics is the fundamental bifurcation it led to in the way one accounts for the deliverances of ordinary experience. Whatever can be verified by the methods of physical science—or perhaps what is universal to all human experience—is given a "cognitive" explanation: The reason these aspects of reality appear to be there is because they actually are there. Whatever appears to be out there but cannot be scientifically verified (or perhaps whatever is not common to all human experience) is given a "non-cognitive" explanation. Naive commonsense is fundamentally mistaken here: These aspects of apparent reality only appear to be out there in the world; they are actually "creations of the human mind," projected onto the external world. What must be explained then, is the act of mental creation, and this is explained in various ways. Adherents of what might be called "Romantic Kantianism"[29] glorify it as the wonderful activity of the creative human spirit, best exemplified in the creative artist. Others give a causal account: Social conditioning or internal psychological dynamics "cause" the mind to attribute certain meanings to events and actions, and the forces governing such production of meaning can be the subject of a social science (Marx, Durkheim), or a psychological science (Freud), or even a biological science (Edward O. Wilson).[30] All agree that culturally variable meanings are subjective creations and projections. This is what I mean by the "subjectivization of meaning."[31]

It is important to see that this new view of things involves some new *ontological*[32] suppositions. Ontological suppositions are assumptions one makes about what *kinds* of real things there are, the basic categories in terms of which one interprets whatever concrete individual perceptions one has. If we compare it to the ontology implicit in ordinary experience, this new view of things involves an ontology that can best be described as "separative." For example, ordinary experience perceives just one thing, "a wedding" happening out there in the world. This new ontology insists that culturally relative perceptions like this are perceptions of two separate and fundamentally different kinds of reality: On the one hand, there are some objective facts about moving physical bodies, and perhaps whatever universal meanings all humans would attribute to such movements. On the other hand, there are some "meanings" created in the mind and projected onto the physical events. This revision of ordinary perception is based on an *ontological* assumption. It is not only that, on some particular occasions, people mistakenly project meanings onto events that do not really have these meanings. This kind of mistake was always widely recognized by everyone. The new ontological assumption is a blanket assumption that culturally variable meanings are never out there in the world. Reality does not include culturally variable meanings out there in the world. We know this before we investigate any particular case. Similar remarks can be made about perceptions of rightness and goodness.

The foundationalist ambitions that have driven much of Western philosophy since Descartes have been severely questioned by the most influential twentieth-century philosophers.[33] One way of putting the argument is this.[34] The foundationalist project can at best be carried out with respect to very limited aspects of the world as we perceive it. After several centuries of attempts and critiques, there have emerged too few things with a plausible claim to represent purely objective facts and/or universal truths to be able to constitute a "world" we can actually live in. Meanwhile, all of our perceptions, thought, and talk centered on these relatively few things take place against a massive backdrop of the culturally conditioned world we actually do perceive, live in, and conduct our business in, the world that German phenomenology refers to as the *Lebenswelt*, the "life-world." Furthermore, without this context our talk about those few things we might plausibly regard as objective/universal truths would not have the meaning that we attribute to it; it would in fact be largely and literally meaningless talk, since meaning is defined in relation to the *Lebenswelt* in which we actually live. This *Lebenswelt* is too massively and pervasively present to our consciousness and beyond its control to be actually regarded as not part of "the real world," as a mental creation or projection, and so on. Inevitably, when we speak of something being "part of objective reality," the "objective reality" we actually have in mind is the *Lebenswelt* we live in. Discourse asserting a separative ontology, asserting the purely subjective origin of all culturally variable meaning in our own *Lebenswelt*, undercuts the very conditions of its own meaningfulness, and so in the end is incoherent. This theoretical self-contradiction is born out in practice. We usually invoke the supposedly subjective origin of culturally variable meanings in a very selective and ad hoc fashion, as a way of discrediting or explaining away those particular aspects of traditional worldviews or the worldviews of others which seem to us implausible or objectionable. We never apply such explanations to our own (empiricist, Kantian, behaviorist, Freudian, etc.) explanations.

One logical conclusion that ought to follow the rejection of foundationalism is a restoration of the ontology implicit in ordinary experience, that is, an acceptance of such things as rightness and goodness, and of "culturally variable meanings out there" as categories of reality.

This would mean an end to philosophical debates about the one correct set of categories appropriate to grasping the truth about the world as it is. Since people in different cultures perceive things and events to have very different meanings, the logical conclusion of accepting "culturally variable meanings out there" is that there is not only one world out there, there are many worlds out there.[35] This assertion about "many worlds" does not, of course, deny that the many cultural worlds there are have massive amounts of elements in common. It only denies that commonality has any decisive *ontological* significance. Those elements which one cultural world has in common with others are not "more real" than those elements unique to it. The "many worlds" theory is simply the logical result of restoring a naive trust in the ontology implicit in ordinary experience, while rejecting the naive ethnocentrism which formerly accompanied this trust.

This "many worlds" theory does not assert that reality is whatever we perceive it to be, that our experience never deceives us, or that we never mistakenly project onto events meanings that they do not have. It only means that detecting such mistakes must be done on a case-by-case basis, rather than settled ahead of time by blanket *ontological* assumptions. This theory must also be distinguished from what might be called metaphysical[36] relativism, the doctrine that there is some fundamental truth which, in an *a priori* way, renders illusory all distinctions between right and wrong or good and bad that appear to be present in the *Lebenswelt*. The restoration of ordinary-experience ontology does away with the fact/value problem by restoring also a class of meanings which I will refer to as "the good": those meanings involved in our perception that certain things matter, are precious, are good, deserve something from us, make a claim on us, and so on. Ordinary experience recognizes a distinction between this class of meanings and the meanings things have for us because of purely self-centered interests, meanings which we consciously create, and so on. This distinction, as a basis for valid obligations, value judgments, ideals, and so on, remains intact in principle (which does not deny the difficulty of avoiding mistakes in many specific cases). Foundationalist thought dismissed our ("subjective," "culturally conditioned") experiential perceptions of the good in principle, and required that any genuine knowledge of the good be based on objective facts or necessary truths. It is an *incomplete* rejection of foundationalist thought that leads to skeptical and nihilist, metaphysical relativism. Such incomplete rejection retains the requirement that knowledge of the good *needs* grounding in objective reality beyond experience to be valid, while rejecting only the possibility of *knowing* any such objective truths.[37]

This thesis about the reality of the good is developed further on pages 270–77. It is ultimately necessary to the present hermeneutics, because it is the foundation of the possibility that we might learn something important in a critical confrontation with the text. On this view, what makes any given text "great" is not that it is founded on universally valid truths, but that it represents an organization of the world which results when one allows one's concernful engagement with the world to be dominated by idealistic concern for some excellent good (see p. 277–80). The good that authors culturally distant from us were concerned with can be generalized and this can open up for us the possibility of being converted to a similar good ourselves. There are a diversity of goods, and focus on some particular good is more appropriate in some contexts than in others. Great texts from distant cultures reveal to us highly developed visions of the good which might not otherwise occur to us. Whether and to what extent the good revealed in any given text is appropriate to take as primary in our modern context, is always a matter for critical discussion.

The above ontology of meaning has fundamental implications for the way we conceive our task in trying to understand the writings of people from other cultures. It undermines both the appeal to the author's intention and the foundationalism that were often central to hermeneutics in the past. Identifying the meaning of a text with the author's intention reflects the subjectivization of meaning described above. That is, "the author's intention" consists of some ideas or meanings in the mind of the author, which (s)he wanted to project onto the world. The goal of interpretation is not to understand the *world* of which the text speaks, but to understand some ideas an author created.[38]

In rejecting this view, the present hermeneutics takes it as its task to understand the world of which the text speaks. But the "many worlds" thesis adopted here means that this "world" is not understood in a foundationalist way.[39] This eliminates the several approaches that are based on the supposition that there is one way the world objectively is and "the meaning of the text" must be measured in relation to this: the naive approach that assumes that the reader's worldview represents the world as it is, and what the text says must be measured in this context; the converse authoritarian view that what the text says represents the one objective truth; and the foundationalist philosopher's view that interpretation must take place in some third realm of objective truth, different both from the unreflective worldview of the naive reader and from the worldview expounded in the text.

But rejecting these underpinnings of traditional hermeneutics does not necessarily leave us with the view that "the original meaning of the text" is an incoherent notion, and so force us to abandon the project of recovering it. There are after all many different *definite* worlds. "The original meaning of the text" consists in what it says about the world, the *Lebenswelt* of the text's author(s). The interpretive task is to approximate as best we can an empathic understanding of this world and how the text relates to it.

In comparison with the way the views of ancient peoples are usually studied, this hermeneutics makes such study a more difficult endeavor, and an endeavor that puts the interpreter's own views more at risk. Non-cognitive explanations of the views of a text's author implicitly privilege the views of the interpreter. For example, a Freudian interpretation explains the views of the author by saying what psychological factors caused him to hold these views. But the interpreter does not explain her acceptance of Freud's ideas by saying what psychological factors caused her to hold these ideas. Implicitly, adherence to these ideas is explained cognitively: She believes them because they are a true account of what happens in the world.

Non-cognitive explanations are also in general easier to devise. One commonly assumes here that human creativity can create almost anything, human beings will arbitrarily believe almost anything, they can be conditioned to believe almost anything, and so on. On these assumptions, almost any beliefs can rather easily be explained. The interpretation envisioned here, on the other hand, often requires a strenuous imaginative effort to imagine a *plausible human world* in which what foreign people say would have some basis in reality. (This does not, of course, rule out non-cognitive explanations, it only means avoiding reaching for this as the first and preferred explanation for any statements in a foreign text that seem out of joint with our own sense of what is real.)

Even if one thinks that the above ontology and the "many worlds" theory is not actually true—that there is only one "real" world—I argue that it is better to provisionally adopt this ontology and many worlds theory as a basis for interpretation. This is because the world that ancient writers are generally talking about, the world to which the words of their text refer, is the world as they experience it. This ought to be our default assumption, the assumption we ought to make in the absence of positive evidence to the contrary. (Such evidence might consist of positive indications that a text's author is specifically making statements that have an ontological scope and directly conflict with the ontology of ordinary experience, for example Galileo's discussion of the reality of color.) To "understand before criticizing" means that one ought first to try to understand *the author's particular* world, which may be different from our own world, and to understand the words in reference to this world. After this, one can use one's supposed knowledge of the real world, "universal truths," and so on, as a critical basis for sifting out what is valid and what is invalid in what the text says.

   Finally, the abandonment of foundationalism and the restoration of ordinary experience ontology brings the present study into accord with the current trend among many Sinologists who emphasize the inappropriateness of studying ancient Chinese texts in the light of the categories, dichotomies, and problems that have preoccupied much Western philosophy. Specific targets of attack here are, for example, the Platonist theory of ideas with its accompanying essentialism,[40] the fact/value dichotomy,[41] mind/body dualism,[42] the idea of a self-contained and self-subsisting transcendent reality.[43] The present hermeneutics would simply situate the criticisms these Sinologists make at a different level. The reason it is important to clear one's mind of these categories when studying Chinese classics is not that ancient Chinese taught philosophical doctrines opposed to them. It is rather that ancient Chinese thinkers were not infected with the foundationalist ambition to build a system of theories to replace the *Lebenswelt* (see p. 14). And it is this ambition, and the consequent denigration of the *Lebenswelt*, that gave rise to so many problematic notions like those listed above. People not infected with this ambition—including many ordinary Westerners outside of scholarly circles—also escaped many of these problems.

2

Philosophical Foundations for Interpretive Method

The two narratives in Chapter 1 lay a partial basis for a reformulated postfoundational hermeneutics. This chapter elaborates further on this basis; it includes some further philosophical foundations for hermeneutic method, some general remarks on the relation of language and verbal form to substantive meaning, and a discussion of the notion of *competence*, which plays a key integrative role in hermeneutic research as envisaged in the present study.

Philosophical Foundations

The discussions in Chapter 1 imply both a negative and a positive relation between philosophy and hermeneutics. On the negative side, one of the main sources of interpretive mistakes is the tendency of many philosophically-minded interpreters to assume that "interpreting" a text means either (1) seeing how it looks when viewed from within some particular philosophical framework (existentialist, behaviorist, Whiteheadian, etc.) favored by the interpreter, or (2) construing what it says as a system of logically articulated philosophical doctrines comparable to those which philosophers generally are trying to construct. This second tendency springs partly from a lack of reflection on the *particularity* of philosophizing as a human endeavor: One assumes that there is something universal about philosophical system-building. All serious thought everywhere has the implicit formal structure characteristic of philosophical systems, and the interpreter is simply making this structure explicit. Both tendencies also often spring from another assumption, not different in principle from assumption underlying "scriptural" hermeneutics: Since the main criterion of a good interpretation is contemporary relevance, not historical accuracy, the philosophically oriented interpreter is justified in interpreting her text as philosophy whether it is the product of philosophical thought or not.[1] On the present view, the question as to whether and to what extent ancient Chinese authors are engaged in the same project modern philosophers are engaged in is a question of crucial importance for interpretation, and it is a question that needs to be decided on historical, not philosophical, grounds (see p. 69–74).

On the positive side, the above discussion should make it clear that hermeneutics needs a sound philosophical basis. Hermeneutics that goes beyond surface detail necessarily involves the interpreter's assumptions concerning what is possibly real. The philosophically unreflective interpreter is very likely simply to assume that the world she lives in is the only real world, and she will tend to interpret everything a text says in the context of this world. Secondly, the hermeneutics envisioned here is a somewhat ambitious hermeneutics, ultimately driving toward more than a purely descriptive account of the ideas presented in a text. It shares the ultimate goal of Gadamer's hermeneutics: *Sachkritik*, not just an uninvolved contemplation of the ideas that a text presents, but a personal engagement with the reality (*die Sach*) of which the text speaks, and a critical understanding of the words and ideas in relation to these realities (see p. 9). This too requires looking at the text from something like a "philosophical" point of view.

Hermeneutics requires some philosophy, but not too much philosophy, and philosophy that enters into interpretation in just the right way. The general solution I will pursue to this problem can be described as follows: Interpretation involves giving second-order description of first-order worldviews. Second-order description of the worldview of a given text needs to take place within a framework that includes some general philosophical assumptions about what is possibly real. But the philosophical framework in question must be as formal and "thin" as possible, in order to allow the greatest possible scope for "thick"[2] description based on empirical historical research. This framework should have no implications concerning first-order substance, favoring one worldview over another. If it does have such implications, the framework itself will be a potential *competitor* with the worldview of the text.

Three developments in twentieth-century thought, suitably generalized and divorced from substantive conclusions, provide the basic elements of the thin interpretive framework I propose: (1) existential phenomenology, (2) semiotics, and (3) pragmatism.

Thin phenomenology. The name "phenomenology" signals an intention to take seriously the *phainomena,* "things as they appear" (from Greek *phainesthai,* "to appear") in our ordinary pre-reflective experience of the world.[3] If some explanation "explains away" things as they appear—as, for example, scientific explanations explain away the meanings of events—this is a sign that these explanations are defective. What phenomenology tries to offer is explanations that preserve the *phainomena,* the "appearances," basically intact.

Martin Heidegger's *Being and Time* is the classic expression of the main phenomenological insight relevant in the present context: Any description of the constitution of the nature of things in the world must include a description of some mode of concernful engagement with these things on the part of a human subject. What things in the world *are* is relative to our concernful engagement with them.[4] When the stool my grandfather left me sits in the corner as a memento and heirloom, it is a different *thing* than it is when someone else simply uses it to sit on, or uses it as kindling to start a fire.

On this assumption, entering the world of another requires that we try to understand and vicariously internalize her concerns and her mode of concernful engagement with her world. We must resist the tendency to view events and actions in another's world through the eyes of someone with *our* particular concerns, which may be quite different from those of the other. It would also be a mistake to think that we can step into some third realm of objective/universal truths and consider these as the text's valid substance, the "real reality" to which it refers, considering the remainder of what the text might say as mental creations and additions projected onto reality by the author.

Thin semiotics. The fundamental notion of semiotics[5] relevant to the present context is the notion of a "differential system." A differential system is a system of mutually defining elements, elements whose content is internally constituted by their relations with (their "differences" from) other elements.[6] Visually and aesthetically, a human face is a good example of a semiotic system. The whole appearance of a person's face is conditioned by the presence of each particular part of the face. If a person goes bald, he does not merely lose one isolated element of his appearance.

The loss of hair gives the entire rest of the face a different appearance. A change in any one part of the face—the loss of an eye, a broken or restructured nose, painted lips—gives all the other parts a different look.

Any explanation of the world that accounts for the way things appear—especially the meanings things appear to have—needs to take into account the way that each thing in our world gets the character and meaning that it has because of its relation to other things in our world. The action of walking barefoot into a Hindu temple is different from the action of walking barefoot into an American Christian church. What the action *is* is determined by the circumstances in which the action occurs. The world human beings experience is not made up of atomistic sense-impressions but (to use Umberto Eco's phrase)[7] "cultural units," things whose being is constituted by their relation to a cultural world. This means likewise that, when trying to enter another's world, we must be careful to understand each element in that world in relation to other elements in that same world, resisting the tendency to take single elements of another's world and see them as they would appear if they occurred in our own world. Semiotic analysis is the opposite of atomistic analysis, breaking everything down into a series of discrete perceptions each independent of all others, as in the "resolutive-compositive" method of Galileo or the atomistic empiricism of Hume.[8]

Phenomenological and semiotic analysis often results in locating at the perceptual level what other philosophers have tended to describe as perceptions plus intellectual beliefs. People do not perceive "bare objective isolated facts" to which they then add some intellectual beliefs. It would not be accurate to say, for example, that Hindus perceive some bare isolated objective facts about bare feet in temples, and then add to this perception an intellectual belief that this is a sign of respect. They rather *perceive* bare feet *as* a sign of respect. This "perceiving X as a Y" is a pervasive feature of all experience, and what X is perceived as depends on the complex of concerns and the semiotic context in which X is experienced. This means that things in a person's ordinary experience are filled with "unconscious" meanings, in the sense that the person involved does not always consciously say to herself, "X has this meaning." It is quite possible that the person may have great difficulty explaining in conceptual form the meanings some things have for her. Such unconscious meanings, of course, can still have a quite definite character. It is an intellectualist prejudice to say that anything difficult to pin down conceptually must be intrinsically vague.

The meanings people experience things to have can seem quite random and "irrational," even to the person experiencing them, and this is even more the case the more we learn how the people in other cultures experience things. Disciplines such as psychoanalysis and structuralism have shown us that there usually is some relatively hidden pattern involved here. For any given person or culture, the world has a meaning-*structure* involving patterned relationships between meanings. Very often people in a given culture are not explicitly aware of these patterned relationships, but they can be detected by careful observation and made explicit by sensitive analysis.

One of the most important implications of semiotics for cultural study is that it provides an explanation of cultural variability that is not functionalist and utilitarian. This is especially important with regard to the good. The conventional assumption has been that the phrase "good in itself" means "good in all cultural contexts," and that the only alternative to this universalist notion of the good is a utilitarian notion in which the term "good" can only mean "instrumentally good for some further purpose." A semiotic account of the good implies that something can be good *for its own sake* because of its semiotic relation to its context.

Semiotic analysis also solves some puzzles that arise in relation to the wonderful yet "ineffable" realities spoken of in some religions, including of course the "nameless Tao" of the *Tao Te Ching*. The fact that some reality cannot adequately be described in words is often taken to mean that there is something indeterminate about the reality itself; it is somehow in its nature a vague reality, or it is without any determinate characteristics because it is infinite, and so on. But this raises the question: Are all things that are vague and indeterminate also wonderful? If not, what is it about these particular indeterminate realities that make them wonderful? Why doesn't "indeterminate" simply mean "without definite meaning," hence relatively meaningless? The solution suggested by semiotics is that the realities encountered in some extraordinary ("mystical") experiences are not in fact indefinite and indeterminate. They are highly packed with definite meaning (with "superlative goodness," I would say), and this meaning is constituted by the semiotic relation of the reality encountered to the rest of the *Lebenswelt* of the person experiencing them. But most realities we encounter can be assigned to some established category within an already structured *Lebenswelt*, and hence it is easy to describe them in the words provided by ordinary language, words which mirror this established structure. Sometimes, however, we experience realities an adequate response to which would cause a reorganization of the *Lebenswelt* itself. No familiar categories exist for describing such realities, and this is why they are experienced as "beyond language" and even "beyond the world" (beyond the familiar *Lebenswelt*). Their definite meaning consists in their semiotic relation to a restructured "world"; it partly consists, in fact, in their semiotic influence in restructuring this world.

Very often both phenomenology and semiotics have been associated with foundationalist attempts to discover some universally valid truths, or to construct some universally valid conceptual frameworks for analyzing all experience and beliefs, as for example early Heideggerian existentialism, Freudian psychology, the structural anthropology of Levi-Strauss, and so on. For the present purposes, the insights of both these traditions must be separated from these foundationalist and systematizing ambitions, and indeed from the substantive contents of any philosophical worldviews associated with specific thinkers in the existentialist, phenomenological, or semiotic traditions. When insights from any of these traditions become foundations from which one draws particular conclusions concerning "the true nature of the world," they become obstacles to historical hermeneutics, since the worldview of the interpreter then becomes a potential competitor to the worldview she is trying to understand. The aspects of these traditions relevant to hermeneutics do not go beyond the very brief descriptions mentioned here. That is, what is universally true is simply *that* what things are is relative to people's concernful engagement with them. The kinds of concernful engagement people might have with the world is indefinitely variable. What is universally true is *that* what things are is constituted by their relationship to other things in their context. The kinds of relationships and kinds of context involved are indefinitely variable. The fact that things have the meaning they do because of *some* modes of subjective engagement and because of *some* mutually defining semiotic relationships has some important, but also very formal and very "thin" implications for method in interpretive research.

Method should not consist in applying some notions about the "universal structure of human existential concerns"[9] for example, or universal structures of conscious experience,[10] or universal structures of discourse, and so on. Theories of this kind always run the risk of having some definite content that is at odds with the actual structures implicit in the world and the writing of cultural others. The substantive content of the concerns underlying the text, and the particular kinds of semiotic relationships defining word-meanings, ought to be a matter for conjecture on the basis of historical evidence.

Separating both phenomenology and semiotics from their foundationalist ambitions also eliminates traditional conflicts between these two points of view. On the one hand, the phenomenological "subject" is now thoroughly situated culturally. On the other hand, the semiotic meaning-structure of the world is not only culturally variable, but is partly constituted by the variable ways that individuals are concernfully engaged with the cultural world they share with their contemporaries. A semiotic analysis of meanings is nothing but an attempt to describe *phainomena*, the world as it appears to a given individual, in a way that preserves its basic character as experienced.

Thin pragmatism. The central insight of pragmatism[11] relevant here is the fact that serious thought varies not only in its contents but also in its structure and validity-criteria. In most other modern philosophical traditions, all valid thought is a disinterested attempt to represent simply "the truth" about the world, and has a certain ideal structure dominated by epistemology and logic. "Well-founded" in this context means "based on objectively verifiable truths." And "consistency" in this context means "adhering to all the conclusions that logically follow from these truths." Pragmatism insists that most thought does and should spring, not from a disinterested search for the objective truth about the world, but from some problem that arises in concrete human life. The meaning of ideas is intrinsically bound up with the implications they have for concrete life. In this context, "well-founded" and "consistent" become relative and variable concepts. Ideas must still have some good basis in reality which supports them, but what counts as a good basis for an idea varies according to the variable roles that ideas play in concrete life. It is still important that one's thinking is coherent and consistent, but this means that one's ideas must fit into a coherent and consistent life; the ways they fit into a consistent life might vary greatly.

Pragmatism must be understood here in a very general and "thin" way. For example, it must be separated from Dewey's tendency to emphasize action-oriented concerns; not all problems that give rise to human thought can be reduced to problems about how to act. It must also be separated from utilitarianism,[12] behaviorism, and from a purely instrumentalist view of language, with which the term pragmatism is sometimes associated. Pragmatist hermeneutics must not be committed *a priori* to the view that all thinkers are themselves pragmatists rather than foundationalist theorizers. It must regard foundationalist theorizing as one possible form of human thought among others, undertaken for its own purposes. Pragmatist hermeneutics offers the possibility of doing greater justice to the thought-achievements of ancient Chinese thinkers, notorious for their concern with practical rather than theoretical thought; still, as hermeneutics it must remain neutral in its initial assumptions as to whether any given Chinese thinker was concerned with theoretical matters, and as to the value of theoretical speculation.

Pragmatism, understood in this general way, provides a basic framework within which to engage in interpretive *Sachkritik*, an attempt to consider critically the question as to whether what a given text says is well-founded. It directs the major questions we ought to ask about the ideas in a given text, namely, (1) what implications did a given text's original author and audience draw from a given idea, and (2) is there some plausible basis in the author's *Lebenswelt* which would support these implications?

This kind of pragmatism has some specific implications for textual analysis, which I would like to illustrate here because it will be central to many discussions in subsequent chapters. My illustrative text is the following statement from the *Mo Tzu*:

> The sage kings of ancient times took great pains to honor the worthy and employ the capable, showing no special consideration for their own kin, no partiality for the eminent and the rich, no favoritism for the good-looking and attractive.[13]

Under the influence of foundationalist ideas about what an ideal argument should consist in, one might try to construe this statement as part of an argument based on the model of a logical deduction from objectively valid facts and principles. The Mohist author believed in some objective historical facts about ancient kings. He also believed in the principle that contemporary kings should follow the example of the ancient kings. From these two beliefs follows the logical conclusion that contemporary rulers should make promotions based on merit rather than kinship, wealth, and so on.

Considering Mohist thinkers in the concrete, however, it is unlikely that this account represents the true implicit logic of their thought. They had little available means for truly objective inquiry into the habits of ancient kings, and little demonstrable interest in such objective historiography. Like most of their contemporaries, they tended to attribute to ancient kings policies they advocated on ideological and practical grounds related to their own present circumstances. It is unlikely they would have changed their mind about these policies if objective historical research had shown that ancient kings did in fact promote people mainly on the basis of kinship.

This does not however, necessarily mean that Mohists were gullible or illogical. Mohists did not generally use statements about ancient kings as a basis for a systematic objective history of ancient China; this is not the pragmatic implication they drew from such statements. The implication they drew from the statement quoted above was that contemporary kings should make merit-based promotions their policy. This recommendation was based on the perceived merits of this policy in current circumstances, a subject they were greatly concerned with and about which they had ample resources to form informed judgments. So the basis they actually had for making the statements quite plausibly supported the main implications they drew from them. As long as they stuck to these implications, it is quite plausible that they were not making any mistakes.

These observations can form the basis for an account of what I will call the "ideal semantic structure" of the Mohist statement. An "ideal semantic structure" is one in which the implications drawn from a statement are plausibly validated by its likely perceptual basis. The ideal semantic structure of the Mohist statement might be diagrammed as shown on page 32.

A foundationalist analysis would take (B) and (C) as epistemologically basic, implicitly constituting a practical syllogism something like: (1) Ancient kings followed wise policies, (2) they promoted the worthy, and (3) therefore current kings wishing to pursue wise policies ought to promote the worthy.

The pragmatic account would instead take (A) as epistemologically basic: The goodness of promoting the worthy in the contemporary context is what needs to be true in order that the Mohist advice (D) be good advice. This contextual goodness is what

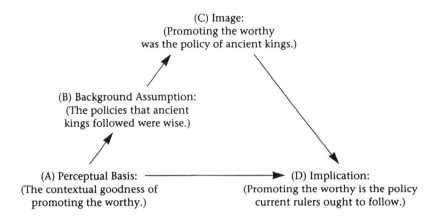

(C) Image:
(Promoting the worthy
was the policy of ancient kings.)

(B) Background Assumption:
(The policies that ancient
kings followed were wise.)

(A) Perceptual Basis: ————————→ (D) Implication:
(The contextual goodness of   (Promoting the worthy is the policy
promoting the worthy.)   current rulers ought to follow.)

Mohists had good reasons to know about. The idea that ancient kings promoted the worthy, (C), is merely an expression of (A). It does not represent anything one knows in addition to knowing (A), nor is it an added foundation for the implication (D). The idea (B), that ancient kings followed wise policies, is not an essential premise here, but merely a background assumption. It is only a *semiotic condition* required in order that "The ancient kings did X" will be understood to make the point "X is wise and good, and we should do X." It is a semiotic condition under which talk about ancient kings becomes a kind of language in which one can speak about the advisability of certain contemporary policies. As a semiotic condition, it need not be actually true, or consistently adhered to in all circumstances, to play its essential role in this semantic structure.

This analysis is partly descriptive, in the sense that it tries to approximate the actual implicit logic of the Mohist statement. Uncovering this implicit logic requires going beyond the apparent surface structure of statements considered in isolation, to consider broader cultural contexts and human experiences and projects that lie behind the statements. The analysis is not entirely descriptive, however. It still considers truth claims, and it requires that any given truth claim be supported by some basis that is relevant to this claim. This results in a critical assessment of the *interpretation* under which a given statement is valid. It may be, for example, that some Mohists took the statement about ancient kings to be objective history. Under this interpretation, they were mistaken. Construed this way, the statement lacks plausible validity. Statements about objective history need to be supported by historical evidence, which it is unlikely that Mohists had.

Thus understood, pragmatist analysis furthers the central ultimate end of the present hermeneutics: A critical grasp of the basis for the truth claims made by the text. But it does this in a way that is more sensitive to the implicit thought processes that most likely lie behind the text historically. It does not reshape these in the name of an unhistorical concern for absolute foundations, standardized logic, and epistemological convenience.

A hermeneutics based in this way on phenomenology, semiotics, and pragmatism leaves a very large scope for, indeed necessitates, historical investigation into the cultural circumstances and the social position and ambitions of the text's author. The present hermeneutics is radically "historicist" in the sense that it regards the meaning of everything said in a text as intrinsically constituted by its relation to historical context. The things spoken of in the text are what they are because of this context, and because of the particular way in which the author is concernfully engaged with his or her cultural world. What serious, well-founded, and coherent thought consists in is relative to the personal and social problematic faced by the text's author. The character of worlds, concernful engagement, and thought, is indefinitely variable, and can only be discovered by historical investigation.

On the other hand, it should also be clear that, for the present hermeneutics, such investigation is necessary for understanding the author's context and concerns, *only* because vicariously entering into this context and internalizing these concerns is a necessary condition for seeing the world as the author saw it. This hermeneutics rejects the kind of "historicism" that attempts to avoid relativism by constructing a comprehensive historical narrative to serve as an "absolute" framework within which one can assign each particular cultural development its appropriate place. Grand historical narratives are by their nature tendentious, choosing some particular issues dear to the historian as organizing principles. "Placing" an author within such narratives is ultimately a way of avoiding opening up one's own selection of "primary issues" to potential challenge by the author's views as to what issues are primary. Even more, of course, the present hermeneutics rejects the idea that one studies social and historical context primarily to understand what factors (conditioning, class interests, etc.) "caused" the author to have the views that he did, enabling one to give a non-cognitive account of his ideas.

Language and Reality

Much interpretation of texts is governed by a very simple—
and, as it turns out, simplistic—view of the relation between language and reality. This view is governed by a normative model of
language as a straightforward representation of objective truths.
The practical result is that one tries as best one can to interpret
whatever a text says as a literal representation of what the interpreter regards as objective truth. Whatever in the text cannot be
so interpreted is to be regarded as either vague and ambiguous, or
as an expression of the subjective associations, feelings, or intentions, of the author. The idea that "the meaning of the text" is
something that can be presented in straightforward literal paraphrase is the straw man that many are attacking when they
declare that texts have no definite meaning. The basis for this
attack is an objection to thinking that there is some set of words,
other than the words of the text themselves, which gives us "the
meaning" of the words in the text. I quite agree with this objection. The present hermeneutics operates with a different view of
the relation of language and reality.

1. Language is often phenomenologically concrete.
That is, it is indeed at least partially representational, but
what it represents is *phainomena*, reality-as-experienced by
the speaker. The speaker's reality may be different from reality as we experience it, or as our theories or beliefs picture it.
We will misunderstand the speaker's words if we try to
understand them as representations of what we regard as
objective truths. Similarly, what might appear to us as objective references plus expressions of feelings, might be regarded by the author as simply descriptions of the way reality
appears to her. This point will be important in the discussion
of the language of self-cultivation in Chapters 8 through 10.

2. People often use words, not only to represent the
world, but also to *do* something: to criticize and correct, to
comfort, to celebrate, to advocate, to convert, and so on.
This "performative" aspect of words as "speech acts"[14] is an
important part of their meaning. To understand what someone says, we must grasp not only the representational content of her words, but the "point" of her speech. We must
ask not only, "What is she saying?," but "What brought that
up?" In addition, like all human acts, speech acts are not

generally arbitrary bare causal events. First, they are generally "motivated"; that is, they have the character of responses
to some perception of the world. Secondly, speech acts have
"meanings"; they represent a speaker "taking a stand" in
relation to live issues in her sociocultural context, and this is
consitutive of the meaning of any given speech act.

3. In contrast to the formalized "academic" speech
characteristic of scientists and philosophers, the speech people use in ordinary conversation and in artful compositions
(proverbs, stories, songs, poems, etc.) usually has a relatively
complex relation to reality. Such speech is often highly contextual. Consider "A watched pot never boils." For those
who use and understand this saying in its normal context, it
will appear to be simple and easy to understand. But this is
precisely because they take for granted the relation of the
words to this context. If we try to make explicit the semantic
structure of such sayings that is implicit in their common
use, this structure turns out to be relatively complex. Points
(2) and (3) will be important in the discussion of the meaning of aphorisms in the *Tao Te Ching*, in Chapters 6 and 7.

4. Writings like the *Tao Te Ching* arose in a society in the
process of transition between an oral culture and a culture
centered on writing, and this means that they require an
interpretive approach somewhat different from that we spontaneously use in approaching books written in later book-centered cultures such as our own. As I will argue in Chapter 12,
most of the material in the *Tao Te Ching* consists of sayings
that once circulated as oral tradition. This means, first, that
each saying needs to be understood first in relation to some
specific and concrete setting in the everyday life of ancient
Chinese, just as bits of our own oral tradition like "A watched
pot never boils" need to be understood in relation to very specific life-settings. Secondly, this means that the brief "sayings-
collages" that constitute the eighty-one "chapters" of the *Tao
Te Ching* need to be understood as layered compositions, consisting partly of oral sayings and partly of additions and alterations to these sayings by those who wove them into artful
collages. This layered character of the *Tao Te Ching*'s composition adds to the complexity of the book's linguistic and
semantic structure. Biblical scholars have developed a special
discipline—"form and redaction criticism"[15]—to deal with
several books in the Bible with a similar complex character

and history, and this discipline will be helpful in the present context as well.

Sometimes today the abandonment of a purely representational view of language results in a kind of linguistic voluntarism epitomized in the phrase, "Language creates reality."[16] This slogan is sometimes interpreted to mean that all worlds are created by language, and people simply use language to create whatever worlds they want. There is no possibility of doing anything else. This eliminates any possibility of a *critical* understanding of people's language by examining its basis in reality. The present hermeneutics rejects this linguistic voluntarism, and takes the ultimate goal of interpretation to be in fact a critical understanding of the words of a text in relation to their basis-in-reality. The "reality" in question does indeed vary. But the "many worlds" theory set forth above ascribes this variability not to arbitrary linguistic "creation" of reality, but to the basic character of reality itself, phenomenologically understood. "Language creates reality" is true only to a very limited extent. The more fundamental truth is that "reality is linguistic." Reality, the *Lebenswelt*, has the character formerly ascribed to language in contrast to reality.[17]

The Idea of Competence

The final crucial element in the present hermeneutics is an elaboration of a theory of competence set forth in Jonathan Culler's (1975) *Structuralist Poetics*.[18] The basic idea of competence can easily be illustrated in the case of sentence grammar. Consider for example, the sentence, "The girl saw the bird." To English speaking persons, the structure of this sentence seems both obvious and objective, something existing in the words themselves. But this is not so. For one who knows only the meaning of English words, but not English grammar, this string of words would be ambiguous as to its structure. For such a person the sentence might equally well refer either to a girl seeing a bird or a bird seeing a girl; the person would not know which. A native English speaker spontaneously structures the words in such a way that the difference is obvious. The reason this happens is that she approaches the sentences *already* implicitly understanding (1) *that* the order of the words in English sentences is significant, and (2) *what* the order of the words signifies (e.g., that a noun preceding a verb is normally its subject). The fact that a native English speaker spontaneously approaches the sentence in this way is part of what makes her "competent" to understand the words. It is part of what is called in linguistics "grammatical competence" in English.

The theory of competence implies that there are two elements constitutive of the meaning of a string of words on the page. There is an objective element, the string of words out there on the page. And there is a subjective element, the assumptions, associations, expectations, and so on, which the "competent" English reader brings to the reading of the words. The two elements in the notion of competence important for hermeneutics are: (1) Competence is "subjective," in the sense that it exists in human minds rather than in the world. But "subjective" here means neither "purely private," nor "arbitrary and vague." Competence in English is something quite definite, and something definite which all English speakers must share if they are to understand each other. (2) In the ideal case, competence exists and operates implicitly and unconsciously. When we are trying to learn a foreign language like Chinese, for example, it might be helpful to make explicit certain elements of competence in Chinese; this is what constitutes "Chinese grammar." But one who has to think consciously of Chinese grammar as she speaks is still a beginner. The ideal is to internalize the rules of Chinese grammar in such a way that they operate implicitly and unconsciously when one carries on conversations in Chinese.

The notion of competence is easily illustrated in the relatively simple case of grammatical competence. But the basic notion can be easily be extended to include many more elements relevant to verbal meaning. Consider the example of a joke, for instance:

> "Did you hear the one about the Texan who was involved in a ten car accident before he left his garage?"

We can speak of "getting" or "not getting" this joke. This means that there is something definite to get or not to get. Getting the joke requires a certain kind of competence, which in this case is somewhat complex. Competence here includes, for example, understanding the contrast in normal circumstances between "ten-car accident" and "garage," and the evocation of ostentatious wealth in "Texan" that explains the contrast. Competence also includes here a certain "mode of engagement" necessary to fully getting the joke: One has to go through a process of expecting the ten-car accident to occur in traffic, and then being surprised on hearing that it occurred in a garage. The elements of competence appropriate to this joke are more complex, but they share the basic characteristics of more simple grammatical competence: They are "subjective" without being arbitrary. They explain how the joke can have a definite content, without identifying this content with some literal statement one can extract from the joke as its "meaning," and tell someone this meaning instead of telling him the joke.

The present hermeneutics extends the notion of grammatical competence by analogy to apply to *all* those factors that need to shape a reader's understanding in order that the words of a text have approximately the same meaning for the reader that they did to the original author and audience. Competence thus serves as a basis for integrating the contributions of phenomenology, semiotics, pragmatism, and linguistics to the interpretive task. That is, research into the original meaning of a given text requires that we make explicit and try to test certain hypotheses as to (1) the semiotic structure of the cultural world in which the author lives, (2) the nature of the author's concernful engagement with her world, influenced by her social position and ambitions in relation to that world, and (3) the potentially complex semantic structure of the author's statements, the complex relation of her language to her world and to her concerns. The notion of competence is thus an integrative notion, specifying the chief goal of all interpretive inquiry: not extracting "the meaning" from the words of the text, or producing other words and meanings by meditating on the text, but discovering the nature of the competence appropriate to this text. When we approximate an explicit understanding of this competence, we need to internalize this understanding and let it implicitly shape our reading. When we are successful, we will engage with the words of the text in roughly the same way the original author and audience did, and the words themselves will have roughly the same meaning for us as they did for them. This is ultimately what it means to "recover the original meaning" of the text.

This Hermeneutics Compared and Contrasted with Recent Trends in Hermeneutics

Recent hermeneutics is generally characterized by a rejection of the goal of recovering the original meaning of texts. This rejection seems motivated by several theoretical difficulties, as well as by a position taken concerning the role played today by interpretation of the classics. The nature and implications of the hermeneutics argued above can be summarized by speaking briefly to each of these points.

One theoretical difficulty concerns the notion of "the meaning of the text" as something objective. The problem is that printed words on a page obviously have no meaning completely in themselves. Words only acquire meaning through readers' subjective involvement with them. The more intense and personal the involvement, the more meaningful the text becomes. Since subjective involvement is an inescapable element in meaning, so the argument goes, the habit of the naive reader who reads the text in the light of her own concerns, questions, and assumptions is not something one can really overcome. Willy nilly, this is what we all do in any case, and what we cannot avoid doing. It is impossible, and in any case undesirable, to approach the text in a completely objective and neutral manner.[19]

This argument ignores a distinction. It is true that we cannot understand a text like the *Tao Te Ching* by approaching it in a completely objective, unengaged way, with no presuppositions or concerns in mind. But we can approach in an objective way the question as to *what* the concerns and presuppositions are that constitute the competence appropriate to this text. We can allow our views on the nature of competence to be governed by rational historical inquiry, rather than choosing the concerns and assumptions that are most important in our own lives. We can then internalize our conclusions about the nature of the concerns and assumptions of the original authors and audience, and let them inform our reading. Recovering the meaning of the text ultimately requires great "subjective" involvement and creative imagination, putting ourselves in the place of the original authors and audience and imagining the force the words of the text had for them. But this requires *disciplined* imagination, imagination disciplined ultimately by internalizing the results of historical inquiry.

My counterargument here only describes the *goal* of interpretive inquiry, a goal we ought to approximate as best we can with whatever evidence is relevant to this goal. This is not to deny the often great historiographical difficulties caused by dearth of evidence. Nor is it to deny the great psychological difficulties involved in actually getting outside of our own perspective and taking on the perspective of others. Such difficulties should make us modest in the claims we make for the results of our inquiry. They are not necessarily reasons for lowering our ambitions.

A second theoretical difficulty concerns the notion of empathic understanding. Romantic hermeneutic theorists in the nineteenth century gave empathy a bad name by conceiving of it as a mysterious communion of the soul of the reader with the soul of the author (usually a great-souled reader with the great soul of the author), and identifying understanding textual meaning with an understanding of the author's subjectivity. The expanded notion of competence remedies this weakness in hermeneutic theory without abandoning the notion of empathy entirely. Understanding the meaning of a text does indeed require some ability to empathically identify with the subjective concerns and associations of a text's author. But (1) this is not necessarily a mysterious process that comes about by a purely intuitive divining of the other's state of mind. As I hope to demonstrate in this book, we can formulate specific hypotheses about the nature of competence appropriate to a given text, and look for evidence for and against these hypotheses. And (2) empathic understanding of an author's mindset does not yet constitute understanding the meaning of the text (any more than an understanding of grammar constitutes an understanding of the meaning of sentences). Such empathic understanding constitutes only the "subjective half" of meaning. Full understanding of meaning only comes about by vicariously engaging with the words of the text, and the reconstructed world of the author, with something approximating the author's mindset.

A third related difficulty concerns the fact that mentioning "method" in the recovery of textual meaning often conjures up the image of a single and fixed series of logical steps; following these steps will infallibly lead one to a sure grasp of the text's original meaning by strict logical deduction. No such implication is intended here. Reconstructing the meaning of texts is always more like detective work than it is like constructing proofs in geometry. It requires creative and imaginative use of whatever evidence happens to be available, coupled with broad historical knowledge and an understanding of a broad range of human experience. Ideally it includes generating many possible good interpretations of the text, and this is a process that can be aided in a number of different ways: discussion with friends, students, and colleagues; reading other commentaries on the text; memorizing the text and repeating it to oneself often; meditating on the text; trying to express the meaning of the text in non-verbal media such as drawing; imagining what following the text's advice might mean concretely in one's own life and trying this on; and so on. One ought then to subject these possible interpretations to critical examination by spelling out all the assumptions involved in them, and then seeing what historical evidence can be found for or against supposing that the original authors and audience shared these assumptions. Finally, like all historiographical work, the end result will never be complete certainty, but an understanding based on the best educated guesses about the best currently available evidence.

A fourth theoretical difficulty concerns the fact that, in the past, the definite meaning of texts was defined in relation to some fixed point of reference assumed to have self-contained meaning, not subject to variation by cultural context. The meaning of a given text was generally defined either (1) in relation to some fixed set of "absolute" truths, or (2) in reference to an author's creative mental act, regarded as an absolute origin of the meaning of the words she wrote. Against this, Jacques Derrida[20] argues that no truths and no "author's intention" escapes the semiotic law that everything gets its meaning from the contingent context of which it is a part. The conclusion many draw from this is that there is no privileged way of construing the words of a text in relation to each other or to the world. There are an indefinite number of ways of doing this, each yielding a different interpretation of the text. In the face of the inevitable "play of differences," all an interpreter can ultimately do is play with the text; some playing is simply more interesting than others to a given modern audience.

This argument ignores the difference between *definiteness* and *absolute grounding*. The present hermeneutics accepts Derrida's idea that nothing escapes the play of (semiotic) differences, and that this means that no meaning is grounded in something absolute. But this does not mean that elements of an author's cultural world, and the words she wrote, were not related in any definite way in her mind. The logical conclusion from Derrida's premises is that there is a plurality of worlds, each of which has a definite character. Each is a semiotic whole consisting of definite elements having a definite structural relationship with each other. The goal of entering into the definite world of the author, and understanding the definite meaning of her words in that world, does not necessarily invoke any absolute grounding or origin.

The final objection that many will have to the present hermeneutics is not a theoretical one. It is rather the attraction still exercised by the practice of interpreting classic texts under traditional assumptions. That is, for centuries in many cultures the interpretation of classic and scriptural texts was a means by which some attempted to exercise control over one of the main sources of legitimation. Battles over what ancient texts mean were battles about whose views would prevail in the present. The idea that authoritative norms for present society are to be derived by the interpretation of classic texts still has a great hold on the popular imagination. It is understandable, then, that many should want to continue to fight their ideological battles on this battleground. Interpretation becomes essentially a struggle for control of classic texts, and for the legitimation they offer to any party able to establish their interpretation as the real meaning of the text.

This strategy, used by cultural conservatives and cultural radicals alike, seems one of the main factors preventing hermeneutics from fulfilling its promise of becoming a genuine tool for cross-cultural understanding, an important project in our modern multicultural setting. When hermeneutics drops the goal of understanding the other as other, it inevitably becomes a tool by which one deliberately refuses to understand the other on the other's own terms. For cultural conservatives like Gadamer, one does this in order to eliminate cultural distance, to suppress the fact that the worldviews of our ancestors were governed by certain assumptions and ideals that are no longer appropriate in our cultural context. Explicitly acknowledging this would legitimate criticism and so undermine the authority of tradition. Cultural radicals, on the other hand, seem to suffer from "the anxiety of influence." They assume there is some necessary connection between "author" and "authority." In empathically entering into the views of our (elitist, anti-democratic, ethnocentric, sexist, racist) ancestors, we will fall under their spell and buy into the authority that tradition accords them. The only way to escape their authority is refusing to understand them. Hence the attraction of "empowering the reader" over against the traditional "power" accorded to the text.[21]

Hermeneutics could become an important tool for intercultural understanding, and a crucial first step in critical evaluation of the various cultural traditions of the world. But it can only do this if it ceases to be understood primarily as a means of colonizing traditional texts, bringing them under the hegemony of the worldview and values of either the conservative or the radical interpreter. The entire institution of "the canonical text" is an obstacle to historical and intercultural hermeneutics. So long as certain texts are accorded an authority beyond rational criticism, simply because of the authority tradition accords them, "interpretation" of these texts in a pluralist and multicultural world is bound to be a rhetorical tool in the service of ideological warfare. If we dropped the idea of a canon, hermeneutics could become a truly universal science and art, applying the same principles to all human discourse whatsoever. It could be useful in all those situations where one person has difficulty understanding another, including especially difficulties which devotees of Western "high culture" have in understanding those whom they have habitually regarded as simply inferior: members of non-Western cultures, subcultures among the poor and excluded in their own countries, the mentally or emotionally handicapped, and so on. Hermeneutics could become an essential ingredient in the rational assessment of the grounds on which some writings originally gained their authoritative status, and a critical discussion as to whether these grounds are relevant in our own context. And it could be an essential ingredient in rationally assessing the claims that radically new works of philosophy or literature might have to be authoritative for us today.

Part II

Sociohistorical Background

Introduction

Interpretations of the *Tao Te Ching* rarely pay much attention to the question of its concrete historical setting, especially its *sociological* setting. Western scholars in the late nineteenth and early twentieth centuries were preoccupied with questions surrounding its supposed author, Lao Tzu, questions they considered crucial to the book's "authenticity."[1] In more recent times attention has shifted to trying to place the *Tao Te Ching* in the context of the "intellectual history" of ancient China, and comparing the philosophical doctrines it teaches to the doctrines of other philosophers in global history. In all these cases, interpretation is implicitly guided by a particular model of how thought develops, a model that largely reflects the way modern scholars think of their own work: Individual thinkers rise above the practical concerns that occupy ordinary people to consider questions of more fundamental and universal importance. These thinkers develop their ideas on these topics in conversation with other thinkers occupied with these same questions. The goal of modern philosophical interpretation is to place the thought of each great thinker in the context of such a conversation, first local conversations within specific cultures, and then the global conversation of world philosophy.

On this model, questions about the original sociological setting of the *Tao Te Ching* have little or nothing to do with the substantive meaning or validity of its ideas. At most, sociological study could offer only non-cognitive explanations such as proposals about the causal influences or personal motives that led to the development of these ideas: class interests, the quest for power or security, and so on.

The present hermeneutics, informed by "thin" pragmatism, semiotics, and phenomenology (see p. 25–33), opens up the possibility of a more intrinsic relation between the meaning and validity of serious thought, on the one hand, and the social setting and practical concerns of thinkers on the other. It *could* of course turn out that historical inquiry would show that the *Tao Te Ching* is the product of philosophical theorizing, carried on in conversation with other contemporary philosophers. But I will argue that, if this is posed as a historical question, rather than assumed as part of one's interpretive approach, the evidence tells against this. In this case, the pragmatist view of truth underlying the present hermeneutics becomes especially important, implying as it does that both the meaning and the substantive validity of ideas is often intrinsically bound up with their sociohistorical circumstances. In this light an attempt to formulate and establish some well founded hypotheses about the circumstances of the *Tao Te Ching*'s origin becomes central to the attempt to recover its original meaning.

On the other hand, this historical inquiry is not undertaken in order to place the *Tao Te Ching* in the stream of Chinese cultural development, nor to explain what factors caused its authors to generate the ideas found in it. Sociohistorical study is ultimately in service to the attempt to enter empathically into the world of the authors and to see reality as they saw it, ultimately to let ourselves be seized, at least vicariously, by the reality (the good) that seized them (see p. 282).

An Overview

Such sociohistorical study is the subject of Part Two. To give a preview of my overall thesis before arguing the details: I will assume, following most recent critical scholars (see p. 301), that the material in the *Tao Te Ching* stems from sometime in the period roughly 350–250 B.C. The material originated in a group belonging to a particular subculture of this period, and the world-as-experienced by men in this particular subculture is the world to which the text refers. This subculture consisted of men whom the contemporary Confucian teacher Mencius calls *shan shih*,[2] "excellent *shih*," and whom I will refer to as *shih*-idealists, or (following Cho-yun Hsu) simply *shih*.[3] *Shih*-idealists had two principal concerns: (1) cultivating moral/spiritual excellence in their own persons, and (2) reforming the practice of contemporary Chinese politics. At the time the *Tao Te Ching* was composed, these *shih*-idealists were still not widely given recognition in the positions of cultural and political leadership to which they aspired; they were still trying to carve out this role for themselves in Chinese society. Drawn from both the lower and upper strata of society, they considered themselves the new nobility, morally and spiritually superior to the traditional nobility and to most contemporary rulers. Yet they did not aspire to overthrow these rulers and take their place, but accepted the established political power structure as it was. They also accepted the traditional role *shih* had had as experts in managerial positions and practical government administration at all levels, although they did aspire in addition to take over the role of moral counselors to kings, a role formerly fulfilled by the nobility. For them there was an intrinsic connection between personal spiritual excellence and good government: Good government can be defined as that kind of government expressive of the spiritual excellence of the ruler.

Shih formed voluntary associations with each other, often under the leadership of some highly respected *shih*-teacher. In these *shih*-"schools" they dedicated themselves to practicing spiritual "self-cultivation" under the master's direction and learning his ideas about how spiritual excellence should ideally manifest itself in the practice of government administration. My argument (p. 118–122) will be that the *Tao Te Ching* (perhaps indeed most of the surviving "philosophical" literature from this period) was initially composed by and for the members of just such a *shih* school. To understand it we need to understand several key aspects of the cultural world in which contemporary *shih* lived and moved, and to understand the complex of concerns that governed their engagement with this world.

The group of *shih* out of which, on this hypothesis, the *Tao Te Ching* arose, is otherwise unknown to us. The *Tao Te Ching* itself is the only evidence of its existence. The thought in it shares many tendencies with the thought of groups of *shih* and *shih* teachers known to us from a roughly contemporary anthology of writings that goes under the name of *Chuang Tzu*. A hundred years later these two books were grouped together[4] and called "Taoist" (products of the *tao chia*/"Tao school"), a term that did not exist in the period these books were written. A. C. Graham has rightly drawn attention to some major differences in the "Taoism" represented in these two books.[5] He also recently suggested a new term, "Laoist" (after Lao Tzu, the legendary author of the *Tao Te Ching*) to refer to the specific thought of the *Tao Te Ching*, in contrast to the somewhat different ("Chuangist") Taoism represented in the Chuang Tzu.[6] I will use the terms "Laoist" and "Laoism" as terms of convenience throughout the present work to refer to the hypothesized group of *shih* that I think is responsible for the *Tao Te Ching*.

I begin this section with a chapter sketching those aspects of the cultural and political climate of Warring States China specially relevant to the position of *shih*, and those social and cultural dynamics which were particularly determinative for the character of their concerns. After this will follow two more chapters focusing on the *Mencius*, a contemporary book that provides an excellent window on the world of Warring States *shih* and the way this world appeared to them. These sections will provide background for the treatment of the sayings and composition of the *Tao Te Ching* in Part Three.

3

The Self Understanding of Warring States Shih

China in the Late Warring States Period

The late Warring States era was a period when China was in the last stages of transition from a feudal society, in which power was shared by the members of noble families, to a centralized state in which a very large group of professional administrators carried out the orders of a centralized government. The developments that will be of most interest to us can be diagrammed chronologically as follows:

Historical Periods	Books referred to below	Socio-Political developments
(Chinese prehistory)		
Yin (Shang) Dynasty		
Chou Dynasty (1122–221 B.C.)	Parts of the *Book of Documents*	
Western Chou period (1122–771 B.C.)		Early Chou Feudalism: Unified rule under one Emperor
Spring and Autumn period (770–464 B.C.)	Confucian *Analects*	Gradual disintegration of Chou feudal order
Warring States period (463–222 B.C.)	The *Mencius* *Tao Te Ching*	Decline of the nobility, rise of the *shih* and the beginnings of centralized bureaucracy
Ch'in Dynasty (221–207 B.C.)		Military dictator as Emperor
Han Dynasty (206 B.C.–220 A.D.)		Establishment of the basis for the enduring Chinese imperial bureaucracy

To explain the chart in more detail: In the late twelfth century B.C. the Chou dynasty established itself as the ruling house in China by defeating a previous group, called in Chou documents the Shang or Yin. Due to the scarcity of reliable sources from the early Chou period, it is not entirely certain how Chou government actually worked.[1] The important factors important for the present study are:

1. The establishment of a political *ideal* something like the feudal[2] order of medieval Europe: In theory, all authority was invested in a single Emperor, the Chou King (*wang*),[3] regarded in his person as the symbolic moral center of Chinese culture and society.[4] The territory of the Chou empire was divided up into many individual states. The ruler in each state, (a *kung*/duke,[5] or *hou*/prince), officially derived his authority from the Emperor. But the Emperor was not free to appoint anyone of his choosing to this office. It was hereditary,[6] belonging to a leading noble family in each state, theoretically "relatives" of the Emperor. Political relationships were largely conceived along the lines of family relationships.[7]

2. The *actual* breakdown of Chou feudalism, while the Chou political ideal was retained.[8] The relevant developments here include, first, the growing independence of the heads of individual states; by 700 B.C. the emperor was in effect just one head-of-state among others.[9] Secondly, during the "Spring and Autumn" period (770–464 B.C.), other families outside of the official ruling family in each state rose in status to become a hereditary nobility, with a hereditary claim to certain high government offices and titles, and became centers of power rivaling that of the ruling family.[10] Finally, power-struggles between both rival families and rival states developed into continuous warfare, from which is derived the name for the next period: "Warring States." In the course of these wars, individuals and families rose and fell from power rapidly. These wars also led to the annexation of weaker states by their more powerful neighbors, so that toward the end of the Warring States period there were only seven large states vying for power with each other (reduced from hundreds of states that had probably existed in the earliest Chou period).[11]

3. Political and military competition in the Warring States period led to such a degree of social mobility, both upward and downward, that the social structure itself was

changed.[12] Power and status derived from family origin and hereditary claims to nobility were greatly weakened. The great families lost their power during this period. Real power and status came to rest in the hands of strong men on top, who rose to power through skill and force, and a large body of supporters—soldiers, advisers, and administrators—drawn from dispossessed nobility and ambitious peasantry. Cho-yun Hsu (1965: 89) uses the term *shih* to refer to men from this strata. Among the *shih* were an important group of idealists—moral and political theorists and advisers—whose writings (including, I will argue, the *Tao Te Ching*) later came to be regarded as repositories of classical Chinese culture.

4. The trend toward political centralization reached its culmination in 221 B.C. when a strong man from the state of Ch'in gathered enough power and supporters to conquer all the other states in a military campaign, to set himself up as new emperor, and to rule all of China through his corps of generals and administrators. This dictator saw the *shih*-idealists as potential rivals to his absolute power, and he tried to destroy their influence, conducting a book-burning campaign to try to rid the empire of "subversive" ideas. The Ch'in were not popular, and their dynasty lasted only fourteen years. It was replaced by the Han Dynasty, who retained the centralized political organization of the Ch'in, but tried to integrate the *shih*-idealists into the government. The *shih* thus eventually became the scholar-officials who staffed the Chinese bureaucracy.[13] The organizational pattern thus established was the basic foundation for Chinese imperial polity which lasted until the coming of Western-style republican government in 1912.

Cho-yun Hsu on the Rise of the Shih

Narrowing our focus now somewhat, it is the rise of the *shih* class during the Warring States period that is of most importance to us, since, on the present view, the Taoists who wrote the *Tao Te Ching* were drawn from this class. Cho-yun Hsu, a modern social-historian of the period, gives an excellent overview (1965: 89-105) of the details most pertinent to our purposes, and I can do no better than gather and arrange here some excerpts from his description of the relevant developments:

The *shih* class . . . originally consisted of stewards and warriors of noble households. The aristocracy and the commoners overlapped in this class. A son of a noble family, who had neither inherited his father's title and office nor had been appointed to a ministerial position, might serve in his own or another noble household as a steward, a warrior, or both. The records mention that a meritorious commoner might expect to be recruited to serve in a noble household and thus gain *shih* status. . . . The *shih* class, consisting of the educated sons of the nobility and the most able and talented of the commoners, was therefore the foundation of the feudal administration. Since they were placed in office because of their ability instead of their heredity, . . . the *shih* produced some quite outstanding persons. . . .

[In the new situation of the Warring States] the noble ministers were forced by their internal conflicts to support their own stewards and warriors and to use them to govern newly taken territory. Thus the *shih* eventually came to hold many positions that had usually been held by noble ministers.(Hsu 1965: 89)

Though formerly composed of stewards and warriors of the noble households, the *shih* class was transformed during the [Warring States] period into a virtually new group. The main difference between the old and the new *shih* groups was caused by the difference between [the earlier type of] feudal noble household and a [much larger and consolidated] state of the new [Warring States] type. . . . A steward who was competent to collect tribute from a few farms of several square miles could have felt completely at a loss in administering a state the size of a major European country. A chariot-warrior of the early [Spring and Autumn] period, who was used to fighting game-like battles with thousands of his fellow knightly warriors, could have felt quite confused if he were asked to lead an army ten times larger in tricky, bloody, and brutal infantry warfare. Statecraft had become so complicated and specialized that the former type of training was no longer useful. New methods of education were needed to turn personnel of many origins into officials able to meet the demands of specialized statecraft. (98–99)

A consolidated state demands that persons of the highest ability be selected as officials and be well controlled to avoid jeopardizing the position of the sovereign. In order to provide such officials, professional education became a necessity. During the [Warring States] period the new type of state reached a high stage of development: an organized administrative staff of well-trained career experts. (93)

The vacuum left by the self-destruction of the middle aristocracy was filled by *shih*, and the main path to advancement for a *shih* lay in education, making him expert in the skills most needed by rulers. This in turn led to the formation of "schools"— groups of men gathered around one or several respected leaders— in which *shih* might learn these very skills. The schools, and the leaders of schools, became in effect new and unprecedented centers of status and power in Warring States society. Hsu again:

> To meet the demand for training the new administrative experts and strategists, a new institution emerged in late [Spring and Autumn] times. This was a school in which a master taught his disciples his own concepts about various subjects. The disciples learned by living with, listening to, and arguing with him. It is generally believed that the first of these masters was Confucius, who established the institutional pattern for those who followed. According to his own statement, Confucius was of humble origin, once served as an accountant, and at another time had charge of some pasture land. . . . He devoted himself to the acquisition of what we may term a liberal education that included history, ethics, government administration, and literature. These studies seem to have been part of his preparation for his final goal, which was to serve in a state government in order to build his ideal society, an opportunity he never attained. In the last years of his life he . . . devoted himself entirely to teaching. The sound moral training that Confucius impressed on his students gave them a dependable moral character, which was no doubt highly appreciated by rulers who had reason to be uneasy about unethically ambitious subordinates. (100–101)

What is most significant is that he opened up a new and lasting path by which any low-born but able young man could gain high office by his own competence. . . . The social vacuum left by the extinction of the aristocratic class had to be filled with the best men available; this provided opportunities for men from the schools of the great masters. (102)

The example set by Confucius was followed by many other masters. . . . Learned masters in the [Warring States] period almost all became leaders of large numbers of disciples and followers. . . . They travelled from state to state with their students and received gifts, respectful treatment, and emoluments. Learned men, like other persons of high reputation, were invited by rulers to fill high offices, though these were sometimes merely consultative positions. . . . King Hsüan of [the state of] Ch'i was the greatest patron of the scholars; he gave about a thousand learned men residences in the Ch'i capital. . . . They lived in luxury, discussing many philosophical problems at their leisure, and were not expected to make any practical contributions to the state. (102–103)

Hsu ends this account by recounting the outlines of the Legend of Su Ch'in, a sort of *shih* Horatio Alger:

After several years of study either by himself or under the tuition of the legendary scholar Kuei Ku Tzu, . . . [Su Ch'in] decided to look to his future. He visited the Ch'in court, where he tried to interest the ruler in a plan for conquering the eastern states, but the ruler was not interested. . . . He ran out of money and had to walk back to Lo-yang, where he appeared like a vagabond, tired and weary, before his family. They turned their backs on the exhausted Su Ch'in. . . . This cruel treatment . . . drove him to work even harder. Day and night for years he worked to learn about the contemporary world and to master the technique of persuasion. He was determined never again to advise a ruler unless he felt that his reward would be riches and glory. . . . [T]his time he succeeded. . . . [W]hen he returned home to Lo-yang he received a welcome so warm that he could not help lamenting over the fickleness of human nature. . . .

The story reveals that a man might, with no aid whatsoever, improve his status by acquiring knowledge and techniques that could be valuable in government service. . . . The successful ones accomplished their goal with such apparent ease and suddenness that others were inspired to follow their example. It is noted in the *Chuang Tzu*, that . . . as soon as people heard of a good teacher they flocked to him, leaving family and occupation and often travelling far to hear his instruction. . . . According to the *Han Fei Tzu*, the appointment of two scholars to official posts stimulated half the population of their native town to sell their houses and lay aside their tools in order to seek education. No doubt this account is exaggerated, yet it reflects the [Warring States] mind. (104–105)

Shih-*Idealists*

Hsu's picture implies but does not make very explicit a division within the *shih*-class. On the one hand, *shih* are a large group, valued for their practical administrative and/or military skills. But among *shih* there exists a smaller group of men one might call "idealists"—men whose aspirations went beyond practical service as "instruments"[14] of higher rulers. They wanted instead to set the practice of government on a fundamentally new basis, often under the inspiration of higher moral or spiritual ideals. Confucius and his followers, described above by Hsu, represent an early paradigm case of this smaller group of *shih*-idealists.

We can cite here a few contemporary examples illustrating the self-conception of *shih*-idealists and the role to which they aspired, drawn predominantly from the *Mencius*, a valuable source of information about the subculture formed by *shih*-idealists:

In one passage (2A/2,4, quoted p. 106), Mencius brings up the example of two professional soldiers, Po-kung Yu and Meng-shih She. What is noteworthy in his description is the way both these men pride themselves not primarily on their *technical* fighting skills, but on their inner cultivation of a spirit of courage and fearless independence, which they show in everyday life even outside of battles. Mencius poses these examples as analogous to his own practice of spiritual self-cultivation, which simply raises their practice to a higher moral level. Mencius' idealism is an extension of an incipient idealism present even among *shih* who were soldiers.

But the emphasis which these soldier-*shih* place on physical bravery makes them not quite "idealistic" enough for other *shih*, and this is illustrated in a story Mencius tells (7B/23, quoted p. 89) about another *shih*, Fang Fu, who was once a famous tamer of tigers, but then "became an excellent *shih* [*shan shih*]." When on one occasion Fang reverts to showing off his skill at taming a dangerous tiger, "The crowd was pleased with him, but those who were *shih* laughed at him." That is, there are some more idealistic *shih* (with whom Mencius identifies) who assume that an "excellent *shih*" ought to be above such vulgar displays of physical bravery, however much the general public might admire this kind of thing. Such ridicule would not have come from soldier-*shih*, or from the broader class Hsu describes.

The great concern of some *shih*-idealists for moral integrity is illustrated in the story of Ch'an Chung, whom Mencius regards (3B/10) as a "thumb among the fingers among the *shih* of [the state of] Ch'i." Ch'an's parents were supported from money which his elder brother earned from service to a local ruler. Ch'an regards the ruler as corrupt, and hence regards his brother's salary as tainted money. His concern to maintain his own integrity in a corrupt society is so great that he is sometimes in danger of starving because he refuses to eat from his brother's table. He does at one time unwittingly eat such tainted food, but when someone tells him about it his reaction is so violent that he throws up his meal.

Mencius himself wants to foster an empire-wide community of *shan shih*/"excellent *shih*": "A *shih* excellent in his village should make friends with all the other excellent *shih* in the village. A *shih* excellent in his state should make friends with all the other excellent *shih* in the state. A *shih* excellent in the Empire should make friends with all the other excellent *shih* in the Empire." (5B/8,1)

The four above examples illustrate something of the personal ideals of idealistic *shih*. Two further examples can be cited illustrating the sociopolitical role to which they aspired.

The *Chuang Tzu* puts the following words into the mouth of a *shih*, Yen Hui, asking permission from his teacher Confucius to go "correct" the ways of a feudal lord: "I have heard that the ruler of [the state of] Wei is very young. He ... thinks little of how he rules his state, and fails to see his faults. It is nothing to him to lead his people into peril. . . . His people have nowhere to turn. I have heard you say, Master, 'Leave the state that is well-ordered and go to the state in chaos!' I want to use these words as my standard, in hopes that I can restore his state to health."[15]

Graham tells a story about the *shih*-teacher Mo Tzu, who while residing in the state of Lu, "hears that Kung-shu Pan has invented a scaling ladder which the great state of Ch'u will use to conquer the little state of Sung. He hurries to Ch'u, demonstrates that he can counter Kung-shu Pan's nine possibilities of attack, and when threatened with death replies that it will be useless to kill him because 300 of his followers are already operating his engines of defense on the walls of Sung."[16] This example shows a very interesting combination of idealism and practicality. Mo

Tzu's motivation seems for the most part disinterested: He has no personal stake in either side in the war, but apparently like Yen Hui sees it as his mission to correct injustices perpetrated by rulers anywhere in the empire. But in this case he does not merely hope that his words will convince the king of Ch'u to change his course. He has three hundred followers, among whom are experts in defensive warfare, whom he uses to enforce his advice on an unwilling king.

The development of a special group of idealists among the larger class of *shih*, illustrated in the above examples, is reflected also in the fact that Mencius sometimes uses *shih* in the broad sense Hsu describes,[17] and sometimes to refer to idealistic individuals. This latter usage is illustrated in his comment, "To have a steady mind without a steady livelihood, only a *shih* can do this" (1A/7,20). Here he has a smaller group of idealistic *shih* in mind, who pride themselves on maintaining their moral integrity even in the midst of trying circumstances. He apparently has this group in mind also when he says (7B/23,2) that the former tiger-tamer Fang Fu "became a *shan shih*/excellent *shih*," and when he says that other *shih* ridiculed him when he lowered himself to a show of physical bravery on one occasion.

Chün tzu and *hsien* are words Mencius uses more frequently to refer to this group. *Chün tzu*, literally "ruler's son," was originally the title for someone of noble birth,[18] but Confucians like Mencius use it to describe morally noble *character* rather than family background. *Hsien* describes someone fit for high office, a man both of fine character and of political competence. Both these terms can be used to designate anyone of high social standing or personal worth, but many passages in the *Mencius*[19] use them to refer more specifically to *shih*-idealists of whom Mencius approves, whom he regards as the new "nobility" *par excellence*. "Promote *hsien*" is a policy often recommended by *shih* to the rulers and high government officials whom they advise.[20] It is a code-phrase meaning that preference should be given to *shih*-idealists when making government appointments. Mencius' advice (2A/4,2) to "honor *te* and promote *shih*" reflects similar underlying assumptions about *shih*: Since the cultivation of *te*/virtue is something *shih* particularly pride themselves on, the two phrases in the advice are parallel synonyms: A ruler shows that he honors *te*/virtue by appointing *shih*-idealists to high government posts.

We should not suppose, of course, that all people who claimed to be *hsien*, *shan shih*, and so on, were actually virtuous. Any social institution to which prestige and power is attached will also attract many charlatans. Sociologically what is important here is: (1) The *claim* to represent and teach high moral standards gave one entrance into a semi-recognized social position—sociologically somewhat similar to the "monk" in medieval Europe, or to the "intellectual" in modern times. (2) The existence of such a position attracted many men who were genuinely idealistic, channeled their ambitions and aspirations in certain directions, and encouraged them to form "schools" of like-minded men pursuing these aspirations and ambitions. I would like now to expand on each of these two points.

How did Shih-Idealists Gain Recognition?

The rise of these *shih* is a rather remarkable phenomenon. As members of the lowest stratum of the ruling class, many *shih*-idealists (including Mencius himself) are persons of relatively low official standing in a very class-conscious society. On the other hand, they have a very exalted view of themselves, and see it as their mission to instruct and correct those in the highest positions. Perhaps most remarkably, they seemed able to win some recognition and material support for themselves on this very basis (recognition and support, not necessarily actual direct influence on policy-makers). How can we account for an evolution in which, from a class of lower-level soldiers, foremen, and clerks, there eventually arose men like Mencius who gain recognition for themselves as teachers of kings? In most traditional scholarship, this question did not arise. For traditional scholars, the greatness of men like Mencius is self-evident, and Mencius' self-image as a teacher superior to kings appears as something his contemporaries ought to have accepted without question. The real question is why Mencius was *not* given the full recognition he deserved from contemporary rulers. (Here one invokes the supposedly extraordinary degeneracy of Warring States rulers, in contrast to the more virtuous rulers of more "normal" times.) But, as we shall see in the next chapter, this retrospective idealization gives us a false picture of the concrete situation which *shih*-idealists actually faced, and causes us to overlook concerns they had about their concrete situation. That is, it causes us to misunderstand the nature of their *Lebenswelt* and important aspects of their concernful engagement with their world.

Warring States *shih* faced difficulties in fulfilling their ambitions for cultural leadership, stemming from their traditionally low class-status and from the fact that the leadership position to which they aspired was still relatively new and not yet fully recognized. These difficulties will be amply illustrated in Chapter 3. Here I want to describe two positive factors that operated in favor of the *shih*-idealists, (1) the importance that moral advisers to the king had in traditional Chou-dynasty ideology, and (2) the need which Warring States rulers had for new sources of legitimation.

The ancient tradition of moral adviser.   A very distinctive feature of early Chou-dynasty ideology is the concept of *t'ien ming*, "the Mandate of Heaven."[21] The Chou claimed that the legitimacy of any given dynasty depended on a mandate to rule which it received from the deity "Heaven." The previous Yin dynasty had lost this mandate through their corruption, and so Heaven had taken it from them and given it to the more virtuous Chou. This Mandate of Heaven was a double-edged sword, however. It could easily be turned *against* any Chou ruler who did not live up to his high moral responsibilities, chief among which was concern for the welfare of the people in his charge.

Connected with this legitimating ideology was the important traditional role that dukes and other high-ranking subordinates of the Emperor had in reminding him of the high moral standards that "Heaven" required of him. A man who became the paradigm for such advisers was the Duke of Chou, brother to the founder of the Chou dynasty and adviser to his successor, King Ch'eng (1117–1079 B.C.)[22] We have in the *Book of Documents* a speech, which several scholars consider to be genuine,[23] by the Duke of Chou to one of his fellow Dukes. The speech is a remarkable statement of the exalted status of the Emperor's subordinates in their role as moral advisers. It pictures the role itself has having important precedents in the previous Yin dynasty:

Text	*Comment*
When Yin ruined its Mandate, we lords of Chou received it. . . . But Heaven is not to be relied upon. . . . If our succeeding grandsons . . . do not know that Heaven's Mandate is not	"Heaven is not to be relied on" means that the Chou rulers cannot rely on the divinity to be on their side no matter what. "Heaven's Mandate is not easy": One must exert great

Text	*Comment*

easy, and that Heaven is difficult to rely on, then they will
ruin the Mandate. . . .

moral effort to retain the Mandate, or Heaven will give it to
some other ruling group.

I have heard that anciently,
when [Yin Emperor] Ch'eng
T'ang had received the Mandate, then there was [an advis-
er] like Yi Yin, who attained to
august Heaven. . . . When the
turn came to [Emperor] T'ai
Mou, then there were [other
advisers] like Yi Chï and Ch'en
Hu, who attained to God on
High. . . . All these [advisers]
were illustrious, and they protected and directed the lords of
Yin. . . . Their *te*/virtue was set
forth, and thus they directed
their princes. Therefore when
The One Man [the Emperor]
had sacrificial performances . . .
there were none who did not
have confidence in him. . . .

Ch'eng T'ang was a ruler of the
previous Yin Dynasty, and Yi
Yin was a close lieutenant and
adviser. (Yi Yin is one of Mencius' heroes as well, see p. 84.)
The Duke is probably reading
his own ideas back into Yin history when he exalts the role of
the advisers to Yin Emperors;
his purpose is to advocate this
role for himself and his fellow
dukes, vis-a-vis the Chou
Emperor. It is very striking that
he claims these advisers
"attained to august Heaven,"
"attained to God on High"; that
is, they had some special access
to the divinity which fit them
for their adviser-role. This is
one important source of the
te/virtue that made them competent advisers; they are the
reason why the Emperor was
able to inspire the confidence
and loyalty of the people.

Formerly God on High . . .
observed King Wen's virtue, and
so it centered the great Mandate
on his person. But, that King
Wen was still able to make con-
cordant the Chinese states in
our possession, was because he
had such [advisers] as Shu . . . ,
Hung Yao . . . , San Yi-sheng . . . ,
T'ai Tien . . . , Nan-kung Kuo. If
they had not . . . brought forward the normative teachings,
King Wen would have had no
te/virtue to send down on the
state's people. They also grandly
helped him to hold on to virtue,

Again, the advisers are the
ones who have primary access
to the "normative teachings"
that should rule government,
and it is only because they pass
these onto the king that he has
such uplifting influence [*te*] on
the society as a whole. "Led
him to understand Heaven's
majesty" probably means they
instilled in him an awe of

and led him forward to understand Heaven's majesty. . . .

Under King Wu four of these men [were still alive and in office]. . . . he looked at them and [so was able to] display his virtue. Now [that they are dead] it rests with me.[24]

Heaven and a fear of losing its Mandate.

King Wu (1122–1116) was the founder of the Chou Dynasty. In Wu's first years, four of the virtuous Yin advisers he mentioned above were still around, and continued to help Wu maintain his *te* as a ruler. Now they are dead, however, and their task has descended to the Duke of Chou.

In the *Mencius* we find this tradition still very much alive: Many passages[25] clearly regard it as the duty of subordinates to correct the top rulers when they are not living up to their moral responsibilities. And Mencius explicitly regards himself as carrying on the tradition of the Duke of Chou: He calls the Confucian tradition that he follows "the *tao* of the Duke of Chou and of Confucius" (3A/4,12, see p. 93).

In former times, the position of moral adviser was filled by the king's relatives or fellow-nobility. But, now that many of the government offices formerly filled by nobility were filled by *shih*, it seems natural that especially the more idealistic *shih* would try to take over the role of moral adviser as well. The tradition of moral adviser provided an established niche for idealistic individuals with reformist ambitions. In a society tightly organized around established social roles, this gave *shih*-idealists an opening, and eliminated the difficulty they would have faced if they had had to carve out a *completely* new position for themselves.

Shih-idealists and the ruler's need for legitimation. Social institutions seldom become established purely on the basis of high moral values. If top rulers of the Warring States era were willing to recognize the claim of lower-class *shih*-idealists to the traditional role of moral adviser to kings, there must have been some reason besides the fact that they admired them for their purported virtue. This is all the more true in the extremely competitive political atmosphere created by the brutal power-struggles of the Warring States period. We can conjecture the following:

Previously, noble families ruled (1) by the physical strength they derived from an extensive kinship system, and (2) ideologically, by the prestige inherent in their very claim to "nobility." Rulers of the Warring States period were losing both these sources of power. For physical strength rulers in this era depended, not on their relatives, but on the support they could gain from large numbers of supporters drawn from the lower social classes. This often forced them into a posture of wooing the support of the peasants and the *shih*, rather than simply commanding them.[26]

Rulers were also in need of a new ideological rationale legitimating their rule. This, we may guess, is why some of them turned to the group whom many people probably respected as having the most plausible claim to represent high moral values and moral leadership, the *shih*-idealists. The prestige of a *shih*-idealist like Mencius is clearly reflected, for example, in one passage (7B/23,1, see p. 89) where rulers show themselves very fearful that Mencius will speak out against their current policy-decisions, influencing the people in this direction. In another passage (6B/14,4) Mencius mentions that a ruler might sometimes offer material support to a *shih* even though he rejects his teachings, because a *shih*-idealist living in poverty in his territory would be a source of public embarrassment ("I would be ashamed to allow him to die of want in my territory"). If the public reputation of some *shih* was a source of anxiety on the part of some rulers, one can imagine conversely that supporting these *shih*, and at least appearing to consult with them and follow their advice, was one of the means by which a ruler without strong hereditary claims to office could gain recognition and support for himself as a legitimate inheritor of political power within the Chou tradition.

The Shih-*School as an Environment for Idealism*

Let us turn now to the other side of this development, the fact that the emerging recognition of a position for *shih* as moral advisers attracted many idealistic men, gave a particular shape to their aspirations, and caused them to band together in *shih*-schools.

First, a rehearsal of the main developments described by Cho-yun Hsu, quoted earlier in this chapter. Hsu describes, (1) the growth in importance of a large group of "well-trained career experts," men who are valuable to top rulers on a purely practical level because of their skills. They have the specialized expertise necessary to manage the newly emerging large-scale and complex sociopolitical units. (2) Because trained experts are in such demand, schools and teachers which provide them with training also grow in importance. Rulers are dependent on trained administrative specialists, who in turn are dependent for their training and their "credentials" on teachers who specialize in teaching administrative and managerial skills. To some extent, these schools become centers of political power and influence in their own right. Unlike later schools for Chinese literati, they are informally organized and beyond state control. Men do not become teachers by state appointment, but simply by gaining the respect of other *shih* who come to study with them, and presumably by the reputation they gain by the competence and subsequent success of the pupils they train.[27] Whatever "authority" these men have is what Max Weber[28] calls "charismatic," rather than institutionalized, authority. (3) The power and influence of *shih* as a large group depends on their practical managerial skills, and it seems likely that this was the primary focus of attention for many, perhaps a majority. However, there are also some high-minded idealists like Confucius who shift their focus from purely practical administrative skills and give primary attention to "liberal education . . . including history, ethics . . . and literature," giving their students "sound moral training," and having utopian hopes to "build [an] ideal society."[29] We can guess at the dynamics here: When a large group gains quasi-independent status on the basis of their own skills, the group itself develops certain standards of excellence for which members of the group admire each other. In the case of Warring States *shih*, a significant number of this group were idealistic, admiring especially those fellow-*shih* who did not focus solely or even primarily on the development of practical administrative skills, but devoted themselves to a rather perfectionist pursuit of the good, both in their own personal lives and in their activities as government administrators and/or advisers.

It is quite possible that most *shih*-idealists had little influence on events in their own lifetime. But by attracting idealistic individuals and providing an environment for developing and articulating their ideals, Warring States *shih*-schools gave rise to a body of ideas and a literature that served as the spiritual foundations for much of subsequent Chinese culture.

To characterize the role their idealism played in this transitional and foundational period in Chinese history, I think some remarks of Max Weber on what he calls "prophetic rationalization" are pertinent. Both "prophet" and "rationality" have special meanings in Weber's sociology. The most familiar case of rationality is what Weber calls "goal-oriented" rationality (*Zweckrationalität*, sometimes now called "instrumental reason"). But Weber also uses the term, as here, to refer to any attempt to develop new *ideals* by giving them conscious attention and working them into a coherent whole, as opposed to simply accepting traditional ideas and norms without much conscious thought.[30] "Prophet," normally a religious term, is used here in a more general sense of fundamentally innovative cultural leadership. The "rationalization" of cultural norms by such "prophets" leads to the development of

> a unified view of the world derived from a consciously integrated and meaningful attitude toward life. To the prophet, both the life of man and the world, both social and cosmic events, have a certain systematic and coherent meaning. To this meaning the conduct of mankind must be oriented if it is to bring salvation, for only in relation to this meaning does life obtain a unified and significant pattern. Now the structure of this meaning may take varied forms, and it may weld together into a unity motives that are logically quite heterogeneous. The whole conception is dominated, not by logical consistency, but by practical valuations. Yet it always denotes . . . an effort to systematize all the manifestations of life.[31]

Warring States China saw "rationalizing" movements of several different kinds. Among the most important factors encouraging a general rationalizing spirit in this period were (1) technological innovations and increased social and economic mobility, which led to more rewards for ambition, creativity, and skill (rather than adherence to traditional roles and methods) in all areas of life;[32] and (2) the new opportunities opened up by the growth of states with very large territories, and the consolidation of centralized political control in each.[33] This latter development provided a much better climate for trade and commerce, and hence opportunities for economic entrepreneurs, who prospered in this period. It also provided a larger scope for social and political planning, and created a demand for social and political theorists able to deal rationally with large-scale and more impersonal organization of the masses. (3) But these first two developments brought about a crisis in the social and personal ideals that undergirded traditional Chou culture, as the contrast between these older ideals and the new social realities became more and more painfully evident. This invited *shih*-idealists, concerned with basic cultural ideals, to engage in another kind of ("prophetic") rationalization: The development of a new fundamental spiritual/cultural vision for China, "a unified view of the world derived from a consciously integrated . . . attitude toward life."

But prophetic, idealistic rationalization, while it often arises in opposition to dominant cultural norms and established political institutions, does not usually arise and take hold without some kind of institutional base. Weber remarks about the development of Western religion: "The rationalization of religious life was fragmentary or entirely missing wherever the priesthood failed to achieve independent class status."[34] We could say: The development of moral and spiritual idealism in Warring States China would have been impossible had Warring States *shih*-idealists and *shih*-teachers not achieved independent class status. On the one hand, the deepening and unification of values among *shih*-idealists involved the rejection of many conventional social standards, and this attitude could scarcely have taken hold among groups completely enmeshed in traditional social roles. As we will see in the *Mencius*, the social position that *shih*-idealists tried to claim for themselves was not one fully integrated into the structure of traditional Chinese society. Their position on the fringes of the power-group invited and stimulated innovative strategies in dealing with the cultural crises of their times. On the other hand, sustained ("rationalizing") attention to matters of no immediate practical value usually takes place only in a social context of a substantial subculture centered on such concerns. And such subcultures generally form only when material conditions give them the leisure for activity that is not immediately practical, and where there is some hope of social recognition and/or of substantial social influence connected with this activity. The partially recognized social function that *shih*-idealists performed in Warring States China encouraged the formation of such a *shih* subculture, and gave this group quasi-independent class status.

The fact that classical Chinese moral and spiritual ideals were formed in this particular social context, in the minds of an essentially "bureaucratic" class, gives them a specific character that differentiates them from the ideals of other cultures which grew up in different social contexts. Consider, for example, some of the main factors that differentiate the position of *shih* from that of social classes aspiring to moral leadership in other cultures. Like their counterparts in other cultures, *shih* are very idealistic men, belonging to a special subculture that values idealism. This gives them some independence and distance from conventional society with its traditional norms, and also from those holding established political power. And yet they depend for their status and their sustenance not only—perhaps not primarily—on their reputation for idealism, but on their practical know-how in governmental administration. This combination of moral idealism and close connection to the practical side of government stands in strong contrast, for example, to the drop-out ascetic monks recognized as cultural leaders in Hindu and Buddhist traditions and in medieval Catholicism. They also stand in strong contrast to "prophetic" figures like Isaiah and Jesus in the Judeo-Christian traditions, and to modern-day academic intellectuals and artists who aspire to cultural leadership. In almost all these other cases there is a strong and institutionalized separation between moral/religious idealism, on the one hand, and practical government on the other. I will argue below that this is a much less acutely felt problem in the *Mencius* and in the *Tao Te Ching*, and the reason is connected with the semiotic/perspectival shaping of ideas mentioned in Chapters 1 and 2. In the thought expressed in these writings, there is less felt conflict between political practice and perfectionist concepts of the good, because the internal content of the latter concepts originally took shape within a framework where both concerns were given fairly equal emphasis.

4

Mencius on the Role of the Shih-*Idealist*

Chapter 3 sketched some of the external conditions determining the position of *shih*-idealists in Warring States China. This chapter and the one following will focus on the *Mencius*, a book dating[1] from roughly the same period as the *Tao Te Ching*. The importance of the *Mencius* for our present purposes lies in the fact that it consists primarily of stories, rich in concrete detail, of the conversations and dealings of the Confucian *shih*-teacher Mencius with his pupils and with contemporary rulers. This narrative form provides us with precisely what the very different form of the *Tao Te Ching* only hints at here and there: concrete and detailed information about the world in which the *shih* moved, the way that world must have looked to them, and the way that at least one group of *shih*-idealists defined themselves in relation to that world.

It is not customary to compare the *Mencius* and the *Tao Te Ching*, especially in any positive way. If one approaches each of these books in the customary way, asking "What doctrines do they teach?," one will indeed find that the content of each is in many obvious respects directly opposed to the other. But this "doctrinal" approach to interpretation is one of the main areas in which, I will argue, traditional scholarship on both these books has been mistaken. A worldview in which "doctrines" play the central role is one kind of worldview, a worldview formally structured in a certain particular way. Philosophically minded interpreters tend to regard this formal structure as normative. My argument will be that, if we ask the *historical* question about the formal structure of the worldview underlying the *Mencius*, the evidence suggests that it is not structured in a way formally similar to doctrine-centered worldviews. Internal evidence both in the *Mencius* and in the *Tao Te Ching* suggests that these two books give expression to worldviews formally different from philosophical systems, but formally similar to each other. Hence one of the primary purposes of the discussions of the *Mencius* in this chapter and the next will be to provide an alternative formal model for the study of the *Tao Te Ching*, offsetting the common tendency to approach the *Tao Te Ching* also asking "What doctrines does it teach?"

The idea of a doctrine-centered worldview will play an important role throughout the remainder of these essays. It will serve as the main foil against which I will try to define, by contrast, the worldviews of the *Mencius* and the *Tao Te Ching*. Because it will play such an important role, I would like to begin by describing here in more detail exactly what I mean by this phrase.

Doctrinal Worldviews vs. the Mencian Worldview

The central feature of doctrinal thought is that it gives explicit attention to the development of ideas as such, trying to construct a system of ideas that will serve as *fixed* standards for guiding evaluation and/or action. Consider, first, the typical case of the person in whose life doctrinal thought plays a minimal role. Such a person's moral judgments will be partly guided by some general maxims like "tell the truth," but in practice she will treat this as a very rough guide to which there are a multitude of exceptions: Cases, for example, in which it is morally permissible not to tell the truth ("white lies"), or even perhaps morally obligatory not to do so (misleading a criminal to prevent a murder).

One weakness of this way of proceeding is that the lack of precise guidelines for applying the maxim makes it easy for non-moral and even immoral concerns to actually be the deciding factors in how the maxim is applied. This weakness is one of the primary motivations for doctrinal moral philosophizing. Moral consistency—letting one's actions be consistently guided by moral considerations—is the personal ideal implicitly motivating doctrinal moral thought. But doctrinal thinkers are not the only ones interested in moral consistency in general. Doctrinal moral thought is further motivated by another, much more specific assumption as to how moral consistency is to be achieved: It is to be achieved by *consciously adhering to a fixed set of moral principles*, applying the principles to concrete situations in a way that is relatively inflexible and highly controlled by the principles themselves, thus leaving minimal scope for non-moral or immoral considerations to enter in. The non-philosopher's moral judgments are based largely on the fact that in specific concrete circumstances, certain things just *seem* right and others just seem wrong. That is, she relies heavily either on rough maxims current in the culture, or on direct impressions she has of the *Lebenswelt*. The doctrinal thinker typically distrusts such "culturally conditioned," "subjective" and changing impressions, and wants a fixed frame of reference that can to a significant degree *replace* cultural tradition and shifting impressions of the *Lebenswelt*, as a guide for moral judgments and decisions.

Maxims that can serve well as *fixed* principles do not occur naturally, but generally require sustained conscious effort at development and refinement. It will not do to simply take rough maxims like "Tell the truth" that come readily to mind, and just decide to apply them in a more inflexible way. The need for *developed and refined* principles provides the key additional stimulus to doctrinal philosophizing. The development of doctrines is a specialized activity. In addressing practical concerns of everyday life, almost everyone invokes a stored set of loosely defined ideas and rough maxims. Not everyone turns away from practical concerns and tries in a systematic way to fashion common ideas and maxims into doctrines universal in their scope and hence well suited to inflexible application to all cases.

Not everyone engages in doctrinal thought. And fixed *doctrines*, as opposed to rough practical maxims, do not play a central role in all worldviews. Generally, the more weight doctrines have to bear in a particular worldview, the more attention people will give to developing and refining the doctrines themselves. This happens sometimes in highly developed traditional cultures such as medieval Christendom, for example, in which a highly developed doctrinal theology served as a central element in a "high culture" theoretically binding on all. In early modern times, on the other hand, great attention was given to developing and refining philosophical doctrines, because rational philosophy had to bear the weight of establishing and legitimating the *independence* of individuals and societies from this traditional religious culture.

When attention is given to the conscious development of doctrines, this seems to take three main forms.

    1. *Refining doctrines* and giving them a verbal form that is conceptually exact. A good doctrine is universal in scope, as opposed, say, to proverbs such as "Slow and steady wins the race," which is useful in particular situations, but is not

strictly true of all cases (see p. 138). Discovery of cases where a doctrine is not strictly true is an occasion for further refining the doctrine.

2. *Developing an extensive system* of doctrines, so that the meaning of every idea and doctrine can be given a fixed definition in the context of this fixed system. This is different from the more normal case, in which the meaning of ideas is greatly influenced by concrete contexts in which the ideas are brought up, so that the meaning of any given idea easily shifts from context to context. Defining ideas within a fixed framework of other ideas typically leads also to the development of a fixed terminology, a set of words fixed in this same way, whose meaning therefore will not vary from context to context as words commonly do in ordinary discourse. All this means that, in the doctrinal ideal, individual ideas are not inserted piecemeal into concrete human life as they more commonly are, but rather affect concrete life by being first incorporated into a system of ideas; the system is what actually serves as a guide. The most ideal case (the "Newtonian" ideal) is the one in which a system of doctrines comprehensively represents "the truth" about the objective structure of reality. There is nothing perspectival or contextual about these truths. They represent a disembodied "view from nowhere," and so are always true everywhere.

3. *Giving the system a solid foundation in objective facts or necessary truths, and deriving all doctrines by strict logic from these foundations.* This ideal is "Descartes' Dream," which dominated modern Western philosophy until recently. Philosophical thought in this tradition often consists largely of making explicit the epistemological bases for one's doctrines, and tracing the logical filiation of all one's ideas, allowing explicit evaluation of epistemological bases and logical consistency. The ideal case is one in which all assumptions concerning the epistemological bases and logical filiation of doctrines have been made explicit and subject to conscious evaluation. This makes the doctrinal system a self-enclosed system, more and more independent of the *Lebenswelt*.

What is important in the present context is the way in which all three of these developments are intimately tied to a particular personal ideal and a vision of the social world. One develops doctrines because these doctrines play a foundational role in one's worldview. In the worldview of Enlightenment philosophers, for example, philosophical doctrines served as a substitute for tradition, convention, and established authority, legitimating the philosopher's independence of these, and establishing his status as an *auto-nomous*, "self-normed" person. Philosophical doctrines also served as foundations for various sociopolitical visions, utopian "Empires of Reason."[2]

My argument is that proper comparisons between Mencius and modern philosophers need to begin at *this* level: personal ideals and social vision. And what the following discussions will try to show is that Mencius' worldview differs at this level from the thought of modern philosophers. It is not only that he "teaches different doctrines," but that doctrines as such are not central to his worldview in the way they are central to the worldview of modern philosophers or to doctrinal thinkers generally. Positively, what I will try to show is that Mencius' social vision centers not on doctrines but on the *person* of the virtuous *shih*, as the pivotal vehicle through which moral values ought to be infused into public life. (Where the modern philosopher prides herself on her superior *knowledge* of moral norms, Mencius prides himself on his actual personal virtue.) This central vision generates two kinds of problems around which Mencius' thought revolves, both of them practical rather than theoretical. The first of these is a *psychological* problem; how the character of *shih* can be molded so that virtue becomes a deeply internalized and completely steady element in their characters, informing even their spontaneous impulses and immediate perception of events in the world, increasing their actual psychological capability of resisting pressures to compromise. A second kind of problem is *political*: How ought virtue to express itself in governmental policy and ruling style, both so that practical governance is infused with virtue, and so that virtuous governance will achieve those political goals commonly assumed to be necessary and proper? And how ought the role and status of *shih* as spiritual leaders of the culture be defined, and how can those in power be persuaded to accord them this status?

These are the primary issues which Mencius thinks *about*, and these are the issues on which he shows himself a most creative thinker. The Mencian worldview is "rationalized" around virtue, in Weber's sense (see p. 66), in that he works out a virtue-centered answer to the above practical problems. One of the most striking contrasts between Mencius and modern philosophers stems from the typical assumption of philosophers that one must begin with some comprehensive theory of morality applicable to all human beings as such. The focal center of Mencian thought, on the contrary, is the concrete situation facing an idealistic *shih* in the conditions of Warring States China. Insofar as he has a "developed" set of ideas, they are developed in relation to these concrete issues. His thought is not highly developed in any of the three doctrinal directions sketched above (refined, systematized, epistemologically well grounded and logically articulated). This is because he does not try to achieve moral consistency by adhering to fixed moral principles, nor does he try to reform society by teaching a comprehensive system of moral principles to others. His personal ideals and social vision are themselves quite different from those that motivate doctrinal thought.

This outlines the general thesis I will argue in this chapter and Chapter 5. Evidence supporting this thesis, I believe, is abundant in the *Mencius* itself. It lies, in fact, very close to the surface of the text, requiring very little sophisticated analysis. The stories that constitute the bulk of the book explicitly depict Mencius dealing with the concrete issues sketched above. What is mainly required is that we simply pay attention to those issues which the narrative form of the book directly brings to our attention, and resist the philosopher's temptation to ignore the book's form and try to extract from the narratives a set of acontextual doctrines.

Because of the above considerations, this chapter will begin discussion of the *Mencius* by focusing on several passages of the kind commonly described as "without philosophical interest." They show Mencius trying to deal with very specific problems which he faced because of the social situation he found himself in, specifically because of the conflict between his very exalted self-image and the exalted leadership role he aspired to play, on the one hand, and the ambiguous and relatively low status he had as a *shih* on the other. I will attempt a close reading of a few longer passages, since this is the best way of illustrating particularities about Mencius' social context and personal ambitions that influence so greatly the meaning of his thought. These longer quotations will also serve the purpose of illustrating contextually the often complex and varied meanings of some special terms, such as *tao* and *te*, which occur also in the *Tao Te Ching*. This focus on a relatively small selection serves well the main purpose here, in that this is the best way to show the concrete situatedness of

Mencius' thought. It cannot, of course, claim to be a fully balanced account of Mencius' thought itself, which is beyond the scope of the present book.

I will present text and commentary in two columns. The reader can grasp the text of the Mencius as a continuous whole by reading only the left-hand column. My comments in the right-hand column will elaborate on ideas in the text of special importance in this study, and also explain some aspects of the text that might present problems for the general reader.

Mencius Stakes Out an Expanded Role for Shih-*Idealists*

The first passages I want to quote show Mencius' concept of the immensely exalted status of his ideal *shih*.

Text	*Comment*
Dwelling in the world's wide dwelling, standing in the position of Norm for the World, practicing the great *tao* of the world. When he gets what he wants [obtaining an official position] to follow [*tao*] for the good of the people. When he does not get what he wants, to practice his *tao* alone.	The ideal *shih* is one spiritually fit to play the traditional role of the Chou Emperor, symbolic *t'ien hsia chih cheng*/"Norm for the World [= the Chinese Empire]."[3] The final line of this passage describes this as the ideal of "the Great Man," but the content here makes it clear that this is not an ideal for people in general, but for *shih*. "What [a *shih*] wants" is an official governmental post where the *tao* that informs his administrative actions will benefit the society. But the *shih*'s *tao* is also a personal "way" of life that one can *hsing*/practice alone. The *shih* must be primarily devoted to his *tao*, rather than to political success, and be ready to practice this *tao* all alone if he happens not to be

Text

Comment

able to gain a governmental appointment.

Honor and wealth cannot corrupt him. Low condition and poverty cannot change him. Power and force cannot make him bend.

These lines reflect a typical concern of *shih* for personal integrity, and some of the societal pressures and forces that a *shih* must resist in order to remain committed to his *tao*.

This is called a great man. (3B/2,3)[4]

The gentleman has three things he delights in, and to be King of the world is not among them. [The first two things he desires are (1) the well being of his parents and brothers, and (2) that he have no personal cause for shame.] (3) That he can get the world's most talented individuals and teach and nourish them. This is his third delight. . . .

"Gentleman" translates *chün tzu* (lit. "ruler's son"), originally referring to members of the hereditary nobility, later describing someone of high personal virtue. The third goal mentioned here makes it clear that the term refers here primarily to *shih*, who might aspire to be teachers attracting other *shih* from all over. (Note the relatively *un*developed, conventional character of the first two moral ideals mentioned.) A highly successful *shih*-teacher will influence large numbers of *shih* who in turn will greatly influence Chinese political and social life. He thus exercises a spiritual leadership, and occupies a spiritual position in Chinese culture superior to the Emperor.

Wide territory and many subjects, a gentleman desires this, but his real delight does not lie here. To stand in the center of

The *chün tzu*/"gentlemen" Mencius is addressing might aspire to unite the Chinese empire under their rule (the meaning of the world and bring peace to the people within the four seas, the gentleman desires this, but what really belongs to his nature does not lie here. What belongs to the gentleman's nature: Just doing great things does not add to it, just dwelling in poverty does not take away from it; these matters of fate are decided elsewhere.

What belongs to the *hsing/* nature of the gentleman: *jen/* Goodness, *i*/Rightness, *li*/Etiquette, and *chih*/Knowledge[5] are rooted in his mind.

When they grow and become manifest, bright-eyed, they show themselves in his face, in the set of his shoulders, manifesting themselves in his four limbs. The four limbs give out a wordless message. (7A/20–21)

"stand in the center of the world and bring peace to all people"). But he wants to morally refine their aspirations. Mencius urges on them a worldview more "rationalized" around personal virtue as something completely separable from external political success. This is contrary to the typical ("unrationalized") worldview of more traditional societies, in which genuine worth and actual social standing are usually more closely bound together (see p. 66).

Mencius is not teaching his audience some doctrines about universal human nature, which he has gained from neutral observation, and which he opposes to particular Chinese "culture." He is trying to get his audience of aspiring *shih* "gentleman" to adopt a certain more refined *ideal* notion of what the *hsing*/nature of a true Chinese gentleman consists in. Mencius' specific concerns and the overall tendencies of his thought give his term *hsing*/nature some special connotations. One's ideal nature is something "internal," in the sense that it is something separable from standing in the external world. On the other hand, it is not something "spiritual" rather than physical. In the ideal case, virtue pervades one's whole being, visible even in one's physical posture.

Next, I want to turn to a group of passages illustrating Mencius' high political ambitions, and the obstacles he faced trying to realize them.

The subsequent fame of great figures like Mencius tends to skew our perception of how they must have been perceived by their contemporaries and, consequently, the actual situation they found themselves in. Later generations assume that Mencius' moral stature must have been plainly visible to anyone willing to look. Any failure to recognize his greatness can only have been due to personal enmity or moral obtuseness. What needs explanation is why he received so little recognition and had such little actual influence on his contemporaries. But stories in the *Mencius* itself reflect a far different and more complex situation.

Apparently in the centuries preceding Mencius, *shih*-idealists and *shih*-schools had become increasingly, but *informally*, recognized as a special group deserving of respect. *Shih* are held in high enough regard that rulers are willing to give material support to individuals and groups simply because they are respected *shih*.[6] On the other hand, contemporary Chinese society was still highly stratified, and an important part of the content of *i*/rightness and *li*/etiquette were rules aimed at dramatizing this stratification by prescribing how members of different strata should behave toward each other. What we see in the *Mencius* is that the respect accorded to *shih* had not yet become fully official by being integrated into the formal rules of social interaction.[7] Formally, many *shih* still occupied an official status at the bottom of the ruling class, barely above the peasants.

This gives rise to some very concrete and crucial problems, to which the *Mencius* devotes considerable space and attention. The key problem is that Mencius' highly exalted self-image (described above) is so greatly at odds with his *formal* status as a lower-class *shih*.[8] This problem is made even more acute by the fact that *i*/Rightness and *li*/Etiquette are two key elements in the moral ideal he claims to uphold. Many passages in the *Mencius* focus on Mencius' attempts to change or bend traditional Rightness-rules to gain for *shih* like himself official recognition as the highest moral leaders of China. Apparently in making this attempt he was going against very entrenched notions, and he was opposed even by some of his friends (as, for example, his friend Ching-tzu in the second story quoted below.)

The first passage I want to discuss is an interchange between Mencius and someone asking his advice, perhaps one of his followers. The interchange partly turns on the meaning of the word *ch'en*. This is a common word for someone who holds a government post, hence someone in authority. But the root meaning of the word is "subject, subordinate." (The *Tao Te Ching* 63[32]:1 says of Tao, "Although it is *hsiao*/insignificant, no one can *ch'en* it," that is, dominate it as something subordinate.) This is a remnant of the feudal order in which, in theory, the Emperor had total power, and everyone else was holding office merely as his "subjects." To accept the position of a *ch'en*, then, was to expressly put oneself in a position as the social inferior to the ruler, one's *chün*/master.

Text

Comment

Wan Chang: I venture to ask: Not [answering a summons to] go to see a prince. Why is this Right?

At issue here is a traditional rule of *i*/Rightness. A feudal head of state summoning[9] someone to "come to see" him is implicitly assigning that person a social ranking considerably below him. This is exactly the official status of Mencius-the-*shih*, so traditional Rightness rules would require him to acknowledge his position relative to a feudal prince by obeying. But Mencius apparently has a well-known policy of refusing to make this gesture of submission. Here Wan Chang asks him to explain this departure from established custom.

Mencius: One dwelling in the city is called '*ch'en* of market-places and wells.' One dwelling in the countryside is called '*ch'en* of grass and plants.' In both cases he is a common

These lines about *shih* charged with very minor responsibilities would not apply to Mencius personally, and probably show that he wants to change the rules for *shih* generally. The pas-

Text

man. A common man, who has not become a [high-ranking][10] *ch'en* by presenting a gift, does not presume to go to see a prince. . . .

Furthermore: Why does he want to see him?

Wan Chang: Either because of his extensive knowledge, or because he is a *hsien*.

Mencius: Because of his extensive knowledge? The Son of Heaven would not order a teacher to come; how much less can one of the princes do this? Because he is a *hsien*? I have never heard of ordering a *hsien* because of a desire to see him. . . .

[Duke Mu once said to Tsu-ssu:] "In ancient times, [rulers of] 10,000-chariot kingdoms have been friends with *shih*. What about this?" Tsu-ssu was not pleased, and said, "In ancient times men had a saying that said, 'Serve him'. Did they only say, 'Be friends with him?'"

Comment

sage seems to reflect the fact that traditional rules accord *shih* a status not fundamentally different from *shu*/peasant-commoners. Mencius ingeniously turns this traditional idea into a support for his innovation, saying it would be too *presumptuous* for a common man to have personal contact with a feudal prince, and that is why a *shih* should not obey the summons.

Next Mencius invokes a second rationale that is apparently the exact opposite of the first: *Shih*-idealists are the rightful inheritors of the traditional role of moral adviser/teacher of the Emperor (see p. 63.) The *shih* merits this role because of his "extensive knowledge" (political know-how) and the fact that he is a *hsien*, a man with fine moral character, wisdom, and leadership ability.

Mencius invokes in his support a story about another famous Confucian *shih*[11] in previous times who also claimed the status of king's adviser/teacher, applying to himself what was apparently a traditional saying regarding the relation between the Emperor and his advisers, advising the Emperor to put himself in the subordinate position of one "in service to" his moral-advisers.

Note that by calling ancient royal advisers *shih*, Mencius is implicitly, but anachronistically, asserting that they and he belong to the same social class. (A similar anachronism can probably be seen in 6[15]:1 of the *Tao Te Ching*.)

[The story says,] "Tsu-ssu was not pleased." Was he not saying [to himself]: "Position-wise, you are the *chün* and I am the *ch'en*. How could I presume to share a *chün's* friendship? Te-wise, you [ought to] serve me. How could you share friendship with me?" So when a 10,000-chariot *chün* wanted to share friendship [with a *shih*], he could not get it. How much less can he order him to come? . . .

Mencius is probably here putting into Tsu-ssu's mouth the double rationale he himself gave above.

The ideal *shih* is the ruler's superior because of his superior *te*/virtue.

Desiring to see a *hsien*-man not according to his *tao* is like desiring someone to enter and then shutting the door in his face. (5B/7)

This interchange shows clearly three of the main factors that enter into Mencius' status and his self-conception: (1) In *traditional* terms, many *shih* belong to the lowest level of the ruling class (shown here in Mencius' first reply to the question). (2) Mencius-the-*shih* claims both for himself and for other *shih*-idealists the exalted traditional role of teacher-adviser to kings, and he uses the word *shih* to refer to one who has this role. (3) The claim of *shih* to this role is based primarily on their claim to be superior in virtue to kings, a status Mencius wants publicly recognized by a change in Etiquette rules surrounding royal visits.

A word must also be said about what the modern reader will probably see as a serious "inconsistency" in Mencius' stated position here. He justifies his idea that *shih* should not obey royal summons, both on the grounds that they are unworthy of a direct audience and on the grounds that they are too worthy to be summoned. But the extremely blatant character of this contradiction should give us pause. If the story's author thought this contradiction was a weakness, it is unlikely that he would let it stand out so strikingly in the way he tells the story. I suggest that there is a strong difference in expectations between a modern and an ancient reader, which accounts for this. For the modern reader, the principal model of the moral idealist is the person who has a logical and clearly thought out set of moral principles to which he adheres consistently and uncompromisingly. But this is not the expectation about the ideal person that underlies the *Mencius*. First, although Mencius is advocating some important adjustments in the social structure to enhance the position of *shih*, he does not (after the manner of Hobbes and Locke) attempt a critical reevaluation of the entire social structure itself. He does not try first to think about the foundations of sociopolitical structure and then use this foundation as the basis for a logically well-founded and consistent vision of the way society should be structured. He accepts many traditional rules regarding Rightness as a framework within which he thinks and acts because they belong to a tradition that he supports, not because he has a theory providing them with a rational foundation. Secondly, the Mencian model of consistency does not center on a set of principles consistently adhered to. The book called the *Mencius* does not consist of essays about moral principles, but primarily of stories about how the *shih*-teacher Mencius handles himself in many different circumstances. What is consistent about the stories is not a set of principles to which Mencius adheres in all of them. What is consistent is Mencius' *tao*, his approach to different situations, the "way" he handles himself in them. What I suggest is that maneuvering, like that illustrated in the above story, is part of Mencius' consistent *tao*. It was something he was skillful at and admired for by other *shih*, for whom the *Mencius* was probably written. The group of *shih* to which Mencius belongs is attempting something difficult: not only aspiring to the position of highest moral leadership in their society, but also trying to gain public recognition for themselves as a class in this role. One way of handling the difficulties involved in this task is to become skillful at maneuvering. For those rulers who refuse to acknowledge the claims of virtue, one learns to invoke other traditional rules by which one's conduct can be justified.

Our next passage opens with a rather amusing series of moves, showing again Mencius' skill at social maneuvering. Mencius is about to go see a local king, when he receives a message from the king. The king says that he had intended to pay Mencius a visit, but he has taken sick and cannot go out today. He says, "In the morning I will hold court. I do not know if I will get to see you then." This message, as Mencius understands it at least, is not a straightforward account of facts, but a very polite way of summoning Mencius to come to court. The statement that the king had intended to pay Mencius a visit is merely a way of conveying the fact that he indeed does have high respect for Mencius, counterbalancing his assertion of superiority by indirectly summoning Mencius to court the next day. This counterbalance is not enough for Mencius. He obviously feels insulted by the summons and replies in kind, sending back a return message that *he* is sick, and so will not be able to come to court. But the next day he rather brazenly goes out to pay a visit of condolence to an acquaintance. We pick up the story when Mencius is staying the night with a friend, Ching-tzu, and Ching-tzu is criticizing him for his conduct.

Text

Comment

Ching-tzu: With *chün*/superiors and *ch'en*/subordinates the rule is respect. I have seen the king's respect for you, but I have not seen your respect for the king. . . . According to the Book of Etiquette, "When the superior's order summons, one should not even wait to harness the horses." You were certainly on your way to court, but when you heard the king's order you did not carry out your purpose. This seems contrary to Etiquette.

Ching thinks that the king's summons was couched in terms as respectful to Mencius as was appropriate, but that Mencius' response was clearly not. Mencius' reply shows that he thinks Ching does not have a sufficiently high appreciation of the status and recognition that a *shih*-idealist deserves.

Mencius: How can you give it that meaning? Tseng-tzu said, "The wealth of Chin and Ch'u cannot be equalled. They have

Mencius brings up the example of one of Confucius' pupils, Tseng-tzu, asserting his equality with the top rulers of two

83

Text

their wealth, I have my *jen*/
Goodness. They have their
noble rank, I have my *i*/Right-
ness. Why should I worry?"
Tseng-tzu said this—shall we
say it is not Right? There is a
tao here. In the world there are
three things recognized as hon-
orable: nobility is one, age is
one, and *te*/virtue is one. At
court, nothing can compare
with nobility. In the village,
nothing can compare with age.
In helping the world and leading the people, nothing can
compare with *te*. How can having one of these be grounds for
looking down on someone
who has two?
Yes, a *chün*/ruler who wants
to accomplish great things has
to have *ch'en*/subordinates
whom he does not order to
come to him. When he wants
advice, he goes to them. Someone who does not honor *te* and
delight in *tao* is not fit to help
accomplish things. Consider
T'ang's relation to Yi Yin: He
hsüeh/Learned [from him] and
only afterwards treated him as
a *ch'en*/subordinate. Yes, and
then he became [a true] King
without difficulty. . . . In the
world today there are many
states equal in size and *te*/influ-
ence. None is able to win out
over the others. Is this not
because [rulers] are fond of
appointing *ch'en*/subordinates

Comment

major Chinese powers of the
time. Note the very explicit
claim here that a *shih's* demand
for recognition above kings rests
on his superior personal virtue.[12]

Note the use of *tao* as "lesson"
here.

Mencius is superior to the king
in age and *te*/virtue, and *te* is
the main spiritual qualification
enabling one to fulfill the functions of a good ruler, "helping
the world and leading the people." (Note that Mencius
implicitly admits here that he is
not of noble lineage.)

The context makes it clear that
"Honor *te* and delight in *tao*"
refers to respect which a ruler
shows to virtuous *shih*,[13] who
possess great *te* and practice *tao*.
T'ang was a pre-Chou ruler
whom we met earlier (p. 62) in
the speech by the Duke of
Chou, along with Yi Yin his
moral adviser. Yi Yin had a
double status: As feudal office-
holder he was the ruler's
ch'en/subject. As moral adviser
he was teacher, superior to his
student the Emperor; in this
capacity the Emperor would
not order him to come to him.
Mencius blames the present
rulers for not seeking out subordinate office-holders [*ch'en*]
who are competent to give

whom they then instruct? They are not fond of creating subordinates by whom they might be taught. T'ang did not dare order Yi Yin to come.(2B/2) them moral instruction. Any ruler who did this would be acting as a true King, and would surely attain supreme power in the empire.

The two preceding passages reflect the rather complicated social position in which a *shih*-teacher like Mencius found himself. On the one hand, he regarded himself as far superior in true personal worth to most contemporary the heads of state. On the other hand, the old social categories were still alive in people's minds, and in traditional terms Mencius-the-*shih* belonged to the lowest level of the nobility. In another passage (1B/16) a king's closest counselors speak with disdain of Mencius as a commoner, and the king, who wants to go visit him, must try to sneak out of his palace to do so. Many of these passages reveal the relative newness and instability of the social category to which Mencius belongs. Mencius could scarcely have gained what recognition he did—or got away with his sometimes high-handed treatment of rulers—if he were the only person of his type, that is, unless he belonged to a social category that was already partly established. On the other hand, if the category were *very firmly* established and had become firmly enmeshed in Chinese Etiquette rules, Mencius would not have had to resort to all the complicated tactics he uses to justify his actions and the claims he makes.

The following two stories illustrate this point very directly. They involve the especially complicated difficulties that arise concerning how *shih* like Mencius, who serve as governmental advisers without official office, can justify the material support they receive from top rulers without violating traditional rules of Rightness, which recognize no such position.

Text

P'ang Kang:[14] Followed by several dozen chariots, with a following of several hundred men, supported by one prince after another—is this not extravagant?

Comment

P'ang may be exaggerating, but it seems probably true that Mencius travels with a rather large number of followers. In 2B/10,3 a king says that he wants to devote a large sum of

Text	*Comment*
Mencius: If it is against the *tao*, then one cannot accept a cup of rice from anyone. If it is in accordance with *tao*, then Shun receiving the empire from Yao would not be considered extravagant. Do you think this was extravagant?	money to the support of Mencius and his followers. Another passage (2B/3,4) describes him as needing protection, a reason for accepting money from a ruler to buy arms. Yao was a legendary Emperor of idealized primordial times; he was supposed to have turned over the empire to Shun, a meritorious commoner.[15]
P'ang Kang: No. [But] a *shih* supported without performing any work—this is not proper.	P'ang is here echoing what must have been a common sentiment of those who did not want to recognize uppity *shih* like Mencius. A passage quoted immediately below has Mencius agreeing with this general principle declared by P'ang. And in 3B/9,9 he himself speaks disdainfully of "unemployed *shih* engaging in unreasonable discussions" (referring to his main opponents, the followers of Yang Chu and Mo Ti).
Mencius: If you do not have an exchange of the products of work, so that surpluses can supply deficiencies, then the farmers will have an overabundance of grain, and the women will have an overabundance of cloth. If you have such an exchange, then carpenters and carriage-makers will get support from you. . . . Why do you honor the carpenter and carriage-maker and make light of	This passage seems to reflect a situation in which rulers support artisans from the produce they collect as tax from farmers.[16] If it is accepted for rulers to support artisans in this way, surely he can support representatives of Goodness and Rightness.

the one who practices Goodness and Rightness?

P'ang Kang: The intention of
the carpenter and the carriage-
maker is to seek to be supported. A *chün tzu*'s doing tao [*wei
tao*]: Is the intention then seeking to be supported?

Mencius: Why are you concerned what the intention is?
He deserves something from
you. It is proper to support
him, so support him.(3B/4)

P'ang tries to catch Mencius
here: So the self-styled *chün tzu*
is "doing *tao*" just in order to
have someone support him?
Mencius does not think support ought to be his motive,
but does think the support
ought to be there.

In the next passage, Mencius himself agrees that it is against
normal Etiquette rules for a *shih* to receive a *regular salary* without
holding office. Here he is forced into some very elaborate conceptual maneuvering to come up with an arrangement that will both
support the *shih* as he thinks proper, and still remain within the
Etiquette rules that form an important part of the framework
within which Mencius thinks.

Text

Wan Chang: Why should a *shih*
not become a [regular salaried]
t'o/dependent of a prince?

Mencius: . . . When a prince
loses his state, and becomes a
dependent of another prince,
this is in accordance with *li*/Eti-
quette. For a *shih* to become
such a dependent is against Etiquette.

Wan Chang: If the ruler
makes him a *gift* of some grain,
does he accept it?

Mencius: He accepts it.

Wan Chang: What is the
i/Rightness in his accepting it?

Comment

Mencius thinks that, according
to Etiquette, normally there are
only two ways in which one
can properly receive regular
support from a feudal prince:
(1) One can be a *t'o*/depen-
dent[17] who receives a regular
stated amount of money or
goods, but this is a category
reserved for a deposed feudal
prince, who becomes "dependent" on the prince of another
state for support. (2) A superior
can *tz'u*/bestow regular pay on
his subordinates, but this category is reserved for people (like

Text

Comment

Mencius: A lord's relation to his people surely requires him to relieve distress.
Wan Chang: If it is relief, then he accepts it. If it is *tz'u*/bestowed [as pay] then he does not. Why?
Mencius: . . . Gatekeepers [for example] . . . have a steady office that is grounds for [regular pay] bestowed by the superior. But for someone without a steady office to receive [pay] *tz'u*/bestowed by the superior— this is disrespectful.
Wan Chang: If the ruler sends a gift, then one accepts it. I wonder if this can be steadily continued. . . .

[Here Mencius tells a story about a former great disciple of Confucius, Tsu-ssu: A ruler supported him by sending him daily "gifts" of food. Tsu-ssu complained about the humiliation this caused him—of having to go through an elaborate "thanking" ceremony every day—and the ruler stopped.]
Wan Chang: If a state's ruler wants to support a *chün tzu*: How should this be done so that he can be said to be [really] "supporting" him?
Mencius: It will be done [the first time] at the ruler's orders. It will be accepted by bowing the head twice to the ground. But after [this first time], the

gatekeepers) doing some kind of regular work for the ruler. *Shih* like Mencius act as counselors to rulers without having any official post that would entitle them to regular support. Mencius does think that such *shih* still ought to receive regular support from the ruler, and in this passage he considers the possibility of preserving Etiquette rules by treating the ruler's support of such a *shih* under the category of "gift," given to "relieve the distress" of the *shih*.

This gives rise to a further difficulty: Gifts sent directly from rulers require an elaborate thanking ceremonial each time, and a *shih* would find this humiliating if he had to do it every time a meal was brought to him.

The solution is to have regular meals sent, but *officially* sent from the storekeeper and the cook rather than the ruler.

storekeeper will continue to
send grain, the cook will continue to send meat, [but] he
will do it [as though] *not* at the
orders of the ruler.(5B/6)

The final story I want to quote illustrating Mencius' conception of his social position is one that shows him backing down
from a confrontation with a feudal lord. This illustrates an important aspect of Mencius' social ideal. That is, although he regards
accomplished *shih* as the highest moral authorities in China, he
does not advocate a revolution that would depose rulers and
replace them with *shih*. At a very basic level, he accepts a situation
in which ultimate political power rests in the hands of people
who are morally inferior to *shih*. The *shih's* primary role is not to
vie with such people for power or for actual leadership, but (1) to
shape public life by their own conduct as administrators, and (2)
to try to influence top rulers by moral suasion. They want rulers
to give them appointments and/or to listen to their advice, but
they must always be prepared for the situation in which a ruler
does not "honor *te* and promote *shih*," and in this case they must
simply withdraw and "practice their *tao* alone."

The story I will quote concerns a famine that is going on in the
state of T'ang. The men in charge have apparently decided it is not
yet time to dip into the grain the state has stored up for such occasions. A government official expresses concern that Mencius will
publicly express an opinion opposing the government on this matter, and so turn the people against the government.

Text	*Comment*
Ch'an Tsin: Everyone in the state is thinking that you, Master, will again ask that the granary of T'ang be opened for them. . . .	This seems to reflect Mencius' prestige and the weight that his opinions carry. The ruler has to fear that a public request on his part would greatly increase public pressure to open the granaries.
Mencius: This would be to act like Fang Fu. . . . [He was]	Mencius answers indirectly by telling a story: A man famous

famous for being an excellent tiger-tamer. Afterwards he became an excellent *shih* [*shan shih*]. Going out once into the wild country, he found people all in pursuit of a tiger. The tiger took refuge in a corner of a hill, where no one dared attack him. But when they saw Fang Fu, they ran and met him. Fang Fu bared his arms and got out of his chariot. The crowd was pleased with him, but those who were *shih* laughed at him.(7B/23)

for skill in taming tigers later entered the ranks of the *shih*-idealists. When he then on one occasion reverted to the role of brave tiger-tamer, the other *shih*-idealists did not find this impressive, but laughed at him. Facing dangerous tigers is not the proper role of *shih*-idealists. The point: Mencius righteously stands up against kings when it is reasonably safe to do so. But risking one's skin in a very dangerous situation is *not* the role of the *shih* in Mencius' mind, and would only make him look foolish.

Mencius decides what to do not only, or even primarily, on the basis of ethical principles strictly adhered to. Primarily, he is a man with a strong and definite sense of the role he wants to play in his society. Quite high-minded motivations underlie the role he is trying to stake out for himself. Nonetheless, his conception of his personal *role*, not ethical principles or ideals, is the ultimate, overriding guiding force behind his decisions. His actions ultimately cohere and are consistent as various parts of a strategy for carrying out this role. This is a role that he has worked out partly with practical possibilities in mind. Some stories show him pushing the limits of the possibilities for a person of his social status. Nonetheless he is very much aware of these limits. The implication of the tiger-tamer story is that Mencius considers political confrontations, opposing force with force, to be beneath the dignity of a *shih*, and it is part of his *tao* to avoid them.

Other Shih-*Schools*

I would like now to turn to a story about Mencius' indirect encounter with another rival *shih*-teacher. Part of my point here is to illustrate the fact that there were other *shih*-teachers who occupy roughly the same *social* position as Mencius, even though they practice rival *tao*'s and are often competing against each other for the minds of pupils and influence over governmental policy. We often find such teachers in the pages of the *Mencius*, discussing and criticizing each other's actions and ideas. In some passages (e.g., 3B/9–10) we find Mencius criticizing other *shih*. In other passages (e.g., 2B/12) we find other *shih* discussing and criticizing something Mencius said or did. The following passage is about Mencius' attitude toward Hsü-hsing, a *shih*-teacher who comes from the southern state of Ch'u.

Text

There was a man named Hsü-Hsing who practiced the words of Shen-nung. He came to T'eng from Ch'u. Presenting himself at the palace gate, he announced himself to Duke Wen, saying, "I, a man from a distant region, have heard that you, master, practice *jen*/Good government. I would like to receive from you a plot of land here and to become your subject." Duke Wen gave him a place to live. His followers numbered several dozen. They all wore haircloth clothes and made hemp-sandals and wove mats for a living.

Comment

Hsü-hsing does not put out his wisdom as his own, but attributes it to a legendary pre-Chou Emperor, Shen-nung, whose name was associated with an agrarian and egalitarian utopia of the past.[18] It was important to *shih*-idealists to find a government that they could respect, and this is why Hsü-hsing mentions *jen*-government as the reason he has come a great distance to Duke Wen's state. He does not ask for any official position, but does ask for support in the form of a plot of land, probably so he can conduct his school in this state, possibly also so he can be available to the ruler for advice. The high respect for *shih* generally is reflected in the fact that the ruler gives him the plot of land, even though he could scarcely have liked Hsü's doctrine that rulers should live simply and make a living by

Text

Ch'en Hsiang, a follower of Ch'en Liang, and his younger brother Hsin, came to T'eng from Sung, carrying their ploughs on their backs. They said, "We have heard that you, My Lord, are practicing Wise-Person-government [*sheng jen*[19] *chih chih*]. This means you are a Wise Person, and we would like to become subjects of a Wise Person."

When Ch'en Hsiang went to see Hsü he was very pleased. He renounced the *hsüeh*/Learning of Ch'en and became a Learner [with Hsü-hsing].

Ch'en Hsiang went to see Mencius and told him what Hsü-hsing said:

The ruler of T'eng is sincere and *hsien*/worthy, but even so he has not yet listened to *tao*. A *hsien* should support himself by cultivating the land with the people, preparing his own morning and evening meals while conducting the government. The ruler of T'eng still has his granaries, arsenals, and storehouses, and this means

Comment

working with their hands. Hsü's followers practice what they preach, probably relieving the ruler of the responsibility of subsidizing their living expenses as well.

Here we find two men from another state who apparently made their living as farmers, but who had been studying for many years under a Confucian *shih*-teacher Ch'en Liang. (He bears the same family name, and may be a relative.)

Ch'en Hsiang had probably left the side of his Confucian teacher hoping to practice and spread this teaching as a *shih* in another state. But in T'eng he goes to listen to Hsü-hsing, and is converted to this new Learning.

This passage illustrates again how the *shih* had a single ideal for themselves and for the ruler; he should practice the *tao*/ "right way" that they practice. He should also be *hsien*, a man of fine character and leadership ability (see p. 59). As often, *tao* serves here as a generic concept, "the right way," though each teacher has a different concept of what the right way is.

he is oppressing the people to provide for himself. . . . [Here there is a long conversation in which Mencius defends a division of labor in which the ruler does his job, ruling, and the people do their job, raising food.]

Mencius: I have heard of using our culture to change the barbarians. I have never heard of being changed by barbarians. Ch'en Liang was born in Ch'u. He found pleasure in the *tao* of the Duke of Chou and of Confucius. He came north to Learn in the Middle Kingdom. Among our northern men of Learning, perhaps there were none who could surpass him. He was what you can call a *shih* of high distinction.

Becoming a *shih* is something in principle open to all, and this provides an avenue of upward mobility in an otherwise somewhat stratified society. By birth, Ch'en Liang was a "barbarian" from the southern fringe state of Ch'u. He was attracted by Confucian Learning, and became an outstanding Confucian *shih* and *shih*-teacher in the northern "Middle Kingdom."[20]

You and your brother followed him for several decades. Your teacher died, and now you turn your back on him. Before, when Confucius died, after the three years [mourning] had passed, his followers . . . were going to return home. Going in to take leave of Tzu-kung [a leading disciple], they looked at each other and wailed till they all lost their voices. After this they returned home, but Tzu-kung went back and built himself a hut on the altar-ground, living alone for [another] three years before he returned home. . . .
Now there is this shrike-

Confucian teaching placed strong emphasis on respect for one's dead parents, shown by mourning rituals and by carrying on the ways of one's parents after they pass away. Mencius thinks the pupils of a *shih*-teacher owe their teacher the same kind of respect. He holds up the example of some of Confucius' followers, who when Confucius died carried out a period of mourning like that prescribed for sons mourning their fathers. He blames Ch'en Hsiang and his brother for not showing similar respect for their dead teacher.

tongued barbarian of the South,
who does not follow the *tao* of
the ancient kings—and you
turn your back on your teacher
and Learn from him.(3A/4)

Shih-teachers like Mencius belong to a social class which
includes many others, such as the *shih*-teacher Hsü Hsing whom
we meet here. He receives the same kind of recognition and support from a feudal lord that Mencius receives, even though it is
explicitly stated that the duke who supported him by giving him
a plot of land did not actually follow his rather utopian recom-
mendations. For all we know the same could be said of the reaction of most rulers to Mencius. Also like Mencius, *shih*-teachers
such as Hsü Hsing have followers who travel with them, live with
them, and receive the same support as they. These students are a
somewhat floating population, however. The students in one
group might go to listen to a different *shih*-teacher, and might
then be persuaded and change groups.

This story shows also that, although *shih*-teachers belong to
the same social class, they do not by any means all look upon
each other as allies. Many are rivals, teaching rival *tao*'s and promoting rival political programs.

One final observation here: much subsequent scholarship
about pre-Han China is excessively book-oriented. Scholars discuss
the few writings that have come down to us from this era as
though they collectively present to us the thinking that would
have been most familiar to all thoughtful men of the time; and
they tend to assume that the authors of these few books developed
their thinking primarily as reactions to the thought we find in
other books (Mohism and Taoism are "reactions against Confucianism," and so on.) There is, of course, some justification for this
approach. But, first, the few books that have come down to us from
this time probably represent a very tiny tip of the iceberg in relation to the thought of the very great number of *shih*-idealists and
shih-schools that existed in this period, like that of Hsü Hsing,
whom extant writings mention only in passing or do not mention
at all. Secondly, although some passages like the one above consist
of direct polemic against other *shih*-teachers, the bulk of material
in the *Mencius*, and in most pre-Han books, shows us thinkers
engaged more in devising practical solutions to practical problems
than in debating theoretical issues with other thinkers.

5

Mencius on Virtue

The discussions of Mencius' personal ideals and his social status and ambitions in Chapter 4 help us understand the central concerns and issues that determine the general structure of his worldview. This chapter will focus primarily on two long passages dealing more directly with the substantive content of his teaching, particularly his ideas about virtue. What I want to examine here is the way that Mencius' ideas about virtue relate to his worldview. Ultimately my purpose is to illuminate the formal structure of this worldview itself, as a helpful starting point for an inquiry into the formal structure of the Laoist worldview in Chapters 6 through 11.

Again a central thread in my discussions will be the contrast between Mencius' worldview, on the one hand, and doctrine-centered worldviews on the other (see p. 70–74). Both passages dealt with extensively in this chapter touch on an idea commonly considered one of Mencius' main "doctrines": that "virtue is natural," or "human nature is good." The following quote from A. C. Graham is a good representative example of this interpretive approach. Graham is commenting on Mencius' concept of *hsing*, the rough Chinese equivalent of our concept of "[human] nature":

> Chinese *hsing* and Western nature do have an important similarity, reinforced on the Chinese side by the assumption that *hsing* is generated by Heaven; they seem to function both as descriptive and prescriptive concepts. . . . *Hsing* is conceived as prescriptive, the course . . . *proper* to a thing . . . [its] *best* [state]. But the *hsing* of a thing is at the same time an observable fact about it, how it will be or become if there is no interference from outside. . . . We can establish man's *hsing* from observing how he develops when free from interference, and then appeal to it in defying current morality. We have the same apparent combination of factual and normative in the Western concept of nature, also a common weapon against traditional morality.[1]

Note the implicit depiction of Mencius here as a thinker concerned with the epistemological bases of moral norms. Like modern philosophers, he wants a basis for deciding on the content of moral norms that is superior to the basis on which traditional morality rests, and that will yield superior norms that contrast with traditional norms. Like them also, he thinks observable facts that can be neutrally described are epistemologically superior to directly prescriptive value judgments, and so provide the epistemological basis for defying conventional morality that one seeks. One could easily[2] take Graham's wording to imply that Mencius has drawn the logical conclusion from this train of thought: He has actually made serious and sustained efforts to "establish man's *hsing* from observing how he develops when free from interference," and has used these observations as the basis for developing new normative notions that contrast with current morality.

This is the kind of interpretation which results from approaching the *Mencius* with the assumption that Mencius is a doctrinal thinker in the modern mode, seeking objective epistemological bases for his thought, and using these as logical first principles from which to deduce normative doctrines. In the discussions below I want to convert this assumption from an *a priori* hermeneutical principle into a historical question. I will argue that a close reading of the *Mencius* itself reveals that the idea "virtue is natural," though it plays a central role, plays a role quite different from the one it plays in modern philosophy.

The Content of Mencius' Instruction to Kings

My first passage opens with a striking question: *Hsüan-wang/* "Hsüan-the-king" asks how he might *wang/*"become-King" *(wang* in the second occurrence used as a verb). *Wang* was once a title reserved for the Emperor, now taken over by some feudal lords, like Hsüan, lord of the feudal state of Ch'i (see p. 52). When King Hsüan asks Mencius how he might *wang/*"become King," he is voicing the ambition of many feudal lords: to reunite the entire Chinese empire under his rule as new Emperor. But for Mencius, *wang* refers primarily to a supreme level of *moral/spiritual* dignity, one whose personal qualities *fit* him to be the normative center of the Empire. I will use "King," capitalized, for this latter meaning. According to Mencius, the first concern of a king should be to cultivate this King-*quality* in himself, and express it in the policies of his government. Then through the power of his own moral character (his *te*), felt in his personal presence and in his policies, he will gain the willing allegiance of all in the empire, and "become king" of all China in actual fact as well. In Mencius' teaching, the primary quality which makes one King is the central Confucian virtue of *jen*, which I translate "Goodness."

Text	Comment

King Hsüan: What *te*/virtue must one have to be able become-King [*wang*]?

Mencius: Becoming King by nourishing and protecting the people—-this is something no one can prevent.

King Hsüan assumes that *te*/virtue is an important qualification for ruling, and he asks what it consists in.

King Hsüan: Is a man like me capable of nourishing and protecting the people?

Mencius: You are capable.

King Hsüan: How do you know? . . .

Mencius: [I heard this story:]

The king was sitting in the upper part of the hall and someone led an ox through the lower part. The king saw it and said, "Where is the ox going?" They replied, "We are going to consecrate a bell with its blood." The king said, "Let it go. I cannot bear its frightened appearance, like an innocent man going to the place of execution."

I wonder if this really happened?

King Hsüan: It happened.

Mencius: This *hsin*/feeling is enough to make you King. . . .

The king clearly understands "loving and protecting the people" in a very strong sense. It is a very high moral achievement and he doubts that he is capable of it. This question sets the agenda for the whole first part of the discussion. What Mencius is trying to show is that the king is indeed capable of the virtue Mencius requires of him. The first move in Mencius' argument is to bring up a case in which the king's spontaneous sympathy for an ox about to be killed was so great that he could not stand it. Modern philosophers sometimes appeal to similar "spontaneous goodness," but the import of such facts is different for them because their concern is different. They are asking foundational questions like "Why be good?," or "How do we know what is good?," and

Text

This is the way *jen*/Goodness works. . . . The attitude of a *chün tzu*/gentleman to animals is this: Once seeing them alive, he cannot bear to see them die. Having heard their cry, he cannot bear to eat their flesh. And so the gentleman avoids the slaughter-house and the kitchen. . . .

King Hsüan: It is said in the Book of Songs, "It is the mind of another man, but I who have read and measured it." These lines apply you. I acted a certain way, but turning inward [*fan*] and inquiring into it, I could not grasp my own *hsin*/feelings. When you, Master, spoke, it struck a chord. How is it that these feelings are sufficient to make someone King?

Mencius: Suppose someone says to the king, "I have enough strength to lift four hundred pounds, but not enough to lift one feather. . . . " Would the king accept this?
King Hsüan: No.

Comment

trying to appeal to "natural instincts" as a foundation for morality. Mencius' concern, and therefore his point in bringing up "natural sympathy," is completely different. His point is that anyone who can feel intense instinctive sympathy for an animal can surely feel it for people. The king cannot get off the hook by claiming that he is incapable of the virtue Mencius requires of him.

Here we see the important role of the *shih*-teacher: He is one who has cultivated a special sensitivity and discernment allowing him to detect the presence of virtue which untrained people like the king here do not perceive, even in themselves. The word *hsin* literally means "heart," but covers the meanings of the English word "mind" as well as "feelings," the meaning suggested by the context here. *Fan*/"turning back" refers here, as often elsewhere in the *Mencius*,[3] to introspective examination of one's state of mind and impulses.

Here Mencius states his main point: To claim that, although one can love an ox, one cannot love one's people, is like claiming one can lift a large weight, but not a feather.

Mencius: Now your kindness is sufficient to extend to animals, but its benefits do not reach the hundred clans.[4] How is this? . . . The king's not becoming-King: It is not that he *can*not do it. He *does* not do it. . . .

Treat your own elders as elders should be treated, so that others will treat their elders properly also. Treat your young people as young people should be treated, so that others will treat their young people properly. . . . Extending kindness will suffice to nourish and protect everyone within the four seas. . . .

Mencius: We take measurements so we can tell the long from the short . . . [and this is true also of the mind:] The king should take measurements on his mind. Gathering war equipment, endangering your *shih*/soldiers and officers, stirring up the resentment of other rulers—do these things bring satisfaction to your mind?
King Hsüan: No. How could I find satisfaction in these things? I am just going after what I desire most.
Mencius: Can I hear what it is the king desires most?

(The king smiles and does not say anything.) . . .

Here we see the common ancient Chinese idea that the ruler sets the tone by his personal conduct, and the *te*/influence of this will spread to all the people. (Another passage [3A/2,4] compares the ruler's influence on the people to the wind blowing on the grass: "When the wind blows, the grass bends.") If the king shows kindness to his family, the people will do this too, and this will ensure that everyone is nourished and protected.

Mencius refers here to king Hsüan's attempts to dominate the other states by force.

Introspective "taking measurements on your mind" for Mencius means discovering what brings one deep mental satisfaction. Here we see another role played by Mencius' idea that Goodness is something "natural": He tries to persuade the king to become Good and exhibit Goodness in his government, because this is something that will satisfy the king's deepest desires, both directly and as an indirect means of winning the allegiance of all, making Hsüan actual Emperor.

Text

Mencius: What the king desires most one can guess: To enlarge your territories, to have Ch'in and Ch'u paying homage at your court, to rule over the Middle Kingdom, to pacify the barbarians on all four sides. But what you are doing to go after what you desire is like climbing a tree to go after a fish. . . . [Mencius reminds the king that his state is about 1/9th the size of the entire empire. How does he expect to conquer a territory nine times the state that he rules?] Turn back to the root.

If the king institutes a government that practices *jen*/Goodness, it will bring about much: The officers of the whole world will all want to have positions in the king's court. The farmers will all want to farm the king's fields. The merchants will all want to store goods in the king's market-places. Travelers will all want to go on the king's roads. Everyone in the world who hates their rulers will want to lay their complaint before the king. And when things start going this way, who could stop them?

Comment

The large states of Ch'in and Ch'u were two of the main competitors of King Hsüan in his struggle for dominance. The "Middle Kingdom" is the Chinese empire, regarded as the Center of the World, surrounded by barbarians, whom it is the Emperor's job to keep "pacified."

"Turn back to the Root," a key phrase in the *Tao Te Ching* (see 28[16]), here seems to mean "return to the fundamentals," though it may have the added connotation in Mencius of turning inward to seek these fundamentals in yourself.

Here we see how practicing *jen*/Goodness is supposed to work. *Jen* being the highest thing there is, everyone "naturally" gravitates[5] toward it, and a king who embodies it will attract the voluntary loyalty and support of all ranks of people in all the states, thus making it a small step for him to take office as Emperor of all China. This is obviously an idealized picture, but it does reflect the necessity of those who sought power to woo supporters from all the lower ranks of society,[6] farmers, merchants, and *shih* (as court officials or advisers).

King Hsüan: I am stupid, and not able to see further beyond this point. I would like you, Master, to assist my *hsin*/mind. Make things clear and instruct me. Though I am not very smart, I will try to carry out what you say.

Mencius: To have a *heng*/steady mind without a steady livelihood——only a *shih* can do this. The people, if they have no steady livelihood, will have no steady mind either. If they lack steady minds there is nothing they will not do: looseness, perversity, viciousness—going completely wild. When they have become involved in crime, to follow them up and punish them—this is to entrap the people. How can entrapping the people be done when there is a Good man in office? And so the clear-sighted ruler, in regulating the material life of the people, must bring it about that, looking at those above, they have enough to care for their parents, and looking at those below, they have enough to support their wives and children. . . . If the king wants to practice this, then why not turn back to the root? Let mulberry-trees be planted in every homestead with five *mu* of land; then those who are fifty can wear

Here again we see the importance of the *shih*-adviser. Those like King Hsüan who wield supreme power are "stupid" when it comes to virtue. They need experts in virtue both to point out to them what virtuous impulses are like, and to explain to them the ways virtue ideally expresses itself in the conduct of government.

The ruler's *jen*/Goodness expresses itself in very concrete ways,[7] such as making sure that mulberry trees are planted (to

Text	Comment
silk. In keeping chickens, pigs, and dogs, let their breeding-times not be overlooked, and those who are seventy can eat meat. . . . When the aged wear silk and eat meat and the . . . people are neither hungry nor cold, it has never happened that [the ruler carrying out these programs] did not become King.(1A/7)	provide silk-worms for silken clothing), and making sure that domestic animals are not slaughtered during breeding season. These concrete acts carrying out *jen* can serve equally well as *jen* itself to describe the "root" which will make a ruler King.

This passage shows clearly Mencius' division of society into three basic groups, and the way his central concept of Goodness relates differently to each: (1) *Shih*-idealists are self-sustaining in their Goodness (they can remain steady in their Goodness without a steady livelihood), and, as experts in and exemplars of Goodness, they teach it to kings. (2) Top rulers who are not *shih* implement policies expressive of Goodness, as taught to them by *shih*. (3) Moral conduct, order, and harmony in the peasant society under the ruler's care is brought about indirectly by the way the rulers conduct their personal lives and their government. Goodness exhibited in both these areas attracts the allegiance of the people, sets a good example for them, and provides the material conditions under which alone the people can be expected to lead law-abiding lives and perform the duties that make for a prosperous and harmonious society.

One of the most interesting features of this passage is the way that it illustrates the framework within which Mencius's concept of *jen*/Goodness is worked out, *intrinsically* affecting the content of the concept itself. Most important is the fact that Mencius looks at everything very consciously and straightforwardly, not from a "universal" point of view, but from the point of view of his own class and its social mission as he conceives it. *Jen*, as he formulates it, is a very high ideal; it is formulated by an idealistic person who stands to a large degree outside of the political establishment, in circumstances more conducive to the development of moral idealism. But Mencius also makes his living by teaching those who are in positions of power and responsibility. So the *jen* he teaches is not the *jen* of monks or other perfectionist dropouts from society. Nor is it a universal ideal to be taught and practiced by all the people, or a normative basis for a legal code binding on all. It is not a general human *jen,* but a ruler's *jen.* It is not, however, *jen* as a king himself might formulate it, something impressive, majestic, divine. It is a *jen* conceived by a manager/administrator, one who knows that the best way to ensure order and harmony in a group is not directly, by imposition or inspiration, but indirectly, by providing the conditions which makes it easier for people to do what they should, and by acting in a way that attracts their willing allegiance and cooperation.

The story occurring early in this passage, about King Hsüan and the ox, is often cited as an illustration of Mencius' attempt to find a "foundation" for his virtue-ideals in some more objective observations about human nature. Mencius' implicit argument is construed to be: "Your spontaneous sympathy with the ox shows that it is part of your human nature to sympathize with suffering. Since it is part of your human nature, it is obligatory." But note, first, that the king's reluctance to follow Mencius' advice is not ascribed in the story to intellectual doubts about whether this is obligatory. He accepts the validity of this ideal, but expresses doubts about his own capacity. Mencius interprets this as moral laziness.

More importantly for our purposes, note the emphasis the story places on Mencius' special personal sensitivity to the implicit presence of virtue in the king's response, a sensitivity that the "stupid" king lacked. Mencius' ideas about "natural virtue" are intrinsically related to his political ideal, involving the key role of the *shih*-idealist. "Natural virtue" is not something that happens by itself if people are left alone. Kings cannot even recognize their own "natural" virtue, much less practice it, without the guidance of *shih* who have become experts in virtue through assiduous self-cultivation.

This point is suggested again by the juxtaposition of two stories in Book 6 of the *Mencius,* worth quoting here. The first story is again one that is frequently quoted as an illustration of Mencius' moral epistemology, his idea that we can discover the nature of virtue objectively, by observing how people act when their nature is not interfered with.

The trees of Niu mountain were once beautiful . . . but they were cut down with axes. . . . Through the nourishing influence of rain and dew, they were not without buds and sprouts springing forth, but then came the cattle and goats and browsed upon them. This is the cause of their bare and stripped appearance. When people see it, they think it was never finely wooded. But is this the *hsing*/nature of the mountain? . . . The way in which a man loses his proper goodness of mind is like the way in which the trees are denuded by axes. (6A/8)

But this story is immediately followed by another, showing the value-laden and partisan character of Mencius' idea of "natural virtue," and the necessity of his own personal influence as a virtuous *shih*, for bringing out this virtue in a king.

It is no wonder that the king is not wise. Suppose you have something that is the easiest thing in the world to grow. If it has one day of warming, then ten days of freezing, it will not be able to grow. *I see the king only seldom.* When I am away, those who "freeze" him come. Although I bring out some buds, what good is it? (6A/9, emphasis added)

The juxtaposition of the passages implies that the influence of other advisers is like the bad influences (of human axes or "natural" weather) that destroy vegetation. The king's *good* "nature" will only thrive under the influence of Mencius' particular virtue-ideals, conveyed in personal audiences with Mencius himself.

Self-Cultivation

My next passage[8] concerns what Mencius calls "self cultivation."[9] This is the moral and spiritual character-formation that constitutes a large part of what Mencius teaches to his *shih*-pupils.

It is important to notice the very practical issue with which this passage begins, and which determines the agenda throughout. We noticed already in the above passage (p. 101) Mencius' idea that "only a *shih* can have a steady mind without a steady livelihood." That is, one of the things *shih*-idealists are intensely concerned about and pride themselves on is their ability to uphold their moral integrity in the face of difficult circumstances, including especially the pressures to moral compromise that anyone faces who aspires to a career in politics (see 3B/2,3, quoted p. 76). In this passage the dialogue begins with a question from one of Mencius' pupils as to whether he could maintain a *pu-tung hsin*/"non-agitated mind" if he were to gain high political office. The first part of Mencius' reply, bringing up examples of people able to stand up unflinchingly against intimidation, shows that he understands the question to be not only about overcoming mental anxiety generally, but specifically about achieving mental steadiness in the face of pressures to moral compromise. (*Pu-tung hsin* can describe a mind that remains "unmoved" by pressures to moral compromise, or a mind that is not psychologically "agitated" by anxiety or excitement. These two meanings are closely connected in Mencius' ideal. I translate "non-agitated" throughout, but the moral meaning seems predominant in the first part of the dialogue, 2A/2,1–8; the psychological meaning is especially evident in 2A/2,10.) This question which begins the dialogue is also brought up again toward the end, in a way that shows it is crucial to the main point Mencius is making. That is, when he is asked about the advantages of his self-cultivation practice over against that of another *shih*-teacher, Kao Tzu, his argument against Kao (2A/2,9–10) largely has to do with the fact that his way is superior in overcoming mental agitation.

Text

Kung-sun Ch'ou: If you were appointed . . . prime minister of [the feudal state] Ch'i, . . . would [this cause you to have] an agitated mind? . . .
Mencius: No. I achieved a non-agitated mind when I was forty. . . . It is not that difficult. Kao Tzu attained a non-agitated mind even earlier.
Ch'ou: A non-agitated mind— is there a *tao*/way for this?"

Comment

The fact that it might take one many years to attain a "non-agitated" state of mind makes it clear that a quite extraordinary state is envisaged here. It seems also implied that once one has achieved this special state it becomes permanent. Mencius has a special method [*tao*] of achieving this state.

Text

Mencius: "There is. [For example] Po-kung Yu nourished his courage [this way:] He did not flinch from blows at his body; he never turned his eyes away [from them]. . . . [He would not stand for the least personal slight, from commoner or nobleman. He was not afraid even of stabbing a nobleman.] Meng Shih-she nourished his courage [another way:] He said,

> To attack only after calculating [one's chances of] victory—this is to stand in awe of the enemy's army. How will I ever be able to make sure of victory? The only thing I am able to do is to have no fear. . . .

I do not know who is more *hsien*/worthy, but Meng Shih-she watched over [*shou*][10] the more important thing. Tsengtzu once said, . . .

> I heard this about great courage from the Master [Confucius]: "If I turn back [*fan*] into myself and find myself not upright, shall I not fear even a poor man in shabby clothes? If I find myself upright, I will go forward against 10,000 men."

Meng shih watched over his *ch'i*/feelings. This cannot compare to the important thing

Comment

Mencius brings up the examples of two other *shih* to compare himself with. These *shih* are professional soldiers, but note that they pride themselves on more than their military skill. They too engage in a kind of "self-cultivation," indicated by such phrases as "nourishing courage," and *shou ch'i*/"watching over *ch'i*". The aim of this self-cultivation is to give one a steadfastness that not only makes for bravery in battle, but allows one a kind of fierce independence, yielding to none in social life as well. Note again the strong psychological, even physical, dimension to the "courage" that Po-kung Yu "nourishes." It is something he gains by practicing so as not to flinch when someone swings at him. Mencius expresses some disapproval of this emphasis on physical bravado, speaking of it as inferior to Meng Shih-she's internal detachment, and even more to the Confucian Tsengtzu's courage springing from "uprightness." He wants to emphasize the strong ethical dimension of his ideal state of mind: Consciousness that one is upright is the most effective means of gaining a "non-agitated mind." But it is important also to keep in mind the continuity between Mencius and Po-kung Yu. Both men reflect a

Tseng Tzu watched over. (2A/2,1–6)

concern of many *shih* to cultivate a source of inner strength that will allow them to maintain their personal independence even when faced with others more powerful than they. And for both this inner strength has a very strong psychological dimension.

The remainder of this passage has to do with Mencius' version of the contrast between himself and another *shih*-teacher, Kao Tzu. It needs further introduction, since two of the key Chinese terms used in the discussion, *hsin* and *ch'i*, have no exact English equivalents and need some preliminary clarification. *Hsin* literally means "heart," but it is the seat of thinking as well as of feeling. *Ch'i*, used already above, is somewhat more bodily than *hsin*, and can encompass internal self-perceptions ranging from what we would call "feelings" to more physiological sensations we might call "bodily energy."[11]

In addition, some of the statements made at the beginning of the discussion are only clarified by what is said later. The key ideas are these:

In the very last section of the discussion Mencius describes the difference between himself and Kao in very practical and experiential terms: The kind of self-cultivation Kao practices, Mencius says, involves imposing moral *i*/Rightness on one's being by will power. (He describes this as the *hsin*/mind "*pao*/manhandling the *ch'i*.") This leads to a feeling of "starvation," by which Mencius means that the mind experiences no concrete sense of satisfaction in this Rightness (2A/2,15-16). The kind of self-cultivation Mencius advocates instead is one in which one's *ch'i*, one's spontaneous impulses and feelings, are internally "nourished" by Rightness, so that Rightness becomes part of them and does not have to be imposed from without. This can only happen by nourishing one's *ch'i* with Rightness gradually, over a long period of time. This contrasts with a sudden "seizing by surprise attack" (2A/2,15), a metaphor he uses to describe the opposite procedure implicitly ascribed to Kao here.

It is in this context that we must understand Mencius' statement that, "Kao does not understand *i*/Rightness, since he thinks of it as something external." That is, we must not rush here to read "external" in the context of our own division "nature" vs. "culture," or "individual" vs. "society." Kao "thinks of Rightness as external" in the sense that in his ideal the individual's own *hsin*/mind imposes Rightness by force on this same individual's *ch'i*/feelings (2A/2,9). Note also the implication that the content of the Rightness one cultivates is intrinsically bound up with the way one cultivates it. A Rightness imposed by will power is a different Rightness than a Rightness informing one's instinctive feelings from within. Kao does not understand what *true* Rightness is—understands it to be something different from what Mencius understands it to be—because he thinks of it as something external, imposed on the *ch'i* from without (2A/2,15).

It is with these considerations in mind that we can discuss, finally, two rather problematic statements that occur earlier in the dialogue: Mencius begins his first answer to the question about how he and Kao differ with a rather enigmatic quotation he attributes to Kao:

What cannot be gotten from word(s), do not look for in the *hsin*/mind.
What cannot be gotten from the mind, do not look for in the *ch'i* (2A/2,9).

Later in this passage (2A/2,11), when the pupil asks Mencius about what it is specifically that makes Mencius outstanding in self-cultivation, he replies, "I understand words. I am good at nourishing my ... *ch'i*." The suggested connection between "understanding words" and "nourishing *ch'i*" again makes this saying somewhat enigmatic. A partial clue to what "understanding words" means is given later in the chapter when a pupil asks him what he means by "understanding words." Mencius replies that he can perceive the state of a person's *hsin*/mind by the way that person talks (2A/2,17).

Taking all the above into consideration, what I suggest is this: Mencius' main point about Kao is that Kao sees no intrinsic connection between ideas and words, on the one hand, and feelings on the other. When a person speaks, or when he has ideas, the entire meaning of his words can be understood on a purely intellectual level, with no reference at all to the person's concrete feelings or mental state. Mencius, on the other hand, denies that one can understand words without relating them to feelings; and he also attributes his own special ability to "understand words" to the fact that he is "good at nourishing *ch'i*." Both these facts are explained because for Mencius, nourishing *ch'i*/feelings requires a double sensitivity: On the one hand, one must be able to understand the feeling-content of words, how the content of words relates to feeling-states. And on the other hand, one must develop a subtle sensitivity to the character of the various feelings a person can have, particularly to the moral dimension of feelings, the way in which various feelings might be said to be imbued or not imbued with virtue. This latter is the kind of skill that Mencius exhibited when he was able to understand King Hsüan's mind better than the King himself could, in the story quoted above (1A/7,9, p. 98).

With all this in mind, we can now resume the dialogue:

Text	*Comment*
Ch'ou: I venture to ask about the master's non-agitated mind, and [its relation to] Kao tzu's non-agitated mind. Can I hear about this? **Mencius:** Kao says,	Note that the pupil Ch'ou brings up again the very concrete problem with which the passage began. He wants to know how Mencius and Kao differ on the issue of the *pu-tung hsin*/"non-agitated mind" which many *shih* strive to cultivate.
What cannot be gotten from word(s), do not look for in the *hsin*/mind.	
What cannot be gotten from the mind, do not look for in the *ch'i*.	
"What cannot be gotten from the *hsin*/mind, do not look for in the *ch'i*." This is alright. "What cannot be gotten from word(s), do not look for in the *hsin*/mind." This is not alright.	Mencius seems to hold that the *hsin*/mind has a moral dimension that *ch'i*, taken by itself, lacks. But *hsin* is more than intellect, with which one could grasp the abstract meaning of words. As we saw in the earlier passage, *hsin* referred to the what we would call the "feelings" of compassion King Hsüan felt for the ox. What Mencius is saying here is that one can only "get" the mean-

Text   *Comment*

ing of words, especially virtue-
words, by understanding their
connection with certain states
of the *hsin*/mind.

The *chih*/will is the *ch'i's* leader.
Ch'i pervades the body. The will
is superior; *ch'i* is subordinate.
So it is said, "Restrain the will,
Do not manhandle the *ch'i*."
Ch'ou: Since you say, "The
mind is superior, the *ch'i* is subordinate," how can you also
say, "Restrain the mind, do not
manhandle the *ch'i*"?

As Legge mentions,[12] *chih*/will
here is more or less synonymous
with *hsin*/mind. The *chih*/will
has a more "spiritual" side,
whereas *ch'i* is more connected
with the physical ("pervading
the body"). Thus the will needs
to guide the *ch'i*. But Mencius'
emphasis on concrete embodi-
ment is developed further when
he says that one must restrain
the tendency of the will to want
to simply impose ideals on the

Mencius: If the *chih*/will alone
[dominates], then it agitates
the *ch'i*. If the *ch'i* alone [domi-
nates], then it agitates the
mind. When stumbling or
rushing, this is *ch'i* [that one
feels]. [This] *ch'i* in turn agitates the mind.

bodily impulses, "manhan-
dling" them by force as it were.[13]
Mencius' objection to Kao's view
is a practical one: Self-cultivation is supposed to bring one a
"non-agitated mind," but when
the mind tries to dominate the
ch'i by will power, this *causes*
more agitation. Of course, it is
also true that *ch'i*, uncultivated,
can agitate the mind as well.
Note Mencius' identification of
ch'i with the quasi-physical
inner turmoil one feels when
stumbling or rushing.

Ch'ou: I venture to ask how
you, Master, are a leader [in
this area].
Mencius: I understand words.
I am good at nourishing my
oceanlike *ch'i*.

We really have here a second
use of *ch'i*. *Ch'i* has a neutral
sense, in which it can refer to
any bodily feelings, such as the
bodily turmoil one feels when
one is stumbling. But then

Ch'ou: I venture to ask what you mean by "oceanlike *ch'i*." **Mencius:** It is difficult to describe:

There is *ch'i*, something exceedingly great, exceedingly strong. If uprightness nourishes it and no harm is done to it, then it completely fills up the space between heaven and earth. There is *ch'i*, an equal partner with *i*/Rightness and *tao*. Without it there is starvation. [A gradual] accumulation is what produces Rightness [i.e., Rightness-imbued *ch'i*]. You cannot "seize it by surprise attack." If the practice [of it] brings no satisfaction to the mind, then there is "starvation." And so I say, Kao does not understand Rightness, since he thinks of it as something external.

We must be in service to it [*ch'i*], without trying to impose correctness [*cheng*] on it. Let the mind not neglect it, but also not try to "help it grow." Not like the man from Sung:

A man from Sung was worried that his young plants

there is *ideal ch'i*, which Mencius claims to have developed in himself by nourishing his ordinary *ch'i* with uprightness. This ideal *ch'i* has a "cosmic" character, it is "oceanlike" and "fills up the space between heaven and earth."[14]

Here we have another practical objection to Kao's self-cultivation practice. If one's Rightness remains a purely intellectual "conviction," it remains abstract. It does not bring the *concretely felt* satisfaction one gets from good qualities thoroughly internalized even down to the level of physical impulses. This feels like a kind of "starvation." Stories in the *Mencius* would suggest that one "accumulates" this special Rightness-imbued *ch'i* simply by upholding one's commitment to it, repeatedly standing up for what is Right in everyday situations. Still, the end result Mencius aims at is not a state in which one is holding oneself to Rightness by will power ("manhandling the *ch'i*"), but one in which it has become a habit, governing one's instinctive reactions.

Some people ignore their *ch'i*/feelings, and they just grow wild. Others try to force them along some pattern or another. To try to force the *ch'i*

Text

Comment

were not growing taller, so he began pulling at them. He returned home all tired out, and said to his family, "I am so worn out today. I have been helping the plants grow." His sons ran to look at them, and found the plants all withered up.

There are few in the world who do not "help the plants grow." Sometimes we think there is no benefit [to *ch'i*], and neglect it; we do not "weed the plants." Sometimes we "help them grow" and "pull the plants out." Not only do we produce no benefit, we do harm.(2A/2,1–16)

to be one way or another by will power (as Kao does), is to act like the man from Sung who tried to make corn grow by pulling on it. This is "harming" the *ch'i*, and produces no benefit of real worth.

Conclusion: The Mencian Shih *vs. the Modern Philosopher*

Philosophically minded interpreters approach the *Mencius* asking, "What doctrines does it teach?" Implicitly or explicitly, they take the project of modern philosophy as an overall framework within which to situate the thought of Mencius. This approach misconstrues the thought of the *Mencius* by taking the *Mencius* apart into separate elements, and reassembling these elements within a structure derived from elsewhere. It fails in the chief task of hermeneutics, which is to try to grasp the other in his otherness (see p. 10). It allows that Mencius might have specific *ideas* that are "other," different from the *ideas* of modern philosophers. It precludes *a priori* allowing Mencius to be an "other" to the philosophical project itself. But this is the area in which philosophers have most to learn from the *Mencius*: critical reflection on the project and social role of philosophizing itself, as compared with the project in which Mencius is engaged.

Tao Te Ching interpretation has suffered from this same tendency, and interpreting the *Mencius* and the *Tao Te Ching* within a philosophical structure has obscured the structural similarities in the thought of these two Chinese classics. I would like to close this discussion of the *Mencius* by comparing and contrasting the structure of Mencius overall worldview with the structure of the worldview of Western Enlightenment philosophy. I choose the Enlightenment because this founding period for modern philosophy was the period in which philosophers gave explicit attention to the distinctive personal ideals and social vision that differentiated philosophers and their followers from their more traditionally minded contemporaries. These personal ideals and social vision are what initially motivated many of the distinctive features of modern philosophy as an intellectual endeavor. And in varying degrees and in varying versions, they still seem to form the implicit background for much philosophical thought today, when this has not become a purely professional activity cut off from any concrete personal or social purpose.

Enlightenment Philosophy	*Mencius*
The personal ideal of the philosopher is an ideal valid for all.[15]	*Mencius' personal ideal* centers on *shih*, and does not apply directly to others.
Autonomy is legitimated through superior rational knowledge. The fact that one's ideas have been arrived at through impartial quest for the truth is the basis for standing up against social convention and entrenched traditions.	Autonomy is legitimated through actual possession of virtue, gained in sustained self-cultivation and verified through self-critical introspection. One's own concrete virtue gives one internal sustenance allowing one to keep one's integrity and stand up against pressures to compromise.
Moral consistency is achieved through adherence to a fixed set of moral principles.	Moral consistency is mainly a psychological issue, becoming internally "steady" through complete internalization of virtue, informing one's sponta-
Intellectual learning and theo-	

Enlightenment Philosophy

rizing is the key activity for which one needs leisure time free of practical concerns.

Intellectual belief in a system of universally valid truths, logically deduced from purely objective foundations, replaces "subjective," emotionally tinged, "culturally conditioned" impressions of the *Lebenswelt*. "Knowing the truth" consists in having a verified set of intellectual beliefs about the world.

The principal focus is on morally correct external actions, logically deduced from moral principles.

Social vision: The "Empire of Reason."

In the realm of social leadership, the aspiration of the ideal philosopher is that in rational debate his *ideas* should be recognized as the most well-founded, and become widely accepted as social norms in this way.

Mencius

neous impulses. Self-cultivation, not intellectual thought, is the key activity for which one needs leisure time free of practical concerns.

Mencius engages in piecemeal criticism of particular conventional ideas. But he makes no *radical* attempt to replace culturally conditioned normative perceptions of the *Lebenswelt* with intellectual beliefs in doctrines derived independently of the *Lebenswelt*. Improvement in moral understanding takes place chiefly through refinement of moral sensitivity gained in introspective self-cultivation. This results in better perceptions, not better beliefs.

The principal focus is on internal virtue, which when internalized automatically expresses itself in good conduct, without logical mediation.

Social vision: Paternalistic government under the spiritual leadership of virtuous *shih*.

The aspiration of the ideal *shih* is that rulers and other *shih* should recognize him as someone who has deeply internalized high moral ideals. Because of this he will gain widespread personal influence, and become in effect spiritual leader of China.

Social life is informed by moral values (1) by universal education transforming all into rationally autonomous persons;[16] (2) by allowing free rational discussion in a free press, which will lead all to grasp and assent to a single set of universally valid moral norms transcending cultural particularity, and (3) by deducing from universal rational principles the nature of the ideal society, its constitution, laws, and institutions.

Social life is informed by moral values through the personal influence wielded by virtuous *shih* both as administrators and as advisers. *Shih* regard as simply given the basic hierarchical structure of Chou-dynasty feudalism, although they do try to carve out an expanded role for themselves within this basic structure. Top rulers, inferior to *shih* in virtue, are instructed by them as to what governing by virtue would mean in any given circumstance. By following their advice, top rulers both set a high moral tone for the society, and provide the material conditions under which alone the masses of the people can be expected to act in a morally upright way.

"Human nature" serves for some philosophers as an epistemological foundation for morality, because (1) human nature is universal, transcending cultural particularity, and (2) one can learn about human nature in a "scientific" way, through neutral observation free of value judgments.

"Human nature" plays an important role in Mencius' thought, but it is in no sense an epistemological foundation from which he deduces the content of his moral ideals. (1) "Nature" is not contrasted with Chinese culture, and the actual content of his moral ideals derives largely from the latter. (2) He makes no attempt to base his ideas about human nature on neutral observation free of value judgments (much less neutral observations about non-Chinese "human nature"). Mencius is not opposed to all civilization as such, nor to traditional Chinese culture in particular. He is

For some thinkers, widespread alienation from established social norms gave rise to the idea that *all* human civilization as such is basically corruptive of human nature, which is perfectly good and pure in its original "uncivilized" state.

115

Enlightenment Philosophy

Mencius

What is most important to the
rationally autonomous philosopher is the *correct content* of
one's ideas about what belongs
to human nature. Whether and
to what extent people's present
spontaneous impulses are in
accord with what is truly "natural," in this sense, is a matter of
indifference. If following actual
("socially corrupted") impulses
would lead to conduct at odds
with the "natural" norms one
has discovered and intellectually believes in, the proper course
is to use education, will power,
or legal coercion to bring
human actions into accord
with these natural norms.

opposed to character formation
that relies on intellectual conviction and will power, and to
social organization that relies on
external coercion. In contrast,
he emphasizes the important
role of already existing spontaneous impulses toward goodness: Psychologically speaking,
virtue will be more thoroughly
internalized and "steady" if cultivating virtue consists in "nourishing" those spontaneous good
tendencies that already exist;
and politically speaking, it is better to rely on people's spontaneous attraction to goodness in
a ruler, than to try to coerce
their cooperation and allegiance. In addition, his political
ideal requires that government
be informed by a high level of
virtue beyond the reach of most
top rulers. Therefore, to counter
their possible rejection of his
political ideal on these grounds,
he insists that the virtue he
speaks of is something already
incipiently present in them
(though it still requires a virtuous *shih* to detect and direct it.)
His point in all these instances is
valid if the spontaneous impulses he appeals to already exist in
most contemporary Chinese. It
is a matter of indifference
whether or not these now spontaneous impulses were originally
formed by specifically Chinese
social conditioning.

Typically, modern philosophically oriented interpreters look at the *Mencius* from within the framework of ideals that have come to be taken for granted in modern philosophy. From this point of view a great deal of material in the *Mencius* appears either unimportant or negative. It is hard not to notice Mencius' ethnocentricity, his failure, except on a few occasions, to transcend cultural particularity to get to universal truths. He is embarrassingly arrogant and self-assertive, placing much more emphasis on his own person than on ideas, as a good philosopher would do. He is elitist, offending the modern egalitarian sense that "one standard fits all." He is inconsistent in the reasons he gives for his actions on different occasions. He accepts too uncritically the political institutions of his time, rather than asking himself what a state truly founded on reason would look like. And so on.

But if, instead of seeing Mencius as a modern philosopher *manquè*, we set his vision side by side with the vision that animated early modern philosophy, we can readily see that Mencius' vision has some important strengths, worth considering today when we have become more aware of the weaknesses of the personal ideal and social vision underlying philosophy as a project. Consider, for example, the interesting ideas that Mencius has to offer on two concrete problems that perennially occur in most societies: (1) The problem facing individuals whose idealism makes them regard conventional social norms as inadequate: How concretely should they relate to the larger society? (2) The question as to the concrete vehicles through which the moral foundations of a society will actually inform public life.

Mencius' answer to the first question is that idealistic individuals ought first to work hard at internalizing their ideals so they become second nature and a concrete source of internal sustenance to substitute for the social support on which they cannot depend. Then they ought to devote themselves to improving the moral state of their society. In doing so, they should not assume that the values most important to them personally are necessarily the ones that should dominate social life for all.[17] They should take into account the actual proclivities and possibilities open to those who have not chosen the kind of life they themselves have. They should normally work in government service. But they should also assume that most of those who hold power in government are at a rather low level morally, and they must know when it is better to compromise to work within the system and when it is better to withdraw and store up spiritual energy for a better time.

Mencius' answer to the second question is that virtuous people in positions of public responsibility (not laws or universal education) are the main vehicles through which moral values ought to influence public life. This should be reflected in a social institution: There should be schools that prepare people for government service. The principal focus of these schools ought to be practical character formation according to very high ideals and the development of ideas about which public policies will, on a pragmatic level, actually result in improving society as a moral environment.

Mencius and the Tao Te Ching

The preceding discussions of Mencius and Warring States *shih* do not by themselves prove anything about the thought structure of the *Tao Te Ching*. But they give us a model culturally close to the *Tao Te Ching*, and hence a point of comparison more adequate than others (such as philosophy) for raising the question about the context and formal structure of its thought. I will end this Part Two by presenting in summary form my main arguments for seeing the *Tao Te Ching* as the product of a Warring States *shih* school and understanding it against the background of a set of concerns, ambitions, and assumptions formally similar to those we see in the *Mencius*. By "formally similar" I mean that, abstracting from the content of Mencius' particular teaching and values, Laoism shares with Mencius most of the characteristics listed in the right hand column of the chart on p. 113–117. It shares with Mencian thought the same contrasts with the formal structure of the worldview implicit in most modern philosophical thought, described in the left hand column. For example, although Laoist *shih* did not cultivate Mencian "virtue," they did cultivate a particular state of mind, and this state of mind plays the same role in the overall Laoist vision as virtue plays in Mencius' vision. It was a source of personal inner sustenance. And it was connected to political practice via the same expressive view of politics we saw in the *Mencius*: Good leadership can be defined for Laoists as that kind of leadership expressive of the ideal state of mind that Laoists cultivated. Although the Laoist vision is motivated by different values than that of Mencius, their basic practical concerns and the formal structure of their worldviews are similar.

I outline my arguments for this parallelism in summary form

here. Many of these arguments will be developed in more detail in the essays to come or in the commentary.

1. In pre-Han China, it had not yet become the custom for individual authors to write books for circulation to the general public (see p. 303). The story that the *Tao Te Ching* itself was written by the sage Lao Tzu rests on completely unreliable legend (see p. 301–02). Hence the *existence* of the *Tao Te Ching* is a piece of historical evidence requiring explanation. What caused the material in the book to be initially preserved? For what purpose and for whom was it initially written? The analyses in Chapters 6 to 12 and in the commentary will point to indications that the *Tao Te Ching* consists mainly of sayings from a relatively homogeneous oral tradition. The sayings have now been artfully combined into brief "sayings-collages" (our eighty one "chapters"), by persons whose thought is not substantially different from the thought expressed in the body of sayings themselves. Much in the book would have been difficult to understand for the general public, and the composers of the book show no concern to provide introductions or explanations to ease this difficulty. In the context of what we know about conditions in the late Warring States period, the most obvious hypothesis that explains this state of affairs is that the sayings in the *Tao Te Ching* are drawn from the oral tradition of a *shih*-school. The sayings-collages were composed by members in this school primarily for use by other members of the school, who would have shared the assumptions and understandings necessary to render the collages intelligible and persuasive. An origin in a *shih*-school best explains the existence and general character of the *Tao Te Ching*.

2. There are quite a few direct allusions in the *Tao Te Ching* itself to teachers, to the activity of teaching, and to relations between teachers and students. See the last six Chapters in Section 4 of the translation and commentary, especially chapter 49[27]. This adds further support to the preceding observations about the *Tao Te Ching*'s probable origin in a *shih* school.

3. Warring States *shih* had a specific and somewhat unique combination of interests, and this combination is reflected in many different ways in the sayings we find in the *Tao Te Ching*.

- *Shih* aspired to implement the strong sense of social responsibility they felt by reforming the conduct of contemporary rulers. We find plentiful advice in the *Tao Te Ching* showing how Laoist values would ideally express themselves in the conduct of rulers. (Almost all the chapters in Sections 5 through 7 of the translation are very obviously advice to someone in a position of authority.) The phrase "one who assists rulers with Tao" in 69[30]:1 indicates that this saying is addressed specifically to one who is acting in the advisory role of *shih*. Advice to rulers includes sharp criticism of those who use their power for their own benefit and oppress the people[18] a traditional theme among Chou dynasty moral advisers, whose role the *shih* appropriated. But despite the critical tone often taken toward those in power, the *Tao Te Ching* does not advocate rebellion or structural reform. Like the *Mencius* it assumes the validity of Chou feudal structures, and it even goes out of its way to affirm the status of the king as one of the pillars of the cosmic order (35[39]:1; 39[25]:4).
- *Shih* also aspired to become government officials themselves. One chapter of the *Tao Te Ching* (18[13]) addresses an audience concerned with the disadvantages as well as the advantages of holding high office, assuming they have some choice. Many sayings assume that accomplishing great *kung*/acheivements:merit is a positive goal.[19] Much of the advice directed at leaders could apply both to top leaders and to *shih* managers and administrators, as for example the advice to "take on the state's misfortunes" (75[78]:4), to "put it in order when it is not yet disordered" 72[64]:2, and to "achieve successes, win the fame, [then] remove yourself" (2[9]:2). Many sayings address an audience with great leadership ambitions, aspiring to "manage things" (37[14]:5), to have the "power to *yung*/manage people" (57[68]:2), to "preside" (27[10]:2), to maintain *chün*/mastery (23[26]:3, to "become leader" (4[22]:5), to "become head of a government" (3[67]:2), to gain the allegiance of all in the empire (46[35]:1), to "possess the state" (26[59]:2), and to "take over the world" (25[48]:3,4, 77[57]:1).
- Sayings in the *Tao Te Ching* that do not address leaders as such still address issues more characteristic of upper class life than the life of the common people. Most notable here

are criticisms of luxury and overstimulation,[20] the desire for fame and wealth,[21] lavish display,[22] and competition over social status.[23] Notably missing are sayings addressing the usual issues of primary concern to people not in leadership positions: cooperation and lack of cooperation with peers; stealing, lying, and cheating; how to deal with hardships; sexual issues; family relationships; how inferiors should deal with those in authority; popular religion; and so on. Concern about "the people" in the *Tao Te Ching* extends only to a concern for their physical well being and a concern to maintain an orderly and harmonious social environment. There is no concern for their inner life (this is especially evident in Section 7 of the translation.) This is in accord with the disjunction we saw in the *Mencius* (p. 102), between what is expected of *shih* in terms of personal virtue and what is expected of the people.

   4. Self cultivation plays an even larger role in the *Tao Te Ching* than it does in the *Mencius*, but it is associated with a similar complex of ideas, and serves the same two basic functions.

• First, even more than the *Mencius*, the *Tao Te Ching* reflects the perspective of people disillusioned with conventional signs of success as a measure of true worth, and hence people seeking a means of inner sustenance. This is the first role which self-cultivation plays in both books. Chapter 13[20] of the *Tao Te Ching* especially reflects both a feeling of alienation and the inner sustenance one finds in the hypostatized quality of mind one cultivates, here called "the nourishing Mother." Chapter 14[23] speaks of the Tao one cultivates as an inner presence "welcoming" the person devoted to it, and 44[41]:4 speaks of Tao as "supporting" such a person. Finally, the many sayings in the *Tao Te Ching* promising that self-cultivation will enable one to "last long" probably reflect a concern for an inner psychological sense of security, similar to Mencius's quest for a "non-agitated mind."[24]
• Secondly, also as in the *Mencius*, self-cultivation practice is intrinsically linked to the practice of government through an expressive theory of politics: Ideal government is defined as that government expressive of an ideal state of mind existing in the ruler. Some passages in the *Tao Te*

Ching speak of cultivating certain qualities of mind such as Softness, Femininity, Tao, and Te, while other passages speak of the way these same qualities express themselves in a certain style of governing; the ruler whose policies and style of governing express these qualities sets the right tone for the society.[25] One advanced in self-cultivation has inherited the spiritual role of Emperor, and has become in his person the symbolic "Pattern for the World" (17[28]:1). Like Mencius, Laoists are optimistic that the people will spontaneously recognize this and "naturally" give such a leader their allegiance and cooperation (55[66]:1, and see p. 100, n. 5) making him, or the one he advises, the new Emperor. (See further p. 537 under Emperor*.)

Part III

Verbal Form and the Structure of
Laoist Thought

Introduction

For a historical hermeneutics—a hermeneutics intent on recovering original meaning—the *Tao Te Ching* is the epitome of a difficult text. Its origins are shrouded in obscurity. The text itself gives no direct indications of the historical contexts to which its sayings apply. Above all, the form of the text—short strings of loosely connected sayings—makes it possible to organize its ideas in any number of different ways, giving rise to any number of different readings.

Approaching this text historically means approaching it wanting to let one's engagement with the text be controlled by historical evidence rather than one's own modern context and personal concerns. But in this case history and the text seem loath to exercise such control. It might almost be supposed that someone has deliberately arranged the text and the circumstances so as to frustrate the historical interpreter, to invite and even demand a "scriptural" approach (see p. 6): either a naive approach in which the reader ignores questions about original meaning and relates each saying to her own life in whatever way is most meaningful; or a more scholarly approach in which the assumed goal is to extract from the text a set of philosophical doctrines answering the kind of questions that modern philosophers customarily ask. The latter approach is also fostered by a still lingering traditional distinction between content and form. The substantive content of any given writing is something that can be stated straightforwardly as literal claims about objective truths. If the text itself does not consist of straightforward literal speech, this is due to its "style," something added on to substantive content as a kind of ornament or rhetorical aid. Interpreting a text philosophically means ignoring style and extracting from the text a doctrinal paraphrase that is the essential "meaning of the text."

The argument in Part Three will be that the *Tao Te Ching* is not an intrinsically vague book. It had a definite meaning for its original audience. Its verbal form is intrinsically related to its substantive meaning. Our primary goal should not be to extract a paraphrase that represents its essential meaning, but to become competent to understand *these* words as they were originally understood (see p. 38). Further, epistemologically, careful attention to verbal form gives us the principal clues we need to reconstruct the nature of the required competence. There are two principal, interrelated facets to the kind of inquiry needed. One is a study of the way verbal form is related to semantic structure. The second is the way verbal form is related to concrete life context. The semantic structure of various kinds of statements will be discussed in detail in Chapters 6 through 10. The relation of verbal form to concrete life context is the subject matter of a discipline developed in biblical studies called "form-criticism," which requires further comments here.

Form-criticism was developed in biblical studies to address problems posed by several biblical books, similar to those posed by the *Tao Te Ching*. Form-criticism supposes (1) that anomalies in some ancient books can be explained by the fact that they are not the work of a single author, but have incorporated substantial amounts of material from oral tradition; (2) that the original oral setting has left traces in the verbal form of this material, traces that can help us reconstruct the oral settings; (3) that the original meaning of the oral material can be reconstructed by understanding it in relation to the original life setting (*Sitz-im-Leben*) so constructed.

Simply put, what this means for *Tao Te Ching* interpretation is that, if form-criticism is appropriate, the definite *literary* setting conspicuously lacking in this book can be supplied by concrete *life* setting. A proper modern book presents us with a set of ideas very explicitly organized into a structured totality, a literary context. We grasp the definite meaning of any given idea in such a book by understanding it "in context," the context being a literary setting consisting of the explicitly organized literary totality which is the book itself. Such an explicitly organized totality is precisely what we are lacking in the *Tao Te Ching*, and this is the chief source of ambiguity, concerning both the meaning of individual sayings and the way in which its many individual sayings are related in a coherent whole. What the form-critical hypothesis suggests is that each individual saying in the *Tao Te Ching* originally belonged in some concrete *life* setting that gave it a definite meaning, and that the coherence of the body of sayings consists in the way that each was functionally related to a concretely coherent way of life.

This form-critical hypothesis is the one I will pursue and argue for in trying to recover the original meaning of the *Tao Te Ching* in Chapters 6 through 12. On this hypothesis, the difficulties and ambiguities that the *Tao Te Ching* presents for historical hermeneutics do not reflect an author's deliberate intention to write a book suitable for scriptural reading for all ages to come. They are rather the result of the historical accident that a body of sayings have been torn from the original life settings that gave them definite meanings, and made their way into a book that can be read in many different settings and hence can be given many different meanings. A chief task of interpretation is therefore to reconstruct the original life settings, place each saying in relation to these settings, and use this as the key to understanding the meaning of the sayings and their relation to each other in a structured whole.

An Overview

The argument of the chapters in Part Three will be somewhat complex, reflecting the complex origins of the book itself. The following overview will give the reader some preliminary orientation to the discussions that follow.

My general hypothesis about the *Tao Te Ching*'s historical origins is the following: Most of the material in this book originated as oral tradition in a small *shih* school of the general kind we see reflected in the *Mencius*, discussed in Part Two. For convenience's sake, I refer to this otherwise unknown group of *shih* as the "Laoist" school (see p. 49). The oral sayings of this school preserved for us in the *Tao Te Ching* consist of two different groups. First, there is a group of proverb-like aphorisms such as "One who shows off will not shine" (1[24]:2). These express the views of the Laoist school on two issues similar to those that most concern Mencius: how an idealistic *shih* should conduct his personal life, and how to reform the political practice of contemporary rulers. These sayings would have originally been brought up in conversation about these topics both among members of the Laoist school and between Laoists and other *shih* and rulers who sought their advice. Because these sayings generally have a strong polemic thrust, criticizing the views of others, I call them "polemic aphorisms."

Laoists also practiced self-cultivation—probably to a more intense degree than the Mencian school—and a second group of sayings is more directly related to self-cultivation practice. Some of these sayings are instructions or exhortations to cultivate a certain state of mind, as in "watch over Femininity" (17[28]:1), *"Fem-*

ininity" being one description of the state of mind cultivated. Many more of these sayings are celebratory, celebrating the wonderful character and cosmic importance of the state of mind cultivated, as in "One who uses [Femininity] will never wear out," and "The [mental] Abode of Mysterious Femininity is the Root of the World" (32[6]:2 and 4).

The unity and coherence of this body of sayings stems from the unity and coherence of the Laoist way of life, which centered on a certain state of mind intensively cultivated by Laoists, partly through meditation exercises. This state of mind was intrinsically linked to a certain stance or attitude toward situations in the world; and this stance in turn expressed itself in a certain style of conducting one's personal life and a certain style of political leadership. This fact provides the essential link between the sayings related to self-cultivation, on the one hand, and the polemic aphorisms on the other: The polemic aphorisms express the attitude connected with the state of mind cultivated, and they give representative examples of the style of personal life and political leadership expressive of this stance. Thus the two major groups of sayings are related via the same "expressive" view of politics that we saw in the *Mencius* (p. 101–02): Proper policy and leadership style can be defined as those policies and that style that express the ideal state of mind (or "virtue" in the *Mencius*) that *shih* cultivate.

The unity and coherence of Laoist sayings consists mainly in the way they are related to the concrete life of the Laoist community. We could probably reconstruct the main features of this unity and coherence even if all we had was a collection of the sayings arranged in random order. But the sayings are not, in fact, arranged in random order. The eighty-one "chapters" of the *Tao Te Ching* are artfully arranged "collages" of oral sayings. (My conjecture is that they were composed by teachers in the Laoist school and given to students to meditate on.) These "composers" (as I will call them) of the chapter-collages frequently altered the oral sayings or added comments to them, making clear their own intentions in composing these collages. The resultant complex nature of these collages is well illustrated in Chapter 78[19]:

Text	*Comment*
Discard "Wisdom," throw away "Knowledge"—	This was originally an oral saying, a polemic aphorism direct-

the people will benefit a
hundredfold.
Discard "Goodness," throw
away "Morality"—
the people will turn back to
respect and caring.
Discard "Skill," throw away
"Profit"—
robbers and thieves will
disappear.

ed against other *shih*-schools,
like that of Mencius, who advocated a government based on
"Wisdom," "Goodness,"
"Morality," and so on. It would
have been brought up in conversations with rulers or other
shih to counter their attraction
to these ideas.

*Taking these three lines as your
text—this is not sufficient.
Give them something to fasten
on to:*

The next three italicized lines
were added by the composer of
the chapter, to connect the previous saying to the following
one.

Pay attention to the Raw,
embrace the Uncarved,
Discount your personal
interests, make your desires
few.

These last two lines were originally an oral saying giving
instruction in Laoist self-cultivation. They would have been
brought up in conversations
between members of the Laoist
school, as for example a conversation in which a Laoist teacher
was instructing a student in
self-cultivation practice.

This example gives a general idea of the kind of study called
for if my hypothesis is correct. One needs to study the body of
polemic aphorisms—like the first saying here—contained in the
Tao Te Ching. This will be the subject of Chapters 6 and 7. One
needs also to study the body of sayings more directly related to
self-cultivation, like the last saying here. This will be the subject
of Chapters 8 through 10. And finally, one needs to study the
work of the "composers" who integrated the oral sayings into
chapter-collages. This will be the subject of Chapter 12.

Form Criticism, Competence, and Ideal Semantic Structure

Form-criticism has often served a hermeneutics focused on
authoritative origins. For example, it has been used to try to separate the original sayings of Jesus from later Christian accretions,

the assumption being that the most important goal of biblical hermeneutics is to understand the ideas as they existed in the mind of Jesus. The present hermeneutics has a different orientation, and this means that form-criticism here will be pressed into the service of a different hermeneutic agenda.

The proximate goal of the present hermeneutics is to become competent to understand the words of the text as they were originally understood (see p. 36–38). Its ultimate goal is to understand the reality of which the text speaks, gaining by this means a critical understanding of the words of the text in relation to this reality (see p. 9, 24, 30–32).

Form-criticism is essential to an understanding of competence in the case of extremely context-bound material, as for example the saying, "It takes two to tango." Modern Americans immediately understand this saying because, even when they see it on the printed page, the saying evokes in their minds the kind of concrete life setting in which the saying is customarily said (a situation in which one is being blamed where two are at fault). The saying is extremely context bound, in the sense that the saying cannot be understood apart from the customary contexts in which it is said. An understanding of the saying's connection with this customary context is an essential aspect of the "competence" necessary to grasp its point. In this respect, form-criticism is a historiographical auxiliary to Pragmatics,[1] that branch of linguistics that studies the effect of concrete context on the meaning of conversational speech.

As the study of the relation of verbal discourse to concrete life, form-criticism is also relevant to the more ambitious ultimate goal of the present hermeneutics, *Sachkritik*, understanding the reality of which the text speaks, understanding in what sense and to what extent it is based on reality and therefore "true." Here the connection with a main tenet of philosophical pragmatism is important, the idea that different assertions relate to concrete life in different ways, and that the "basis in reality" any assertion needs to be well founded varies with the different kinds of point made by different assertions. This is meant to counter the foundationalist assumption that there is only one ultimate test of well-foundedness, the test as to whether a given statement is ultimately based on some accurate picture of reality-as-it-is.

The relevance of pragmatism to textual interpretation was illustrated in Chapter 2 (p. 30) by means of a Mohist statement that ancient kings promoted the worthy rather than their kin: On the surface the statement seems to be an assertion about historical facts, and therefore to need historical evidence warranting its truth, which Mohists did not have. But neither were Mohists interested in reconstructing history for its own sake. The point of this statement is to present a policy Mohists wanted to urge as a wise policy in the present. Not only this, but their perception of the wisdom of the policy in the present is arguably the basis on which they ascribed the policy to ancient kings in the first place. The point made by the statement has a plausible basis in Mohist experience and reflection.

But this analysis also yields a critical understanding of the Mohist statement. If a statement needs some basis in reality to be well-founded, then that basis in reality also constitutes a restriction on what the statement can validly be construed to mean. Insofar as Mohists interpreted their statements about ancient kings literally, they were mistaken; such an understanding goes against the plausible basis they actually had.

This kind of analysis gets at what I will call the "ideal semantic structure" of a given statement. An ideal semantic structure is one in which the main point made by a statement is plausibly proportionate to the basis that a person has in making the statement.

So in the present hermeneutics, form-criticism stands in service to "Pragmatics" in the linguistic sense, the study of the way concrete context affects the meaning of spoken discourse. But form-criticism and linguistic Pragmatics stand in further service to philosophical pragmatism, the view that well-foundedness is relative to contextual purpose. And philosophical pragmatism is linked to *Sachkritik*, an attempt to understand the reality of which the text speaks, and to interpret its words critically in relation to this reality. This complex of viewpoints will lead to a unified focus in the following chapters: Ultimately all discussions will center on the question as to the ideal semantic structure of various kinds of verbal forms in the *Tao Te Ching*.

Many of the issues that concerned us in discussing the *Mencius* will continue to be of concern here. The doctrinal approach will continue to be the main foil over against which I will try to define the more contextual-pragmatist interpretation I think is more appropriate. The main difference lies in the fact that the main focus of our Mencius discussions was the relation between substantive content and social context. Now, while continuing to draw on ideas about the social situation of *shih*, our interest will shift to the relation between substantive content and linguistic form.

The Semantic Structure of Aphorisms

The Proverb as a Special Genre of Speech

Holmes Welch makes this comment on the saying, "A violent man will not reach his natural end" (36[42]:6):

> Lao Tzu is wrong about it, of course. Violent men usually die natural deaths, but not always. In our day the dictatorial score is two to one—assuming Stalin was not done in by his doctors.[1]

Welch's comment implicitly assumes that sayings like this belong to the genre of "general laws." Their formal structure is "A always leads to B," and so they belong formally to the same linguistic genre as Newton's, "For every action there is an equal and opposite reaction." The competence required to understand the structure of these statements, their relation to reality, and their basis in reality, is formally the same. Fung Yu-lan[2] is even more explicit in asserting that much of Laoist wisdom consists of attempts to formulate general "laws of nature." This approach has a certain initial appeal, both because it is straightforwardly literal and hence apparently the "simplest" approach, and also because it assimilates Laoist thought to modern scientific and philosophical thought.

When interpreted this way, however, the *Tao Te Ching* seems to contain many implausible propositions dogmatically asserted without argument.[3] It also contains many contradictions (see p. 157). The fact that there are many ways in which the text does not make sense when interpreted this way should serve as an initial suspicion, at least, that this may not be the most plausible hypothesis about the way language is being used here. And it is relevant to note here that, in their form, Laoist aphorisms[4] resemble proverbs in general use, and also that many proverbs in common use would be subject to Welch's objection if they were interpreted as general laws. Consider such wildly implausible general laws as, "When it rains it pours," and "A watched pot never boils." And consider such contradictory pairs of general laws as "Absence makes the heart grow fonder" vs. "Out of sight, out of mind"; and "You can't teach an old dog new tricks" vs. "It's never too late to learn." If people really regarded these as general laws predicting what will always or even probably happen, only extremely thoughtless people would ever use them.

In what follows, I will argue (1) that the practical and polemic element in Laoist wisdom is cast largely in the form of aphorisms that have the same *formal* semantic structure as proverbs generally. And (2) in our everyday use of familiar proverbs, we implicitly understand them as having a formal structure very different from the formal structure of general laws, and we construe them as having a different relation to reality. It is only when the unfamiliarity of a Laoist proverb prevents such spontaneous implicit understanding that we revert to the "simple" model of literal discourse. A first step in understanding the proverb-like polemic aphorisms in the *Tao Te Ching*, then, will be to develop a general account of the kind of competence implied in the way we commonly use and understand proverbs generally. In order to develop such an account, we need to begin with proverbs familiar to us. As Jonathan Culler argues,[5] when undertaking a formal linguistic analysis of *how* statements mean, it is important to base one's fundamental analysis on examples where one is reasonably sure of one's intuitions about *what* they mean. Without this, one's hypothesis about semantic structure lacks any meaningful test and runs the risk of being circular: One arbitrarily imposes a particular structure on the statements, and then just declares the resultant meaning to be their true meaning.

I begin here, then, with a discussion of the formal semantic structure of some familiar proverbs that is implicit in our ordinary understanding of them, drawing on some insights from ordinary language philosophy and from the related discipline of Pragmatics, the study of language as used in ordinary conversation. I will make the provisional assumption here that Laoist polemic aphorisms have the same formal semantic structure as proverbs in most cultures, including our own. This assumption will receive further support in the next chapter, where it will be shown that construing Laoist aphorisms on this formal model makes sense of many aspects of the *Tao Te Ching* that are otherwise difficult to make sense of.

Conversational Implicature

One notion helpful in understanding proverbs is an idea developed by the philosopher H. P. Grice,[6] which he called "conversational implicature." Stephen Levinson uses the following example to illustrate Grice's main point:

—Where's Sue?
—Well, there's a yellow VW parked outside Bill's house.[7]

In the context of this conversation, the primary intent of the second statement is clearly to convey the information that Sue is at Bill's house, even though there is nothing about the statement taken literally that actually says this. Grice asked the question: What specific linguistic mechanism makes this phenomenon possible? His answer: In conversation, our general habit is not to take every statement at face value, and accept or dismiss it accordingly. Our habit rather is to begin with the initial assumption that every statement does in fact make sense in its context, and first try to *construe it in such a way* as to make it make sense. In the present case, the normal person would not just take the statement about the VW at face value, and dismiss it as irrelevant. She would first try to construe it in a way that *makes* it an answer to the question asked. This habit has become one of the assumptions underlying our carrying on of conversations. It is according to this assumption that the statement can be declared to clearly and unambiguously *mean* that Sue is at Bill's house, even though this is not what it literally says. This mechanism is what Grice calls "conversational implicature": Meanings that are not *logically* implied by some statements are nonetheless taken *in conversation* to be assuredly and very clearly implied by them.[8]

A similar linguistic phenomenon seems to be common in our understanding of aphorisms. Consider "A watched pot never boils." Taken literally, it is clearly false. But we do not take it literally. Rather, we try to imagine some way of understanding it which would make it make sense. We try to imagine a plausible connection between "watching" a pot, and its "never boiling." This causes us to give a special meaning to each of the terms. "Watching" is not taken to mean just any kind of watching (say, leisurely contemplation), but *anxious* watching. And "never boiling" is taken psychologically rather than physically; anxious watching will make it *seem as though* the water will never boil.

Because of the mechanism described above, these very narrowly defined and somewhat unusual meanings of the words can be said to be an integral part of the saying's primary meaning, even though they are not explicitly indicated. In this respect, bringing up a proverb is more like telling a story than it is like telling someone a general law. "A watched pot never boils" evokes a brief vignette: A person sitting by a stove, anxiously watching a pot, wanting it to boil, and annoyed that it seems to be taking so long. The implicit message conveyed by one who says the proverb to another is: "Consider this vignette. It makes a point relevant to your situation." To say that a saying evokes a vignette is to say that it evokes an experiential complex, a complex of elements interrelated in a particular kind of experience. The proper way to understand the vignette is to empathically identify with the human experience involved: here, the experience of anxious watching, which causes a sense that the expected event will "never come." In this situation one experiences elements of reality related in a certain way. Empathic identification is necessary in order to perceive the specific experienced connection between "watching" and "never boiling" that the saying means to evoke.

It is important to differentiate this experienced connection from the "necessary connections" dealt with in logic and the sciences. In the latter contexts it is important (1) that the elements connected be definable independently of each other, and (2) that the connection be a necessary, or at least probable one. Our present saying does not really consist of a prediction that something independently definable as "anxious watching" will necessarily or even probably lead to a sense that the awaited event will "never come." Rather, it evokes an experience in which these two things happen to be internally related to each other, as one experiences them. The point of the saying is not to declare with what degree of probability two independent things are connected. What is spoken of is an experiential complex made up of several mutually defining elements: That-kind-of-watching-which-produces-"never boiling," and that-kind-of-"never boiling"-which-is-produced-by-watching. What the saying asserts is that this is a *significant* complex or vignette. The vignette implies something significant about the situation in which one says the saying. This element of the meaning of sayings is perhaps most accurately called the "significant experiential complex" evoked by the saying. For convenience's sake, I will refer to this element more briefly as simply the "image" evoked by a saying.

Speech Acts

A second notion helpful in understanding aphorisms is the idea of a "speech act," first developed by the philosopher J. L. Austin.[9] The central insight here is that conveying information is not the only purpose for which we use language. Some sentences cannot be adequately understood as representations of some truths about the world. When someone says, "I do" at a wedding ceremony, for example, the person is not conveying some information about pre-established facts. What the person is doing is best understood as "taking an action," i.e., committing herself to a marriage.

Aphorisms are not "speech acts" in the same sense that wedding vows are. But in some crucial respects they resemble "taking an action" more than they resemble attempts to represent something about the world. Consider the case in which someone in a risky situation says to another, "Better safe than sorry." The speaker might also have said in the same situation, "Nothing ventured, nothing gained." Both sayings evoke some "experiential complex," and both complexes seem to represent something potentially true about reality. But, as we saw above, the point of such sayings is not to assert the truth of a given complex. It is to assert that some particular complex has some special *significance* in the situation addressed. We perceive the speaker as having "made a choice" about what particular image to bring up in the present situation. In making such a choice one "takes a stand" about what is important in the situation. One says either that this is a situation in which the image of being-sorry-for-not-having-played-it-safe is the crucial image to keep in mind; or that it is a situation in which it is better to bring up the image of losing-an-opportunity-for-profit-by-playing-it-safe. In making these choices one expresses an attitude toward the situation; a "conservative" attitude is expressed in the former case, an "adventurous" attitude in the latter case.

The two sayings involved in this example do not speak *about* the stand taken or the attitude expressed. The stand taken is something "performed" by the one saying the saying. To say the saying *is* to take a stand on the situation addressed. The one saying the proverb is taking a stand by saying it, and the stand taken is motivated by a particular value-orientation that makes one see the situation from a certain perspective. The person saying the proverb is inviting the person she addresses to share this perspective and take up the same stance toward it.

Every stand one takes has a particular content, identical in this case with the meaning of the act one performs by bringing up a particular saying. The meaning of the act which a saying performs can generally be further broken down into two elements: First, the meaning-content of "taking a stand" can be defined partly by what one takes a stand *against*. Let us call this the *target* of the proverb. The meaning of what one does in taking a stand can also be defined by what one takes a stand in favor of, what it is that positively motivates the stand one takes. Let us call this the *attitude* expressed in the saying.

The Target of Proverbs

As to the target of proverbs, note first that a proverb does not normally directly state what its target is, but every proverb nonetheless has a definite target, and understanding this target is essential to understanding its meaning. People in a given culture normally learn the targets of specific proverbs by hearing them used in situations where their target is clear. But imagine a foreigner trying to understand the meaning of "It takes two to tango," if all she knew was the literal meaning of the sentence.

The customary target is often the most essential thing one needs to know about a proverb. If one knows the target it is often easy to fill in the rest. For example, a foreigner could probably guess the meaning of "It takes two to tango" if we told her, "We say this on occasions where one person is being blamed but two are actually at fault."

A proverb's target is also essential in that the meaning of a proverb consists essentially in the fact that it is corrective. Consider, for example, the fact that "Slow and steady wins the race," is a common proverb although it is not reliable as a general law about who wins races. "The race usually goes to the swift" is more true, but is not a proverb. Why? People have a tendency to assume that being swift is *always the only* way to win races, and "Slow and steady wins the race" corrects this tendency. It wakes people up to a different possibility. Its point, which is its meaning, is to compensate for this tendency. But there is no tendency to think that fast people will not win. "The race is to the swift" has nothing to compensate for, and so it has no point that is very useful in ordinary life. *As a proverb* it lacks significant meaning, because proverbs are essentially corrective, compensatory wisdom.

The meaning of an aphorism is exhausted in making a point against a particular target. The scope of its claims is limited to the situation in which it is said. This is a major difference between proverbs and general laws. In evaluating a statement proposed as a general law—say, a law of physics—it is important to compare it to a body of established laws to see if it is logically compatible with them. An individual general law needs to be logically connected to and consistent with a system of general laws. Proverbs are not like this. A person might say on one occasion, "Absence makes the heart grow fonder," and on another occasion, "Out of sight, out of mind." There is no contradiction here, because the meaning of each proverb is exhausted by making a point against a particular target in a particular situation. "Absence makes the heart grow fonder" does not really make any claim about necessary or even probable connections between things that could conflict with similar general claims made by "Out of sight, out of mind." The meaning of both sayings is completely context-bound, narrowly limited in scope rather than making general claims. Proverbs are extremely "context-bound" in one sense, if by "context" we mean the concrete *life setting* in which they are said. But in another sense their meaning is extremely self-contained and free of context, if by "context" we mean some further body of general *theories* to which they are connected.

The Attitude Expressed and the Value-Orientation Motivating It

Turning now to the positive stand one takes by saying a saying, the *attitude* it expresses, here again it is important to note that this is a definite and essential meaning element, even though it is something suggested rather than explicitly spoken about. A child who says in a particular situation, "Sticks and stones may break my bones, but names will never hurt me," is "posturing," assuming a certain posture or attitude toward a situation, insisting on seeing it in a certain perspective. One could understand the literal meaning of the sentence but not understand the posture or stance which the child is adopting toward her situation by bringing up this proverb. Such an understanding would fail to grasp an essential part of the meaning of the proverb.

Further, it seems true to say that the *character* of the stance taken is the main basis on which a given proverb hopes to persuade. For example, what is the ultimate reason that a child would bring up the sticks-and-stones saying in a given situation, and why would we think it is good for her to bring it up? The main reason seems to be that the child who says this saying is taking up a stance toward the situation that is a good and admirable stance to take. Taking this stance shows a certain amount of courage and maturity, the ability to "rise above" the cycle of human hurting. The goodness of this stance contrasts with other stances we would not admire as much, such as sulking, on the one hand, or vengeful counterattack on the other.

To analyze further what this goodness consists in, it is helpful to consider the connection between stance and *perspective*, and the way both stance and perspective potentially represent a response to some perceived good.[10] In a situation where one is being called names, there are certain elements already given and beyond one's control. But one is still left a certain amount of freedom in the way one *construes* the situation. What about this situation will one focus on and allow to dominate one's perspective on the situation? Being called insulting names threatens a person's sense of self-esteem. But although this is often a keenly *felt* threat, it is a threat without substance. Only actually *being* a bad person—not just being spoken of badly—really warrants a lowered sense of self-esteem. The child who sulks or shouts retaliatory insults implicitly accepts the unwarranted threat at face value. The child who "rises above" the threat is motivated by a sense of her own dignity and worth. She shows maturity by standing by this actually untouched dignity and worth. She courageously stands up for it in the world, acting out the position of a self that has not really been affected.

One could analyze this as a mini-"conversion."[11] First we have a situation of name-calling, a situation in which children normally feel drawn either to sulking and self-pity or to vengeful counterattack. This is the "target mentality" against which our saying is directed. The saying gives evidence of a "conversion" from this mentality to a different one, a change in mentality which also brings about a transformation in the situation-as-perceived. The saying gives evidence that the child has let concern for something genuinely good—her own untouched human worth—dominate her perspective on the situation. Sensitivity toward and concern for this good is what she is expressing by insisting on setting up the image of names-not-hurting as an organizing center governing her perception of this situation. Saying the saying to others is an attempt to sensitize them to this same good, and to let this sensitivity govern their perspective on the situation.

What ultimately makes our saying well-founded, then, is the fact that it enacts a stance and a perspective governed by concern for something truly good. What has to be true about the world in order for the saying to be well-founded is that what elicits this concern *is* actually something genuinely good.

Several aspects of this analysis can be further clarified by considering a twist on the traditional saying that appeared in a recent school poster. The poster shows children of different races shouting at each other, and the caption underneath says: "Sticks and stones will break my bones, but names will *really* hurt me." The "image" brought up here is the opposite of that brought up in the traditional saying. It asks us to imagine the possibility that people can experience name-calling as *more* hurtful than stone-throwing. Furthermore, we implicitly understand this image to be related to the situation addressed in a different way. The traditional saying asks the one being hurt to take the image of names-not-hurting as a possibility she might try to realize. This saying asks the one doing the hurtful namecalling to take the image of the *other*-greatly-hurt-by-names as an organizing center for the situation. What is she supposed to see in this way of construing the situation, to motivate her to adopt this way of construing it? This way of seeing the situation allows something truly deserving of respect—the feelings and self-esteem of others—to dominate her perspective on the situation.

The traditional proverb and this modern twist on it represent two stances adopted toward a similar situation. The two are different stances but both good. Let us now imagine a teacher making posters and deciding whether to call attention to the traditional saying or to the new version. We can see here that a single situation can be construed in a number of good ways. One might let one's perspective on the situation be determined by several different good concerns. The teacher might be concerned to develop her students' ability to rise above name-calling, and print the traditional saying. Or she might be concerned to develop their sensitivity toward others, and print the new version.

One point this example illustrates is the diversity of good concerns. The fact that in the present situation these two concerns would tend to conflict with each other does not mean that they cannot both be good in themselves. But we can also sense some cultural preferences at stake here. Older American culture placed a priority on the concern that children develop a "stiff upper lip," and this value orientation would lead them to appreciate the traditional form of our saying more than the modern alteration. Recent trends toward a more humanistic culture, emphasizing sensitivity to human feelings, have produced subcultures in America whose value orientation would lead them to appreciate more the modern alteration of the saying.

While there is a diversity of good concerns and good ways of construing the situation addressed by our saying, there are also ones that are clearly not good. Goodness remains an aspect of reality-as-experienced, not an aribitrary subjective creation (see p. 14–18, 274). Suppose, for example, one child deliberately calls another hurtful names, and then offers as an excuse: "Sticks and stones will break her bones but names will never hurt her." We cannot make the stance expressed here a good one by arbitrarily labelling it "good." In normal human experience this particular speech act *has* a particular meaning—trying to excuse the inexcusable—and this meaning makes it not-good. There is a limit to the number of good ways one can construe a certain situation, and some situations call on us to give priority to certain values rather than to others. In the concrete, the goodness of any given perspective and value orientation is also partly a function of the situation in which one decides to take up this perspective.

The results of this discussion can now be summarized in terms of the several goals of the present hermeneutics outlined in the introduction to Part Three. First, aphorisms have their normal place, not in books or systematic treatises, but in the ongoing stream of concrete human life, and this means that the analytical tools provided by form-criticism and Pragmatics are the most relevant here. Specifically, there are two aspects of concrete life situations that are essential in determining the meaning of aphorisms: (1) A given aphorism is pertinent to a particular situation in which its central purpose is to counter a particular target mentality; and (2) a given aphorism expresses and invites a certain "conversion" of one's mentality, resulting in a transformed way of perceiving the situation addressed. The meaning of the aphorism must be perceived in relation to this concrete transformation of one's mentality and perception of the situation. This differentiates an aphorism, for example, from a philosophical doctrine, which can be understood in a more objective fashion as an attempt to represent some non-perspectival objective truth about the world.

Secondly, the above discussion gives us an account of the kind of *competence* required to understand aphorisms. That is, it makes explicit the essential elements that implicitly structure the way people understand aphorisms in their common use. People who understand a given aphorism implicitly

1. understand it in relation to a specific situation in which it counters a specific target;

2. understand the image or experiential complex that the saying means to evoke, and appreciate what it would mean to allow this image to serve as an organizing center structuring one's perception of a situation;

3. perceive the goodness motivating the stance and perspective on the situation which the saying expresses or "performs."

Inquiry into the meaning of unfamiliar aphorisms from foreign cultures requires that we first form and test hypotheses about these three meaning elements and then internalize them and let them implicitly shape our understanding of the words. This is what it would mean to be "competent" to understand the words as they were originally understood.

Finally, these discussions have also given us an account of the *ideal semantic structure* of aphorisms. An ideal semantic structure is a model in which a statement's basis in reality and the way it affects one's perception of reality are mutually proportionate; the basis is one that validates this changed perception, and the changed perception does not go beyond what is validated by this basis (see p. 131). Consider our saying, "Sticks and stones will break my bones but names will never hurt me." The ultimate basis for this saying is the perceived goodness of the maturity and courage expressed in it. This goodness does validate the changed perception of reality which, in its normal understanding, the saying advocates. That is, this goodness makes the changed perception a good change. Someone could, however, interpret the saying as a prediction and a promise that name calling will never hurt anyone. What the saying says on *this* interpretation needs a different basis. One could not know that names will never hurt based on one's perception of the goodness of maturity and courage. Even though it is possible that some given group of people might interpret the saying in this way, they are making a mistake. This account of ideal semantic structure is based in part on a purely descriptive account of competence, an account of the way people normally *do* understand a given statement. But it also goes beyond a purely descriptive account, to arrive at an account in which the basis and the changed perception are actually proportionate. This is what enables a descriptive account of competence to become a normative *Sachkritik*, a critical evaluation of meaning based on the real reality to which a given statement draws our attention.

Understanding Laoist Polemic Aphorisms

It is often supposed that an interpreter has only two alternatives. One is to interpret her text literally. And, since the opposite of literal speech is "suggestive" speech, the other alternative is to focus on intuitive guesses as to the substance of what the author is trying to suggest, not giving too much weight to the details of linguistic form. This is what is often called "divinatory hermeneutics," which relies purely on an intuitive feeling that one is communing with the spirit of the text's author.

The account given in Chapter 6 of the semantic structure of aphorisms, if it is indeed appropriate to the *Tao Te Ching*, allows for a third alternative in this case. Aphoristic speech is not literal speech. It does not have the simple and straightforward semantic structure characteristic of literal speech. And yet for the "competent" listener—one who has an implicit grasp of the semantic structure of aphorisms, and understands the appropriate context—they have definite meanings, and the words of the aphorisms themselves are a rather exact guide to this meaning. An explicit account of this normally implicit understanding, if it is accurate, thus ought to yield an explicit analysis of a saying's meaning that accurately replicates the understanding of the original competent listener.

But this brings us to the matter of what counts as evidence that the account of competence in Chapter 6 is indeed applicable to the polemic aphorisms in the *Tao Te Ching*. Merely showing how a group of statements looks when construed in a certain way does not by itself constitute evidence that this is the way they were construed by their original author and audience. We face here a kind of "hermeneutic circle" that cannot be completely avoided, but can be mitigated. The main argument I have to offer in this chapter is that, consistently applied to the entire body of Laoist aphorisms, the model of aphoristic meaning outlined in

Chapter 6 is able to make very good sense of them. The assumptions behind this argument are as follows.

An interpreter ought to approach any given text with the working hypothesis that it makes sense; that is, that the writer intended to say something definite, plausible, and coherent, and that the words the writer chose are roughly apt for saying what she wanted to say. This ought to be our initial hypothesis, first, because people usually are trying to say something that makes sense to them. Secondly, it is important to approach every text in this way in order to counteract our natural tendency to dismiss as nonsensical any text that does not at first sight seem to make sense. More exactly, then, our initial hypothesis should be that, if any given text does not at first appear to make sense, it is we who are at fault. It appears to us not to make sense because we have not yet become "competent" readers of this particular text. The only way to know whether a given text makes sense or not is to try as hard as we can to devise and formulate an account of competence in light of which it does make sense.

On the other hand, the possibility of failure in this endeavor is important. Any method that can make sense of any text whatsoever is not a good method, because we know of possible ways that writings can be generated that do not make sense. The key fact that makes failure possible in a competence based hermeneutics is that normally *competence is a constant* with respect to any given text (just as grammatical competence is a constant throughout any text written in English, while the *meaning* of the various sentences involved might vary greatly.) Hence, any competence-based analysis must be carried through systematically and consistently throughout the entire text. And one test of its validity is whether, when so carried out, it yields a plausible interpretation for each statement in the text, as well as of the text as a whole.

The importance of this principle can be illustrated by an analogy to the deciphering of unknown alphabets such as Linear B. It is possible easily to make sense of a series of unknown marks simply by attributing some plausible message to them. But this is only easy if one is free to shift the meaning attributed to individual marks in an ad hoc way from passage to passage to fit whatever substantive meaning one wants to attribute to the passage in question. If one has to assign the same meaning to the same mark consistently and systematically wherever it occurs, this cuts down enormously on the possible ways one can make sense of the marks as human language.

Similarly, in the case of any given text whose meaning is initially unclear, it is easy to make sense of the words if we are free to shift the implicit model of semantic structure we are using from passage to passage in an ad hoc way, to fit whatever substantive meaning we want to attribute to a given passage. It is possible in this way to make sense of any text in any number of different ways, including texts that are severely corrupted and do not really make sense. If we have to work with an explicit model of competence and apply it consistently to the entire text, this limits considerably the ways in which one can make sense of any given text. While we should be open to an indefinite variety of possibilities as to the competence appropriate to any given text, we also have to keep in mind the possibility that for some given text, no account of competence consistently applied will yield an interpretation that makes sense. This is the definition of a genuinely nonsensical text.

The linguistic basis for the above principle is that, to be understandable, any given text has to rely on some specific kind of competence that remains a constant throughout the text. If the nature of the appropriate competence changed, this would be the equivalent of a coded message in which the alphabet was used normally in some parts, but the values of the letters were changed arbitrarily in other parts.

These observations give us a partial basis for testing the appropriateness of the above account of aphoristic meaning-structure to Laoist aphorisms. That is, initial appearances give some justification for supposing that Laoist aphorisms have the same formal meaning-structure as proverbs generally. But this leaves us still uncertain, for example, as to whether Laoists might be using aphorisms in some way that draws on other possibilities of meaning not well described in our formal model. The fact that, when consistently applied to the entire body of aphorisms, this formal model yields an interpretation that makes sense of them as a body, is supportive evidence that this model is indeed a good account of the competence appropriate to these sayings.

In order to make the concept of "making sense" more precise, I suggest five main elements:

    1. *Definiteness.* When people speak, they normally intend their words to have some definite content (though this content can be complex, "performed" rather than stated, not subject to direct praphrase, and so on.) Applying a given account of competence to a Laoist saying ought to result in specifying some definite content for it.

2. *Plausibility*. When people speak, they are normally implicitly appealing to some basis on which they expect their audience to accept what they are saying. One test of an account of competence appropriate to Laoist aphorisms is therefore that the meanings it yields would seem, to a likely Chinese audience, to have some plausible basis in their *Lebenswelt*, reality as they experienced it.

3. *Coherence*. The various things people say are usually relatively coherent, in *some* meaning of the word coherent. Unless we have some other positive evidence that there are conflicting voices in the text, we ought to prefer that account of competence which leads to an interpretation of the body of Laoist sayings according to which they form a coherent whole.

4. *Appropriate wording*. When people speak, they generally choose wording that is roughly suited to saying what they want to say. Oftentimes interpreters make sense of a given text by ignoring its form and extracting from it some content that makes sense. But fully making sense of a text requires that we not only derive from it some content that makes sense, but also say why it is that the text's author would express this content in precisely this way.

5. *Historical plausibility*. The competence required to understand the original meaning of a text is always identical with part of the mind-set of some concrete historical persons. A further test of some account of competence appropriate to Laoist aphorisms is therefore how well this account can be tied to a plausible narrative of the text's origins and original milieu, given what else we know about late Warring States China.

The commentaries and the Topical Glossary in Part Four apply the above account of aphoristic meaning structure to the entire body of Laoist aphorisms, showing in detail how this account makes good sense of them by the above criteria. But some ways in which this is true can better be discussed in a general fashion, and this is the subject of the following observations.

Definiteness

It is sometimes said that the author of the *Tao Te Ching* deliberately made his text vague and ambiguous.[1] Anything is possible, of course, but this should be an explanation of last resort. Normally when people speak or write they have something definite to say. ("Definite" does not mean "capturable in straightforward language." As illustrated in the case of jokes [p. 37] language might convey some substantive content that is definite, even though this definite content can only be conveyed suggestively.) We ought to try first to devise an account of competence able to draw definite meanings from the words of the text, and only conclude that it is vague if this attempt fails.

Consistently applied to the body of Laoist polemic aphorisms, the present account of the meaning-structure of aphorisms is able to provide a plausible account as to how Laoist aphorisms would have had definite meanings for their originally intended audience. It also provides an account as to why these originally definite meanings were not apparent to subsequent readers of this book, and what in general we need to do to try to recover their original definite meanings.

The main point here is that aphorisms have definite meanings when they are used in their normal context, oral conversation in concrete life settings. Such life settings, and repeated use in similar life settings, give participants enough clues to enable them to fill in the three main elements of aphoristic meaning (the image, the target, and the attitude expressed. See p. 136–42). So, for example, "It takes two to tango" has a definite meaning when said in an appropriate life setting. It would lose this definite meaning if it were written down on a page and then came into the hands of someone unfamiliar with the life setting in which this saying is normally used. Taken in conjunction with our hypothesis about a community of Laoist *shih* (p. 127), this suggests something similar about the body of aphorisms preserved in the *Tao Te Ching*. That is, these sayings represent the oral tradition of a community of *shih*. Each saying was originally brought up orally in concrete settings to which it was appropriate, and which provided enough clues to the audience to fill in the necessary three meaning elements. The sayings took on the appearance of being vague and ambiguous when they became part of a written book and passed into the hands of those unfamiliar with these original life settings.

This hypothesis also suggests in general what we must do to try to recover the original definite meanings of these sayings: It will not do to stare at the words and try to read their meaning off the surface of the words themselves. We must rather try to reconstruct a plausible life setting for each saying, and reconstruct the three essential meaning elements suggested but not stated by the words. Our account of the semantic structure of aphorisms, of course, only tells us about *formal* structure, the general nature of the three crucial meaning elements and how they are formally related to each other. It does not make us fully competent to understand any given aphorism, which requires that we fill in these three formal categories with the appropriate substantive contents, reconstructing *what* exactly is the image, the target, and the attitude implied in this particular aphorism. So, while providing more control than purely intuitive approaches, the present approach does not eliminate conjecture. On the contrary, it implies that we must make conjectures on matters about which, in many cases, we have only slight historical evidence. If it is true that the image, the target, and the attitude are implied but definite and *essential* meaning-elements in any given aphorism, then interpreting any given aphorism requires that we fill in these three elements with some particular contents, even if in some cases this means making guesses on the basis of slight evidence. To try to "stick with what we know" in these cases would not be to avoid conjecture. It would be to conjecture that the saying we are dealing with does not have an aphoristic meaning-structure.

The formal structure of aphorisms suggests at least the *kind* of information we need in order to understand the meaning of any given Laoist aphorism. One of the main things we need to fill in, for example, is the "image" suggested in a given saying. For example, as an aphorism, "He does not show off, so he shines" (4[22]:5) should not be taken as a dogmatic but implausible statement to be accepted blindly, to the effect that whenever a person does not show off she will surely shine. Our initial assumption should be that the saying means to evoke an image, an experiential complex, in which there is some realistically plausible connection between "not showing off" and "shining." As we saw earlier (p. 135), understanding the image evoked by an aphorism frequently involves giving special meanings to the terms involved. Very often, plausible images come fairly readily to mind if we simply consult our own sense of how things generally happen in human affairs. In the present case, for example, it is not too difficult to imagine a kind of "not showing off" that will cause a person to "shine." That is, it is indeed sometimes true that a person who already has admirable qualities will be more admired if she is also self-effacing about these qualities. This special meaning given to "not showing off" also gives "shining" a different sense. A self-effacing person shines in a different way than one who is boastful and self-assertive. This means that a purely utilitarian interpretation of this saying[2]—an interpretation that construes the saying as advice on the most effective way to gain social admiration—is a mistake. What is implied is rather a sublimation of the desire of *shih* to shine, substituting attractive self-effacement as an ideal in place of boastful self-assertion.

Sometimes a number of plausible images might suggest themselves if we consult only our own experience and insights. But comparison with other Laoist aphorisms often helps us narrow down the number of possibilities. This is especially true of those sayings consisting of parallel lines on a common theme, as for example,

The five colors make people's eyes go blind
the five tones make people's ears go deaf
the five flavors make people's mouth turn sour.
Galloping and racing, hunting and chasing,
    make people's minds go mad.
Goods hard to come by corrupt people's ways. (21[12]:1)

"The five colors make people's eyes go blind" is at first sight implausible, but we can assume that this apparently implausible statement means to evoke some plausible experiential complex. What causes the implausibility here is hyperbole. That is, what comes easily to mind here as a plausible image is the way that prolonged sensory stimulation results in diminished sensitivity or sensory confusion. "Colors" here can then be taken to represent visual stimulation, and "blindness" can be seen as an exaggerated reference to diminished sensitivity. The saying does not advocate banning all colorful objects, therefore. It is a warning against sensory stimulation *when and insofar as* it is desensitizing and/or brings about mental disturbance.

This line by itself is susceptible to other interpretations,[3] but other lines in the saying tend to confirm the one just given. The third line of the saying in particular, "The five flavors make people's mouths turn sour," pretty clearly evokes the image of spicy food leaving a bad taste in the mouth. The fourth line, "Galloping and racing, hunting and chasing, make people's minds go mad" evokes an image in which stimulating activity causes mental disturbance, suggesting that stimulation damaging the senses is the point of the first line as well.

Sometimes we must look to sayings in different parts of the book to illuminate especially difficult or paradoxical sayings. Consider, for example, the paradoxical lines

> Compromised—then upright
> Empty—then solid
> old and spent—then young and sprightly. (4[22]:2)

What we need to conjure up here is an image of someone of whom it would be plausible to say, "He is compromised, so he is upright."[4] It is at first difficult to discover a plausible image that these lines might mean to evoke. But in this we are helped by a string of other sayings. Begin, for example, with "Elegant words are not sincere" (8[81]:1). Although paradoxical in its expression, this saying evokes an image easily accessible to ordinary understanding, the image of elegant speech which is insincere. This reflects the commonsense observation that appearances are often deceiving, a point made also by commonsense sayings like, "You can't tell a book by its cover." Next, consider the saying

> Reside with the substance, [not] with what is thin.
> Reside with the fruit, [not] with the flower. (11[38]:7)

The parallelism between *flower* and *thin* here, and the contrast with fruit/substance, suggests a point of view in which what is showy and impressive (flower-like) is associated with what lacks substance, an obvious parallel with the image of elegant but empty speech. One can see how this view might be developed in such a way that one would come to think that the purest images of good qualities are examples in which substantive worth is divorced from potentially deceptive fine appearances. This is the kind of image directly evoked by two juxtaposed sayings in 5[45]:1–2:

> The greatest perfection will seem lacking in something. . . .
> The greatest solidity will seem Empty. . . .
> The greatest uprightness will seem compromised. . . .

Here we have wording identical to or synonymous with our original saying, which needed clarification, "Compromised—then upright/ Empty—then solid." These comparisons suggest that the image this paradoxical saying means to evoke is the case in which someone has a great deal of integrity but appears to others to be compromised. The image means to present to us an ideal, a person devoted to integrity for its own sake rather than for the sake of appearances. This is why she holds onto this integrity even when it makes her appear to others as someone compromised.[5]

But extremely paradoxical sayings like "Compromised—then upright" pose a problem regarding the historical dimension of

competence. Competence in understanding this difficult oral saying must have required more of an ancient Chinese audience than
simply consulting common experience of how things happen in
human affairs. It probably required a special familiarity with the
special Laoist themes and values just described. How would it
come about that some historical persons in Warring States China
would acquire a mind-set which would cause these words to evoke
the image described above, without the careful comparison to
other sayings that was necessary for us?

This is a common problem one faces in interpreting the sayings in the *Tao Te Ching*. Sayings on many topics range from those
expressing ideas easily accessible and relatively commonsensical,
to those very difficult to make sense of.[6] The present theory solves
this problem by joining the formal semantic account of the structure of aphorisms with a historical hypothesis about the concrete
life setting of these particular sayings in a Warring States *shih*-
school. A *shih*-school offers several different concrete forums in
which aphorisms might be used. As we see from the *Mencius*,
members of a *shih*-school would sometimes engage in conversation with others who were not members of the school, for example rulers whom they wanted to advise (see p. 97), and other *shih*
curious to understand the message of this particular school (see p.
92). Those Laoist aphorisms which are relatively easy to understand would be well suited to use in such conversations. But the
school itself also contains some long-term members, teachers,[7]
and "advanced" students.[8] Conversations within this "inner circle" would be a forum well suited to the use of those sayings more
difficult to understand. To some extent, such sayings represent
esoteric wisdom. Insiders would be competent to understand
them, but not relative outsiders.

Making Sense of the Paradoxical Style of Laoist Aphorisms

We come next to the problem as to why it is that Laoists used
such paradoxical and exaggerated language in expressing themselves. The fact that aphorisms are corrective, compensatory wisdom, designed to wake people up to a possibility they are over-
looking, provides a partial explanation here. The exaggerated
language in some proverbs can be understood as a heightening
and strengthening of this element. One who says, exaggeratedly,
"Never believe anything you hear and only half of what you see,"

is countering a common human tendency to be gullible. The exaggerated language heightens and strengthens this counteractive element in the saying's meaning.

The exaggerated language of this saying is also related to the attitude that it expresses. One finds the exaggerated language attractive insofar as one shares a suspicious attitude and finds gullibility an important danger to look out for. The attitude reflects a certain perspective on life, a certain heightened sensitivity to particular issues. This seems true of hyperbole generally. Of two people looking at the same room, one might say, "It's a little bit messy," while the other might say, "It looks like a cyclone hit it." The difference lies in perspective, differing levels of sensitivity to order and disorder.

The exaggerated language of Laoist aphorisms similarly reflects a heightened sensitivity to certain issues. "The five colors make people's eyes go blind" (21[12]:1) expresses extreme opposition to people's attraction to stimulating things, an opposition motivated by an extreme sensitivity to the condition of one's mental faculties, an extreme care to keep them intact and healthy rather than disturbed and exhausted (see p. 531 under *Agitation**). "Extreme" here is relative, extreme in relation to what would conventionally be regarded as a normal level of sensitivity.

This is where the historical aspect of the explanation comes in: Several passages in the *Tao Te Ching* suggest that Laoist *shih* felt more than usually alienated from their society, felt their views, their values, and their teaching to be more than usually in opposition to what appeared to their contemporaries as well-established and commonsensical views, habits, and norms.[9] The exaggerated language of Laoist aphorisms expresses an attitude motivated by this feeling. As in all aphorisms, the character of this attitude the language expresses is not peripheral. It is a central aspect of the substantive meaning of the aphorisms, the principal basis on which one might agree with them or reject them. Laoist *shih* found the attitude expressed by hyperbole attractive because of their extreme opposition to conventional social norms. Here we can see the way that aphorisms, particularly paradoxical aphorisms, offer a very apt medium for the substantive content of Laoist wisdom. And accordingly, full competence in understanding the paradoxical aphorisms involves not only understanding the formal structure of aphorisms in general, but identifying with or empathically understanding the kind of alienation Laoists felt.

These observations apply to the use of paradox and hyperbole in Laoist aphorisms and also to a recurring figure of speech which is best described as *ironic self-caricature*, exaggerated negative language used to portray positive ideals. "Grandma's *Sinful* Sweets," a brand-name for a line of pastry, is an example of ironic self-caricature. "Sinful" is a normally negative word describing the sweets as someone with a very puritan mentality might caricature them. But the negative term is meant here ironically, and the underlying positive intent is clear: The phrase is meant to be a deliberate affront to the puritan mentality, and suggests on the positive side that anything condemned by a pleasure-hater must be very pleasurable indeed. Similarly, when Laoists advocate "watching over what is disgraceful" (17[28]:1), praise the "dull and incompetent" ruler (59[58]:1), and compare an ideal state to a prostitute (56[61]:1), this is intended as a deliberately shocking affront to their moralistic contemporaries. The statements that those ancients who practiced Tao " . . . kept the people stupid," and "By 'Ignorance' govern the state—a boon to the state" (80[65]:1 and 3) can probably also be put in the same category.[10] In each case, conjuring up a plausible image for such sayings requires that we understand the negative terms ironically rather than seriously, and imagine for each of the negative terms some underlying positive content.

It is important to note here that although ironic self-caricature is meant as a direct affront to conventional norms, it implicitly accepts conventional norms as a framework within which to describe oneself. One describes the most important qualities as "disgraceful" because that is how they appear to others. This points to a further explanation as to the intimate connection between aphorisms as a medium of expression and the substantive character of the Laoist worldview. Laoists held a worldview that was at odds with contemporary conventional views and standards, not on one or two particular points, but fundamentally and on a fairly large scale. Developing a new system of doctrines is one strategy for handling this situation. Newtonian physics presents a paradigm case: It developed a whole new set of technical terms and a system of propositions. This system was intended to *entirely replace* ordinary-experience impressions as a framework within which to discuss the causal structure of the world. Philosophers also frequently try to provide a system of doctrines that provide a straightforward positive account of "the truth" about life, intended to replace impressions delivered by ordinary experience (see p. 14). Ironic self-caricature reflects a Laoist decision not to build another whole system of beliefs and concepts in which their own attitudes would appear in a positive light. (This decision is made explicit in their rejection of "naming" knowledge; see p. 545 under *Naming**.) Laoist aphorisms accept the concrete conventional world as the basic framework within which one lives and speaks, and they also accept *appearing* "low," "shameful," "insignificant," and so on, as a permanent condition of the ideal way of being.

The widespread use of paradox, hyperbole, and irony have an essential relation to this basic Laoist strategy. That is, if one is creating an alternative system of ideas meant to replace conventional thinking, one will ordinarily try to use direct speech to represent those ideas. Such speech invites a certain mode of engagement. It invites an audience to accept these ideas as foundational truths from which to draw conclusions for one's life. Paradox, hyperbole, and irony are indirect speech, and invite a different mode of engagement. They provoke the listener herself to stretch her mind to create images or vignettes representing new and different ideal ways of being and acting. Such images are definite in character; the sayings do not mean to evoke just any image. Yet they are not images one grasps by listening to the direct meanings of some words. It is important to try to perceive the difficult-to-express and subtle substance beneath the attention-getting exaggerated language. It is in this sense that what we have in this book is "wordless teaching" (47[43]:2; 42[2]:3) and a "nameless" Tao (37[14]:3; 39[25]:2; 43[1]:1 and 2; 44[41]:4; 63[32]:1; 81[37]:2). The substance of the teaching is conveyed *by* words, but is not "*in*" the words after the manner of literal speech.

The Problem of Coherence

Coherence has been a major problem for traditional interpretation of the *Tao Te Ching*. And indeed a common opinion among interpreters is that the book is not in fact coherent, but contains some serious inconsistencies.[11] From the present point of view, the major cause of this difficulty is insufficient attention given to the question as to what *kind* of coherence we should expect from the *Tao Te Ching*. Interpreters tend to come to this work with the *a priori* assumption that, if it has a coherent structure, its structure and coherence are the type we look for in philosophical thought-systems. That is, one comes to the text looking for one or several fundamental truths, which can be regarded as the basis of Laoist thought. And one tries then to construe the rest of Laoist ideas as logical conclusions from these fundamental truths. It is these assumptions which cause the text to appear inconsistent in several places. The following is a sample of apparent internal conflicts.

• Many passages seem to suggest or imply that society would be "naturally" good if rulers simply stopped interfering and left people alone (62[29]:1–2; 77[57]; 78[19]; 59[58]:1; 60[49]:1; 81[37]:1,2:1–2,3). This is the interpretation many interpreters give to the recurrent Laoist slogan *wu wei*/"not working." On this view one would think that Laoists regarded the entire existence and social role of rulers as superfluous at best. And yet there are overwhelming indications that this book is a manual of government (see Sections 5–7 of the translation and commentary). It assumes that reaching high governmental office is a desirable goal (3[67]:2:9; 4[22]:5:4); like Mencius (p. 96), it gives advice on how to become a True King (see p. 537 under *Emperor**); it advocates hard work at governmental tasks (75[78]:4, 71[63]:2,4); it gives advice on how to intervene to stop undesirable developments in society (72[64]:1–2; 73[36]:1; 79[3]:2–3; 80[65]:1,5; 81[37]:2:3–7); in contrast to those passages that advocate *wu wei*/"not working," there are other passages that explicitly advocate *wei*/doing:working (72[64]:2, 8[81]:3–4; 27[10]:2).

• Several passages seem to criticize value judgments in general (42[2]:1–2; 13[20]:1–3), and criticize attempts to work at any personal ideals (11[38]:2; 25[48]:1; 33[55]:4:2). And yet many passages give instruction in self-cultivation or have self-cultivation as their most likely context (see p. 191–99 and Section 3 of the translation). The *Tao Te Ching* advocates cultivating certain specific qualities, and pictures these as greatly superior to their opposites: Femininity is superior to masculinity, Softness is superior to hardness, mental Stillness is superior to excitement, Emptiness is superior to solidity.[12] It contains strong moral condemnations of abuses on the part of the rich and powerful (50[53]; 51[75]; 52[77]:1; 53[72]:2); and it advocates stopping certain "progressive" tendencies which go against specific Laoist social ideals. (See Section 7 of the translation.)

• Many passages advocate self-effacement ("remaining concealed," 6[15]:5), and seem to warn against all desire and effort directed to gaining personal advantage or high status for oneself (see p. 548 under *Self-Promotion**). Yet others assume that gaining admiration and political status and power is a desirable goal (2[9]:2:2; 3[67]:2:9; 59[58]:4:5), and advocate certain ways of acting partly on the basis that they will help one achieve this goal (4[22]:5-6; 10[7]:2; 55[66]:1,2,4; 56[61]; 57[68]).

From the present point of view, the main source of these apparent inconsistencies in the *Tao Te Ching* is the habit interpreters have of trying to find some fundamental truth *of unlimited scope*, and expecting the coherence of Laoist thought to consist in the fact that it adheres to all the logical conclusions that would follow from the unlimited application of this truth. This is a mistake, because aphorisms as such are extremely context-bound. Their meaning is exhausted in the point they make about a specific situation that they address. And a major part of their meaning and their validity consists in correcting and counteracting some tendency in this situation which they oppose (see p. 138–39, 153–54).

This suggests one major way to resolve apparent contradictions among sayings in the *Tao Te Ching*. Laoist polemic aphorisms are meant to be understood within a particular context, a framework of several taken-for-granted goals and assumptions common to Warring States *shih* presented in Part Two. They are compensatory wisdom within this framework, working to counteract many ideas that usually accompany these goals and assumptions.

The main assumptions involved are: That reforming society by gaining positions of political and cultural influence is a primary goal (p. 58, 75–76); that cultivation of one's character is the primary means of fitting oneself for such leadership positions (p. 104); that social order depends on the existence of a good paternalistic government, and that the ideal society has a single head who represents in his person the symbolic normative center of the Chinese world (p. 52, 75); that the main goals of a ruler are gaining the allegiance and cooperation of the people, setting the proper tone for the society (p. 99–100), and performing the administrative tasks necessary for the society to function smoothly and efficiently, thereby providing the basis for material prosperity and social harmony (p. 101–02). While working within these assumptions, Laoist aphorisms try to counteract such things as the boastful self-assertion by which some *shih* tried to gain positions of influence, conventional notions about what good character means, the tendency of rulers to project an impressive presence and to coerce obedience, and so on. Because the aphorisms are basically compensatory, they frequently seem to be injunctions against any quest whatsoever for higher social status, against the very existence of an authoritative ruler, against any attempts by rulers to influence the society, and so on. But the case here is like the case in which one advises a college student, "Forget about grades and diplomas, and just concentrate on doing your work well." This advice takes place within a framework in which fulfilling degree requirements is taken for granted. It does not really advocate leaving college altogether, but tries to compensate for certain tendencies that very often accompany degree-seeking.

On the positive side, the account of aphorisms given in Chapter 6 suggests the particular kind of unity and coherence we should expect to find in a body of aphorisms. We should expect their coherence to be centered around the three chief meaning elements of aphoristic meaning structure: the target, the images suggested, and the attitude expressed and value orientation motivating this attitude. The commentaries and the Topical Glossary in Part Four demonstrate in detail that this is indeed the case. Laoist aphorisms are partly unified by the fact that they are addressed to a small interrelated group of major concerns. These concerns are the main basis for my rearrangement of the chapters in the seven sections of the commentary (except for Section 3, and parts of Section 4). And several major topics in the Topical Glossary show the unity of several groups of aphorisms that have the same target.

Discussions in the Topical Glossary under *Appearances** and *Confucianism** show the unity of one group of aphorisms whose target is the tendency to admire and cultivate fine appearances, and the topic *Self-Promotion** does the same for a group whose target is boastful self-promotion in peer-competition among *shih*. The discussion in each case shows that sayings having the same target, present a similar or closely related set of images, and are motivated by the same value orientation. These three topics are the main themes in the chapters grouped together in Section 1 of the translation. The main theme in Section 2 is Laoist thought about psychobiological health and peace of mind. The unity of aphorisms in this group is shown in discussion under the topics *Agitation** and *Desire** (again the names of the two major targets of aphorisms on this subject). Aphorisms expressing Laoist views about the nature of true understanding occur mainly in chapters grouped together as the first four chapters in Section 4, and their unity is shown in discussions under the topics *Naming** and *Understanding**. Aphorisms dealing with Laoist ideals for the ruler are grouped together in Sections 5 through 7. Their unity is shown in the discussion under topics that describe the main targets of these sayings: Essays under the topics *Impressive** and *Strict** discuss the main topics of those chapters grouped together in Section 5. The essay under the topic *Improvements** discusses the main topics of those chapters grouped together in Section 7.

These two sets of observations provide a partial account of the unity of thought in Laoist aphorisms, and of how some apparent contradictions in them can be resolved. But the main positive factor that gives to the *Tao Te Ching* the feeling of unity that many feel in it lies in an additional factor suggested by the analysis of aphoristic meaning structure given in Chapter 6. There it was argued that the main basis for whatever validity an aphorism expresses is the goodness of the value orientation expressed. One would expect from this that, if a body of aphorisms is highly unified, their unity would consist in the single value orientation that all the aphorisms "perform." This I believe turns out to be the case with the body of Laoist sayings contained in the *Tao Te Ching*. This topic needs more extended discussion.

The Unifying Basis for Laoist Thought:
A Concern for Organic Harmony

Most readers sense a unity in the *Tao Te Ching*. The main modern attempts to describe the single basis that gives this thought its unity are influenced by the foundationalist assumption that all valid thought needs a basis in some objective reality that can be defined in an absolute way: Here the main proposals are that Laoist thought is founded in observations about objective "nature,"[13] or that it is founded in some metaphysical absolute similar to the Hindu Brahman.[14] The other main alternative is that it teaches the modern opposing counterpart of foundationalism, metaphysical relativism,[15] resulting in a skepticism toward all value judgments and all claims to truth.

These explanations contain assumptions contrary to the semantic structure of aphorisms presented in Chapter 6. Aphorisms are not based on objective observations of "natural laws" (see p. 133–34). They are not deductions from more fundamental principles that provide their epistemological and logical basis; they are rather self-contained, suggesting by themselves the basis on which they hope to persuade (see p. 139–40). This basis is generally some value-orientation "performed" by the aphorism, which has a positive and definite character. One could, of course, imagine a *body* of aphorisms designed to inculcate skepticism: Such a body would need to contain aphorisms expressing directly opposing value orientations. But, although there is an abundance of paradox in Laoist aphorisms, most commentators have been struck by a certain unidirectionality in these paradoxes,[16] suggesting a single positive value orientation.

I can most economically present my proposals about this unifying value orientation by first giving an abstract and synthetic account, and then showing how this account is supported by the dominant themes present in the text.

One fundamental phenomenon on which my proposals are based is the ability of human consciousness to create a mental space separated off from the physiological, psychogical, and experiential whole of which it is a part, and which is its concrete sustaining substrate. This manifests itself, for example, in analytical and conceptual thought—the ability to represent certain aspects of reality by means of ideas, which in turn enable us to mentally organize our world in a deliberate way, to orient ourselves in this world, to conceptualize certain goals, and to manipulate reality to attain these goals. Another illustration of this ability is the phenomenon of deception, which seems ultimately dependent on an ability to formulate concepts that are separated off from our actual perceptions and experience of reality, and to create "artificial" appearances contrary to reality as actually experienced. These abilities are partly rooted in a pervasive phenomenon in the psychology of perception: The tendency of all sensation and consciousness to split experience into a "foreground" that stands out as a focus of awareness, over against a taken-for-granted "background." The separate mental space we create for ourselves seems a development of what is foregrounded in perception, split off from what appears as background.

This phenomenon of individual psychology has an analogy in social life. Individual identity is itself a social phenomenon, in that each person's self-image is defined in relation to the social whole of which she is a part. But here again human consciousness has the ability to split itself off, to ignore its taken-for-granted dependency on this sustaining social whole, and to see itself as an individual consciousness with an interest in asserting itself over against the whole. The leadership roles that are part of many social organisms provide special opportunities for this kind of self-assertion. Such self-assertion is often partially supported by the social group as a whole, for whom some people appear to "stand out" as especially noteworthy and admirable against the relatively "ordinary" social whole considered here as background.

These tendencies are the basis for some things we nowadays value highly in life. But for present purposes we have to consider also some of their negative aspects and results. We need to try especially to define carefully what positive values might be damaged by the tendencies described, positive values that one might try to develop and cultivate instead. I suggest three things that "separated" consciousness can be contrasted with: wholeness, concreteness, and a sustaining substrate. Separated consciousness is one part existing in a whole human being, but it tends to value its ability to stand out in contrast to this whole. Separated consciousness is a "mental" reality, contrasted with the more concrete reality of the person as a psychological, biological, and physical being. The whole of a person's concrete being is a sustaining substrate for separated consciousness: Our ability to function well mentally, and find satisfaction in our lives, depends greatly on the healthy condition of the whole of our concrete being.

What is especially noteworthy here is the fact that when separated consciousness gives overwhelming emphasis to its own specific value and its aims and activity, it can easily damage the quality of the concrete whole that is its sustaining basis, and thus damage the quality of its own existence and its own ability to function well. The specific damage done here seems to be the damage done to the organic goodness and the organic harmony of the whole concrete being. "Organic" here refers to the fact that a human being is a complex whole, made up of elements and forces each of which has some spontaneous intrinsic tendency to coordinate itself with other elements in the whole. Organic goodness is the kind of goodness that arises as a result of these tendencies, and organic harmony is the kind of unity that comes about through these tendencies. What is organic to any given being can be contrasted with the kind of goodness or order that comes about through an enforced subordination of some elements to others, or through the imposition of a conscious plan external to the elements themselves. Separated consciousness is in a privileged position to damage organic goodness and harmony: Although it is one element in a whole human being, it has the ability to dominate the whole and organize the whole around itself, its ideas, and its goals.

A human being simply *is* always a concrete whole; this is a fact that cannot be diminished or increased. Organic harmony is, however, subject to degrees; one can have more of it or less of it. While human beings, like all living organisms, have some intrinsic tendencies toward internal organic harmony, organic harmony is also something that can be deliberately fostered. This cannot be done directly, by first devising a conceptual model of what organic harmony would mean and then imposing it on one's being. But it can be done indirectly, by combating those tendencies (sometimes equally spontaneous) that tend to destroy it, and by providing conditions that support and foster spontaneous tendencies toward organic harmony already present in one's being.

One can gain some understanding of the possible goodness[17] involved in a state of highly developed organic harmony by extrapolation from more ordinary examples. One can easily see, for example, that the quality of a person's existence is damaged by severe cases of overstimulation and exhaustion, or by severe cases of psychological repression. One can imagine how progress in ridding oneself of such psychologically damaging conditions would result in improvements in the quality of an individual human existence itself. Imagine also making progress in gaining more and more of the specific kind of goodness involved here, until this goodness was present in a very superlative degree. Imagining this might be difficult, not because we have no experience at all of this kind of goodness, but because the Western cultural heritage offers us few models or ideas about organic harmony as something one might want to achieve to a very high degree for its own sake. It tends to have a relatively low and subservient place in our list of priorities.

There is also a further intrinsic difficulty, however, in imagining organic harmony in its perfection: in most models of perfection, some quality clearly stands out to capture our attention against a background of ordinariness. By comparison, the greatness one would feel in great organic harmony would be somewhat mysterious, in that one could feel the greatness but could not locate this greatness in the usual way by identifying it with some one or few attention getting element(s). (The closest Western analogy here might be the beauty of some classic Greek statues, which consists in the perfect proportioning and harmony of the parts, rather than in any one outstanding beautiful feature.)

My claim is that this description of organic harmony as a good best explains the particular combination of themes that we find in Laoist aphorisms. Let me begin with aphorisms dealing with the Laoist equivalent of Mencian "virtue"—those that attack certain models of what it means to be a great human being and propose other models instead. If my thesis is correct, Laoist thought on this subject is based on the fact that any given human personality has a tendency to develop in such a way that the various qualities making up the personality form a spontaneously integrated and harmonious whole. Laoists are particularly sensitive to certain other human tendencies that damage this organic integration. One important negative tendency here is the tendency of separated consciousness to take impressing others as a primary goal. Thus it will give special emphasis to fostering those individual qualities that are socially impressive, and to repressing those qualities that appear negligible or negative in a given social environment. Another negative tendency is the tendency of separated consciousness to develop *conceptually* formulated ideals, and to think of "becoming good" as a matter of shaping one's being and conduct according to these conceptual ideals. Both these tendencies will typically lead to a development of personality that is "unbalanced" from the point of view of one who takes as her norm an organic balance and integration of qualities rising from within. They will also lead to a certain kind of permanent internal strain, as consciousness has to continually work against the tendency of some repressed instincts and elements of the personality to assert and integrate themselves into the whole.

On the present thesis, these two tendencies are the main targets of Laoist aphorisms on this subject. This group of aphorisms is motivated by a value orientation in which organic harmony is the primary value, and some of them suggest ways in which organic harmony can be fostered. My argument for this thesis is that (1) it best explains the dominant themes (the most commonly repeated themes) in Laoist aphorisms on this subject; (2) it best explains the particular combination of themes we find here; and (3) it does justice to certain ideas other commentators have emphasized, while overcoming some of their shortcomings, especially the internal contradictions that appear in Laoist thought in other interpretations. I will list my arguments here, citing evidence in footnotes except where only one passage is involved, or in the case of references to entries in the Topical Glossary (marked with asterisks), beginning p. 531.

This thesis explains the strong Laoist attack on the tendency to admire and cultivate impressive *Appearances**; Laoist thought characterizes such appearances as the result of artificial attempts to impress others (see *Self-promotion**) that typically lack real substance. Real substance has an important "natural" (i.e., organic) element, not able to be produced by deliberate conscious planning and effort. This thesis explains the attention Laoists give to quiet (3[67]:2) and subtle (44[41]:3) virtues, and the advice to cultivate even qualities most people would consider "disgraceful"; this is necessary in order to counter the tendency of separated consciousness to emphasize those qualities that impress others, and in order to cultivate instead a more organic wholeness by reintegrating those aspects of personality that get repressed in this process. A highly developed reintegration makes for a great person, "the Pattern for the World" (17[28]:1).

This thesis explains the continuity between Laoist values and certain commonly admired "quiet" virtues, but also the apparently radical Laoist attack on conventional values in general, and the associated habit of defining Laoist values in ironic or negative terms. Organic harmony is by nature something that will never stand out as especially good to ordinary consciousness, and so its goodness cannot be described in positive terms taken from language shaped by conventional usage. To a conventional mentality that pays attention to what stands out, the goodness of organic harmony will appear "Empty," "Nothing."[18] But a highly developed internal organic harmony will be experienced by its possessor as a state of being that is very sustaining and satisfying. Hence the Laoist contrast between what impresses others and an endlessly "useful"[19] Nothing. The permanent internal strain resulting from conscious development in opposition to organic harmony explains why Laoists characterize cultivation of fine appearances as negative *wei*/"working" (11[38]:1). A state of organic harmony lacks this kind of strain, and so can be characterized as "not doing" (25[48]:1–2) and as "Still" (5[45]:1–4). It has a self-sustaining quality and so feels more "lasting" (10[7]:1) than those states that require constant internal discipline motivated by external goals. (This is connected with the theme of a hypostatized, internally nourishing "Mother," discussed in Chapter 9 [p. 218]).

This thesis explains above all why Laoists can express such radical skepticism of conventional values, and apparently advocate being "natural" (14[23]:1), and at the same time advocate sustained and intensive efforts at self-cultivation[20] aimed at achieving high ideals. Although organic harmony bears some resemblance to what we ordinarily call "being natural," organic harmony cannot be identified with whatever happens through following just any spontaneous impulses. The tendencies destructive of organic harmony described above are as "spontaneous" and universal as the tendencies that foster organic harmony.[21] And organic harmony is something one can have more or less of, and can try to foster in oneself through creating conditions that bring it about to a higher degree. Perfect organic harmony is a "high excellence" (7[8]:1) that is "natural" and at the same time goes radically contrary to the tendency of human beings and human societies to admire most those ideals developed by separated consciousness.

This explanation can be extended to explain the dominant Laoist themes in those aphorisms whose target is the tendency of *shih* toward self-promotion*, "contending*" with others for social status. The organic reality that is involved here is social rather than individual: A society also has a certain organic order to it, and the worth of individuals is partly measured by the place of each in this organic whole and his or her contribution to it. Certain individuals might "shine" as leaders in this organic social order (4[22]:5), but for one who values the organic most highly this must always be because of the genuine contribution such an individual makes to the organic social whole, not through any direct self-assertive efforts to stand out. Such "artificial" standing out is precisely what is destructive of organic social harmony. Seen against the normative horizon of an organically ordered whole, deliberatly self-assertive and boastful self-promotion is an "excess" that has no solid grounding in "things" (1[24]:1–4). This analysis explains why Laoists can both strongly attack deliberate and direct attempts to shine socially, and also take it as their ambition to become leaders of their society.[22]

This analysis can also be extended to Laoist thought about gaining true knowledge. The "organic organization" relevant here is that of multidimensional human experience involving the whole person, facing ever new and uniquely configured situations. This stands in contrast to the mode of knowledge characteristic of separated consciousness, in which reality is grasped through the medium of relatively fixed analytical concepts. The reality (the *Lebenswelt*) perceived by holistic human experience is a complex but organically organized and rich totality whose character is always shifting and taking on unique configurations. By contrast, the reality we grasp by concepts is relatively thin and abstract. And the fixed set of concepts and value terms we usually employ will tend to bias our perception so that we will fail to appreciate certain kinds of goodness that we might otherwise perceive in the world. Perceiving reality as an organic whole requires that we maintain an organic harmony within ourselves, rather than letting our beings be dominated by separated consciousness (43[1]:3–5). The deeper the organic harmony we attain within ourselves, the deeper will be our perception of organic order and goodness in the world. Allowing our awareness to be dominated by conceptual thought damages the quality of our consciousness, and so the quality of the *Lebenswelt* we perceive (see Understanding*). This analysis explains why Laoists can mount a radical attack on the use of value terms *("Names"*), and still claim to possess a superior evaluative understanding of reality that is the basis for certain obvious value judgments they make themselves.

One can also speak of an organic harmony on a psychological and physiological level. What damages organic harmony on this level is alignment around some external stimulus or goal, as for example prolonged excitement, prolonged work under pressure to acheive a certain goal, or anxiety caused by perceived threats to something one values very highly (a job, social status, self-image, etc.). These are all examples where something that is foregrounded in one's attention causes an unbalanced internal alignment that damages the healthy and organic harmony of our psychological and physiological being that is the necessary sustaining substrate of consciousness.[23] Laoists aim to reduce the stress caused by external stimulation and attachments. But the ultimate goal here is not (as in early Hinduism and Buddhism) the achievement of internal freedom for the spirit through detachment, but a kind of "higher hedonism," the ability to find deep and subtle satisfaction in the simple things of life (contentment in what satisfies one's internal "belly," in contrast to what catches one's eye [21[12]:2]).

Finally, we can apply this analysis to Laoist thought about ruling well. The main assumption here is that the individual members of longstanding social groups also have a spontaneous tendency to define and conduct themselves in a manner harmonious with the characteristics and conduct of other group members. There thus develops a kind of goodness and order that is relatively unique and organic to any given social group. Laoists assume (with all their contemporaries we know about) that a ruler plays a central role in the organic harmony of any organized society, both as a unifying focus of allegiance[24] and as someone who provides the conditions that maintain and foster this social harmony.[25] However they also perceive the ruler as the primary potential threat to organic harmony. Rulers damage the organic harmony of the society when they insist on overt dramatization of the difference between themselves and their subjects, fostering a polarization between themselves and the rest of society. Seen against the normative horizon of an organically ordered society, the dominating presence of such a ruler will appear a foreign intrusion. This will be more true, the more the ruler himself allows his perspective to be dominated by a separated consciousness: valuing qualities and appearances that make him stand out as impressive* and awesome, letting his leadership style be governed by strict* and sharply conceptualized norms, and emphasizing the importance of human agency in bringing about improvements* in the world. One important manifestation of his foreignness will be the fact that the people (who have an instinctive feeling for the unique organic order proper to their society) will feel him as a burden, and so will resent him and refuse him their allegiance and cooperation (54[17]:1). Emphatic and egoistic assertion of his personal superiority will also set a tone encouraging others to compete ("contend"*) with him and with each other for dominance (57[68]:2).

The contrasting Laoist ideal is not an anarchist society without a leader, nor a society in which the ruler literally does nothing. On the negative side, the ideal Laoist ruler or administrator/manager is one who avoids or minimizes any overt dramatization of the difference between himself and his subjects. Organic social harmony depends on people identifying with and taking pride in the social units to which they belong; this is weakened when the admiration of group members is directed toward someone outside the group, and even more weakened when fear of power intrusions from outside the group exerts a strong influence on group life. The ideal ruler will also not focus on direct enforcement of fixed standards of right and wrong. He will be sensitive to the unique and shifting conditions in any social group, and will flexibly pursue policies designed to foster the kind of organic harmony appropriate to each unique situation.[26] He will perform his necessary administrative work in such a way that it blends in as unobtrusively as possible with the ongoing processes of the society (54[17]:3). If he has to take action in opposition to some of his subjects, he will try to do so in a way that is as non-confrontational as possible.[27] He will resort to physical violence only very reluctantly and as a last resort.[28]

The main positive ideal the ruler should strive to attain is that he should represent in his person and in his policies the organic spirit of the society in its most ideal form (60[49]:1). In this case the people will recognize in him the same goodness they instinctively feel in their group life. This will be the source of his Te/charisma, and it will feel "natural" to the people to give him their allegiance and cooperation (55[66]:1). He will simply be a symbolic focus for their spontaneous attachment to the spirit of their own group.

All this explains why Laoists can express strong criticism of conventional assumptions that rulers should aim for "great" achievements and project a powerful and majestic image, and why at the same time they can take as their ambition becoming spiritual heir of the Chou Emperor as Norm for the World.

Despite Laoist distaste for oppositional intrusion on the part of the ruler, there is one set of tendencies they perceive in their society that they think must be strongly opposed, because these tendencies are disruptive of organic harmony. Among these are especially several tendencies others undoubtedly looked upon as great social improvements*: tendencies toward emphasizing instrumental and conceptual rationality both in the technological/economic sphere and in political/legal sphere; the growth and encouragement of individual ambition; and attempts to make Confucian virtues the official norm for all. Advocating active intrusion in opposition to these tendencies is not an inconsistent contradiction of Laoist strictures against the intrusive (*wei*/"working") ruler. Such opposition shows, rather, a consistent devotion to the central value of organic harmony.

The ideal of organic harmony as applied to the social and political order is an ideal that other commentators have remarked on as a common concern among ancient Chinese generally. This is especially true of Joseph Needham,[29] who also quotes the following interesting passage from Marcel Granet:

People like to talk about the gregarious instinct of the Chinese, and to attribute to them an anarchic temperament. In fact, their spirit of associativeness, and their individualism, are rustic and peasant qualities. Their idea of Order derives from a healthy country feeling for *good understanding*. . . . This feeling, wounded by excessive administrative intrusions, equalitarian constraints, or abstract rules and regulations, always rested . . . upon a kind of passion for autonomy, and upon a need, no less strong, for comradeship and friendship. State, Dogma, Law, were powerless as compared with Order. Order was conceived as a Peace which no abstract forms of obedience could establish, no abstract reasoning impose. To make this Peace reign everywhere, a taste for conciliation was necessary, involving an acute sense of compromise, spontaneous solidarities, and free hierarchies.[30]

Granet's view that the concern for organic harmony stems from a "rustic and peasant" worldview seems one quite likely partial explanation of the cultural origins of Laoism.

One further way of summing up the kind of goodness that unifies and motivates Laoist practical wisdom is by comparing it with the modern concern for the "quality of the environment." Many of our specific modern problems seem to have to do with the way that our narrow focus on certain apparently good *individual* aims causes us to ignore the way that pursuing these individual aims damages the environment on which the quality of our lives and even our productivity depends. The *Tao Te Ching* does not express direct concern for the "natural environment" as we understand it: trees, rivers, wildlife, and so on.[31] But consider other kinds of "environment."

A personality is an environment for the various virtues and good qualities that go to make up the personality. Western tradition typically emphasizes choosing rightly *which* particular virtues to develop. But we can also see that being a good person does not only mean having *some* collection of individual good qualities. In the concrete, we will generally perceive a given collection of good qualities to be more good if the qualities are highly integrated with each other, harmonious, and balanced. "Balance" and internal harmony are things we can perceive as good for their own sake, although they are not usually given much priority in the Western hierarchy of goods. Laoism makes this the *highest* good. Harmonious balance in a personality is what makes that personality a high quality "environment" for individual virtues.

Similarly, a state of mind is a physical/psychological "environment" in which particular experiences occur. We normally pay more attention to *which* individual experiences occur, preferring more meaningful and more "intense" individual experiences. But we can see that, all other things being equal, experiences that occur in a high quality physiological and psychological environment have a greater richness of meaning than those that occur when we are physically exhausted or psychologically agitated.

Our total mental state and our total relation to reality also constitute an environment in which understanding occurs. We can see that excessive reliance on conceptual knowledge can give a person a certain abstract and stilted relation to the world, damaging the general mental environment in which perceptions of the world occur. All other things being equal, our perceptions of and relation to the world will be of higher quality when they take place in an overall mental environment that involves our full being.

Finally, we can consider the quality of the social environment. We tend to think most about the *contents* of public policy and social conduct, and so focus on whether we think the authorities and/or the people are acting according to correct moral principles. But we can recognize also that a leader's narrow focus on the correctness of her policies, and emphasis on her own authority, can cause her to ignore the effect that her *style* of implementing these policies has on the general atmosphere in the group, as a social atmosphere in which policies are realized. All other things being equal, group life and interactions are of a higher quality the more they take place in a social environment characterized by organic harmony.

My argument is that organic goodness and harmony is a specific kind of goodness that is the unifying basis for the Laoist worldview. But Laoist sayings do not give us a system of ideas or theories that explicitly lay out for us what organic harmony consists in. This is because Laoists were not interested in a conceptual and theoretical elaboration of their ideal such as I am attempting here. The polemic aphorisms "peform" a concern for organic harmony in their selection of targets and images. I will show in Chapters 8 through 10 that Laoists also engaged in self-cultivation practices aimed at developing personal qualities (like Stillness and Oneness) that foster organic harmony within, and other qualities (like Softness) that make for a leadership style fostering organic harmony in the society.

On the above account, speaking in general, Laoist advice is *good* advice, at least in some contexts, because the perspective it urges is motivated by concern for something good and deserving of respect, organic harmony. The goodness of organic harmony is the ultimate unifying subject matter (*die Sach*) that Laoist sayings call to our attention to and try to convert us to.

Organic harmony is, however, *a* good among many possible goods. How important a good it is, and what priority it deserves with respect to other goods, is something that might vary according to varying cultural contexts. Discussing how important this good is in our own cultural context is a matter beyond the scope of this book. (I offer some comments illustrating possible directions such a discussion might take on p. 294–300.)

Appendix: Sayings about Nature, Heaven, and the Ancients

There are two issues related to the interpretation of Laoist aphorisms that require some further brief comment here. The first issue concerns the common opinion that Laoists took it as a fundamental truth that nature is to be imitated. The implicit assumption here is that this basic doctrine led Laoists to undertake impartial observations to determine the patterns or laws underlying natural phenomena, and from these observations they derived models for human conduct.[32]

This is implausible. First, the kind of understanding Laoists aim at decidedly precludes the emphasis on detailed observation and exact conceptualization that is necessary for really understanding the laws underlying natural phenomena (see 41[47], and comments under *Naming** and *Understanding**).

Secondly, Laoists were clearly quite selective rather than neutral in their "observation of nature." If they really held the doctrine that they should imitate nature, and if they were seriously seeking to discover the laws that predominate in nature, surely the advantage of height would have attracted at least as much attention as the value of "lowness," and the value of strength as much as the value of weakness, the value of fullness as much as that of emptiness, and so on. There are two sayings that draw attention to natural phenomena implicitly pictured as *negative*: Violent but short-lived phenomena like whirlwinds and heavy downpours (14[23]:2), and the seasonal flourishing-and-withering-away of plants (33[55]:5), serve as images of the human cycle of artificial-stimulation-and-exhaustion which Laoists want to avoid. This suggests that observations about natural phenomena are not really the basis for Laoist thought. Rather, what we find is that there are many Laoist sayings of a basically aphoristic nature which involve nature images. Like all images presented in Laoist aphorisms (see p. 136), these images were selected because they make some important point that Laoists wanted to make for reasons given above, quite independently of any genuinely neutral observations of nature.

The main thing about nature-sayings that needs additional comment here is the fact that they often present a more complex, *extended* metaphor in the place of the simpler images typical of the shorter sayings. For example 7[8]:1 uses phenomena connected with water to make two separate points, that it flows downward "settling in places everyone else avoids," and that it "benefits the thousands of things" (i.e., nourishes plants). These two points are connected in Laoist wisdom in a different way than they are in the natural world: Laoists emphasized that *shih* should not "contend" for high status for themselves, but instead should cultivate a self-effacing devotion to the betterment of the society, even if this means accepting personal obscurity ("low" status) and lack of social recognition. (See commentary on 7[8] and 8[81].)

There are two other kinds of sayings that one might also be tempted to regard as proposing fundamental doctrines, but that ought to be interpreted along the same lines as nature sayings. These are sayings invoking the way "Heaven" acts, (as in "The Way of Heaven is to benefit and not to harm" 8[81]:4), and sayings invoking an idealized ancient golden age of Chinese civilization (as in "The men of old who were Excellent at doing Tao—it was not to enlighten the people, but to keep them stupid" 80[65]:1 [see further examples under *Ancient**]).

Here again the form of the sayings might lead one to think that Laoists *began* by taking it as a fundamental truth that people ought to imitate Heaven and the ancient sages. They then seriously tried to discover the habits of Heaven and these sages, and *deduced* from these truths some guidelines about the way they themselves should act. But there is no indication that Laoists engaged in such inquiries. These sayings too have an essentially aphoristic structure. One *begins with a point* one wants to make, and then one selects, or one creates, images connected with Heaven or with ancient sages that will get across this point. Laoist sayings asserting or implying facts about Heaven or about an idealized ancient time have the same basic semantic structure as the Mohist statement about ancient kings analyzed on p. 30–32.

A few further remarks can be made about Heaven. First, it is sometimes asserted that Laoists based their views on *t'ien chih*

Tao/"Heaven's Tao," which they learned by observing the processes of nature (governed by Heaven as cosmic ruler). This is one basic difference between Laoism and Confucianism, which based itself on a "Tao of mankind," that is, the values of human civilization.[33] But 52[77]:1 is the only saying in which "Heaven's Tao" certainly refers to observable natural processes. The saying in 2[9]:2 says that to "achieve successes, win the fame, withdraw yourself" is "Heaven's Way"; what is described here is clearly the conduct of an ideal Laoist *shih*, not nature processes. Other passages describing Heaven's Way (8[81]:4, 9[79]:4, 58[73]:5) are more ambiguous, but in any case the content is surely derived from Laoist ideals, not from neutral investigation of nature.

Secondly, the many fragments of lore about Heaven scattered throughout the *Tao Te Ching* are sometimes in conflict with each other. For example, the sayings invoking "Heaven's Way" suggest that Heaven acts according to a consistent pattern that one should imitate. But 58[73]:1–3, after implying that "Heaven's hatred" is the reason for deaths of individuals on the battlefield, says that this hatred is unpredictable ("What Heaven hates—who knows the reason?"). The saying in 16[5]:2 asserts that Heaven is "not Good," but indifferent to what goes on in the world; but 8[81]:4 says that "The Way of Heaven is to benefit and not to harm"; and 52[77]:1 says it is the Way of Heaven to intervene to take away from the "haves" in order to help the "have-nots"; and 9[79]:4 says, "Heaven's Way [is] . . . to be invariably good to all" (or alternatively: "Heaven's Way is always to be with the good man.")

On the present reading, what these apparent conflicts indicate is not that Laoists were illogical or inconsistent, but rather that lore about Heaven served them only as a store of images to be put to various uses. They were not interested in *doctrines* about Heaven for their own sake, much less as a foundation for their own views of life.

8

Sayings and Self-Cultivation

Introduction

Chapter 7 dealt with Laoist aphorisms on the basis of an analysis
of the meaning-structure of aphorisms generally, assuming a constant meaning-structure for aphorisms as a genre across the cultural boundaries that separate us from ancient China. There are other
sayings in the *Tao Te Ching*, however, which cannot be dealt with
in this way, and these are the subject of Chapters 8 through 10.
The sayings treated here do not have such clear parallels in our
own culture, and quite clearly assume some different and more
specialized kind of context. These are sayings like:

> The world has a Source, the Mother of the World. (29[52]:1)

> Tao produced the Oneness
> The One produced Two
> Two produced Three
> Three produced the thousands of things. (36[42]:1)

> The Tao that can be told is not the invariant Tao. . . .
> Nameless, it is the source of the thousands of things.
>   (43[1]:1–2)

These sayings, usually described as "cosmological" or "metaphysical,"[1] have attracted widespread attention, especially sayings
about Tao. There is a nearly universal tendency, especially among
scholarly interpreters, to treat the content of these sayings as foundational doctrine. The *Tao Te Ching* teaches a certain set of metaphysical doctrines about the world that are in competition with other
metaphysical doctrines claiming to represent reality as it is, and
these sayings are especially important because they state the *epistemological* foundation of Laoist doctrine. They state what must be
objectively and uniquely true in order for the rest of Laoist thought
to be well-founded. And they present to us the *logical* foundation for
Laoist thought, in that the rest of Laoist thought can in principle be
logically deduced from truths expressed in these sayings.

Benjamin Schwartz' recent interpretation[2] of this area of Laoist thought serves as one good representative example of this general approach. This is how Schwartz describes the place of Tao in the thought of the *Tao Te Ching*:

> [In the thought of the *Tao Te Ching*] a major characteristic of this world is its determinate finitude. The *tao* in its aspect of the ineffable eternal is nondeterminate and nameless. It cannot be identified with anything nameable. It is nonbeing (*wu*). . . . *Wu* is a reality which corresponds to no determinate finite entity, relation, or process which can be named. Yet it is eminently "real" and the source of all finite reality. (197)

Although according to Schwartz, strictly speaking the concept of Tao has no definite content, being beyond all finite determinations, this *teaching* about Tao still teaches something definite and potentially controversial. It asserts (1) that reality has two layers, reality immediately perceived vs. "ultimate" reality, and (2) that all valid truths about phenomenal reality must be grounded in the character of ultimate reality. Therefore, (3) since the ultimate reality, Tao, is beyond all finite determinations, including the determinations "good" and "evil," our perceptions of good and evil in the world are ungrounded and hence are invalid. In Schwartz' words, since *tao* is "beyond all determinations," (193) and "the sage is himself modelled on the mystery of the Tao," it follows that the sage "is not consciously 'good'. . . . We have here an aspiration to look at nature without any value judgments." (202)

On Schwartz' interpretation, the *Tao Te Ching* arose out of a speculative mysticism comparable to Neoplatonism and to Hindu Vedanta.[3] It is *speculative* mysticism in that extraordinary mental states are looked upon as a source of insights into foundational truths, "direct knowledge of the ineffable source of all that which lends existence meaning." (193) This knowledge is knowledge of a foundational truth, from which one can and should draw conclusions about the nature of the phenomenal world.

Schwartz's view of this Tao doctrine as a foundational truth shows very clearly in the way he handles those passages in which, as he himself sees, the *Tao Te Ching* clearly does make value judgments: For example, it favors Femininity over masculinity, and Softness over hardness (203); it "attack[s] the . . . evils of civilization in a prophetic spirit" (209); it fosters one specific type of social order over against other possibilities (212–23). If Laoist thought is indeed founded on the doctrine about the transcendent but indeterminate Tao with which Schwartz begins his discussion, these are all serious inconsistencies, a failure to adhere to all the logical implications of this foundational doctrine. This is exactly Schwartz' judgment: These aspects of Laoist thought represent an "unexpected moralistic torque, which would create a problem from . . . a 'mystical' point of view" (203). It reveals "an impulse which is in deep tension . . . with [Lao Tzu's] mysticism, to the extent that mysticism points to a realm 'beyond good and evil'. . . . Lao-tzu had not entirely freed himself from 'value judgment'" (204). Despite all one can say to try to resolve the "basic inconsistency" caused by the *Tao Te Ching*'s "moralistic torque," "this contradiction remains unresolved" (213).

Schwartz is following a basic line of interpretation that goes back to the earliest Chinese commentator on the *Tao Te Ching*, Han Fei Tzu.[4] Another form that this doctrinal approach takes is the attempt to treat some key Laoist terms—Tao, Te, The One, The Mother, Femininity—as references to some systematically differentiated conceptual system.[5] One assumes that Tao and Te, for example, are different realities that stand in some specific and fixed relation to each other in some conceptual system that is consistently adhered to. One also tries to figure out whether *mu*/"[The] Mother," or *i*/"[The] One" are realities different from Tao in this system, or just other names for Tao. And so on.

As I remarked in Chapters 4 and 5 on the *Mencius*, the assumption that there is some body of theory that underlies the thought of pre-Han Chinese classics is usually an assumption that scholars bring to these works. One does not come to the works asking first *whether* some system of doctrines is present, one sets out right away trying to piece together what the doctrines are. But, as also argued in Chapters 4 and 5, "constructing doctrinal systems" is a very specific human project requiring sustained conscious attention, usually undertaken for some specific purpose. We cannot assume that this is the focus of all serious thought, but we must in each case ask the historical question whether we have evidence that any given text reflects specifically doctrinal thought. My argument in this chapter and the one to follow is that the evidence counts against this thesis with respect to the *Tao Te Ching*.

My argument instead will be that sayings about Tao, Te, and The Mother in the *Tao Te Ching* are part of a large group of sayings that have as their background not doctrinal speculation but the concrete practice of self-cultivation. In general these sayings are those that use a special set of recurrent terms: Stillness, Emptiness,

Femininity, Softness/Weakness, Harmony, Clarity, The Merging, The Oneness, the Uncarved Block, The Mother, Tao, Te, and Excellence. These terms are descriptions or hypostatizations of a state of mind that Laoists cultivated. Laoist self-cultivation was more intense and introspective than that reflected in the *Mencius*, and it involved meditation exercises that probably led to some extraordinary experiences that could be called "mystical." But the mysticism involved was not unitive mysticism, aiming at union with some supreme reality, undertaken for its own sake. Nor was it speculative mysticism, regarding extraordinary experiences as a source of direct insight into the ultimate structure of reality. Laoists cultivated an extraordinary state of mind ultimately, like Mencius, for practical purposes: This state of mind made them internally self-sustaining, not having to rely on worldly success; and it expressed itself in a certain style of personal conduct and of political leadership that they valued for its own sake. Sayings about Tao as world-origin are not doctrinal teaching, but celebrate the cosmic importance of the state of mind Laoists cultivated, and the fact that it is something that transcends the conventional world. To simplify, using a contemporary analogy, "Love makes the world go 'round,'" does not answer the question "What makes the earth spin?" but rather the question "How great is love?" In the same way, "Tao . . . is the origin of the thousands of things" does not answer the question "How did the world begin?" but rather the question, "How great is the Tao we cultivate?"

This thesis involves a related thesis about the use of language in the relevant sayings. This thesis requires noting the difference between the way language is used when one is invoking a set of established theories, as opposed to the way language is used in ordinary conversation where no theories are at stake. As an example of a statement invoking a theory, consider the statement a doctor might make to a heart patient, "The pain you feel in your chest is caused by insufficient blood flow to the outside of the heart, due to cholesterol buildup in one of your coronary arteries." I will call such a statement "analytically explanatory." The doctor is analyzing a felt pain into its constituent elements and causes, invoking established and systematized medical theories about these elements and causes (e.g., that the heart is a muscle and that insufficient blood flow to a muscle causes pain). The validity of the statement depends on the truth of these theories.

Contrast this with a statement one might make in ordinary conversation, "An idea just came to me." This statement is not analytically explanatory. It does not mean to explain to others the elements or causes of an experience. We could call it, rather, "experientially evocative." The words are trying to convey a particular common experience to others, using words that evoke similar experiences they have had. Pragmatically speaking, the statement does its work in this conversation if others have had similar experiences and recognize the words as a reference to this kind of experience. People could perfectly well and validly go on talking this way even if someone proved that all psychological theories positing the objective existence of entities called *ideas* are false. The term *idea* names something phenomenologically concrete, a *phainomenon*, part of the "appearances" of the world, rather than a set of entities whose existence we have established by critical reflection on that experience.

We make many statements like this in ordinary conversation, statements like: "She is full of energy today"; "He has a big ego"; "She has a bad case of nerves"; "Part of me wants to go, and part of me wants to stay"; "Use your will power"; "I'm smiling on the outside, but sad on the inside"; "These feelings are very deep"; "I felt touched at the center of my being"; and so on. A foreigner who did not recognize the experiential referents of the phrases involved here might easily take them as analytically explanatory, and think that these statements reflect some doctrines that are all part of a psychological theory: Doctrines about "energy," "egos," "nerves," and "will power"; doctrines about internal divisions of people into various "parts," or into an "inside" and an "outside," or into a "center" and a "periphery"; doctrines about different layers of feelings, and so on. But all we have here is a collection of familiar concepts and images that people use to describe to others some aspects of reality as they perceive it. The concepts and images involved do not get their meaning by being part of some overall system of doctrines in which each has a fixed place. They get their meaning by being inserted piecemeal into conversations about concrete circumstances. This is especially true of terms people use to speak of "internal" experiences, perceptions of their own mental state that have no obvious external behavioral correlates. These are terms like *feelings, ideas, self, mind, will, attitudes* and so on. Sometimes these are spoken of as elements of "folk psychology," but this is misleading if it implies that they are elements in some attempt at systematic psychological *theory*. In ordinary conversation, they are simply terms we find helpful in speaking to others about elements of our perception of ourselves that are not externally observable.

To give another example, somewhat closer to our subject matter, T'ai Chi instructors frequently use the word *ch'i* in instructions they give. An instructor might say, for example,[6] "Do not move your arms with your arm muscles, but with the *ch'i* which comes from your stomach." This language needs to be understood in the experiential and pragmatic context of T'ai Chi practice. The T'ai Chi teacher may or may not be invoking some particular theory about an entity or force called *ch'i*. What he is primarily doing is giving concrete directives concerning a physical exercise. His language is primarily experientially evocative. People practicing T'ai Chi need to develop a highly acute and differentiated sensitivity to certain internal sensations that occur while moving slowly in a certain way, and these sensations are the phenomenologically concrete reference of the term *ch'i*. The teacher's directives do their work and are valid if the term *ch'i* has some intelligible relation to internal sensations that the pupils actually have, and if moving one's arms *as if* they were being moved by this *ch'i* achieves some of the aims which T'ai Chi sets out to achieve. From a pragmatist point of view (p. 29–32) it does not essentially matter whether *ch'i* has any objective reference that goes beyond what is merely phenomenologically concrete. If someone shows conclusively that *ch'i* is simply not a reality of the kind one finds described in modern scientific essays on physiology, this would not in the least affect the meaning of talk about *ch'i* in the context of T'ai Chi practice.

My thesis about the use of language in the Laoist sayings treated in these chapters will be that references to Tao, Te, The Mother, and so on, are not analytically explanatory, but experientially evocative. These terms represent a collection of familiar concepts that Laoists used to talk about experiences connected with self-cultivation. Laoists did not use these experiences as a basis for constructing any set of doctrines either about psychology or about the structure of the cosmos.

My argument for this thesis will be a basically form-critical one, understanding form-criticism as the twin investigation into original life setting, and into the relation of verbal forms or genres to this life setting (see p. 126, 130). The present chapter will prepare for a form-critical study of various genres of sayings in the *Tao Te Ching* related to self-cultivation, by looking at passages from another document roughly contemporary with the *Tao Te Ching*, and reflecting a similar background, the *Nei Yeh*.

The Nei Yeh

The *Nei Yeh*, "Inward Training" is a writing that dates from sometime in the fourth century, preserved for us in an ancient miscellany entitled the *Kuan Tzu*.[7]

The main advantages of the *Nei Yeh* in the present context are that, first, the relation between verbal form and concrete setting is quite clear in this writing. And secondly there are many similarities between this work and the *Tao Te Ching*, both in form and in substance, giving us some assurance that it can appropriately be used to illuminate the background of the *Tao Te Ching*.

In several recent studies of the *Nei Yeh*,[8] Harold Roth has pointed out the important contribution this document has to make to our knowledge of self-cultivation in early Taoism. But Roth tends to come to the study of the *Nei Yeh* assuming that the special terms used in this work are parts of a psychological theory about the human makeup. This leads him to try to establish the precise relation between terms like Tao, *ch'i*, and *ching*/"vital energy" that play an important part in this book. We need to begin one step back from this, and ask what the evidence shows about *whether* any systematic psychological theorizing underlies the use of these terms in the *Nei Yeh*. I will argue that the evidence runs counter to this assumption. As Roth emphasizes, the *Nei Yeh* shows clear positive evidence of self-cultivation practice as its concrete life setting. But there are no positive indications of an interest in developing a systematic psychology. The unsystematic use of the terms in this work, which I will point out (and which Roth partly recognizes), argues against this.

What can first be pointed out is clear evidence that many passages in the *Nei Yeh* refer to the practice of self-cultivation. The self-cultivation involved is similar to that reflected in the *Mencius*, but it has a somewhat different object: What one cultivates is not virtue but what might be called a certain "state of mind," specifically a state of mental calmness. The following three stanzas are an example of the kind of passages involved.[9]

Always:
The mind's Form
is self-sufficient, reaching fullness by itself
self-producing, self-perfecting.

What we lose it by:
It is always sorrow, happiness, joy, anger, desire for profit.

If we are able to get rid of sorrow, happiness, joy, anger,
   desire for profit,
then the mind turns back to completeness.
What profits the mind's feelings: Peacefulness brought on
   by rest.

No trouble, no confusion,
then Harmony will perfect itself.

"Peacefulness brought on by rest" is a clear description of a
desirable state of mind. And it seems clear that the stanza previous to the one where this phrase occurs refers to a means by
which one might achieve this mental peacefulness. One should
try to get rid of strong, "disturbing" emotions and desires. Further,
although the term the term *Harmony* is not in itself necessarily
connected with peacefulness, the context here indicates that *Harmony* refers concretely to a peaceful state of mind. The same could
be said of *completeness* in the second stanza quoted.

All this leads to a similar interpretation of the first stanza. One
might at first think that this section means to teach us a doctrine
about the *hsin chih hsing*/"the mind's Form," a concept that is part
of the author's "theory of psychology." But the theory is difficult
to understand: The first lines give the impression that this Form
automatically perfects itself with no effort on our part; the following lines say that we can lose this Form by emotional disturbance.
The only thing that seems clear, then, is that *Form* is a concrete
reference to an ideal state of mind,[10] concretely identical with the
peaceful state of mind spoken of in the rest of these stanzas. Note
that harmony is also "self-perfecting" when we have freed the
mind of trouble and confusion.

The passage as a whole offers us enough clues to piece together the kind of concrete psychological experience the text has in
mind: One tries to eliminate sources of mental disturbance in
one's life, and when one prepares one's mind this way, a state of
mental calm seems to be brought about by some further process
that is relatively autonomous, not under direct conscious control.
Although the text hypostatizes Form and Harmony as quasi-
autonomous forces, this does not automatically mean that statements involving Form and Harmony are analytically explanatory,
invoking a set of psychological theories involving these concepts.
They might well be simply experientially evocative, ways of speaking about certain experiences people have who cultivate the state
of mental calm that the text speaks of.

Consider now the following stanzas occurring shortly after the ones quoted above:

Tao is what perfects the Form
but men cannot make it stand fast:
[sometimes] it goes and does not return
[sometimes] it comes and does not stay. . . .

Always:
Tao has no [fixed] place
it will peacefully settle in a good mind.
The mind still, the *ch'i* right,
then Tao can stay.

We note right away here another "contradiction." The earlier statement said that "The *hsing*/Form reaches perfection by itself," but now we hear that "Tao perfects the *hsing*/Form." This I think is even stronger evidence that these statements are not analytically explanatory, invoking a consistently held system of doctrines in which Tao, Form, and Harmony are concepts with fixed meanings standing in a fixed relation to each other. What is constant here is a certain experiential background. One makes ordinary efforts to calm one's mind, but this is a preparatory stage for further internal developments that appear to be driven by forces beyond one's conscious control. This second development can be described by picturing something like an ideal mental Form that perfects itself; but alternatively it can be described by picturing another force, Tao, that brings the Form to its ideal calm state. Further examples of this unsystematic use of terms are evident in the passage quoted below: Te makes the *ch'i* peaceful; but Te is also what results when one "watches over [*ch'i*] and does not lose it," as well as what results from Harmony. And Harmony is what results from a peaceful mind. Tao is also what stays when the mind is peaceful and the *ch'i* is right.

At one point in his study of the *Nei Yeh*, Roth recognizes this unsystematic and sometimes "contradictory" use of terms, and the difficulty this presents for his attempt to outline the "psychological theory" proposed in the *Nei Yeh*. He then suggests something like the experiential solution to this problem that I am proposing. He says:

We see the Tao (and the vital essence [*ching*]) conceived of as constantly moving into and out of the human mind. But if this Tao is the ultimate ground of the cosmos, how can it ever be separate from any one part of it? Rather than taking these descriptions literally, I interpret them as metaphorical references to one's experience of the Tao. That is, . . . when the mind is still, it seems as if Tao is present, and when the mind is agitated, it seems as if Tao has departed. Also the Tao is so intimately associated with the vital essence [*ching*] . . . that . . . identical metaphors are used to describe them.

I would simply take this last suggestion one step further and say that the terms in the *Nei Yeh only* describe a certain experience. Tao and *ching* are not part of any systematic theory, but are simply two experientially evocative terms referring to what is essentially a single state of mind.

The above remarks give the essential features of my argument. Let me now expand on them and present the main elements of my thesis about the *Nei Yeh*, which I think will be borne out by the close reading of the opening passage of the *Nei Yeh* given below. This, with some adjustments, will be my thesis about the *Tao Te Ching* as well.

First, sayings in the *Nei Yeh* have their concrete life setting in the self-cultivation practices of a particular group. The self-cultivation this group engaged in engendered a kind of mental calmness that was different in its intensity from normal mental calmness. And, as is usual in groups engaged in prolonged introspective exercises, these exercises engendered an awareness of internal states, sensations, and movements that was more acute and differentiated than ordinary internal self-awareness. As is also often the case with such groups, this group developed a special vocabulary to speak of these sensations and states. Among the main terms they used were those encountered above: Harmony, Completeness, Tao, *ch'i*/breath:energy,[11] and *hsing*/Form. They also use other terms we will meet below: *te*/virtue:power, *ching*/"vital energy," and *shen*/ghost:spirit. These terms had a phenomenologically concrete reference. They referred to what appeared to be concretely perceived realities in the world (the *Lebenswelt*) of those engaged in self-cultivation. Sayings using these terms are not analytically explanatory but experientially evocative.

Secondly, using Frege's *Sinn/Bedeutung* distinction[12] in modified form, we could say that each of these special terms has a different meaning-content, or *Sinn*, deriving from the different meanings of the terms. But they all have the same *Bedeutung*, taking *Bedeutung* here to mean not their reference to discrete objects, but their *phenomenologically* concrete reference to felt shifts in one's state of mind. For example, the term Tao does not have the same *Sinn* as the term *Harmony*. But the statement, "The mind still, the *ch'i* right, then Tao can stay" is *experientially* equivalent to, "No trouble, no confusion, then Harmony will perfect itself." Both statements refer to the same felt shift in one's mental state. Tao and Harmony have the same phenomenologically concrete *Bedeutung*.

Thirdly, phrases like "Tao stays" and "Harmony perfects itself" imply a linguistic and imaginal, but not a doctrinal and ontological hypostatization of Tao and Harmony. *Hypostatization* refers to cases where we conceive and speak of something as though it were an independent entity or energy. "Let nature take its course" hypostatizes "nature." "The weather is acting strange today" hypostatizes "the weather." "Let the music flow through your fingers" hypostatizes "music." Such hypostatizations treat "nature," "music" and so on *linguistically and imaginally* as separate entities or energies. Sometimes linguistic and imaginal hypostatization has a phenomenologically concrete basis. "Let the music flow through your fingers," for example, reflects an experience frequently reported by musicians ("I am not playing the music; the music is playing me.") But in experiential contexts like this, such hypostatization is seldom theoretical and ontological. *Speaking* as though "music" were an independent force does not necessarily imply a doctrinal belief in such a force. Similarly, if the present hypothesis is correct, phrases in the *Nei Yeh* like "Harmony perfects itself," "store *ching* in the breast," "watch over *ch'i*," and "Tao stays" represent linguistic and imaginal, but not doctrinal, hypostatizations of Harmony, *ching*, *ch'i*, and Tao. These hypostatizations very likely have some experiential basis. That is, the people whom the text envisages cultivating an extraordinary mental calm probably have fleeting internal sensations which they refer to by the special names, *ching*, Tao, and so on, and these seem to come and go after the manner of quasi-autonomous forces over which one has no direct control.

Finally, the hypostatization of these mental states makes possible a particular kind of statement which describes the immense, "cosmic" importance of the mental states, by making "cosmic" statements about Tao, *ch'i*, and so on.[13] We already saw something similar in Mencius' ideas concerning *ch'i* (p. 111): *Ch'i* can refer both to a relatively ordinary internal "feeling," and also to a cosmic presence that "fills up the space between Heaven and Earth."

It *becomes* a cosmic force when it is properly cultivated: It fills up the space between Heaven and Earth "when it is nourished by Rightness and when no harm is done to it." This statement suggests the origin of Mencius' cosmic image of *ch'i* pervading the space all around us: Mencius experiences Rightness-imbued *ch'i* as something of supreme importance, and this makes it feel like *ch'i* is some kind of pervasive force in the cosmos.

A good comparison here is the eulogy of *li*/ceremony:etiquette as a "cosmic" force found in the *Hsün Tzu:*

By this Heaven and Earth join,
By this sun and moon shine,
By this the four seasons proceed,
By this the stars take their course,
By this the Yangtse and the Yellow River flow,
By this the myriad things flourish.[14]

No serious scholar would suggest that this passage is the result of Hsün Tzu's attempts to satisfy people's curiosity about what makes the sun shine and the seasons proceed. They are clearly celebrations of the cosmic importance of *li*.

The *Nei Yeh* opens with a similar cosmic statement about *ching*/"vital energy."

The *ching* of things is what gave them birth
below, it gave birth to the five grains
above, it gave birth to the many stars.
Floating in the space between Heaven and Earth,
    we call it *shen*/spirit.
[The one who has it] stored in [his] breast
    we call the Wise Person.

This text presents *ching* as something that is the origin of everything, but also something that only some special people have: Having it makes one a *sheng jen*/"Wise Person." On the present interpretation, the last line presents the experiential basis of the "cosmic" lines that precede it. *Ching* is a very special internal "energy" one develops in self-cultivation. The supreme importance of this extraordinary energy makes it feel like something "cosmic." Again, the lack of *doctrinal* belief about *ching* as world origin shows in the unsystematic character of cosmogonic descriptions in the *Nei Yeh*. In addition to the above cosmogony centered on *ching*, we have sayings like, "Heaven develops [man's] *ching*, Earth develops his *hsing*/Form,"[15] and "What gives birth [*sheng*] to all things, what completes all things, this is called Tao."[16] People seriously holding doctrinal beliefs are usually more careful about the consistency of the various beliefs they hold. For people celebrating the cosmic importance of something, the power of the various images they use to express this is more important than consistency among the images.

Let me now quote and comment on the opening passage of the *Nei Yeh*. Literally, this writing bears some resemblance to the *Tao Te Ching*. That is, it does not appear to be written by a single hand as a continuous composition. It consists of relatively short, self-contained sayings. Sayings about *ching* are followed by sayings about *ch'i*, and then by sayings about Tao, with very abrupt transitions between these groups. Many of the individual sayings resemble each other stylistically and/or in content. Some of the individual sayings are difficult to understand, and little help is given in this by the present literary context. All this suggests a good possibility that this writing is made up primarily of sayings from the oral tradition of some group engaged in the self-cultivation practices described above. (See comments on similar features in the *Tao Te Ching*, p. 128–29, 306–07.)

Text

Always: {1}
The *ching* of things is what
    gave them birth
Below, it gave birth to the five
    grains. Above, it gave birth
    to the many stars.[17]
Flowing in the space between
    Heaven and Earth, we call it
    spirit
[the one who has it] stored in
    [his] breast we call the Wise
    Person.

Comment

The text opens by speaking of the cosmic importance of *ching*/"vital energy," expressing this by saying that *ching* gave birth to the grain and the stars. But the phrase "Store [*ching*] in the breast" is also one among many ways of describing the goal of self cultivation in the *Nei Yeh*. Those who cultivate this *ching* feel it as a ghostlike presence, a *shen*/spirit, pervading the space around them (like Mencius' *ch'i*).[18] As we shall see below, the *Nei Yeh* and the *Chuang Tzu* appropriate *shen*/ghost:spirit, a term from popular religion, to speak also

Text	*Comment*
	of the internal "spirit" one cultivates.
And so people's *ch'i*: {2} A bright sun! like something rising high in the heavens. Dark! like something descending into an abyss. Vast! like something residing in the ocean. Fully complete! like something residing in itself [alone].	A saying about *ch'i* follows, with only a formalized transition (*shih ku*/"and so"). No further transition is needed, because in the *Nei Yeh*, *ching* and *ch'i*/breath:energy are two names referring to the same hypostatized mental state. Stylistically, this saying is similar to sayings {9}, {11}, and {12}. These seem to represent a sayings-form connected with self-cultivation, remarking on the elusive yet wonderful quality of mind one is trying to cultivate internally. (See p. 196–97. The exclamation marks represent the exclamatory particle *hsi*.) This is obviously a special *ch'i*, not just the "breath" which everything possesses.
And so: {3} This *ch'i* cannot be made to stay[19] by force, but it can be made peaceful by Te, cannot be summoned by calling, but can be welcomed by the mind.[20]	The object of this self-cultivation can partly be described as trying to get a special kind of *ch'i* (described in {2}) to "stay" in oneself. It can equivalently be described as producing a peaceful *ch'i* by using some gentle internal force called Te here, which is the opposite of the forceful approach (criticized also in the *Mencius* [p. 112] and the *Tao Te Ching* 33[55]:4.)
Watch over It {4} with care and respect, and do not lose it.	Because this saying uses Te also, but in a different sense (as the *result* of self-cultivation), I

This is called "complete Te."[21]
Te complete, wisdom emerges,
the thousands of things reach
    fruition.[22]

Always: {5}
The mind's Form[23]
is self-sufficient, reaching
    fullness by itself,
self-producing, self-perfecting.

What we lose It by: {6}
It is always sorrow, happiness,
    joy, anger, desire for profit.
If we are able to get rid of
sorrow, happiness, joy, anger,
    desire for profit,
then the mind turns back to
    completeness.

What profits the mind's   {7}
    feelings:
peacefulness brought on by
    rest.

No trouble, no confusion,   {8}
then Harmony will perfect
    itself.

suspect it was originally independent of {3}. Here we see the
term *shou*/"watch over," used
also in the *Mencius* and the *Tao
Te Ching* to refer to self-cultivation (see p. 226). If this is an
oral saying, it would have been
used in contexts where it
would have been clear what
the "It" that one watches over
refers to.

Now we have a saying about
hsing/Form, again introduced
with no transition, except for
the introductory[24] *fan*/always.

This saying again refers to the
object of self cultivation as "It,"
which the juxtaposition of sayings here identifies as the
hsing/Form, another term referring to an ideal state of mind.
One loses it by emotional
excitement or disturbance, suggesting that Form here means
something like "the mind's true
form," the mind in its prime
condition. Note the use of the
further descriptive term "completeness" to refer to the quality
of mind one is cultivating.

Here a hypostatized *ho*/Harmo-
ny is pictured as a quasi-independent force that
autonomously "perfects itself"
when one gets rid of mental
disturbances.

Text	*Comment*

So lowly! like something {9}
   residing in a place
   disdained.[25]
So minute! like something one
   could never *te*/get.
So vast! like something that
   exhausts the limitless.
This is found close at hand—
   use its Te everyday.

This saying belongs to the same genre as {2}, {11}, and {12}. The juxtaposition here suggests that Harmony is its subject; but as we have seen Harmony is just one more term referring to a hypostatized mental quality one is trying to mentally *te*/get through self-cultivation. The descriptions are experiential: One feels this quality as something barely perceptible which others might disdain, and yet to the one cultivating it, it fills infinite space. It has a Te/power one can *yung*/use everyday; that is, this mental quality will express itself in one's everyday conduct.

Tao is what perfects {10}
   the Form
but men cannot make it
   stand fast:
[sometimes] it goes and
   does not return
[sometimes] it comes and
   does not stay.

Silent! no one hears {11}
   its sound.
Fully complete! it resides
   in the mind.
So obscure! we cannot see
   its form.
So vast! born together
   with me.

We cannot see its form, {12}
we cannot hear its sound,

Finally, we have some sayings speaking of *tao*. The juxtaposition, and the line about *tao* "staying" or "not staying" makes it clear that *tao* is here one more term referring to the elusive quality of mind one is trying to cultivate. (A later passage uses almost identical language about *shen*/spirit.[26]) Note that although *tao*, the elusive presence internally cultivated, is pictured as being beyond our *direct* control, this does not lead to the conclusion that we just have to leave things alone and hope it will come. The text later[27] urges strenuous efforts to "keep clean its abode," and promises that if this is done *tao* will indeed come and stay.

but we sense its completeness.
[This is] called *tao*.

Always: {13}
Tao has no [fixed] place,
it will peacefully settle in a
    good mind.

The mind still, the *ch'i*   {14}   In {2} and {3} above, the term
    right,   *ch'i* served as a name for the
then Tao can stay.[28]   ideal mental quality one is cul-
                                       tivating. Here the term is used
                                       to describe a mental state one
                                       should try to bring about (make
                                       the *ch'i cheng*/right) in order to
                                       get a hypostatized mental quali-
                                       ty *tao* to come and stay.

Some Parallels between the Tao Te Ching and the Nei Yeh

There is evidence in the *Tao Te Ching* that the practice of self-cultivation is the concrete life setting for many of its sayings also. I will show below that it too has a special vocabulary to speak about what it is that one cultivates, although its vocabulary is somewhat different from that of the *Nei Yeh*. Folk-psychological terms like *ching* and *ch'i* play only a minor role. Their place is partly taken by a group of adjectival terms descriptive of the state of mind cultivated—Stillness, Emptiness, Steadiness, Clarity, Harmony—and partly by terms hypostatizing this state of mind as The Mother, The Oneness, Tao, and Te. Because these are all special terms I always capitalize them when they occur in *Tao Te Ching* passages.

As evidence of self-cultivation in the *Tao Te Ching* we can cite first some sayings that appear to be direct instructions in self-cultivation, like:

Push Emptiness to the limit,
watch over Stillness very firmly. . . . (28[16]:1)

Close your eyes
shut your doors.
Dampen the passion
untie the tangles (30[56]:2–3)

> Pay attention to the Raw, embrace the Uncarved
> discount your personal interests, make your desires few.
> (78[19]:2)

Similarly, "overcoming oneself" in 24[33]:1 seems to reflect some kind of inner struggle with oneself; "Increasing one's store of Te" by "getting dressed early" (26[59]:2) also seems to have in mind some strenuous efforts to acquire a mental quality called Te. The *Tao Te Ching* also frequently uses the term *shou*/"watch over," which we saw used of self-cultivation both in the *Mencius* and the *Nei Yeh*: It speaks of "watching over" Weakness (29[52]:5), Femininity (17[28]:1), Tao (63[32]:2; 8[37]:2), and The Mother (29[52]:2). In addition, we have a reference to *hsi heng*/"cultivating Steadiness" (29[52]:7); references to *chih*/experiencing Steadiness and Harmony (28[16]:3-4; 33[55]:3); and references to *yung*/using Femininity (32[6]:4), Tao (31[4]:1; 46[35]:2–3; 34[40]:1), and the Uncarved Block (17[28]:2).

In addition to these phrases scattered throughout the *Tao Te Ching*, there are two passages that seem fairly clearly to be meditation[29] instruction. One is a brief saying in 6[15]:3:

> Who is able, as muddy water,
>   by Stilling to slowly become clear?
> Who is able, at rest,
>   by long drawn-out movement to slowly come to life?

What is described here does not seem to be something that would happen in the course of everyday life. It seems to picture someone whose mind is at first "muddy," stirred up and confused. A period of time is spent gradually stilling the mind until it becomes very still and clear. And then another period is pictured in which the mind slowly becomes active again, probably in a more harmonious way for having gone through this period of stillness. Note the use of rhetorical questions ("Who is able . . . ?") to give instructions, a stylistic feature we will meet again below.

The second passage is a longer meditation instruction given in 27[10], also using rhetorical questions. Because this passage is parallel to an illuminating passage in the *Nei Yeh*,[30] let me cite and comment on the latter first:

Text

Concentrate *ch'i*, spirit-like,
The thousands of things lie
   there all in order.
Can you concentrate?
Can [you be] One?

Can you know good and bad
   fortune without divination?

Can you halt, can you stop?
Can you stop seeking it from
   other men and get It in
   yourself?

Comment

Chuan ch'i/"concentrate *ch'i*"
occurs in the *Tao Te Ching* also
(see immediately below). In the
light of the unsystematic use of
ch'i in the *Nei Yeh*, it seems
unlikely that this phrase reflects
a doctrinal belief about *ch'i* (that
one first believes something
about *ch'i* and then devises
techniques to manipulate this
ch'i). The *Nei Yeh* also speaks of
chuan hsin/"concentrating
mind,"[31] a phrase that Mencius
uses of a chess player.[32] This is a
concrete directive, assuming no
more than that one know how
to perform the internal activity
referred to, which can also be
described simply (in line 3 here)
as "concentrate." Concentrating
eliminates distraction and makes
one's mind more unified, "One."

Foretelling the future without
divination (the usual means in
ancient China) is said to be the
result of attaining perfect sincerity in the Confucian *Doctrine of the Mean* (24), and of
practicing Tao in 11[38]:6 of
the *Tao Te Ching*. Such a claim
is often associated with religious traditions having developed meditation techniques.[33]

"Stop" here is explained as stopping the tendency to seek for
what one desires outside oneself.[34] The fulfillment of one's
desires lies in something one

Text	Comment
	can *te*/get within oneself, through the concentrative meditation exercise spoken of here.
Set your mind to it! set your mind to it! Seriously set your mind to it again! If you set your mind to it and cannot penetrate It, the spirit penetrates It. [It is] not [penetrated] by the strength of the spirit [*kuei-shen*],[35] [but by] the utmost perfection of *ching* [and] *ch'i*.[36]	In another context, one might interpret these lines in reference to attempts to gain an intellectual grasp of some truth. In the context of the *Nei Yeh*, however, "It" is the hypostatized quality of mind that one is trying to mentally *te*/get in oneself. Only one with a highly perfected consciousness and way of being is capable of this.

Compare now the beginning of 27[10] in the *Tao Te Ching*, the clearest case of meditation instruction in this book:

Text	Comment
When 'carrying your soul,' embracing the Oneness, can you be undivided? When 'concentrating *ch'i*,' bringing about Softness, can you be like an infant? When 'cleansing and purifying the mysterious mirror,' can you be without blemish? . . . [37] When 'the Doors of Heaven open and shut,' can you remain Feminine?	"Embracing the Oneness" occurs also in 4[22]:4; but *ying p'o*/"carry [your] soul" occurs only here. This observation is true also of the next three stanzas. The first phrases in these stanzas (placed in quotes) probably refer to some internal meditation techniques which the original audience knew how to perform, or experiences with which they were familiar. The technique involves purifying one's mind of distractions: *Chuan ch'i*/"concentrating *ch'i*," becoming "undivided,"

194

When 'Clarity and bareness
penetrate everywhere,'
can you remain not doing?

"cleansing and purifying" one's consciousness so that a clarity also seems to pervade the external world. Following these phrases referring to meditation techniques in each stanza, other phrases are used that mention certain qualities or states of mind—Softness, infancy, Femininity, not doing, Clarity—which are mentioned frequently elsewhere in the *Tao Te Ching* as qualities or states one ought to foster in oneself.

The reference to "Heaven's Doors opening and shutting" in the fourth stanza here has no parallel in the *Nei Yeh*, and requires some further comment. The closest contemporary analogy seems to be the tradition of the "spirit journey," probably a survival of Chinese shamanism,[38] in which a person in a trance state feels himself to be journeying in spirit to other worlds. A Heavenly Gate is mentioned in one description of a spirit journey that occurs in a later Taoist poem included in the *Ch'u Tzu* anthology.[39]

I ask the Lord's Gateman to open up for me; He leans against the Ch'ang-ho gate and looks at me. I ask the Gateman of Heaven to open the gate; He pushes open the Ch'ang-ho portals and looks out at me. . . . [The poem ends:] . . . I transcend Non-action and come to Purity. . . . I draw near the Great Beginning.

Another passage in the *Chuang Tzu* involving a spirit journey (quoted p. 207–08) also mentions passing through a "Dark and Mysterious Gate." If these parallels are relevant to our context, they suggest that the Laoist meditation instruction quoted above envisioned the possibility that the meditator might go into a trance and experience a spirit journey. What is important in our present context is that the instruction makes no mention of any revelatory insights gained in such a trance. The primary goal of the meditation practice seems to be the cultivation of a particular state of mind. As will be pointed out later (p. 318), the composer of the chapter where this saying now occurs has added material to the saying that suggests that Laoist meditation is primarily preparation for ruling well, not a means of learning esoteric truths.

One can scarcely doubt that 27[10]:1 does represent meditation instruction, and further indications suggest that it is an oral saying. The main indication is that it uses phrases like "carrying the soul" which would probably have been almost as difficult for ancient Chinese to understand as they are for us, and no explanation is given either here or elsewhere in the *Tao Te Ching*. This is not what one would expect of a single author addressing himself to the general public. The most likely explanation is that this passage assumes an audience who already understood these phrases, or who heard them in some concrete context where their meaning would be made clear: students learning meditation from Laoist teachers, as part of the self-cultivation practice of the Laoist school.

This passage and the others quoted above serve as indirect evidence of their own original life setting, Laoist self-cultivation practices. And this life setting in turn indicates something about how the sayings are to be understood. For example, if we know that "concentrating *ch'i*" and "carrying [the] soul" are meditation instruction, we know that their most important reference is to some internal movement that Laoist meditators would know, or would have to learn, how to perform. They may or may not have had any reference to doctrines concerning *ch'i* or the *p'o*/soul.[40] In the absence of any indication of doctrinal speculation in the *Tao Te Ching*, either in general or specifically about these terms, I think our assumption should be that there are no further doctrines involved. Like *ch'i*/breath and *ching*/"vital energy" in the *Nei Yeh*, *p'o*/soul here is probably just a term of folk psychology appropriated to speak about sensations experienced at meditation. We can see something also about the Laoist use of language. When we see that *pao i*/"embrace [the] Oneness" occurs in parallel with a phrase with an obviously experiential reference like "bring about Softness," this suggests that "embrace the Oneness" also had a concrete reference to something one does internally at meditation.

In addition to the above parallels, there is another genre of saying that occurs both in the *Nei Yeh* and in the *Tao Te Ching*. Here, for example, are three samples of this genre that occur in the opening passage of the *Nei Yeh* quoted above.

People's *ch'i*:
A bright sun! like something rising high in the heavens.

Dark! like something descending into an abyss.
Vast! like something residing in the ocean.
Fully complete! like something residing in itself [alone].

So lowly! like something residing in a place disdained.
So minute! like something one could never get.
So vast! like something that exhausts the limitless.

Silent! no one hears its sound.
Fully complete! it resides in the mind.
So obscure! we cannot see its form.
So vast! born together with me.

Observations about the *Nei Yeh* above indicate that these sayings have as their background concrete attempts to foster in oneself a certain state of mind, hypostatized as a certain internally felt but elusive presence. The descriptions in the above passages are therefore phenomenologically concrete. "Bright," "dark," "vast," "minute," and "silent" are attempts to describe what this elusive presence feels like to one trying to cultivate it.

Chapters 37[14] and 38[21] of the *Tao Te Ching* contain several passages exhibiting similar features:

"Look for It, you won't see It: It is called 'fleeting'
Listen for It, you won't hear It: It is called 'thin'
Grasp at It, you can't get It: It is called 'subtle'."[41]

Its top is not bright
Its underside is not dim.

Always unnameable, It turns back to nothingness.
This is the shape of something shapeless
the form of a nothing
this is elusive and evasive.

Encountering It, you won't see the front
following It, you won't see Its back. (37[14]:1,3,4)

Evasive, elusive![42]
in it lies the *hsiang*/Pattern.
Elusive, evasive!
in it lies something substantial [*wu*].
Shadowy, dim!
in it lies vital energy [*ching*].
This energy is very strong
in it lies true genuineness. (38[21]:2)

Taken by themselves, these sayings could be understood in the context of a speculative mysticism. They represent frustrated attempts to achieve an *intellectual understanding* of some revelatory truth or some "ultimate reality" that eludes such understanding. But indications of self-cultivation meditation instruction quoted earlier, and other arguments below, suggest a different life setting, similar to that suggested by similar sayings in the *Nei Yeh*: People are engaged in introspective meditation, aimed at cultivating a certain state of mind. Experientially, they sometimes feel as though they are trying to get hold of an elusive hypostatized presence, and this kind of experience is what the sayings reflect. Sometimes this elusive presence might be named—the final saying quoted calls it Tao (as in the *Nei Yeh*)—but other times it is referred to simply as "It" (again as in the *Nei Yeh*). The final saying also reflects the experience of the wonderful character of this elusive presence: It is something of substantive worth, giving to its possessor a personal genuineness, strength, and *ching*/"vital energy," and putting him in touch with the true norm (the *hsiang*/Pattern)[43] for the world.

If this analysis is correct, then there are two more sayings in the *Tao Te Ching* that probably belong to this same genre:

Text	*Comment*
Look for It: you will not be satisfied looking Listen for It: you will not be satisfied listening Put It into practice: you will not be satisfied stopping. (46[35]:3)	The first saying seems to be a version of 37[14]:1, quoted above. "Put it into practice" (lit. *yung chih*/"use it") indicates again that the "It" that one is trying to grasp is a hypostatized state of mind that can animate one's actions in everyday life. (Compare the *Nei Yeh*'s statement, quoted above p. 190, about *yung*/using in everyday life the Te/power of the internal presence one cultivates in meditation.)
You cannot get close you cannot stay away	This second saying probably belongs to the same form-criti-

you cannot help It
you cannot harm It
you cannot treasure It
you cannot look down on
    It.(30[56]:4)

cal category, although its content is somewhat different from the other sayings quoted here. That is, it has in mind a meditator cultivating a hypostatized internal presence (identified as The Merging in 30[56]:3), and it wants to assert that this presence acts as an autonomous being beyond the meditator's control. This is in accord with those sayings in the *Nei Yeh* which insist that the presence one is cultivating cannot be directly controlled but can only be indirectly "welcomed" by the mind.

These parallels between the *Nei Yeh* and the *Tao Te Ching* serve as preliminary support for the thesis that self-cultivation practice provides the concrete background for many sayings in the *Tao Te Ching*. Observations in this chapter also begin to establish a certain view concerning the use of language in relation to self-cultivation. Both of these points will be further developed and reinforced in the two chapters to come.

9

The Vocabulary of Self-Cultivation in the Chuang Tzu *and the* Tao Te Ching

Discussions in Chapter 8 involved some preliminary observations about certain special terms—Femininity, Softness, Tao, etc.—that on the present view describe the focus of self-cultivation in the *Tao Te Ching*. This chapter will consist of a more systematic treatment of all these recurrent special terms. Partly, I would like to look at the various contexts in which each term occurs and point out what these contexts tell us about the meaning of the terms, their relation to each other, and their concrete background.

Self-Cultivation Vocabulary in the Chuang Tzu

Since the *Tao Te Ching* is such a brief work, however, some of the special terms are used too seldom in it to give us good contextual evidence as to what connotations they had for Laoists. This deficiency of the *Tao Te Ching* can be partly made up for by first examining some passages in the *Chuang Tzu*, which uses many of the same special terms used in *Tao Te Ching* and often gives us better contextual clues as to what the terms might have meant to those involved in self-cultivation. Although the overall message of many chapters in the *Chuang Tzu* differs in some ways from the message of the *Tao Te Ching*,[1] the brief passages I will quote here contain no obvious conflicts with sayings in the *Tao Te Ching*. I take this as some indication that these passages stem from Taoist circles engaged in self-cultivation practices not substantially different from those reflected in the *Tao Te Ching*, and so they can be used as appropriate parallels.

The terms to focus on in these selections are *hsü*/Empty, *ching*/Still, *ming*/Clear, *p'u*/Uncarved, *i*/One, *t'ung*/Merged, *wu*/nonbeing, *wu wei*/not-doing, *Tao*, and *Te*. One thing important to notice is the unsystematic use of these terms and indications that they all describe different aspects of a single state of mind.

I will give each of the *Chuang Tzu* selections a number, followed by the reference to chapter and HYC[2] line number, for ease in referring to these passages in later discussions. I generally follow Watson's translation, but revise it in many places in the light of the Chinese text.

Text	*Comment*

1.(4/26–33)
[Yen Hui wants to go correct the ways of a feudal lord. Confucius is skeptical of his intentions and abilities.]

The opening of this passage is quoted p. 58. Confucius is pictured here as giving very "Taoist" advice.

[Yen Hui said:] If I am *tuan*/proper and *hsü*/Empty, *mien*/hard-working and *i*/single-minded, won't that do?

[Confucius rejects several of Yen Hui's plans, then advises him to "fast," and then explains that he means "mind-fasting."]

[Yen Hui said:] May I ask about "mind-fasting?"

Hsü/Empty probably means not "coming on strong" in trying to correct the king (see p. 58), but being deferential, proper conduct toward a king. *I*/One in this context seems to mean working single-mindedly at his purpose.

Confucius said: Unify your will [*i chih*]. Don't listen with the ears, listen with the mind. Don't listen with the mind, listen with the *ch'i*. Listening stays in the ears; the mind stays with recognition. *Ch'i* is *hsü*/Empty, and waits for things. Tao accumulates in Emptiness. Emptiness is mind-fasting.

Here we see the internal self-cultivation necessary to conduct oneself well in advising kings. One has to have an internal *i*/Unity, not full of one's own ideas but waiting very receptively and "Emptily" for impressions and perceptions about events. Tao is a hypostatized presence that "accumulates" in this mental Emptiness. (For the meaning of *ch'i*/breath:energy see p. 534.)

Yen Hui said: Before I heard
this, I was sure I was Hui. Now
that I've heard it, I'm not sure I
am Hui. Can this be called
Emptiness?

Confucius said: That's all there
is to it. You can go play in the
[feudal lord's] bird cage, but
don't be moved by fame. If he
listens, then sing; if not, stop.
Have no gate, no opening.
Make *i*/Oneness your abode,
and live with what cannot be
avoided. Then you will be close
to success. Not walking at all is
easy; what is hard is walking
without touching the ground. .
. . You have heard of the
knowledge that knows; you
have not heard of the knowledge that does not know. Look
into the closed room, the
hsü/Empty chamber where
brightness is born. (Watson
1968: 57–58)

The experience evoked by Confucius' words makes Hui feel he
has lost his normal identity
(see 29[52]:3), and he calls this
feeling "being Empty."

"Make Oneness your abode" is
Watson's translation of *i che*,
which could also be translated
"[have] one home." This
phrase, and even more obviously the later mention of an
"empty chamber," seem to picture an internal mental
"abode" where one can mentally dwell. The *Nei Yeh* also
speaks of an internal *shê*/abode.
It is on this basis that I translate *men*/door:dwelling as
"[internal] abode" in 32[6]:2
and 43[1]:5.[3]

2.(7/30–33)
[Hu Tzu's pupil, Lieh Tzu, is
impressed with a local shaman
who claims supernatural abilities such as clairvoyance and
direct intuition of people's
internal state. Hu Tzu demonstrates his ability to show the
shaman an internal state that is
beyond the shaman's abilities to
understand. The shaman takes
fright and runs away. Hu Tzu
explains the shaman's fright:]

Text	Comment

Text

Just now I appeared to him
as Not Yet Emerged From My
Source. I came at him *hsü/*
Empty, wriggling and turning,
not knowing anything about
"who" or "what," now dipping
and bending, now flowing in
waves—that's why he ran
away. . . .

[Lieh Tzu was impressed:] He
went home and did not go out
for three years. . . . He showed
no preferences in the things he
did. He *fu/*turned back from
being *tiao/*carved and *cho/*pol-
ished to being *p'u/*Uncarved. . . .
In the midst of entanglement
he remained sealed. [He
remained in] *i/*Oneness to the
end of his life.
    Do not be an embodier of
fame; do not be a storehouse of
schemes; do not be an under-
taker of projects. . . . Hold onto
what you have received from
Heaven [fate], but do not regard
this a gain. Be *hsü/*Empty, that
is all. The perfect man uses his
mind as a mirror—going after
nothing, welcoming nothing,
responding but not
storing.(Watson 1968: 97)

Comment

The phrasing here suggests the
image of a deeper layer of consciousness that is completely
intangible, and the source of
the person as a tangible and
socially involved entity. Hu Tzu
shows this "Empty" part of his
being to the shaman.

This passage brings out the
concrete reference of *p'u*
to an uncarved block of wood.
"Carved" evidently refers
metaphorically to Lieh Tzu's
previous life according to "civilized" social conventions. *I/*One
here seems to refer to the
extreme simplicity of his new
life.

Emptiness is associated here
with a mind that sees things
clearly and without preferences.
(This may be different from the
Tao Te Ching, where there is
only one mention of this
notion (27[10]:1:5–6,11–12),
and no mention of *Emptiness* in
connection with it.)

3.(12/39–40)
To have a trained nature is to

(Taoist) Te is a quality of mind
one gets by merging with the

fan/turn-back to Te. To perfect Te is to *t'ung*/merge with the Beginning. *T'ung*/Merged then *hsü*/Empty, Empty then *ta*/vast. (Watson 1968: 132)

deeper layer of one's consciousness, the source/beginning of one's being. *T'ung*/Merged in its second occurrence may have an association with a mental oneness where everything is merged together (as in the passage that follows), and this is also an Empty state of mind that has a vast, "cosmic" quality to it.

4.(28/54–55)
You have only to rest in *wu wei*/not-doing . . . , spit out hearing and eyesight, forget you are a thing among other things. [This is] the Great Merging [*ta t'ung*] with the deep and boundless. Undo the mind, slough off the spirit, and the thousands of things one by one will turn back to the root. (Watson 1969: 122)

Ceasing all mental activity and releasing one's connection with the external world brings about a state of mind called *ta t'ung*, "The Great Merging." This brings about a shift in the way one experiences the world: Things in the busy world calm down and appear as though they spring from a single root (see p. 247).

5.(13/2–10)
The thousands of things are insufficient to distract his mind, so he is *ching*/Still. Water that is Still gives back a clear image. . . . When water is Still it is *ming*/clear; how much more is [this true of clear] spirit [*kuei shen*]. The wise person's mind is Still, the mirror of Heaven and Earth . . . *hsü*/ Empty, *ching*/Still, limpid, silent, not doing [*wu wei*] . . . these are the substance of Tao and Te. Therefore the Emperor,

Stillness is the attribute of a mind that is not disturbed by events in the world. A Still internal spirit is Clear like still water.

As sometimes in the *Nei Yeh*, *kuei-shen*/spirit:ghost is used of a person's internal "spirit."
     Clarity and Stillness are associated with Emptiness and not-doing. (Note that *not-doing* describes here an *internally* inactive, still mind.) These

Text

the King, and the sage rest in them. Resting here they are *hsü*/Empty.
Empty, then full; full, then complete.
Empty, then Still; Still, then moving; moving, then gaining.
Still, then not doing [*wu wei*]. . . . In your Stillness you will be *sheng*/wise; in motion you will king, in not doing you will be honored. *P'u*/Uncarved, you will have a beauty no one can compete with. (Watson 1968: 142)

Comment

qualities are the essential characteristics of the Tao and Te that Laoists cultivate.

Uncarved is another word to describe this same Still/Empty state of mind. The mention of beauty probably evokes a contrast with the "carving" usually assumed to be necessary to produce beautiful objects and beautiful people.

6.(15/13–15)
His *shen*/spirit is pure and clear, his soul never worried. In *hsü*/Emptiness, *wu*/non-being, clarity, he joins with Heaven's Te. . . . When the mind is without sorrow or joy, [this is] the perfection of Te. An *i*/Oneness without change, [this is] the perfection of *ching*/Stillness. When there is nothing it grates against, this is the perfection of *hsü*/Emptiness. . . .

Emptiness is here associated with lack of internal mental disturbance. *Wu*/non-being here seems to refer to the lack of anything perceptible going on in the mind. As in the *Nei Yeh* (p. 182), stilling of all strong emotion brings the desired state, here described as "Heaven's Te." Oneness refers to the singleness of this state of mind, unaffected by emotional changes, therefore described also as Still. The Emptiness of this state of mind refers to the fact that it finds itself in opposition to nothing.

When the body is made to labor and take no rest, it will wear out. If the *ching*/vitality is made use of without ceasing, it will grow weary. Wearied, then exhausted.

It is in the nature of water that when it is not mixed with other things, it will be clear . . . , but if it is dammed and hemmed in, and not allowed to flow, then it cannot be clear. This is an image of Heaven's Te. Yes, it is said: To be pure, clean, and mixed with nothing; *ching*/Still, *i*/One, and unchanging, limpid and not doing [*wu wei*], moving with the ways of Heaven [*t'ien hsing*]. This is the *tao*/way to care for the *shen*/spirit. (Watson 1968: 169)

Here we see the more ordinary meaning of *ching* as one's felt "vital energy," which can become used up through continuous exertion.

When the mind is "mixed" with disturbing external impressions, or restrained by too much effort at self-control, it will become agitated and not clear, like churned up muddy water. The opposed Taoist ideal is a spirit that is Still and has an unchanging *i*/singleness to it. It is "inactive" in the sense that it is not "working" at anything, yet it still moves in its own spontaneous "Heavenly" ways.

7.(11/35–43)
The Extreme of Perfect Tao is mysterious and hushed in silence. Let there be no seeing, no hearing; *pao*/embrace the *shen*/spirit in *ching*/Stillness, and the *hsing*/Form will become *cheng*/correct by itself.

You must be Still, you must be pure. Do not labor your Form, do not churn up your vital energy [*ching*], and then you can live a long life.

When the eye does not see, the ear does not hear, and the mind does not know, then your spirit will watch over [*shou*] the Form. With this Form will come long life.

Tao here refers to something one finds in a silent and mysterious place in one's own mind. "Embrace the spirit" probably means concentrate your attention on your own mental state (compare "carry the soul" in 27[10]:1, p. 194). In the *Nei Yeh*, *hsing*/Form refers to an ideal condition of the mind, and this is probably the meaning here also. But "vital energy" [*ching*] here is not used in a special sense; it is only the bodily energy that must not be agitated, to avoid exhaustion and achieve Stillness.

Text	*Comment*
Be cautious of what is inside; block off what is outside. . . . Then I will lead you up above the Great *ming*/Clarity, to the Source of Perfect Yang; I will guide you through the Dark and Mysterious Gate, to the Source of the Perfect Yin. . . . I watch over the *i*/Oneness, so as to reside in the *ho*/ Harmony. . . . So I will take leave of you, to enter gate of the Inexhaustible and wander in the limitless fields, to form a triad with the light of the sun and moon, to partake in the *ch'ang*/Steadiness of Heaven and Earth. (Watson 1968: 119)	After the preceding mental preparations comes a spirit journey; a guide leads the meditator through various mental "places," called *Ta Ming*/"The Great Clarity," "The Source of the Perfect Yang and Yin," "The Dark and Mysterious Gate." (Compare "Heaven's Gate" in 27[10].) One stays in this ecstatic state of mind by *shou i*/"watching over [the] Oneness," that allows one to reside in a hypostatized mental Harmony.

The Vocabulary of Self-Cultivation in the Tao Te Ching

With these passages and comments in mind, I now turn to some detailed observations about the use of the special recurrent terms in the *Tao Te Ching*. These observations will attempt to support various aspects of my overall thesis about the meaning of the sayings in which they occur, their relation to self-cultivation, and their relation to the rest of Laoist thought.

First, some observations will support the thesis that the terms have a concrete reference to a certain state or quality of mind. My argument here will be this: In the case of the descriptive terms used in this work—like *Stillness, Emptiness, Clarity, Harmony, Softness*—the fact that these terms refer to certain ideal qualities or states of mind Laoists want to develop in themselves is fairly obvious. With others like *The Mother* and *Tao* this is not so obvious. My thesis is that these latter terms are hypostatizations of this same state of mind, and one of my main arguments here consists in a certain parallelism I will point out between the use of the descriptive terms like Stillness and Femininity, on the one hand, and the use of the substantive terms like *The Mother* and *Tao* on the other: On the one hand, descriptive terms like *Softness* are sometimes treated as hypostatizations (for instance in the saying "Softness overcomes hardness" see p. 231). This shows that in the Laoist milieu there did exist a general tendency toward linguistic[4] and imaginal hypostatization of the personal quality cultivated. On the other hand, substantive terms like *The Mother, The Oneness*, and *Tao* are sometimes used in contexts which show that they refer to a concrete state or quality of mind being cultivated. For example, "embrace the Oneness" is part of a meditation instruction, where it is parallel to directives like "bring about Softness." One passage speaks of *shou*/"watching over" the Mother (29[52]:2), or Tao (63[32]:2), in the same way another speaks of *shou ching*/"watching over Stillness" (28[16]:1). Some passages speak of *yung*/using Tao (31[4]:1, 46[35]:3) in the same way another saying speaks of *yung*/using Femininity (32[6]:4). And so on.

A second point I want to make concerns the unsystematic use of these special terms in the *Tao Te Ching*. Like the *Nei Yeh*, the terms are related to each other in various ways in various passages, and the same or similar statements are made about different terms. I take this as an indication that sayings involving these special terms neither teach nor invoke any system of doctrines. All the terms have basically the same phenomenologically concrete reference (*Bedeutung*), to the ideal state of mind Laoists cultivate. The different meanings (*Sinne*) of the various terms represent different aspects of this single ideal state.

Thirdly, I want to point out the relation of each of the special terms to the dominant themes of the polemic aphorisms, as for example the fact that the ideal of mental Stillness is the direct contrast to the mental agitation that is the target of one group of polemic aphorisms.

Finally, these observations will point out evidence that Laoists connected the quality of mind they cultivated with certain patterns of action. An internal Softness, for example, expresses itself in a "Soft," non-confrontational way of dealing with opposition (73[36]:1-2).

Some of the observations here draw on discussions of further sayings-forms using the special terms in Chapter 10, and on arguments in Chapter 12 showing that the juxtaposition of sayings in the various chapters is not random but indicates certain definite associations of ideas.

Stillness (ching). Chuang Tzu 5.(13/2–10)[5] and 6.(15/13–15) picture Stillness as the opposite of a mind simulated by external impressions. ("The thousands of things are insufficient to distract his mind, so he is *ching*/Still").[6] Chapter 23[26] in the *Tao Te Ching* also contrasts Stillness with the mental stimulation of sightseeing. The Laoist ideal of Stillness is thus related to the polemic against stimulation and excitement, which wears one out and gives one a "light," superficial way of being, as opposed to the dignity and *chün*/mastery of the Still person (23[26]). In 77[57]:5 "loving Stillness" describes the style of a ruler who also practices "not-desiring" and "not-doing." His internal Stillness expresses itself in a ruling style that brings about a *p'u*/Simple people. Like the *Chuang Tzu* passages, 28[16]:3 suggests a close connection between Stillness, Emptiness, and Clarity. It also associates Stillness with Steadiness, (Stillness and Steadiness are closely connected to Harmony in 33[55]:3), and suggests that being Still gives one the cosmic status of *wang*/King, Heaven, and Tao. In 5[45]:3 Stillness is a hypostatized *te*/force that "overcomes" its opposite (see p. 231), and 5[45]:4 ascribes to hypostatized Stillness the cosmic status of "Norm of the World." (Saying 17[28]:1 ascribes a similar status to one who cultivates Femininity, and 35[39]:1 says that the *wang*/king(s) became the Norm of the World by "getting the Oneness.") The juxtaposition of sayings in 6[15] suggests that following the meditation instructions to gain Stillness and Clarity (6[15]:3) is part of what it means to "hold on to this Tao" (which makes one Empty, 6[15]:4). Saying 56[61]:2 says that Femininity overcomes masculinity by Stillness.

Emptiness. Three synonyms meaning "empty" occur in the *Tao Te Ching*: *Hsü* (16[5]2; 28[16]:1), *ch'ung* (31[4]:1; 36[42]:3; 5[45]:1), and *wa* (4[22]:2). *Hsü*/empty often has the same negative associations that *empty* has in English, meaning "worthless"; this is evident in "Is this a *hsü*/empty saying?" (4[22]:7). See also *Mencius* (7A/37), which says that a state without *jen*/Goodness becomes *hsü*/empty; and *Analects* (7/36), which describes hypocritical people who "are *hsü*/empty but act *ying*/full." *Hsü*/empty also has a more neutral sense in which it refers to a certain way one's presence feels to others, as when the *Chuang Tzu* speaks of a swordsman who "makes a display of emptiness, drawing one out with hopes of advantage."[7] Presenting an "empty" appearance seems here the opposite of an attempt to directly overawe one's opponent by presenting a forceful appearance. This seems similar to the meaning of "I came at him empty," quoted in *Chuang Tzu* 2.(7/30–33). The *Tao Te Ching* (6[15]:2 and 4) likewise describes the "timid, cautious, yielding, vacant" ideal men as *pu-ying*/"not-full." Emptiness as an external ideal is thus probably associated with the Laoist polemic against admiring fine appearances, which feel solid ("full"), by comparison with the subtle, apparently negligible qualities which Laoists cultivate (see 4[22]:2; 5[45]:1–2). For this reason I think *ying*/full, the opposite of Empty in 4[22]:2, 5[45]:1, and 31[4]:1, is better translated "solid." The ordinarily positive connotations of *ying*/solid and negative connotations of *hsü*/Empty:worthless are probably important in the *Tao Te Ching*: Laoist paradoxical wisdom emphasizes the fact that the qualities they value most highly are ones that seem empty/worthless from a conventional point of view (see p. 154). In the Laoist ideal this externally felt Emptiness is connected to an internal state of mind also described as Empty. Most of the occurrences of *Empty* in the *Chuang Tzu* passages quoted above have this internal, mental Emptiness in mind (although these passages also associate Emptiness with mental receptiveness, an association probably not present in the *Tao Te Ching*). Internal Emptiness is probably intended in 28[16]:1, which associates Emptiness with Stillness. The juxtaposition of sayings in 6[15]:3–4 also suggests that Emptiness is associated with achieving internal mental Stillness and Clarity. Saying 16[5]:2 celebrates the inexhaustible energy that comes from an Empty state of mind (compare also 5[45]:1); this seems associated with the theme that agitation wears one out, while a Still/Empty state of mind is more lasting. (Not wearing out is a characteristic of Femininity in 32[6]:4, and it is implied of Tao in 33[55]:5.) Tao is called Empty in 31[4]:1, and both in this saying and in 6[15]:4, "using" or "holding onto" Tao makes a person Empty (*pu-ying*/"not-solid"). Section 36[42]:3 speaks of a *ch'ung*/Empty *ch'i*, which brings Harmony. *Chuang Tzu* 1.(4/26–33) also speaks of a *hsü*/Empty *ch'i*, and pictures Tao as a hypostatized force or quality that "accumulates in Emptiness."

Clarity (ming). Ming can also mean "bright" (44[41]:2), "shine" (4[22]:4), "to understand," or "to enlighten [= to educate]" (80[65]:1). The *Book of Documents* emphasizes the importance of kings having *ming te*/"bright te." In *Chuang Tzu* 5.(13/2–10) Clarity is the property of a Still mind, compared to still water; saying 6[15]:3 uses the same water image to picture clarity brought on by stilling the mind at meditation. Clarity is also associated with Stillness in 28[16]:3. Chapter 27[10] suggests that *ming*/Clear describes the way the world appears to someone proficient at meditation, and 24[33]:1 says that Clarity is the result of knowing oneself. The juxtaposition of sayings in 73[36] suggests that a *ming*/Clear state of mind expresses itself in a Soft/Weak style of overcoming opposition. Chapter 49[27]:4 probably hypostatizes Clarity by speaking of "putting on Clarity," and the juxtaposition of 49[27]:3 and 4 suggests that the subtle but effective teaching style of the Laoist teacher is an expression of this Clear state of mind. (This makes it a parallel to the subtle but effective "teaching done by not talking," and to Softness, Nothing, and Not-Doing, in 47[43]:1–2.) In 29[52], turning back to Clarity parallels turning back to the Mother and is associated with watching over Weakness.

Nothing (wu or wu yu). *Wu* is usually a verb meaning "there is no . . . ," in contrast to *yu*/"there is." But *wu* and *yu* are also contrasted as meaning "lacking" and "having," or nominally "absence" and "presence." "Non-being" is an approximate translation; *wu* does not necessarily refer to literal non-existence. It can also refer to something relatively intangible, a *seeming* "absence." *Chuang Tzu* 6.(15/13–15) uses *wu*/non-being as a partial description of an Empty and Clear state of mind. This suggests an experiential meaning for the word, referring to the fact that the state of mind involved is so intangible. In 37[14]:3, the elusive internal presence one is trying to grasp is experientially described as "turning back to *wu*/nothingness," meaning that it recedes into intangibility. In a similar way, in 47[43] *wu yu*/"non-being" describes a Soft and Not-Doing way of operating and "teaching without words." So *wu*/Nothing is probably very similar in meaning to *Emptiness*, as a very intangible quality of one's mind, and of one's presence as felt by others. (Compare *Chuang Tzu* 2.[7/30–33], in which Hu Tzu reveals an "Empty" layer of his mind, "not yet emerged from its source.") Chapter 15[11] celebrates the "usefulness" of *wu*/Nothing, suggesting a parallel with the "useful" Emptiness of 5[45]:1. The juxtaposition of sayings in 34[40] suggests that Nothing is associated with a *jo*/Weak state of mind, another term referring to the relative intangibility of the state of mind Laoists cultivate. The juxtaposition of sayings in this chapter also suggests that Nothing is associated with using Tao, and with the internal motion of *fan*/"Turning Back." This hypostatized Nothing is the origin of the cosmos (like Tao, The Mother, The Oneness, and Femininity).

The Merging (t'ung). *T'ung* can mean "to agree with," or "unite with." *Chuang Tzu* 3.(12/39–40) and 4.(28/54–55) use this term to refer to an internal state, "The Great Merging [*ta t'ung*][8] with the deep and boundless." As a state of mind, *t'ung*/Merging seems close in meaning to *i*/Oneness. In 30[56] *t'ung*/Merging also seems clearly a hypostatization of a calm state of mind. Section 30[56]:3 first speaks of calming one's mind, causing the "dust to settle" in the external world, described as "*t'ung*/merging the dust." Then it says, "This is called the Mysterious Merging [*hsüan t'ung*]." This is followed by a saying about trying to grasp an elusive internal presence (see p. 198), in this case a hypostatized "Merging." The chapter ends, "It [The Merging] is the Treasure of the World" (a saying used of Tao in 48[62]). Chapter 43[1] speaks again of *hsüan t'ung*/"[the] Mysterious Merging," probably identified with a state of "not desiring." It pictures this as an internal mental space (*men*/abode) in which one can see the hidden essence of things in the world. This same basic idea is expressed in different terms in 29[52]:2 by saying that "getting the Mother" allows one to rightly understand things in the world, the Mother's "children."

Oneness (i). The *Chuang Tzu* passages quoted earlier show several interconnected uses of the term *i*/One. In *Chuang Tzu* 1.(4/26–33) it probably means "single-minded" in one occurrence; in another occurrence, *i chih*/"unifying [your] will" is associated with "mind-fasting," having an "Empty *ch'i*" not preoccupied with external things. In *Chuang Tzu* 2.(7/30–33) it describes the state of a person undistracted by engagement with the world. *Chuang Tzu* 6. (15/13–15) associates a "Oneness without change" with *ching*/Stillness. *Chuang Tzu* 7.(11/35–43) pictures *shou i*/"watching over the Oneness" as part of the mental preparation for a spirit journey. Similarly in 27[10], *pao i*/"embrace the Oneness" is part of a meditation instruction, connected with becoming internally "undivided," and with *ying p'o*/"carrying the soul." This passage and the *Chuang Tzu* passages just listed suggest that *i*/One refers to single-mindedness and lack of distraction, hence I render it as "[mental] Oneness" in the translation, rather than "The One" as many other translators prefer.[9] *Pao i*/"embracing the Oneness" is said in 4[22]:4 to make one spiritual Emperor ("Shepherd of the World"). (Gaining Emperor status is the result of cultivating Femininity in 17[28]:1, and of cultivating Stillness in 28[16]:1–5; Stillness is itself called the Norm of the World in 5[45]:4.) *Te i*/"getting the Oneness," then, is one way of describing the goal of Laoist self-cultivation, and 35[39]:1 celebrates the cosmic importance of this achievement by saying that an ordered cosmos came about when all the principal elements of the universe "got the Oneness." The saying following this cosmogony pictures the Oneness as something "lowly," so that getting the Oneness expresses itself externally in the adoption of a "low," deferential attitude in one's dealing with others. (Chapter 56[61] suggests that this posture expresses a Feminine quality of mind.)

Uncarved Block (p'u). P'u can mean "simplicity," but the mention of "cutting" associated with this term in 17[28]:2 and 63[32]:1–3 evokes the concrete association of the word with raw material like jade or wood before it has been carved into some artistic shape. This association is also suggested in *Chuang Tzu* 2.(7/30–33), by the mention of *tiao*/carved, describing a state opposite that of *p'u*/uncarved. (*Uncarved* describes the state of the recluse Lieh Tzu after he had withdrawn from involvement in the world). In *Chuang Tzu* 5.(13/2–10) *p'u*/uncarved describes the "natural" beauty of a spirit that is *ching*/Still, *hsü*/Empty, and *ming*/Clear. The *Mencius* (6A/1) uses a similar image, attributing to Kao Tzu, a rival teacher, the idea that making a person's character Good and Right is like carving a block of willow to make a cup or a bowl. (Mencius criticizes the image, as implying that cultivating virtue does violence to our *hsing*/nature.) Chapter 17[28] suggests that *p'u*/"Uncarved Block" refers to a way of being that has not been "carved up" by the social pressure to identify with only fine appearing qualities. Chapter 63[32] suggests that it is also related to Laoist polemic against "naming": carving up the one true but nameless normative reality (Tao) into many specific rules. Section 63[32]:1 says that Tao is the Uncarved Block, while the juxtaposition of sayings in 17[28] suggests that gaining Te by cultivating Femininity is equivalent to "using" the Uncarved Block. In 78[19]:2 *pao p'u*/"embracing the Uncarved Block" describes part of the Laoist ideal, along with "diminishing one's desires, lessening what is personal." In 6[15]:3 the Uncarved Block is associated with an intangible and undefined state of mind in which everything is mixed together and "muddy" (similar to The Merging), and "vacant" (similar to Empty). In 81[37]:2 *p'u* describes an internal state of the ideal ruler that expresses itself in the manner in which he restrains ambitious and disorderly people, a tactful manner that does not humiliate them.

Harmony (ho). The *Nei Yeh* pictures mental *ho*/Harmony as a hypostatized autonomous force when it says "Harmony perfects itself" (p. 182). Similarly, *Chuang Tzu* 7.(11/35–43) hypostatizes mental *ho*/Harmony when it says "I watch over the Oneness to abide in the Harmony [*ch'u chih ho*]"; it pictures this mental Harmony as one of the conditions necessary for the spirit journey. One Laoist association with Harmony is illustrated in 33[55]:2 by the Soft/Weak infant, full of *ching*/vitality, whose inner forces are working together so well that he "can scream all day without getting hoarse." This Harmony brings Steadiness and Clarity. The saying in 36[42]:4 says that an Empty *ch'i* brings Harmony.

Steadiness (heng in MWT, ch'ang in WP).[10] *Heng* is common in the *Tao Te Ching* meaning "always, invariably," and it is sometimes used (like *fan*/always in the *Nei Yeh*)[11] as an introductory or concluding particle. Mencius (1A/7,20) says "To have a *heng*/steady mind without a steady livelihood—only a *shih* can do this." He is referring to the *pu-tung hsin* (2A/2,1), the "unmoved mind" of the ideal *shih*, able to remain true to its own inner values in the face of external pressures. *Heng*/Steady probably has a similar meaning when it occurs in the *Tao Te Ching*, except that here it is connected to the ideal Laoist Still state of mind as a source of internal steadiness. Steadiness is associated with *ching*/Stilling the Mind and with *ming*/Clarity in 28[16]:3. In 29[52] the statement "This is cultivating Steadiness" ends a long chain of sayings preceding it, one saying advocating withdrawal from tiring activities, and other sayings that include phrases like "turn back and watch over the Mother," "Watch over Weakness," "turn back to Clarity." Thus Steadiness is probably most closely related to the Laoist polemic against stimulation and excitement; a Steady mind is the opposite of an agitated mind. In 17[28] *heng* is used as an adjective to describe Te (achieved by cultivating Femininity); and 43[1]:1 uses it as an adjective describing (Laoist) Tao. Especially in the last passage, many understand *heng* to mean "eternal," Absolute, assimilating Laoist thought to Western metaphysics or to the speculative mysticism of Hindu Vedanta (see p. 176). The trend of the observations being made here runs counter to this assimilation. It suggests instead that *heng*/Steadiness should be understood against the background of a practical concern to maintain concrete mental stability, in contrast to mental agitation and worry. The *heng*/invariant Tao is not an element in a doctrine about the two-tiered structure of reality. It is a concretely felt reality one feels within oneself, a true and unchanging internal standard one can always rely on amid the changing circumstances and pressures of the world.[12]

Not-working (wu wei) and Not-desiring (wu yü). Chuang Tzu 5.(13/2-10) speaks of *wu wei* as an inner state: "*hsü*/Empty, *ching*/Still, limpid, silent, not-doing [*wu wei*] . . . these are the substance of Tao and Te. . . . Still, then not doing [*wu wei*]." Something similar is implied about the meaning of *wu wei* in 4.(28/54-55) and 6.(15/13-15). *Wu wei* is mentioned in the meditation instruction in 27[10], were it seems likewise to describe an internal, Still state of mind. This internal state of mind expresses itself in a certain style of leadership also described as *wu wei*. See especially: 47[43]:1 where *wu wei* describes a style of managing or teaching, also described there as animated by *ju*/Softness and *wu-yu*/Nothing; 81[37]:1, which says that the Tao animating the ideal ruler's actions "always does nothing"; and 77[57]:5, which associates *wu wei* with Stillness, and not-desiring. In 43[1]:3 *wu yü*/"not-desiring" describes a state of mind (probably associated with The Merging) that gives one knowledge of the hidden truth (like "getting the Mother" in 29[52]:2); in 78[19]:2 having few desires is associated with embracing the Uncarved Block.

Soft and Weak (jou jo). Among three "bad friendships," *Analects* 33/16/4 lists friendship with a *shan jou*, "one good at being *jou*/soft," probably referring to a person who is too suave and ingratiating. (Confucians themselves, however, were known as *ju*, a possible cognate of *jou*/soft.)[13] *Jo*/weak is normally a negative term, regularly used in the phrase *lao jo*/"old [and] weak." As with *hsü*/Emptiness, the negative connotations of these two terms are probably important to the paradoxical wisdom of Laoism, which emphasizes the necessity of cultivating qualities others look down upon. Chapter 27[10] pictures *jou*/Softness as an internal quality of mind one cultivates at meditation, speaking of this as the result of "concentrating *ch'i.*" (It is also associated here with "embracing Oneness," "remaining Feminine," "not-doing," "not knowing," and achieving *ming*/Clarity.) Chapter 34[40] says that *jo*/Weakness is a characteristic of one who *yung*/uses Tao. The juxtaposition of sayings in 29[52] suggests that *shou jo*/"watching over Weakness" is closely associated with "watching over the Mother," with "turning back to Clarity," and with "cultivating Steadiness." But cultivating this Weakness also results in an inner strength. Chapter 33[55] uses the infant as an image of an ideal person who is *jou jo*/"Soft and Weak," and yet also strong. (This chapter implies a close association between Softness/Weakness, Te, *ching*/vitality, *ho*/Harmony, *heng*/Steadiness, and *ming*/Clarity.) Chapter 74[76] associates the *jou jo*/"Softness and Weakness" Laoists cultivate with an internal aliveness (in contrast to the "deadness" of those who are *ch'iang*/

hard:strong:forcing). The above passages speak of Softness and Weakness as characteristic of an internal state of mind. The juxtaposition of sayings in 73[36] suggests that Softness/Weakness also describes an attitude that expresses itself in a non-confrontational style of overcoming opposition, a style which in 72[64] is said to express a "Not-Working" state of mind. Chapter 47[43] implies that the terms Softness and Not-Working both refer to the same style of conduct, associated with *wu yu*/"Nothing" and "the teaching done by not talking." Hence Softness/Weakness as an ideal style of action seems most closely related to the Laoist polemic against a confrontational style of interaction. (See Section 6 of the translation and commentary.) Sayings in 73[36]:2, 75[78]:2 picture Softness and Weakness as hypostatized *te*/forces that overcome their opposites (see p. 231). Soft and Weak never occur in the *Chuang Tzu* as special terms referring to the object of self-cultivation; this seems one difference between the Taoism of the *Tao Te Ching* and that represented in the *Chuang Tzu*.

Femininity. Two synonyms meaning *Feminine* occur in the *Tao Te Ching*: *p'in* (32[6]:2-3, 56[61]:2), and *tz'u* (27[10]:1, 17[28]:1). The parallelism with "disgraceful" in 17[28] indicates that "being Feminine" would have been looked down upon among men in Warring States China. This is confirmed by Mencius' (3B/2,2) disparaging comparison of other *shih* to women; his point is that the role of women is to be compliant, but the role of *shih* is to stand up against bad rulers, which these *shih* fail to do. This suggests that Femininity as a Laoist ideal is connected with *jou*/Softness, which also means pliant, flexible (the opposite of hard/strong masculinity). *P'in chih men*/"the [internal] abode of Femininity" suggests that Femininity is a characteristic of an internal mental "space" (compare the mention of an "Empty [inner] chamber" in *Chuang Tzu* 1.[4/26–33]). Chapter 56[61] suggests that Femininity expresses itself in a deferential ("low") style of diplomacy. (The juxtaposition of sayings in 35[39]:1–2 suggests that adopting a deferential posture is equivalent to "getting the Oneness"). The saying in 56[61]:2 assimilates Femininity to a hypostatized *te*/force that overcomes masculinity (see p. 231), and associates Femininity's power with Stillness. Chapter 32[6] pictures Femininity (like Tao) as a cosmic origin, and pictures it as a hypostatized quality one can "use"; it is an inexhaustible source of energy to one who "uses" it (like Emptiness in 16[5]:2). Femininity, like Softness, does not occur in the *Chuang Tzu* as an object of self-cultivation. The *Chuang Tzu*[14] mentions one woman teacher ("Woman Crookback," who may, however, be a fictitious person); otherwise I know of no evidence suggesting that the Laoist group included women.[15]

The Mother (mu). Chapter 29[52] speaks of internally *te*/getting and *shou*/"watching over" the Mother, which is thus a hypostatized internal presence. But (like Femininity, Tao, and Te) this internal presence is also a cosmic origin, "the Mother of the World." The phrase, "I treasure the nourishing Mother" (13[20]:5), suggests that this Mother is an internal presence which Laoists find nourishing, similar to the "welcoming" presence of Tao/Te in 14[23] and the "sustaining" Tao in 44[41]. The juxtaposition of sayings in 26[59] suggests that gaining great public influence by "storing up an abundance of Te" is equivalent to "possessing the Mother of the State." (Since *t'ien hsia*/"the world" usually refers to the Chinese Empire, "the Mother of the World," and "The Mother of the State" are probably equivalent phrases. In the Laoist view, "the Mother of the World" they cultivate is the foundation of true Chinese culture.)[16] The juxtaposition of sayings in 29[52]:2–6 suggests that "turning back to watch over the Mother" is parallel to "turning back to Clarity," and is associated with withdrawal from the world, "watching over Weakness" and "cultivating Steadiness." Tao is said to be the Mother of the World in 43[1] and 39[25]. Again, the use of *Mother* as a special term is peculiar to Laoism; it does not occur in the *Chuang Tzu*. It is probably related to the fact that Laoist values focus on establishing a nourishing "environment," both internal and external (see p. 170), connected with their opposition to inspiring/challenging ideals. (Contrast the inspiring/challenging character of the Judeo-Christian-Islamic male divinity.) The uniqueness of this concept makes one wonder whether Laoism derives ultimately in part from some more feminine-oriented local culture in China—a subject worth further investigation.[17]

Tao. As we saw in the *Mencius* excerpts in Chapters 3 and 4, Tao/road:way was a common term in ancient China, used especially among Warring States *shih* to describe the "Way," both personal and political, that each advocated. Mencius (3B/4,4) uses *wei tao*/"doing tao" to describe the specific occupation of *shih*, in contrast to the occupations of carpenters and carriage-makers. The *Nei Yeh*, the *Tao Te Ching*, and the *Chuang Tzu* are the first writings to give the term Tao the pregnant meaning that eventually made it an important term in subsequent religious thought in East Asia, and more recently in the modern West. Its popularity in later cultural contexts has also, however, tended to make it a rather amorphous term. If one tries to determine the meaning that the term Tao originally had in the *Tao Te Ching*, paying attention to its cultural context, the verbal context in this work, and to evidence given above concerning its concrete life setting, I think the main meanings can be summarized under the following five points.

1. Some Laoist sayings use phrases that assume, following contemporary Chinese usage, that Tao means "the right Way" generally. The point of most of these sayings is to assert that some aspect of Laoist teaching is this right Way.

2. Some sayings use phrases that do not assert, but already assume, that Tao refers specifically to the Laoist Way. "Doing Tao" (25[48]:1), for example, can be paraphrased as "engaging in Laoist self-cultivation," and the point of the saying using this phrase is to contrast Laoist self-cultivation with Confucian self-cultivation.

3. Some sayings use phrases that assume that Tao refers to the *internal spirit* that expresses itself in the Laoist way of being or acting. "Ruling by Tao" (70[60]:1) means letting the spirit of Tao inform governmental policy and leadership style.

4. Some sayings picture Tao as a hypostatized power or elusive internal presence. "Tao is good at supporting [a person] and bringing [him] to perfection" (44[41]:4) speaks of Tao as a kind of force that sustains a person and perfects his being.

5. Some sayings picture Tao as a cosmic reality, the origin of the world.

The continuity observable between these various uses of the term Tao suggests the probable lines of development leading from common Chinese to specifically Laoist meanings. Sayings in the first group use Tao in the ordinary sense current among ancient Chinese generally. Sayings in the second group show Laoists appropriating the term Tao to refer to their specific Way, *in contrast* to the Ways of other schools. (Presumably we see here the beginning of a development which led to the use of Tao to name a particular school of thought [*tao chia*/"[the] Tao school"] in contrast to other schools.) Laoist emphasis on the cultivation of a certain internal state of mind that expresses itself in a style of conduct probably led to the meaning it has in the third and fourth group of sayings. This suggestion is supported by the fact that Tao is the name of an elusive internal presence or force in the *Nei Yeh* and the *Chuang Tzu* also, writings which likewise reflect internal self-cultivation. Finally, the hypostatization of Tao, and the fact that it became the predominant name for what was existentially foundational in the Laoist universe (see p. 243–49), are conditions making possible and motivating those sayings picturing Tao as a "cosmic" reality, as *ch'i* is in the *Mencius* (p. 111), and as *ching* is in the *Nei Yeh* (p. 186). There are no strict boundaries between the five categories of sayings; they represent a continuum.

1. The first group of sayings does not depart at all from common usage in ancient China. This group assumes that there are general debates among various *shih* schools about what the right Way consists in, and their point is to identify certain aspects of Laoist advice with this "right Way." The term Tao in these sayings has no necessary connection with specifically Taoist meanings of the word, and non-Laoists hearing the sayings would have no difficulty understanding what point was being made. The point of 20[46]:1 is to assert that Laoist contentment (contrasted with acquisitiveness) is in accord with the right Way; section 50[53]:6 asserts that the conspicuous consumption of the wealthy is *fei Tao*/"contrary to [the right] Way"; saying 80[65]:1 asserts that the right Way of ruling (*shan wei Tao*/"excellent doing Tao") is to "keep people stupid"; saying 69[30]:1 asserts that a *shih* who claims to be advising rulers about the right Way should not urge the use of military force; saying 43[1]:1 asserts that any Way that can be told is not the *heng*/invariant Way, the true Way one ought to adhere to under all circumstances; saying 44[41]:1:1–5 describes *shih*-students listening to teaching about the right Way (in the original saying this could have referred to the teaching of any *shih*-school; see the commentary).

2. The second group of sayings seems to assume an audience who already understand Tao as a reference to the specifically Laoist Way. 25[48]:1 contrasts *wei Tao*/"doing Tao" with *wei hsüeh*/"doing [Confucian] Learning," a contrast Mencius would certainly not have agreed to. The description of the Tao one teaches as "flat . . . no taste" in 46[35]:2, and the celebration of the greatness of "sitting and presenting this Tao" (48[62]:5) presume that it is the *Laoist* Way that is being taught. "Great Tao" in 50[53]:1,3 and 12[18], the bright/smooth Tao in 44[41]:2 must be the Laoist Way; "knowing the

ancient origins" describes the main thread of *Laoist* Tao in 37[14]:6 (see p. 254–55). It is only the paradoxical Laoist Tao that will *necessarily* appear laughable to a *shih* with poor insight (44[41]:1:6). The fact that the behavior of water metaphorically models ideal Laoist attitudes and conduct means that it *chi yü tao*, "approximates the (*Laoist*) Way." In the light of these passages it seems likely that "in Tao" (1[24]:3) means "from the Laoist point of view." Foreknowledge is the flower of Tao" (11[38]:6) means that clairvoyance is one product of Laoist self-cultivation practice. "Turning back is Tao's movement" (34[40]:1) means that "turning back" describes an internal movement characteristic of Laoist self-cultivation. In the sentence "one devoted to Tao is a Tao man," (14[23]:3) *tao che*/"Tao man" can be paraphrased "a true Laoist." The phrases "the Tao of the ancients" (37[14]:5), and "Heaven's Tao" (2[9]:2; 8[81]:4; 9[79]:4; 41[47]:1; 52[77]:1; 58[73]:5) likewise refer to the Laoist Way (see p. 173–74; and compare "Heaven's Te" in *Chuang Tzu* 6.[15/13–15]).

3. Even for other schools, Tao is usually not the name of a specific set of *rules* prescribing the right way of acting. It usually refers to a more generalized conception of a right spirit that ought to animate one's way of acting. In this sense it might be better to speak of Mencius' Tao[18] as Mencius' "approach" to life and politics. This is even more true of Laoists, both because of their opposition to rules and "naming" and because of the central place they gave to cultivating a certain state of mind. The assumption that Tao refers to the spirit that animates the ideal Laoist way of being and acting is evident in sayings like "Being Weak is the practice of Tao [*tao chih yung*]" (34[40]:1) and "Tao being Empty, one who uses it will not yearn for solidity" (31[4]:1): The character of Tao as an internal spirit manifests itself in the fact that one who *yung*/uses it will appear to have a "Weak" and "Empty" (*pu-ying*/"not solid") way of being and acting. "The impression made by magnificent Te comes from Tao" (38[21]:1) means that Laoist Tao as an internal spirit manifests itself in a certain kind of external *Te*/charisma. This use of Tao probably explains the statement that the seasonal flourishing and dying of things is an example of something *pu Tao*/"un-Tao-ish":[19] the internal spirit Laoists cultivate is Still and lasting, in contrast with the cycles of excitement and exhaustion characteristic of some others. "Ruling by Tao" (70[60]:1) and kings *shou tao*/"watching over Tao" (63[32]:1)

refer to letting the spirit of Tao inform governmental policy and conduct. The sayings "Great Tao drifts, it can go right or go left" (64[34]:1) and "Tao always does nothing, and nothing remains not done" (81[37]:1) also refer to Tao as an internal spirit that animates a ruler (see p. 235). "The norm of Tao is things as they are [*tzu jan*]" (39[25]:4) probably means that Tao is identical with the feeling one has when one is in a "natural" (organically harmonious) state. Most sayings in this category would be fully understandable only to those who had some familiarity with Laoist self-cultivation and the specific state of mind cultivated.

4. The *Nei Yeh* says (p. 190–91) "Men cannot make [Tao] stand fast: [sometimes] it goes and does not return, [sometimes] it comes and does not stay . . . so obscure! we cannot see its form, so vast! born together with me . . . *Tao* . . . will peacefully settle in a good mind. The mind still, the *ch'i* right, then *Tao* can stay." This illustrates the use of Tao in the context of meditative self-cultivation, to speak of the spirit one cultivates as a hypostatized internal presence. *Chuang Tzu* 1.(4/26–33) also pictures Tao as a hypostatized internal force or quality that "accumulates in [mental] Emptiness," brought about through "mind-fasting." Chapter 38[21], and probably chapter 37[14], speak similarly of Tao as a hypostatized internal presence one tries to grasp mentally. And Tao is also pictured as a hypostatized internal presence in the statements that "one who merges with Tao, Tao welcomes him" (14[23]:3), and "Tao . . . is good at sustaining[20] [a person] and completing [him]" (44[41]:4). Tao is pictured as a hypostatized power able to protect and rescue people who are not good in 48[62], and "Tao's name" in 38[21]:3 probably refers to Tao as a hypostatized power that can bring people a true understanding of things. Only those involved in specifically Laoist self-cultivation would have understood these sayings.

5. Tao is pictured as something that everything in the cosmos "naturally" treasures and obeys in 65[51]; 63[32]:4 (cp. 55[66]:1); and 48[62]:7 (cp. 30[56]:5). It is pictured as a cosmic norm in 39[25]:4. The saying in 28[16]:5 does not assert but assumes that Tao is a cosmic norm superior to Heaven and Earth. These passages probably draw on traditional Chou-dynasty ideas about the Emperor as cosmic norm. Passages picturing Tao as the origin of the cosmos (31[4]; 43[1]; 36[42]; 39[25]; 65[51]) will be commented on in detail in Chapter 10

(p. 251–56). All of these sayings are esoteric, in the sense that only Laoists involved in self-cultivation would have understood the hypostatization of Tao assumed in these sayings and would have appreciated the basis on which cosmic importance is accorded to Tao.

As with the other terms described above, Tao is not related to other special terms in any consistent and systematic way. Tao is described as Empty (31[4]:1; cp. 6[15]:4), an Uncarved Block (63[32]:1), the Mother (39[25]:1–2, 43[1]:1–2), doing nothing (81[37]:1). Becoming Tao is the result of becoming Empty, Still, Steady, and Clear (28[16]:5). Cultivation of Tao is described as "being Weak" in 34[40]:1. Although Te seems subordinated to Tao in 65[51]:1, 38[21]:1, and 11[38]:4, it is parallel to Tao in 65[51]:2, 14[23]:3 and in Chapter 70[60]. Tao is something hsiao/"of no account" (63[32]:1; cp. 29[52]:5), "left out" (14[23]:3) of conventional social life, just as the Mother is something that nourishes the alienated person (13[20]:4–5) and the Oneness is said to be something "lowly" (35[39]:1–2, 4). Both Tao and t'ung/"the Merging" are said to be the "Treasure of the World" (48[62]:7; 30[56]:5). Tao's name (its power) gives one true knowledge (38[21]:3), which can also be gained by attaining a Merged state (43[1]:5) and by "getting the Mother" (29[52]:2). One can yung/"use" Tao (31[4]:1; 46[35]:2–3) just as one can use Femininity (32[6]:1–2, 4) and the Uncarved Block (17[28]:2), and one can shou/"watch over" Tao (63[32]:2; 81[37]:2) just as one can watch over the Mother (29[52]:2), Weakness (29[52]:5), Femininity (17[28]:1), and Stillness (28[16]:1). All these are indications that, although it has a different meaning-content (Sinn) than the other terms, Tao has the same phenomenologically concrete reference to the single hypostatized state of mind that Laoists cultivate.

Te. In passages quoted in earlier chapters, one can see te used in three principal senses: (1) The Book of Documents says that, if the Emperor were not well advised "he would have no te to send down on the people." This is probably connected with the statement about the opposite case: If an emperor had good advisers, "when . . . he had sacrificial performances, there were none who did not have confidence in him." Public sacrificial performances ideally serve the function of sustaining the Emperor's symbolic normative role by inspiring the people with awe at their grandeur. It gives the Emperor genuine "charisma." This passage says the Emperor will only have genuine charisma if he really stands for something good, manifest in the truly beneficial public policies his wise advisers urge on him. *Te* thus stands for something good about the Emperor's person and policies, but has special reference to the positive impact that this has on the people, the subtle but effective political "power" that it gives him by gaining their respect. See also the use of *te* to refer to the invisible influence of a ruler (contrasted with punishment) in the story of Ch'i Tzu (quoted p. 554). When Mencius says that many states in his time "are equal in size and *te*," he is probably using *te* in a similar meaning: It refers to the "greatness" of the various states, as concretely felt in their reputation and influence. (2) Mencius more often gives a meaning to *te* that is closely connected to the moral ideal he advocates as proper to *shih*. An ideal *shih* cultivates various virtues (Goodness, Rightness, Etiquette). *Te* can serve as a summary reference to the resultant "virtuous" character of the *shih* that is his special claim to respect and social position. *Te* can thus be contrasted with official position, and with hereditary nobility or age, as a claim that a *shih* has to the respect of others. Said of a top ruler, "honor *te* and delight in *tao*" is a code phrase referring to the ruler's giving "virtuous" *shih* the respect, and the employment, they deserve. (3) In the *Nei Yeh* passage quoted p. 188–90, *te* is used in the context of self-cultivation practice to refer to an internal force one relies on in self-cultivation, (*"ch'i* can't be made to stay by force, but it can be made peaceful by Te"), a good quality of one's being that is the result of self-cultivation, ("Watch over [*ch'i*] . . . and don't lose it. This is called 'Complete Te'"), a power that one can *yung*/use in everyday life ("Use its Te every day"). In this context traditional meanings of the term *te* are not as important to its meaning as is the fact that it describes the calm state of mind one is cultivating. That is, these sayings seem to rely on the fact that (as in the *Mencius*) *te* is a general word that can refer to anything someone thinks of as central to human goodness. Something similar seems true of the *Chuang Tzu* passages quoted above that refer to self-cultivation. Here we have statements like "To have a trained nature is to *fan*/turn back to Te. To perfect Te is to *t'ung*/merge with the beginning" (3.[12/39–40]); "*hsü*/Empty, *ching*/Still, limpid, silent, not-doing [*wu wei*] . . . these are the substance of Tao and Te" (4.[28/54–55]); "In *hsü*/Emptiness, *wu*/non-being, Clarity, he joins with Heaven's Te . . . when the mind is without sorrow or joy, [this is] the perfection of Te. . . . It is in the nature of water that when it is not mixed with other things, it will be clear. . . . This is an image of Heaven's Te" (6.[15/13–15]).

In the *Tao Te Ching*, two passages (11:[38]:1–2; 44[41]:3) probably use *te* in something like its Mencian sense of "virtue" in general: Their point is that true *te*/virtue does not look like what people ordinarily consider virtue. And unlike Confucian virtue, Laoist virtue is something one does not "work" at according to conscious ideals (11[38]:2). The saying in 38[21]:1 seems also to be using *te* in the normal sense of impressive virtue when it speaks of "the impression made by magnificent Te." The saying in 61[54]:2 also seems to be using *te* in a relatively conventional sense when it speaks of the Te of families, villages, and states—that is, their general goodness or greatness, as manifest in their reputation. (This comes about by cultivating "It," that is, the Laoist spirit.) The saying in 71[63]:3 is a common saying (quoted also in *Analects* 14/36) that uses *te* in the sense of "kindness," in contrast to doing injury. This seems connected to two other sayings (9[79]:3, 60[49]:2) that picture Laoist Te as a personal quality that expresses itself in selfless generosity to others, regardless of their merit.

Several other passages picture Te as a personal quality of the ideal Laoist ruler, one that expresses itself in the specifically Laoist style of his ruling: gently preserving harmony (70[60]:4); opposing disquieting "improvements" (80[65]:4–5); being self-effacing (27[10]:2); adopting a deferential posture toward subordinates (57[68]:2). (In this last passage, Te is specifically a kind of effective charismatic "power" one gains as a manager through one's deferential and "non-contending" managerial style.) Chapter 27[10] suggests that the Te that expresses itself in a Laoist ruling style is something gained at meditation. Self-cultivation practice is probably also referred to in the statement in 26[59] that speaks of "getting dressed early to store up an abundance of Te," a Te that gives one great political charismatic power ("no one knows the limit, one can possess the state.") And "one devoted to Te, merges with Te. . . . Te welcomes him," implies a meaning of Te similar to its meaning in the *Nei Yeh* and the *Chuang Tzu*: a hypostatized internal force one can have a relation to. So when 33[55]:1 speaks of the magical invulnerability of one "who has an abundance of Te," this probably refers to a kind of inner power one gains through self-cultivation (the latter part of 33[55] refers directly to self-cultivation practices).

In 27[10] Laoist Te is something gained through cultivating Oneness, Softness, not-Doing, not-Knowing, and Femininity; it is associated with Femininity and the Uncarved Block in 17[28]; with being Soft and Weak, Harmonious, Steady, Clear in 33[55].

Te is sometimes subordinated to Tao (11[38]:4, 38[21]:1, 65[51]:1), but also sometimes parallel to Tao (14[23]:3, 65[51]:2). Chapter 70[60] and 80[65] imply that ruling by Tao and ruling by Te are the same thing, and chapter 44[41] implies that Tao and Te are two names for the same personal quality taught to and developed by members of the Laoist school. Magical invulnerability is ascribed both to "possessing an abundance of Te" in 33[55]:1, and to "fostering life *shan*/Excellently" in 22[50]:3.

Excellent (shan). Shan is very common in Chinese, meaning both "morally good" and "competent" ("good at. . . ."). Like *tao* and *te*, and like the English word "good," it is a generic concept: It refers to something the *speaker* approves of, although different people have different ideas about what actually is "good." *Shan* is used very frequently in the *Tao Te Ching* to refer to the ideal Laoist way of being. In several passages it seems to refer to a *very high degree* of Laoist "goodness": For example 49[27]:3–4 speaks of the Taoist teacher as a *shan jen*, and his pupil as a *pu-shan jen* (compare 48[62]:2, 4]). It is unlikely that the latter phrase means a "no-good man." It means rather one who is not highly advanced in goodness like the teacher: hence my translation "Excellent man" and "not-excellent man." This understanding of the word is supported by three other passages (49[27]:1–3; 61[54]:1; 22[50]:3), which attribute wonderful and quasi-magical effects to actions done *shan*/Excellently. Chapter 7[8] describes the important Taoist ideal of non-competitive lowness as "high *shan*/Excellence." Hence where *shan* refers to the Laoist ideal, I generally translate it with the English "Excellence" or one of its cognates: See 7[8]:1–2; 6[15]:1; 49[27]; 69[30]:4; 22[50]:3; 61[54]:1; 58[73]:5; 9[81]:1. I translate it "the best" in 57[68]:1, and "good" in 48[62]:2, 4; 9[79]:1, 4, and [49]:2 (in the latter two passages it means "kind"). The use of this common term for "goodness" to describe their ideal is one indication that Laoists did not really aspire to get beyond all value judgments.

Besides the special terms describing what it is Laoists cultivate, there seems to be also something of a special vocabulary describing the act of cultivating itself.

We saw especially the term *shou*/"watch over," used frequently in the *Mencius*,[21] the *Nei Yeh*[22] and the *Chuang Tzu*[23] to describe the practice of fostering and "guarding"[24] in oneself certain qualities or states. In the *Tao Te Ching, shou* is used of Stillness (28[16]:1), Femininity (17[28]:1), Tao (63[32]:2; 81[37]:2), The Mother (29[52]:2), and Weakness (29[52]:5). *Shou chung*/"watch over [what is] inside" in 16[5]:4 probably also refers to self-cultivation.

Yung/use is another recurring verb, probably referring to another aspect of self-cultivation: Letting certain qualities inform one's way of being and acting. Thus the *Nei Yeh* speaks (p. 190) of "*yung*/using every day" the Te one gains through internal cultivation. The *Tao Te Ching* speaks of *yung*/using Tao (4[31]:1; 34[40]:1; 46[35]:3; in the last passage using Tao is contrasted with trying to grasp it with one's mind), using Femininity (32[6]:4), and using the Uncarved Block (17[28]:2). *Yung huang*, lit. "use the lights" in 29[52]:6 probably means "engage with the flashing [stimulating] things" in the world, the opposite of "turning back to [internal] Clarity."

Pao/embrace is a term used in the phrase *pao shen*/"embrace the spirit" in *Chuang Tzu* 7.(11/35–43), speaking of internal self-cultivation. The *Tao Te Ching* speaks of *pao i*/embracing Oneness (27[10]:1; 4[22]:5), and *pao p'u*/"embracing the Uncarved" 78[19]:2. *Pao* as a description of qualities one embraces is also probably implied in the phrase *pao yang*/"embrace *yang*" (in contrast to *yin*) 36[42]:2.

Te/get is a term used by the *Nei Yeh* (p. 190, 196) when speaking of an elusive internal presence one is trying to mentally grasp or "get"; the *Tao Te Ching* shows a similar use in 37[14]:1. It also speaks of *te*/getting the Mother (29[52]:2), and the Oneness 35[39]:1. (The similar cosmogony in the *Tao Yüan*, quoted p.265, speaks of the cosmic order as a result of things *te*/getting "It.")

Finally, several words meaning "return" occur in the *Tao Te Ching* that refer to ideas related to self-cultivation. We saw the use of *fan*/return in the *Mencius* to refer to introspective "turning inward." The *Nei Yeh* (p. 189, Sect. 6) says that when we become calm the mind *fan*/"turns back" to completeness. Similarly *Chuang Tzu* 3.(12/39–40) says that "To have a trained nature is to *fan*/turn back to Te."; in *Chuang Tzu* 2.(7/30–33) the recluse Lieh Tzu is described as *fu*/turning back from being *tiao*/carved and *cho*/polished to being *p'u*/Uncarved; *Chuang Tzu* 4.(28/54–55) says, "Undo the mind, slough off the spirit, and the thousands of things one by one will turn back to the root." (This probably describes a felt shift one's experience of the world: when one's mind becomes Still, things in the world seem to reach a singleness also. See p. 247.)

In the *Tao Te Ching*, *fan*/"turn back" describes the movement of self-cultivation in 34[40]:1, and a cosmic movement imitative of this in 39[25]:3. In 28[16]:2:2 *fu*/"turn back" describes Stilling one's mind, in contrast to the *tso*/activity of things in the world; saying 72[64]:7 speaks of *fu*/"turning back" to the "place all others have gone on from"; *fu ming* in 28[16]:3:2–3 probably evokes the image of a soldier "returning to his commander" to report in, a metaphor for turning inward in self-cultivation; *fu shou mu*/"turn back [and] watch over the Mother" in 29[52]:2 also contrasts with occupying oneself with worldly affairs in 29[52]:4. Line 28[16]:2:4 speaks of *fu-kuei*/"turning back" to the Root; 29[52]6 uses this same phrase of turning back to Clarity; 17[28]:1 uses it of turning back to being an infant, unlimited, and an Uncarved Block; 37[14]:3 describes the apparent movement of the elusive internal presence one is trying to grasp as *fu-kuei yü wu*/"turning back to Nothingness." In 28[16]:3:1 *kuei*/"turn back" is used in the phrase *kuei pen*/"turn back to the root" to refer to the act of Stilling one's mind; 4[22]:7 speaks of *kuei*/"turning back" to true maturity.

Two Laoist notions condition the meaning of "turn back" in the *Tao Te Ching*: The first is the idea of an "original" and superior state (see p. 252) of mental Stillness we ought to "turn back to." The second is the idea of an unfortunate human tendency to become mentally active and direct energy outward (see 36[42]:3); in this context Laoist self-cultivation involves a "reversal" of this tendency, "turning back to the place all others have gone on from" (72[64]:7). See comments on "knowing to stop" at 63[32], a phrase that I think evokes similar Laoist ideas.

10

The Wonderful and Cosmic Tao

Chapters 8 and 9 presented evidence of self-cultivation as the background for many sayings in the *Tao Te Ching* and showed how some of the special terms that occur in these sayings describe the state of mind Laoists cultivated. Two sayings-forms were dealt with in the discussions in Chapter 8:

    1. Direct instructions in self-cultivation (p. 191–95).

    2. Sayings about an elusive presence (p. 197–99).

The present chapter will consist of form-critical analyses of six further sayings-forms in which the special terms occur, and show the way these sayings are related to self-cultivation as their life setting.

    3. Sayings using the formula "*X sheng*/overcomes *Y*," borrowed from speculation about the conquest cycle.

    4. Sayings linking one quality to another.

    5. Normative descriptions of the way Laoist Tao or Te expresses itself in conduct.

    6. Sayings describing the wonderful benefits that flow from the qualities Laoists cultivate.

    7. Sayings ascribing a "cosmic" status to qualities Laoists cultivate, or to the person who cultivates them.

    8. Cosmogonic sayings, describing the origins or foundations of the world.

I will draw on evidence already presented in Chapter 8 that self-cultivation is the proper life setting for all of these sayings. I will also add several more arguments related to individual forms.

It is especially the *combination* of forms involved, and their relation to each other, that provides additional evidence of this background in self-cultivation. Consider, for example, the fact that the same terms occur both in instructions "Watch over Femininity" (17[28]:1), "Watch over Stillness" (28[16]:1), and in sayings attributing cosmic importance to Femininity and Stillness: "The abode of mysterious Femininity is the Root of the World" (32[6]:2), and "Stillness is the Norm for the World" (5[45]:4). This shows that the latter statements have the same probable origin we have observed in the *Mencius* and the *Nei Yeh*, the tendency to attribute cosmic importance to the quality of mind one cultivates internally, because of the supreme importance one feels it to have.

"Softness Overcomes Hardness"

A first sayings-form I want to treat is one that uses the formula, *"X sheng*/overcomes *Y,"* as in "Softness overcomes hardness" (75[78]:2). Understanding this form requires a brief excursion into a current in ancient Chinese thought concerning the basic forces responsible for observable changes both in people and in the physical world.[1] This thought is somewhat comparable to that which gave rise in ancient Greece to the theory of "four elements" (fire, air, water, and earth) conceived of both as the basic constituents of things and also the basic dynamic forces responsible for change. A familiar theme connected with this thought in ancient China was the idea of a hierarchical ordering among the forces, expressed by saying that one force *sheng*/"overcomes" another, as in "Water overcomes fire," or "fire overcomes metal."[2] A. C. Graham (1989: 326) calls the hierarchical order expressed in these "overcomings," the "cycle of conquests."

The following example, which Alfred Forke quotes from the *Shuo Wen*, gives a good idea of the kind of thought involved:

South produces heat, heat produces fire, fire produces bitterness, bitterness the heart. . . . Joy injures the heart, but fear *sheng*/overcomes joy. Heat injures the breath, but cold overcomes heat, and bitterness injures the breath, but salt overcomes bitterness. . . . North produces cold . . . water . . . salt . . . kidneys. . . . Fear injures the kidneys, but desire overcomes fear . . . cold injures the blood, but dryness overcomes cold.[3]

Note the interweaving of external/physical with internal/ psychological terms. Some forces that "overcome" others are psychological, like fear and desire, but others are physical, like cold, salt, and dryness. Both the psychological and the physical terms seem to represent quasi-independent energies or forces. Passages like this represent a hypostatization of psychological categories like desire and fear, picturing them as manifestations of the same kind of forces that underlie physical phenomena.

Sometimes five particular hypostatized forces are named—water, fire, metal, wood, and earth—and these are called *wu te*, "the five powers," or later[4] *wu hsing*, literally "the five goings."

The formula *"X sheng/overcomes Y"* occurs four times in the *Tao Te Ching*:

Softness and Weakness overcome hardness and strength.
(73[36]:2)

Softness overcomes hardness
Weakness overcomes strength. (75[78]:2)

Femininity always overcomes masculinity by Stillness.
(56[61]:2)

Agitation overcomes cold
Stillness overcomes heat. (5[45]:3)

The last saying listed here is probably a direct borrowing from the speculation described above. That is, although the second line mentions "Stillness," a special term in Laoist vocabulary, the first line about agitation overcoming cold seems to lack any relevance to subjects Laoists elsewhere show an interest in. The most obvious explanation is that this entire saying was coined outside Laoist circles, and is being quoted here only for the sake of its second line.

A fifth saying uses somewhat different terminology, but is possibly an example of this same form:

Heaviness is the root of lightness
Stillness is the master of agitation. (23[26]:1)

There may have been some[5] in pre-Han China who tried to develop thought about the conquest cycle into a genuine explanatory scheme, an attempt to develop a consistent theory about the set of forces in terms of which physical and psychological changes can be explained. There is no indication that genuine systematic speculation of this kind underlies the above sayings in the *Tao Te Ching*. Aside from the one line (5[45]:3:1) mentioned above, all sayings using this formula can easily be explained on the supposition that Laoists cultivated the mental qualities of Femininity, Softness, and Stillness because of their perceived intrinsic value, and that they merely used this formula to express this perceived value, pictured as the superiority of these qualities over their opposites. The *Mencius* (6A/18,1) provides us with a fairly clear parallel here: "Goodness overcomes the not-good [*jen sheng pu-jen*], just as water overcomes fire." Mencius cultivates Goodness because of its perceived intrinsic value, not because systematic inquiry has led him to a foundational theory in which Good is a power that always wins out over its opposite.

This is the key to the ideal semantic structure of these sayings, the structure they have when the implications drawn from them are proportionate to their perceptual basis (see p. 131). That is, they do not have the perceptual basis—systematic and objective observation of natural processes—that general physical laws need. But neither did Laoists draw from them the kinds of conclusions one draws from general laws. Their perceptual basis suggested by the above discussions is the perceived supreme importance of certain personal qualities—Stillness, Softness, and Femininity—as experienced by "converted" Laoists engaged in cultivating these qualities in themselves. The thrust of the sayings is celebratory, celebrating this experienced importance by picturing these qualities as "conquering" all contrasting qualities opposed to them.

Sayings in the *Tao Te Ching* using this formula show that Laoists assimilated certain mental qualities or states they cultivated—Stillness, Femininity, Softness, and Weakness—to the hypostatized *te*/forces that ancient Chinese sometimes invoked to explain physical or psychological phenomena. Thus they are further evidence of a general Laoist tendency to hypostatize the qualities they cultivated. But if the above remarks are correct, this is a linguistic and imaginal, not a doctrinal and ontological, hypostatization.

Sayings Linking One Quality to Another

Another sayings form, one requiring little comment, is a form in which one mental quality Laoists cultivate is linked to another, as in "Experiencing Steadiness is Clarity" (28[16]:3). These sayings are one more indication that the terms involved do not describe entirely different mental qualities, but rather different aspects of a single state of mind which Laoists cultivated. Their thrust is probably also celebratory, celebrating the way that, in Laoist practice, cultivating one quality brings others with it. (Further examples of this form are 29[52]:5; 33[55]:3; and 36[42]:3.)

Normative Descriptions

Another sayings form is one that describes how (Laoist) Tao or Te expresses itself in conduct, as for example:

One who assists the people's rulers with Tao
does not use weapons to force changes in the world. (69[30]:1)

One who has Te is concerned with fulfilling [his side of] the
    contract.
One who does not have Te concerns himself with collecting
    his due. (9[79]:3)

Those who are good, I am good to them
those who are not good, I am also good to them—
Te is good. (60[49]:2)

Produce but don't possess
work but don't rely on this
preside but don't rule.
This is mysterious Te. (27[10]:2)

The point of these sayings seems partly dependent on the fact that the terms Tao and Te were generic terms used by different Warring States *shih*-schools. For each school they designate some normative way of being and acting, but schools were in conflict over exactly what ought to be considered the normative way of being and acting, and consequently the specific contents of these terms varied from school to school. In this context, to say that one who has Tao or Te acts in such and such a way is simply to assert that this way of acting is the right way. In this respect the main point of the sayings could be paraphrased without using the terms Tao or Te. The sayings above also belong in the category of polemic aphorisms.

In a context where Tao and Te are also names of a hypostatized mental quality one cultivates, however, these sayings are an explicit indication of the close connection between this quality of mind, on the one hand, and certain ways of conducting oneself thought to be expressive of this state of mind. When through self-cultivation one "increases one's store of Te," (26[59]:2) this Te expresses itself in a leadership style described in 27[10]:2 "Produce but don't possess/Work but don't rely on this/Preside but don't rule"—"This is mysterious Te."

This facet of Laoist thought is suggested also by the juxtaposition of sayings in several chapters. For example, 73[36]:1–2 suggests that the "Softness" one cultivates in meditation (26[10]:1) expresses itself in a "soft," non-confrontational style of defeating opposition. Chapter 56[61]:2–3 suggests that a "Feminine" state of mind expresses itself in a deferential ("low") style of diplomacy. Chapter 81[37]:2 suggests that the *p'u*/Uncarved state one cultivates internally expresses itself in a leadership style that is able to restrain people without making them feel humiliated.

If this analysis is correct, it gives us a basis for including several other sayings in this form-critical category which one might not otherwise think of including.

> Whoever holds onto this Tao
> does not yearn for solidity. (6[15]:3)

> Tao being Empty,
> it seems one who uses it will lack solidity. (31[4]:1)

"This Tao" in the first saying is the Laoist "way" ("this" implies that there are other Tao's as well), but also the name for the hypostatized quality of mind that animates this way. One who "holds onto" this quality of mind does not yearn to project a tangibly powerful, *ying*/solid presence in the world. The second saying is probably a version of the first (a common phenomenon in oral traditions.) Here it is clearer that Tao is a hypostatized mental quality which one *yung*/uses (internalizes). "Emptiness" is a name describing this same quality, so one who "uses" *Laoist* Tao has a way of being that is not felt by others as a tangibly "solid" presence.

> Turning Back is Tao movement
> being Weak is Tao practice. (34[40]:1)

Jo/Weakness is another name for the quality of mind Laoists cultivate, and the second line of this saying says that *yung*/using (Laoist) Tao means taking on a way of being that appears "Weak."

("Tao practice" translates *tao chih yung*, lit. "Tao's use.") "Turning Back" elsewhere describes the internal movement of Laoist self-cultivation (see p. 227–28). So the first line can be understood as parallel with the second if we understand "Tao" to mean here the Laoist way in self-cultivation. "Tao movement" (*tao chih tung*) refers to an internal movement characteristic of Laoist self-cultivation practice.

> The ability to know the ancient sources,
> this is the main thread of Tao. (37[14]:6)

I will argue below (p. 254–55) that "knowing the ancient sources" probably means gaining a true understanding of situations in the world. So *Tao* here probably stands again for the Laoist self-cultivation project itself (as it probably does also in 11[38]:6; compare Mencius' use of Tao as "method" [2A/2,3, p. 105]). The state of mind cultivated gives one a perspective from which one sees situations in their "true" light, and this is one of the principal aims of self-cultivation.

> Great Tao drifts—it can go right or go left. (64[34]:1)

Tao here is the hypostatized mental quality that animates the government of the ideal Laoist ruler (compare 63[32]:1–2). The saying describes the very flexible leadership style expressive of this ruler's way of being and conducting himself.

In the context of Laoist life, the point of sayings in this genre seems to be to define a kind of Laoist "orthopraxy": True Laoist Tao can be known partly by a person's general way of being and style of conducting himself. If a person has a way of being and conduct very different from that described in these sayings, this is a sign that he has not internalized *true* (Laoist) Tao. Note that there is no *logical* mediation between Tao and action here, no truths about Tao from which one intellectually "draws conclusions" about how to act. Like Mencius' *jen, Tao* concretely refers to a particular state of mind that immediately expresses itself in certain patterns of conduct.

These sayings reflect the fact that, like Mencius, Laoists have an expressive theory of politics: Good government is that government expressive of the ruler's character, or state of mind. Rather than taking extraordinary mental states as a source of revelatory insights, the basis for a metaphysical system, Laoists cultivated these states of mind primarily as a means of personal transformation, leading to a better style of conducting oneself both in one's personal life and in one's role as a political leader.

Sayings Describing the Wonderful Benefits
of the Qualities Laoists Cultivate

The next sayings-form is a very common one in the *Tao Te Ching*. The general characteristic of this form is that it describes the great benefits that flow from self-cultivation or from the quality of mind cultivated. These are sayings like:

If the princes and kings could watch over It [Tao],
the thousands of things would on their own be as deferential
    as guests.
Heaven and Earth would join together to send sweet dew.
The people on their own would share equally without anyone
    giving orders. (63[32]:2)

The benefits described in some of these sayings seem relatively mild and realistic, like "Keep to the Tao of the ancients, and so manage things happening today" (37[14]:5). Others seem extravagant and magical, like "One who Excels at fostering life / 'travels on land without meeting rhinoceros or tiger / enters combat without armor or weapon'" (22[50]:3). Some use phrases referring to self-cultivation practice (e.g., "fostering life Excellently," 22[50]:3). Some use one of the special recurring terms (e.g., "Once you get the Mother, then you understand the Children" 29[52]:2). Some speak simply of "It" (e.g., "Cultivate It in your person, its Te will be pure"⁶ 61[54]:2). Four sayings (15[11]:1; 16[5]:2; 10[7]:1; 47[43]:1) use nature images as metaphors to describe the wonderful benefits of the quality Laoists cultivate.

There is some overlap between this sayings form and certain polemic aphorisms. "Do not-doing and nothing will remain not done," for example, ascribes marvelous benefits to "Not-doing." Accordingly in some cases (in accord with the "experiential complex" implied in aphorisms, see p. 136) there seems to be some strong particular connection between the two parts of a given saying, as for example, "I have no desires, and the people become Simple"; on the assumption that the ruler sets the tone for his people, one can see a definite connection between "desire-less-ness" on the part of a ruler and *p'u*/simplicity on the part of the people.

In many sayings describing marvelous benefits, however, there does not seem to be any strong particular connection implied. For example, 32[6]:4, 16[5]:2, 26[59]:3, and 10[7]:1 all speak of the same wonderful results, "lasting long," but the first saying attributes lasting long to "It" (in the context, "It" is Femininity), the second to Emptiness, the third to "possessing the Mother of the State," and the fourth to "not living for oneself." The reason for this, suggested by discussions in Chapter 8, is that the state of mind and way of being cultivated by Laoists is basically single. Different phrases all refer to a single state of mind from which the same benefits flow.

Finally, one can note that many of the benefits described are those that would have been typical desiderata for Warring States *shih*: lasting long and steadiness (32[6]:4; 16[5]:2; 26[59]:3; 29[52]:4); internal harmony (33[55]:2; 31[4]:3); protection in combat (3[67]:3; 22[50]:3); effective speech (14[23]:4); gaining true understanding (29[52]:2; 43[1]:3,5; 38[21]:3); effective teaching (49[27]:1–3), managing (37[14]:5), and governing (81[37]:1); reuniting the Empire (25[48]:3); gaining allegiance (46[35]:1); social harmony (63[32]:2; 70[60]:3; 77[57]:5); public service benefiting all (52[77]:2); success in diplomacy (56[61]:3).

We come now to the question as to how we should understand the claims made by these sayings, and the basis for these claims. What role did these sayings probably play in the life of Laoists, and how did this affect the way they were originally understood? Can we devise an account of their ideal semantic structure (see p. 131) that approximates their original understanding and at the same time points to some interpretation under which these sayings say something true which Laoists are likely to have known about?

On a literal reading, these sayings might seem to invite utilitarian calculation: Some people greatly desire the benefits offered, and these sayings inform them about the means to achieve their desires. But this does not give us a very plausible account of the origin of these sayings. First, at best, cultivating Tao could plausibly be considered only one among several methods of achieving the goals mentioned. If genuine utilitarian interest lies behind these sayings, one would expect them to provide one with a "cookbook" of various methods. Why do they mention only cultivating Tao? Secondly, on what basis would these assertions of causal connections be made, and on what basis would one expect anyone to believe them? On what basis would any sensible person believe that "fostering life Excellently" in the Laoist manner would allow him to enter combat without armor or weapon and come out unharmed? Did the original author and audience of the sayings regularly witness miracles like this? Were they gullible people who had a propensity to believe extraordinary claims with no basis? If this is true, did they believe all extraordinary claims anyone made, or just those made about cultivating Tao? Must we just say that they simply were not people like us, and that therefore we have no possibility of empathically understanding any humanly plausible basis for these sayings?

These observations suggest that we need to look for a different way of construing these sayings. What I suggest is a semantic structure formally similar to the Mohist passage analyzed in Chapter 2:

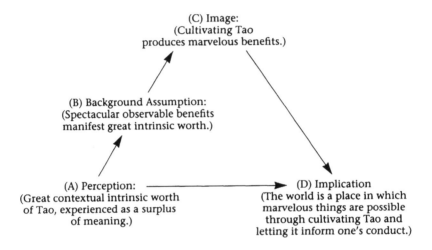

Let us begin with (D). On this model, the main implication of sayings in this group has to do with the changed character of the *Lebenswelt*, as a field for action, brought about by Laoist self-cultivation. Consider a possible "before/after" scenario that would dramatize the character of this change. Before the change let us imagine some individual Warring States *shih*-idealist facing a world which seems to offer very limited scope for meaningful action. A personal life satisfying idealistic standards cannot be achieved; neither can political life be reformed in any way satisfactory to an idealistic person. A *Lebenswelt* of this kind is depressing, offering little grounds for hope and little stimulus for ambitious efforts at personal or social improvement. But then we can imagine a dramatic change brought about in the *Lebenswelt*, the world-as-perceived by this *shih*. After the change, he perceives the world as a place where marvelous things are possible. The primary marvelous thing possible is a personal way of being and a style of political leadership that is both practically viable and informed by something of high intrinsic worth. An intensely meaningful way of life is possible. This is a *Lebenswelt* that encourages optimism and strenuous efforts to achieve ambitious and idealistic goals.

What could serve as a valid perceptual basis for this changed view of the world (*[A]* in the diagram)? We need a *cognitive* basis, something real that motivates the new optimism, not merely a decision to become more optimistic because it feels better psychologically. For an idealistic person, *meaningfulness* is the primary issue. An available opportunity to gain total power by brute force would not be grounds for optimism. What would be grounds for optimism and ambitious effort would be something concretely experienced to be of high intrinsic worth, and something also capable of informing one's efforts to meet the practical problems one faces in concrete personal and social life.

This is what might plausibly have been provided by Laoist self-cultivation. In this context Laoists might plausibly have experienced the state of mind cultivated as something of high intrinsic worth. *Tao*, the hypostatized quality of mind cultivated, served as source of internal sustenance (a "Mother"), answering the quest of *shih* for personal integrity and psychological "steadiness," and it also expressed itself in an effective style of political leadership. (I will use "Tao" in this chapter as a simplified designation for the quality of mind Laoists cultivate, referred to in some sayings by other terms.) Adopting a style of personal life and political leadership informed by Tao may have produced some improvements observable on a purely psychological and political level, but these were unlikely to have gone spectacularly beyond what could have been achieved on this external level by other means. The goodness of the Tao a Laoist leader practiced did not consist primarily in its instrumental usefulness in effective ruling. On the contrary, the effective ruling it led to was perceived to have an extraordinarily high intrinsic worth because it was informed by the Tao he cultivated. The possibility that one's leadership style could be informed by something of such high intrinsic worth is what transforms the *Lebenswelt* of the Laoist *shih* into a place encouraging optimism and strenuous effort to achieve ambitious goals.

A plausible account of the high intrinsic worth involved was suggested in our earlier description of the good stance motivating Laoist polemic aphorisms. The ultimate basis here is the high intrinsic worth of organic harmony. The state of mind Laoists cultivated was one that led to an *internal* state of organic harmony, and was also connected to an administrative attitude motivated by a concern for organic harmony in the society. In the context of the *Lebenswelt* of Laoist *shih* "converted" (see p. 278) to this kind of goodness, it is easy to see that this could make the Tao cultivated a focal center, a reality highly charged with a "surplus of meaning" (see p. 288).

This gives us an account of a historically plausible perceptual basis which would also serve epistemologically as a valid basis for the changed vision of the world and of the changed (optimistic and ambitious) attitude described above. This implies also, then, an account of the restricted interpretation under which sayings in this genre might plausibly be well founded. They are well founded if what they lead one to expect is that an intensely *meaningful* life as a *shih* is possible. They are not well founded on a literal interpretation, that is, if they lead one to expect that the exact benefits they describe can reliably be expected to result from Laoist self-cultivation.

The background assumption semiotically necessary in order for our sayings have the meaning just described (*[B]* in the diagram) is the assumption that spectacular observable phenomena symbolically represent high intrinsic worth. In general terms, what is involved here is the human tendency to picture symbolic relationships as causal ones. For example, when a country happens to prosper materially under a strongly ideological leader, this material prosperity will tend to take on a symbolic value as a visible sign of the greatness of the less visible ideological vision involved. This symbolic relationship then tends to be pictured as a causal one: The greatness of the ideological vision will be pictured as having "caused" the material prosperity. This picture need not be supported by accurate perception of actual causal connections. The picture of the causal relationship will "feel right" because it mirrors a perceived symbolic relationship. The background assumption involved in the present model presumes the same kind of causal-symbolic connection, played in reverse: The spectacular and utopian benefits pictured in the sayings symbolically match the perceived intrinsic greatness of the Tao cultivated, and thus the picture of Tao causing these great benefits felt right to Laoists. (This background assumption, being only a semiotic condition, need not be either a true belief or a consistently held belief in order for what the sayings say to be well founded.)

Another way of making this same point is to say that sayings describing marvelous benefits take realistic perceived results of

Laoist self-cultivation and extrapolate from them to completely idealized, "perfect" images in which Tao solves all of life's main problems. These images become a key organizing element in the *Lebenswelt* of a Laoist *shih*. Even though in real life he realizes these benefits only in a much more realistic, moderate, and imperfect way, the realistic benefits he does see take on added meaning because they "participate in" these perfect images. "Participate" is a concept used by Plato[7] to describe the way that the imperfect virtues of actual people "participate in" the Perfect Forms of virtue. But there are also more everyday examples of this phenomenon: The play of a young basketball player takes on added meaning because what he is doing "participates in" the play of great basketball stars who are his heroes; the everyday interactions of lovers takes on added meaning because of the perfect love that is "bigger than both of us," which they feel they are participating in. In these examples "participation" describes a semiotic, not a logical or causal relationship.

Thus these sayings are useful in furthering the Laoist verbal strategy described in Chapter 7 (p. 155–56). The center of the Laoist message itself is something that is by nature relatively intangible and not very attention getting. Laoist sayings do not *directly* describe the greatness of the reality on which Laoist life is centered, but they create an attention-getting set of images—such as those in these sayings—that indirectly point to this hidden greatness.

On this interpretation, sayings describing marvelous benefits do make serious claims, and these claims have implications for the way we interpret other parts of the body of sayings in the *Tao Te Ching*. That is, sayings describing marvelous benefits need to be "motivated," in something like the way that climactic actions or events in a good novel need to be sufficiently "motivated" by prior events. What we need to ask is, "Under what interpretation would other sayings in the *Tao Te Ching* provide sufficient motivation for these sayings describing marvelous benefits?" The polemic aphorisms provide part of this motivation by evoking for us the kind of highly admirable goodness that animates the Laoist perspective on the world, and to which Laoists were "converted" (see p. 278). Instructions in self-cultivation suggest additional motivation, in that they indicate very *intensive* cultivation of certain good personal qualities, cultivation that could be expected to produce these qualities in highly excellent forms. (This is especially true of the meditation instruction 27[10], which probably suggests practices of such intensity that they might result in trance states.) What we have, then, is a relation of mutual semiotic dependency between the groups of sayings involved. Sayings about marvelous benefits suggest that the goodness that motivates Laoist polemic aphorisms, and that is the focus of instructions for self-cultivation, was experienced by Laoists as a very extraordinary and superlative kind of ideal goodness. These latter sayings in turn fill in for us a motivating basis that makes plausible the extraordinary claims made by sayings describing marvelous benefits.

From a historical perspective, the above account implies that the original audience which would have been "competent" to understand these sayings (see p. 148) was a rather specialized one. The general public in ancient China could not have been expected to understand in any depth what Laoists meant by phrases like "watch over Tao." Nor could they have been expected to have had a perception of Tao's great intrinsic worth that would have made plausible the strong assertions made in these sayings. The sayings themselves do not provide, but assume, these understandings. They are to this extent esoteric sayings. Their point is not instructional, giving instruction or information to an audience who is not yet aware of their basic message. They are rather celebratory. That is, they assume that the audience they address is a group of people who already have certain shared experiences of the wonderfulness of the Tao they cultivate, and they celebrate this wonderful character.

Finally, it is worth recalling here a point made with regard to Mencius in Chapter 5. One might initially suppose that a saying like 63[32]:2, promising that universal order and peace will come when a ruler "watches over Tao," advocates cultivating Tao *instead of* doing normal administrative work. Laoists somehow expected that simply cultivating the proper state of mind, without taking any further action, would magically ensure social order. But we saw earlier (p. 101) that, when Mencius promises King Hsüan that he can gain the allegiance of all Chinese just by becoming *jen*/Good, he does not have in mind cultivating Goodness *instead of* attending to administrative tasks. Mencius assumes that this Goodness will express itself in the way the king takes care of very nitty-gritty matters like silk production and animal breeding. Similarly, looking at the *Tao Te Ching* as a whole, we should remain aware that the phrase "watching over Tao" probably refers both to cultivating a state of mind through introspective meditation exercises and also to letting this state of mind inform one's policies and one's leadership style in carrying out routine administrative tasks. The many references in the *Tao Te Ching* to leadership ambitions and to the performance of managerial tasks (see p. 120–21) reflects the fact that this material is meant to serve as a spiritual guide for an audience who took these tasks for granted.

Cosmic Sayings: A General Thesis

The two remaining sayings forms that need discussion are forms that ascribe a "cosmic" status to the state of mind Laoists cultivate. One form is exemplified in the saying, "Stillness is the Norm of the World" (5[45]:4). The other form speaks of Tao as world-origin, as in "Nameless, It [Tao] is the origin of the thousands of things" (43[1]:2).

In the analysis I will argue for,[8] both these forms have a similar basis and make a similar point. Their basic thrust can best be explained by introducing the idea of an "evaluative context." That is, prior to reflective thought, everyone evaluates her experiences and actions in the world in the light of some view of the world-as-context. This takes place on a small scale when one reacts to someone's behavior in a restaurant as "appropriate" or "inappropriate" in this context. It takes place on a larger scale when one perceives oneself as a "success" or a "failure" in one's social environment. A "social environment" operates as a large scale evaluative context, which greatly shapes people's implicit evaluative perceptions of themselves in any given culture.

It is important to note that a social environment does not consist only of the individual people and objects materially surrounding us. It consists of a certain perceptual *organization* of these people and objects, an organization partly determined by values, ideals, and concerns. Identical material surroundings might form different social environments for people in different cultures or subcultures. In more technical language, the world-as-evaluative-context is a semiotically and perspectivally organized totality.

Consider now a major problem facing a Laoist cultivating Tao. As seen *within* the conventional social environment, the *Lebenswelt* organized by ordinary concerns and perspectives, Tao appears to be something insignificant, of no account (63[32]:1). For the Laoist, however, this picture of Tao is false and needs to be reversed. Tao has the highest experienced worth in the world. Tao, or alternatively the one who embodies Tao, has become the new

"Norm of the World," replacing the Chou Emperor, and inheriting his "cosmic" role.

Another way of imaginally representing this aspect of Laoist experience is by picturing a dimension of reality, dominated by Tao, that is evaluatively, axiologically, "more ultimate" than the conventional social environment. Imaginally, Tao can be presented this way by taking advantage of the common feeling that civilized society occurs in the context of a wider natural world, and picturing Tao as a more ultimate origin of even this enveloping natural world. Tao is "not part of" the normal world, in the sense that its real worth cannot appear when it is seen within the conventional social environment. But this reality that is not part of the world is axiologically "beyond," superior to, the world (the conventional *Lebenswelt*) as a whole. This again is what it means to say that Tao is a "cosmic" reality, or to say that Tao has an existence "prior" to the existence of the physical universe.

In earlier chapters we saw several examples of realities connected with self-cultivation pictured as having a "cosmic" status. Thus Mencius says of the "ocean-like *ch'i*" he cultivates: "If uprightness nourishes it, and no harm is done to it, then it completely fills up the space between heaven and earth." (see p. 111) The *Nei Yeh* attributes a cosmic importance to *ching* and to *tao* (see p. 185–86), hypostatized mental qualities whose cultivation is described in that book. *Hsün Tzu's* eulogy of *li*/Etiquette (quoted p. 186) pictures it as something that makes the sun and moon shine, and makes the myriad things flourish.

One major problem for us moderns in understanding this cosmic language and imagery is that the imaginal and linguistic habits they reflect—shared by many ancient peoples—are no longer common among us today. Perhaps the closest analogy in our culture, which can help us to empathically enter into the particular relation between experience and language these sayings reflect, are ways of speaking about falling in love. Consider the following stanza from a modern love song by Ewan McColl:

> The first time ever I saw your face,
> I thought the sun rose in your eyes,
> And the moon and stars were the gift you gave,
> To the dark and the empty skies.

This song celebrates the "cosmic" significance that the loved one takes on for the lover. Our understanding of the underlying experience allows us to be more precise about what "cosmic" means here. One thing that makes falling in love different from ordinary experiences is that ordinary experiences take place within a "world" that is the stable backdrop for our lives. Falling in love is an experience strongly affecting the backdrop itself, making it seem as though the world itself is radically changed. It is now a *fundamentally* different place, a place in which love and the loved person have a central place on the "largest" possible scale. Love seems to be "more ultimate" than the encompassing sky itself, and this is expressed by saying that it is "the source" of this encompassing reality. The spatial image of the "large encompassing" sky serves to represent the way that the context in which one leads one's life is changed in a very fundamental way.

Drawing on all these observations, the ideal semantic structure of most sayings about Tao as cosmic norm or origin can be described in the following way. The main point of these sayings is to counteract what would happen if a Laoist *shih* allowed the conventional *Lebenswelt* to serve as an evaluative context, and allowed this context to determine the image he had of the Tao that he cultivated and practiced. In this context, Tao appears something "lowly" (35[39]:2) and *hsiao*/"of no account" (63[32]:1). Images of Tao as a "cosmic" norm or origin correct this "false" picture of the evaluative context in which human life takes place and the false picture of Tao that results from it. In the new picture of the world they present, the phenomenologically concrete Tao one feels within oneself is a concrete manifestation of a reality that also dominates the more ultimate evaluative context in which human life takes place, a context normatively more ultimate than the conventional Chinese cultural world.

But this picture of Tao dominating our evaluative context on a cosmic level is not an *epistemological and logical* basis in Laoist thought. Laoists had no independent basis for knowing that the world objectively has an axiological structure dominated by Tao at the ultimate level. And there is no evidence that they regarded cosmic images of Tao as a logical foundation from which to draw conclusions about the world. Rather, images of a normative and cosmic Tao represent the "true" picture of the world as it appears to a person "converted" to Tao, a person who lets Tao become the dominant focus of his concernful engagement with the world and his perspective on it. (This can be compared to falling in love as a "conversion" experience, reflected in the love song quoted above.) What needs an epistemological basis is this conversion experience itself. The discussions above suggest that the ultimate basis is the extraordinary and superlative goodness of Tao directly ("subjectively") perceived in Laoist self-cultivation.:

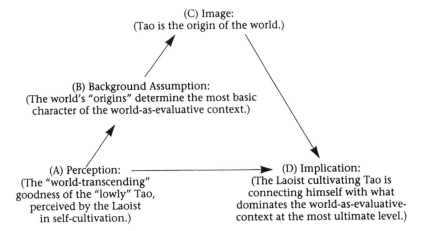

(C) Image:
(Tao is the origin of the world.)

(B) Background Assumption:
(The world's "origins" determine the most basic
character of the world-as-evaluative context.)

(A) Perception:
(The "world-transcending"
goodness of the "lowly" Tao,
perceived by the Laoist
in self-cultivation.)

(D) Implication:
(The Laoist cultivating Tao is
connecting himself with what
dominates the world-as-evaluative-
context at the most ultimate level.)

The perception (A), not the image (C), is the ultimate epistemological basis for the implication (D). (C) represents the character of the world as seen by someone who is "converted" by letting the experienced goodness of Tao dominate his concernful engagement with the world.

In the above remarks, "the world" that cosmic realities are beyond is more or less identical with the *Lebenswelt* of ordinary perception. The point of the cosmic language is to assert that some highly meaningful reality is axiologically beyond this world that everyone sees.

But Laoists have also a second and somewhat different view of "the world" that also figures in some cosmic sayings. This is a world different from the world perceived by all; it is the "true" world, the world as seen from the perspective of the ideal Laoist. That is, cultivating Tao brings about an inner personal transformation that also brings about a transformation of the *Lebenswelt*; the world now becomes a world reorganized semiotically in many of its details by Tao as an organizing center, and perspectivally by Tao as a central focus of concern.

One passage in the *Chuang Tzu*, paralleled by one in the *Tao Te Ching* and one in the *Nei Yeh*, gives a particularly helpful illustration of this point:

You have only to rest in *wu wei*/not-doing, and things will transform themselves. Smash your form and body, spit out hearing and eyesight, forget you are a thing among other things. [This is] the Great Merging [ta t'ung] with the deep and boundless. Undo the mind, slough off the spirit, and the thousands of things one by one will turn back to the root.[9]

Many phrases in this *Chuang Tzu* passage refer to attempts to cultivate a state of mind (see p. 205). This transformation of one's state of mind causes a transformation of the world-as-perceived. This transformation of the *Lebenswelt* is described by saying that "the thousands of things turn back to the Root." That is, to a still mind the world itself appears a more "quiet" place. It has been semiotically reorganized in perception, and this new semiotic organization can be pictured by saying that the world has a new single semiotic organizing center, a single "root." This "root" is not a reality permanently existing in an unseen world that one believes in intellectually. This root comes into being in the experience itself. It is a hypostatized feeling one perceives as the "source" of the felt character of the newly quieted world. The passage is implicitly celebratory, implying that a world in which "things have returned to the root" is a more richly meaningful world, and "the root" is (semiotically) the source of this meaning.

Next a parallel passage in the *Tao Te Ching*:

Push Emptiness to the limit,
watch over Stillness very firmly.

The thousands of things all around are active—
I give my attention to Turning Back.
Things growing wild as weeds
all turn back to the Root.

To turn back to The Root is called Stillness. (28[16]:1–3)

This passage begins with instruction in cultivating a mental Stillness and Emptiness. Stilling one's own mind can be described as "turning back to the root." But, as in the *Chuang Tzu* passage, "turning back to the root" also describes the perceptual stilling of the external world that happens with the stilling of the mind. The old *Lebenswelt* was a world of confusing multiplicity (the point of the "weeds" image). The new *Lebenswelt* has a more peaceful and unified feeling, that seems to stem from a single source, identical with the Stillness one cultivates internally.

Finally, some brief lines from the *Nei Yeh*:

> Concentrate *ch'i*, spirit-like,
> the thousands of things lie there all in order.
> Can you concentrate? Can [you be] One?

These lines from the meditation instruction in the *Nei Yeh* quoted earlier (p. 192), probably reflect a similar experience: An internal transformation from mental distraction to mental "oneness" also causes a transformation of the *Lebenswelt* from confusion to orderliness.

Note that the "Root" spoken of in the first two quotations is not something separate from the transformed world. It has no content that could be set off over against the world itself, no content that could serve as a first principle from which one could draw logical conclusions about the world. It is a hypostatized feeling or spirit that pervades a world *perceptually* restructured by the transformative "conversion" experience gradually engendered by Taoist self-cultivation and meditation exercises. This pervading spirit is directly experienced as semiotically determining the character of world it pervades, the semiotic "source" of the character and meaning-structure of the world. Thus (unlike Schwartz' metaphysical Tao, p. 176), this non-conceptual reality is not a metaphysical principle undermining all determinate characteristics and values. The transformed *world* has a definite character and meaning, stemming semiotically from a reality which also has a definite character, however inexpressible in words it might be.

Besides being a more "Still," peaceful and harmonious world pictured in the above saying, this transformed world is also one in which situations and events are interpreted in a certain way. This is what it means to say that "The world has an origin . . . the Mother of the World. Once you get the Mother, then you know the children" (29[52]:1–2). The "children" are situations and events in the world as perceived when their meaning-structure has its source ("Mother") in the state of mind one *te*/gets in Laoist self-cultivation. This is the way one comes to understand the "true" meaning of the events. In the absence of any other likely candidates for the content of such knowledge, we ought to assume that such a perception is identical with the perception one has of various situations and events when one lets one's perspective on them be dominated by the images offered in the polemic aphorisms (see p. 140). Again, there is no independently verifiable, unique and objectively true meaning to these events, "getting the Mother" serving merely as an instrumental means of gaining this understanding. Far less is there some objective truth *about* the Mother one learns, that then serves as a logical first principle from which one deduces true interpretations of situations. The "true" meaning of events is implicitly *defined* as the meaning one sees who has achieved a certain state of mind ("gotten the Mother"), a state of mind acted out by the polemic aphorisms.

This is my overall thesis about the ideal semantic structure of the cosmic sayings in the *Tao Te Ching*. This account can now be filled out with more specific remarks about the two groups of sayings involved.

"Stillness Is the Norm of the World"

Most sayings in the first group employ the formula "*X* is the *Y* of the World" (*X wei t'ien hsia Y*), as in "Stillness is the Norm of the World." These sayings need to be understood in the context of the ambition of *shih*, visible in the *Mencius*, to replace the traditional Chou Emperor as the highest spiritual leader of the Chinese Empire. Traditionally, the Chou Emperor was considered "The One Man," symbolic normative "center of the world" (see p. 52). This tradition is reflected in two passages in the *Tao Te Ching* itself (35[39]:1, and 39[25]:4), in which the Emperor is regarded as one of the pillars of the cosmic order. But in Chapter 4 (p. 75) we saw that it is now Mencius' ambition to "stand in the norm-giving position of the world," and his associated claim to be superior to all the feudal lords because of his self-cultivation. The underlying assumption is that one who personally embodies the highest ideals in Chinese culture by that fact deserves to *spiritually* replace the Emperor as normative spiritual leader, although it was apparently characteristic of *shih* not to aspire to top *political* leadership. Laoist sayings often seem to reflect a similar background assumption, using phrases evoking the traditional role of the Emperor: The ideal Laoist "can be entrusted with the world" (18[13]:4) and is "the Shepherd of the World" (4[22]:4), "The Counterpart of Heaven" (in ruling the empire, 57[68]2), and so on. We must keep in mind here that it was naive ethnocentrism, rather than anything like modern attempts to discover transcultural truths, that led ancient Chinese in general to assume that the normative center of the Chinese Empire and the normative center of the world are the same.

The sayings belonging to this group are listed here, with some comments.

Text	*Comment*
Purity and Stillness are the Norm of the World. (5[45]:4)	The hypostatized Stillness that Laoists cultivate takes the place of the Emperor (called "norm of the world" in 35[39]:1), as the normative center of the Chinese Empire.
It [Tao] is the Treasure of the World. (30[56]:5) It [The Merging] is the Treasure of the World. (48[62]:7) Among the thousands of things there are none that do not honor Tao and treasure Te. (65[51]:2)	"Treasure of the World" probably reflects the idea (found both in the *Tao Te Ching* and the *Mencius*[10]) that everything "naturally" gravitates toward that which is truly normative. The hypostatized quality of mind Laoists cultivate is this attractive normative center in the transformed world of the Laoist.
Tao is the honored center for the thousands of things. (48[62]:1)	"Honored center" translates *ao*, the shrine for household gods that was the center of the house. Tao is a cosmic *ao*.
Heaven gives the rule for Earth Tao gives the rule for Heaven. (39[25]:4)	Tao is a cosmic norm more ultimate than the conventional ultimate norms, the cosmic powers Earth and Heaven.
Embrace The Oneness, and become the Shepherd[11] of the World. (4[22]:4) Watch over Femininity— and become the Valley of the World. . . . Watch over what is dark and black— and become the Pattern for the World.	Equivalently, it is the *person* who cultivates "The Oneness," and "Femininity" (hypostatized qualities that appear "disgraceful" from a conventional point of view) who takes the place of the Emperor, "Shepherd" or normative "Pattern" for the world. This parallelism reflects the emphasis on the person of the *shih* that we saw reflected in the *Mencius*. *Shih* in both

Watch over what is
  disgraceful—
and become the Valley of the
  World. (17[28]:1)

schools expect their ideals to affect public life, not as doctrines taught to all, but primarily through the persons of *shih* who internalize these ideals and let them inform their own political practice (see p. 115).

Experiencing Steadiness, then
  one is all-embracing
all-embracing, then an
  impartial Prince
Prince, then King
King, then Heaven
Heaven, then Tao. (28[16]:5)

This saying shows even more clearly the normative cosmic status of the one who internalizes Laoist Steadiness. This person *becomes* the equivalent of the chief cosmic powers, the *wang*/king:emperor, Heaven, and Tao.

It is unlikely that any differentiated and systematic set of doctrines underlies these sayings (for example, that Laoist belief held Stillness to be the Norm of the World, whereas Tao was the Treasure of the World). The sayings simply express the ultimately normative status of the hypostatized quality Laoists cultivate.

Cosmogonies

The final sayings form we need to consider, sayings about world-origins, is a subject of some importance in the interpretation of the *Tao Te Ching*, and needs more extended discussion here. The semantic structure of such sayings has been sketched above (p. 246). I want first to deal in more detail with the probable "background assumptions" that Laoists associated with origin imagery. These associations would have determined what perceptions origin images would be taken to express, and what point cosmogonic sayings would be taken to be making. Fortunately, ideas and images utilizing or implicitly evoking origin imagery occur in many passages in the *Tao Te Ching* besides the cosmogonic sayings themselves, and these passages can give us helpful clues concerning specifically Laoist associations. The following are some observations about these other passages.

Text	Comment
When Great Tao vanished, we got "Goodness" and "Morality." (12[18]:1)	These lines implicitly evoke an image in which "original" is equivalent to "ideal." The "original" state of the world was an ideal one in which Tao prevailed. Current (Confucian) concern for Goodness and Morality is pictured as a chronological "decline" from this original ideal state.
Desire to be desireless . . . learn to be un-Learned, turn back to the ["original"] place all others have gone on from. (72[64]:7)	This saying implicitly evokes the same picture, on an individual level: The "original" state is one in which the mind is still (not stirred up by desires) and "undeveloped" (un-Learned), but everyone has an unfortunate tendency to "pass on from" this ideal original state.
Watch over Femininity. . . . Turn back to being an infant. . . . Watch over what is disgraceful. . . . Turn back to being an Uncarved Block. (17[28]:1)	This saying implies again an "original" state of an individual, "before" social pressures caused her to try to develop "desirable" qualities. This represents an unfortunate "carving up" of a previously more ideal "uncarved" personality. One "turns back" to this more ideal state by cultivating and recovering qualities society regards as "disgraceful."
Heaviness is the root of lightness Stillness is the master of agitation. (23[26]:1)	A heavy/Still state of mind is here pictured as the original and superior "root" state, in relation to which mental agitation and mental "levity" repre-

sent a decline. Note the apparent equivalence between *pen*/root—an origin-metaphor—and *chün*/master, a metaphor portraying superiority in worth.

Note that the equation of "ideal" with "original" operates here as a background assumption, not a foundational belief. As with the Mohist saying about ancient kings discussed earlier (p. 30–32), it is highly unlikely that Laoists first began (for unknown reasons) to believe that what is chronologically prior is also superior, conducted objective research to discover the original states of individuals and societies, and based their ideals on the results of such research. What is much more likely is that the ideals of Laoist *shih* were determined by their own contemporary concerns and context, and the equation between "ideal" and "original" led them to *express* these ideals by means of origin images. Origin images constitute a language within which one can indirectly express one's views about what is ideal.

A second set of passages illustrates the use of origin imagery to describe the single "source" of Laoist wisdom.

Text	*Comment*
My words are very easy to understand, very easy to practice. No one in the world can understand, no one can practice them. The words have an ancestor the practice has a master. They just do not understand and so they do not understand me. (45[70]:1–2)	People "do not understand me" because they do not understand a difficult-to-understand "ancestor of the words." If we take seriously the Laoist polemic against "naming" as a polemic against conceptual knowledge in general, it is unlikely that this "ancestor" is a foundational *doctrine* from which the rest of Laoist thought is derived by logical deduction.
What another has taught, I also teach:	It is unlikely that the *content* of the popular saying quoted here

"A violent man will not reach his natural end." I will make of this the father of my teaching. (36[42]:6) serves as the *logical* foundation of Laoist thought. Something else is being referred to as the "parent" of Laoist teaching.

The discussion of polemic aphorisms in Chapters 6 and 7 suggests an explanation of both the above sayings. The single "origin" (ancestor/father) of Laoist wisdom is the state of mind and attitude that Laoists cultivate. This state of mind gives one a certain perspective on the world, and this perspective is the motivating basis for Laoist wisdom expressed in the aphorisms. (This perspective is the motivating force the composer of 36[42] feels present in the saying "A violent man will not reach his natural end," and this is why he can say that this saying conveys the "father" of his teaching.) So there is no conceptual *doctrine*, separable from what the aphorisms say, that serves as the foundation for the aphorisms. To be competent to understand the body of aphorisms correctly is to understand the single attitude they all express.

So to call something the "father/ancestor" of Laoist sayings is to assert that this something is the "basis" of the sayings. This is in accord with Graham's linguistic observation that the Chinese word *ku*/ancient is related etymologically to another *ku* that means "a reason," "a basis," used by Mohist logicians to refer to the factual assertion that is the "basic core" of a sentence's meaning.[12] It is just that in the Laoist case, this "basis" cannot be a truth to be grasped intellectually, but a spirit and perspective to be cultivated.

In two other sayings, origin imagery seems to be used to describe understanding not Laoist teaching, but the world itself. These two sayings are:

The ability to know the ancient sources,
this is the main thread of Tao. (37[14]:6)

From ancient times until today
Its name has not been forgotten
allowing us to see the beginnings of everything. (38[21]:3)

It is unlikely that "know the ancient source" refers to intellectual knowledge of some reality or truth. In addition to the unlikelihood that such an intellectual truth is the basis of the Laoist understanding of things, one can point out that the only plausible "beginning of everything" one would learn about would be Tao. But these sayings picture Tao as the *means* by which one knows the source of everything. In the first saying, *Tao* seems to serve as a shorthand designation of Laoist self-cultivation. In the second saying, Tao's "name" probably refers to the power of Tao. Tao informs one's consciousness and perspective on the world, and this allows one to understand things as they "truly" are. One uses origin imagery to *describe* this true understanding. Just as a true understanding of Laoist sayings can be described as an understanding that grasps the spirit that is their "ancestor," so a true (Laoist) understanding of events in the world can be described as "seeing the source of everything" in the world. If this analysis is correct, then "the world" that one understands by means of "knowing its source" is not the conventional world, but the *transformed* world of the "converted" Laoist. These sayings reflect the same basic experience as the sayings quoted above (p. 247) in which a Stilling of the mind changes the character of the *Lebenswelt*, experienced as a Still world stemming from a single Still Root/source. A related passage, already mentioned above, can be dealt with in more detail here:

The world has a Source, the Mother of the World.

Once you get the Mother
then you understand the children.
Once you understand the children
turn back and watch over the Mother. (29[52]:1–2)

As we saw earlier (p. 227), "*te*/getting the Mother" describes the object of self-cultivation, "the Mother" being the hypostatized mental quality of mind Laoists cultivate. "Getting the Mother" gives one a "*true*" understanding of the world. That is, it transforms one's consciousness so that one sees the events in the world world in their true (Laoist) perspective. The meaning-structure of the world experienced in this transformed way appears to stem from a single "source," here called "the Mother of the world." Situations and events in the world, "truly" understood, are the "children" of this "Mother."

This is the meaning of the saying "Once you get the Mother, then you understand the children." The composer of this passage has added a line to the saying that is not completely in accord with its original meaning. In this addition, "children" takes on a negative meaning, referring to the *conventional* world one might allow oneself to be concerned with in a worldly way, *in contrast with* "The Mother" one might cultivate internally. Thus this passage aptly illustrates the two meanings that "the world" has in Laoist thought, and two corresponding meanings that images about the origin of the world might have.

These observations can be summarized as follows:

1. The conventional world (the conventional *Lebenswelt*) is an evaluative context. To picture Tao as an origin, existing prior to the world and causing its existence, is to picture it as the dominant reality in an overarching evaluative context superior to and "more ultimate" than this conventional world.

2. Similarly, to assert that some state of an individual or society is chronologically prior is a way of asserting that it is more ideal. Imaginally, what comes first is pure and perfect. What comes later represents a "decline" from this original ideal state. So to picture Tao as "prior" to the world—or to the cosmic powers "ruling" the world—is to picture Tao as pure and perfect, in contrast with the inferior realities that develop later.

3. But "the world" can also refer to the transformed *Lebenswelt* of the ideal "converted" Laoist. To say that Tao is the source of *this* world is to say that it is the semiotic source of the meaning structure of this more "true" world.

Laoist origin sayings themselves call upon the above associations in somewhat diverse ways. The interpretation of them that follows from the above discussion can best be presented in comments on the sayings themselves. Additional light is often thrown on these sayings by seeing the way the composers of various chapters have used the sayings. (Chapter 12 argues that deliberate intentions lie behind the juxtaposition of sayings.)

Text	*Comment*

32[6]
The Abode of mysterious {2}
  Femininity:
This is the Root of Heaven and
  Earth. . . .
 	
One who uses it never {4}
wears out.
	"Abode" translates
	men/door:house. It refers to an
	internal "abode," a mental
	"space"[13] in which Femininity
	resides. Femininity is an ideal
	spirit more fundamental than
	the forces "Heaven and Earth"
	that rule the world in conventional belief. "*Yung*/use It" in

{4} indicates that this cosmic reality is a hypostatized state of mind that one can internalize and practice in everyday life.

31[4]

Tao being Empty, {1}
it seems one who uses it will
  lack solidity.

An abyss, {2}
it seems something like the
  ancestor of the thousands of
  things.

It dampens the passion {3}
it unties the tangles
it makes the flashing things
  harmonious
it makes the dust merge
  together.

Deep, {4}
it is perhaps like an enduring
  something.

I don't know of anything {5}
  whose offspring it
  might be—
it appears to precede God.

Sections {1} and {3} make it clear that Tao is something concrete, a hypostatized state of mind. Because it is "Empty," the person who *yung*/uses Tao (lets it inform his way of being) will appear to others to lack solidity {1}. Tao as an internal presence also has the effect of transforming, calming down, the world-as-experienced {3}. For one who "uses" this Tao, it is experienced both as an internal presence and as a "deeper" dimension of reality. What is expressed by the spatial images *deep* and *abyss* can be equivalently expressed in chronological imagery as "ancestor." This Tao is the *most* pure and perfect, axiologically ultimate, reality, more ultimate than even the high God *ti*.

43[1]

The Tao that can be told is not
  the invariant Tao
The names that can be named
  are not the invariant Names.

Nameless, It is the source of the
  thousands of things
(named, it is 'Mother' of the
  thousands of things).

Tao here is probably Tao as the normative "Way" that individual *shih* should follow, which is also the norm for the society, and which they should represent in their capacity as government officials. This norm consists in an internal spirit or attitude that informs their actions. It cannot be put into

Text	*Comment*
	words because it is a spirit/attitude, not a propositional principle to be conceptually grasped, and also because its true nature cannot be described in ordinary words and verbal forms, closely tied as these are to the conventional worldview. But this hidden reality is a norm axiologically more ultimate than the enveloping physical context ("the thousands of things") in which social life takes place.
34[40] Turning back is Tao movement. Being weak is Tao practice. "The thousands of things in the world are born of Being" Being is born of Nothing.	Laoist self-cultivation consists in "turning back" to a more pure and perfect "original" state, which appears in the conventional world as something very "Weak," an insignificant "Nothing." But this insubstantial Nothing deserves (semiotically) to dominate our concept of the most ultimate context in which we live. It is axiologically more ultimate than "Being," which here serves as a hypostatized principle of the apparent solidity of the conventional world.
36[42] Tao produced The Oneness {1} The One produced Two Two produced Three Three produced the thousands of things.	The world of multiplicity ("Two . . . three . . . thousands") has a double relation to the One source of meaning in this world: (1) It is a meaningful multiplicity, semiotically

The thousands of things: {2}
Turn their back on the quiet
and dark,
and embrace the aggressive and
bright.

deriving its meaning from the one Tao that is more ultimate even than the enveloping physical world. But (2) one can easily get lost in the multiplicity itself (becoming preoccupied with "The Mother's children," 29[52]:2). In this respect multiplicity potentially represents a fall and a decline from a more "original" ideal Oneness. People have an unfortunate common tendency to "fall" from this ideal original state, the *yin*/"still and dark" Tao, and embrace the *yang*/"active and bright" world of multiplicity. This tendency is what produces the conventional *Lebenswelt*, which we can now see as a secondary and derivative, rather than "ultimate" context for our lives.

39[25]
There was a chaotic {1}
    something, yet lacking
    nothing
born before Heaven and Earth.
Alone.
Still.
Standing alone, unchanging.
Revolving, endlessly.
It can be thought of as Mother of
    the World.

I do not know its name, {2}
One can call it 'Tao.'
The name of its powerful
    presence:
One can call it 'The Great One.'

Form-critically, the kernel of {1} is probably a report of a vision someone had at meditation. The fact that what was seen was "chaotic" yet perfect reflects the character of the state of mind Laoists cultivate, experienced as an undifferentiated and "muddy" Uncarved Block (6[15]:3) which is yet harmonious and superlatively good. The composer's added comments (italicized) picture this chaotic something as extremely primordial (an "ultimate" normative reality completely transcending the enveloping natu-

Text

Comment

ral/historical world.) It first existed by itself alone, prior to the cosmic powers Heaven and Earth, and then the entire cosmos arose out of this primordial "Mother." This Mother is the Great Tao that Laoists cultivate.

Great means going forth {3}
going forth means going far
   away
going far away means turning
   back.

"Great means going forth" suggests an emanationist cosmogony, in which the universe represents an "overflowing" of this Great primordial reality. As in 36[42], there is also a suggestion that this development of the universe was a kind of Fall, an alienation ("going far away") of the world from the source of its meaning. This alienating movement is what is reversed in the "natural" turning back movement of Laoist self cultivation.

Heaven gives the rule {4}
   for Earth
Tao gives the rule for Heaven
the rule for Tao: things as they
   are.

There is a reciprocal semiotic relation between Tao and the world in its ideal, "natural" (organically harmonious) state: Tao can be pictured as the "source" of the meaning-structure of this world. But alternatively, as in {4} here, Tao can be defined simply as a hypostatization of this *tzu jan*/naturalness, which is thus the "norm for Tao."

35[39]
Those that of old got The
   Oneness:

"Getting the Oneness" describes the goal of Laoist self-cultivation. This long passage

The sky got The Oneness,
and by this became clear.
The earth got The Oneness,
and by this became steady.
The spirits got The Oneness,
and by this obtained their
    powers.
The rivers got The Oneness,
and by this became full.
The thousands of things got
    The Oneness,
and by this came to life.
The princes and the King got
    The Oneness,
and by this became the
    Standard for the World.
This is how things came about.

The sky, without what makes it
    clear,
is likely to crack.
The earth, without what makes
    it steady,
is likely to quake.
The spirits, without what gives
    them powers,
are likely to vanish.
The rivers, without what makes
    them full
are likely to dry up.
The thousands of things,
    without what gives them
    life,
are likely to perish.
The princes and kings, without
    what makes them eminent
    and noble,
are likely to fall.

celebrates the cosmic greatness
of this project, by picturing it
as the foundation of the order
of the world. This passage differs from the other cosmogonic
sayings above in that it is an
order-from-chaos cosmogony:
It assumes that all the elements
of the cosmos first existed in a
disordered state, then, by getting the Oneness, gained the
characteristics on which world-
order depends. The Oneness is
not a previously existing source
from which things came. Primordial chaos here has a *negative* character, as something
that would constantly threaten
still, were it not for The Oneness that keeps everything stable. The Laoist experience of
The Oneness as more ultimate
than the world makes the
apparently solid world seem
fragile, dependent for its solidity and order on something
beyond it. The cosmic order
pictured here reflects the standard worldview of contemporary Chinese. This shows especially in that the Chou feudal
rulers take their place here
among the pillars of the cosmic
order. (Laoists would hardly
have held that contemporary
rulers had already achieved the
goal of Laoist self cultivation.)
The point of the saying is to
portray the cosmic greatness of
The Oneness by picturing it as
the reality on which this whole
conventional world depends.

Text

Yes, the eminent takes the
   common and ignored as a
   root
the noble takes the lowly as a
   foundation.
And so, the princes and kings
   call themselves
'the orphan . . . ,' 'the poor . . .
   ,' 'the unfortunate. . . . '
Is this not using the common
   and ignored as a root?
Is it not so?

Comment

The Oneness is a hypostatized
state of mind intrinsically connected to a certain attitude or
posture one adopts toward the
world. Hence, "getting The Oneness" and assuming a low and
deferential posture in the world
refer to different aspects of one
and the same goal of Laoist self-
cultivation. Again we see the
assertion that what would be
regarded as "lowly" in the world
(by those engaged in power politics) is a more ultimate reality on
which the order of the enveloping universe depends.

65[51]
Tao produces them   {1}
Te rears them
events shape them
talents complete their
   development.

The Tao and Te that Laoists cultivate are pictured in {1} as the
very first in a series of factors in
a developmental process that
makes things what they are.
This seems to be a picture of
how individual things continue to come into existence, not
how the cosmos began.

And so: {2}
Among the thousands of things
   there are none that do not
   honor Tao and treasure Te.
This honoring Tao and
   treasuring Te—
no one commands it, it always
   happens naturally.

Tao and Te are pictured in {2} as
cosmic rulers: Things "naturally" honor them, as Laoists and
Mencius suppose people will
"naturally" (in the ideal case)
honor a true human ruler.
Although it might seem as
though "what rules" in the
world-as-evaluative-context is
raw power, empty show, and so
on, one sees the world truly
when one sees it as a place

where "Tao rules." On the assumptions outlined above (that chronological priority = normative superiority, etc.) the picture of Tao/Te as creator and that of Tao/Te as cosmic ruler express the same basic point.

Tao produces them,   {3}
Te rears them
makes them grow, nurses them,
settles them, heals them,
sustains them, protects them.

Section {3} reflects the paternalistic ideal of human government common among ancient Chinese. It pictures Tao/Te as a benevolent source of cosmic well being (similar in this respect to 35[39]:1).

Produces but does not   {4}
    possess
works but does not rely on this
presides but does not rule.
This is mysterious Te.

Section {4} originated as a saying about how the Te of an ideal Laoist ruler expresses itself in his style of ruling. The point it makes in this context is that the ruler who rules in this way is putting himself in accord with "what rules" in the universe truly understood, as explained above. This is the same point made by Chapter 64[34] as a whole, which consists of a pastiche of themes originally describing the ideal Laoist ruler, but now pictured as describing Tao as cosmic ruler.

Contradictions and Non-Literal Understanding

One can note several conflicts that would appear if one took all the cosmic images in the above sayings straightforwardly as a literal picture of reality.

First, two different pictures of the world seem involved, the conventional world "inferior" to Tao, and the transformed world whose meaning structure has Tao as its source.

Secondly, several different cosmogonies are given, whose details do not easily mesh: One might guess from 43[1]:1–2 that there are two phases of Tao, one in which it is an unnamed *shih*/origin, and another in which it is a named Mother.[14] But this is not easily harmonized with 29[52]:1, which pictures a one-phase creation in which the Mother *is* the *shih*/origin. In 36[42]:1 we have a four-phase creation, the details of which are not easy to correlate with the one-phase origin-sayings in 43[1]:2 and 29[52]:1, and the different four phases described in 65[51]. The Oneness in 36[42]:1 is something different from Tao, whereas in 35[39]:1 The Oneness seems to be a name for the ultimate reality. In 65[51] Te, rather than The Oneness, is the other reality that enters the picture to complete the process of creation alongside Tao. This account in 65[51] seems entirely separate from the ones in which The Mother (29[52]:1; 43[1]:2), The Oneness (36[42]:1; 35[39]:1), and Being (34[40]:2) play a part. The order-from-chaos cosmogony in 35[39]:1 seems to involve suppositions entirely different from the creationist or emanationist cosmogonies that prevail elsewhere.

One could also note that "Being was produced by Nothing" in 34[40]:2 contradicts 42[2]:2, which says that Being and Nothing produce each other. Some sayings (28[16]:5; 39[25]:4) picture Tao as more ultimate than Heaven, while other sayings speak of the Laoist Way as "Heaven's Tao."

With some ingenuity it might be possible to fit all these elements into a rather complex but consistent picture of cosmogonic origins. But the nature of the material makes one question whether any single cosmogonic doctrine, consistent on a literal level, actually does underlie these sayings in all their diversity. For comparison, I offer a roughly contemporary passage that does apparently reflect a rather consistent cosmogonic picture. The passage is from a newly found document from the Ma-Wang-Tui excavations, entitled *Tao Yüan*, "Tao the Origin."

At the beginning of the eternal past,
　　all were undifferentiated from and were identical with
　　the great vacuity.
Vacuously identical with the One,
　　and at rest in the One eternally.
Fluid and undifferentiated,
　　there was no distinction of dark and light.
The spirit was subtle and full all around.

The essences were peaceful and unexcited.
Therefore, it had no application.
The ten thousand things did not use it. . . .
It had no form in ancient times.
    It was undifferentiated and nameless.
Heaven could not cover it, Earth could not bear it up.

The small ones became small because of it,
    the big ones became big because of it.
It overflows all regions within the four seas,
    it further wraps them from the outside. . . .
Birds fly when they *te*/get it, fishes swim when they get it
Animals walk when they get it,
    the ten thousand things are born when they get it.[15]

Here we see various images arranged in a clear progression: A first section presents images describing a primordial reality existing by itself. A second section then presents images describing how things in the world get their characteristic form by "getting" this reality. All the details fit together very easily into a consistent literal picture of the origin of things. It would be difficult to arrange all the cosmogonic sayings in the *Tao Te Ching* in such a consistent and orderly progression.

If my overall form-critical and semantic analysis of Laoist cosmogonic sayings is correct, then the lack of comparable consistency in these sayings is not a sign of carelessness. As we saw in Chapter 4 (p. 70–72), concern for consistency on a literal level normally accompanies doctrinal thinking. If one is trying to develop a system of doctrines that will be a fixed representation of the objective truth about the world, then one will take care that all the individual statements one makes fit together to form one consistent picture. The lack of concern for consistency is evidence that Laoist cosmogonic sayings do not reflect any attempt to formulate a set of cosmogonic or metaphysical doctrines. The Laoist worldview remained centered on the phenomenologically concrete Tao that they cultivated, a Tao that expressed itself in their style of life and leadership. Cosmogonic sayings express an important aspect of this Tao, the fact that, despite its apparent "insignificance" in the conventional world, it is axiologically transcendent to this conventional world. But these sayings present simply an overlapping series of images all pointing to this one aspect of the Tao that was a phenomenologically concrete presence in the lives of committed Laoists. This concretely felt Tao remained the focal center of the Laoist worldview. It is unlikely that this worldview included, as a major element, any *fixed* picture of the way the world began (as say, the worldview of the modern fundamentalist Christian includes, as a major element, a fixed picture of divine creation).

All this should not be taken to imply that Laoists *consciously* thought of the language in these sayings as symbolic language. In the absence of any competing, scientifically established, theories of world origins, it even is quite likely that they took cosmogonic language literally (even though, on the present view of the ideal semantic structure of the sayings, such a literal understanding was a mistake; they are not well founded under a literal interpretation). What does seem true is that (1) the *main* Laoist interest in such sayings was not the literal information they offer to persons curious about cosmic origins (the lack of consistency is evidence of this). And (2) the main implications they drew from cosmogonic sayings—the world-transcending *importance* of Tao—was plausibly substantiated by their direct experience of its superlative goodness in the context of their culture and their concerns.

11

A Pluralist but Critical Theory of Worldviews

The interpretation of Tao presented in Chapters 8 through 10 runs counter not only to prevailing interpretations of Tao, but to some prevailing assumptions in the philosophy of religion as well. That is, it is common to regard not only Tao, but the focal centers of religions in general (God or gods, Brahman, etc.) as also the epistemological foundations of their respective religions. On this common assumption, religions are inescapably foundationalist, in that they offer absolute certainty about all-important absolute truths that transcend the world of culturally conditioned experience. This is the *crucial* claim made by any given religion, and so this is the claim that ought to be the focus of attempts either to support or to critically evaluate any religion.

I have argued throughout that foundationalist concerns and assumptions are foreign to Laoist thought (I think they are foreign to the founding generation of most religions) and lead to a fundamental misconstrual of this thought. On the other hand, I have tried in various places to offer an alternative account of the actual "basis in reality" that Laoism must have in order to be valid. Ultimately this endeavor requires an alternate, non-foundationalist philosophy of religion. Various elements of such a theory have been presented in several places in the preceding chapters.[1] In this chapter I offer the outlines of this theory in more systematic form. I begin by situating this theory in relation to some major problems in the interpretation of religions and to some other attempts to address these problems.

The Dilemmas of Ethnocentrism and Diversity

The approach to understanding other religions and cultures that comes most naturally is one governed by a naive ethnocentrism. People regard their own worldview as a simple representation of reality as it is. Thus they do not set the worldview of another culture side by side with their own, as something to be first understood in its own right and then compared to their own worldview on an equal basis. Rather, for Christians, the Christian worldview becomes the framework within which one understands and evaluates Buddhism; and Buddhists, of course, do the same with Christianity. This is a kind of cultural imperialism.

One way of overcoming cultural imperialism is to try to separate understanding from criticism entirely. One adopts a "methodological agnosticism" on the question as to whether and to what extent the worldview one is studying has some valid basis in reality, and sticks to pure, neutral description of the ideas and beliefs that constitute the worldview of the cultural other.[2] This posture is difficult to maintain in practice. It is difficult to read descriptions of others' beliefs without forming an implicit picture of concrete human beings holding these beliefs. When we do this, we either fill in for ourselves some plausible bases (cognitive or noncognitive) for the beliefs, or else we imagine the cultural others as strange beings who hold beliefs for no reason whatsoever.

This highlights a central dilemma one faces in the study of the diversity of worldviews that exist and have existed on our planet. Fully understanding the worldviews of other human beings means forming some ideas about the basis that these worldviews have in reality. And yet, in doing this, it is difficult to avoid the position that there is one true version of reality within which all worldviews need to be evaluated. And is this not in turn a merely more sophisticated version of the ethnocentric mistake, leading to cultural imperialism, a critical interpretation of other worldviews within a single framework that the interpreter regards as true?

One currently popular way of resolving this dilemma is to say that the apparent diversity in the images of transempirical reality offered by different religions is due to the fact that these images are all culturally conditioned attempts to represent some absolute but ineffable Reality that transcends all cultural particularity.[3] (The first line of the *Tao Te Ching*, referring to "The Tao that cannot be told," is often held to be a reference to this ineffable absolute.[4]) This Reality transcends all cultural particularity, and this one Reality is the real basis for all the different religions. But since it itself is beyond all cultural particularity, beliefs about it cannot come into conflict with the particular beliefs of various specific religions.

I am in sympathy with the intentions behind this view, but ultimately it is an illusory solution. Most often the teaching about a transcultural Absolute Reality does have some definite content that is in potential conflict with the teachings of various religions (see the discussion of Schwartz' Tao interpretation, p. 176). In this case this solution represents a subtle and sophisticated cultural imperialism, interpreting all religions within the framework of this one superreligion.[5] If this teaching really has no content at all, then neither can it be the foundation of anything. Its only function is to make possible the assertion that all religions teach the same universal truth. But it makes this possible only by depriving the teaching of any pragmatic "cash value": There is no test by which it could be shown to be true or false, and no definite practical conclusions can be drawn from it.

A central feature of the alternative solution I propose to the above problems and dilemmas is the abandonment of the almost universal assumption that the focal centers of religions are also their epistemological foundations. (The view, for example, that Christianity is true if, and only if, God exists as an entity or metaphysical principle, in objective and absolute reality-as-it-is. Taoism is true if, and only if, Tao exists as an element in reality-as-it-is. And so on.) On the present view, religious worldviews do need (and generally have) some epistemological foundation. We never get something for nothing. If they are well founded, there must be something that is true about the world that makes them well founded, something that might in principle be false. And if this is so, one must be able to give reasons for or against the truth(s) involved. The theory I propose (1) substitutes the good, an aspect of cultural *Lebenswelten*, for the transcultural objective Absolute, as the epistemological foundation for worldviews and religions. It holds (2) that well-foundedness in worldviews is a basically a moral rather than a metaphysical issue: Worldviews should be looked upon as well founded to the extent that they are what results when one is "converted," that is, when one lets one's concernful engagement with the world be dominated by concern for something truly good. It holds (3) that the focal centers of some religious worldviews are properly regarded by believers as focal centers for their personal commitment, but this is because such commitment is a major way in which they remain faithful to their conversion, not because they have metaphysical certainty about such realities.

This theory implies a critical pluralism with respect to worldviews[6] and religions. It is a genuinely and radically *pluralist* theory: It holds that there can be a plurality of worldviews, fundamentally differing from each other at the most ultimate level, and yet that each of these can have a cognitive basis in something real. This pluralism is made possible by the fact that there are many different kinds of good. This theory is also, however, a *critical* theory: It holds that, while there is a possible plurality of well founded worldviews, not all worldviews are equally well founded. This critical element is founded on the fact that not just anything is good. This critical pluralism is thus also particularist. Rather than regarding cultural particularity as a defect, and locating the basis for religious belief in some transcultural universal truth, it takes as its motto: "Divinity lies in the details." It is also a critical *and contextual* pluralism: While in the abstract there are a multitude of good ways, no one lives in the abstract. The question as to whether the values that guide my life have universal validity is unimportant—what is important is that I respond in the best way I can to the particular cultural situation I find myself in.

I will now discuss each of these topics in more detail, beginning with a general theory of "the good."

A Broadened Theory of "the Good" as an Irreducible Ontological Category

All worldviews to some degree serve as evaluative contexts. At least implicitly and indirectly, they have some normative force, providing a basis for the way people evaluate their lives. Our worldview determines what we regard as important or unimportant, what deserves our respect and commitment and what does not, what we ought and ought not do with our lives, what counts as a "successful" life or a "wasted" life. This is especially true of religious worldviews.

"Ought" questions are notoriously difficult to deal with rationally. Although we are constantly making judgments about what we ought to do, it seems difficult to provide such judgments with any basis in "objective" reality. Modern apologists for religion frequently appeal to this difficulty to assert the superiority of religious over "secular" worldviews. The views of believers about oughts are objectively "grounded" in a cosmology or a metaphysics. Knowing cosmological and metaphysical truths does not involve us in the difficulties that normal ought-questions involve us in. But these truths can somehow serve as the epistemological and logical foundation for our knowledge about what is truly important and deserving, what we ought to do, and so on. Even apart from the question as to how believers come by their cosmological or metaphysical knowledge, these claims involve the lapse in logic that Hume first pointed to in his famous dictum that one cannot derive an "ought" from an "is."[7] To put it in more formal terms: If an argument has nothing but neutral facts in its premises, no facts that do not already involve an "ought," then these premises cannot serve as the basis for any conclusion involving an "ought."

If our judgments about what we ought to do are to have any basis in reality, they must have a basis in some reality that is not axiologically neutral. There must be a dimension of reality giving rise to "oughts" that is not reducible to any reality that is neutral with respect to oughts. It will not do to point, for example, to some reality that is cosmologically "larger," metaphysically basic and "necessary," or "universally" held by all of mankind. If one can show that something is larger, basic, necessary, or universal by purely neutral and objective inquiry involving no value judgments, then these assertions cannot be made the basis of value judgments.

This is why any critical and cognitive theory of religions or evaluative worldviews must assume that there is some irreducible dimension of reality itself that gives rise to "oughts." On the other hand, if we are to avoid the ethnocentric mistake and cultural imperialism, we must formulate a conception of this dimension that is very "thin," very formal and abstract. We need a description of the broad ontological category, the *kind of reality* that is the basis for judgments involving "ought," "deserving," "important," and so on, but this description must not be based on some specific substantive criterion for saying what exactly *is* important and deserving, or what we ought to do. To make the theory dependent on a specific substantive definition would be to evaluate all worldviews by a single substantive criterion. The theory would be *methodologically* committed to the view that a given religion could never disclose to us something *new* about what is truly important, something we had not already established before being exposed to this religion.

One obstacle to the formulation of a sufficiently general theory of the good is that philosophers have not usually concerned themselves with this dimension of reality at a sufficiently abstract level, as a matter of *formal* ontology.[8] Any given philosopher is generally most concerned to establish some *particular* substantive criteria for deciding ought questions. (Should the criteria be "the good" rather than "the right"? Should it emphasize social duty or individual self-fulfillment? Should it favor Apollonic or Dionysiac values? and so on.) Our language itself has been shaped by this concern, so that we have numerous words and concepts relating to specific conceptions, but no words sufficiently general to serve as the name of the abstract category to which all these words belong.

Wittgenstein's "Lecture on Ethics" deals partly with this problem. Wittgenstein says he wants to use the term Ethics in a much broader sense than is customary. (For example, he says that "Ethics" for him includes "the most essential part of Aesthetics.") There is no single established term that describes this field, and so he says he will try to describe it by using a number of more or less synonymous expressions, "so if you look through the row of synonyms . . . you will . . . be able to see the characteristic features they all have in common." In this context "Ethical enquiry" can be described as "enquiry into what is good . . . into what is valuable . . . into what is really important . . . into the meaning of life . . . into what makes life worth living . . . into the right way of living."[9] I would add to Wittgenstein's list a number of further terms and phrases: *deserving, meaningful, enriching; the basis for duties, obligations, and oughts; what is of intrinsic worth; what makes a claim on us; what is truly admirable and deserving of respect; what is deserving of service, commitment, loyalty; valid grounds for self-esteem; what would make life truly worthwhile.*

For convenience, let us call the dimension of reality dealt with in all these phrases "the axiological dimension" of reality, or simply "the good." We must only be careful to understand the term "the good" as a broad and formal ontological category much wider than the particular kinds of good that Plato has in mind. And we must not assume any specifically Platonic associations with the term "good." Some plausible candidates that might belong to this broad ontological category of "the good" are: *human dignity or worth*, in that "human dignity" is one name for what it is about a child in danger that founds my obligation to come to its aid; *virtues or good human qualities*, in that these deserve my respect and are valid grounds for self-esteem; *good impulses*, in that I ought to follow my good impulses rather than my bad ones; *self-realization*, insofar as what is "realized" are potential good qualities that I have; *friendship or romantic love*, in that these might enrich my life and make it true that something really worthwhile is happening in my life; *meaningful or uplifting experiences,* such as those we have with nature or art, that enhance the quality of our lives; what is now sometimes called the *quality of life; the "call" of specific situations,* in the sense that in some situations I feel "called upon" to stand up against injustice, help someone in need, realize some great opportunity for good, and so on. If we think of valid authority as what truly deserves our respect and obedience, then all valid authority is ultimately based on something good.

We can also define the axiological dimension of reality by differentiating it from other dimensions that are different but appear similar. "Important," "deserving," and "ought," when used in their strict axiological sense, refer to a dimension of reality different from what we refer to when we say that something is customary, or is socially accepted and expected; that something is instinctive among humans; that something is conducive to psychological well being; that something is conducive to the smooth functioning of society.

As a dimension of reality, the good has one peculiar characteristic that makes it epistemologically probably the most difficult dimension to deal with, but that can also serve to differentiate it from other aspects of reality. In other areas, mistakes will typically have some relatively evident and incontrovertible consequences that will reveal to us that a mistake has been made. If I deny that a two-ton boulder is heavy, and if I try to put my denial into practice by lifting it, my inability will provide incontrovertible evidence that I was wrong. If I deny that child abuse is psychologically damaging to the child, the child's subsequent psychological state could in principle prove me wrong. If however I could easily save my dying child but refuse to recognize my *moral* duty to do so, nothing comparable will occur that will show me to have been *morally* mistaken. The only "consequence" of my refusal that matters axiologically will be that I will be wrong. I will just have failed in what I ought to have done. If someone tries to point to some other more objectively measurable fact (the strength of my parental instinct, my grief, the disapproval of my neighbors, etc.) as evidence that I was mistaken, she will be pointing to something outside the axiological dimension, therefore to something that has no axiological force. To put it another way: To the extent that my motivation for saving my dying child is something *other* than that I owe it to her, my response lacks moral goodness. I am not responding to the child as the child deserves because she deserves it. "For its own sake" is a phrase commonly used to express this point: Something or someone is "deserving" in a strictly axiological sense when it is true that it deserves something from me "for its own sake."

Another obstacle to the formulation of a general theory of the good is the almost universal assumption in modern philosophy that general principles or standards are the epistemological basis for all well founded knowledge of what is good or right. To illustrate, consider the following case: I am walking along with an ice cream cone in each hand, come across a child playing on a railroad track, and see a train coming. Modern philosophers tend to say that I do not really *know* for sure that I have an obligation to save the child unless I have a verified belief in some true principle that founds my obligation. Such true general principles are the necessary foundation of all well founded moral judgments. But this view faces the further problem about how such principles are themselves to be verified. (It is the difficulty of such verification that leads to much moral skepticism among philosophers today.) My proposal is that there are some cases, illustrated in the above example, in which we directly perceive some good that gives rise to an obvious obligation. Such direct perceptions in obvious cases are the ultimate epistemological basis for moral judgments. General principles are generalizations from these perceptions, and are epistemologically dependent on them.

On this view, "the good" is an aspect of the *Lebenswelt*. It is an irreducible aspect of *phainomena*, reality-as-it-appears in human experience. I argued in Chapter 1 (p. 16–17) that the *Lebenswelt* is the only coherent referent of the term "reality." It is "the world" we actually live in and speak about, so to say that the good belongs to "appearances" implies no defect in relation to some further more real "reality." As also argued in Chapter 1, the logical conclusion of this equation of the *Lebenswelt* with reality is that there are many realities, corresponding to the ways that the world is experienced by different people, especially in different cultures. This "many worlds" theory in turn makes possible a genuinely pluralist theory of the good.[10] As an abstract and formal ontological category, "the good" is a dimension of all *Lebenswelten*. But there is no specific set of categories that describe what goods there are in all possible worlds. Different cultures divide up the pie of axiological experience in different ways, giving rise to different kinds of experienced goods. Learning to empathically understand a different culture typically means learning to perceive certain kinds of goods one was not previously familiar with.

The assumption that directly perceived realities in the *Lebenswelt* are epistemologically foundational makes possible a genuinely pluralist theory of the good, which is generally not possible when one assumes that general principles are foundational. Positive moral theories assuming that general principles are epistemologically foundational almost inevitably assume also that there must be a single universally valid set of such principles.

Saying that the good is an irreducible and directly perceived aspect of reality is not to say that our perceptions of the good are never mistaken. It is only to say that the only bases for evaluating the validity of axiological perceptions are further axiological perceptions, just as support for perceptions of roundness can only appeal to further perceptions concerning shape. If the good is an irreducible ontological category, then the epistemological problem of verifying our perceptions of the good is not a problem of providing a more objective "foundation" for such perceptions. We make mistakes about the good, not because our "subjective" perceptions lack more objective foundations, but because we mistake various simulacra of goodness for true goodness itself. Rational evaluation of such perceptions does not involve foundational reasoning but discriminating reasoning, not reaching beyond the *Lebenswelt* to more "objective" reality, but discriminating the truly good from the apparently good.

A full development and defense of this theory would need some well defined methods of such rational discrimination. But this is a subject requiring more space than I can give it here.[11] I can offer some brief suggestions as to how the "for its own sake" can become the basis for rational methods of discriminating between true good and apparent good.

First, on the phenomenological view pursued here, all valid thought about the good is based ultimately on a certain kind of perception, a perception that something "matters." Normally, such perceptions "move" us in some way. But, psychologically speaking, we are moved to feel that something matters for many other reasons besides that it is truly good for its own sake (our pride is hurt, we feel personally flattered or threatened, etc.). Epistemologically, our primary problem is discriminating between those occasions when something moves us and appears to matter because it is truly good, and those occasions when something moves us for some other reason. We can discriminate by a process of elimination: Suppose something moves us and appears to matter, but this *phainomenon* can be explained without remainder by tracing its source to some neutral "hard facts" (physical, psychological, social). This is evidence that we are not perceiving something that "matters for its own sake," evidence that it does not belong to the category of the good. Conversely, if it cannot be so explained, and if it does not contradict our other perceptions about what is good, this is evidence that it moves us because it is indeed good for its own sake.

The second way that this "for its own sake" can become an epistemological criterion has to do with the particular relationship in which we stand toward the good. Other realities and aspects of reality can become instruments to use in furthering goals extrinsic to them. Standing in a "using" relationship toward the good always puts us in the wrong. The good deserves that we in some sense put ourselves in service to it (I would include here realizing some meaningful good in our lives or experience). We become "good" ourselves when we put ourselves in this relation to the good.

Finally, "for its own sake" can become an epistemological criterion in that true commitment to the good must be a generalized commitment, a commitment to the good wherever it appears, with no partiality for *my* good. The modern concern for "self-realization" or "the quality of life" is often criticized, for example, as being intrinsically narcissistic, in contrast to the more traditional emphasis on duties and the help we owe to others. But the difficulty is not that human self-realization is not a good. The difficulty is that, when I am exclusively concerned with *my own* self-realization, this is an indication that I am not really concerned with human self-realization for its own sake. I am concerned with what it can instrumentally contribute to my own comfort, my own *feelings* of self-esteem, my own feelings of superior social status, and so on. Conversely, one sign that a person values human self-realization for its own sake is that she will be willing to sacrifice her own comfort, status, and so on, in order to provide an environment conducive to self-realization for her neighbors.

Rejecting any single, universally valid *substantive* definition of what is good solves some old problems. But it also introduces a new difficulty into our attempts at a critical understanding of other cultures and religions. If we know ahead of time what is good, this gives us a definite point of reference for understanding what is good in a particular worldview. We simply have to compare the contents of this worldview to our single definition. Deprived of this, what will be our new point of reference for understanding the goodness, or lack thereof, in any worldview we are studying? What will be the bridge between the reality we are familiar with and the foreign reality we are trying to understand?

My solution to this hermeneutic problem hinges on analogies between elements of our *Lebenswelt* and the *Lebenswelt* of the text. That is, most often the strangeness of another worldview is not due to the fact that it values highly something that we ourselves perceive to be *completely* without intrinsic value. It is rather that it takes something with a very low and subservient place in our hierarchy of goods, and makes it into a high priority. Doing this also reorganizes and restructures the entire *Lebenswelt*, generating different categories and different polarities. This means that the process of understanding involves first locating aspects of our own experience that are good but perhaps relatively neglected in our world. It means, secondly, imagining what this goodness would be in its most perfect and ideal form. Thirdly, it means imagining the hierarchy of goods and the reorganization of the world that would result from taking this as the highest good.

Chapter 7 (p. 160–72) outlined an interpretation of Laoist values in which "organic harmony" constitutes the highest intrinsic good to which Laoists were devoted. Descriptions in that chapter utilize the strategy just described. They draw on relatively ordinary examples of organic harmony we might experience today, and use these as points of departure for entering empathically and imaginatively into a world organized around this as the highest and ideal value. Organic harmony is something whose goodness we already perceive to some extent, but we do not let it dominate our perspective on the world the way Laoists did. Organic harmony is one particular kind of good. The mere fact that it is *a* good does not necessarily mean that it deserves to be made a priority in everyone's view of the world.

Conversion and the Transformation of the Lebenswelt

Philosophers typically not only try to make explicit the epistemological bases for their worldview. The very *structure* of the worldview of a systematic philosopher is determined by epistemological and logical concerns. The contents of this worldview are arranged in a structure that makes clear to a critical mind what exactly is the basis of the claim to validity of any part of the system. We have seen above (p. 70–73, 113–117) that not all world-views have the structure of a philosophical system, and the attempt to construe them this way amounts to a misinterpretation. It is a mistake to examine the elements of a religious believer's explicit thoughts, assuming *a priori* that somewhere in this collection of thoughts will be found a thought that is the episte-mological foundation for the rest, which stand to it as logical deductions. This is the mistake made by most philosophies of religion, as well as by most religious apologetics: They assume that the explicit focal center of a given religion must also be its episte-mological and logical foundation.

All valid worldviews need some epistemological basis. Something which might in principle be false has to be true instead, in order for any particular vision of the world as evaluative context to be well founded. But in order to do justice to the actual structure of the vision of non-philosophers, we have to realize that their real basis is very often implicit rather than explicit, and that the relation of explicit thoughts to this basis may not be a strictly logical one. The formulation I think is more adequate for world-views generally is this: A given view of the world as evaluative context is well-founded insofar as it is a view that results from allowing some good, something of truly high intrinsic worth, to predominate in our concernful engagement with the world.

This formulation is partly based on a generalization of the traditional religious notion of "conversion."[12] A conversion is a fundamental psychological transformation that results in a corresponding fundamental transformation of the *Lebenswelt*. People need to maintain a sense of self-worth, and most people depend on some relatively fixed way of doing this through a certain definite personality structure that is defined in relation to a certain system of social relationships. Sometimes a person is very moved by something of very high intrinsic worth, but responding to this as she feels she ought would result in a restructuring of her previous personality integration and social identity, a reorganization of the structures through which she previously maintained her sense of self-worth. Her sense of self-worth is now more completely dependent on her relation to the superlative good that has entered her life. Yielding to this "conversion" is not a matter of changing some intellectual beliefs, but potentially involves wrenching psychological change, confusion, and a sense of "losing one's self." Such a conversion involves an equally fundamental change in a person's mode of concernful engagement with the world, a new "perspective," which changes the basic character of the world she lives in, her *Lebenswelt*. Conversions that happen suddenly exemplify these basic phenomena in highly dramatic form. But of course the same changes can take place gradually and less dramatically over longer periods of time. Meditation techniques such as are practiced in Buddhism, Hinduism, and Taoism are essentially techniques for deliberately inducing such "conversions," often in a very gradual fashion.

Religious writings like the *Tao Te Ching*, written by the founding generation of a particular tradition, often aim to picture the way reality appears to a converted person. That is, such writings are not primarily proposing to us a set of intellectual beliefs or doctrines that a person could adopt in the same way we intellectually adopt new theories about the ozone layer. They aim to represent the transformed *Lebenswelt*, reality as it is *immediately experienced* by the converted person. They mean to present this world as a whole in such a way that its superlative goodness will be felt by the reader, thus converting her to this world. This is why the foundational canonical "scriptures" of any given tradition (in contrast to later systematic and apologetic writings) typically plunge one right into this new *Lebenswelt*, rather than leading one into it in step by step fashion, beginning with "fundamental" truths and proceeding to deductions from these truths.

The idea of a psychological transformation that also transforms the character of the *Lebenswelt* does justice both to the "subjective" element in worldviews and to their variability, over against those theories that require some completely objective and universally valid basis for religious belief. At the same time it avoids the voluntarism of the more usual attempts to do justice to subjectivity and variability in worldviews. By "voluntarist" I mean theories in which worldviews are essentially mental creations based ultimately on an arbitrary (though perhaps unconscious) act of will.[13] One crucial difficulty such theories face is how it is that a person can owe something to realities that are the creations of her own mind. To say that a worldview is the result of a conversion is to say that the system does indeed have an important basis in something subjective. But the subjective event of conversion, unlike the subjective event of mental creation, is a *response* to something out there, something which *is* superlatively good, something whose existence and goodness are not dependent on the creative mind. The diversity of religious beliefs stems from the fact that each represents a response to a different good, in a different context, rather than the fact that different groups have arbitrarily decided to create different visions of the world.

This formulation not only accepts, but makes central, the semiotic and perspectival variability of reality, but it does this without entailing skeptical relativism. For every given person, the world as evaluative context has some axiological structure. Everyone is always already "converted" to some view of reality as an evaluative context. There are no axiologically neutral worlds, but neither is there some one way the world is objectively structured axiologically.[14] For the traditional criterion of objective truth, the present theory substitutes the criterion of conversion to the good. Some axiological visions of the world *are* better than others, but the reason they are better is a moral reason: They represent the way the world is structured for one more converted to something more good. Conversion to the good, and the consequent well-foundedness of worldviews, is not an either/or issue, but is subject to degrees. The fact that there are many kinds of good makes it possible also that there can be many genuinely different axiological visions that are roughly equal in their goodness.

This reverses the usual view of the relation between goodness, conversion, and the structure of reality. On the usual view, immediate perceptions of goodness are unreliable and need some "grounding" in a view of the objective axiological structure of the world. One can test the validity of psychological conversion experiences by the extent to which the vision of the world they lead to is objectively true. This objective truth is the source of the "necessity" the believer is under to remain faithful to her conversion. On the present view, the validity of a psychological conversion experience should be tested by whether it is a response to something genuinely good or not. And the validity of some view of the axiological structure of reality should be tested by asking whether it is the result of a genuine conversion to something good. The "necessity" the believer is under to adhere to this vision is a moral necessity: This is the way she remains faithful to the good to which she is converted.

This theory allows for extreme variability, not only in the elements that make up different well founded visions of the world, but also in their semiotic structure. The theory gives no favored position to those visions (like Plato's) that arise from philosophizing, those that take the form of a progressive historical narrative (ancient Judaism, early Christianity, Marxism), those that consist of a picture of a stable cosmic order, or those that accord cosmic importance to spiritual self-development. In all these cases, well-foundedness is a property of the vision as a whole. It is not that belief in some one element (e.g., God, Tao) is well founded and serves as a free-standing foundation for the rest. The relation of the more central elements to less central elements will typically be semiotically complex, and not reducible to clear logical relationships. All this is reflected in the fact that the typical way of making new "converts" to a religion is to present them with the vision as a whole, because this is the whole within which the particular superlative good involved can best be experienced. The vision as a whole is what is inspiring, and the vision as a whole represents what one is to be converted to.

The semiotic structure of any given vision of the world as evaluative context has a perspectival basis. And this applies to the religious believer's way of *construing* the elements of her own beliefs. Well-foundedness consists more in the way of construing these elements than it does in the elements themselves. A Christian whose view of afterlife beliefs is dominated by self-centered concern for personal reward does not have a vision of the world as evaluative context that results from conversion to something superlatively good. Showing that the Christian vision is well founded under some interpretation does not show that any vision that includes many individual "Christian beliefs" is also well founded. Concern for something superlatively good must dominate one's way of construing the beliefs themselves, and determine the way these beliefs form a structured whole. In the Laoist context, it would be possible for a person to let his approach to the *Tao Te Ching* be dominated by concern for gaining political success, for maintaining power over others, or for achieving personal long life or immortality. In Laoist language, a person who did so would fail to "understand the ancestor of the sayings" (45[70]:2), would not perceive the sayings structured around the superlatively good center that dominates the whole for one wholeheartedly devoted to this good for its own sake.

In terms of hermeneutic theory, this last point places *Sachkritik* (see p. 9) at the center of the interpretive endeavor. The ultimate goal of the interpreter of a religious text is not to understand some ideas in the mind of the author, but to understand the substantive subject matter (*die Sach*) of which her text speaks. The interpreter's understanding of the subject matter can serve also as a *critical* principle, allowing her to understand under what interpretation what the text says is wellfounded. The preeminent subject matter of which wellfounded religious texts speak is some kind of good. The ultimate goal of the interpreter is to place herself in a position to appreciate this good, to let herself be vicariously seized by this good as it seized the original authors. And she should let her understanding of this good inform her understanding of the text as a whole. This good is the basis for whatever valid "authority" a given text can claim to have.

Sachkritik makes possible an internal critique of Laoist views, a critique based on a criterion internal to Laoism rather than a criterion to be applied to all religions. Although we have to learn about the nature of this good from the *Tao Te Ching*, the goodness of this good is something independent of the mind of Laoists. It is not simply whatever they say it is, but something to which they are responsible, something they may be more faithful to or less faithful to, more faithful to in some passages than in others. (It seems evident, for example, that the goodness of organic harmony provides no justification for the view [56(61):5] that it is good for large states to take over small states. This is not necessarily a sign that the "inspired" authors of the *Tao Te Ching* did not write this passage. Inspired authors have their lapses like the rest of us.)

Besides letting our vicarious engagement with the text be dominated by the good of which the text speaks, *Sachkritik* also has a second aspect. It means also considering what can be known on the basis of this knowledge of the good. It seems obvious, for example, that knowledge of the good is not a good source of information about how the world began. So if it seems probable that the perceptual basis of Laoist cosmogonic sayings is the superlative goodness of Tao (see p. 239), then these sayings are not well-founded under a literal interpretation. This does not require us to suppose that, in the ideal case, Laoists consciously thought to themselves, "These sayings are symbolic rather than literal." It means that in the ideal case, Laoists understood the main point of such sayings to be, not to give information about ancient events, but to celebrate the superlative goodness of Tao.

Transcendence

Tao is, in an important sense, a "transcendent" reality in the *Tao Te Ching*. But in contemporary usage the term "transcendent" also has several connotations that do not apply to Tao under the present interpretation. The notion of *transcending*, going beyond, is a relative notion whose content is defined in relation to what it is that is "gone beyond." There are at least four separable elements in the usual meaning of transcendence, only one of which applies to Tao.

First, *transcendent* is sometimes opposed to *immanent*, both terms understood in a quasi-spatial sense. The Judeo-Christian God is "transcendent" in the sense that believers feel him to be external to themselves, as opposed to the Hindu Atman/Brahman which Hindu meditators find "immanent" within themselves. Tao is more immanent than transcendent in this sense.

Secondly, for Kant[15] and post-Kantian philosophy, the term *transcendent* is often used in discussions about whether we can know only "appearances"—reality as it appears in our experience—or whether we know reality as it is in itself, reality that "transcends" our experience of it. On the present view, "the good" is a dimension or aspect of the *Lebenswelt*, reality-as-it-appears. No axiological vision of the world could be founded on reality that transcends the *Lebenswelt*, even if we could know such a reality.

Thirdly, since early modern times philosophy has taken on itself the task of solving interreligious and intercultural conflict by discovering universal, transcultural truths that "transcend" all cultures and are valid for all peoples of all eras.[16] Laoists probably claimed for Tao something like transcultural validity in this sense. But, first, this was not the main claim they made about Tao, nor did any part of the Laoist worldview crucially depend on this claim. And, secondly, this claim was due to the same naive ethnocentrism that caused all ancient Chinese to refer to the Chinese Empire as "the world," and to regard all non-Chinese as barbarians. The basis for Laoist ideas about Tao was not sufficient to warrant this claim. This is arguably true for the "transcendent" claims of all other religions and philosophies. This is no defect whatsoever, because there is no necessary connection between goodness and universality. On the contrary, the goodness of Laoist Tao, Hindu Brahman, and the Christian God is intimately bound up with characteristics particular to each of these realities, characteristics semiotically determined by their relation to a particular cultural world. (The idea that it is better to "transcend the narrowness" of one's own cultural context and try to live in some realm beyond culture does not really make sense. Everyone lives in some particular cultural context and ought to be devoted to some particular good that deserves to be made a priority in this context. Even if one could transcend all particulari-ty, doing so would seem to mean not responding to the particular needs of the particular situation one lives in.)

In a fourth sense, the term *transcendent* is used to describe what it is people appeal to when they criticize some norms, insti-tutions or authorities commonly regarded as final authorities by the society at large. Transcendence in this sense is often proposed as a characteristic of certain movements of the "axial age."[17] Ancient Israelite prophets, for example, represented one such movement: The God they appealed to in criticizing Israelite kings and priests was a God who "transcended" these established social authorities, rather than a (non-transcendent) God who was previ-ously assumed to stand in support of them. Laoist Tao is transcen-dent in this sense, more transcendent than the *jen* of ancient Con-fucians, and this is a crucial element in the Laoist worldview.

It is often thought that the third meaning of transcendence (transcultural) is a precondition for the fourth. One cannot under-take a fundamental critique of the norms of one's own culture unless one achieves some standpoint *completely* outside this cul-ture. This does indeed describe the ambition that gave birth to much modern philosophy and is prominent also in religious apologetics. But an account of transcendence in the fourth sense is possible that does not include the idea of a transcultural absolute.

Let me begin with a quote from Jacques Derrida, criticizing the notion of a transcendent center that lies outside the structure (the structured worldview) of which it is the center.

> The structurality of structure . . . has always been neutralized or reduced . . . by . . . giving it a center or referring it to a point of presence, a fixed origin. . . . It has always been thought that the center, which is by definition unique, consti-tuted that very thing within a structure which governs the structure, while escaping structurality. . . . The center is at the center of the totality, and yet since the center does not belong to the totality . . . the totality *has its center elsewhere.* . . . [18]

This is a criticism of the notion of transcultural transcendence from a semiotic point of view. Semiotically, the meaning of any given reality is defined by its relation to other realities in the same worldview. The idea of a transcultural center is an attempt to avoid this mutual definition, an attempt to picture an *asymmetric* semiotic dependency between a structured worldview and its center.[19] All other elements of the worldview get their meaning by their relation to this center. But the meaning of the center is somehow self-contained, not dependent for its meaning on its relation to the rest of the worldview. The center "governs the structure while escaping structurality."

Derrida's argument is indeed persuasive against construing the transcendent centers of some religions (God, Brahman, Tao) as transcultural absolutes. On the other hand, it does not undermine the alternative account of transcendence proposed here. The notion of "center" that Derrida criticizes calls to mind an opposite notion that can serve as part of this account, the notion of a semiotically *symmetrical* relation between structure and center. This in fact describes a familiar aesthetic phenomenon. Some paintings have a unified visual center that decisively determines the aesthetic impact of other elements of the painting. Yet one can see that this visual center would not have the aesthetic value it has if it were taken out of this painting and put in another visual setting. There is a symmetrical, mutually defining relation between the painting as a whole and its center. This phenomenon is easy to see in visual arts like painting and architecture. But something similar is true in the case of music that builds to a climax. The climax dominates the aesthetic meaning of what precedes it, but it would not have the aesthetic meaning it has to one who heard it without the buildup. Jokes have the same structure: A punch line appears to be "the funny part," making the buildup funny in retrospect—but of course the punch line would not be funny without the buildup. There is a relation of mutual semiotic dependence between buildup and punch line.

Tao is a "center" of the Laoist worldview in this same sense. The relation between the worldview and this center is this same kind of mutual semiotic dependence. The fact that it is a "transcendent" center does not mean that it has a self-contained meaning independent of any context. The character of transcendence as a religious category can be described rather as follows.

Every social environment is an evaluative context determining the evaluative perceptions people have of their own lives and those of their neighbors. Normally, everything is taken to have the value it is perceived to have in this context. This means, for example, that religious activities and motivations will appear in a positive light if they conform to people's sense of what is "normal." If they go against the conventional sense of normalcy, they will appear negative, deviant. This normative "social environment" does not consist simply of a collection of individual elements (people, buildings, events, etc.). It is a collection of elements structured in a certain specific way, in a structure that is partly determined perspectivally, by the dominant concerns of the people. We generally call this the "conventional mentality," closely connected with "conventional morality" in any given society. In most societies, the conventional mentality is dominated by several kinds of concerns closely integrated with one another: Concern to maintain the status quo, concern for various kinds of self-interest, as well as concerns for things that are good for their own sake.[20] As long as these concerns are integrated, people assume that conventional signs of success (wealth, status, power) are also signs of genuine goodness, and they are for the most part right. But sometimes "cultural crises" arise in which this integration breaks down. Idealistic people become alienated. That is, they do not perceive a continuity but a disjunction between customary signs of success on the one hand and real goodness on the other.[21] This disjunction between genuine goodness and practical ("worldly") success tends also to mean that goodness itself is perceived in its most "pure," ideal form, giving rise to utopian visions.

This kind of crisis can produce a split between the conventional mentality that continues to determine the character of the social environment, and the mentality of various idealistic minorities. The latter will appear to others merely deviant when measured against the standard of "normalcy" inherent in the conventional social environment. But to themselves, the good that these idealists are devoted to will appear to "transcend" this same social environment. Its full reality cannot appear within the conventional social environment, considered as an *evaluative* context. And yet it appears to them a superlative good, vastly superior to anything that does appear in this conventional context. It transcends all other reality in its *goodness*.[22] Personal conversion to this transcendent good transforms the axiological structure of the social environment for the converted person. It is now an environment dominated semiotically by a different center.

This center does not escape the semiotic law of mutual definition. The world of the Laoist is a world whose character is semiotically dominated by Tao, its transcendently good center. But the center and the totality are mutually defining. Tao only has the goodness that it has because it is the center of the particular cultural world of Warring States *shih*, with their particular concerns and ambitions (see p. 293).

It should be obvious that, on this account, transcendence is a not an either/or issue, but is susceptible of degrees. Worldviews can have centers that are more transcendent and less transcendent. For example, transcendence is a characteristic feature of "axial age" movements. But in several of these movements one can observe a split in traditions, one centering on something "more transcendent" to conventional society than another. For example, early Buddhism centered on the cultivation of a mental state very similar to that which is the focus of interest in contemporary Upanishadic Hinduism. But Buddhism was more radical in emphatically rejecting any connection of this mental state with traditional religion or with the traditional caste system. The *Bhagavad Gita*, on the contrary, shows us a Hindu mind bent on integrating higher meditation practice with traditional religion and a social order organized around caste.[23] In the sense described above, the Buddhist ideal was "more transcendent" than that described in the *Bhagavad Gita*, in that there is a stronger polarization between this ideal and the conventional social environment of the time. Similar remarks could be made about early Pauline Christianity. Paul's Christianity represents a development of tendencies toward transcendent social criticism already present in contemporary rabbinic Judaism. But the rabbis strove to integrate these tendencies with Jewish ethnic culture with its legal prescriptions, whereas in Paul's mind these ideas and values had become "more transcendent"— that is, more polarized over against Jewish cultural forms.

This model also seems to work to some extent for early Confucianism and Taoism as well. Confucian *jen* is a moderately transcendent ideal, in the sense that for early Confucians it names a perfect, scarcely attainable, way of being that puts one at odds with contemporary society.[24] But at the same time it is an ideal that Confucians were at some pains to present as continuous with the traditional culture and customs of the Chinese ruling class. Laoist *shih* share many basic values with Confucian *shih* (organic harmony plays some part in the Confucian ideal as well), but the Tao that is the center of their worldview was pictured as something much more fundamentally at odds with the values of the Chinese elite of the time, "more transcendent" in the present sense of that term.

Needless to say, using "transcendent" in this sense requires that we abandon the notion that a higher degree of transcendence is necessarily the sign of a superior religion or worldview.

Finally, the idea of a semiotic or aesthetic center of meaning provides a solution to the familiar problem of religious symbolism.

It is frequently said that specific images of God, Brahman, Tao, and so on, are not adequate to the reality that they mean to represent. They are rather "symbols that point beyond themselves." But since we most often assume a referential theory of symbols, the natural question is, then, what are they a symbol *of?* What is this reality beyond themselves to which they point? The idea of an aesthetic center offers a non-referential theory of symbolism. In an aesthetic center properly perceived, we feel a depth and an intensity of meaning going far beyond the surface, a depth of meaning beyond what a purely objective, unengaged observer could perceive. But this depth of meaning does not consist in some further reality for which the center is a substitute symbol. The depth is rather a "surplus of meaning," deriving semiotically from the fact that we always experience an aesthetic center as more "packed with meaning" than the totality of which it is the center, and we always experience the climax as more packed with meaning than the buildup. But again this surplus of meaning will be perceived only by the person concernfully engaged, very fully and in the right way, with a picture, a musical piece, a joke, or a religion.

This surplus of meaning is what makes Laoist Tao (and the focal centers of many other religions) "ineffable." Tao is not a symbol whose real referent is a metaphysical reality or principle. (This implies that the metaphysician has a direct grasp of what Laoists grasped only through a veil darkly.) Far less is it ineffable because the metaphysical reality it represents has no determinate content. (Such a reality could found nothing positive.) Tao's "surplus of meaning" has a definite content. It is "unnameable" in the sense that no possible word or set of words by themselves can guarantee that a person reading the words will grasp this surplus of meaning. The word Tao will convey this surplus of meaning only to the "competent" reader or listener. And this competence includes understanding Tao as a semiotic, aesthetic center of the rest of the Laoist worldview. More importantly, it includes allowing an intense personal involvement with a particular kind of good to inform the way one perceives and implicitly organizes this worldview, and the way one understands Tao as its center.

Subject's View and Outsider's View

The above theory has many advantages in solving central problems in the philosophy of religion. Its biggest weakness for most readers, especially religious believers, will probably be the way the theory seems to contrast strongly at several points with the self-understanding of most believers. It must be admitted that it is difficult both to hold this theory and to maintain some traditional faith unchanged. I argue that there is indeed a psychological difficulty involved here, but not a logical one. It is roughly similar to the difficulty one has in thinking explicitly of the grammar of a sentence as one speaks it, or finding a joke funny at the same time one analyzes it.

Perhaps the most crucial difficulty here is the present theory's assertion that all worldviews are essentially semiotic systems of *mutually defining* elements. Taken seriously, this implies that the very reality of Tao is constituted by its relation to the rest of the Laoist worldview. Likewise, the very reality of the Christian God is constituted by God's relation to the rest of the Christian worldview. The Christian God is real in the Christian world, but is not real in the Laoist world, unless the Laoist "converts" to Christianity, and her entire world changes accordingly. Similarly, Tao is not real in the Christian world, unless the Christian converts to a world that has Tao as its semiotic center. Tao and God become elements in real worlds in and through the process of conversion.

These assertions seem to conflict in the strongest possible way with the conscious views of believers. The true Christian regards God's existence as independent of her conversion, and indeed the cause of her conversion. And she regards God as the self-subsisting foundation of other elements of the Christian worldview, like creation and redemption. God is not dependent for his existence on these other elements. Similar things could be said about the Hindu attitude to Brahman, and probably about the Laoist attitude to Tao.

My answer to these problems hinges on the difference between an awareness *implicitly* shaped by certain factors, and an awareness that makes these same factors explicit for itself. For example, when listening to a joke, one is usually led through a series of steps that "set one up" for experiencing the punch line as very funny. But all of these steps generate a *background, implicitly* shaping one's perception of the funniness of the punch line. In the act of perceiving the punch line as funny, one does not think explicitly of all of these background factors lying alongside the punch line, nor does one think explicitly of the semiotic relationships existing between these background factors and the punch line. In the ideal case, when the punch line comes, it absorbs one's entire conscious attention and simply seems funny in itself. Thinking *explicitly* of all the background factors that actually make the punch line seem funny would actually prevent one from perceiving it as funny. This is what we do when we "explain a joke," and everyone knows that an explanation of even the funniest joke will not itself be funny.

In theoretical terms, we can make a distinction here: There is, first, an "insider's" view of a punch line, the way the punch line looks to a person who lets her perception be implicitly shaped by the buildup. And there is an "outsider's" perception of the punch line, the perception of one who tries to make explicit all the factors implicitly shaping the insider's perception, explaining why the punch line appears to be funny. The outsider's perception may be perfectly accurate. And in fact it takes an outsider's analysis to explain why the punch line, which appears to be funny in itself, would not be funny if heard in a different context. And yet it is also a mistake to think that there is something inherently defective about the insider's perception, that she is not perceiving "the full truth" about the punch line. It is a mistake to think that the insider ought to try to integrate the outsider's perception into her own, that this would somehow make her view "more true."

Jokes are of course very different from religious writing. What makes the above analogy appropriate, however, is that finding jokes funny and finding religious beliefs moving and compelling both require intense subjective involvement. This means that they both require a strong absorption in an "insider's" view. In each case one needs to let one's attention be completely focused on a focal center, and *conscious explicit* attention to background and to semiotic dependencies will interfere with this.[25] (Note also that what one gets when one gets a joke is "ineffable," in formally the same sense that the content of Tao is ineffable: It is not something that can be directly presented in a paraphrase to be objectively grasped by an uninvolved person.)

This solution to the problem can be described in terms of a pragmatist view of truth (see p. 29–30). The central cause of our difficulty can be explained by saying that religious beliefs are an answer to one kind of question, and the above theory is an answer to a different question. Religious beliefs answer the question, What is life like? How is the world to be viewed as an evaluative context within which to evaluate success and failure? The best answers to this question come through conversion, attending to and devoting oneself to the highest good that appears in one's experience. Conversion and adherence to some vision of the world take intense personal involvement.

The above theory of religion is an attempt to answer different kinds of questions. In general, these are questions about the relation of religious knowledge to other kinds of knowledge, and about the relation of one religion to other religions or to non-religious worldviews. Many try to give these problems a religious solution (a "Christian view of Islam," a "Hindu view of Christianity," an "Islamic view of science," and so on), but this is a mistake. Answering these kinds of questions requires that we step back from our involvement in any given worldview, try as best we can to see other worldviews from the inside, and devise some relatively neutral framework for making comparisons and picturing relationships. This is a work for dispassionate objective analysis.

It is, of course, somewhat disturbing that things look different to dispassionate analysis than they do when we are passionately engaged. But this is wholly to be expected, just as we expect that a joke will be funny but an accurate analysis of a joke will not be funny. And just as it is a mistake to try to give a religious solution to all theoretical problems in comparative religion, so it is a mistake to assume that each person committed to a vision of the world should try to integrate the above theory into her vision.

It is psychologically difficult to live with the idea that the apparently conflicting views of the insider and the outsider are both true. This is a psychological problem our ethnocentric ancestors, including Laoists, did not face. What we need to try to achieve is "a second naivete." We lose our initial ethnocentric naivete when we learn to appreciate another religion, and begin to theorize about the relationship between religions. We should recognize that such theorizing has a comparatively limited usefulness, for those relatively infrequent occasions where we have to deal with interreligious or crosscultural comparisons. We ought to learn, in most of our daily life, to drop our theorizing and take up again a naive commitment to the particular idealistic vision to which we each commit ourselves wholeheartedly. We need to drop our naive ethnocentric absolutism, but also to stop living in the shadow of the Absolute that preoccupied Enlightenment thinkers, stop allowing ourselves to be worried and paralyzed by the fact that there are other excellent visions we ourselves are not committed to.

The Laoist "System"

We now have assembled all the elements necessary for sketching the overall character of the Laoist worldview as a semiotic system of mutually defining elements in specific relation to each other. The formal structure of this system can be described roughly as follows.

The selection of targets and of many negative images in Laoist polemic aphorisms is an expression of a certain perspective. Laoists picked out certain elements of conventional culture as particularly negative because they were in direct opposition to a certain good which they held in highest esteem, organic harmony. Many positive images in the polemic aphorisms give representative examples of some ways that concern for this good might typically manifest itself in concrete conduct.

The collection of images presented in the polemic aphorisms taken together represent the "true" Laoist picture of the world. One sees the world as it ought to be seen when one lets one's perspective on various situations addressed be governed by these images. "Truth" here is axiological truth. Epistemologically, the reason the Laoist view of the world is well-founded is an axiological reason: This view is the one that resulted when Laoists let their concernful engagement with the world be dominated by concern for organic harmony.

Aphorisms are speech acts performing the attitude of one who is converted to this good. The goodness of this attitude is the ultimate basis on which they hope to persuade, and the proper epistemological basis on which they should be evaluated. It also determines their ideal semantic structure, and so should govern their interpretation.

Laoists did not hope to make their conduct good by formulating and following certain guidelines. Rather, they cultivated a certain attitude that then would express itself in their conduct and make their conduct good. The way they cultivated this attitude was partly governed by the fact that, in the concrete, this attitude was closely connected to a state or quality of mind. This state of mind was described as Soft and Weak, Empty, Feminine, Still, Clear, Merged, and Harmonious. They made direct efforts to cultivate this state of mind, by getting in touch with these qualities in themselves and fostering them, partly through meditation exercises. Cultivating these mental qualities probably also meant being continually conscious of the ways that these qualities might inform one's everyday dealings with the world, and making efforts to ensure that they do so inform one's dealings.

This state of mind became the focal center of the Laoist worldview. Laoists expressed and maintained their commitment to organic harmony primarily by fostering this state of mind and letting it inform their conduct.

The reasons why a *state of mind* became the center for the Laoist worldview are connected to the cultural context and concerns and Warring States *shih*. This was partly a development of the traditional Chinese focus on the *person* of the Emperor as symbolic normative center of Chinese culture, and more specifically of the emphasis Chinese political thought placed on the idea that the Emperor ought to set the tone for the society. Those Warring States *shih* who aspired to reform politics by assuming cultural leadership found a cultural niche already prepared for them. Their aspirations thus led them to cultivate characteristics in their own persons that, when these expressed themselves in an administrative style, would set the proper tone for the people they influenced in their administrative and advisory roles. Laoists hoped that the people would "naturally" perceive the goodness of the characteristics they cultivated as something ultimately normative, and this would attract their spontaneous allegiance and cooperation and would set a tone fostering the organic harmony of the society.

The second major reason why a state of mind became a focal center for Laoists had to do with the concern of *shih* to develop an internal source of spiritual and moral sustenance to substitute for the support that their social environment failed to provide for moral idealists. The fact that Laoists were more alienated than many other *shih* is probably one reason why they attended to and fostered the experience of an *hypostatized* internal presence animating the state of mind they cultivated.

Laoists felt this hypostatized state of mind to be "transcendent," in that it appeared to them both at odds with the dominant social environment and vastly superior to this environment. This is what they expressed in the cosmic sayings about Tao. The fact that this superlatively good state of mind expressed itself in plausibly successful ways of dealing with practical problems led to utopian images of the hoped-for success. Modest successes actually achieved became more meaningful because of their (semiotic) participation in these idealized images.

Some Comments on Contemporary Relevance

The foregoing section concludes my proposals about the sub-stantive meaning that the *Tao Te Ching* had for its original authors and audience. The present hermeneutics envisages, in addition, another stage in the interpretive process. The goal of the first stage, just completed, is to enter vicariously into the world of a text's author, to be able to understand and appreciate the good that attracted this author, suspending temporarily our own sense of what is real and important in our own world. This needs to be supplemented by a second stage, a critical evaluation of the rele-vance of the good the text presents to those concerns that are important in our present cultural context.

This second stage depends on the ability to conceive of the good presented in the text in a generalized form, in which it can be adapted and applied to cultural circumstances different from those of the text's authors. This generalizability of the good is not neces-sarily the same as universality, if "universality" implies normative validity in all cultural circumstances. While something good is always good, not every good deserves to be taken as a priority in all cultural circumstances. Different cultures divide up the pie of moral experience differently, and differ in the priority they accord to certain goods over others. This is as it should be: Different cul-tural heritages embedded in a people's psychology and in their social structure, as well as different material conditions, means that people's experience of the good changes from era to era, and that the priorities accorded to certain goods should also change. If the good conveyed to us in the *Tao Te Ching* deserves to be given an important place in our culture today, this is not because it deserves to be given priority in all cultures whatsoever, but because of coin-cidences—that is, because cultural circumstances today make it appropriate to give this good a priority in our lives. It need not be appropriate, of course, because this good is in *accord* with domi-nant cultural trends today. It might deserve priority because giving it priority would counter some particularly deleterious trends today—because it is a good antidote for our particular poisons.

I would like to make some suggestions here as to some ways that Laoist thought might be relevant today. I offer these not as a definitive statement but only as an illustration of what the "sec-ond stage of interpretation" in my hermeneutics might look like. On my own account (see p. 9), the *Tao Te Ching* might be relevant to different people in different ways.

Proposals about relevance involve first of all some analysis of modernity. In this light I suggest that a central problem today is the following: Modern industry, technology, and capitalist economic organization make possible a relatively high standard of living for large masses of people, thus providing the material conditions in which the dream of an individually fulfilling life for all becomes possible on a large scale. But at the same time the reign of technology and economics produces a relatively impersonal and often dehumanizing environment that people experience as something in direct conflict with the human self-fulfillment that modern life seems to make possible.[26] One result of this conflict is an extremely deep and widespread feeling of alienation from "the system," an alienation that in some form appears to be a permanent feature of modern industrial and technological society.

This alienation is not simply a psychological condition, but has a moral basis: The dehumanizing features of modern socioeconomic structure *should* be resisted. But all moral resistance is implicitly motivated by something positive held to be precious but currently threatened. This is an area in which modern Western thought, especially in recent times, has experienced difficulties. The most common critical analyses of modern alienating social structures take as their positive basis the Enlightenment ideals of freedom and rational autonomy, or the Romantic ideal of emotional self-expression;[27] modern conditions are negatively alienating precisely because they run counter to these ideals. But these ideals have proven difficult to provide with positive and critical moral content. As a result modern "radical" social criticism tends toward a voluntarist skepticism that protests the obstacles modern society puts in the way of freedom, rational autonomy, and self-expression, but has difficulty giving a positive moral content to these ideals themselves.[28]

Laoist organic harmony provides an interesting alternative here. Consider the possibility that organic harmony—not freedom, autonomy, or self-expression—is the ideal condition which one needs to protect and foster, against the main forces in the modern social environment destructive of the organic good particular to each person and group. What we mean by a "dehumanizing" social environment is precisely an environment that grossly distorts the organic, internally balanced, human growth of persons and communities. The overwhelming reign of instrumental rationality, the pressure to conform to stereotyped roles, and the constant stimulation of excitement and acquisitive desire are well recognized problems today. On this view, they are problems *because* they distort organic goodness, and organic goodness is what we positively need to foster in opposition to these negative aspects of our cultural environment. A respect for individual differences and individual freedom is important, not because all ways of being and all exercises of freedom are equally good, but because what an organically harmonious development consists in is different for different people, and needs to be determined internally. Democracy is good, not because whatever the majority votes for is good by definition, but because voting is one of the best channels through which a community's instinctive feeling for its own organic goodness can shape the political environment in ways that foster this goodness.

One could imagine here also a merging of the Laoist ideal of organic harmony and modern ideals of emotional self-fulfillment: The quality of one's life is partly dependent on emotional richness, but also on a balanced integration of qualities and impulses that brings deep internal satisfaction. The resultant ideal is arguably close to the positive value that actually motivates much current popular dissatisfaction with certain elements of Western civilization: the revolt against abstract rationality in the name of sensual and emotional life; the emphasis on discovering one's own ideals as opposed to living by standardized norms; the importance of small communities in contrast with the individualism of classical liberalism; an appreciation of the natural environment in contrast to civilization. In short, in its own time Laoism represented one last voice protesting the advance of "civilizing" tendencies, which depended on the development of a separated consciousness valuing itself and its projects over against the organic harmony that is part of the given world. This movement has reached its apogee today, and people instinctively feel that further "progress" in the same direction is self-destructive. We need to "turn back" to recover many things lost in the progress of civilization, things that radically "conservative" Laoists were trying to protect. At the same time, we ought to take this as compensatory wisdom, realizing that its very attractiveness to us depends on the existence of many things brought about by the progress of civilization.

This is what Laoism might offer in the way of a general analysis of one of the main problems in modern society. Let us next address the topic that modern readers will probably find most objectionable in the *Tao Te Ching*—its acceptance of a hierarchical class structure, aggravated by the fact that the ethos it develops is intended only for a small segment of the ruling class, and that it opposes rationally directed ambition on the part of the masses of the people.

First, it is clear that today we need to take for granted the interrelated developments of modern technology and economic organization, of modern democracy, and of modern reason-based education. This also means accepting the need for rational planning to handle complex large-scale social and economic enterprises, and probably means also accepting continued fundamental change. This means giving up organic harmony as the overwhelmingly primary value it was for Laoists, and also means that this is not a value applicable to human communities larger than small subcultures, work groups, and neighborhoods. Giving priority to organic harmony as an *individual* ideal, integrated with the ideal of personal self-fulfillment, means also rejecting those kinds of social structures involving such things as the subordination of women, even though these structures might be an organic part of the traditional culture of some communities. (This is one way that the organic ideal I envision here differs from some ideals of organic order proposed by conservatives such as Edmund Burke.)

But with this taken for granted, let us address the issue of the ethos of those who are today the rough equivalent of *shih*-idealists. We should not think primarily here of high elected officials. Nor should we think only of "government," as opposed to private enterprise (these were not distinct in ancient China). Job-wise, we should think rather of all those people, at all levels, whose responsibilities give them some degree of authority over others: foremen in construction, factories, and farms; supervisors in restaurants, hospitals, and hotels, in small and large businesses; shop-stewards in labor unions; social workers, teachers, lawyers, police, accountants; government workers in charge of maintaining roads, collecting taxes, enforcing environmental protection laws, administering unemployment compensation, taking care of the poor and of severely disturbed families; and so on.

But we also have to think, not of all people in such positions, but of idealistic individuals, people who strive for high ideals in their personal life, and who also want to give extended thought to the good of society as a whole, and to work actively to shape the social environment so as to make life better for other people. Here our democratic egalitarianism produces some conflicts. Our egalitarian instincts make us suspect anyone who claims to be better than other people. Our democratic instincts make us suspect anyone who claims to know what is good for the people as a whole, better than the people themselves. But this suspicion tends to dampen idealism itself, inhibiting the ambition to strive for high ideals in one's personal life, and to formulate highly developed ideas about what would actually be for the common good. Those on the Right today tend to react directly against these inhibitions, adopting an explicitly elitist and paternalist stance toward society. Those on the Left tend to solve the dilemma by imagining themselves to be champions of "the people," saying what the people would say if their minds were not clouded by oppressive social conditioning. But in practice this usually means projecting onto the people the values of certain kinds of intellectuals.[29]

One could imagine applying some Laoist ideas, in modified form, to come up with a different approach to this situation. First, the idealistic person should not begin with a utopian theory about what an ideal society would look like, but should begin with her own actual predicament. There is no theory that says the majority *cannot* be idealistic and give extended thought to developing ideas about the common good. One ought to try to make these ambitions as widespread as possible. On the other hand, it seems unlikely that, in the near future, these ambitions will be widespread enough to be a strong influence on public culture. The idealistic and public minded person who is also realistic faces a situation in which she and people like her form a rather small subculture somewhat alienated from the dominant culture.

The Laoist advice here would be to concern oneself both with overcoming personal alienation and also with helping to create a less alienating social environment for others, but to conceive of these as two different projects. One ought to overcome personal alienation by developing a personal devotion and relation to an internal goodness, an organic harmony in one's person that can be felt as an internally nourishing and "Mothering" source of spiritual sustenance. This internal world-transcending Mother allows one to achieve some independence from the alienating modern socioeconomic environment. It is arguably better in this respect than the forms of transcendence more common in both the religious and philosophical traditions in the West, which tend to increase one's feeling of being a separated consciousness, alienated from any reality one can feel as *concretely* sustaining.

Establishing a personal relationship to this internal sustaining transcendence will diminish the felt need to try to confirm the worth of the values one finds most precious by struggling to make these values prevail over others in the public arena. It will not, however, cause one to reject any sense of responsibility to try to make the world a better place. But improving the quality of life for individuals and groups will mean fostering the flourishing of the particular good, and the configuration of goods, that is organic to concrete individuals and groups. The kind of goodness organic to other persons or groups might be very different from the kind of goodness organic to the way of life of the public minded alienated idealist. (Imagine, for example, a social worker educated in humanistic therapy, dealing with a crisis situation in a family group not accustomed to open expression of their feelings toward one another; or a university educated philosopher teaching students in a community college, who are not themselves going to become philosophers.) The influence one wields should always be measured by its pragmatic effects in the overall incremental improvement it brings in the goodness organic to particular real groups. And the style of one's concrete interactions matters here as much as, if not more than, the appropriateness of the goals one is trying to achieve.

Finally, Laoism has an interesting approach to the problem of elitism. What we now call elitism seems to have been a pervasive feature of most premodern ("inegalitarian") cultures. It was connected with the fact that social life in traditional societies tended to be a kind of morality play in which specific standards of excellence had highly visible representatives, and in which these standards were continually reaffirmed symbolically by the privileged position of these representatives and the enforced deference shown to them. Human excellence was identified with certain virtues and external forms specific to the life of a particular "upper" class, and these forms were defined specifically in opposition to characteristics common among the "lower" classes. Such elitism inevitably produces a certain kind of alienation among the lower classes: They look upon true goodness as something by definition located outside themselves and their way of life. The only recognized way they can improve themselves morally is by aping certain forms of life among the upper class that are in no way organic to their own way of life.

An egalitarian culture like ours that attempts to reject such elitism faces the difficulty that then there will be no focus for public reaffirmation of any standards of excellence whatsoever. The culture will be tempted to adopt mediocrity almost as an official ideology, rejecting as elitist all claims that any way of life is better than any other. This seems to be one motive for a revival of elitist social ideals by cultural conservatives today.

Laoism is interesting in this context because it developed highly idealistic standards of excellence, but defined these standards specifically in radical opposition to elitist social drama. This opposition shows itself in their opposition to boastful "contention" for social status among their fellow *shih*, to the Confucian exaltation of "refined" and admired virtues and conduct, and to an "impressive" leadership style that dramatized its importance by strong handed imposition of norms from above. This opposition was partly motivated by their feeling that dramatization of the ruler's superiority damages the social order made up primarily of lower classes, even that it hurts their feelings. The best leader will not even try to win the admiration of the people, because this alienates them from themselves and will ultimately cause resentments. She should rather be so low key that her influence will be invisible, and people will attribute social order to themselves. On the other hand, Laoists are not skeptical relativists but strive to cultivate in themselves a very high excellence—an excellence that they hope will have a leavening and uplifting influence on their culture, through the personal presence and leadership style of those who exemplify it.

Our uneasiness with the very idea of authority over others, and our dislike of managers and "bureaucrats" in general, stands in some conflict with the fact that the well-being of our very complex society depends on a very great number of people performing both efficiently and humanely in positions of responsibility at all levels, from the highest CEO to the night supervisor at MacDonald's. Our uneasiness does not do away with our dependence on people in these roles. It has only prevented us from formulating a highly developed and idealistic ethos for such people. In the *Mencius* and the *Tao Te Ching* we see the beginnings of the development of the ideal of the idealistic "virtuoso bureaucrat," a rather unique and distinctive feature of traditional Chinese civilization that may also be one of the most important things the Chinese tradition has to offer to global culture today.

12

The Art of the Sayings Collage

The previous chapters have assumed two interrelated hypotheses about the composition of the *Tao Te Ching*: (1) That the bulk of material in the book consists of sayings from the oral tradition of a Warring States *shih* school, and (2) that these sayings have been deliberately arranged in artfully composed collages of sayings. The present chapter will present evidence and argumentation supporting these hypotheses.

Most modern critical scholars now date the *Tao Te Ching* to sometime between roughly 350 and 250 B.C.[1]

The *Tao Te Ching* is customarily divided into eigthy-one numbered *chang*/"chapters," grouped in two books (though there is some discrepancy in the manuscript tradition on this issue).[2] Each chapter is typically composed of three or more brief units with fairly clear boundaries marked by changes in style and/or substance. Many of these units have the appearance of proverbs that could easily be understood and function alone, outside of their present literary context. Some of the individual "chapter"-units are composed of sayings evidently closely related to each other;[3] in others the relation between sayings seems at first sight tangential at best.[4] Aside from few cases where similar chapters are placed together (e.g., 71[63] and 72[64], 69[30] and 67[31]), the chapters are arranged in no readily discernible order.[5]

Chinese tradition[6] has it that the *Tao Te Ching* was written by an individual author, Lao Tzu. According to one legend, Lao Tzu was a sage who despaired of his countrymen. On his way leaving China a gateman begged him to leave some account of his wisdom behind, upon which he sat down and produced the *Tao Te Ching*.[7] Despite this and other charming legends that have grown up around the figure of Lao Tzu, modern scholarship has shown that we have no reliable historical evidence at all either concerning Lao Tzu himself or concerning his authorship of the *Tao Te Ching*. The earliest attempt at a "biography" of Lao Tzu, that of Ssu-ma T'an (d. 110 B.C.),[8] consists of a report of several different stories the historian has heard, some introduced by "some say . . . ," and accompanied once by the comment "people today do not know who is right."[9] As Waley remarks, "Ssu-ma T'an's 'biography' of Lao Tzu consists simply of a confession that for the writing of such a biography no materials existed at all."[10]

For earlier modern scholarship, Lao Tzu's authorship seemed somehow crucial to the worth (the "authenticity") of the book itself.[11] But this assumption rests on a peculiar logic. That is, it is not that Lao Tzu first gained a reputation for wisdom, and then people began holding the *Tao Te Ching* in high esteem because it was written by this wise person. Lao Tzu's supposed authorship of the *Tao Te Ching* is in fact his only serious claim to fame. Lao Tzu's reputation is based on the reputation of the *Tao Te Ching*, not vice versa. To suppose that to question Lao Tzu's authorship is somehow to remove the basis for the book's claim to greatness goes completely against the situation reflected by the historical evidence, and seems merely to reflect an emphasis of later ages on individual genius and authorship.

There is, however, another question regarding the *Tao Te Ching*'s origin that is potentially much more important than the question of Lao Tzu's authorship. This is the question as to whether the *Tao Te Ching* is a book written after the manner of modern books: Was it written by a single author to introduce his thought system to the general public for the first time? If it is a book of this kind, then to understand any given idea in the *Tao Te Ching* "in context" is to understand it in the context of a thought system existing in the mind of its author. This is contrary to the interpretive approach pursued throughout the preceding chapters, in which the meaning of any given saying is determined by its place in the concrete *community life* of a Laoist *shih* school. The precise issue at stake here is not whether the *Tao Te Ching* was written by a single author: The interpretive approach pursued here is compatible with the idea that this work was composed by a single member of this school for use by other members of the school. It is not compatible with the idea that it was written by a single isolated author to introduce an original system of thought to the general public for the first time.

Indirect External Evidence

We have no reliable direct accounts of the *Tao Te Ching*'s origin, but at a very general level, external evidence suggests two facts indirectly relevant to this issue, both counting against the supposition that the *Tao Te Ching* was written after the manner of modern books: First, Warring States China was in general still an oral, rather than a book-centered culture.[12] Influential thinkers did not yet automatically reach for the pen (or ink-brush) as a means of disseminating their ideas. The dominant mode of communication was personal conversation. Contemporary literature speaks frequently of people travelling long distances to listen to a famous teacher. We seldom hear of a contemporary teacher sitting down to write a book directed to the general public, or of others trying to acquire a book written by a contemporary teacher.[13] Mencius, for example, is a self-styled follower of "the Tao of Confucius," living three or four generations after Confucius. He quotes many sayings that are also contained in our *Analects*,[14] but there is no evidence in the *Mencius* that Mencius has learned these by reading a *book* of Confucius' sayings.

Secondly, the nature of the writings that have come down to us from this period also counts in general against the thesis that they were written by single authors to introduce original ideas to the general public. Many of the books that originated in pre-Han China are anonymous.[15] Others are clearly pseudonymous.[16] Critical scholarship has shown that most books attributed to a single author are in fact composite.[17] Of those books like the *Mencius* that are connected to the name of a great teacher, probably the majority are primarily the work of the great man's disciples.[18]

The probable conclusion is that, in general, people in pre-Han China who did write books did so not to present something original, but to collect in one place and to preserve existing lore already familiar to some particular group who had reason to want to collect and preserve it. Such groups seem to be a necessary condition in any case for the preservation of such works: In the absence of general commerce in books, collecting them in libraries, and so on, how else would they have been preserved? This also is a likely source of anonymity and pseudonymity in pre-Han works: Since the writers were not the source of the ideas in these books, there was no reason why they should sign their names to them.[19] The *Tao Te Ching* itself may well have been originally anonymous: The manuscripts recently found which date from the second century B.C. bear no author's name (or title).[20] One chapter (32[6]) is quoted in the *Lieh Tzu* as something taken from "The Book of the Yellow Emperor."[21]

The contrary tradition, strongly established in Han (206 B.C.–220 A.D.) and post-Han times, picturing pre-Han books as the works of individual authors is not difficult to explain: It simply reflects the habit of scholars—still prevalent today—of projecting their own self-image and social roles onto the men of ancient times.

Internal Evidence that the Tao Te Ching Is Composed of Sayings from an Oral Tradition

This general external evidence would incline us against supposing that the *Tao Te Ching* was written after the manner of a modern book. And internal evidence—its internal composition—points in the same direction. I will first consider here evidence indicating that the bulk of the material in the book consists of sayings that originated and circulated as oral tradition prior to being incorporated in this book. After that I will consider evidence that these sayings have been deliberately and artfully arranged in sayings-collages.

The thesis that the *Tao Te Ching* consists mainly of sayings that preexisted the book seems to be the opinion of most modern critical scholars.[22] The following are the main characteristics of the *Tao Te Ching* that point in this direction.

Individual chapters of the *Tao Te Ching* are typically composed of short units whose boundaries are relatively clear both because they show clear differences in style and/or content, and because the wording of each unit can easily be understood independently of any reference to surrounding units. Many sayings easily fall into groups that resemble each other either substantively[23] or stylistically. But sayings in such groupings occur scattered throughout the book rather than together.

Consider, for example, 10[7]. Even though there is a clear unifying theme in this chapter, indicating deliberate composition, the chapter is composed of several very distinct units. Each unit could stand by itself, none has any wording that needs to refer to the other units. Each unit is also closely related stylistically and/or in substance to sayings elsewhere in the book.

Text	*Comment*
Heaven is lasting, Earth endures. {1} What enables Heaven and Earth to last and endure? Because they do not live for themselves— so it is that they can live so long.	Section {1} belongs to a common genre in the *Tao Te Ching*: metaphorical images, usually taken from nature, illustrating Laoist ideals. (See p. 544 under Metaphorical*.)
And so, the Wise Person: {2} Puts himself last, and so finds himself in front. Puts himself in the out group, and so maintains his place.	Section {2} is written in a different style, also frequent in the *Tao Te Ching*: Lines in parallel construction, often rhyming with each other. Substantively and in its wording, the first line is very close to 55[66]:2:4–5, and makes a point similar to quite a few more sayings.[24] This unit is introduced by a very standardized introduction, *shih i sheng jen/*"And so the Wise Person."
The personal {3} doesn't exist for him— isn't this how he can perfect what for him is most personal?	Section {3} again is marked by a clear change in style. Its wording is similar to a saying that occurs twice elsewhere, in 64[34]:5 and 71[63]:5.

The features noted might represent stylistic peculiarities of an author, but they are unusual, differing considerably from the usual features of writing in which everything was composed to go together (such as the present paragraph.) In this case we generally see more uniformity of style, rather than units with marked stylistic traits that sharply differentiate one unit from those next to it. We also tend to see more phrases in one unit that have a necessary reference to surrounding units. But the noted features are very typical of oral traditions. The substantive similarities observable in groups of sayings reflect the fact that group wisdom consists of variations on a relatively small number of themes. Stylistic similarities reflect the fact that popular tradition in a given sub-culture often expresses itself in relatively standardized forms.

Further:

1. Some sayings are repeated verbatim two or more times in the book.[25] And many sayings appear to be similarly word-ed versions of other sayings.[26] This could represent an author repeating himself, but it is more easily explained if one sup-poses that the *Tao Te Ching* is made up of sayings from an oral tradition.[27] Duplicate sayings represent simply the fact that the same oral saying found its way into the book in two differ-ent places. Different versions of the same saying reflect a phe-nomenon common in oral tradition, differently worded ver-sions of the same basic saying.

2. Often the wording of an individual unit is such that it would probably not have made clear sense to the general pub-lic in ancient China. But in many of these cases no gloss in the present literary context explains the meaning, as one would expect if an author were introducing ideas to the general pub-lic. On the other hand, discussions in Chapters 6 to 9 have shown that each saying would have a complete and self-con-tained meaning if said in one of the concrete life settings connected with a Laoist *shih*-school whose character I have reconstructed. For example, the meaning of some extremely paradoxical polemic aphorisms[28] is clarified if we compare them to other less paradoxical sayings on the same theme. But typically these clarifying sayings occur widely separated from the sayings they clarify. The gradation in polemic aphorisms, from commonsensical ones to extremely paradoxical ones, fits well the situation in a Warring States *shih*-school, in which such aphorisms would be used in conversations both between Laoist *shih* and relative outsiders or newcomers, and between more long-term members of the Laoist school themselves. In addition, discussions in Chapter 8 have shown that phrases in some sayings assume a specialized audience already familiar with certain self-cultivation practices and with special terms related to self-cultivation.[29] We can learn about these practices by paying careful attention to indirect indications given in other sayings in the *Tao Te Ching*, but again these other clarify-ing sayings occur in other widely separated passages. And in any case the clarifying indications they give are indirect. They

are not given in the form of direct clarifications such as one would expect if an author was trying to explain matters unfamiliar to a general audience. Finally, discussions in Chapter 9 show that many sayings involving recurrent special terms (Tao, Femininity, The Mother, etc.) assume special meanings of these terms that would probably not have been familiar to a general audience in ancient China. Sayings celebrating the marvelous benefits or the cosmic importance of Tao, Femininity, The Mother, and so on (see p. 236–43), would appear unmotivated and implausible to an audience who had not already experienced the wonderful character of the realities named by these words. But again, frequently[30] nothing in the immediate context of these sayings suggests this experiential background.

3. Some passages clearly intended as a meaningful unit still give evidence that they were probably not written from scratch as a single unit, but involve either two originally separate units, or two layers of composition. For example, it is fairly clear that 81[37]:2 and 29[52]:2 consist of an initial saying, followed by comments that are in conflict with the point of this saying. It is unlikely that the same person wrote both the saying and the comments. In several instances we can see that only one line of a given saying is really pertinent to the context, but one or more other lines irrelevant in this context are included (e.g., 62[29]:2; 5[45]:3). The obvious suggestion is that someone is quoting a saying he himself did not write, and only one part of which he finds useful for his purposes.

Internal Evidence for Deliberate and Artful Composition of the Chapters

Considerations like those above have convinced most modern critical scholars that a large proportion of the *Tao Te Ching* consists of sayings that antedated the present book, and that the tradition of single authorship therefore has to be severely modified if not abandoned. There is widespread disagreement, however, about the extent to which the arrangement of sayings in their traditional order is the result of any deliberate design. There seem to be roughly four plausible hypotheses on this issue, each of which has found scholarly representatives.

1. The *Tao Te Ching* was from the beginning nothing but a collection of sayings loosely thrown together. Sometimes sayings on a similar topic, or sharing some terms, are juxtaposed, but we should not look for any connections beyond the obvious ones. Many times there are no connections. This is the position of D. C. Lau.[31]

2. The sayings in *Tao Te Ching* were originally arranged in an orderly and logical fashion, but this original order was lost very early and so is not reflected in any of the surviving manuscripts. (A common explanation is that, after the ancient custom, the *Tao Te Ching* was written on short bamboo strips tied together with leather thongs, and at some early date the thongs broke, and the original order of the strips was lost.) The modern Chinese critical scholar Ma Hsü-lun, a prominent representative of this view, attempted to reconstruct the "original" order, leading to a fairly radical rearrangement of the entire text.[32] This rearrangement has influenced the translations of Karlgren, Ch'u, and Duyvendak.

3. The *Tao Te Ching* as we have it was composed in several different stages by several different people with somewhat different ideas. This is the view of the modern Japanese scholar Kimura Eiichi.[33]

4. The chapters of the *Tao Te Ching* that we find in the traditional text consist of oral sayings that have been deliberately and artfully arranged according to some coherent and unified intention. The individual chapters are poem-like collages of sayings, "poem-like" in that part of the meaning of these chapters lies in connections between different sayings that are often implied and suggested rather than directly stated. This is Arthur Waley's view.[34] The present chapter tends to corroborate Waley's basic view with more extensive argumentation, and to provide grounds for a more systematic and methodical analysis of the text on these lines, presented here and in the commentary.

The question of deliberate arrangement in the chapters of the *Tao Te Ching* presents us with a rather difficult issue in interpretive method. The order we see in a text is always to some extent an order we create in reading it. The perennial temptation for interpreters is to make sense of some given passage by imposing a certain pattern on it,[35] and then present the passage so interpreted as "evidence" of the existence of the pattern. Such circular reasoning is the main charge that Waley's approach must defend itself against, and this requires more than the suggestive and intuitive comments he actually offers us. Attempts like Ma's to recover a supposedly lost order in the text suffer from a related weakness: Such attempts suppose that we have some way of knowing, independently of the text we now have, the original principles of order according to which it was arranged.

My solution to this dilemma involves some observations connected with the notion of competence invoked already in several earlier chapters. That is, first, we can phrase the present question as a question about competence: Does competence in reading the *Tao Te Ching* include coming to the text looking for certain patterns of order in the individual chapters that make it up? Secondly, although order is always a product of the way we read a text, not just any way of reading a given text is appropriate to it (see p. 37). Just as understanding an English sentence means sharing a particular kind of competence (internalized grammatical understanding) with the sentence's speaker, so understanding the chapters of the *Tao Te Ching* means bringing to them a competence that matches the formative intentions of whoever put the *Tao Te Ching* together. Finally, one way of learning the nature of the competence proper to a given text is careful attention to those passages which do show clear signs of deliberate arrangement. We can derive models of order from these passages, which we can then use to construe other passages whose organization is not clear by itself.[36] This will subject our intuitions to some methodical control, overcoming the weakness of Waley's approach. And it will correct the tendency of Ma's approach to rearrange the text according to models of order not derived from the text itself.

This solution elaborates on an approach known in biblical studies as "redaction criticism" (see p. 35). Once "form-critical" studies of some biblical books made it clear that they incorporated large bodies of oral material, scholars turned their interest to the techniques and intentions of those ("redactors") who integrated this material into more complex compositions. Redaction criticism usually relies on careful study of internal evidence to discover signs of artful composition, and to discover the techniques and the substantive ideas and thought-associations that guided the redaction of various works. (I prefer the term "composer" to "redactor." Although it is not perfectly satisfactory, it is better suited to convey the creative work that is sometimes involved here.)

As noted in earlier discussions, any account of the competence appropriate to a given writing must be tied to some plausible account as to how such competence could have developed in some concrete historical group. In the present case, the evidence of deliberate organization presented below implies that the chapters of the *Tao Te Ching* belong to a genre whose general character and organizational modes were recognized by some historical group, who thus would have had the "competence" required to understand them. The most plausible hypothesis here is that the chapters represent a genre of composition that arose in a Warring States *shih* school. The sayings that make up the bulk of the material were sayings that circulated orally in this school, through frequent repetition in the settings described earlier (p. 48–49, 127–28). I show below and in the commentary that the thought of those who composed collages out of these oral sayings is not substantially different from the thought expressed in the sayings themselves. Thus historically what seems most likely is that, in the second or third generation after the sayings were coined, they came to be not just repeated but reflected on[37] as repositories of group wisdom. This in turn led some to compose brief collages of sayings. Members of this school were the originally intended audience of these compositions, and they would have been competent to understand their genre because they would already have been exposed to its oral use in school settings where the character, intentions, and organizing techniques of these compositions would have been clear. The most likely hypothesis seems to be that the collages were composed by teachers for use by students.

Note that this rather tenuous hypothesis about the occasion for the composition of the collages is not the *basis* for the thesis about the genre of the chapters. The conventions of this genre can be gathered from internal evidence presented below. The above hypothesis is based on this evidence of deliberate artfulness in the composition of the chapters, and its purpose is only to show that a very plausible account is available showing how a historical group could have arisen who would have been competent to understand this genre.

Evidence of Deliberate "Framing"

One compositional device that offers good opportunities to illustrate the method described above is a device that might best be called "framing": Placing closely related sayings at the beginning and end of a given chapter, or before and after other material, thus "framing" the intervening sayings. There are a number of passages in which this device is very clearly present and deliberate. There are a number of other passages in which this device appears quite likely. Knowing from passages in the first group that this device is one surely used in some places in the *Tao Te Ching* makes us more sure that framing is also intentional in passages in the second group. There are altogether roughly seven passages in the first group, and fifteen more in the second group. These twenty-two examples serve as evidence, not that all chapters must somehow exhibit this pattern, but that part of the competence appropriate to these compositions is to come to them *being alert to possible signs* of framing. (As an analogy: Not all English sentences follow the pattern subject-verb-object, but part of competence in English consists in coming to sentences with this pattern implicitly in mind as a prime possibility.) When we look at the chapters specially alert to possible instances of this pattern, we can see that framing is quite likely in several other passages where, taken in isolation, internal evidence would not be sufficient to convince us that intentional framing was present.

Let me first present several very obvious cases of framing.

Text		*Comment*

4[22]

"Bent—then mature."   {1}

Compromised—then   {2}
   upright
Empty—then solid
old and spent—then young
   and sprightly.

. . .

What the ancients said: {7}
   "Bent—then mature,"
is this an empty saying?
This is true maturity,
   turn back to it.

Comment for 4[22]:
This chapter ends with an explicit reference to the saying that begins it. One might suppose that some of the five intervening sayings are "interpolations," but it is difficult to suppose that {7} originally followed *directly* on {1}. Someone clearly intended {1} and {7} to frame *some* of the intervening material.

23[26]
Heaviness is the *root* of   {1}
   lightness

Comment for 23[26]:
The last section of this chapter contains clear and unmistakable catchword references to

Stillness is the *master* of
   agitation.

And so the Wise Person: {2}
Travels all day, not departing
   from the heavy baggage
   wagon. . . .

Light, then lose the *Root*   {3}
agitated, then lose the *mastery*.

the first section. It is clearly
more closely related to this section than it is to the saying
that comes between them.

31[4]
An abyss,   {2}
it seems something like the
   ancestor of the thousands
   of things.

It dampens the passion   {3}
it unties the tangles
it makes the flashing things
   harmonious
it makes the dust merge
   together.

Deep,   {4}
it is perhaps like an
   enduring something.

Two stylistically similar lines
here ({2} and {4}) frame a saying that occurs between them.
The intervening saying is stylistically different, and occurs verbatim also in 30[56]. A similar
pattern is observable in 76[80],
where stylistically similar sections ({2} and {4}) frame another saying with different stylistic
traits.

Other clear cases of framing are: chapter 7[8], in which the
catchword "contend" links 7[8]:1 and 3, but is not found in
7[8]:2; chapter 22[50], in which the catchphrase "death spot"
links 22[50]:2 and 4, but is not found in 22[50]:3. Cases in which,
taken by themselves, framing would seem likely but not clear are:
chapter 9[79]:1 and 4, linked by the catchword "good"; chapter
11[38]:1–2 and 4, linked by the catchword "Te"; chapter 29[52]:2
and 6, linked by the catchphrase "turn back" and similar ideas;
chapter 32[6]:1 and 3–4, linked by the idea of lasting long; chapter 50[53]:1–3 and 6, linked by "Tao" and the idea of
display/boast; chapter 58[73]:1–3 and 6, linked by "Heaven";
chapter 63[32]:1 and 3, linked by the fact that 63[32]:3 refers to

cutting up the Uncarved Block mentioned in 63[32]:1; chapter 67[31]:1 and 4, linked by the reference to ill-omened weapons; chapter 67[31]:3 and 7, linked by the reference to a custom involving left and right; chapter 67[31]:6 and 8, linked by reference to victory gained through slaughtering people; chapter 72[64]:4–5 and 8, linked by the catchphrase "not working"; chapter 79[3]:1 and 3, linked by equivalent references to *hsien*/wise and *chih*/knowing government administrators; chapter 79[3]:2 and 4, linked by the catchword "govern."

The cumulation of evidence in these cases makes it fairly clear that framing is a deliberate technique in common use in these chapters. When we then actively look for signs of framing in other cases, taking this as one element of the competence appropriate to these chapters, we find a number of other passages where framing is probably present also, as in 14[23]:

Text		*Comment*
Speaking little is what is natural.	{1}	At first sight, {4} seems to have no connection at all to any of the other sayings in this chapter. (It is missing in MWT.) A little detective work, however, suggests that its presence in precisely this spot is indeed intentional. First, sayings in 8[81]:1 and 7[8]:2 connect *hsin*/sincerity specifically with sincerity in *speech*. Secondly, {4} occurs also in 54[17], followed immediately by a reference to being sparing with words. These observations, and the observation that framing is a common device in the chapter-compositions, reinforce each other in this case. The fact that sincerity in {4} is elsewhere connected with sincerity and parsimony in speech suggests that {4} was put here because it is connected with {1}. The fact
Yes:	{2}	
A whirlwind does not blow a whole morning a downpour does not fall a whole day. And who causes these things?—Heaven and Earth. If even Heaven and Earth cannot make things last very long, how much less can man.		
Yes:	{3}	
One devoted to Tao: Is a Tao man, merges with Tao is a Te man, merges with Te is a man left out, merges with What Is Left Out.		
One who merges with Tao, Tao welcomes him		

Comment   *Comment*

one who merges with Te, Te
   welcomes him
one who merges with What Is
   Left Out
What Is Left Out welcomes him.

When sincerity does not   {4}
   suffice,
it was not sincerity.

that a competent reader should
come to each chapter *looking*
for possible signs of framing
gives additional reason to suppose that this potential connection between the two sayings is indeed intentional.

Alterations and Additions Copying the Style of the Sayings into Which They Are Inserted

Besides the above evidence of deliberate arrangement of sayings in some of the chapters, there is also considerable evidence of
alterations and additions to sayings, alterations and additions
written specifically for the present context. Consider, for example,
the following passage from 35[39]:

Text   *Comment*

Things that of old got The   {1}
   Oneness:
The sky got The Oneness, and
   by this became clear.
The earth got The Oneness,
   and by this became steady.

. . .

The princes and kings got The
   Oneness,
and by this became the
   Standard for the World.
This is how things came about.

The sky, without what makes it
   clear, is likely to crack.
The earth, without what makes
   it steady, is likely to quake.

All the lines of the second half
of {1} are parallel to the corresponding lines of the first half,
until we come to the last line.

. . .

The princes and kings,
without what makes them
eminent and noble,
are likely to fall.

Yes, the *eminent* takes the {2}
common and ignored as a
root
the *noble* takes the lowly as a
foundation.

Where parallelism would lead one to expect "without what makes them the *Standard for the World,*" we find instead "without what makes them *eminent and noble.*" The words "eminent" and "noble" appear in {2}, a stylistically common saying consisting of two lines in parallel construction.

It seems fairly clear that section {1} originally consisted of a celebratory saying with completely parallel lines. Section {2} was a polemic aphorism on a common Laoist theme. Considering the sayings by themselves, there is no obvious connection between them. The most likely explanation of "eminent and noble" in the last lines of {1} is that whoever juxtaposed these sayings has altered {1} to connect it better to {2}. (The substantive thought here is explained on p. 214.)

This example also illustrates well the general criteria by which the presence of this device can be detected. That is, we have reason to believe that a given phrase or line is a composer's alteration or addition to a saying if:

1. It is somewhat unexpected in the section in which it occurs,

and if also

2. It serves to connect one section of the chapter to another.

"Unexpected" generally means unexpected in relation to certain recurrent characteristics observable in Laoist sayings. Many sayings, for example, consist of lines in fairly strict parallel construction, and the fact that "eminent and noble" in the above example departs from parallelism of the rest of the saying is reason to say that it is "unexpected." Other recurrent characteristics of Laoist sayings are:

1. *Rhyme.* Many (not all) parallel lines also rhyme.[38] Breaks in an established rhyme pattern are also cause for suspicion.

2. Most sayings are *succinct and strikingly phrased*. Like parallelism and rhyme, this feature makes them "catchy" and memorable, usually a necessary condition for preservation through repetition in oral tradition. If a unit in the text is not catchy or memorable in any way, this is cause to suspect that it is compositional.

3. Most sayings are *single-pointed*. One can observe that if a saying in this book has more than one or two lines, the several statements made typically involve various concrete examples of a single general point being made. This also probably reflects the use of the sayings in life settings: they are more versatile and more easily inserted into various situations if the point they make is relatively simple. If a unit makes more than one point, then, this is cause to suspect that compositional work is involved (or perhaps that there are really two different sayings involved).

4. The sayings are relatively *self-contained*. The ability to use a saying in a variety of situations requires that it cannot be dependent on very specific ideas preceding or succeeding it in order to make sense. If a line seems to require some reference to a specific idea contained in another nearby passage, this is reason to suspect that it is the work of a composer.

I have spoken each time here of "cause for suspicion" (rather than of decisive signs) of compositional alterations. Most often, we can speak with some assurance of compositional work only when a number of considerations all point in the same direction in a specific case. In the examples below I will always use the above criteria in combination with each other and with the other criteria mentioned above: the fact that the "suspect" element also connects the saying in which it occurs to another saying nearby. Occasionally also simple awkwardness in the wording of a passage will serve as supportive evidence that an alteration has been made.

We can now proceed to look more closely at several more relatively clear examples of connective alterations and additions to oral sayings.

Text		*Comment*
69[30]		
One who assists the people's rulers with Tao	{1}	Section {4} is made up primarily of parallel lines, but its sec-

does not use weapons to
  ch'iang/force [changes in]
  the world. . . .

Excellence consists in: {4}
Being resolute, that is all
not venturing to take control
  by *ch'iang/force*
being resolute, but not boastful
being resolute, but not
  overbearing
being resolute, but not
  arrogant
being resolute, when you have
  no choice
being resolute, but *not forcing.*

ond line interrupts this parallelism. Its reference to "forcing" also awkwardly duplicates
the same term in the saying's
final line. This line provides a
connecting link to the saying
in {1}.

56[61]
The great state is a *low* and   {1}
  easy woman for the world
the one the whole world
  unites with.

Femininity always   {2}
  overcomes Masculinity,
  by Stillness,
in Stillness it *takes the low place.*

Yes: {3}
A great state, by *putting itself
  lower* than the smaller state,
will win out over the smaller
  state.

The first line of {2} uses a formula connected with the conquest cycle, found elsewhere in
the *Tao Te Ching* (see p. 230).
The second line is without parallel in other sayings of this
kind, but it serves to connect
this line to the unifying theme
of this chapter, *hsia/*"[being]
low." Section {2} would otherwise have no apparent connection to these other sayings.

27[10]
When 'carrying your soul,'   {1}
  embracing the Oneness,
can you be undivided?

From a form-critical point of
view, section {1} is meditation-
instruction, speaking about

Text	Comment
When 'concentrating *ch'i*,' bringing about Softness, can you be like an infant?	internal states. But, although it is stylistically parallel, the fourth stanza (italicized) is substantively quite different from the rest. It is not meditation instruction, but speaks of a different topic, being a good ruler.
When 'cleansing and purifying the mysterious mirror,' can you be without blemish?	
When 'loving the people and caring for the kingdom,' can you be without knowledge?	The chapter also ends with a saying about an ideal ruler. (This saying is found in several variations elsewhere [42(2):5; 52(77):3; 65(51)4].) Especially in the light of the other examples cited above, it seems likely that the person who juxtaposed sections {1} and {2} in this chapter composed and added the fourth stanza to {1}, specifically in order to connect {1} and {2}. The substantive connection this suggests, that meditation is preparation for ruling well, is suggested by the juxtaposition of sayings at the end of 37[14] as well.
When 'the Doors of Heaven open and shut,' can you remain Feminine?	
When 'Clarity and bareness penetrate everywhere,' can you remain not doing?	
Produce and nourish. {2} Produce but don't possess. Work but don't rely on this. Preside but don't rule. This is mysterious Te.	

These are passages in which connective alterations and additions clearly occur as deliberate techniques for bringing more unity to the sayings gathered in the respective chapters. Once we see that this technique is clearly present in some chapters, we can add to our account of competence a special sensitivity to possible signs of connective alterations and additions in other chapters. Developing the historical hypothesis introduced earlier, what suggests itself here is that the original audience would already have been familiar with the oral sayings making up the chapters, and so additions to or alterations of these sayings would have been immediately evident. (For comparison: Most Americans immediately recognize the sign "In God we trust, all others pay cash," as a traditional saying plus an addition.)

Two other instances where connective alterations and additions are fairly clear are the following: The first three lines of 57[68]:1 are about soldiering; the fourth line, though formally parallel, switches to speaking about "managing men," the subject also of the lines immediately following in this chapter. Parallelism in 67[31]:7:1–2 would require the second line to speak of "unfortunate times," which is indeed the reading of WP; MWT, however, substitutes "mourning" for "unfortunate," thus connecting these lines to the main theme of mourning in the rest of 67[31]:7–8. What is historically likely here is that WP gives a saying (67[31]:7:1–2) in its traditional oral form. MWT represents someone's alteration of this saying to give it more connection with the present context.[39]

Once these clear examples show us that alertness to possible signs of connective alterations and additions belongs to reading competence, other examples suggest themselves that would not be clear cases if taken by themselves:

The lines in 44[41]:3:5–8 all make sense when taken in reference to physical objects; for example, "a great square has no corners" can be taken to refer to a drawing of a square where the sides stop just short of joining at the corners. The corners are delicately suggested then, rather than drawn in. However, the last line, "the great image has no shape" is difficult to take in the same way. But the phrase "Great Image" is found in 46[35]:1, where it refers to Tao,[40] said to be "without shape" in 37[14]:3. This line is most likely a connective addition or alteration to 44[41]:3, to connect it to the lines about Tao that immediately follow it.

The first and third stanzas of 51[75]:1 are a polemic against the lavish life of the upper classes, and the damage that this does to the society as a whole. The second intervening stanza contains no reference to lavish living, but to "working." The meaning of this "working" is spelled out in 51[75]:2, "working at living." (For a similar ellipsis involving "working" see 8[81]:3–4.) The most likely explanation of this somewhat awkward composition is that the composer of this chapter is trying to relate social criticism, not a dominant theme in the *Tao Te Ching*, to the recurrent theme of "not working."

The saying in 7[8]:2 consists of parallel lines, all of which also rhyme, except for the first line, "Excellence in a house: the ground." This is also the only line in the saying that is metaphorical. It provides a link between 7[8]:2 and the implied theme "being low" in 7[8]:1, if we understand it to mean that a house's excellence lies in its "low" foundation. There is otherwise nothing specifically Laoist about 7[8]:2: Taken without its first line, and out of this context, it could as easily be taken as Confucian wisdom (see the commentary).

The saying in 6[15]:2:3–6 consists of four parallel lines that follow a consistent rhyme scheme and use metaphors taken from everyday life to describe the presence of an ideal Laoist. The three final lines of this section, however, depart slightly from the rhyme pattern of the preceding four lines.[41] More importantly, they depart from everyday metaphors to using special Laoist terms like "Uncarved Block" and "Valley" (see 32[6]:1, 17[28]:1). The last of these three final lines connects this section to the next, by means of the catchword "muddy water."

Wu shih/"no-work" in 77[57]:5:6–7 duplicates *wu wei*/"do nothing" in the first line of this section. It also connects this section to *wu shih*/"not-working" in the first section of this chapter.

The introductory line 79[3]:2:1 alters the standard formula, "and so the Wise Person" to "and so the *chih/government* of the wise person." This matches a probable alteration in the final line of this chapter: The catchy saying, "Do not doing and nothing will remain not *done*" occurs in 25[48]:2, altered here to "and nothing will remain not *chih/governed.*

Finally, the cumulative evidence provided by these examples renders it likely that connective alterations or additions are present in places where we might not otherwise suspect them.

Section 11[38]:4 appears to be mainly a saying criticizing Confucians, parallel to the saying in 12[18]. But the first line is implicitly critical also of Te, normally a positive term in the Laoist vocabulary. But the first two sayings in this particular chapter are also critical of a certain kind of Te. It seems likely that a reference to Te has been added to 11[38]:4 in order to connect this saying to 11[38]:1–2 (also framing one intervening saying).

The first three lines of 58[73]:5, speaking of the cosmic ruler, Heaven, each speak of omitting some direct effort to achieve a particular result with its subjects, but achieving it anyhow. The last line of this saying continues the same general subject, but interrupts the parallelism: It leaves out the negative (*pu*), speaks only of the general quality of the ruler's policy ("lax"),[42] and does not mention directly the results achieved, as do the first three. "Lax" in this line also creates a link between this saying in 58[73]:5 and the idea of the "loosely woven net" of 58[73]:6. This latter also represents the deceptive "laxity" of Heaven's rule.

In 38[21]:2:1, "Tao is a *wu*/something" awkwardly duplicates a line occurring later in this same saying, "in it is *wu*/"something substantial." It seems likely that 38[21]:2 was originally a saying that lacked the two lines that now begin it (see p. 197). The reference to Tao in these opening lines connects this saying to Tao in the saying that precedes this one.

The final line in 59[58]:4 departs from the geometric images of the previous lines, and probably connects substantively with the "dull and incompetent" ruler mentioned in 59[58]:1.

The final line of 39[25]:4, though formally parallel, breaks with the buildup (Earth-Heaven-Tao) of the preceding lines.

Additional Connective Lines
Written by the Composer of a Passage

The passages discussed above represent cases in which some-one has smoothly worked additions or alterations into previously existent sayings, so that the added lines would appear to the casual reader to be part of the sayings themselves. There are also many instances, however in which someone has apparently simply added some lines, without making them appear to be part of sayings that surround them. Again we can point to a few relatively clear examples of this phenomenon. These will establish that there are some lines in the *Tao Te Ching* deliberately written as just described. We can use observable patterns in these clear cases to help us analyze cases which by themselves would not be so clear.

Text		*Comment*
11[38]		
Etiquette is loyalty and	{5}	Taken by themselves, sections
sincerity spread *thin*		{5} and {6} here are not very
and the first sign of disorders.		closely connected with each
		other. Each could easily stand
Foreknowledge is the	{6}	alone as a saying repeated in
flower of Tao		oral contexts. Section {7} picks
and the beginning of folly.		up "thin" from {5} and "flow-
		er" from {6}. Although substan-
And so the great man:	{7}	tively it could stand alone as an
Resides with the substance		oral saying, it is an unlikely
does not stay with what is *thin*.		coincidence that another oral
Resides with the fruit		saying should just happen to
does not stay with the *flower*.		contain these two catchwords

Text	*Comment*

linking it to {5} and {6}. It is much more likely that it was written specifically for the present context. That is, part of its intention is to link the previous two sayings to each other.

28[16]
Push Emptiness to the limit, {1}
watch over *Stillness* very
   firmly.

The thousands of things   {2}
   all around are active—
I give my attention to
   Turning Back.
Things growing wild as weeds
   all *turn back to the Root.*

To *turn back to The Root* is
   called *Stillness.*   {3}

Again, this passage contains two sayings ({1} and {2}), unconnected with each other, each of which could stand alone in an oral context. It seems an unlikely coincidence that {3} happens to share catchwords ("turning back to the Root" and "Stillness") that link it to these two sayings. It is more likely that it was written specifically to link the two previous sayings to each other.

6[15]
The Excellent *shih* of   {1}
   ancient times
penetrated into the most
   obscure, the marvelous,
   the mysterious.
They had a depth beyond
   understanding.

They were simply beyond   {2}
   understanding.
The appearance of their forceful
   presence:
Cautious, like one crossing a
   stream in winter

Section {1}, and the lines beginning, "Cautious, like one crossing . . . " in section {2}, could each stand alone as oral sayings, not closely connected to each other by means of content or terms. Parallelism in the last lines also differentiates them strongly and obviously from section {1}. So this passage was most probably not written from the beginning as a single composition. The words "They were simply . . . their forceful presence" were fairly clearly written specifically for

timid, like one who fears the
  surrounding neighbors
reserved, like guests
yielding, like ice about to melt.

the present context, to join
these two units originally unrelated to each other.

37[14]
"Look for It, you won't   {1}
  see It: It is called 'fleeting.'
Listen for It, you won't hear It:
  It is called 'thin.'
Grasp at It, you can't get It:
  It is called 'subtle'."

These three lines   {2}
are about something that
  evades scrutiny.
Yes, in it everything blends and
  becomes one.

Section {1} was originally a saying about spirits,[43] that probably did not originate in Laoist
circles. The phrase "These three
[lines]" in section {2} is an
explicit reference to {1}, hence
{2} could not have stood alone
as an oral saying independent
of {1}. It was clearly written
specifically for this context.

81[37]
Tao invariably Does Nothing,
  and nothing remains not
  done.   {1}

If the princes and kings can
  watch over it   {2}
the thousands of things will
  change by themselves.
If they change, and become
  desirous and active,
I will restrain them with the
  Nameless One's Simplicity. . . .

The first two lines of section {2}
were originally celebratory of
the marvelous benefits of ruling by Tao, hence *hua*/change
in "The thousands of things
will change by themselves"
must originally have had the
positive meaning (positive
social "transformation") it has
in 77[57]:5. The lines beginning "If they change . . . ,"
however, give a negative meaning to *hua*/change, as something leading to *yü*/desire and
tso/activity that need to be
restrained. These latter lines
could not stand by themselves
as an independent saying, but
neither could they have originally been a part of a saying
begun by the first two lines.

Generalizing from the above examples, the following are the main signs indicating that some given lines are additions written specifically for the present context:

1. The lines in question depart significantly enough from the surrounding sayings, either in style or substance, so that they do not appear to be part of these sayings.

2. The lines do not appear to be themselves an independent oral saying, but appear to have been written specifically for the present context. This could either be because some phrase in the lines refers necessarily to another saying in the context (as with "these three [lines]" in 37[14]:2), or because the lines contain references to two or more words or ideas in other sayings, and this is unlikely to be a mere coincidence.

One can observe several different patterns in passages exemplifying this phenomenon, and accordingly I list examples here under several different categories. Within each category I will again attempt to list examples in an order that proceeds from more clear to less clear cases.

Additional Lines Referring Back to Previous Sections

First, there are many cases in which the composer's additional lines refer back to preceding lines or sayings in the same chapter. The lines involved frequently serve to connect two previous sections to each other, typically by repeating one catchword from each, as in the clear example of 11[38]:7, analyzed above. The following exemplify this pattern.

Section 67[31]:4 is not single-pointed, and seems specifically written to link "ill-omened instruments" from 67[31]:1 and "gentleman" of 67[31]:3.

Lines 67[31]:7:1–2 could have been a common proverbial "rule of thumb," but 67[31]:7:3–5 refers to a different custom than the previous two lines, and is unlikely to have been a saying. These lines seem specifically written to connect certain prescribed battle positions to the mourning custom mentioned in the previous lines. Similarly, the following passage, 67[31]:8, seems specifically written to pick up "victorious" and "slaughter" from 67[31]:6, and "mourning ceremony" from 67[31]:7, thus linking these two previous sections.

The lines in 22[50]:4 depart from the parallelism of the previous lines, and they appear specifically written to connect these lines with the theme of being vulnerable to death in 22[50]:1–2, via the catchword "death spot."

Lines 35[39]:2:3–4 could not stand by themselves as a saying, although they make what is evidently a common Laoist point (see 36[42]:4, which is also unlikely to have been an independent saying; it is rather prosy and lacks an obvious point if taken by itself). The following lines, 35[39]:2:5–6, explicitly present these lines as an illustrative example of the saying that precedes them.

Although it is introduced by *i*/"in order to," 72[64]:8 is not likely to have been an original part of the saying that precedes it. It seems to have been written specifically to connect this saying to the theme of "not-working" mentioned in 72[64]:4–5.

The lines in 79[3]:3 are not single pointed. "Without knowledge and without desires" probably refers to the "empty minds" and "weakened ambitions" of the saying that precedes it, and "knowing ones" probably refers to the *hsien*/"wise and worthy" of 79[3]:1:1. Thus it seems specifically written to connect the two sayings that precede it with each other.

In 50[53]:6, *shih wei*/"this is," refers to what comes before; "robbers boasting" refers to ideas in 50[53]:2, 4, 5; and "not *the Way*" is a catchword connection to 50[53]:1 and 2.

Lines 45[70]:2:3–4 depart from the parallelism of the previous saying; "understand" (introduced by *wei*/just) refers back to 45[70]:1 and links this to the saying in 45[70]:2:1–2.

Section 41[47]:3 appears to refer to and link two ideas, "going" and "looking," from the previous two sayings. Its last line connects the unusual Laoist ideal of knowledge to the central theme of "not-doing."

Line 8[81]:4:2, although stylistically parallel to the preceding line, is only loosely connected with it in substance; its phrase "work and not contend" probably intends to link together the ideas of several previous sayings: "Work" is an elliptical reference to "work for others" in 8[81]:3, and "not contend" is connected with the criticism of impressive appearances in 8[81]:1. ("Contending" is connected specifically with contention for social status also in 4[22]:5–6 and 55[66]:1–4.)

The line 32[6]:3 departs from the parallelism of 32[6]:2, but needs to get its subject from this previous saying, and so could not stand alone. "Endure" in it probably refers back to "immortal" in 32[6]:1.

In 6[15]:5, "He simply lacks solidity, and so . . . " repeats words from the previous saying and leads into "remaining concealed," a probable connection with the "unfathomable" wise men mentioned in 6[15]:1.

Lines 43[1]:4–5 open with an explicit reference to the previous saying ("These two [lines . . .]"); and these lines link the third and the first saying of this chapter by means of the words *ming*/name and *miao*/"secret essence."

Section 44[41]:4 is not single pointed or catchy enough to have been an independent saying. "Concealed" probably repeats the theme of the previous saying, and "Tao" refers back to the first two sayings in the chapter.

Section 29[52]:7 links "Clarity" of the preceding saying to "turn back" of 29[52]:2, and seems to repeat the ideas of this latter section (see commentary).

"Cut up" in 63[32]:3 is a comment on "Uncarved Block" in 63[32]:1, and the remaining lines of this section lead into the saying in the last line (which occurs verbatim in 19[44]:4).

Shan/good in 9[79]:4 probably refers back to the same word in 9[79]:1:3; this line is itself probably a comment on the previous saying.

Lines 55[66]:3:4–5 depart from the parallelism of the previous two lines, and are probably connected substantively to the idea of the people's "natural" allegiance in 55[66]:1.

Sections 60[49]:3 and 4 do not have any stylistic features usual in Laoist sayings. "Muddled" in 60[49]:3 is probably connected substantively to the "man without a mind" mentioned in 60[49]:1.

"In opposition to things" in 80[65]:5 probably refers to the way that the ideal Laoist attitude (Te) is opposed to the development of "knowledge" criticized in 80[65]:2-3.

Additional Lines Serving as a Transition to Sections That Follow

These are cases in which some lines appear to have been specifically written to provide a transition from one saying or thematic section to the next, exemplified most clearly in 6[15]:2:1–2, analyzed above.

Lines 53[72]:2:1–2 are too prosy and lacking in striking stylistic features to have been an independent saying by themselves. There is a likely substantive connection between these lines and "majesty" in the previous saying, and they connect this saying to the following catchy lines by means of the catchword "tire."

The phrase "these three [lines]" in 78[19]:2:1–2 refers to the saying that precedes it, and leads into several originally unconnected lines that follow.

The phrase "these two [lines]" in 80[65]:4 refers to the saying that precedes it, and it leads into the lines about Te that follow.

Section 39[25]:2 needs the previous lines to provide its subject, and "great" in its last line leads into the following saying.

Section 26[59]:2 repeats words from the previous saying (introduced by *wei*/"just") and leads into the following saying by means of "possess the state."

The last line of 30[56]:3 departs from the parallelism of the previous lines and is not part of this saying as it appears in 4[31]:3. It is introduced by *shih wei*/"This is," and repeats *t'ung*/merge from the previous line. In the present context, it provides a subject for the saying that follows.

Section 17[28]:2 repeats "Uncarved Block," and the reference to "head of the government" leads into the following saying.

The final lines of 23[26]:2 appear specifically written to lead from the previous metaphorical image to 23[26]:3, by leading back to the catchword *ching*/light.

The saying in 47[43]:1:1–3 belongs to a genre of metaphorical models, celebrating the wonderful character of the "Nothing" that Laoists cultivate; the last line of this section introduces a new idea, "not doing," that does not fit smoothly into the preceding image, and joins this saying to the lines that follow.

Expanding Comments

Some lines appear to offer interpretations or expansions on the thought of a saying that precedes them.

Section 49[27]:5 departs from the parallelism of the previous lines, but the term "material" in it would probably not be understandable without the previous characterization of students as "material."

Lines 59[58]:2:3–6 depart from the parallelism of the previous lines and appear to comment on and expand upon them.

Section 56[61]:5 appears to be an interpretive gloss on the saying that precedes it ("get what they want" interprets "win out.") But this "interpretation" departs considerably from the original point of the saying, and so was not originally part of it.

Section 1[24]:3 makes a comment on the previous saying, explicitly referring to it ("This is. . . . ").

Section 70[60]:2 is a celebratory saying; 70[60]:3 continues the thought, but departs from its simple celebratory point to say something more qualified and complex.

Lines 39[25]:4:5–7 interrupt the parallelism of the previous lines to make an extended point about the king's greatness, introduced with an "also."

Lines 52[77]:1:7–8 repeat the point of the lines that precede it, and so the entire section 52[77]:1:6–11 is more likely an interpretive explication of these lines than an original part of the same saying.

Section 15[11]:2 interrupts the parallelism of the previous lines, but refers to the "useful nothingness"; this is an unlikely coincidence, making it unlikely that these lines were originally a separate saying.

Lines 71[63]:4:3–4 could possibly have been a separate saying, but more likely these lines are an expanding comment on the saying that precedes them.

Line 43[1]:2:1 belongs to a genre of sayings celebrating nameless Tao as cosmic origin; the line following it makes a different point—not a not celebratory one—that Tao has some names, such as "Mother."

Lines 12[18]:1:3–4 interrupt the strict parallelism of the other lines coming before and after it; they appear to comment on the Confucian virtues mentioned in them, as "the Great Shams."

Section 47[43]:2 cannot easily stand by itself as an independent saying; it is joined to the preceding saying by a connective line, 46[43]:1:4. Its point is celebratory.

Line 57[68]:1:4 departs from the subject matter of the previous lines and links these to the lines that follow. These subsequent lines, 57[68]:2, do not seem single pointed enough to have been an originally independent saying themselves. Their point is celebratory.

It is perhaps significant for the style of these chapter collages that the greater number of these added compositions[44] occur at or near the end of chapters, rather than at the beginning.

Sayings Used as Take-Off Points for Comments

There seems to be a number of cases in which a saying is brought up primarily, not because it makes some point the chapter's composer wants to make, but rather in order to serve as a starting point for a rather different comment.

This is perhaps most obvious in those cases in which a saying is followed by a comment that goes against the original point of the saying: Chapter 18[13] begins with a two-line saying, most likely from a "Yangist" source. This is followed by an explicit interpretation of each line separately. The Laoist "interpretation" of the second line probably goes against the original point. Sections 29[52]:2 and 81[37]:2 both begin with Laoist celebratory sayings, which are then commented on in a way that goes against their original celebratory point. Chapter 58[73] opens with a saying about the failure of the "daring" as opposed to the non-daring soldier, probably without specifically Laoist content. This is followed by two lines about unpredictability, apparently criticizing the implication of the opening saying that success/failure in battle is predictable. The lines in 67[31]:3 and 7:1–2 seem to be parallel lines stating etiquette rules with no specifically Laoist content. The composer's "interpretation" of the sayings departs from their original intention. Line 13[20]:3:1 is probably a Confucian saying, followed by a sarcastic Laoist rejection. Line 25[48]:1:1 is also likely to be a Confucian saying, followed by a paradoxical Laoist contrast. Lines 66[74]:1:1 and 51[75]:1:1 and 7 probably present a common complaint of rulers about their subjects, followed now by Laoist comments that seem distinct from them (see commentary).

In other cases, we seem to have non-Laoist sayings that seem mainly to serve as take-off points for introducing Laoist comments or sayings only loosely related to them: Lines 77[57]:1:1–2 are a saying contrasting the tactics appropriate for normal government and for wars, respectively. There is nothing specifically Laoist about this, and the line that follows makes a completely unrelated Laoist point, celebrating the power of "not-doing." The only function of the first two lines seems to be to serve as a take-off point for introducing a Laoist idea. Chapter 4[22]:1 begins with a saying that could be a common proverb, characterized later in the chapter as a "saying of the ancients." Its main function seems to be to serve as a take-off point for introducing some specifically Laoist sayings that happen to have a parallel construction. If 32[6]:1 were a single pointed saying, it would say "Mysterious Femininity is undying"; so it probably consists of a non-Laoist saying about an immortal Valley Spirit, followed by a composer's identification of this with Femininity (introduced by "this is . . . ," which leads into a saying following this). Lines 9[79]:1:1–2 seem to be a saying about leftover hostility, without specifically Laoist content; it serves as a take-off point for introducing Laoist ideas about Te as self-forgetting generosity toward others. Line 8[81]:4:1 has no specifically Laoist content, and its imperfect parallelism with the Laoist comment following it seems to mark it as primarily a take-off point for the comment. Line 34[40]:2:1 speaks of "Being" as a cosmic origin; this idea plays no part elsewhere, and Being is usually contrasted

with Laoist "Nothing," so this line is probably non-Laoist speculation, placed here as a take-off point for a Laoist comment emphasizing the priority of Nothing over Being (compare 15[11]). The
wording of both 22[50]:1-2 and 40[71]:1 presents problems for
interpretation, problems that can be solved if we assume that these
passages consist of sayings introduced as take-off points for quite
different comments (see commentary).

Some passages initially appear to be a single unit, but a closer
look shows that the specifically Laoist point occurs only in the
last line: Section 13[20]:4 is an uncharacteristically lyrical lament,
with nothing specifically Laoist about it until some final lines
(13[20]:5) about "the nourishing Mother." Lines 44[41]:1:1-5 are
about reactions of different grades of students to the *tao* taught in
a *shih*-school, any school; only the final line, making a completely
new point about Tao as "laughable," are specifically Laoist. Lines
50[53]:5:1-3 speak in glowing terms of the finery at a banquet;
only the final line seems at all critical. Sections 59[58]:2 and
72[64]:6 seem to represent non-Laoist sayings, followed by Laoist
comments expanding on their point. We know from the *Doctrine
of Mean* (16,2) that 37[14]:1 was originally a saying about elusive
spirits; it is now followed by Laoist sayings interpreting it as a reference to elusive Tao.

The Incorporation of Non-Laoist Sayings

At several points in the above observations, mention has been
made of the incorporation of non-Laoist sayings, and this subject
requires a few comments here.

First, several passages explicitly characterize specific sayings as
something borrowed from elsewhere: Section 4[22]:7 refers to a
"saying of the ancients"; Section 36[42]:6 speaks of a saying as
"what another has taught." Line 68[69]:1:1 introduces what follows as "a saying of military men"; line 22[50]:3:1 introduces
what follows as something "heard"; and 48[62]:6:2 introduces a
saying as something "said." Sections 18[13]:2 and 3 specifically
ask what the preceding saying means. In all these cases there is
nothing specifically Laoist about the sayings involved. (Section
44[41]:2 introduces what looks like a Laoist saying, possibly as
something taken from a collection entitled "Well-founded Sayings"; the phrase could also, however, simply characterize the following saying as a well-founded saying.)

There are many sayings in the book that have no specifically
Laoist content and could easily be common proverbs. These

include: 1[24]:1; 9[79]:1:1–2; 9[79]:2:2–3; 26[59]:1; 58[73]:2:2 and 3; 59[58]:2:1–2 and 3; 66[74]:2:7; 67[31]:3,7:1–2; 69[30]:2; 72[64]:6:1–2; 73[36]:3. Several sayings (7[8]:3:2–7; 13[20]:3; 25[48]:1:1) seem to be Confucian sayings. Saying 5[45]:3 seems to be taken from speculation about the conquest cycle (see p. 231); its first line has nothing to do with Laoist thought. Two sayings are known to be non-Laoist sayings because of quotations in other books: 37[14]:1 (quoted in the *Doctrine of Mean* 16,2]) and 71[63]:3 (quoted in *Analects* 14/36.) The saying in 3[67]:3:2–3 could apply to anything; the mention of gentleness seems external. Likewise, 54[17]:2:3 is unlikely to be either an independent saying or a composer's comment, so I judge it to be a quotation.

Analyses above show the following to probably to consist of a non-Laoist saying followed by a Laoist comment: 13[20]:4; 22[50]:1; 25[48]:1; 32[6]:1:1; 34[40]:2:1; 40[71]:1:1; 44[41]:1:1–5; 50[53]:5:1–3; 58[73]:1; 66[74]:1:1 (= 51[75]:1:1); 77[57]:1:1–2.

We have to consider the general character of oral tradition in the Laoist *shih*-school, our hypothetical origin of sayings in the *Tao Te Ching*. What we can see here is that there is a large core of sayings that are similar to each other in content, vocabulary, style, and genre. In saying that a saying has specifically Laoist content, I generally mean that at least two other sayings or passages in the *Tao Te Ching* make a similar point when analyzed according to the general principles discussed in Chapters 6 through 10. The saying in 16[5]:2 about nature's indifference, for example, has no parallel elsewhere in the book; this is why, although it is clearly "Taoist" in a more general sense, I judge it to be at best peripheral to specifically Laoist thought, and the composer probably interprets it in a way that differs somewhat from its original intent (see the commentary).

The fact that many sayings are similar to each other in content and style is an indication that these sayings arose in a very homogenous group, coined perhaps by a relatively small number of men. But of course at some points, Laoist wisdom resembles what could easily be common wisdom, expressed in popular proverbs. Although there are some specifically Laoist themes, there is no strict line dividing Laoist thought from common wisdom on some issues, and so there are some sayings that could be popular proverbs as easily as they could be sayings coined specifically by Laoists. It is very likely that Laoists liked and used sayings that did not originate in their own community.

We must also keep in mind that there were other "Taoist" groups besides Laoists. Sayings from these other groups may well have been familiar to and used by Laoists. Thus, although there is a large core of rather specifically Laoist sayings, the composers of the chapter-collages are probably drawing on a much larger store of sayings, with no strict boundaries between very specifically Laoist sayings, on the one hand, and popular proverbs or sayings of other Taoist groups on the other.

A Contemporary Stylistic Parallel

In order to show that compositional techniques described above are not without parallel in contemporary writing, let me cite a brief example from the Confucian *Great Learning*:

Text	*Comment*
What is meant by *"making thoughts sincere"* {1} is not deceiving oneself: as when we hate the hateful, as when we love the lovely.	The *Great Learning* consists of a very brief text at the beginning. This is followed by longer passages, each of which is presented as a commentary on this opening passage. "Making
This is called enjoying {2} oneself. *Yes, the gentleman must be watchful [even in] his solitude.*	thoughts sincere" is a phrase from the opening text, which the present passage takes as a subject for commentary.
A *hsiao*/petty man, {3} [when he] is alone doing wrong, there is nothing he will stop at. [But] seeing the gentleman, he immediately tries to put on a disguise, covering up his wrongdoing and presenting himself as someone good.	The "commentary," however, is clearly not written from scratch. It consists of disparate short units, whose relation to each other would, however, not be at all clear if the person who composed the passage did not link it together with the repetition of "making thoughts sincere" and "a gentleman must be watchful [even] in his solitude."
[But] the other sees as {4} though he looked into his heart. What use is the disguise?	This is most clear in sections {3} to {5}: The story told itself is about the *"petty man"* not

This is the meaning of:
"Sincerity on the inside [is
    equivalent to] enforcement
    on the outside."

Yes,   {5}
the *gentleman must be watchful
    [even in] his solitude.*

Tsang Tzu said: {6}
"What ten eyes see, what ten
    hands point to, this is to be
    respected."

Riches adorn a house   {7}
virtue adorns a person.

The mind is expanded   {8}
the body is at ease.

And so the gentleman   {9}
    makes his thoughts sincere.[45]

being careful in his solitude,
but the composer turns its
point into an admonition on
his theme addressed to the gentleman.

Section {6} is introduced explicitly as a saying of someone
else's. The last lines of {4} are
also a version of a saying found
elsewhere (see p. 554). Section
{7}, and perhaps {8}, also seem
to be independent sayings.

Section {9} frames the whole by
referring back to {1}.

One could also point to the opening passage of the *Hsün tzu*
as an example of this kind of compositional technique. In general,
late Warring States China seems to have been a transition period
from a culture centered almost entirely on oral communication to
one in which writing and reading books took on much more
importance as a means of communication between thinkers. The
kind of compositional style we see here reflects this transition,
showing us a composer who is not yet an "author" in our sense of
the term, but someone who is trying to put together an extended
composition with the use of previously existent oral materials
that represent a tradition he wants to carry on.

Substantive Associations of the Composers

The many detailed observations given above serve as sufficient
evidence, I believe, that all of the chapters of the *Tao Te Ching* are
probably deliberate, artfully arranged collages of sayings, some-

times augmented by the comments of those who put the collages together.

The fact that there are so many signs of deliberate composition, using standard techniques, serves as justification for supposing that there are intended connections between sayings, even in those passages in which, taken by themselves, such connections would not be at all obvious. If the juxtaposition of sayings in any given passage is motivated by particular associations, this means that part of competence in reading these compositions is an ability to "read between the lines," and to understand associations implied but not stated. On the hypothesis pursued here, the original readers would have been competent to perceive such associations, because they were members of a community in which these shared associations were familiar. We are helped to become competent to understand these substantive associations partly by study of the dominant themes in the body of oral sayings themselves, and by the general reconstruction of Laoist thought presented above.

There are also a number of cases in which sayings seem to be juxtaposed in different passages because of the same association between them. These can also help control the way we read between the lines and help us avoid simply reading our own associations into the text. The following are the principal cases one can point to:

The same saying (33[55]:5 = 69[30]:5) occurs following a criticism of "forcing" in two different passages, even though the saying itself is not obviously about forcing;[46] sayings that mention "talking" in a critical way are followed in two places (30[56]:1-3; 14[23]:1-2) by sayings critical of excitement, though the sayings about talking in the two cases are not about excited talking (excited talking is the subject of 16[5]:3). Sayings about "turning back" to the Root or to the Mother, are associated in two places (28[16]:2,6; 29[52]:2-3) with the same saying about "the self being destroyed." Chapters 1[24], 2[9], and 3[67] characterize showing off as an "excess." Chapters 4[22], 7[8], 8[81], 55[66], and 57[68] associate a willingness to be "low," or cultivate non-impressive qualities, with "not contending." Being content is associated with lasting long both in 19[44] and in 24[33]. Weakness and Nothingness are associated both in 47[43] and 34[40]. "Not rejecting" is associated with not making rigid value judgments in 42[2] and 64[34]. "Not working" is associated with careful attention to detail both in 71[63] and 72[64]; "not working" is associated with polemic against social "progress" in 62[29], 77[57] and 79[3]. Extreme subtlety in Laoist teaching methods is suggested by the juxtaposition of material in both 47[43] and 49[27]. A saying about not rejecting people (i.e., students) is associated with other sayings about teaching in both 49[27] and 48[62]. Chapters 50[53] and 53[72] both associate oppressive luxury of rulers with their tendency toward boastful display. The same saying about sincerity is associated with sayings about speaking little in 14[23] and 54[17]. The juxtaposition of sayings in both 53[72] and 55[66] suggests that the "high" "majestic" ruler *yen*/tires the people. Sayings emphasizing the unpredictability of the world are associated with sayings criticizing the overconfident and overassertive ruler in 58[73], 59[58] and 62[29]. In both 67[31] and 68[69] sayings critical of aggressive warmaking are associated with the opposing image of the "mourning" soldier.

There are a few places in which the juxtaposition of sayings, or comments on them, indicates that the composers interpret the sayings in a way different from their original intention. For example, 29[52]:2:2–4 makes a different point than 29[52]:1–2. This is true also of 81[37]:2:3 vs. 81[37]:2:1–2, of 58[73]:2–3 vs. 53[73]:1, of 30[56]:2–3 vs. 30[56]:1, and of 14[23]:2 vs. 14[23]:1. The association of 69[30]:5 with "forcing" in 69[30]:4 and 33[55]:4 also probably goes against the original intention of the saying. But in these cases, the composers express thoughts found elsewhere in Laoist sayings; they do not introduce new ideas fundamentally different from those found in the body of sayings. (This is part of my argument that the composers were members of the same school in which the sayings circulated, writing not more than two generations after the sayings were coined. See p. 310.)

All of this constitutes sufficient evidence for the general supposition that (1) all the chapters of the *Tao Te Ching* are collages of sayings deliberately composed with specific associations in mind, and that (2) the person or persons composing the various chapters did so with the same set of associations in mind, associations that in general follow the contours of Laoist thought expressed in the body of oral sayings. Thus we are justified in attempting to reconstruct what the associations were that motivated the composer of each chapter to select and juxtapose the sayings the way he did. Sometimes we are helped in this by alterations and additions inserted by the composers. Often we are helped by likely associations more visible in some of the sayings or in other chapters. There are some cases[47] in which there seem to be neither explicit indications nor likely associations to guide our conjectures. In these cases I have still proceeded in the commentary on the assumption that there probably were some intended connections more clear to the original audience than they are to us, because of their greater familiarity with Laoist thought and with the material itself. I have tried in these cases to make some guesses based on the character of Laoist thought reconstructed in these discussions.

Part IV

Translation, Commentary,
and Topical Glossary

Introduction

Part Four consists of a complete translation of the *Tao Te Ching*, a detailed commentary on each chapter, and a Topical Glossary containing brief essays on topics that occur with some frequency in the *Tao Te Ching* or the commentary.[1]

The traditional text of the *Tao Te Ching* consists of eighty-one numbered "chapters." On the view argued in Chapter 12, it is probably an anthology of once-independent chapter/collages, arranged in no readily apparent order. I take this as partial justification for my rearrangement of the chapters in a topical order that allows for more continuity in the commentary, and that I think is better suited to introduce the modern reader to Laoist thought. For ease of reference, I have also renumbered all the chapters according to this new sequence, keeping the old number in brackets. Thus 1[24] indicates chapter 24 in the traditional arrangement, which is chapter 1 in my new arrangement. (Pages 641–42 gives a list of chapters in the traditional order, matched with my new numbers and with page numbers where they are found in this translation.)

In general this new rearrangement proceeds from the personal to the political. Chapters are grouped in seven Sections, mainly on the basis of the predominant targets of Laoist aphorisms discussed in Chapter 7 (see p. 164–69). Chapters grouped together in Sections 1 and 2 concern two central facets of Laoist personal ideals, the cultivation of an unconventional and often negative-appearing kind of goodness (Section 1), and the cultivation of what we would perhaps call "mental/physical health" (Section 2). Chapters in Section 3 are more directly concerned with the practice of self-cultivation and the mental qualities cultivated. Chapters in Section 4 deal with teacher-student relations in the Laoist school, and the kind of understanding of reality taught there. Chapters in Sections 5-7 are about ruling. Chapters in Section 5 express the principal Laoist ideals concerning the person and general role of the ruler/administrator. Chapters in Section 6 concern more particularly the "Soft" style of ruling Laoists advocate, and chapters in Section 7 express Laoist ideals developed in opposition to contemporary social "improvement" programs. Further explanations of the rationale for the arrangement of chapters within each section will be found in the last paragraphs of the commentaries on chapters 2[9], 5[45] 7[8], 9[79], 12[18], 15[11], 18[13], 21[12], 23[26], 24[33], 31[4], 34[40], 37[14], 39[25], 40[71] 45[70], 50[53], 53[72], 59[58], 61[54], 64[34], 66[74], 70[60], 74[76], 76[80], 81[37].

According to the thesis argued in Chapter 12, most "chapters" of the *Tao Te Ching* consist of two layers of material. The first layer consists of short sayings, taken mostly from the oral tradition of a "Laoist" *shih*-school (see p. 49). The second layer consists of alterations and/or additions, most likely made by teachers in the Laoist school who gathered and arranged the sayings, whom I call the "composers" of the chapters. I have used typographical conventions in the translation to indicate different types of material in the chapters:

• Sayings I believe to stem from this oral tradition are printed in plain print in the translation.

• Sayings I believe to be borrowed from other sources are printed in plain print enclosed in double quotes.

• Comments and alterations I believe to be the work of the teacher/composers are printed in italics.

The first part of the commentary on each chapter consists of a paraphrase representing my view of how a Taoist would present the message of this chapter in modern terms.

A second part of the commentary on each chapter, following a dividing line, is more analytical. Besides explaining specific details necessary to understanding specific lines, it tries to support the interpretation offered by giving many cross-references to other passages in the *Tao Te Ching*, to analytical categories discussed in Part Three, and to essays on special topics given in an alphabetically arranged Topical Glossary (p. 531–58). Terms followed by an asterisk (e.g., Tao*) mark entries in this Topical Glossary, where a more systematic treatment of the topic is given.

The translation divides each chapter into several sections, and each section is given a number (placed in braces in the right margin), so that the commentary can refer to sections by number. References to other chapters use square brackets and colons: For example, 28[16] refers to chapter 16 in the traditional arrangement, which is chapter 28 in my new rearrangement, and 28[16]:1 refers to the first section of this chapter. (28[16]:1:2 refers to the second line of this first section.)

The translation given here is based on the standard traditional Chinese text of the *Tao Te Ching* given in the commentary of Wang Pi, as printed in Ho Shih-chih's *Ku pen Tao te ching hsiao k'an*. When I accept a reading not from Wang Pi, I always mention this in the textual notes. Most of these other readings are from the newly discovered Ma-wang-tui manuscripts, as printed and discussed in Henricks.[2]

This translation was done over a period of eighteen years, during which I went carefully through the Chinese text a number of times, comparing it to the principal available scholarly translations in Western languages, especially those of Paul Carus, Wing-tsit Chan, Ch'en Ku-ying, Ch'u Ta-kao, J. J. L. Duyvendak, Carmelo Elorduy, Robert Henricks, Bernhard Karlgren, D. C. Lau, James Legge, Victor von Strauss, Arthur Waley, and the translations of Chinese commentators given in Erkes (1950), Julien, and Rump (see Reference List). Phrases in my translation and ideas in my commentary too numerous to mention are borrowed from these previous works. On matters having to do strictly with the meanings of individual words I often give special weight to the very literal translation by Bernhard Karlgren, a scholar with little interpretive expertise, but a foremost expert on ancient Chinese language and lexicography and the author of a standard dictionary of ancient Chinese. Ninety-five percent of the time, my basic understanding of the text is one found in at least one of these translators. In cases where I am consciously departing from all of the above authors in my basic understanding, I mention either in the commentary or the textual notes that this is a "new" translation and/or interpretation of the text (i.e., new in relation to the above authors), and try to give some reasons.

My method of translation is a compromise between two main principles. The first principle is that it is good where possible to give a fairly literal translation, approximating one English word for one Chinese word and approximating also the Chinese word order. (The first goal is rendered difficult because the Chinese of the text is so succinct. The latter goal is often made relatively easy because Chinese syntax resembles that of English in many respects.) This literal approach yields translations like "not-Tao, soon gone" (69[30]:5).

Literal translation[3] would sometimes, however, give the wrong impression in English, or read too awkwardly, or be too succinct to make sense to an English-speaking reader. Where this seemed to be the case I have drawn on a different approach to translation: One ought to try first to get a concrete sense of what the Chinese probably means, keep this concrete sense without words, and then try to think how one would express this sense in contemporary English today. So, for example, in 3[67]:1 a very literal rendering would read something like,

> I great seem not resemble . . . if resemble long-time the insignificance.

I translate

> I'm 'great—but not normal' . . . if I were 'normal,' I'd have been of little worth for a long time now.

I have deliberately avoided the somewhat formal style characteristic of older translations, considering more colloquial English closer to the Laoist spirit. I have especially tried to maintain the colorful, sometimes "shocking" character of the Chinese, which is sometimes smoothed out by other translators.

Both in the translation and in the commentary I have construed everything in some way that I can make some sense of. I have strongly resisted forcing the text to say what I would like it to say; the theories discussed in Part Three about this book's composite character and complex origins provide many options for solving difficulties for which others often propose solutions I tend to adopt only as a very last resort (like textual emendation without manuscript support).[4] On the other hand, even where the text is difficult to make sense of, I have generally chosen some conjectural rendering that makes some sense, rather than giving a literal translation and leaving the reader to make sense of it however she can. For the sake of brevity, I have also generally given only one interpretation of each passage, rather than discussing several other plausible ones, even where this means sometimes choosing on the basis of rather slight probabilities inclining in one direction rather than another. Where I am conscious that my translation is more than usually conjectural, I have tried to mention this fact either in the commentary or the textual notes.

Excellence That Is Not Outstanding

1[24]

"A person on tiptoe is not firmly planted   {1}
a person in a rush will not go far."

One who shows off will not shine   {2}
one who promotes himself won't become famous
one who boasts of himself will get no credit
one who glorifies himself will not become leader.

In Tao   {3}
this is called 'stuffing oneself,' 'overdoing it.'

Things seem to detest this,   {4}
so the ambitious man does not dwell here.

(Paraphrase:)[1] Some people try to manufacture increased public stature for themselves by deliberate attention-getting tactics {2}.[1] This is like a simpleton who is on tiptoe because she[2] thinks that standing higher must necessarily be standing better {1}. Such a manufactured image, like standing on tiptoe, is precarious, an "excess" {3} added above and beyond any solid grounding in reality. Such a person cannot have any genuine success. It is as though her pretentious claims are detested by "things," by reality itself {4}.

(Analysis:) Saying {1}[1] looks like a common proverb against overextending oneself. Saying {2} is a Laoist*[4] saying countering[3] the tendency of *shih**[4] toward self-promotion*,[4] by posing the image[3] of the person whose deliberate efforts to impress only turn people off and inhibit his success. Saying {4} is a Laoist saying that could apply to many areas of life, depending on the context in which it is said.

Sections {1} and {3} implicitly characterize the "showing off" of {2} as an "excess." This implies a background view of reality in which there is a "normal" amount of importance and recognition given to each individual, based on true substantive worth and the part each plays in an organic social whole. The self-promoting person is "excessive" in trying to get more for himself above and beyond this. The rejection of the show-off by "things*"[4] {4} is related to this same idea: *Things* here refers to normative reality as seen from a Laoist perspective, that is, reality as an organically*[4] ordered whole. This is the reality that "detests" the show-off who violates this organic order by deliberate attempts to "stand out." Compare the occurrence of {4} in 67[31]:2.[1] "Things detest" weapons of war, and so the soldier out for personal glory by killing others "cannot achieve his purposes in the world" (67[31]:6). This has a quasi-superstitious*[4] basis. In the Laoist view, people in various ways put themselves out of joint with reality, and reality in turn turns against them. *Tao**[4] in {3:1} has an adjectival sense, referring to the specifically Laoist way of looking at things.

---

1. For the arrangement, numbering system, and typographical conventions followed in the translation and commentary, see p. 340–41.

2. Paraphrases are partly intended to indirectly suggest the modern relevance of the *Tao Te Ching,* so I freely use *she* in the paraphrases (to counterbalance *he* in the analysis). So far as I know it is unlikely that members of the Laoist school included women.

3. Terms like *counter, criticize, directed against,* etc. indicate that the saying being commented on is a Laoist polemic aphorism. The target of the aphorism is being countered by "posing an image." On these elements of the meaning-structure of aphorisms, see p. 136–43.

4. Asterisks mark topics explained and discussed further in the Topical Glossary, where the key words so marked are listed in alphabetical order.

2[9]

In filling, if you keep on and on—   {1}
better to have stopped.
In sharpening, if you keep trying—
the edge won't last long.
When gold and jade fill the halls,
no one can guard it all.
Rich, famous—and conceited:
leading to a downfall self-caused.

Achieve successes,   {2}
win the fame,
remove yourself:
Heaven's Way.

A person who gets caught up in the quest for wealth and fame is like a person who keeps pouring after the jar is full, or who keeps filing after the blade is sharp {1}. Such a person is fooled by the momentum of her attraction, pursuing what is attractive beyond the point where it is still really useful. So likewise, when you distinguish yourself in public service, don't avidly capitalize on this for self-promotion. The highest Way is to do a great job and quietly move on {2}.

Saying {1} is a rhymed saying presenting both accumulated wealth and pride in one's success, as a kind of "excess" that is precarious (similar to the Greek concept of hubris. Compare 1[24]). Saying {2} counters the tendency toward self-promotion* by posing the image of the *shih** who quits his government post just when he is becoming successful. The contrast between the two sayings has a specific basis in Laoist thought: Real worth is typically hidden worth, whereas those qualities that win public recognition typically are less solid and genuine. A person who tries to capitalize on the attention-getting aspect of his accomplishments to further his career {2} is relying on the *less* solid part of what he has done. The person who gets his self-esteem from being rich and famous {1} is a more extreme example of this same tendency and so puts himself in an even more precarious position.

The first three chapters in this Section 1 (1[24], 2[9], 3[67]) all have to do with precarious "excess." (See also 19[44]:2, 62[29]:4).

3[67]

Everyone in the world says of me: {1}
  'great—but doesn't seem normal.'
It's just 'greatness'—
  that's why it does not seem normal.
If I were normal,
I'd have been of little worth for a long time now.

I have three treasures,   {2}
I protect and keep hold of them.
The first is called 'gentleness'
the second is called 'frugality'
the third is called 'not presuming to act
  like leader of the world.'

Gentle, so able to be bold
frugal, so able to be lavish
not presuming to act like leader of the world,
  so able to become head of a government.

Now:
To be bold without being gentle
to be lavish without being frugal
to act like leader without putting oneself last:
This is death.

Yes, gentleness: {3}
"Attack with it and you will win
defend with it and you will stand firm."

When Heaven wants to rescue someone,   {4}
it surrounds him with a wall of gentleness.

There are loud and outgoing qualities (being bold, lavish, self-assertive), and there are quiet and retiring ones (being gentle, frugal, self-effacing). When outgoing qualities exist by themselves, they are typically the result of artificial effort, and so lack grounding in reality. An identity founded on this is precarious, insecure, "death" inviting. But the outgoing qualities are not wrong in themselves. One whose basic identity resides in the quiet virtues has a safe and solid basis for herself. Such a one can be bold and lavish on occasion, or occupy the highest social positions, without danger {2}. Quiet virtues like gentleness have a quality about them that acts as a magical protection, whatever situation one is in {3–4}.

Quiet virtues intensely cultivated—"taken to an extreme" by normal standards—make one appear not only quiet but odd {1}. But it is normal standards that are at fault in this: "Extremism" in the service of what is truly good is the right way. There is reason to worry if one is *not* a little odd.

Saying {1} is related to sayings countering the tendency to admire only impressive appearances*. The "I" is anonymous, but the image of the "great but not normal" person probably has primary reference to teachers* in the Laoist school, held up as models for others (compare 45[70]:2–3). Saying {2} is a saying against the tendencies of the upper classes toward assertiveness, conspicuous consumption, and self-promotion*. "Death" is hyperbole, portraying the "dangerous" precariousness of this. There seems no *practical* basis for the implication that the quieter virtues give one's life a "safe" foundation. The most likely basis is rather the one suggested in 1[24]: Loud self-assertion is precarious because it lacks a firm basis in (normative) reality.

In juxtaposing {1} and {2}, the composer draws on the Laoist association between personal qualities that attract little notice at all {2} and qualities that make one appear positively odd or disreputable {1} (see 4[22]). Saying {3:2–3} looks like it could be a common saying applicable to a variety of things. In their thrust, both {3} and the composer's addition in {4} function as celebratory sayings that portray the marvelous benefits of the quality "gentleness," which Laoists cultivate. (See "Benefits*" for further notes on this genre of sayings.)

4[22]

"Bent—then mature."   {1}

Compromised—then upright   {2}
Empty—then solid
old and spent—then young and sprightly.

A little—then a gain   {3}
a lot—then confusing.

And so the Wise Person: {4}
Embraces The Oneness,
and becomes the Shepherd of the World.

He does not show off, so he shines   {5}
he does not promote himself, so he becomes famous
he does not boast of himself, so he gets the credit
he does not glorify himself, so he becomes leader.

He just does not contend   {6}
and so no one can contend with him.

What the ancients said: "bent—then mature,"   {7}
is this an empty saying?
This is true maturity, turn back to it.

There are two parts to human goodness: The part that makes a good impression in the social world, and the part that is simply good. The part that makes a good impression is easily counterfeited. So the "purest" image of goodness is found in those persons who are good but do not appear so: A person who has great integrity but who appears compromised, a person of substance who appears "empty," and so on {1–2 and 7}. One who rests in this kind of goodness does not join the social competition for high status {5–6}. She realizes, for example, that a little bit of knowledge deeply understood may not impress others, but is actually more valuable than simply memorizing a lot of information {3}. Quantity impresses, but what one needs is only to turn back to the One Simple Thing, a certain quality of mind embodying pure but hidden goodness—this is the Center of the World {4}.

I believe {1} is a folk proverb to the effect that the negative, "bent" appearance of old people is a sign of something positive, their maturity. Saying {2} is a Laoist saying against admiring only impressive appearances*, posing the counterimage of fine qualities that appear negative on the surface. (Some of the wording, such as "compromised/upright," recalls similar sayings in 5[45]:1–2, see comments there). *Confusing* in {3} suggests that, despite the parallelism with {2}, this saying is on a different topic. It criticizes the view that gaining understanding* consists in widespread study or information gathering, posing the counterimage of the person whose multifarious knowledge only confuses him (compare 41[47]:2). Saying {4} celebrates the cosmic* importance of Laoist self-cultivation, described here as "embracing* the Oneness*." ("Shepherd of the World" is a traditional designation of the Emperor*.) Sayings {5} and {6} are sayings against self-promotion*. Saying {5} (a version of 1[24]:2) evokes the image of the person whose self-effacing manner elicits the admiration of others and wins influence. Saying {6} (= 55[66]:4) expresses the Laoist view that the ideal person, by refusing to compete (contend*) for social status, becomes in fact superior to all.

The image evoked in {2}, of great qualities hidden under negative appearances, expresses in more extreme fashion the advocacy of a self-effacing attitude in {5} and {6}. "The Oneness" that Laoists cultivate in themselves was felt by them to be something conventionally looked down upon (see 14[23]:3, 35[39]:2), and this association connects {2} and {4}. A connection between embracing this *Oneness* ("a little"), on the one hand, and having a multifarious store of impressive knowledge on the other {3} also may be intended. The composer frames* the chapter with a reference to the same traditional saying in {1} and {7}.

5[45]

The greatest perfection will seem lacking in something   {1}
but its usefulness never ends.
The greatest solidity will seem Empty
but its usefulness is inexhaustible.

The greatest uprightness will seem compromised   {2}
the greatest ability will seem clumsy
the greatest eloquence will seem tongue-tied.

"Agitation overcomes cold   {3}
Stillness overcomes heat."

Purity and Stillness are the Norm of the World.   {4}

Cultivating personal qualities that impress others takes constant effort, and so is mentally tiring. And in the absence of an audience, what good are they really? Look within for qualities of mind that are inherently satisfying to yourself, and cultivate these instead. These qualities will always appear in the conventional world as something worthless or not quite right {1–2}. But they sustain themselves, and so will be an inexhaustible source of real satisfaction to you {1}. In them your mind can find rest and stillness—that Stillness which is the Center of the world {4}.

Sayings {1} and {2} counter the tendency to admire only impressive appearances*, posing contrasting images of a kind of true internal greatness that, however, has a negative external appearance. *Perfection* in {1} is more literally "completeness," that is, a personal character "brought to completion" (see 10[7]:3, 44[41]:4, 65[51]:1:4, 71[63]:5). *Solidity** is more literally "fullness": I take it to describe a person whose presence seems "substantial," in contrast to someone who appears worthless, Empty* (see 6[15]:2 and 4). The Laoist contrast to the showiness of fine appearances is "usefulness," which probably refers to a concrete sense of personal satisfaction in one's own being. (Compare the image of inexhaustibly useful Emptiness in 16[5]:2, the useful Nothingness in 15[11], and the fruit/flower image in 11[38]:7). *Upright/compromised* in {2} is more literally "straight/bent," but the *Mencius*[1] uses these same words to describe moral integrity and moral compromise, respectively. Saying {3} is a celebratory* saying borrowed from contemporary speculation about the "conquest cycle," concerning which physical/psychic energy "overcomes" ("conquers") which other. Here a two-line saying is quoted from this speculation, of which only the second line—about how the energy Stillness* conquers its opposite, agitation*—is relevant to Laoist thought (see "Conquest*"). Saying {4} is celebratory, celebrating Stillness as a cosmic* norm.

The composer's associations between {1–2} and {3–4} here probably depend on the fact that achieving an impressive appearance requires "working*" (see 11[38]:2–3), that is, a mind stirred into activity, as opposed to the deep mental Stillness Laoists associate with a more "natural*" (but less impressive) way of being. This same association underlies the juxtaposition of sayings in 6[15]:2–3.

Three chapters grouped together here (4[22], 5[45], and 6[15]) urge cultivation of good personal qualities that appear negative or Empty*/worthless from a conventional point of view.

---

1. 3B/1.

6[15]

The Excellent *shih* of ancient times   {1}
penetrated into the most obscure,
        the marvelous, the mysterious.
They had a depth beyond understanding.

They were simply beyond understanding,   {2}
the appearance of their forceful presence:
Cautious, like one crossing a stream in winter
timid, like one who fears the surrounding neighbors
reserved, like guests
yielding, like ice about to melt
unspecified, like the Uncarved Block
all vacant space, like the Valley
everything mixed together, like muddy water.

Who is able, as muddy water,   {3}
        by Stilling to slowly become clear?
Who is able, at rest,
        by long drawn-out movement to slowly come to life?

Whoever holds onto this Tao   {4}
does not yearn for solidity.

He simply lacks solidity, and so   {5}
what he is capable of:
Remaining concealed, accomplishing nothing new.

Cultivating mental depth {1} means fostering a deep Stillness {3}, and coming to exist at a level of mind that, from a conventional perspective, seems to have no existence {4–5}. It appears vacant, unspecific, un-definite {2:7–9}. The person who has it has a magically forceful presence, which however typically presents an appearance of hesitance and timidity {2:3–6}. Her great achievement is to blend in perfectly, to do nothing that appears strikingly new and different {5}.

Saying {1} reflects one of the ideals of Laoist *shih**: To become a person who understands* things "in depth," which for them meant primarily cultivating the depths of one's own mind (see 43[1]:5). Here this ideal is projected onto an idealized ancient* time, when immensely "deep" *shih* advised the legendary great emperors. Saying {2:3–6} is related to sayings against self-promotion*, countering the common admiration of an aggressive and forceful presence by posing somewhat exaggerated images of the opposite kind of person. Lines {2:7–9} are probably added by the composer. (They interrupt a rhyme scheme, and they switch from describing external appearances to describing an internal state and from everyday metaphors to the more technical Laoist terms, *Uncarved* Block* and *Valley**. Line {2:9} may be a connective* link to {3}. My translation of *ch'iang wei* [lit. "strong working"] as "forceful presence" in {2:2} [and in 39[25]:2:3] is new. Others translate "[I will] *ch'iang*/try to *wei*/render their appearance....") Saying {3} is meditation* instruction: One first brings the mind from a state of busy-ness to Stillness*, and then gradually returns to being mentally active (see comments on 33[55]:2.) Saying {4} (a version of 31[4]:1) is an instructional saying giving a normative* description of what one is like who embodies Laoist Tao*—he will not yearn for a "solid*" (lit. "full") social presence.

The juxtapositions here suggest that "not...solid" in {4} is a description of the person of shy and retiring presence described in {2} and the person who remains unnoticed in {5}. *Concealed* also seems connected with the image of the ancient *shih* in {1}, whose minds existed on such a mysterious and deep level that no one could understand them. This is the state of mind and hidden/Empty way of being aimed at by one who cultivates Stillness {3–4}. The sayings in this chapter connect the internal state of the ideal person {1, 3, 4, 5} to a certain kind of external appearance {2:3–6}.

7[8]

The highest Excellence is like water.   {1}
Water, Excellent at being of benefit
    to the thousands of things,
does not contend—
it settles in places everyone else avoids.
Yes, it is just about Tao.

Excellence in a house: the ground   {2}
"Excellence in a mind: depth
Excellence in companions: Goodness
Excellence in speaking: sincerity
Excellence in setting things right: good management
Excellence on the job: ability
Excellence in making a move: good timing."

Simply do not contend   {3}
then there will be no fault.

What makes for a good house is not what gives it a striking appearance, but the solidity of the unseen foundation. Look out for this in other areas of life as well: For example, sincerity in speech and depth of mind do not get as much attention as eloquence and brilliance, but they are more solid {2}. Cultivating truly solid qualities means forgoing social competition and a willingness to accept the lowest rung on the social ladder. But these also are the qualities of most actual benefit to others. Cultivating these should be the main business of anyone truly devoted to helping others in public service, rather than just making a name for herself {1}.

Saying {1} is a saying against self-promotion*, using a nature image as an extended metaphor*. The fact that water flows downward and nourishes plants serves as an image illustrating the Laoist ideals of (a) not contending* with others for high social status, (b) willingness to accept being in a low* and unnoticed position ("which all others avoid"), and (c) devoting oneself to public service ("benefiting the thousands of things") as a *shih** in government office. To act like this is to identify with the role of Tao* in the world. Saying {2:2–6}, in its idealization of *jen*/Goodness,[1] sincerity, and "good timing,"[2] reads best as a rhymed saying from some school with a Confucian* bent. Saying {3} is a saying using an oracle* formula to present not-contending* as a "lucky" way to act.

Because the first line of {2} alone is metaphorical, and because it does not rhyme with the rest, I mark it a connective* addition by the composer. The "lowness" of the house's foundation connects this saying to the theme of lowness (water flowing downward) implicit in {1}. (Compare the low foundation image in 35[39]:2. The composer probably sees the virtues praised in {2} as examples of good qualities that are relatively unimpressive externally (as in the paraphrase). This is why he associates this saying with the Laoist polemic against contending for high social standing {1 and 3}, and with the advice to accept a social position low and unnoticed {1}. He "baptizes" this Confucian saying by relating it to the Laoist theme of "lowness*," an association facilitated by the occurrence of "depth" in {2:2}.

The same associations apparent in this chapter—criticism of fine appearances, devotion to public service, and "not contending"—also link sayings in the next chapter, 8[81].

---

1. Words printed in this format represent a Chinese word (*jen*) and an English equivalent ("Goodness"). For further explanation see p. 567 n.5.
2. See *Mencius* 5B/1,5.

8[81]

Sincere words are not elegant   {1}
elegant words are not sincere.
Excellence is not winning arguments
winning arguments is not being Excellent.
Understanding is not wide learning
wide learning is not understanding.

The Wise Person does not store up for himself.   {2}

By working for others   {3}
he increases what he himself possesses.
By giving to others
he gets increase for himself more and more.

"Heaven's Way: to benefit and not to harm."   {4}
The Way of the Wise Person: to work and not contend.

People pretend to be striving for Excellence when they are really just egotistically trying to store up points for themselves by impressing others. These are the people who value elegance over sincerity in speech, and prefer impressive learning to real understanding {1–2}. But the real route to personal worth is not storing up points for oneself in social competition. It lies in selflessly trying to be of service to the people {3–5}.

Saying {1} is a saying against admiring only impressive appearances*, countering this tendency with a series of contrasting images: good qualities that are not impressive on the one hand, and impressive qualities that are empty show on the other. (Saying {1:5–6} is also related to sayings about true understanding*.) Sayings {2} and {3} are sayings against self-promotion*, countering the tendency of shih* toward a self-centered focus on their own personal ambitions. The contrasting image posed in {3} is that of the shih who perfects his own being by selfless service to his society. (The first line of {4} looks like a common saying: Its sentiment is not specifically Laoist, and the parallelism with the last line is very rough.)

In the composer's final line, wei/work* is an elliptical reference to "working for others" in {3} (compare the similar ellipsis in 51[75]:2]). And "not contending*" is a reference back to the polemic against impressive qualities in {1}. As in 7[8]:1, the contrast is between cultivating impressive qualities with the intention of self-promotion, on the one hand, and self-effacing public service, on the other.

9[79]

"When great hostilities are smoothed over   {1}
there is always some hostility left."
How could this be considered good?

And so the Wise Person: {2}
"Keeps hold of the left-hand contract tally,
and doesn't make demands on others."

One who has Te is concerned with fulfilling his contract   {3}
one who does not have Te concerns himself
     with collecting his due.

Heaven's Way: {4}
Not to have personal favorites,
but to be invariably good to all.

Even when people make up after a fight, hurt and hostile feelings remain. How can the cycle of hurting be broken? The person concerned about her self-importance will always insist on her rights. The person secure in herself can afford to be generous all the time—careful of her responsibilities, but willing to overlook what others owe her. So she can be an agent of peace.

Saying {1}, and possibly {2}, appear to be common sayings, used by the composer as take-off* points for more specifically Laoist ideas. Commentators generally interpret "holding the left-hand tally" to mean being mindful of one's own obligation. (Contracts in ancient China were sometimes sealed by breaking a tally, each partner keeping one half.) Saying {3} is a normative* description of what one is like who has Te*/virtue:charisma,[1] related to sayings against self-promotion*. The tendency to insist on one's own rights is countered by the image of the ideal person whose behavior expresses the Te he has inside. Te is associated with self-forgetting generosity with no thought of reciprocation also in 60[49]:2 and 71[63]:3. This idea seems to be the connecting thread throughout for the composer here as well. (Most other translators understand *t'ien heng yü shan jen* in {4} to mean something like "Heaven is always *yü*/with the *shan*/good man." I understand *yü* in the sense of "bestow" and *yü shan jen* as "bestow kindness on [all] others," connecting this line to *shan*/good in {1:3} and the theme of unreciprocated generosity to all in {2–3}.)

Three chapters are grouped here (8[81], 9[79], 10[7]) that share the theme of selflessness.

---

1. Words printed in this format represent a Chinese word before the slash, followed by two or more English equivalents, separated by colons. See p. 567 n. 5.

10[7]

Heaven is lasting, Earth endures.   {1}
What enables Heaven and Earth to last and endure?
Because they do not live for themselves—
so it is that they can live so long.

And so, the Wise Person: {2}
Puts himself last, and so finds himself in front.
Puts himself in the out group, and so maintains his place.

The personal does not exist for him—   {3}
isn't this how he can perfect
     what for him is most personal?

A person focused on furthering her own interests has to do it all herself, with constant effort. This produces a sense of precariousness—if she rests, everything will fall down. The person who can be unconcerned about whether she is "getting hers" can also realize the natural goodness in her being {3}. And she can rest secure in something that is just there, lasting all by itself, like the earth and the sky {1}. Give up trying to be recognized, and others will recognize it {2}.

Saying {1} is a saying using a metaphorical* nature image. "Heaven* and Earth" sometimes serve as quasi-divine cosmic powers in the *Tao Te Ching,* but here the image may well mean to evoke also a concrete sense of the still permanence of the physical sky and the ground underneath us. In content all three sayings are aphorisms against self-centeredness and self-promotion*. "Perfect what for him is [most] personal" probably describes perfecting one's character through self-cultivation (see 5[45]:1). For Laoists, to achieve the kind of selflessness described in {2} *is* to perfect one's character.

Saying {2:3} reads literally "outs his *shen*/self but *shen*/self preserves." In the context, this seems to mean that he preserves his social standing by, paradoxically, being willing to be considered someone in the "out" group. The use of *shen* here to refer to a person's social standing is the basis for my similar interpretation of *shen*/self in 18[13]:3. Note that, as in the case of many other words, *shen* has no uniform meaning consistently adhered to in the *Tao Te Ching.* For example, in 19[44]:1 and 23[26]:2 *shen* has a positive ("Yangist*") sense, referring to one's own basic being as something to which one ought to pay primary attention, in contrast to fame, wealth, and exciting things in the world. But 18[13]:3 and 28[16]:6 speak of *losing* one's *shen*/self as something positive—in these latter passages *shen* seems to refer to one's "sense of self" as a socially acknowledged participant in the ongoing life of the world. This "inconsistent" use of terms is a common characteristic of everyday conversational speech, in contrast to the more specialized and technical use of language by philosophers intent on grasping reality by means of a comprehensive and consistent conceptual system. See further comments under "Naming*."

11[38]

The finest Te is not Te-like, so it is Te	{1}
the poorest Te never leaves off being Te-like,	
so it is not Te.	

The finest Te: no working at it, no goal in mind   {2}
the poorest Te: people work at it, with a goal in mind.

The finest Goodness: People work at it,   {3}
    but with no goal in mind
the finest Morality: People work at it,
    with a goal in mind
the finest Etiquette: People work at it,
    and, when none pay attention,
    they roll up their sleeves and go on the attack.

Yes: {4}
Losing Tao, *next comes Te*
losing Te, next comes Goodness
losing Goodness, next comes Morality
losing Morality, next comes Etiquette.

And now Etiquette is loyalty and sincerity spread thin   {5}
    and the first sign of disorders.

Foreknowledge is the flower of Tao   {6}
and the beginning of folly.

And so the great man: {7}
Resides with the substance
does not stay with what is thin.
Resides with the fruit
does not stay with the flower.

Yes: {8}
He leaves 'that' aside and attends to 'this.'

Some human qualities are like flowers: They are striking and attract a lot of attention, but they are thin on substance and so bring no real satisfaction to the one who has them {7}. They are really pseudo-virtues, just the product of conscious efforts to impress other people {2–6}. Other qualities are like fruit, dull and uninteresting in appearance, but deeply nourishing to the possessor. These need to be cultivated for their own sake, with no hope to "get something out of it" {2–3}.

Saying {1} is a saying against impressive appearances*. Saying {2} is about cultivating Te*/virtue in oneself and contrasts the spirit of Laoist self-cultivation with the spirit of other *shih** schools who also cultivated Te. Sayings {3–5} are sayings against schools of a Confucian* bent. (Sayings {2} and {3} are separate sayings; there is no implication that "poorest Te" is equal in rank to "finest morality.") That the goal others "work" at is public impressiveness comes out in {3:7}, an exaggerated image of the person who does not get the recognition from others he wants and so turns nasty. "Not working" describes the *spirit* of Laoist self-cultivation—getting in touch with and drawing out one's own inherent "natural*" goodness, rather than "working" according to conscious ideals. Saying {4} denigrates Confucian virtues by presenting them as the result of the progressive decline from an ancient* Utopia (compare 12[18]). In {6} "foreknowledge" refers to extraordinary powers to see into the future, a result of intensive mental self-cultivation.[1] The saying recognizes that this might happen, but criticizes the tendency to make much of it. Saying {8} (= 21[12]:3 and 53[72]:4) advocates attending to the quality of one's own being ("this"), in contrast to a concern for the external impression one makes on others ("that"). (See "This*.")

The composer's comments in {7} pick up the words *thin* and *flower* from {5} and {6}. The association flower/thin and fruit/substance is important because it suggests the *positive* basis of Laoist thought about good-but-unimpressive qualities: Showy qualities ("flowers") are associated with lack of substance ("thin"), whereas substantive worth ("fruit") lies in what does not attract much attention. The "fruit" image probably also means to evoke the "usefulness"—that is, the satisfying quality—of unimpressive virtues, mentioned also in 5[45] and 15[11]. Showy-but-thin qualities must be "worked" at, whereas the useful-but-unimpressive ones are associated with "not working." This is in accord with the underlying Laoist assumption that the "natural*" goodness organic to one's being is more real and substantial, whereas virtues imposed by a planning mind out of touch with this organic* goodness are less real and "thin."

---

1. Similar claims are made in the *Doctrine of the Mean* and the *Nei Yeh*, see p. 193

12[18]

When Great Tao vanished   {1}
we got 'Goodness and Morality.'

When 'Wisdom and Know-how' arose
we got the Great Shams.

When the six family relationships fell into disharmony
we got 'Respect and Caring.'

When the states and the great families
     became all benighted and disordered
we got 'Loyal Subjects.'

Some people try to be virtuous only because they sense the need to have some qualities that will gain the respect of others, qualities that they now lack. But instead of turning back to the neglected goodness inherent in their being, they try to go forward, to "make progress" in applying their know-how to developing qualities that everyone admires. This will succeed only in producing artificial substitutes of no real worth. So when people start *talking* a lot about "Goodness," you know something is wrong. Run the other way.

Couplets 1, 3, and 4 here criticize Confucian* self-cultivation, which focused on the virtues mentioned in the second line of the first, third, and fourth couplets. As in 11[38]:4, these sayings evoke the image of an ideal ancient* Golden Age when everyone was "naturally*" good. (The "six [main] relationships" are father/son, husband/wife, elder-brother/younger-brother. "Respect" and "caring" are the virtues proper to children and parents respectively.)

Because of the lack of parallelism, I believe that the second couplet was added by the composer: The virtues Confucians cultivate are a product of calculating reason ("know-how") pressed into the service of self-interest in impressing others and hence are "Shams," artificially created to cover up for the lack of the more real and natural, "original" state of being Laoists cultivate.

This is one of three chapters criticizing Confucianism, grouped together here (11[38], 12[18], 13[20]).

13[20]

Break with Learning, and there will be no trouble.   {1}

'Yeah' and 'yes sir'—   {2}
is there a big difference between them?
'Excellent' and 'despicable'—
what's the real difference between them?

"What others hold in respect, we can't fail to respect."   {3}
Craziness. Aren't we over this yet?

"All the others are beaming and beaming   {4}
like people enjoying a great ceremonial feast,
like people climbing an overlook tower in the spring.
I am alone still—
no indications at all yet
like an infant who hasn't yet even smiled.
So sad. Like someone with no place to go home to.

All the others have a superabundance
I alone seem to have missed out.
Oh my simpleton's mind! So confused.

Ordinary men are so bright
I alone am so dull.
Ordinary men are so sharp
I alone am so stupid.
Churned up like the ocean,
blown about, like someone with no place to rest.

All the others all have their function
I alone am thick-headed,
        like someone from the back country."

I am alone, different from others—   {5}
treasuring the nourishing Mother.

There is an ongoing vibrancy to the social life that everyone wants to be a part of. But it is sustained by the constant effort of everyone to be "up" and outgoing {4} and to show off their refined manners {1–3}. One who cultivates the hidden substance of goodness inside has to accept often appearing and feeling "out of it." But there exists a nourishing and sustaining internal presence one can feel inside, that substitutes for the loss of a feeling of social support {5}.

Sayings {1} and {2} criticize Confucian* self-cultivation. Saying {1} uses an oracle* formula to picture the abandonment of Confucian Learning as a very "lucky" thing to do. Saying {2} refers to one of the main objects of such Learning, knowing proper *li*/Etiquette—how to distinguish proper from improper conduct and when to use formal or informal ways to say "yes." Saying {3:1} is probably a Confucian saying advising respect for accepted social conventions. (Compare the similar saying in the *Great Learning*,[1] "What ten eyes behold, what ten hands point to, is to be regarded with reverence.") The composer follows it here with a sarcastic rejection. Section {4} is uncharacteristically lyrical. I suspect it is from a non-Laoist source, perhaps a popular song, or a lament like those found in a roughly contemporary book called the *Ch'u Tz'u*.[2] Laoists like it because it mirrors an important aspect of their own experience—feeling "left out" of normal life because the quality of being which they value most highly seems like "nothing" from a conventional point of view. It is "left out" of the conventional world, as the next chapter 14[23]:2 describes it. (This in contrast to the Confucians, whose Etiquette seems to Laoists to be itself part of conventional society. Hence the connection between the first and last parts of this chapter.) Note the important twist in the composer's line at the end, showing that in his mind the lament is not a real lament. It only pictures the social alienation that typically accompanies something very positive, the Laoist way of being in which one develops a satisfying relation to "the nourishing Mother*"—the hypostatized* quality of mind one cultivates, felt as a sustaining internal presence that substitutes for the lack of external social support.

This chapter shows well the Laoist feeling of alienation, in contrast to the much less alienated Confucians. This I believe is the primary reason why Laoists developed and stressed a relation to a world-transcending Tao/Mother. (Not, as some suppose, because unlike Confucians, Laoists were interested in cosmological/metaphysical speculation.)

1. Comm. 6,3, quoted p. 333.
2. Hawkes 1985.

14[23]

Speaking little is what is natural.   {1}

Yes: {2}
A whirlwind does not blow a whole morning
a downpour does not fall a whole day.
And who causes these things?—Heaven and Earth.
If even Heaven and Earth cannot make things last very long,
how much less can man.

Yes: {3}
One devoted to Tao:
Is a Tao man, merges with Tao
is a Te man, merges with Te
is a man left out, merges with What Is Left Out.

One who merges with Tao, Tao welcomes him
one who merges with Te, Te welcomes him
one who merges with What Is Left Out,
What Is Left Out welcomes him.

When sincerity does not suffice,   {4}
it was not sincerity.

Some try to be out there all the time, talking {1}, impressing {4}. But even nature cannot force a wind to blow forever {2}. People need to mentally drop out sometimes, drop into the space that by its nature can never look like anything important in the world. Pay attention, and there exists a presence that will welcome and sustain you there {3}.

Saying {1} is related to a group of sayings against excitement and agitation*—prolonged talking takes effort and wears one out (16[5]:3) and so, from a Laoist perspective, is not "natural*." Saying {2} is also related to sayings against mentally agitating* activity. It uses metaphorical* nature images as *negative* examples to make a common Laoist point—that intense human activity exhausts one's energy and is short lived (see also 69[30]:5, 29[52]:4, 22[50]:2). This contrasts with Laoist advice to conserve one's energy in order to "last* long." Saying {3} celebrates the wonderful benefits* of the internal quality cultivated by Laoists. We see here several uses of Tao*: (a) adjectival— one who cultivates (Laoist) Tao has a Tao quality to his being (*tao che*/"[is a] Tao-man");[1] (b) as an hypostatized*, entitylike quality with which one can "merge"; (c) as a supportive presence one feels inside, "welcoming" one (compare the "nourishing" Mother* in 13[20]:5, and the "supporting/completing" Tao in 44[41]:4). *Tao* and *Te* are equivalent names for the same presence, here called also the *shih*/"Left-Out [One]," because it generally goes unrecognized in the world (compare 13[20]:5, 35[39]:1–2). Saying {4} is related to sayings against impressive appearances*. Like 8[81]:1, it means to emphasize sincerity rather than eloquence in speech, correcting the tendency to think that sincerity alone will not suffice to convince an audience. Laoists are confident that *real* sincerity has a subtle power that will surely be felt.[2]

The composer's associations in this chapter are probably as follows: Whirlwinds and downpours {2} are metaphors for intense human activity, of which lengthy talking {1} to impress others {4} is an example. Such talking is also a form of very active participation in the ongoing life of the world. But, as in 13[20]:4–5 and 29[52]:3, Laoist self-cultivation is often accompanied by a sense of losing this normally vital social connection. Hence the connection with "merging with What Is Left Out" in {3}. (My new understanding of sincerity *in speech* as the reference in {4} has the advantage of relating {4} to {1}, framing* the chapter as a whole. Saying {4} also occurs in 54[17]:2, immediately followed by a saying praising reticence in speech.)

---

1. Karlgren's translation. Compare *mo che*/"Mo-man" (= a disciple of Mo Ti), *Mencius* 3A/5,1.
2. Compare *Mencius* 4A/12,3.

15[11]

Thirty spokes unite in one hollow hub— {1}
in this 'nothing' lies the wheel's usefulness.

Knead clay to make a jar—
in its 'nothing' lies the jar's usefulness.

Cut out doors and windows in making a house—
in their 'nothing' lies the house's usefulness.

Yes: {2}
'Being' makes for profit
'Nothing' makes for usefulness.

Social admiration gives certain qualities a feeling of solidity, and makes others feel like "nothing." But think of all the cases—wheel centers, pots, windows, and doors—in which some "nothing" makes the thing functionally worth something {1}. If you are not looking for social "profit," but for what is of genuine worth and brings real satisfaction {2}, pay attention to those parts of your being that seem like "nothing."

Stylistically {1} is related to sayings using metaphorical* nature images. In content, the images celebrate* the great "usefulness" of the Nothingness* Laoists cultivate. (Compare 16[5]:2 and the similar "useful Emptiness*" in 5[45]:1.) The Being/Nothing contrast in {2} is not philosophical but concrete, equivalent to the contrast solid/Empty*; that is, *Being* refers to those aspects of one's personal being that feel tangible (like the tangible sides of a jar) because they are socially admired (hence *li*/profitable, a negative term here, as it is in 78[19]:1. It is an especially negative term in the *Mencius*,[1] too. The term *li*/profit figures prominently in the utilitarian social thought of the Mohists*[2]). *Nothing*, like Emptiness, refers to those aspects that feel intangible because they make no impression on others.

In this interpretation, *Nothing* in this chapter is related to the *Emptiness* celebrated in the next chapter, 16[5], and to the social alienation implied in the previous two chapters—the socially "lost" person in 13[20], and the person cultivating "left-out" Tao/Te in 14[23]. Chapter 17[28], the last one in this Section 1, is a climax, advocating the cultivation of qualities that appear "disgraceful" and relating this theme to the central Laoist concept of the "Uncarved* Block." (See comments on climaxes at 39[25].)

---

1. 1A/1,1–6.
2. Graham 1989: 37–41.

16[5]

"Heaven and Earth are not Good   {1}
they treat the thousands of things like straw dogs.
The Wise Person is not Good
he treats the hundred clans like straw dogs."

The space between heaven and earth   {2}
isn't it like a bellows?
Empty, but not shrivelled up,
set it in motion and always more comes out.

Much talking, quickly exhausted.   {3}

It can't compare to watching over what is inside.   {4}

Why do we spend so much time talking {3}? Is it not because this gives us a tangible sense of our identity, confirmed by being part of social life? Sometimes this also is the motivation of the self-important person in authority, anxious to appear to her people as someone "Good" {1}. By contrast, if we are just looking into ourselves, by ourselves {4}, we easily lose a tangible sense of our own existence. Our being seems evanescent and empty. But this Emptiness is worth holding onto. Attended to and cultivated {5}, it is a potential source of endless energy {2}.

Saying {1} is a saying against Confucian* *jen*/Goodness as an ideal for the ruler.[1] It mocks the Confucian emphasis that the upper classes should have a strong sense of social responsibility, making fun of Confucian seriousness by posing an exaggerated image of the opposite attitude—having no concern whatsoever for the people—and appealing to nature's indifference in support of this. ("Straw dogs" is a reference to a religious ceremony described in the *Chuang* *Tzu*,[2] in which dogs made of straw were first given a place of honor, then later discarded and trampled.) But this saying has no parallel elsewhere in the *Tao Te Ching*, and Laoists elsewhere advocate selfless devotion to the good of society (8[81]:2-4, 7[8]:1, 9[79]:2-4, 75[78]:4). So, although many commentators focus on {1} as central to Laoist teaching, I doubt that this is a Laoist saying. The composer of this chapter likes it because it mocks the sense of *self-importance* he thinks motivates the Confucian sense of "responsibility." But he contrasts "Goodness," not with indifference, but with the "Emptiness" of {2}. Saying {2} is a saying celebrating the wonderful benefits* of this "Emptiness*" Laoists cultivate—the fact that this Empty state of mind is a source of boundless energy. (It is thus related also to sayings against mentally agitating* excitement, which is "exhausting.") The metaphorical* nature image employed seems to envision the "empty" physical space around us as continuously and endlessly producing all the living things that fill it up. Saying {3} is a saying against stimulating and mentally agitating* activity (talking-as-exhausting suggests excited or prolonged talking). Saying {4} celebrates* the importance of self-cultivation (internally "watching* over" qualities one wants to develop.) The composer's probable associations are described in the paraphrase.

---

1. Compare *Mencius* 1A/7,1-24, quoted p. 97-102.
2. Watson, 1968: 159.

17[28]

Be familiar with Masculinity   {1}
but watch over Femininity—
and become the Valley of the World.
Being the Valley of the World,
invariant Te will not leave you.
Turn back to being an infant.

Be familiar with what is pure and white
but watch over what is dark and black—
and become the Pattern for the World.
Being the Pattern for the World,
your invariant Te will be constant.
Turn back to being limitless.

Be familiar with what is praiseworthy
but watch over what is disgraceful—
and become the Valley of the World.
Being the Valley of the World,
your invariant Te will be sufficient.
Turn back to being an Uncarved Block.

When the Uncarved Block is cut up   {2}
then it becomes a government tool.
When the Wise Person instead uses it
then it becomes head of the government.

Yes: {3}
A great carver does no cutting,
a great ruler makes no rules.

There is a conflict between what our being tends to be if left to itself and the direction of growth it takes under the influence of social competition. The desire to be "praiseworthy" causes an artificial emphasis on some particular qualities and the repression of others that we become ashamed of. This does not result in a genuinely better personality, but in a loss of wholeness, a lessening of being and true worth. In practice, recovery of our own full and unique being requires that we find and cultivate the goodness in those parts of ourselves the conventional world ignores or looks down on. Such a fully recovered being is the center of the world.

Saying {1} is related to sayings against admiring impressive appearances*. But it also celebrates the way that Laoist self-cultivation gives a person the spiritual status of cosmic* norm. (The capitalized special terms describing these results are explained in the Topical Glossary.) *Femininity** and *dark and black* both refer to qualities that would be looked down upon by contemporaries, as is evident from the parallel with "disgraceful." The negative connotations are important, as part of the thrust of this passage is to shock, and to emphasize the reversal of conventional values. In {3} I have used two lines where the text has one, to capture the play on words: The word translated "carver" also means "ruler." The basic implied image is the woodcarver, who brings out the beautiful form already inherent in a piece of wood, doing as little cutting as possible. This is a metaphor* for the ideal ruler, who imposes as few explicit rules as possible on his society, drawing out instead its intrinsic goodness. (See "Naming*" and "Strict*.") Here "the great ruler" probably refers to the ideal person generally.

In the composer's comments in {2}, the *Uncarved* Block* serves as an image of a personality before it is "carved up" into standardized, socially desirable qualities (compare 63[32]:1–3). Recovering an "uncarved" personality is described as "using*" the Uncarved Block, whose great status is described in political metaphors: *Tool* describes a minor official—an "instrument" used by his superiors—in contrast to the exalted status of "prime minister." Reading {1} as aphoristic*, *corrective* wisdom, one would say that for Laoists, what it takes to recover "wholeness" is not (as in later *yin*/yang* Taoism) *equal* attention to both Masculinity and Femininity. One should rather cultivate Femininity. (One could see the difference as more apparent than real, however; because the universal tendency of everything is to "embrace* *yang*" [36[42]:2], *yang* Masculinity takes care of itself.)

2

Stillness and Contentment

18[13]

"Favor and disgrace: this means being upset   {1}
high rank does great damage to your self."

What does it mean,   {2}
"favor and disgrace: this means being upset"?
Favor is degrading:
Gaining it you will be upset
losing it you will be upset.
This is what it means,
"favor and disgrace: this means being upset."

What does it mean,   {3}
"high rank does great damage to your self"?
What is the source of the great damage done me?
It is because I have a self.
If I had no self, what damage could be done me?
This is what it means,
"high rank does great damage to your self."

Yes: {4}
A valuing of one's self
    that regards the self the same as the world—
this means one can be entrusted with the world.
A loving of one's self
    that regards the self the same as the world—
this means one can be given the world.

Being in the public eye disturbs your peace of mind. You might feel fine during those times when you're well liked and successful. But as long as your identity is wrapped up in your success there will be some underlying anxiety {2}. The answer is not to withdraw from public life. It is rather to cease to identify yourself with your public image {3}. A person who doesn't insist on being treated as someone special, is after all the best kind of person to have in charge {4}.

The text of this chapter is difficult and translations vary widely. My understanding is new in many places and more than usually conjectural. (See "Additional Textual Notes.") I believe that {1} is a saying from a "hedonist" thinker like Yang* Chu. The original saying advises *shih** not to seek public office, because this disturbs one's peace of mind.[1] Saying {4} is related to sayings against self-promotion.* It celebrates* the supremely high status of spiritual "Emperor*" that a self-effacing person deserves (the meaning of "can be entrusted with the world.") In {4:3 and 7}, I take *i shen wei t'ien hsia/*"treat self as world" to mean: Attribute no special status to your self over against the rest of the world.

Sections {2–3} are "interpretations" of the Yangist saying by the Laoist composer. Section {2} captures fairly well the sense of the original: It is not only disgrace that is upsetting. Even if you are currently "in favor," you will be anxious about losing favor. (Compare the similarly worded 19[44]:1, which implies that "gaining" fame, not losing it, is the real cause of pain.) Section {3} however, turns the original meaning of the Yangist saying completely around. The saying advocates entirely avoiding high rank. But Laoists aspire to public office, and accordingly the composer's "interpretation" says that what is "damaging" (upsetting) is not occupying high office but "having a self"—that is, being concerned with one's public image or persona (see comments on this meaning of *shen*/self at 10[7]:2). The composer's thought in {2} and {3} is related to the sayings against desire* for status as something disturbing one's peace of mind. One who is not preoccupied with maintaining a public reputation can maintain peace of mind while in public office, and in fact this attitude will make one deserving of the highest leadership role {4}.

Three chapters are grouped here (18[13], 19[44], 20[46]) that speak of the way desire* for fame or wealth is mentally agitating* and so "damaging" to our being. (19[44] and 20[46] also share the theme of content/discontent.)

---

1. Compare *Mencius** 2A/2,1, quoted p. 105.

19[44]

Your fame or your self, which is closer to you?   {1}
Your self or your possessions, which counts for more?
Gaining or losing, which brings the pain?

Indeed: {2}
Very fond, much expended
much hoarding, heavy loss.

Be content and there will be no disgrace.   {3}
Know to stop and there will be no danger.   {4}

And you can last very long.   {5}

It might seem that, when you acquire more possessions or make a name for yourself, you are "adding" to what you are—all you need to worry about is losing these things. But the real problem lies in gaining, not in losing. In attaching so much importance to gaining these things, you are really just expending energy and wearing yourself out {2}, making your existence anxious and precarious by staking so much on what can easily be lost {1}. You should learn to stop this flow of your energy outward, and to rest content in your own being {3-4}. This is the ultimate security {5}.

Saying {1} counters the desire* for wealth and fame by calling to mind that loss of these things is painful only because one first became attached to gaining them. Saying {2} counters the same desire* by calling to mind the cost in energy and resources and by evoking the quasi-superstitious* feeling that the person who hoards wealth is setting himself up for a downfall. Sayings {3} and {4} (= 63[32]:3:4) use an oracle* formula. "Knowing to stop" in {4} refers to "stopping" the outward-directed mental activity of desiring fame and possessions mentioned in {1} and {2}, hence it has a meaning here similar to resting content* in yourself {3} and to the recurrent term *turning* back.* See further comments on the phrase *knowing to stop* in 63[32]:3.

The composer's comment in {5} evokes the Laoist idea that remaining content within oneself conserves one's energy and so allows one to "last* long."

20[46]

When the world has Tao,   {1}
    they have no use for saddle horses,
    using them to haul manure.
When the world has no Tao,
    they raise war horses on sacred ground.

Nothing is more crime producing than desirable things   {2}
nothing is a worse misfortune than not being content
nothing makes for more guilt than desire for gain.

Yes: {3}
Be content with enough, and there will always be enough.

"Desirable things"—everyone wants them, but what do they do? They ruin your peace of mind {2} and set you at greedy war with your neighbors {1:4–5}. Rather than paying attention to what everyone considers "desirable," think of what is of solid practical use {1:1–3}. Contentment is an attitude, and the main key to being content is finding contentment in what you already have {3}.

Saying {1} is a normative* description of a society imbued with the spirit of Tao*, countering the desire* of Warring States rulers for territorial expansion and high living standards. It poses contrasting images: On the one hand, the ruler whose greed for more territory causes him to raise war horses wherever he can, even (sacrilegiously) on sacred ground. On the other hand, an ideal state in which people live simply and place no special value on luxury items like saddle horses. ("Hauling manure" is an extremely practical, "useful" task, in contrast to the luxury of pleasure riding. Compare 76[80]. "Sacred ground" in {1:5} follows Waley's understanding of *chiao* as a reference to a sacred mound outside the capital city that figured in ancient Chinese ritual. Others translate *chiao* as "suburb.") Saying {2} also counters the desire* for wealth. As in 79[3]:1, its three lines are complementary: "Desirable things" stir up "desire for gain," causing discontent, leading to the misfortune of crime and guilt. Note the emphasis on the damaging *personal* effects of desires—crime and guilt are added "misfortunes" for the discontented greedy person. Saying {3} counters the desire* for more by suggesting that contentment is a matter of one's state of mind, not how much one has.

21[12]

The five colors make people's eyes go blind   {1}
the five tones make people's ears go deaf
the five flavors make people's mouths turn sour.
Galloping and racing, hunting and chasing,
        make people's minds go mad.
Goods hard to come by corrupt people's ways.

And so the Wise Person: {2}
Goes by the belly, not by the eye.

Yes: {3}
He leaves 'that' aside, and attends to 'this'.

In the midst of ordinariness, stimulating things seem very attractive, apparently promising to enrich our lives. But this is like foods that excite the eye then pain the belly {2}. If you're looking for real enjoyment of the world, the most important thing is to preserve a healthy state of mind {3}, capable of subtle pleasures and a deeply satisfying relation to things—and this is what constant stimulation destroys {1}.

Saying {1} counters the desire of the Warring States upper classes for an exciting and luxurious life: Colorful clothes and decorations, fine music and food, horse racing and hunting, collecting rare objects. (*Five* is merely a conventional categorization, without special significance here. The colors: red, blue, yellow, white, black. The tones [of the ancient Chinese scale] are C, D, E, G, A. The flavors are sweet, sour, bitter, acrid, salty.) Note that the negative images posed in {1:1–4} are not moralistic, but call to mind the way overindulgence agitates* and damages one's mind and senses, an obstacle to the deep enjoyment and satisfaction in things possible to a Still* mind and healthy senses. (Rare goods corrupt people by arousing criminal desires; see 20[46]:2 and 79[3]:1. The parallelism implies that this corruption too is seen as a kind of "damage" to one's mind.) "The belly" in {2} is probably a metaphor for what is truly satisfying, as opposed to what is eye-catching but also ultimately agitating*. I believe that *this* in {3} originally referred to internal self-cultivation as opposed to a concern for external effectiveness ("that"). (See discussion under "This*".) The composer of this chapter probably is stretching its meaning here to refer to concern for one's state of mind (maintaining healthy senses), in contrast to concern for eye-catching but agitating* things out there. This reading makes the contrast this/that very similar to the contrast belly/eye.

This chapter and the next, 22[50], are directed against the attraction to a luxurious and exciting life.

22[50]

"Setting out to live is entering into death." {1}

"Thirteen are the life givers {2}
thirteen are the death bringers."
The thirteen body parts are also death spots
    in people's life and activity. Why?
Because they live life so lavishly.

So we hear: {3}
One who Excels at fostering life
"travels on land without meeting rhinoceros or tiger
enters combat without armor or weapon."

The rhinoceros finds no place to jab its horn {4}
the tiger finds no place to lay its claws
a weapon finds no place where its point can enter.
Why?
Because he has no death spot.

Sometimes the marvelous health of the body sustains a person and seems to make everything in life go right. Sometimes the body is what makes us vulnerable to every passing disease and danger. The difference? Some people protect and foster their life energy. Some people waste it in lavish living.

The wording of this chapter is difficult and has been variously translated. My understanding is new and conjectural. I think {1} was originally a pessimistic folk-saying to the effect that coming into the world at birth is also the first step toward death. The original point of {2:1–2} was that the same thirteen body parts that sustain our life also make us susceptible to death. ("The thirteen" are the four limbs and the nine apertures of the body mentioned in the *Nei* Yeh*.[1]) Lines {2:3–5} are an addition by the composer. They reinterpret *live* in {1}, so that "setting out into life" becomes "setting out to live it up" (to *sheng sheng chih hou*/"live life's thickness," compare the similar phrase in 51[75]:1). *This* ruins one's health and so is a first step toward death. The composer also reinterprets the saying in {2:1–2} so that the body parts are not *by nature* points of vulnerability ("death spots"), but become so because people "live it up." *Fostering life* {3} probably refers to a particular aspect of Laoist self-cultivation: Getting in touch with one's life-energy and fostering it, perhaps through some kind of meditation* (see further comments under "Life*" and "Yang* Chu"). Here this is contrasted with "living life lavishly." The marvelous benefits* ascribed to this in {3–4} indicate that Excel* has a strong meaning here, referring to highly developed self-cultivation. (Saying 33[55]:1 also pictures magical invulnerability as one result of self-cultivation.) The composer's thought here is related to Laoist criticism of mentally agitating* excitement as exhausting and the contrasting Laoist ideal of "lasting* long" by conserving one's health and energy.

The connection of the "state of mind" Laoists cultivated with *physical* health, evident here, is a point of connection between early Taoism and later Taoist groups who made physical self-cultivation much more central, through the use of diet, physical exercises, breathing techniques, herbs and drugs, and so on.[2]

---

1. Quoted in Waley, 1958:48.
2. See Welch 1957: 101–112; Maspero 1981: 445–554; Kohn 1989 passim.

23[26]

Heaviness is the root of lightness   {1}
Stillness is the master of agitation.

And so the Wise Person: {2}
Travels all day, not departing from the heavy baggage wagon
although there are grand sights, he sits calmly aloof.
Why is this?
A 10,000-chariot lord,
mindful of his self, takes the world lightly.

Light, then lose the Root   {3}
agitated, then lose the mastery.

A mind needing constant stimulation is a shallow mind, a light-weight mind. Stimulation is a shallow space. Deep Stillness is where one's true worth lies. Even though it seems a heavy space, rest there.

Saying {1} probably borrows a formula from the speculation concerning the "conquest* cycle," to celebrate the superiority of the heaviness/Stillness* that Laoists cultivate over their opposites, lightness and agitation*. The metaphorical* image in {2:2–3} is that of a gentleman of very high status, traveling in a caravan. Where one might expect him to be sightseeing with others along the way, he unexpectedly plods along with the baggage wagon—something one would expect of the servants. The image serves as a metaphor for the ideal Laoist attitude, resting in a Still/heavy state of mind, in contrast to a mind attracted to exciting things.

The composer plays on several meanings of *heavy* and *light*. *Chung*/heavy also means "dignified." The heavy wagon is associated with the lord's "heavy" dignity, which in turn is an image for the value/dignity of the *shen*/self cultivated for its own sake. (Compare the contrast between *shen*/self and fame/possessions in 19[44]:1, and further comments on *shen* at 10[7]:2.) One who gravitates toward exciting but agitating* things loses the Stillness that is for Laoists the Root of the self's true dignity and its high status as *chün*/master {3}. An excited person becomes a "light" person of little consequence, as opposed to the person who learns to value his self and take the exciting external world lightly.

This chapter links the theme of mental agitation*, the target of the preceding chapters in Section 2, to the special recurrent term *Stillness**. Achieving mental Stillness is one of the central goals of Laoist self-cultivation, the theme of Section 3 to follow. Stillness and contentment are especially central ideas in Chapters 28[16], 29[52], 30[56], and 31[4].

3

Self-Cultivation

24[33]

One who understands others is clever   {1}
one who understands himself has Clarity.
One who wins out over others has power
one who wins out over himself is strong.

One who is content is wealthy   {2}
one strong in his practice is self-possessed.

One who does not leave his place is lasting   {3}
one who dies and does not perish is truly long lived.

Occupying yourself with figuring out the others and beating them, you lose the centeredness in yourself {1}. Gaining self-possession and contentment in yourself {2}—this takes practice, but brings real security {3}. Make this your project.

All three sayings here refer directly to self-cultivation. Saying {1} advises *shih** to give priority to self-cultivation over political achievement. (Compare 53[72]:4. "Understanding others" probably refers to the political skill of being a good judge of others.) Based on the use of *li hsing/*"vigorous practice" in the *Doctrine of the Mean*[1] to describe self-cultivation, I believe *ch'iang hsing/*"strong practice" in {2} is a reference to persevering effort in self-cultivation, leading to self-possession (*yu chih,* lit. "possess mind"). This gives one the internal "wealth" of a contented* mind. (This new interpretation gives {2} a strong connection to {1}.) I take *not leave* [your] *place* in {3:1} to mean something like "stay centered in yourself," in contrast to "losing yourself" in external preoccupations (see remarks on "Dwelling*" and on "know to stop" at 63[32]:3). This conserves one's energy and leads to "lasting*" longer. Line {3:2} may be an indication that some Laoists extrapolated from the enhanced vitality and deep sense of inner security self-cultivation brought them to an expectation of surviving death. (This is not, of course, the same thing as saying Laoists undertook self-cultivation *for the primary purpose of* achieving immortality, as Maspero[2] suggests.)

The connections suggested here between *being content* {2}, *not leaving one's place,* and *lasting* {3} are similar to the train of associations in 19[44]. One might think from other passages that Laoists advocated "being natural*," in the sense of leaving one's own being alone, not consciously trying to be any particular way. But the state of mind they tried to achieve clearly was an extraordinary one, and the phrase *winning out over oneself* in {1} shows that the process of achieving Laoist "naturalness" involved also some inner struggle with oneself.

Section 3 on self-cultivation opens with three chapters (24[33], 25[48], 26[59]) that speak primarily of the importance of self-cultivation and the great benefits to be gained from it. After this follow four chapters (27[10], 28[16], 29[52], 30[56]) that contain more instruction in the practice of Laoist self-cultivation.

---

1. 20,10.
2. 1981: 416, and see p. 237.

25[48]

"Doing Learning, one profits everyday."   {1}
Doing Tao, one suffers a loss everyday—
loses, and loses some more
and so arrives at not doing anything.

Doing nothing, nothing will remain not done.   {2}

Taking over the world: only by not working.   {3}

A person who sets to working,   {4}
doesn't have what it takes to take over the world.

Confucians say that doing Learning brings one some benefit every-day. One could say, cultivating Tao makes one suffer a loss—something is subtracted from one's being—everyday. Subtract over and over, and you will come to live in a space where there is no trying, no doing. Rule from this space, and everything will take care of itself. Only the Non Worker shows herself fit to be in charge of the world.

I think {1:1} is a Confucian* saying in praise of Learning, quoted as a take-off* point for a tongue-in-cheek Laoist reply: Laoist practice consists partly in stripping away those qualities people develop to win social admiration. There is probably an intended play on "doing*": "Doing Learning...Doing Tao*...not doing [anything]"; the last phrase describes a state of mind that is the goal of Laoist practice. (*Yi*/profit and *sun*/loss in {1} are usually translated by more neutral words like *add* and *subtract,* the meaning I give them in 36[42]:5. The composer's comments take advantage of this connotation of the words. But two passages in the Confucian *Analects*[1] use *yi/sun* in the more evaluative sense of "profit/loss," and this is the basis for my translation and interpretation here.) Sayings {2} {3} and {4} counter the tendency of rulers to want to "work* on" society; that is, to impose plans on it from without (see 62[29], 72[64]). Sayings {2} and {3} (a version of 77[57]:1:3) celebrate* the marvelous benefits* that come from ruling in a "not-doing*" spirit. The results of this are pictured in exaggerated utopian imagery: "Take over the world" suggests that this leadership style will attract the allegiance of all, and enable the "not-doing" ruler to become the new Emperor*, reuniting the Empire under his rule.

---

1. 16:4 and 15:30.

26[59]

"When it comes to governing the people and serving Heaven,   {1}
there's no one like a farmer."

Just being a farmer—   {2}
this means getting dressed early.
Getting dressed early means increasing one's store of Te
increasing one's store of Te, then nothing is impossible
nothing impossible, then no telling the limit
no telling the limit, then one can possess the state.

One who possesses the Mother of the state   {3}
can last a long time.

This means having deep roots and strong foundations,   {4}
the Way of 'lasting life, good eyesight into old age'.

Getting to that quality of mind is not a matter of just thinking about it. It is like farming—a lot of hard work and very slow results. But the results are solid; they put you in possession of the one thing necessary, the foundation of the world. With it you can manage anything.

I think {1} was originally a paradoxical saying to the effect that a (simple? hard-working?) peasant farmer would make the best ruler. ("Governing the people and serving Heaven*" is a conventional way of describing the ruler's task.) But in {2} the composer takes the "farmer" as an image of someone working hard at self-cultivation, "getting dressed early" to store up Te*/charisma:power. (Mencius* also speaks[1] of "rising at cockcrow" to practice virtue.) Saying {2} celebrates the marvelous benefits* of this accumulated Te, which translates into irresistible political power (here described in idealized and exaggerated terms. Further marvelous powers are ascribed to accumulated Te in 33[55]:1.) Saying {3} celebrates the marvelous *personal* benefits* ("lasting* long") gained by "possessing the Mother* of the State." I take *kuo chih mu*/"State's Mother" as equivalent to "Mother of the World" (29[52]:1): Both phrases refer to the ideal foundations of Chinese society and culture. Laoists felt that the quality of mind they were cultivating *was* this foundation. I take {4:2} to be a conventional description of a ripe and healthy old age, that is, lasting* long by conserving one's energy.

1. 7A/25,1.

27[10]

When 'carrying your soul,' embracing the Oneness,　　　　　{1}
can you be undivided?

When 'concentrating *ch'i*', bringing about Softness,
can you be like an infant?

When 'cleansing and purifying the mysterious mirror,'
can you be without blemish?

When 'loving the people and caring for the kingdom,'
can you be without knowledge?

When 'the Doors of Heaven open and shut,'
can you remain Feminine?

When 'Clarity and bareness penetrate everywhere,'
can you remain not doing?

Produce and nourish.　　　　　{2}
Produce but don't possess
work but don't rely on this
preside but don't rule.
This is mysterious Te.

About meditation: At first you are nervous, your mind at odds with your body energy. Give the energy all of your attention. Think of embracing it, "carrying" it with your mind. Slowly identify with it, becoming less divided in yourself. Things will feel softer, infantlike, womanlike, gentle. With softness gradually comes mental clarity, things press less insistently. With long practice the mind becomes fresh, a clear mirror for reality seen plainly and without trouble. Sometimes you will hear or see things, or travel in your mind—like passing through the gates of Heaven. What is important is to retain the femininity of your soft mind. With this you can manage all your responsibilities well and selflessly {2}.

Saying {1} is the most explicit and detailed instruction for meditation* in the *Tao Te Ching*. Many of the terms are common ones: *Embracing the Oneness*, Softness*, Clarity*, Femininity*, not doing*, infancy** (for *without knowledge* see comments on "Understanding*"). Unfortunately, there also seem to be many esoteric phrases (placed in single quotation marks), whose concrete reference is now lost to us. Groups of people who meditate regularly often develop a highly differentiated awareness of inner states and movements and a special vocabulary to describe them, which outsiders always will have difficulty understanding. The paraphrase gives my best conjectures (based partly on attempts to practice what I think is being said). I think the primary reference of words like *p'o*/soul is to concrete internal self-perceptions, perhaps in this case to bodily energy concretely felt by someone in introspective meditation. (If this is so, ancient Chinese *theories* about the *p'o*/"bodily soul" and *hun*/"spiritual soul" are not important to the meaning in this context.) *Chuan-ch'i*/"concentrate *ch'i**" may refer to some special meditation technique, but it may mean simply "[mentally] concentrate."[1] "Heaven's Gate" may reflect the theme of the "spirit journey," a feeling of being mentally transported through spiritual realms. This is common in shamanistic traditions, of which some survivals reflected in the contemporary *Chuang* Tzu*[2] and the *Ch'u tz'u*[3] mention passing through heavenly gates. Saying {2} (a version of 42[2]:5, 52[77]:3, and 65[51]:4) counters the desire of rulers to capitalize on their achievements for self-promotion*. Laoist Te*/virtue expresses itself instead in a self-effacing spirit.

The stanza in {1} beginning "when 'loving the people'" is advice for the ruler, so I believe it was not an original part of the meditation instruction, but a connective* addition added by the same person who added {2}. The purpose of both additions is to emphasize that meditation is preparation for ruling (compare 26[59]:1–2, 37[14]:5).

1. See *Mencius** (6A/9,3) where *chuan-hsin*/"concentrate mind" describes the concentration of a chess player.
2. See Watson, 1968: 119, quoted and discussed p. 208.
3. Quoted p. 195.

28[16]

Push Emptiness to the limit,   {1}
watch over Stillness very firmly.

The thousands of things all around are active—   {2}
I give my attention to Turning Back.
Things growing wild as weeds
all turn back to the Root.

To turn back to The Root is called Stillness.   {3}
This is 'reporting in'
'reporting in' is becoming Steady.
Experiencing Steadiness is Clarity.

Not to experience Steadiness   {4}
is to be heedless in one's actions—bad luck.

Experiencing Steadiness, then one is all-embracing   {5}
all-embracing, then an impartial Prince
Prince, then King
King, then Heaven
Heaven, then Tao
Tao, then one lasts very long.

As to destroying the self,   {6}
there will be nothing to fear.

Everything wants to be active. The mind is active, things are active {2}. Caught up entirely in activity, they lose the Still center—Still, Empty, Steady, Clear {1, 3}. Turn back to this stillness and the world around will also become still {2}. In gaining it, you will feel like you are losing the self that is part of the active world {6}. But activity passes. This is the enduring root of everything worthwhile, the center of the world {5}.

Saying {1} is a brief instruction* in self-cultivation. Saying {2} is instruction in "turning* back," one description of what one does in Laoist meditation* (compare 34[40]:1). Based on a passage in the *Chuang* Tzu[1] I believe the saying pictures a shift* in the world as perceived, due to a shift in one's own mental state: To a racing, agitated* mind, the world seems full of nervous activity too. (*Tso*/active is the negative opposite of Stillness in 81[37]:2.) "Turning back" describes Stilling* one's active mind, so that one perceives the agitated multiplicity of the world as though it stems from a single Still origin (see "Origin*"). "Growing wild as weeds" [lit. "weedy weedy"] evokes a sense of disordered multiplicity. Saying {3:4} (= 33[55]:3:2) celebrates the way that Steadiness* is linked* to Clarity*. Saying {4} uses an oracle* formula to picture a life "out of control" because it lacks Steadiness*. Saying {5} celebrates the cosmic* importance of Steadiness: One who achieves it occupies the spiritual status of the Emperor*, and is one with the cosmic principles Heaven* and Tao*. Saying {6} also occurs in 29[52]:3 in close conjunction with a saying about "turning* back," suggesting that Laoists sometimes experienced the movement toward Stillness, away from external activity, as one threatening a loss of *shen*/self, a loss of a tangible identity as part of the world (compare 13[20]:4–5, 14[23]:1–3 and comments on *shen*/self at 10[7]:2). This saying (using an oracle* formula) is reassurance in the face of this frightening experience.

Line {3:1} is a connective* addition by the composer, connecting {2:4} to "Stillness" in {1:2}. In {3:2–3} "reporting in" translates *fu ming,* a phrase sometimes used of a soldier or emissary reporting back to his superior,[2] suggesting that the Still quality of mind is a "command post" to which one returns from "action in the field." Line {5:6} departs from the images of the rest of {5}, and so I think it is another connective* addition by the composer. "Lasting*" refers to the security one finds in Tao, in contrast to "losing oneself" {6} which might seem to threaten.

---

1. Watson 1968: 122, quoted and discussed p. 246–47.
2. See Legge 1891 ad loc. Compare *fan-ming* in *Mencius** 3A/2, 3.

29[52]

The world has a Source, the Mother of the World. {1}

Once you get the Mother {2}
then you understand the children.
Once you understand the children
turn back and watch over the Mother.

As to destroying the self, {3}
there will be nothing to fear.

Close your eyes {4}
shut your doors,
till the end of your life you will not get tired.
Open your eyes
carry on your business,
till the end of your life you will not be safe.

Keeping your eyes on the Small Thing is called Clarity {5}
watching over Weakness is called strength.

Engage with the flashing things {6}
turn back to Clarity
do not deliver yourself to disaster.

This is cultivating Steadiness. {7}

Being constantly outgoing, living on the surface, wears you out. And you never truly understand the truth about things in the world. It is not safe. Withdraw sometimes, shut your door, go inside {4}. Find that space where the truth of everything resides {2}. In contrast to the active world, what is there will at first appear small and weak {5}, and you will feel like you are losing your self being there {3}. But there you will find a sustaining presence—strength, Clarity, and Steadiness {5,6}.

Saying {2:1–2} celebrates the benefits* of *te mu*/"getting [the] Mother*," one description of the goal of Laoist self-cultivation. This puts one in touch with the foundation of all meaning in the world, and thus gives one an intuitive true understanding* of all worldly situations (the Mother's "children." Compare 43[1]:5). Saying {3} reassures one against the fear of losing oneself one might experience in Laoist self-cultivation. (See comments on this saying at 28[16]:6.) Saying {4} is instruction in Laoist self-cultivation, which sometimes requires withdrawing from the world to Still* one's mind. It is closely related to sayings picturing excitement and agitation* as exhausting. Saying {5} celebrates the way that cultivating one quality of mind is linked* to the achievement of other ideal qualities as well. (The *hsiao*/"small thing" is the frail-feeling quality of mind cultivated. Compare the *hsiao*/small:insignificant:"of-no-account" Tao in 63[32]:1 and 64[34]:4.)

I think the origin* statement in {1} is the composer's lead into {2}. The composer's warning in {2:3–4} goes against the original celebratory point of the saying in {2:1–2}: Don't get too caught up in the "children" (worldly affairs) and forget to turn* back to the [internal] Mother. I think *huang*/"flashing [things]" in {6} refers to lively events in the world (compare the same word in 30[56]:3). Hence, this term parallels "children" in {2} (and "carrying on your business" in {3}). Correspondingly, "turning* back to [internal] Clarity" parallels "turning back to the Mother" in {2}.

30[56]

Those who understand are not talkers   {1}
talkers don't understand.

Close your eyes   {2}
shut your doors.

Dampen the passion   {3}
untie the tangles
make the flashing things harmonious
make the dust merge together.
This is called the mysterious Merging.

Yes: {4}
You cannot get close
you cannot stay away
you cannot help It
you cannot harm It
you cannot treasure It
you cannot look down on It.

Yes: {5}
It is the Treasure of the World.

Excited, talking away, the mind in tangles, the world all heated up
{1–2}. But there is something else, something always there whether
you are attending to it or not {4}. This something will untangle the
world. It is a place where everything merges together harmoniously
{3}. It is the world's treasure {5}.

Saying {1} criticizes admiring only impressive appearances*, posing
the contrasting images of impressive but empty speech, on the one
hand, and silent wisdom, on the other. Saying {2} is a fragment of the
saying in 29[52]:4, urging regular withdrawal from the world to Still*
the mind. Saying {3:1–4} (= 31[4]:3) functions here as meditation*
instruction. *Tangles, flashing things,* and *dust* describe the agitated and
confused state of the world as it appears to an agitated* state of mind.
If one can bring about a shift to a calmer state of mind, this causes a
corresponding shift* in the character of the world as experienced.
Saying {4} is also about meditation*, criticizing the dominating,
"doing*" attitude a meditator might take, thinking of the quality of
mind cultivated as something produced by one's own action. The
saying reflects instead the Laoist feeling that this hypostatized* quality of mind (left unnamed here) has an autonomous existence, which
one tries to find within and identify with, rather than "produce"
(compare the criticism in 33[55]:4). In its genre this saying resembles
37[14]:3,4, 38[21]:2, 46[35]:3. Saying {5} (= 48[62]:7) celebrates the
cosmic* importance of Tao.

As in 16[5]:3 and 14[23]:1–2, the composer probably takes "talking" in {1} as an example of excited* and exhausting activity (somewhat contrary to the original intention of the saying). Sayings {3} and
{4} are important for showing the meaning of *t'ung*/Merging*, used as
a special term here and in 43[1]:4–5. Line {3:4} uses *t'ung* as a verb,
"*make* the dust *merge* together." The composer's connective* addition
then describes the resultant state of mind as *hsüan t'ung*/"mysterious
Merging," implying that when the "dust" of the world settles in our
experience, the internal forces of our mind also are "merged together" rather than in conflict, because we withdrew from the world and
quieted our strong feelings. But then, by his placement of {4}, the
composer indicates (as in 43[1]:4–5) that he takes "The Merging" also
to refer to the hypostatized* quality of mind Laoists cultivate, pictured in {4} as having an autonomous existence.

31[4]

Tao being Empty,   {1}
it seems one who uses it will lack solidity.

An abyss,   {2}
it seems something like the ancestor
    of the thousands of things.

It dampens the passion   {3}
it unties the tangles
it makes the flashing things harmonious
it makes the dust merge together.

Deep,   {4}
it is perhaps like an enduring something.

I don't know of anything whose offspring it might be—   {5}
it appears to precede God.

Some things are inspiring, stirring, exciting. They also heat up the world and make it feel more tangled. Tao feels different: subtle, hardly perceptible {1}, but deep and fundamental, more fundamental than God {2, 4, 5}. Its subtle presence does not make the world more exciting and disturbing, but more quiet and filled with harmony {3}.

Saying {1} gives a normative* description of the way of being of one who has Tao: Because Tao is very intangible ("Empty*"), such a one does not project a "solid*" presence in the world. (I follow Karlgren's construal of these lines, departing from most other translators; see "Additional Textual Notes." See also comments on 6[15]:4, a version of this same saying.) Saying {2} is about Tao as the origin* of the world. ("Ancestor" in China not only referred literally to earlier progenitors of a noble family, these symbolized its idealized foundational spirit. So the unified spirit behind Laoist sayings can be called in 45[70]:2 "the ancestor" of the words.) Saying {3} (= 30[56]:3) functions here as a celebration of the great benefits* of cultivating Tao. (The same Chinese verbs can function as either indicatives or imperatives, and this allows the same words to describe benefits here and function as directives in 30[56]:3.)

By following {1–2} with {3}, the composer indicates that internally cultivating the "Empty" (subtle and very intangible) Tao produces a shift* in the world as experienced, calming it down. He also emphasizes the association between Tao as something "deep," and the image of Tao as primordial origin, "preceding God." I believe these two ideas have the same basis in Laoist experience: What is experienced as "deeper" and foundational is expressed via the imagery of chronological priority (see further under "Origin*"). (Ti/God in {5} is a pre-Chou name for the supreme deity. Chou usage favored the name Heaven* instead, but ti continued to be used also, as here. In this period some kings began to claim Ti as a title for themselves.[1]) Note that the composer repeats words throughout this chapter that emphasize tentativeness: Huo/seems, ssu/perhaps, jo/"something like" "I don't know"). This is probably associated with the elusive character of the "Empty" Tao.

This chapter shares a saying, {3}, with the previous chapter, 30[56]. Instead of centering on instruction in self-cultivation like the previous four chapters in this section, its intent is primarily celebratory*, celebrating the cosmic* importance and wonderful benefits* that flow from the hypostatized* quality of mind cultivated. It shares this celebratory intent with the remaining chapters of this Section.

---

1. Bodde 1981: 105.

32[6]

"The Valley Spirit is undying."   {1}
This is mysterious Femininity.

The Abode of mysterious Femininity: {2}
This is the Root of Heaven and Earth.

It seems to endure on and on.   {3}

One who uses It never wears out.   {4}

There is a mental abode within that is like a valley: feminine, misty, low lying, empty space. It is the foundation of the world, and an inexhaustible source of energy for you.

Saying {2} celebrates the mental space ("abode") where Femininity* resides as a cosmic* foundation and origin*. ("Abode" translates *men*, more usually translated as "gate." See comments on "Dwell*," and on 43[1]:5 where *men*/abode also occurs. Because Femininity is an hypo-statized* mental quality, there is no significant difference between Femininity and the mental "space" that feels Feminine.) Saying {4} celebrates one of the great benefits* of the mental quality Laoists cul-tivate—inexhaustible energy, enabling one to last* long. (Compare 16[5]:2. This theme is related to sayings against agitated*, "exhaust-ing" excitement.)

I believe that {1} was originally a folk saying about the spirit of a certain valley (ancient Chinese believed in many such nature spirits). But among those devoted to self-cultivation,[1] *shen*/spirit was also used to refer to the mind or to a certain quality of mind. (See also the saying about spirits in 37[14]:1, applied there also to the quality of mind Laoists cultivate.) And "Valley*" is associated in 6[15]:2 and 17[28]:1 with the ideal Laoist state of mind (and see 44[41]:3). Hence the composer reinterprets the popular saying to refer to the "Valley Spirit" that Laoists cultivated internally, associating it with the quali-ty "Femininity" {2}. The "immortality" mentioned in the saying is reinterpreted in {3–4} as reflecting the Laoist theme that the mental quality they cultivate is a lasting*, inexhaustible source of energy.

---

1. See discussion p. 194 n. 5.

33[55]

One who has an abundance of Te   {1}
is like a newborn child:
Poisonous bugs will not bite it
fierce beasts will not snatch it
birds of prey will not attack it.

Its bones are Soft, its sinews Weak,   {2}
but its grip is firm.
It has not known the union of man and woman,
but its organs get aroused:
Vital energy at its height.
It will scream all day without getting hoarse:
Harmony at its height.

To experience Harmony is called being Steady   {3}
to experience Steadiness is called Clarity.

'Increasing life': ominous   {4}
'the mind controlling the *ch'i*': forcing.

Things are vigorous, then grow old: {5}
A case of 'not-Tao'.
Not-Tao, soon gone.

How do you increase vitality? Not by forcing yourself to be up; this will quickly fade {4–5}. Find the softness in which strength lives, the energy that is self-generating. Learn steady smoothness in intense activity {2}. This makes you an innocent in the world—harmless, attracting no harm {1}.

Saying {1} celebrates the marvelous benefits* attributed to the Te*/virtue Laoists cultivate. Laoist Te can be described partly as a kind of fresh innocence that radiates peace, conveyed here in the image of the innocent child safe from dangerous insects and wild animals (compare 22[50]:3). Saying {2} uses the infant* image as an extended metaphor*, illustrating several aspects of the quality of mind Laoists cultivate: Softness*/Weakness, Harmony*, and vital energy. The arousal of sexual organs without sexual contact is probably an image of ching/"vital energy" generated completely from within rather than through external stimulation. (Ching/"vital energy" occurs in 38[21]:2, and is also a focus of self-cultivation in the Nei* Yeh[1]). "Screaming all day without getting hoarse" is an important corrective for the tendency to take Laoist mental Stillness* literally, as though it signifies the simple absence of any vigorous activity. Here we have the ideal of a very vigorous action that is yet smooth and Harmonious* (not "agitated*"), because it arises out of a different (unstimulated, basically "Still") state of mind. (Compare 6[15]:3, which describes first stilling the mind and then slowly returning to being active.) Saying {3} celebrates the link* between various qualities of mind Laoists cultivate ({3:2} = 28[16]:3:4). In {4}, I take "increasing sheng/life" and "the mind controlling the ch'i*" as descriptions of the self-cultivation practices of others, who attempt to increase their internal energy (ch'i) directly, by will power. (Such practices also are criticized in the Mencius*,[2] as attempts to artificially "force*" things.) "Fostering sheng/life" describes a Laoist goal, too (see "Life*"). But this must be the indirect result of cultivating internal Softness and Stillness. Saying {5} (= 69[30]:5) takes the seasonal flourishing and dying of plants as a negative metaphorical* image of what happens in human life when things are done in a pu-Tao*/"un-Tao-[like]" spirit: One gets a short-lived flash in the pan rather than a "slow burn," the lasting* inexhaustible energy associated with Tao (see 16[5]:2). (Saying {5} follows a criticism of "forcing*" in 69[30] as well. In content it is related to sayings critical of exhausting agitation* and excitement.) The composer's point here is that a forcing* approach to self-cultivation will not produce the kind of internal Softness/vital-energy/Harmony Laoists aim at.

---

1. See discussion p. 187.
2. 2A/2, 9–10 and 16, discussed p. 111–12.

34[40]

Turning Back is Tao movement   {1}
being Weak is Tao practice.

"The thousands of things in the world are born of Being"   {2}
Being is born of Nothing.

What is the essential practice? Reverse the striving for strength, for tangible Being. Turn back to what feels weak, Nothing. This space is the essential source.

Saying {1} gives a normative* description of Laoist self-cultivation. I think "Tao*" has an "adjectival" meaning here, referring to specifically Laoist practice and goals. Read this way, "Tao* practice" (*tao chih yung,* lit. "Tao's use*") is a description of Laoist self-cultivation—here, the cultivation of Weakness*. (Compare the connection of "using Tao" with being Empty* in 31[4]:1.) The parallel phrase "Tao's movement" would then refer to the internal movement characteristic of one engaged in Laoist practice. Because "Being" plays no positive role elsewhere, but is contrasted with "Nothing*" in 42[2]:2 and 15[11]:2, I think that the first line of {2} is a bit of non-Laoist speculation, placed here only as a take-off* point for a Laoist line using origin* imagery to celebrate the "priority" (the more foundational importance) of the "Nothingness*" they cultivate, pictured as a cosmic* force. I believe my understanding of both sections here is new.

If *wu*/Nothing in {2} is understood experientially, to refer to scarcely tangible internal qualities, it is close in meaning to "Weakness" in {1}. (*Wu yu*/"No Being" is connected with Weakness also in 47[43]:1.).

This chapter and the two to follow (35[39], 36[42]) celebrate the cosmic importance of the quality of mind Laoists cultivate by picturing it as the origin* of the world.

35[39]

Those that of old got The Oneness: {1}
The sky got The Oneness,
    and by this became clear.
The earth got The Oneness,
    and by this became steady.
The spirits got The Oneness,
    and by this obtained their powers.
The rivers got The Oneness,
    and by this became full.
The thousands of things got The Oneness,
    and by this came to life.
The princes and kings got The Oneness,
    and by this became the Standard for the World.
This is how things came about.

The sky, without what makes it clear,
    is likely to crack.
The earth, without what makes it steady,
    is likely to quake.
The spirits, without what gives them powers,
    are likely to vanish.
The rivers, without what makes them full,
    are likely to dry up.
The thousands of things, without what gives them life,
    are likely to perish.
The princes and kings,
    without what makes them *eminent and noble,*
    are likely to fall.

Yes, the eminent takes the common and ignored as a root   {2}
the noble takes the lowly as a foundation.
And so the princes and kings call themselves
'the orphan...,' 'the poor...,' 'the destitute...'
Is this not using the common and ignored as a root?
Is it not so?

Yes, enumerate the carriage parts—still not a carriage.   {3}

He doesn't wish to glitter and glitter like jade   {4}
he falls like a stone, falling into oblivion.

418

The one thing necessary is something that does not glitter in the world. Cultivating it means being willing to go unrecognized, take the low place. But this nothing is the foundation of the order of the world.

Saying {1} is an origin* saying, picturing the present world order as the result of everything at the beginning having "gotten the Oneness*." (It is an order-from-chaos cosmogony, different from most other Laoist origin sayings, which picture how things first came into existence.) Te i/"get* [the] Oneness" is primarily a description of the goal of Laoist self-cultivation (compare te mu/"get [the] Mother" in 29[52]:2). Saying {1} celebrates the cosmic* importance of this project, picturing it as what gave rise to and sustains the order of the cosmos. (Note that here the earthly rulers of China take their place as fundamental elements of the cosmic order, an important part of Chou dynasty Emperor* ideology.) Saying {2:1-2} speaks against impressive* appearances, posing the counterimage of the ruler who gains true nobility and respect by his deferential and self-effacing manner (see "Low*"). Lines {2:3-4} give a stock Laoist example of this idea, commented on at 36[42]:4. Saying {4} criticizes self-promotion*. The last line reads literally "fall fall like stone." But lo/fall means also "die," which I take metaphorically as the opposite of "glittering," that is, falling out of sight so far as the conventional world is concerned. (This is connected also with "low" in {2}). The translation of {3} (lit. "count carriage not carriage") is very conjectural. I think that the point is this: What makes a carriage one unified thing is not identical with the collection of tangible carriage parts, but is something single yet intangible—"the Oneness" of {1}. (Compare 45[70]:2, which implies that a single but difficult to grasp principle constitutes the unity behind the multiplicity of Laoist sayings. The parts of a horse are the basis for a similar image in the Chuang* Tzu.[1] And see the very similar use of the chariot image in the early Buddhist Questions of King Melinda.[2])

In the final lines of {1}, "eminent and noble" interrupt the parallelism with the first stanza and provide a connection with {2}. These words are a connective* alteration by the composer, suggesting an equation between adopting a "lowly" stance in society, on the one hand, and "gaining the Oneness," on the other. These are two aspects of the quality of mind and way of being Laoists cultivate.

---

1. Watson 1968: 290.
2. Stryk 1969: 90–93.

36[42]

Tao produced The Oneness   {1}
The One produced Two
Two produced Three
Three produced the thousands of things.

The thousands of things: {2}
Turn their backs on the quiet and dark
and embrace the aggressive and bright.

An Empty *ch'i* brings Harmony.   {3}

What people look down upon: {4}
to be orphaned, poor, destitute.
But the kings and princes
    make these names into titles.

Yes, things: {5}
Sometimes you reduce them, and they are enlarged
sometimes you enlarge them, and they are reduced.

What another has taught, I also teach: {6}
"A violent man will not reach his natural end."
I will make of this the father of my teaching.

Man runs to escape what he has forgotten.[1] All want to enlarge themselves—to become strong, to win, to make a name. People flee from what appears soft, weak, empty in themselves. But this is the foundation, the source of everything important. Turn back to it.

Saying {1} is an origin* saying, celebrating Tao as the single foundation of meaning in the world of distracting variety and multiplicity. (Many commentators try to identify what "Two" and "Three" stand for, but no contemporary source I know of gives any solid clue about this.) Saying {2} describes the tendency of "things*" (people) to embrace* the yang/aggressive:bright, socially desirable qualities, and to shun the yin*/quiet:dark ones—an unfortunate tendency in Laoist eyes. (Yin and yang, which became central to later Taoism are mentioned only here in the Tao Te Ching.) Saying {3} links* two qualities: Cultivating an internal Empty* ch'i*/energy also brings mental Harmony*. Saying {5} counters the desire of rulers to project an impressive* presence, posing contrasting images of the person whose deferential (self-"reducing") manner enhances ("enlarges") people's respect for him, and the person whose attempts to impress diminish this respect. Section {4} refers to what was apparently a custom among some Chinese nobility whereby a King Wu, for example, would refer to himself self-deprecatingly as "the poor Wu." The composer here (and in 35[39]:2) refers to this custom as an example of how a self-deprecating manner gains one true respect. Saying {6:2} is introduced as a non-Laoist saying, probably of popular origin (compare, "He who lives by the sword will die by the sword.")

The composer gives no direct hint of the connection he sees between these various sayings, and so my reconstruction is more than usually conjectural here. I think {2} is the pivotal saying that unites the piece: The tendencies toward self-glorification and violence criticized in {4–6} count as "embracing* yang," the masculine aggressiveness implicitly deplored in {2}. Violence, as the extreme of yang, here represents yang qualities in general. This is why the composer can claim that the popular saying against violence is the main principle behind (the "father" of) all Laoist teaching*. All this contrasts with the yin Feminine Emptiness Laoists cultivate {3}. To reverse the general gravitation toward yang, turning back to yin, is also to identify with the most fundamental cosmic reality, Tao as the source of all true meaning in the world {1}. This turning back to the yin Tao is a reversal, on a psychological level, of the original cosmogonic process described in {1}. (According to Girardot,[2] just such a reversal played a part in meditation practices in later esoteric Taoism.)

---

1. I owe this line to a student whose name I have forgotten.
2. 1983: 282–292.

37[14]

"Look for It, you won't see It: It is called 'fleeting'.   {1}
Listen for It, you won't hear It: It is called 'thin'.
Grasp at It, you can't get It: It is called 'subtle'."

These three lines   {2}
    are about something that evades scrutiny.
Yes, in it everything blends and becomes one.

Its top is not bright   {3}
Its underside is not dim.
Always unnameable, It turns back to nothingness.
This is the shape of something shapeless
the form of a nothing
this is elusive and evasive.

Encountering It, you won't see the front   {4}
following It, you won't see Its back.

Keep to the Tao of the ancients   {5}
and so manage things happening today.

The ability to know the ancient sources,   {6}
this is the main thread of Tao.

When you're sitting, trying to get in touch with the Softness, the One important thing, it evades your grasp—like a spirit that appears here, then there, then is gone {1}. You think you see it, then it recedes into nothing. This is the only way to describe the presence that is formless {3}. But in this practice we achieve a oneness {2}. And we come in contact with the deep sources of all things {4}, the ancient sources that enable us to handle whatever comes to us today {5}.

Saying {1} is a version of a saying about spirits, quoted also in the *Doctrine of the Mean.*[1] (Compare a similar use of a saying about a spirit in 32[6]:1.) Sayings {3 and 4} describe the experience of trying to grasp an elusive mental quality one is cultivating in Laoist meditation* (compare 38[21]:2, 46[35]:3, 30[56]:4). Saying {5} describes a benefit* of cultivating Laoist Tao, here pictured as the true Tao taught in the ancient*, idealized Golden Age. This will enable *shih** to handle any contemporary problems they encounter as government administrator-advisers. Saying {6} is a normative* description of what Laoist self-cultivation entails. As in 11[38]:6, *Tao* here probably is short for "cultivating Tao." I take "know the ancient source(s)" of things to mean gaining an intuitive understanding* of the deep truth about affairs. (As often, "ancient" serves to express what we more commonly express by images of "depth." See further under "Origin*." Note that here *Tao* is not the name of the ancient source that one knows, but of the practice by which one comes to know it.) Section {2} reads more literally: "these three, cannot be scrutinized, yes blend and become one." It seems very unlikely that "these three" refers to three different *things* mentioned in {1}, which "become one." It makes more sense to suppose that "these three" refers to the three-line *saying* in {1}, which is *about* a presence or mental quality incapable of being grasped through close mental scrutiny. In this mental space everything is Merged*, "blends and becomes one." This observation is a partial basis for my solution to the puzzle about the meaning of 43[1]:4:1, reading literally "these two, merged." That is, it refers to the previous two-line *saying* in 43[1]:3, which is (partly) *about* the state of "not desiring," which 43[1]:4 identifies with a mentally Still* state called *t'ung/*"the Merging*." Mencius[2] shows a similar use of "these two." Compare also "these two" and "these three" in 80[65]:4 and 78[19]:2.

---

1. 16,2, discussed p. 197 n. 41.
2. 4A/7,1.

38[21]

The impression made by magnificent Te   {1}
comes only from Tao.

Tao is a something   {2}
but elusive, but evasive.
Evasive, elusive,
in it lies the Pattern.
Elusive, evasive,
in it lies something substantial.
Shadowy, dim.
In it lies vital energy.
This energy is very strong
in it lies true genuineness.

From ancient times until today   {3}
Its name has not been forgotten
allowing us to see the beginnings of everything.

How do I recognize the form   {4}
    of the beginnings of everything?
By this.

Sitting, trying to grasp it, it eludes your mind. But this elusive something is also the most substantial and real thing there is. In it lies the key to recovering the normative pattern, vital energy at its best, human genuineness in its perfection {2}. If you want to radiate goodness, this is where to be {1}. Being there gives insight into the nature of whatever you meet {3}. What's the secret? Polish the mirror of your pure mind, and look {4}.

Saying {1} celebrates one of the benefits* of Tao: One who has it radiates a subtle but powerful presence (Te*). Saying {2:3–10} describes the experience of one at meditation*, trying to grasp an internal presence which one feels as elusive but also as yet containing in itself the highest qualities. *Ching*/"vital energy" is an object of internal cultivation in the *Nei* Yeh,[1] and Laoist cultivation in 33[55]:2, illustrated there by the image of the self-generating sexual energy of an infant. In {2:4} I translate *hsiang* (translated "Image" in 46[35]:1) as Pattern, on the basis of the *Chuang Tzu*'s use of this term as a normative pattern for action.[2] Saying {3} celebrates one of the benefits* of cultivating Tao: Tao's "name" (=its power) enables the mind to see the "beginnings" of things; that is, to understand them "in depth," to understand the foundations of their true meaning (compare 37[14]:6, and further comments on origin*-sayings). In {4}, I think "How do I know...? By this." is a stock Laoist reply to demands for arguments in support of their opinions: "By this" refers to the powers of one's own mind, developed through self-cultivation. (See further under "This*." The formula occurs also in 61[54]:4 and 77[57]:2.)

I mark {2:1–2} as a connective* alteration by the composer mainly because of the repetition of *wu*/thing:substance in {2:1} and {2:6} ("a something" and "something substantial," respectively). This addition identifies the evasive something described in {2} as "Tao," and thus connects {2} to {1}. The juxtaposition of {3} and {4} implies that intuitions springing from the right state of mind (gained at meditation {2}) are the same as intuitions springing from the power given by Tao. This chapter and the previous one (37[14]) picture Tao as an hypostatized* internal presence which eludes the grasp of one who tries to grasp it introspectively. Both chapters end with the suggestion that cultivating this elusive presence enables one to understand* the truth about reality, seeing everything in relation to its source/foundation.

---

1. See the discussion p. 187.
2. See p. 198 n. 43.

39[25]

There was a chaotic something, yet lacking nothing   {1}
born before Heaven and Earth.
Alone.
Still.
Standing alone, unchanging.
Revolving, endlessly.
It can be thought of as Mother of the World.

I do not know its name,   {2}
one can call it 'Tao.'
The name of its powerful presence:
One can call it 'The Great One.'

Great means going forth   {3}
going forth means going far away
going far away means turning back.

Yes: {4}
Tao is great
Heaven is great
Earth is great
(the king is also great
In the universe there are four great ones
and the king takes his place as one of them).

Earth gives the rule for people
Heaven gives the rule for Earth
Tao gives the rule for Heaven
the rule for Tao: things as they are.

Sitting still, she saw something. Everything mixed together, but perfect. Nothing else existed. It circled around, forever. A vision of Tao, the Mother of the World {1–2}. Its greatness overflowed, and the world came to be. The present world has gone far from it, but everything secretly wants to return to Tao {3}, the ultimate cosmic norm. Where do we find this norm? By looking at concrete things in their naturalness {4}.

Saying {1} reads best as a description of a vision someone saw at meditation* (perhaps in a "spirit journey" like that evoked in 27[10]:1). If this is so, the cosmogonic, nonvisual comments ("born before Heaven and Earth...the Mother of the World") are probably additions to the original vision-description. "Chaotic" probably is associated with idea of the "Uncarved* Block." Saying {3} seems to encapsulate a basic aspect of the Laoist vision of reality: Tao is the origin* and foundation of everything (everything has "gone out" from its greatness). But the social atmosphere in which we now live represents an alienation ("going far") from that source, due to the development of superficial social conventions. The true inner desire of everything is to "turn* back" to Tao (the object of Laoist self-cultivation). Sayings {4:2–4 and 8–10} celebrate the status of Tao as supreme cosmic* norm, above the principles of Heaven* and Earth conventionally thought to be supreme.

The lines about the *wang*/Emperor:king in {4:5–7} seem to stray from the main point of the saying in {4}, going out of the way to reaffirm the traditional Chinese belief that the Emperor is one of the pillars of the cosmic order (see 35[39]:1). These lines may have been added to please a royal patron who claimed the title of Emperor*,[1] or perhaps to correct genuinely "anarchistic" tendencies within the Laoist school itself. The final line of {4} seems anticlimactic, and I suspect it was added by the composer of this chapter to make a point similar to that of 38[21]:4. After the mystical flight in {1}, he wants to emphasize the very concrete, everyday character of Tao as it appears in our experience: *Tao* is just the name for a quality we perceive in things when they (and we) are in an ideal *tzu-jan*/natural state of Stillness.

Placing this chapter last in this section reflects my view that cosmic images are best understood as "climaxes" following on the "build-up" provided by the more mundane and practical aspects of Laoist wisdom. This stands in contrast to traditional interpretations of the *Tao Te Ching* that treat cosmic ideas first, as the "foundation" of Laoist thought and an essential basis for understanding the practical "conclusions" deduced from this foundation.

---

1. See p. 96.

4

Knowledge, Learning, and Teaching

40[71]

"Aware but not aware of it: a high thing."   {1}
Not aware but aware of it: sick of this.
Simply sick of the sickness—and so no longer sick.

The Wise Person's lack of this sickness: {2}
He became sick of being sick, and so he's no longer sick.

Some say to have true awareness but to be unselfconsciously unaware of this is a high achievement. One could also say: It is a great thing if a person lacking true awareness is painfully aware of her lack. Is not the pain at not having it, a sign that she actually does have it?

Lines {1:1–2} read literally: "Know not know high / not know know sick." I believe the puzzle as to their meaning is best solved if we regard the first line as a saying quoted here only as a take-off* point for the second line, which plays with the same words to make a completely different point. Line {1:1} is a saying in praise of the modest person who has great understanding but is unpretentious about this—he makes nothing of this and ignores it. Line {1:2} is about the person who has come to realize that he lacks true understanding* and is distressed by ("sick of") the lack. This line then leads in to a Laoist saying in {1:3}, repeated in {2}. This saying suggests a cure for the "sickness" (lack of true understanding) that afflicts us all: Recognition that one's conventional views are defective, and distress at this, can only spring from something in oneself that has in germ a different, better way of seeing things. If this intuitive wisdom becomes strong enough, it creates enough revulsion at defective views to throw them off and replace them.

The first four chapters of Section 4 (40[71], 41[47], 42[2], 43[1]) deal with Laoist views about how one gains a true understanding* of the world, and what such an understanding consists in.

41[47]

Understanding the world   {1}
    without going out the door.
Understanding Heaven's Way
    without looking out the window.

Traveling very widely, understanding very little.   {2}

And so the Wise Person: {3}
Knows without any going
names without any looking
accomplishes without any doing.

How is it that some people can travel the world and end up understanding nothing of life {2}? They develop no depth of understanding; they do not engage deeply with things they meet. A person who develops this depth can understand the true nature of things while hardly stepping out of her door {1, 3}.

Sayings {1} and {2} counter the assumption that to be a knowledgeable *shih** one must travel widely and learn about many different things. Saying {2} poses the negative image of the person whose wide travels have left him with a superficial understanding of things. Saying {1} evokes the exaggerated image of the person who develops the ability to intuitively understand* things in depth without ever leaving home; that is, by devoting himself to mental self-cultivation. For an example of the view these sayings oppose, see the opening passage of the *Hsün Tzu*.

The composer's images in {3} are even more exaggerated. For example, "naming*" things here probably means understanding the truth about issues and events, which for Laoists is the same thing as seeing them from the right perspective, in the right state of mind (43[1]:1:2 also seems to use *names* to mean the real nature of things). So "names without looking" is hyperbole, expressing this ideal by exaggerated contrast with the person who thinks that close inspection of details will give him true understanding. In the final line— "accomplishes [knowledge] without any doing [close examining]"— the composer stretches the meaning of *not doing* to apply to this area of life as well (see comments on 51[75]:2).

42[2]

| When everyone in the world | {1} |
| recognizes the elegant as elegant... | |

When everyone in the world   {1}
   recognizes the elegant as elegant...
then ugliness has just appeared.
When all recognize goodness as good...
then the not-good has just appeared.

Yes: {2}
'Being' and 'nothing' give birth one to the other
'the difficult' and 'the easy'
   give full shape to one another
'what excels' and 'what falls short' form one another
'the noble' and 'the lowly' give content to one another
the music and the voice harmonize with one another
the back and the front follow one another.
Always.

And so the Wise Person: {3}
Settles into his job of Not Doing
carries on his teaching done without talking.

The thousands of things arise and are active—   {4}
and he rejects none of them.

He is a doer but does not rely on this   {5}
he achieves successes but does not dwell in them.
He just does not dwell in them,
and so they cannot be taken away.

"If only we could teach everyone to label *elegant* only what is truly elegant," they say. But what would really happen? A person would learn to mark certain things off as outstandingly elegant—and suddenly her world also would be filled with many more ugly things standing out by contrast {1}. Some things appear to "excel" only if the world gets cut up into a few eye-catching things that "excel" and many rejects that appear to "fall short." Really, what "excels" stands on the shoulders of what is rejected as "falling short" {2}. Some things then are unnecessarily rejected {4}; and the world loses its fullness, becoming less than it was. People come to dwell in these half-realities, taking pride in their "noble" activities and their "excelling" status {5}. The person who understands this teaches without using names like *elegant* and *noble* {3}. She aims for success but does not depend on appearing "successful." She never rests on her laurels, and that is why no one can take them away {3} and {5}.

Sayings {1} and {2} are probably directed against "rectifying names*," the attempt to establish and enforce one correct way of using judgmental names like *good* and *bad*. I believe that {1} twists a common slogan favoring that program, which originally described a positive result. The Laoist twist describes a negative result instead: Conscious and pronounced evaluative labeling produces a negative shift* in the way people experience the world. Both {1} and {2} have as their background the Laoist idea of the Uncarved* Block: The ideal state of mind is a state in which one experiences reality directly—not overlain with conscious conventional judgmental concepts, not "cutting up" the world and pigeonholing things (see 63[32]:1–3). In this state one will see conventional good-bad opposites as parts of a whole, complementing each other like voice and musical accompaniment. Like the flexible Tao in 64[34]:2, one will not then "reject" those things one finds annoying {4}. (*Tso*/arise:act is a negative term in 28[16]:2 and 81[37]:2:3, so I believe {4} evokes an experience of things in which they assert themselves annoyingly.) Saying {3} (a version of 47[43]:2) emphasizes the "wordless" character of Laoist teaching* in contrast to the "naming" criticized in {1} and {2}. Saying {5} (a version of 27[10]:2, 52[77]:3, 65[51]:4) counters the tendency toward self-promotion*: The person who does not "dwell* in" (build his identity on) his external successes is the one who truly deserves the merit. One who relates to reality without accentuating conscious value judgments also will not focus on the public impression made by his work.

43[1]

The Tao that can be told is not the invariant Tao   {1}
the names that can be named are not the invariant Names.

Nameless, it is the source of the thousands of things   {2}
(named, it is 'Mother' of the thousands of things).

Yes: {3}
Always: being desireless,
    one sees the hidden essentials.
Always: having desires,
    one sees only what is sought.

These two lines are about The Merging—   {4}
it is when things develop and emerge from this
that the different names appear.

The Merging is something mysterious—   {5}
mysterious, and more mysterious,
the abode of all the hidden essences.

There is a place in the mind that is Still, desireless, where there are no concepts, no separate perceptions, just engagement with reality as a whole. There resides Tao, the source and norm of the world {1–2}. Residing here, one sees things the way they are {1, 5}. But something about the mind desires clear and separate things to see, labeled by clear and definite concepts {1, 3}—the beginning of life on the surface. People who live on the surface of their minds live on the surface of the world. Out of touch with the depths of their mind, the depth of things and events is hidden from them.

Saying {1} is directed against rectifying names*. Any Way that can be spelled out in concepts is not the true (Laoist) Tao. Situations in the world have a true nature ("name*"), but this needs to be understood in direct experience rather than grasped through concepts ("names"). Saying {2:1} pictures the nameless Tao as the origin* of the world. The interpretation of the rest of this chapter is very controversial and the following interpretation is new. Saying {3} celebrates a benefit* of the ideal "desireless*" state Laoists cultivate. Being in this Still* state causes a shift* in the way one experiences the world, allowing one to understand* the true inner meaning (*miao*/"hidden essentials") of events and situations. One whose mind becomes active, stirred up by desires and conceptual thinking, perceives only in categories that satisfy the seeking mind but cover up the real truth.

"Different names appear" in {4} refers back to the attempt in {1} to name things correctly and give a conceptual definition of Tao. Hence {4} is essentially an account of the unfortunate process by which conceptual naming arises out of a superior mental state described as *t'ung*/"[the] Merging" (compare 30[56]:3), which the composer identifies with the state of "not desiring" mentioned in {3}. (On the phrase "these two *lines*," see comments in 37[14]:2.) This is a Still*, desireless and conceptless, mental space (*men*/dwelling*) in which one knows Tao, the foundational "source" of the world, which is the same as knowing the true natures of things (see 38[21]:3)—knowing their *heng*/invariant Names {1} (see "Steady*"), which is the same as knowing their *miao*/"hidden essences" {3, 5}. (On *miao*, see 49[27]:5; and compare 63[32]:3, which describes a similar unfortunate process of "names" coming to be when one "cuts up" Tao as norm, an originally "nameless" "Uncarved* Block.") The contrast between named and nameless Tao in {2:2}, which many make much of, plays no part elsewhere. I believe {2:2} makes the relatively simple point that Tao also has some "names," such as the name *Mother.*

44[41]

"When the best *shih* hears Tao,   {1}
    he puts out great effort to practice it.
When the average *shih* hears Tao,
    he will keep it sometimes, and sometimes forget about it.
When the poorest *shih* hears Tao, he just has a big laugh."
If he does not laugh, it must not quite be Tao.

Yes, the 'Well-Founded Sayings' has it: {2}
The bright Tao seems dark
the Tao going forward seems to be going backward
the smooth Tao seems rough.

The loftiest Te seems like a valley   {3}
great purity seems sullied
abundant Te seems insufficient.

Well-founded Te seems flimsy
what is pure and natural seems faded
the best square has no corners.

A great bronze takes long to finish
great music has a delicate sound
the Great Image has no shape.

Tao is something concealed, nameless.   {4}
It is just Tao,
    good at sustaining a person and completing him.

The Tao and Te taught in our school don't look like very much at first. Our Tao is a backward, dark, and rough road {2}. It's like natural beauty that looks to some only crude and faded, like subtle music that appeals only to a delicate ear, like a square whose corners are suggested rather than drawn in, like a great ceremonial bronze whose beauty comes about so slowly {3}. Many who come think it's laughable {1}. But to one who makes the effort to cultivate it, this Tao is a sustaining presence, fulfilling her best potential {4}.

---

*Shih** in {1} refers to men aspiring to careers as government officials or advisors, who traveled to study with respected teachers in *shih* schools. Saying {1:1–5} is about the varying aptitudes of students in such schools for appreciating moral and spiritual teaching. Other schools also referred to their teaching as *Tao**, so there is nothing specifically Laoist about the saying before the final line. I think this is added by the Laoist composer to make a point very different from the original: It is in the nature of true (Laoist) Tao that it will appear ridiculous to a conventional mind. Saying {2} describes the paradoxical character of Laoist self-cultivation, playing on the meaning of Tao as "road." (It apparently quotes from a now-lost sayings collection.) Saying {3} is related to the sayings against impressive appearances*. In the background here is the idea that attempts to achieve strikingly positive appearances always result in something rather artificial. Genuine, "natural" goodness typically will not be striking in its appearance, but subtle, even appearing negative at times. Lines {3:6–8} use various metaphorical* images illustrating this idea, described in the paraphrase. Because {3:9} is difficult to make sense of as a metaphor, I think it is a connective* alteration written by the composer: As in 46[35]:1, "The Great Image" is Tao (called *shapeless* in 37[14]:3), and so this line leads into {4}.

The composer's comment in {4} pictures Tao as an hypostatized* inner presence, felt as elusive and "nameless*," beyond one's mental grasp, yet supportive of the one who cultivates it (see 14[23]:3, 13[20]:5). The chapter as a whole, then, is about the character of the Tao/Te taught in the Laoist *shih* school—not a doctrine but a subtle way of being animated by an intangible but sustaining inner presence.

45[70]

| My words are very easy to understand, | {1} |
| very easy to practice. | |

No one in the world can understand,
no one can practice them.

The words have an ancestor   {2}
the practice has a master.
They just do not understand
and so they do not understand me.
(So few understand me—a rare treasure indeed.)

And so the Wise Person: {3}
Dressed in shabby clothes, jade under his shirt.

The Tao that we teach: It's nothing strikingly unusual. It is found in the middle of ordinariness—in some ways the easiest thing to grasp, in some ways the hardest {1}. All our sayings and ways of doing things are expressions of only one thing, but this one thing cannot be put into words {2}. A student has to sense it—but most do not. A good teacher is like the Tao she teaches: precious jade under grubby clothes {3}.

Sayings {1} and {2:1-2} reflect on the nature of Laoist teaching*—the relation between the words used to teach and the spirit taught, which can't be directly captured in words. Lines {2:3-5} and saying {3} reflect on what it is like to be a teacher teaching the Laoist way (compare 3[67]:1).

The preceding chapter (44[41]) and the following four (46[35], 47[43], 48[62], 49[27]) center on the teaching and learning that takes place in the Laoist *shih** school, including especially reflections on what it is like to be a Laoist teacher* and the special style of teaching that matches the character of the Tao being taught.

46[35]

Grasp the Great Image and the world will come   {1}
it will come and not be harmed—
a great peace and evenness.

For music and cakes, passing strangers stop   {2}
Tao flowing from the lips—
flat. No taste to it.

Look for it: you will not be satisfied looking   {3}
listen for it: you will not be satisfied listening
put it into practice: you will not be satisfied stopping.

Music and pastry at a fair will catch people's attention. When someone is teaching Tao it will appear as though nothing is going on {2}. And yet, given time, it attracts everyone {1}. Practiced over time, it is like a nourishing but unspiced meal—it leaves you like you are, only much better {1}. You will not want to stop {3}.

"Grasp the Great Image [= Tao]" in {1} describes an ideal ruler who mentally keeps hold of Tao and lets it inform his leadership style. The saying celebrates the benefits* of this. "The world will come" refers to the desire of each feudal prince in Warring States China to establish a great social order that would attract people from all over China wanting to be part of it.[1] "Not harmed" is brought up because of an implied contrast with the "impressive*" ruler: Striking and inspiring ideals stir people up but also "hurt*" them; that is, cause them to feel bad and guilty about the contrast between the ideal and their present state. (Compare 55[66]:3, 81[37]:2:6–7.) But when one rules by the spirit of Tao, one exercises a subtle rather than striking and "inspiring" influence. This spirit brings out the natural goodness already present, rather than confronting people with something they are not. Saying {2} reflects on what it is like to be a Laoist teacher, teaching* a subtle "tasteless" Tao. Saying {3:1–2} is a version of 37[14]:1, describing what it is like to try to grasp Tao at meditation*.

The composer probably intends {1} here as a description not of a ruler but of the Laoist teacher, whose Tao attracts students from all over.[2] "You will not be satisfied stopping" is a new and conjectural understanding of {3:3}. I think this is probably a composer's twist added to {3:1–2}, celebrating one of the benefits* of cultivating (*yung*/using) Tao, subtle but deep satisfaction.

1. See p. 100.
2. Compare *Mencius** 7A/20,4, quoted p. 76.

47[43]

The Softest thing in the world   {1}
rides right over the Hardest things in the world.
What-has-No-Being enters what-leaves-no-opening.
This makes me realize the advantage of Not Doing.

Teaching done by not talking   {2}
the advantage gained by Not Doing—
few things in the world can match this.

Sometimes a student is very set in her ways, a hard nut to crack. Closed up tight, words bounce off of her. What will get through is only the teaching that is not really in the words, but exists between the lines. Don't act as though teaching is a big project that needs a lot of "doing." Appear as a nondoer. Present to her the subtle Nothing that will get through.

Saying {1} uses a metaphorical* nature image (water eroding rocks, or perhaps penetrating and cracking them as ice) to celebrate the power and benefits* of Softness* and Nothing*, mental qualities Laoists cultivate. ("Rides over" refers to riding down hunting prey, and evokes the idea of *sheng*/overcoming, a recurrent formula in the *Tao Te Ching* borrowed from speculation about the "conquest*" cycle. Compare 75[78]:1–2.)

I think that teaching* {2:1} is the main subject here for the composer: Laoist teaching is "Soft*" (nonconfrontational), and it feels like "Nothing*"; that is, it has little definite *surface* content that can be presented directly in words or "names*" (see 42[2]:3, 43[1]:1, 45[70]:1, 46[35]:2). This is why it can penetrate the "hard" surface of the resistant student (compare 49[27] on the magical and irresistible effectiveness of imperceptible, "trackless" Laoist teaching). Note the equivalence implied here between *Softness*, No-Being, no words,* and *not doing**. All these have an equivalent experiential reference, describing the subtle presence of the Laoist teacher as felt by others. This passage is important in showing that "no-being" is not intended literally or philosophically, but experientially, as hyperbole referring to something experienced as relatively intangible.

48[62]

Tao is the honored center for the thousands of things.   {1}

The treasure of the good   {2}
what protects the not good.

Elegant words can buy and sell   {3}
fine conduct gets people promoted.

People who are not good,   {4}
why are they rejected?

Yes: {5}
When they are enthroning the Son of Heaven
or installing the Three Ministers—
although they are presenting in tribute
      jade medallions out in front of four-horse teams,
this cannot compare to sitting and setting forth this Tao.

What was the reason that the ancients treasured this Tao?   {6}
Is it not said:
"By it the seeker obtains
by it the guilty escapes."

Yes: {7}
It is the Treasure of the World.

It's a difficult world. People ashamed of their lives, looking for something, wanting to become what they should be (and rejected by some teachers, who offer only elegant words that profit themselves {3–4}). Tao is this world's secret desire, the thing that will get for the seeker what she wants, that will turn around the life of the person gone wrong {2, 6}. One can do nothing in the world that is better than teaching people this Tao {5}.

Sayings {1} and {7} (= 30[56]:5) celebrate the cosmic* importance of Tao, as that which all things instinctively cherish above all. (*Ao*/"honored center" refers to the religious shrine in a house for the household gods, the central place of honor in the house.) Sayings {2} and {6} celebrate Tao's great benefits*, its power to "save" by mere contact those *shih** who come to the Laoist school looking for something better than their wayward or mediocre life. Saying {5} celebrates the greatness of teaching* Tao, by comparing the Tao taught to the expensive gifts offered in tribute at grand court ceremonies. ("Son of Heaven" is a title of the Emperor*.) On the basis of similar wording in 49[27]:3 and 4, I believe that {4} is directed against the practice of some *shih** teachers who refused to accept as students those they judged unfit. (*Pu-shan*/"not good" may mean not immoral but inexperienced in self-cultivation, as in 49[27]:4. To judge from 49[27], the connection here is that Laoist Tao is so effective that it can penetrate even the poorest student, hence rejection would be groundless. Mencius* also is said[1] not to have rejected even criminally inclined *shih* who wanted to study with him.) Saying {3} counters the admiration of fine appearances* by picturing eloquence and refined manners as serving only the selfish and commercial interests of their possessors. (I am guessing the composer intends a contrast between eloquence and teaching "tasteless" Tao [see 46[35]:2]. But this saying may have crept in here by mistake. My understanding of it is new.)

This chapter is the one with the most "religious" flavor, assuming that there are "guilty" people who need to be "saved" by Tao. I take this as a measure of Laoist alienation: One cannot find meaning by participating in conventional social life, but finds it instead in the Laoist *shih* school. The Tao that is the focus of community life there takes the place of the Emperor* and the ceremonial surrounding him, the traditional cultural center of meaning, now replaced by teaching and learning self-cultivation which takes place in the Laoist school.

---

1. 7B/30,2

49[27]

Excellent traveling: no tracks or traces   {1}
Excellent speaking: no blemish or blame.

Excellent counting does not use counting slips.   {2}
Excellent locking: no bolt or bar,
    but the door cannot be opened.
Excellent tying: no cord or rope,
    but the knots cannot be undone.

And so the Wise Person: {3}
Always Excels at rescuing people
    and so does not turn anyone away.
Always Excels at resolving things
    and so does not turn away from anything.
This is called 'being clothed in Clarity.'

The Excellent person   {4}
    is the teacher of the person who is not Excellent.
The person who is not Excellent
    is material for the Excellent person.

Not to treasure one's teacher   {5}
not to love one's material,
though 'smart,' is a great mistake.
This is an important secret.

Some teachers have something very definite and forceful to teach. Some students accept it, but many resist—the teachers can do nothing with them. The Tao we teach is different. It gets into people subtly, without them knowing it—like a good hunter who can walk leaving no tracks, like a magician who can tie up people using no ropes, or fasten a door using no lock {1–2}. This is a Tao for all occasions— the one who teaches it needs to turn down no person and no problem {3}. Teaching it requires an atmosphere in which students look up to teachers who embody Tao, and teachers love the students whom they mold {4–5}.

Saying {3} celebrates the great powers and benefits* of teaching* done by an accomplished Laoist teacher, enabling him to cope with any student or problem. (Compare 48[62]:4. I take *wu*/things* in {3:4} to mean "affairs, problems," hence I translate *chiu*/rescue as "resolve" in this line.) The images of {1–2} here serve as analogies to the quasi-magical influence, imperceptible but irresistible, of his style of teaching (compare 47[43].) Saying {4} is about the respective roles of teachers* and students in the Laoist school. *Shan*/Excellent* throughout this chapter has a strong meaning, referring to people who are "experts" in what they do, including especially {3–4} expert teachers well advanced in Laoist self-cultivation ("clothed in Clarity*" {3:6}). Hence I translate *pu shan* as "not Excellent"—that is, a relative beginner—although the phrase also could mean "not good" (see 48[62]:4).

Sections {4–5} give the most direct indication in the *Tao Te Ching* of sharply defined roles of teachers and students in the Laoist school. Section {5} seems intended to correct some bad tendencies the composer sees among both students and teachers within the school. It seems unlikely that the composer would direct general criticism at teachers unless there was more than one, hence I take {5:2} as indirect evidence that in fact there was more than one. "Secret" in {5:4} is *miao*, translated "hidden essences/essentials" in 43[1]:3 and 5. The use of *miao* here shows that advice such as that given in {4–5} is the kind of thing Laoists mean by "understanding the hidden essence" of situations.

5

Majesty That Is Not Awesome

50[53]

If I had the least bit of understanding	{1}
I would walk on the great Way.	

Only display will be dangerous.	{2}

The great Way is very smooth	{3}
but people love bypaths.	

The court is very well kept	{4}
the fields are very weedy	
the granaries very empty.	

"Their clothes are fine and colorful	{5}
on their belts are sharp swords,	
they are filled with food and drink"	
a superabundance of expensive goods.	

This is robbers boasting,	{6}
certainly not the Way.	

People admire the parties of the rich: the fine clothes, the abundance of great food {5}. But what are they doing? They take great care of the court (for themselves), but neglect their responsibilities: they ignore weedy fields, and fail to see that grain is stored against famine {4}. What are their parties really like? A gang of thieves showing off booty stolen from the people {6}.

Sayings {1} and {3} contrast the obvious importance of the "easy" Tao*/Way with its neglect by the unthinking majority. Saying {2} speaks against self-promotion*, using an oracle* formula. Saying {3} criticizes contemporary rulers who give their attention to the elegance of court life at the expense of their public responsibilities, like managing agriculture and storing grain against famine (compare 52[77]:1). Because lines {5:1–3} seem so glowing, I suspect they are a quotation. Line {5:4} expresses the composer's disapproval of the banquet scene described.

The saying criticizing "display" in {2} is connected with the criticism of conspicuous consumption in {5} and "boasting" in {6}. It is placed near the beginning to frame* some of the material, giving this composition more unity. Section {6} further unifies the composition: "Robbers boasting" characterizes the court's conspicuous consumption in {4–5}, and "the Way" refers back to {1} and {3}.

In {2} most translators emend *shih*/display to *yi*/"go astray," yielding "[I would] only fear going astray," which might seem to make much better sense in the immediate context of talk about the "Great Way" and the "bypaths" (see Duyvendak). But (a) the catchy *wei shih shih wei*/"only display will be dangerous" makes sense as an independent saying using an oracle* formula, and (b) the location of this saying at the beginning follows a unifying "framing*" technique visible elsewhere. This is a good example of the way form and redaction criticism[1] sometimes can provide solutions to textual puzzles without resort to emendations.

This Section 5 begins with three chapters (50[53], 51[75], 52[77]) expressing Laoist protest against the unjust distribution of wealth and the luxury the upper classes enjoy at the expense of the peasantry.

---

1. See p. 126, 309.

51[75]

'The people are starving.'   {1}
It is because those high up eat too much tax grain,
this is why they are starving.

'The people are hard to govern.'
It is because there is Working among those high up,
this is why they are hard to govern.

'The people take death lightly.'
It is because they pursue a lavish life,
this is why they take death lightly.

Simply: {2}
Those who do not Work at 'living'—
these are better men than those who 'love life.'

People in office are always complaining, "the people are hard to govern"; "the people are uncontrollable"; "the people are starving." Can't they see that they themselves are the cause? If they tax the people so heavily, of course the people will starve. If they themselves are reckless in pursuit of pleasure, do they think the people are not going to be {1}? The poor farmers who do not waste all their efforts trying to live it up are better than the all those officials who "love life" {2}.

I think the first lines of the first three stanzas here are quotations of common complaints by rulers (compare 66[74]:1). The criticism of wealth derived from burdensome taxation in {1:1–3} is similar to that in 50[53]:4, 52[77]:1, and 53[72]:2. As to {1:7–9}: 76[80] mentions, as part of its description of an ideal society, that the people in this society "take death seriously and do not travel far distances." Hence the opposite here "taking death lightly" probably means that the people are reckless, or perhaps that they can't be controlled by fear of capital punishment. (The criticism of capital punishment in 66[74]:1 mentions people's lack of "fear of death.") Hence the overall meaning here is that rulers are responsible for the people's recklessness because their own reckless quest for high living sets a bad tone for the society.

"Work" in {1:4–6} doesn't go well with the criticism of luxury in the other two stanzas. I take it to be the composer's addition. As in 8[81]:4, *work* is an elliptical reference, spelled out in {2}: People are hard to govern because those high up set a bad tone by "working *at living*"; that is, at living luxuriously, which they claim manifests their "love of life." (Compare the similar criticism of lavish living in 22[50]:2, where *sheng sheng chih hou*/"live life's lavishness" matches *chou sheng chih hou*/"pursue life's lavishness" here.) The composer here seems to be stretching the more usual meaning of the key Laoist term *working**, to cover "working" at luxurious living (see also 41[47]:3). I'm guessing that "those who don't work at living it up" are peasant-farmers, objects of the complaints in {1}.

52[77]

Heaven's Way is like the stringing of a bow: {1}
It pulls down what is high
it lifts up what is low
it takes away from what has an abundance
to give to what has not enough.

Heaven's Way:
Take away from what has an abundance
help along what has not enough.
People's way is not like this:
Take away from what has not enough
to offer it to what has an abundance.

Who can have an abundance to offer the world? {2}
Only the one who has Tao.

And so the Wise Person: {3}
Works but does not rely on this
achieves successes but does not dwell in them
has no desire to show off his worth.

Look at nature's leveling: High river banks get pulled down, low-lying ravines get filled in. What do people do? Those who are on top get lifted higher. Rulers demand that the lowest people in need feed the coffers of those who already have more than enough {1}. The abundance they receive is a source of pride for them. But what is real "abundance"? What is the "abundance" that will benefit the people? It is the Tao that one has inside, the spirit that enables a leader to make a real contribution {2} without puffing herself up over it {3}.

Saying {1} uses a metaphorical* nature image, described in the paraphrase. In its criticism of wealth as imbalance, it is similar to 50[53]:4–6, 51[75]:1, and 53[72]:2. Underlying these sayings is a feeling for the social whole that Laoist *shih** wanted to promote among contemporary leaders. When "the rich get richer," this is bad because it means that resources are diverted from those who need it most to those who need it least, and that resources are spent on luxuries rather than on what is most useful to the society (50[53]:4). Saying {2} celebrates the benefits* one who has Tao* can confer on his society. Saying {3} criticizes the tendency toward self-promotion*, by posing the image of the ideal *shih** who is very competent and successful in his managerial tasks, but does not rely on them for his sense of self-worth, and so is not possessive of them and does not "dwell* in" (identify himself with) them. (Versions of this saying occur also at 42[2]:5, 65[51]:4, and 27[10]:2.)

In the second half of this chapter, the composer shifts the focus away from wealth as imbalance, to a contrast between the implied "false abundance" of wealth {1} and the more real spiritual "abundance" of the *shih* who possesses the spirit of Tao {2}, spreading this spirit by the self-effacing style of his leadership {3} (see comments in 7[8]:1).

53[72]

When the people are not in awe of your majesty   {1}
then great majesty has been achieved.

Do not restrict where they can live   {2}
do not tire them out by taxing what they live on.
Simply do not tire them
and they will not tire of you.

And so, the Wise Person: {3}
Knows himself
does not make a show of himself.
Loves himself
does not exalt himself.

Yes, he leaves 'that' aside, and attends to 'this.'   {4}

Some rulers need to make their importance felt {1} by constant assertion of their privileges: Staking out "royal lands" where the people
aren't allowed to live, taxing heavily the farm produce the people live
on {2:1-2}. The people know this does not represent true "majesty."
They'll soon tire of such a person, and that will be the end of his rule
{2:3-4}. Rulers indeed ought to know and love themselves better, paying more attention to developing their own character {3-4}. Then
they could be easier on the people. Then *true* "majesty" will have
arrived {1}.

Saying {1} counters the desire of Warring States rulers to awe their
subjects with an impressive* and commanding presence. The image
of the nonawesome ruler it presents, evokes the Laoist idea that the
internal spirit he cultivates {3-4} fits a ruler for true greatness—and
this spirit is not something that makes a striking external impression.
(Compare 54[17]:1. The translation of {1} here is new, based on a passage in the *Mencius*[1] using the same words for *awe* and *majesty* in the
sense I give them here.) Saying {2:3-4} counters the tendency of these
rulers to impose burdens on their people, picturing not burdening
the people as the best way to keep their allegiance (a constant worry
of Warring States rulers). Saying {3} urges introspective concern for
the quality of one's own being, in contrast to self-promotion*. I think
that "this" in {4} refers also to concern for one's own being, as
opposed to concern for the external impression one makes on others
("that"). (See discussion under "This*." This saying also occurs in
11[38]:8 and 21[12]:3.)

The "burdensome" restrictions and taxation referred to in {2:1-2}
have not only a practical purpose, but are a means of imposing recognition of the ruler's special status and "majesty" {1}. (Compare the
criticisms of similar practices in *Mencius*[2].) The composer redirects
the ruler's attention to introspective care for and development of his
own being {3-4} in contrast to a preoccupation with gaining public
recognition (compare 24[33]:1). His own inner spirit thus cultivated
will win more subtly, but more effectively, the respect and allegiance
of the people.

This chapter shares the social criticism of the previous three
chapters, but relates this also to the main theme of the following four
(54[17], 55[66], 56[61], 57[68]): Laoist opposition to the "impressive*"
ruler.

---

1. 1B/3,3.
2. For example, 1A/5,3, 1B/2, 1B/5,3.

54[17]

The greatest ruler: those under him only know he exists   {1}
the next best kind: they love and praise him
the next: they are in awe of him
the next: they despise him.

When sincerity does not suffice   {2}
it was not sincerity.
("Reticent—he is sparing with words.")

He achieves successes   {3}
he accomplishes his tasks
and the hundred clans all say: We are just being natural.

Why do rulers want so much to impress their people? First the people give them love and respect, but this is only one step removed from awe—and awe is only one step removed from resentment and hatred. The ruler who stands out is a burden {1}. Why give impressive speeches? Real sincerity will always be sufficient, even when it's not impressive {2}. The best turn of events: You work hard, but your work is invisible—people think things are just going well naturally {3}.

Sayings {1} and {3} counter the ruler's desire to be impressive*—to gain the love and respect of his people, and to have them credit him with the society's order and prosperity. The idea behind the progression in {1} is that when the ruler is so exalted in the people's mind this "hurts*" them (55[66]:3) and causes them to feel inferior (81[37]:2:6), which eventually leads to resentment. The contrasting image is the ideal Laoist ruler whose greatness consists in the intangible and unimpressive spirit he cultivates, which expresses itself by keeping an extremely low profile. Thus he actually works hard and competently at social organization {3:1-2}, but calls so little attention to himself that the people think social harmony came about spontaneously {3:3}. Saying {2:1-2} (= 14[23]:4) counters the feeling that speech will be effective only when it is eloquent, sincerity will not suffice to convince. I think {2:3} probably is a quotation about some great "man of few words." (Its presence here is one reason that I think {2:1-2} is about sincere *speech*. See further comments at 14[23]:4.) For Laoists, sincere speech counts as something relatively unimpressive in contrast to eloquence (see 7[8]:2:4, 8[81]:1), hence the connection of this saying with the idealization of the unimpressive ruler in {1} and {3}.

55[66]

The Yang-tze and the ocean: {1}
How are they able to be Kings of the hundred streams?
Because they excel at being low—
this is how they are able to be Kings
    of the hundred streams.

And so: {2}
Wishing to be high above the people,
    you must by your speech put yourself at the bottom.
Wishing to be out in front of the people,
    you must put your self in the last place.

And so, the Wise Person: {3}
Stands above, but the people are not weighed down
stands out in front, but the people are not harmed
and so the world delights in praising him,
    and does not tire.

Because of his not contending   {4}
no one in the world can contend with him.

With some leaders, every word they speak, every action they take, says, "I am someone of great importance. You are my lowly subjects." Such a person is an oppressive weight on the people, hurting them by casting them always in a bad light, as "inferior." People will not accept this. Weighed down, they weary of her. The people wearied, she loses their support {3}. She becomes just one more individual, joining in society's quarrelsome competition for honor and status. (And she wonders why people become so contentious and quarrelsome with her {4}.) Look at the ocean and the Yang-tze, greatest of rivers. Did they become great because of their talent for being impressive? No, their uniqueness among rivers lies in their surpassing lowness, occupying the place toward which all the water naturally flows {1}. This is an image of the weightless authority of the one who occupies the Central place, but also the lowly place.

Sayings {1}, {2}, and {3:2–3} criticize the ideal of the impressive* ruler. The metaphorical* nature image in {1} represents the idea that the quality Laoists cultivate gives a ruler true claim to Emperor* status and will attract the spontaneous allegiance of all the people, but this quality expresses itself partly in a deferential manner, a willingness (as in {2}) to adopt the stance characteristic of someone of low* social standing in dealing with others. (See 35[39]:2. *Mencius**[1] also uses water's gravity flow as an image of the people's "natural" allegiance for a true ruler, but without the emphasis on lowness. Not just any kind of "being low" is involved here: The ideal ruler has a greatness *all the more* attractive because it expresses itself in a deferential manner in dealing with his people.) Saying {3:2–3} reflects the Laoist ideal for the ruler, setting a high tone for the society, yet doing so in such a way that his presence is not felt as overbearing or in any way hurtful* or accusatory (see also 81[37]:2:6.) Line {3:2} plays on *chung*/heavy, which also means "dignified": The ideal ruler is one whose great weight/dignity does not "weigh on" the people (compare 53[72]:1, 54[17]:1). Saying {4} (= 4[22]:6) criticizes the tendency to *cheng*/contend*:quarrel with others for high social standing. ("Lowness" and "not contending" are connected also in 7[8]:1 and 57[68]:1–2.) The noncontentious person "has no competition" in the contest for *real* worth.

Line {3:4} interrupts the parallelism of the previous two lines, it is introduced by the standard introduction *shih yi*/"and so," and its point seems equivalent to the universal attractiveness theme of {1}—this is why I think it is a connective* addition by the composer.

---

1. See p. 100, n.5.

56[61]

The great state is a low and easy   {1}
woman for the world
the one the whole world unites with.

Femininity always overcomes Masculinity, by Stillness,   {2}
in Stillness it takes the low place.

Yes: {3}
A great state,
    by putting itself lower than the smaller state,
    will win out over the smaller state.
A small state,
    by putting itself lower than the great state,
    will win out over the great state.

Yes: {4}
One puts itself lower so it will win out,
if the other gets lower, then it will win.

(A great state has no further desire   {5}
than to embrace and protect other states.
A small state has no further desire
than to enter and serve other states.
So both get what they want.)

The greatest should be the lowest.   {6}

Some hope to make their state great by forming grand plans and gaining a reputation for high ideals, thinking that in this way they will attract people from all over. But what state will really attract the world? The one that imitates the prostitute: Feminine, Still, low, loose, and easy. In dealing with other states, diplomacy that plays the lower part wins out in the long run over arrogance.

Several individual states were competing with each other in this period, each wanting to restore unity to the Chinese empire under *its* leadership. More powerful states regularly swallowed up their weaker neighbors. A favorite strategy was for one ruler to try to attract the allegiance of a rival state's people. Saying {1} criticizes the ideal of the strict* ruler, one who hopes to attract people and make his state great by upholding the highest moral standards. The saying means to shock by proposing the extreme opposite ideal: Attract the people's allegiance by being like a prostitute who has no moral standards. (Seeing a prostitute image underlying this passage is new. See "Additional Textual Notes.") A positive Laoist ideal underlies the negative prostitute metaphor*: The ideal ruler rules by a spirit that is just the spirit of an ideal organic harmony already potentially present in the society, needing just to be brought out (see 60[49]:1). This is why it will be attractive to the people, but will not be experienced by them as a moral norm imposed from without. Saying {2:1} borrows a formula from thought about the "conquest* cycle," to celebrate the superiority of the Femininity*/Stillness* Laoists cultivate over the Masculine spirit. (I take {2:2} to be the composer's connective* addition, linking {2:1} to the theme of lowness, the leitmotif for this chapter.) Saying {3} celebrates the power and benefits* of Laoist lowness*, which here expresses itself in a deferential manner when conducting interstate diplomacy (a common task of Warring States *shih**). Saying {6} also advises deference, as especially suited to those (people or states) with great power and status (compare our principle of noblesse oblige).

Section {5} seems to be in conflict with {1–4}. Sayings {1–4} suggest that even small states can win out in struggles with larger states if their rulers cultivate Laoist Femininity/Stillness/lowness. Section {5} only appears to uphold this idea, by a contorted interpretation of "winning out": A small state now "wins out" by "getting what it wants," and this turns out to be annexation by its larger neighbors! Note also the way that the meaning of *ta*/great changes. In {1} it means "great in stature," in {3–6} it means "large in size." Perhaps {5} was added as propaganda defending the ambitions of some large state to take over its smaller neighbors.

57[68]

The best soldier is not warlike   {1}
the best fighter shows no anger
the one best at defeating the enemy does not engage him
the one best at managing people puts himself below them.

This is the Te of not contending   {2}
this is the power to manage people.
This is being the Counterpart of Heaven
equalling the very best of the ancients.

Managers should take a lesson from the soldier: The good soldier puts aside his personal stake in the fighting, doesn't get angry or go looking for a fight. She does only what she has to do {1}. The best supervisor has no stake in being boss, but treats her people as though she is there to serve them. The workers feel it {2}.

Saying {1:1–3} counters excessively aggressive tendencies among solders, posing the opposite image of one who is more effective because his judgment and actions are not distorted by anger, and he is willing to use indirect tactics (the point of the exaggerated image in {1:3}; compare 58[73]:1, 68[69]:1–2).

The composer uses the saying about soldiering to present a model for being a good *supervisor*, the ambition of many *shih**. The association is aided by the connotations of *cheng*/contend*:quarrel, which can refer to both physical fighting and the social struggle for status. The ideal supervisor is not "contentious" in his desire to establish himself as the boss {2:1}, but is able to treat those under him as though he were their social inferior {1:4}, someone "lower*" than they. "Te*" here has the meaning of subtle influence and power, emanating from the supervisor's "noncontentious" spirit. Such a one, even if he is only a minor administrator, achieves the *spiritual* status of the idealized ancient* Emperors*, the "Counterparts of Heaven*" in ruling the world {2:3–4}.

58[73]

"One who shows bravery by being daring will get killed   {1}
one who shows bravery by not being daring will survive."

But in both these cases: {2}
"Sometimes it helps, sometimes it harms."

"What Heaven picks to hate—who knows the reason?"   {3}

And so the Wise Person: {4}
Treats things as difficult.

Heaven's Way: {5}
Not contending, but excels at overcoming
not speaking, but excels in getting answers
not summoning, but people come of themselves
lax, but excels at organization.

Heaven's net is very wide—   {6}
loosely woven,
but it lets nothing slip by.

Some rulers are at the people all the time, watching every move, summoning them, demanding answers—as though at war with the people {5}. But this isn't the way the world works. Consider fate. It appears unpredictable—now taking a life, now sparing a life {1–3}; but in the end, justice prevails. The best ruler is like that, appearing easy, planning and managing things quietly, so order is maintained but she never has to play the policeman {5–6}.

Saying {1} speaks against aggressive soldiering, posing the opposite image of a brave but smarter soldier. Sayings {2:2} and {3} look like common proverbs about our inability to predict what brings good or bad fortune. (Saying {3} invokes an idea common in ancient China that bad fortune is a sign of Heaven's* hatred toward someone.) Saying {4} is a fragment of the saying found in 71[63]:7, advising caution rather than carelessly making light of things. Saying {5:2–4} counters the ideal of the strict* and aggressive ruler, posing exaggerated images of the opposing ideal: The low-key ruler who elicits cooperation and overcomes opposition by indirect means and the subtle power of his Te*.

The composer takes {1} not as an aphorism*, but a literal prediction of who will survive and who will die. He uses this as a take-off* point for criticism of confidence in predictability, expressed in the sayings about uncertainty in {2} and {3} (compare 59[58]:2, 62[29]:3, and comments on "Understanding*"). Saying {4} counters confidence in simplistic predictive laws, advising that one treat the course of events as difficult to understand*. Saying {6} and the composer's addition in {5:5} interpret the unpredictability of "Heaven" {1–3} as apparent laxity in enforcing justice, a laxity that is *only* apparent, however: In the long run no one gets away with anything. (I mark {5:5} a connective* addition because it interrupts the parallelism of the previous lines and leads into the image of {6}.) The chapter thus outlines a "Way of Heaven" that is a model for the ideal ruler, who will often *appear* easy and "lax," rather than a strict policeman. But this is because of his subtle *style* of ruling, flowing from the state of mind and attitude he cultivates, a style that ultimately has the effect of enforcing justice. This chapter makes it clear that the policy of being "low and easy" advocated in 56[61], and the "nonintervention" some other chapters might appear to recommend, are not to be taken literally as a description of the ultimate *goal and effect* of the ideal Laoist ruling style, which still aims at enforcing justice.

59[58]

When the ruler is dull and incompetent,   {1}
the people are pure and simple.
When the ruler is sharp and alert,
the people are a bad lot.

"Bad luck: good luck depends on it   {2}
good luck: bad luck hides in it."
Who knows where this ends?
There is no norm.
What accords with the norm turns around and becomes weird
what is excellent turns around and becomes ominous.

"People's blindness—   {3}
it has been going on so long now."

And so the Wise Person: {4}
Is square and honest but does not cut
is pointed and exact but does not hurt
is straight and direct but not tactless
shines but does not dazzle.

Some rulers think they know exactly what's right and what's wrong, which plans will succeed and which will come to ruin {2}. They keep a sharp and constant watch {1}, judging everyone and everything by their sure knowledge. They try to dazzle their people {4} with the inspiring high standards of their government, but their self-assurance makes them abrasive {4}. This is a very old kind of blindness {3}. Better is the ruler who remains always aware of uncertainty and who emphasizes tact, managing to uphold high standards without hurting anyone's feelings {4}. She accepts the risk of appearing dull and incompetent {1}—this is so much better than a "dazzling" ruler who constantly makes the people feel lacking.

Sayings {1} and {4:2-4} counter the ideal of the strict* ruler. The image of the "dull and incompetent" ruler in {1} (Karlgren's translation) is an exaggerated self-caricature emphasizing the opposite Laoist ideal—a ruler who actually stands for high standards, but who is not dramatic and confrontational about this and so sometimes appears not to know what is going on. The "sharp" ruler provokes a rebellious attitude in his people, whereas the "dull" Laoist ruler fosters organic* social harmony. Saying {4:2-4} poses the image of the person whose interactions manage to combine honesty and uprightness with tact, so as not to hurt* anyone. (It uses metaphors taken from measurements in carpentry: The word for "square" also means "honest," the word for "right-angled" also means "scrupulous, exacting," etc.) Saying {2:1-2} looks like a folk proverb emphasizing uncertainty, countering the human tendency to construe one piece of apparent good or bad luck as a "trend" (see comments on "Understanding*"). The saying that follows in {3} deplores this tendency as a manifestation of all-to-common ignorance (compare 13[20]:3:2).

The composer adds {2:3-6} emphasizing our inability to know easily and name* correctly what is lucky or unlucky, good or bad. Such knowledge would give a person in authority a good basis for taking an uncompromising moral stance toward his subjects, hence the connection to the criticism in {1} and {3}. (Compare similar implied associations in 58[73] and 62[29].) *Dazzle* in the final line refers to the striking moral impressiveness* some rulers strive for, contrasted with the subtle shining of the tactful Laoist.

This chapter belongs to a group of three chapters (58[73], 59[58], 60[49]) criticizing the ideal of the strict* ruler.

60[49]

The Wise Person is always a man without a mind—   {1}
he takes the mind of the hundred clans as his mind.

Those who are good, I am good to them   {2}
those who are not good, I am also good to them—
Te is good.

Those who are honest, I am honest with them
those who are not honest, I am also honest with them—
Te is honest.

The Wise Person   {3}
lives in the world all drawn in
for the world's sake he keeps his mind muddled.

The hundred clans   {4}
all strain their eyes and ears toward him.
The Wise Person treats them all as his children.

Some officials have a very set mind regarding good and bad {1}. They find it easy to recognize which people they meet are insincere and no good—and they know that such people should be dealt with in kind {2}. This attitude is hurtful. The best official is like someone who has no mind of her own. She takes the mind of the people as a guide to policy {1}. In her respect for the people she shows unwavering goodness to all, good and bad alike {2}, like a loving parent {4}. She does not inhabit the world like something with bristles all extended, constantly waiting to puncture those doing wrong in her eyes. Rather she appears drawn in, "muddle minded" some might say—all so she will not hurt the people {3}.

Saying {1} counters the ideal of the strict* ruler who thinks it is *his* role to represent high mindedness in contrast to the people who are lacking in this. It poses instead an exaggerated counterimage of a man with no mind of his own at all. The ideal he holds up for the society does not *confront* them as something coming from outside. It is nothing but an idealized version of the organic* goodness already inherent in the society ("the hundred clans"). Saying {2} counters the tendency to respond to others in kind, giving a normative* description of the way one acts who has Te*. Laoist Te expresses itself in a selfless generosity to all, regardless of their deserts. (A similar quality is ascribed to Te in 9[79] and 71[63]:3).

"Keeps his mind muddled" in {3} is an exaggerated image of the ruler who keeps his mind free of sharply defined moral standards to impose on his people. (This would "hurt*" them [see 81[37]:2:6], hence the statement that he does this "for the world's [society's] sake.") He also presents the appearance of someone "drawn in," rather than aggressive (compare 6[15]:2). ("Muddled" and "drawn in" follow Karlgren's understanding of the Chinese words involved.) In {4} I take "strain their eyes...toward him" to mean that people look to him for moral guidance, and "treats them all as children" to signify a protective attitude. The Chinese phrase could mean instead that he "acts like a child."

61[54]

Excellently founded: it will not be uprooted   {1}
Excellently embraced and cared for: it will not slip away
so sons and grandsons
    will never cease to offer the sacrifices.

Cultivate It in your person, its Te will be pure   {2}
cultivate It in the clan, its Te will be abundant
cultivate It in the village, its Te will be lasting
cultivate It in the state, its Te will be ample
cultivate It in the empire, its Te will be all-embracing.

Yes: {3}
Judge a person taking that person as the measure
judge a clan taking that clan as the measure
judge a village taking that village as the measure
judge a state taking that state as the measure
judge the world taking the world as the measure.

How do I know the nature of the world?   {4}
By this.

Like individuals, groups and societies also have a spirit that needs cultivation {2}. Some great families last and last because they are founded on a solid spirit {1}. How do you know what to cultivate? Pay attention to that inner something which is this group at its best—it differs from group to group, and it cannot be known by any grand plan {3}. How do you come to know it? Cultivate the right state of mind, and look {4}.

Large family clans were an important element in ancient Chinese society, and {1} is about building up and maintaining the greatness of the clan to which one belongs.[1] The enduring greatness of a clan is made manifest here in the fact that clan descendants continue to offer sacrifices to clan ancestors for generation after generation. If this is a Laoist saying, *shan*/Excellently* refers to cultivating clan greatness according to Laoist ideals, and the saying celebrates the wonderful benefits* of this. Saying {2} also celebrates the benefits* of cultivating this spirit (here called simply *It*) at all levels of society. (Te* here probably refers to the character of the social unit as it makes itself felt in its reputation.[2]) Saying {3} reads, literally, "By person examine person, by clan examine clan, etc." My conjecture is that the target of the saying is the tendency to judge smaller social units in the light of larger ones, all according to some normative scheme. Against this, the saying advocates understanding* and judging each individual unit on its own, and furthermore viewing each in its uniqueness ("measured by itself"), rather than according to some single norm applied to all. This understanding makes it easy to connect this saying with {4}, which employs a recurrent Laoist formula found also in 38[21]:4 and 77[57]:2. I think it is a stock answer to questions by opponents about the source of Laoist views, by appealing to immediate experiential intuition ("this*"), in the proper state of mind. The connection then would be that {3} also recommends evaluating a person just by one's direct experience of that person, without reference to other, external criteria. The ultimate point is similar to that in 60[49]:1, that norms should be derived from characteristics already in some sense inherent in social units, rather than from some scheme external to them.

This chapter belongs to a group of six (58[73], 59[58], 60[49], 61[54], 62[29], 63[32]) sharing a common opposition to the ruler who wants to base his policies on sure conceptual knowledge of norms and general laws governing social life.

---

1. Compare *Mencius** 1B/14,3.
2. As in ibid. 2B/2,9, and see also p. 84.

62[29]

When someone wants to take over the world   {1}
    and do some work on it,
I can see he won't be able.
The world is a spirit-thing, it can't be 'worked' on.

One who works ruins   {2}
one who grasps loses.

Yes, things: {3}
Sometimes they will go ahead, sometimes follow after
sometimes they will be snorting wildly,
    sometimes breathing easily
sometimes they will be strong, sometimes weak
sometimes they will break, sometimes destroy.

And so the Wise Person: {4}
Avoids excess, avoids extravagance, avoids being grandiose.

Some people have grand plans for reforming the world. They possess the key to how the world really works, and they think "If only I were completely in charge." But the social world is always beyond our grasp and control, a sacred thing {1} with an unpredictable mind of its own {3}. People with the ambition to "work it over" stand out as grossly superfluous on the face of the world {4}. Wherever they go they ruin the irreplaceable goodness of the given {2}.

Saying {1} counters the ambition of some Warring States thinkers and rulers to get control of the entire Chinese Empire ("the world") and make it over according to some grand design. The term *shen-ch'i*/"spirit thing" probably means to evoke not only awe for something sacred, but the common ancient Chinese fear of spirits—the "superstitious*" feeling that offending them could easily bring retaliation or bad luck. (*Shen-ch'i* could also mean "spirit vessel," a sacred vessel used in religious ceremony.) The phrase conveys a Laoist feeling for the world that underlies their polemic against "working*": The "worker" typically thinks his own plans and efforts are all important, considering what he is working on as mere raw material. By contrast, Laoists emphasize reverence and respect for the givenness of things. Saying {2} (= 72[64]:4) criticizes the attitude of those who want to control things by their own efforts, suggesting that what is most valuable about things cannot be possessed by direct grasping and typically is ruined by attempts to work* on or "improve*" on them. Saying {3} counters the confidence in our ability to predict and control things in the world, posing as a counterimage the unpredictable behavior of barnyard animals (indicated by "snorting," etc.) Saying {4} is probably related to those criticizing self-promotion* as "excessive" (see 1[24] and 2[9]).

As in 58[73] and 59[58], the composer here associates emphasis on uncertainty {3} with criticism of ruling with a strong hand {1-2}. That is, this attitude on the part of a ruler typically results from self-assurance that he understands* things perfectly—a "grandiose" attitude. The emphasis on the unpredictability of events in the world is part of the Laoist insistence that the world always eludes our conceptual ("naming*") grasp. One who realizes this will not be so confident that implementing his reforming plans will actually be successful and beneficial.

63[32]

Tao will always be nameless, an Uncarved Block   {1}
although it is a thing of no account,
no one in the world can make it his subject.

If the princes and kings could watch over It,   {2}
the thousands of things
    would on their own be as deferential as guests.
Heaven and Earth would join together to send sweet dew.
The people on their own would share equally
    without anyone giving orders.

When you begin making decisions and cutting it up,   {3}
rules and names appear.
And once names appear, you should know to stop.
Knowing to stop, you can be without fear.

A comparison: {4}
Tao's presence in the world
    is like the relation of small river valleys
    to the Yang-tze and the ocean.

What is the Center of the World—the supreme thing which everything naturally wants to obey, the thing toward which all things naturally flow {4}, the thing that brings spontaneous peace to the world {2}? It is something that by its nature will always appear small, of no account in the world {1}. If those at the top could only cultivate and maintain it in themselves, what a world this could be. But what do they do instead? They feel it is too intangible. The Norm needs to be named. They chop up this simple and natural thing into a thousand pieces, relying on a thousand laws to keep people in line {3}. They've lost it.

Saying {1} celebrates* the Tao* Laoists cultivate, something of great power and importance although it appears insignificant in the conventional world. Saying {2} celebrates the marvelous benefits* brought to a society by a ruler who "watches* over" Tao and lets it animate his government. Saying {3:4} uses an oracle* formula to advocate "knowing to stop." This phrase occurs in a similar context in the Nei* Yeh,[1] "Life then thought, thought then knowledge, knowledge then stop." On the basis of this, and the occurrence of this saying in 19[44]:4, I believe this phrase has a meaning similar to "turn* back." It is based on the image of an "original" Still* state of mind that can become stirred up into various kinds of outward-looking mental "activity," like conceptual ("naming*") thought or desire for fame or possessions (as in 19[44]:1–2). When one becomes aware of such negative mental "activity," one should "know to stop" it. Saying {4} uses the same metaphorical* image as 55[66]:1 to represent the natural gravitation of everyone toward the "low*" Tao.

"Cutting up" in {3:1–2} refers to the Uncarved* Block of {1} and is directed against other contemporary shih* schools that advocated explicit formulation of moral and legal norms (see "Naming*"). Chi/"cut up" also means "govern": Explicit legal naming and "decisions" deprive the ruler of real authority by making destructive "incisions" in the real Norm of the World, the Tao as Uncarved Block. When instead the ruler governs by the spirit of the insignificant/low/uncarved Tao, it exerts a subtle but powerful influence that attracts the allegiance of all {4} and produces social harmony and prosperity {2}. See 17[28]:2, where the Uncarved Block refers to one's person as a whole, before it is "cut up" into good and bad qualities. (These are the same: For Laoists, Tao functions as a Norm through its existence in the person of the ideal ruler.)

---

1. See p. 193 n. 34.

64[34]

Great Tao drifts—it can go right or go left.   {1}

The thousands of things depend on it for life,   {2}
it rejects nothing.

It achieves successes,   {3}
     but does not hold tight to the fame.
It clothes and feeds the thousands of things
but does not act the ruler.

Always: {4}
Desiring nothing, it can be called 'of no account.'
The thousands of things turn back to it
     but it does not act the ruler—
it can be called 'Great.'

Because in the end   {5}
it does not insist on its own greatness,
yes, it is able to achieve its full greatness.

The spirit that rules the world is like the spirit that animates the best ruler: All-accepting, infinitely flexible {1–2}. Everything depends on its loving care, everything obeys—yet it acts like the lowest person, daring to desire nothing for itself or impose its will {3–4}. Is this not its greatness {5}?

Saying {1} counters the ideal of the strict* ruler with a normative* description of the flexible Tao* that informs the actions of the ideal ruler, adhering to no fixed rules (see 56[61]:1, 60[49]:1), but able to bring out the best in every new and different circumstance, "rejecting nothing" {2}. Sayings {3:1} and {5} (= 71[63]:5) speak against self-promotion*.

The composer's additions in {2}, {3:3–4}, and {4} take the ideals expressed in these sayings, originally ideals for the human ruler, and project them onto Tao as cosmic ruler—which in turn is a model for the earthly ruler. As in 65[51], the net effect is to express the ultimate, "cosmic*" character of Tao as the norm for a government. These additions are a pastiche of motifs and phrases found elsewhere in Laoist sayings. (For "rejecting nothing" in {2} see 42[2]:4; for hsiao/"small:of no account" in {4} see 63[32]:1; for "not acting the ruler" in {3} and {4} see 27[10]:2; for "not desiring*" in {4} see 72[64]:7, 77[57]:5; for "turning* back" to Tao in {4} see 28[16]:2.) Note the association of "not desiring" with hsiao/"of no account" in {4}. Hsiao means "small," but also refers to a socially "insignificant" person. The underlying (conventional) assumption here seems to be then that "great" people can legitimately impose their desires on the society—Tao's lack of such desires is a sign of its smallness/insignificance.

This and the next chapter share the theme of Tao as cosmic ruler. Chapter 63[32] is related to this, picturing the cosmic importance of the Tao that is an hypostatization* of the spirit animating the government of an ideal human ruler. As in the case of the final chapters of Sections 1 and 3, placing these "cosmic" chapters last in this section reflects my view that they are "climaxes" of Laoist thought on this topic, rather than "foundations" (see comments on 39[25]).

65[51]

Tao produces them   {1}
Te rears them
events shape them
talents complete their development.

And so: {2}
Among the thousands of things
        there are none that do not honor Tao and treasure Te.
This honoring Tao and treasuring Te—
no one commands it, it always happens naturally.

Tao produces them,   {3}
Te rears them,
makes them grow, nurses them,
settles them, heals them,
sustains them, protects them.

Produces but does not possess   {4}
works but does not rely on this
presides but doesn't rule.
This is mysterious Te.

The ruler who cultivates Tao and Te participates in the force that rules the universe. It is a generating, sustaining, selflessly giving force—which also animates her government. It is the secret spontaneous desire and treasure of all the world.

Sayings {1} and {3} are origin* sayings, celebrating the foundational importance of Tao* and Te* by picturing them as the cosmic source and ideal cosmic ruler. The qualities of Te as a cosmic ruler in {3} are a projection of paternalistic Chinese notions about the role of the ruler as loving parent. Saying {4} (= 27[10]:2) speaks against self-promotion*, picturing the way Laoist Te expresses itself in a self-effacing attitude toward one's political accomplishments. Saying {2:2} celebrates the cosmic* importance of Tao as that which everything spontaneously treasures (compare 48[62]:7).

Several Laoist feelings and assumptions are merged here. Tao is that good toward which everything "naturally*" gravitates {2}. Hence, on the Chinese assumption that people "naturally" give their allegiance to someone who truly merits being ruler, Tao is something easily imagined as the "ruler" of the world. But Tao is also the name of the spirit that animates the ideal human ruler, who is caring {3} and self-effacing {4}, and who does not try to force allegiance {2}. Tao/Te as world ruler, "setting the tone" for the world as perceived by Laoists, must have this same character.

The Soft Way

66[74]

"The people are always lacking in the fear of death."   {1}
Then why frighten them with death?

Supposing the people always had the fear of death,   {2}
and we could catch law breakers and kill them—
who would dare?
There is always The Executioner—he does the killing.
Doing the killing in The Executioner's place,
this is like
"doing the cutting in the master carpenter's place."
One who cuts in the master carpenter's place—
seldom it is he does not cut his hand.

Some rulers complain, "My people are reckless, not even afraid of death. I can do nothing with them." And what solution do they reach for? Executions, to scare these fearless people into line by threatening them with death! {1} They don't realize the death of a person is very serious. Taking it on oneself to kill is assuming a position above anyone's reach. It will come back on the person who does it {2}.

I believe {1:1} quotes a common complaint on the part of rulers (quoted also in 51[75]:1, see comments there), used as a take-off* point for comments by the composer. "The Executioner" {2:4} is probably either a personification of Death or a reference to the deity Heaven*. This chapter reflects the quasi-superstitious* side of Laoist thought, the sense that the ruler who becomes self-important and high-handed enough to presume to take lives is showing hubris, and this will somehow come back on him. He is letting his position as ruler go to his head and not showing enough respect for the givenness of the social world in his charge, a "spirit thing" (62[29]:1) he must stand in awe of. This quasi-superstitious feeling is especially evident in Laoist thought about violence.

Section 6 begins with four chapters (66[74], 67[31], 68[69], 69[30]) expressing Laoist views on capital punishment and war. Their negative view of violent confrontation is related to their positive ideal of the "Soft," delicate, and nonconfrontational style they think ought to guide all a ruler's actions and policies. This positive ideal is the subject of the remainder of the chapters in this section, after these first four.

67[31]

'Fine weapons' are ill-omened instruments.   {1}

Things seem to detest them   {2}
so the ambitious man does not dwell here.

"The gentleman at home favors the left   {3}
when at war he favors the right."

Weapons are ill-omened instruments   {4}
not instruments for the gentleman
he uses them when he has no choice.

What is calm and quiet is highest.   {5}

When victorious, he does not think this a fine thing   {6}
because to think it fine is to delight in slaughtering people.
One who delights in slaughtering people
    cannot achieve his purposes in the world.

"In fortunate times, prefer the left   {7}
in *mourning,* prefer the right."
The lower officer takes his stand on the left
the higher officer takes his stand on the right.
This says: He takes his stand as at a mourning ceremony.

At the slaughter of such masses of men,   {8}
    he weeps for them, mourning and lamenting.
When victorious in the battle—
he takes his stand as at a mourning ceremony.

Some glory in their fine weapons {1} and look for the day when they can show their strength in glorious battle. But what is this? It is delight in slaughtering people {6}. There sometimes comes a day when battle cannot be avoided, but the superior person looks on this as the most unfortunate of days {1,3,4}. In the attack, tradition assigns the right flank of the army to the superior officer. Why? Because this is also the place assigned when one is in mourning {7–8}.

Saying {1} counters the admiration of "fine weapons" by casting them as "unlucky." Saying {2} (= 1[24]:4) is a quasi-superstitious* Laoist saying that can apply to many ways in which people put themselves at odds with reality ("things*"). Saying {6} counters the admiration of war, again on a quasi-superstitious* basis. I think {3} and {7:1–2} are common sayings reflecting customs as to how gentlemen of the nobility should place themselves differently at gatherings during peacetime and wartime, normal times and mourning times.

The composer's main point is given in {7:5}: He reinterprets the traditional custom of placing the highest officer on the right in battle ({7:4}), to mean that the superior man should look upon battle, even victory in battle, in an attitude of mourning (compare 68[69]:4). He makes this point by conflating and reinterpreting three different customs, related to differences in peacetime and wartime etiquette {3}, to battlefield positions {7:3–4}, and to mourning {7:2, 8:4}. (He is probably reading new meanings into old customs here. Saying 75[78]:4 also reads a new "hidden" meaning into ancient custom, and this practice is reflected in the Confucian *Doctrine of the Mean*[1] as well.)

The arrangement of the sayings here leads many commentators to suspect textual corruption of some kind. I think it shows many techniques used by the composers elsewhere: The composer here frames* his material, by placing {3} at the beginning and picking it up again in {7}. (Compare the placing of 50[53]:2, picked up in 50[53]:6). He also makes use of many catchwords to connect the different sayings: Section {4} repeats {1} and *gentleman* from {3}, thus connecting {1} and {3}. The contrast in {7:1–2} probably was originally "good fortune/ill fortune"—the composer has changed "ill fortune" to "mourning," as a connective* alteration linking this saying to {7:5} and {8} (see "Additional Textual Notes"). Section {8} picks up *slaughter* and *victorious* from {6}. I think the repetitions in this chapter express a sense of pathos.

*Shih** sometimes served as soldiers or military officers. This chapter and the following two seem partly addressed to *shih* considering this possibility.

---

1. 19/6.

68[69]

Military men have a saying: {1}
"I do not presume to act as master, I act as guest
I do not presume to advance an inch, I retreat a foot."

This is like   {2}
"going forward without going forward
rolling up the sleeves but baring no arm
attacking without showing hostility
drawing with no sword."

Nothing brings greater disaster than the motto: {3}
"The enemy is nothing."
Thinking, "the enemy is nothing":
close to losing my Treasure.

Yes, when they cross weapons and attack each other   {4}
the one in mourning will win.

Some soldiers take every occasion to show off how strong and fearless they are, charging the enemy recklessly at the drop of a hat. But there is a better way: Playing the submissive one {1}. Advancing in such a way that they will think you are retreating. Attacking them in such a way they will not even know they have an opponent {2}. The "fearless" soldier likes to attack with the attitude, "The enemy is a nothing!" With such bloated self-importance one loses the essential thing one should never lose {3}. The best soldier is not the one who treats the enemy as nothing, but who respects life and goes into battle reluctantly and with great sadness {4}.

Saying {4} counters the attitude of glorying in war, posing the contrasting ideal of the one whose great respect for human life makes him approach battle in mourning (compare 67[31]:7–8).

I think {1} and {2} are sayings borrowed from contemporary military strategists, which recommend very indirect and deceptive tactics as the way to succeed. I take it that the images in these sayings describe how one's actions appear to the opponent; for example, "drawing with no sword" describes in concrete and highly exaggerated terms the deceptive and confusing appearance of the general strategy involved. "Motto" in {3:1} is not in the text. I add it because I take *wu ti*/"there is no enemy" in {3} as a motto, meant to convey complete lack of fear of the enemy. (Compare Mencius's description[1] of the bravado of the *shih** Po-kung Yu.) The interest of the composer is not so much in military success through deceptive strategy as in the connection between fighting style and *attitude:* Some soldiers take fighting as a chance to prove their own personal superiority. (They want to act the "master" rather than the deferential "guest.") This kind of soldier will prefer direct and dramatic confrontations, allowing him to show off his strength and courage. He will also take the attitude expressed in the motto "[For me] the enemy is nothing." Taking this attitude means that the person has lost what Laoists consider to be the essential "Treasure" {3:4}: the respect for others and the *non*-self-assertive spirit they cultivate. (Compare the three non-assertive virtues praised in 3[67]:2, which are also called there *my three treasures.*) The person who maintains this spirit will also be one who approaches war in the attitude of mourning {4}.

---

1. 2A/2,4, see p. 106.

69[30]

One who assists the people's rulers with Tao   {1}
does not use weapons to force changes in the world.

"Such action usually backfires."   {2}

Where troops camp, thorns and brambles grow.   {3}

Excellence consists in: {4}
Being resolute, that is all
      not venturing to take control by force
being resolute, but not boastful
being resolute, but not overbearing
being resolute, but not arrogant
being resolute, when you have no choice
being resolute, but not forcing.

Things are vigorous, then grow old and weak: {5}
A case of 'not-Tao.'
Not-Tao, soon gone.

Some high counselors urge rulers to take over the world by force of arms—and they themselves lead troops into battle {1}. But violent armies are a blot on the face of the world: Brambles grow where they camp {3}. Forced success is always short lived {5}, and violence always comes back to visit the violent {2}. This is not the right Way. The excellent counselor must put aside masculine pride and boasting, and simply stand steadfast, doing battle when circumstances leave no choice {4}.

Saying {1} is a normative* description of what one does who has Tao. It counters the readiness of some *shih**-advisers ("assisting rulers with Tao") to advocate war or lead armies themselves, as a means of gaining political objectives. (Mencius[1] also criticizes such *shih*.) *Ch'iang*/forcing* is often a negative term in the Laoist vocabulary. It is one of the words elsewhere translated as "hard," the opposite of Laoist *jou-jo*/Softness*-Weakness. Saying {2} looks like a common saying that might apply to many things. Saying {3} probably has a quasi-superstitious* basis: Brambles growing where troops camp is an image of the "unlucky" character of war. Saying {4} is related to sayings against boastful self-promotion*, countering the boasting/forcing* attitude of those who glory in war as an occasion for proving personal prowess, posing instead the ideal attitude of the soldier who is just resolute, fighting only when he must. In {5} the seasonal flourishing and dying of vegetation serves as a negative metaphorical* image of the short-lived nature of human actions that are "forced*." (Originally this saying was probably related more to sayings against "exhausting" excitement and agitation*. But it occurs following a criticism of forcing also in 33[55]:5.)

The composer's point lies in the association between (a) "boastful" self-assertion {4}, (b) a "forcing*" attitude expressed in the readiness to resort to violence {1}, and (c) the idea that such forcing can have no lasting* good results {2-3, 5}. On the connection between (a) and (b), compare the associations linking 71[63]:5 with the rest of 71[63]. Underlying (c) is an insistence that human action should be integrated into reality as given. Violence is the extreme case of something extraneous imposed on given reality from without. (Because {4:3} interrupts the parallelism and duplicates {4:8}, I believe it is a connective* addition. The catchword *forcing* connects {4} to {1}.)

---

1. 7B/4,1.

70[60]

Governing a large state is like cooking a small fish.   {1}

Rule the world by Tao   {2}
then ghosts will not take to haunting.

It is not that the ghosts will not haunt   {3}
their haunting will cause no hurt to humankind.
(It's not only that their haunting will not hurt humankind,
the Wise Person also does not cause hurt to them.
These two do not hurt each other.)

Yes, Te unifies and restores.   {4}

Some rulers think that a large state can endure rough handling. But no matter how large, a society is a delicate thing, requiring a soft touch {1}. Heavy-handed intrusion can throw everything out of balance, stirring up even the ghosts of the dead to roam around doing mischief {2–3}. To avoid hurt of any kind, what is needed is rule by subtle Tao, and by the gentle Te that unites and restores everything in the world to its natural harmony {4}.

Saying {1} counters the tendency of rulers toward heavy-handed intrusion, calling to mind instead the delicacy needed to cook a small fish as the appropriate attitude (compare 71[63]). Saying {2} celebrates the benefits* of ruling by Tao. It has a quasi-superstitious* basis: Ancient Chinese believed in ghosts of the dead who if provoked might use their supernatural power to hurt people. There was also a belief, apparently shared by Laoists, that the ruler has a powerful but invisible effect on the structure and dynamics of all parts of the world: If he rules wrongly, it can throw everything out of kilter—society, nature, and ghosts. Ruling by the subtle spirit of Tao, the ruler blends in with the organic harmony of society and causes no disturbance in the order of things. Saying {3} celebrates the powers and benefits* of Te*.

Section {3} is difficult to make sense of. I tentatively take {3:4–5} to mean that the ruler does not "hurt" the ghosts by his bad rule, and so they don't hurt him either (personally? by hurting his people?). Note the composer's implied equivalence between (a) ruling delicately {1}, (b) ruling by Tao {2}, and (c) ruling by Te {3}.

For the effect of the ruler's conduct on the world in general, see the mention of "phantom women coming out after dark" in the quotation cited under "Superstitious*," and also the *Chuang Tzu*'s description of a good king's reign, "gods and ghosts did no harm, the four seasons were perfectly proportioned...all that lived escaped an untimely death."[1] The king's effect on nature is also vividly dramatized in the *Yüeh Ling* section of the *Li Chi*,[2] which prescribes that, on the day beginning each season, the king should enter a certain palace with specially arranged rooms. He should ritually enter the proper room, wear certain clothes, and eat certain foods appropriate to the season just beginning. Doing the wrong thing will throw the seasons out of kilter; for example, if he eats "winter food" in summer, he might cause summer snowstorms.

This chapter begins a series of four chapters (70[60], 71[63], 72[64], 73[36]) dealing with the Soft*—delicate, careful, subtle, nonconfrontational—style of ruling that Laoists advocate.

---

1. Quoted in Graham 1989: 305.
2. Legge 1885: 249–310.

71[63]

Be a Non Doer {1}
work at Not Working
acquire a taste for what has no taste.

Treat small things as though they were great {2}
treat few things as though they were many.

"Reward what is injurious, with kind Te." {3}

Plan difficult things focusing on the easy parts {4}
do great things focusing on the small details.
Difficult tasks in the world always begin from what is easy
great tasks in the world always begin from what is small.

And so the Wise Person: {5}
Does not 'do great things'
and so is able to fulfill his greatness.

Yes: {6}
Light agreement is never very trustworthy
considering everything easy makes everything difficult.

And so the Wise Person: {7}
Treats things as difficult,
and in the end has no difficulty.

People full of themselves are always anxious to "do great things" {5}. They think only the great and difficult result is worthy of them; they are too important to be bothered with the "easy" details. What difficulties they will have {6}! The smart person is not full of herself, as a great "doer" {1}. She submits herself to the task, developing a subtle appreciation for the importance of what seems barely noticeable to others {1}. She begins with the most insignificant details and approaches these with the care one gives to what is most difficult {2, 4}. She treats everything as almost beyond her and in the end brings everything under control {7}.

Saying {1} is instruction* in Laoist self-cultivation. Note the connection between "not doing*" and developing an extremely subtle sensitivity—opposite the "doer," who is typically preoccupied with putting his stamp on reality, rather than sensitive to the subtle particularities of always-new situations. Sayings {2}, {6}, and {7} speak against underestimating the difficulty of tasks, and hence being careless. "Treat things as difficult" means dealing with them carefully (see also 58[73]:4). Saying {4:1–2} counters the tendency to focus attention on the great results one hopes to attain, neglecting attention to the small tasks necessary to get there (compare 72[64]:3). Saying {3} is a common saying, quoted also in the Confucian *Analects*.[1] (See the similar association with Te* in 9[79] and 60[49]:2.) In {5} I take *wei ta/*"do great things" to suggest a person attracted to impressive projects as a means of self-promotion*. The saying poses instead the ideal of a self-completion associated with a self-effacing attitude. (Saying {5} is a version of 64[34]:5.)

By placing {5} with the other sayings here, the composer suggests that the person who wants to focus only on "great" things, neglecting small beginnings, does so because of his own sense of self-importance. Like 72[64], this chapter is important in showing the particular, nonliteral meaning of *not doing*. *Doing* here means doing something obviously *significant*, something that stands out as great over against the ordinary routine of things, allowing the doer also to stand out. Conversely, *not doing* describes the attitude and style of one who can take his eyes off of the outstanding results that will bring him personal glory and submit himself entirely to the practical demands of the task, including especially subtle sensitivity {1} and painstaking attention to its most insignificant details. (Compare the idealization of the person willing to take on his state's "dirty work" in 75[78]:4.)

---

1. 14/36.

72[64]

When sitting still, they are easy to hold down   {1}
no omens yet, it is easy to plan
when fragile, they are easy to break
when small, they are easy to scatter.

Work on it when it isn't yet   {2}
put it in order when it is not yet disordered.

A tree you can barely get your arms around,   {3}
    grows from a tiny shoot
a nine-story tower begins as a heap of earth
a thousand-mile journey begins under your feet.

Working ruins, grasping loses.   {4}

And so the Wise Person: {5}
Does not work, so does not ruin
does not grasp, so does not lose.

"When the people are engaged in some task,   {6}
they are always on the point of finishing when they ruin it."
Careful at the end just as at the beginning
then there will be no ruining of the work.

And so the Wise Person: {7}
Desires to be desireless
does not prize goods hard to come by
learns to be un-Learned
turns back to the place all others have gone on from.

So as to help along the naturalness   {8}
    of the thousands of things
without presuming to be a Worker.

A natural state of society is not achieved easily. People start being disruptive, things start going in the wrong direction, and soon the organic harmony of the world is gone. Something must be done. And yet "working ruins"—the solution can be as disruptive as the problem {4–5}. The answer is this: Pay careful attention all the time, as though you were always at the beginning of something {6}. Catch problems in their smallest beginnings. Head off the difficulty before anything seems really to have gone wrong {1–3}. Then you will never have to be disruptive yourself. Acting in this way requires a certain state of mind: A constant returning to that deep state before desires have arisen, before the mind has become "Learned"—the place everyone else has long since run away from {7}.

Note that (like 73[36]:1) {1} and {2} assume it sometimes is necessary to take strongly intrusive measures against movements in the society that the ruler judges to be harmful. Saying {3} (like 71[63]:4) counters the tendency to focus on great goals, neglecting the necessary small beginnings. Saying {6} looks like a common complaint among managers about the way workers become careless toward the end of a job. Saying {4} is the same as 62[29]:2. Saying {5} celebrates the benefits* of operating with a "not working*" attitude. Saying {7} gives instruction* in Laoist self-cultivation. The "place all others have gone on from" is the Still* state of mind before it has been stirred up by desires* and become active in conceptual Learning* (see also comments on "Dwelling*").

"Working" in this chapter describes the *attitude* of one who sees things in terms of "my important work" versus inert things to be worked on. Having no respect for things to be worked on, such a person will tend to be inattentive to the subtleties of the issues he is dealing with. "Not working" by contrast, describes not literal nonintervention, but the attitude of one strenuously attentive to the smallest details, able to nip things in the bud and so avoid the kind of *overt and dramatically disruptive intervention* necessary when things have gotten very out of hand. This kind of intervention will ruin the *tzujan*/naturalness* {8} of the social world, the organic* harmony deeply rooted in the given state of affairs. This "natural" organic harmony is an *ideal* state of things brought about by the extremely careful work of a "not working" ruler. Saying {7} implies that this acute sensitivity and subtle style of intervention is possible only to one who has "turned* back" to a deeper state which the conventional mind tries always to get away from.

73[36]

When you want to shrink something   {1}
    you must always enlarge it.
When you want to weaken something
    you must always strengthen it.
When you want to neglect something
    you must always involve yourself with it.
When you want to deprive something
    you must always give to it.
This is called 'Subtle Clarity.'

Softness and Weakness overcome what is hard and strong.   {2}

"The fish must not leave the depths   {3}
the state's 'sharp weapons' must not be shown to others."

Confrontation is not the way. When something goes wrong, do not oppose it directly. Build it up, let it overreach itself and come to its own ruin {1}. This is the Soft Way {2} of the Clear-sighted {1:9}. (It only works if they do not know you are doing it, {3}).

Saying {1} corrects the tendency to react to opposition by using the most obvious and direct methods of attack. It relies on the strategy expressed in our proverb, "Give them enough rope and they'll hang themselves." Saying {2} celebrates the superiority of Softness*/Weakness over its opposite, using a formula borrowed from speculation about the "conquest* cycle." (Ch'iang/hard also means "forcing*," the opposite of the "Soft" tactics advocated in {1}.) Because of the context here, I take "sharp weapons" in {3} to be a metaphorical reference to clever stratagems devised by a ruler or his counselors, such as that described in {1}, which the saying says must be kept secret. (The same phrase occurs in 77[57]:3.)

For the composer, the indirect strategy of {1} is an example of how a Laoist ruler's Soft/Weak quality of mind expresses itself in dealing with opposition. "Soft/Weak" describes an indirect and nonconfrontational *style* of acting, which might also be very intrusive however and even "destructive" in the results aimed at. (Compare Japanese "judo," derived from the Chinese *jou-Tao*/"Soft Tao.") I take "subtle Clarity*" in {1:9} to refer to the intuitive insight the composer sees manifest in {1} and {2}. (Compare 49[27]:3:6.)

74[76]

People begin life Soft and Weak   {1}
when they are dead they are hard and firm.
Among the thousands of things:
Grass and trees begin life Soft and tender
when they are dead they are withered and brittle.

Yes, strength and hardness accompany death   {2}
Softness and Weakness accompany life.

And so: {3}
With a battle axe too hardened, you cannot win
when a tree becomes hard, then comes the axe.

The strong and the great stand lowest   {4}
the Soft and Weak stand highest.

"A great man is a strong man and a hard man. An unyielding man who makes clear decisions and carries them out with an absolutely firm will. A man who lets nothing get in his way."

Or so some think. But consider infants, with fresh life in their young bodies: They're Soft and Weak. The most "unyielding" kind of body is the stiff corpse. Likewise with plants—the young shoot most full of life is also the most flexible and tender. Dead branches are "hard" and "strong" {1}. The "hardest" tree is the one that has died and is ready for the axe. And axes—the "hardest" axes just chip and shatter when you try to use them {3}. To become really Alive, it's necessary also to cultivate what seems Soft and Weak in yourself {2}. Hard men are dead inside.

Saying {1} uses some metaphorical* images to celebrate the felt character of Softness* as an internal energy: Like fresh *sheng*/life* newly begun. Saying {2} makes the same point as {1} only more briefly. Saying {3} uses two metaphorical* images to picture the negative character of a "hard" state of mind: Brittle and short lived. (It reads literally: "Axe hard then not win, tree hard then axe." Because of "win" in the first line I think *ping*/axe:weapon there refers to a metal weapon—it has been tempered incorrectly and so is too brittle and breaks in battle. My understanding of both lines is new. For the short-lived character of what is *ch'iang*/hard:forced* see 69[30]:4–5.) Saying {4} celebrates the superiority of Softness over hardness. The connection between "strong" and "great" in this saying provides a good suggestion as to the kind of person Laoists have in mind when they criticize being "hard and strong."

This chapter and the next (75[78]) celebrate directly the greatness of the hypostatized* Softness/Weakness Laoists cultivate internally. The four chapters immediately preceding them (70[60], 71[63], 72[64], 73[36]) give examples of how this internally cultivated Soft/not-working state of mind expresses itself in the governing style of the ideal ruler.

75[78]

Nothing in the world   {1}
is Softer or Weaker than water.
But when it attacks what is hard and strong
none of them can win out,
because they have no way of affecting it.

Softness overcomes what is hard   {2}
Weakness overcomes what is unyielding.

Everyone in the world understands it   {3}
no one can practice it.

And so the Wise Person says: {4}
Taking on a state's dirt makes one lord of its earth altars
taking on a state's misfortunes makes one King of the world.

Right words seem the opposite.   {5}

Some present a rigid and unyielding front. But a stiff front is most easily chipped at. The smart person is firm underneath, but completely Soft and flexible on the surface. Being flexible means having no fixed shape that others can hammer at {1}. Inside, everyone already knows that this "Weak" way is the most effective way—but carrying it out is another matter {3}.

What does it mean to cultivate this Weakness? It means also learning to be the Weak one in the government, the one who has to take on the difficult and unglamorous jobs others do not want to dirty their hands with. But while others are enjoying themselves, this one is doing the job that fits her to be true ruler of the world {4}.

Like 47[43]:1, {1} uses water as a metaphorical* image to celebrate the powers and benefits* of Softness*/Weakness. The "Weakness" of water here seems to refer to its infinite flexibility: Because it identifies itself with no fixed shape, neither can it be negatively affected (*yi*, lit. "changed") by piercing, breaking, bending, and so on. I take the "hard and strong" things that water wins out over to be rocks on the riverbank (compare 47[43]:1). Saying {2} celebrates the superiority of Softness/Weakness over their opposites (using a formula borrowed from speculation about the "conquest* cycle"). Both {3} and {5} are sayings about the paradoxical character of Laoist teaching*. (Saying {3} is a version of 45[70]:1.) In the background of {4} is a Chinese investiture ceremony at which the Emperor symbolically entrusted a particular territory to a local feudal lord by giving him a clod of earth from a special mound.[1] "Receiving this dirt" made the recipient official master of the Earth altars set up to the god of the soil of that particular territory. But *kou*/dirt also means "garbage, filth," and this allows the person who coined this saying to reinterpret the entire ceremony: What makes one a true ruler is to take on oneself the "garbage" of the state; that is, its most "unlucky" happenings, its most difficult problems. (Compare the importance ascribed to hard work at governmental tasks in 71[63] and 72[64].) This gives one the spiritual status not only of feudal lord, but of Emperor*, King of the world. (Compare the reinterpretation of traditional customs in 67[31].)

Both {1-2} and {4} are examples of paradoxical wisdom {5}. *Jou*/Soft and especially *jo*/Weak have negative connotations (greatness is conventionally connected with overt strength, see 74[76]:4). This may also be involved in the composer's association between being "Soft/Weak" and lowering oneself to do a state's dirty work.

---

1. See E. Chavannes 1910: 452–453.

Against Disquieting "Improvements"

76[80]

Oh for a small country with few people!   {1}

Supposing there were men   {2}
    with the talents of dozens and hundreds,
    but no one employed them.
Supposing the people took death seriously,
    and did not travel far distances.

Although there exist boats and carriages,   {3}
    they have no occasion to ride in them.
Although there exist armor and weapons,
    they have no occasion to show them off.

Supposing people returned to knotting cords,   {4}
    and using this as writing.

They find their food savory   {5}
they find their clothes elegant
they are content with their homes
they are fond of their folkways.

Neighboring states are in sight of one another   {6}
so they hear the sounds of each others' dogs and roosters—
but people reach old age and die
with no comings and goings between them.

The dream of some rulers is a large territory with a huge population; the latest in carriages and boats and military gear; talented men arriving by the hundreds from all over, wanting to serve in the government; the whole state abuzz and ambitious for progress. But if you want to dream, why not dream peace: A small country with a few contented people {1}. They might have talents and contrivances to spare, but they like simplicity so much that they find little use for them. Everything they want is in their backyard—what need is there to invent new things or travel to new places {2–6}?

This chapter counters the desire* of Warring States rulers to encourage "progressive" improvements*. Saying {1} is intended paradoxically: In place of the usual ambition to reign over large territories and population,[1] it suggests the ambition of ruling over "a small country, few people." Saying {3} criticizes the desire for better equipment for travel and war (the sign of an "advanced" state), posing the counterimage of a society which has such things in abundance but ignores them (compare 20[46]:1:1–3). Saying {2:1–3} counters the desire to attract skilled people from all over,[2] posing the same kind of counterimage as in {3}. "Traveling far distances" in {2:5} describes a restless and ambitious, mobile population, contrasted with the exaggerated image in {6} of people so content they never even visit the next village nearby. "Take death seriously" in {2:4} probably describes a sober rather than reckless people (see comments at 51[75]:1). According to legend, "knotting cords" {4} was a primitive recording device prior to writing, hence {4} poses an exaggerated counterimage of a people deliberately becoming more "backward." Although there were some literal "primitivists" in ancient China,[3] I doubt if this chapter describes a literal program advocated by Laoists. For example, why would there be modern contrivances in abundance in a primitive society? This "unrealistic" touch shows that the whole is an aphoristic*, exaggerated corrective image, not a literal description.

This chapter, presenting an idealized and exaggerated contrast to "improvement" programs others advocated, is followed by four others (77[57], 78[19], 79[3], 80[65]) criticizing specific programs Laoists are opposed to, and proposing an ideal governing style that runs directly counter to these programs.

---

1. See *Mencius** 7A/21,1.
2. See ibid. 1A/7,18, quoted p. 100.
3. See p. 91–92, and see Graham 1989: 64–74.

77[57]

"Rule the kingdom by the norm   {1}
wage war by the unexpected."
Take over the world by Not Working.

How do I know it is so?   {2}
By this.

In the world: The more rules and restrictions there are   {3}
    the poorer the people will be.
The people: The more 'sharp weapons' they have,
    the more disordered the state and the clans will be.
Men: The more clever and skillful they are,
    the more weird things will start to happen.

The more you publicize rules and laws,   {4}
the more robbers and thieves you will have.

Yes, the Wise Person says: {5}
I Do Nothing,
    and the people transform themselves.
I love Stillness,
    and the people bring themselves to correctness.
I do No Work,
    and the people enrich themselves.
I have no desires,
    and the people by themselves become Simple.

Rulers are becoming more ambitious and clever. They have schemes for making better laws. Schemes for improving job skills among the people by education and encouragement {3}. They think such programs will eventually make them King of the world {1}.

But all this 'doing' is interference in the natural harmony of the world. People are restrained, on the one side, making them poor. People are encouraged, on the other side, making them overambitious and unruly. Hemming them in with rules just makes them resentful and rebellious {3–4}. What the society really needs is a nondoing ruler who is most Still and content in herself, and who spreads her Still spirit to all the people. Then the people's natural goodness and energy will come out, and this will be fully sufficient to transform the society and enrich the state {5}.

I believe {1:1–2} is a common proverb contrasting tactics appropriate for peacetime governance, with tactics best suited to war. This is used as a take-off* point to introduce a Laoist motto about not doing* in {1:3} (= 25[48]:3). Saying {2} is a stock reply of Laoists to the demand for reasons for their views—"by this" means by intuitive insight (see comments under "This*"). Sayings {3:1–2} and {4} protest attempts to improve* the social order by publicizing written laws (see further under "Naming*"). On *li ch'i/*"sharp weapons," see 73[36]:3. The prediction of "weird" things resulting from raising people's skill levels {3:5–6} reflects a quasi-superstitious* sentiment: Attempts to introduce fundamental changes will disrupt the established ("natural*") order of things and cause weird things to happen (ghostly apparitions, deformed animals, and so forth, see 70[60].) Saying {5} celebrates the great benefits* that occur when the ruler sets the proper tone for the society by ruling it in the right spirit—"not doing*," "not-desiring*," "Still*." (*P'u/*Simplicity in the last line is elsewhere translated "Uncarved* Block." Because *wu shih/*"not working" in {5:6} duplicates *wu wei/*"not doing" in {5:2} and repeats the *wu shih* in {1:3}, I think it is a connective* addition by the composer of this chapter.)

As in 79[3] and 62[29], the composer here characterizes various social improvement programs {3–4} as a negative "doing" {1, 5}. As in 71[63] and 72[64], one can see that here *doing* means doing something significant that stands out against the ordinary routine—here, doing something that introduces new "improvements" in the society—in contrast to a "not doing" style of administration that actively strives to preserve the "natural" organic* harmony of the given (see 72[64]:8).

78[19]

Discard "Wisdom," throw away "Knowledge"—   {1}
the people will benefit a hundredfold.
Discard "Goodness," throw away "Morality"—
the people will turn back to respect and caring.
Discard "Skill," throw away "Profit"—
robbers and thieves will disappear.

Taking these three lines as your text—   {2}
    this is not sufficient.
Give them something to fasten on to:
Pay attention to the Raw, embrace the Uncarved
discount your personal interests, make your desires few.

Everyone urges new government mottoes: "Be a Wise Person!" "Goodness and Morality!" "Calculate what is Profitable!" "Encourage Skill!" But what does this do? Children and parents cultivate artificial Goodness—and lose the respect and caring that comes naturally to them. You begin looking for profit and encouraging skill—and the people also look for profit and become skillful thieves. Dropping all these programs is the best thing you can do for your state {1}. But this is not really enough. Give the people something concrete to hold on to: Cultivate the subtle spirit that comes from getting rid of your desires and ambitions. Put "civilizing" projects out of your mind and show how much you care for things in their raw state. Embrace the Uncarved Block {2}.

Saying {1} criticizes several movements Laoists lump together as attempts to improve* the world according to some ideal plan. The capitalized words designate mottoes that summarize programs advocated by others. *Knowledge, Goodness,* and *Morality* are keywords for Mencius*,[1] but Laoists lump these with *li*/profit, a key word in Mohist utilitarian thinking,[2] which Mencius also viewed negatively.[3] *Sheng*/wisdom normally describes the Laoist ideal *sheng jen*/"Wise Person" (an "inconsistency" in Laoist word use, see "Naming*.") Note also that *respect and caring* represent artificial Confucian virtues in 12[18], but here represent "natural" goodness.) Saying {2:4-5} is instruction* in Laoist self-cultivation. The composer's introduction in {2:1-3} is probably intended somewhat ironically and humorously: Following it, one expects a description of a very tangible basis for social order that the people can hold on to. Instead we get something *less* tangible, the subtle internal spirit of the ruler who sets a tone for society by cultivating the mental state called *not-desiring** and *Uncarved** Block. (*Wen*/text in {2:1} also means "culture," allowing for the alternate reading, "not sufficient to take as refined culture.")

Section {2} raises the question: Did Laoists expect rulers to engage in self-cultivation? My conjecture about this is based on a passage[4] which pictures Mencius as an indispensable guide[5] for a king who wants to practice *jen*/Good government, because Mencius has made a project of cultivating Goodness, and the king has not. Mencius must instruct the king on *policies*[6] that express an ideal Goodness that the king himself has only incipiently. If the analogy holds, Laoists did not expect kings to practice self-cultivation, but advised them to implement policies expressive of the state of mind which Laoist *shih* cultivated.

1. See for example *Mencius** 6A/6,7, 7A/21,4, quoted p. 77.
2. Graham 1989: 41.
3. 1A/1,1-6, 6B/4,5.
4. 1A/7, quoted and discussed p. 97–102.
5. 1A/7,19-20.
6. 1A/7,22-24.

79[3]

Not promoting the wise and worthy   {1}
    brings it about that the people are not contentious.
Not prizing goods hard to come by
    brings it about that the people do not become thieves.
Not paying attention to the desirable
    brings it about that the people's minds
    do not become disordered.

And so, the government of the Wise Person: {2}
Empty their minds, fill their bellies
weaken their ambitions, strengthen their bones.

Always bring it about that the people   {3}
    are without knowledge and without desires.
Bring it about that the clever ones
    do not presume to set about doing.

Do Not Doing   {4}
and nothing will be left un-*governed.*

"The way to build a great society is to provide incentives," they say. "Promote the learned and outstanding and you will encourage people to excel in learning." They do not realize what they are doing. "Providing incentives" will turn people into social climbers, and quarrels will start where once there was peace. They are stirring up the destructive forces, neglecting the society's organic unity and harmony for the sake of the grand plans of some thinkers {1 and 3}. The ruler must have a Still, not-doing, not-desiring mind—a mind not active and ambitious for change. She and those she appoints must be the Still spirit of the contented society, and spread not ambition but Stillness and contentment, by everything they do {3-4}.

Saying {1} opposes the tone set for society by a ruler who accords special recognition to what appears especially "desirable" {1:5-6}—especially desirable goods (1:3-4), or especially desirable administrative staff {1:1-2}. This promotes social disharmony by stirring up disorderly desires in the people, causing both thievery and a *cheng*/quarrelsome:contentious* spirit among those competing for government appointments. *Shang hsien*/"promote wise and worthy [*shih**]" is a policy advocated by many contemporary *shih*.[1] It is unlikely that Laoists, who aspire to public office, are entirely opposed to promotion on the basis of merit. Line {1:1-2} is an aphoristic* corrective warning, rather than a rejection of the entire policy. (Mencius explicitly advocates promoting *hsien*, but he also[2] warns against the same negative side-effect mentioned here. Laoists may have regarded *hsien* as a description of *shih* they disliked—*hsien*/worth is used negatively in 52[77]:3.) Saying {2} is directed against contemporary "improvement*" programs encouraging an ambitious peasantry. It evokes the exaggerated counterimage of a program fostering a healthy peasantry whose contentment is not disturbed by such programs (see 76[80]). Saying {4} is a version of 25[48]:2. (*Chih*/governed is a connective* alteration, a link to *chih*/government in {2:1}, which in turn is an alteration of the standard introduction "And so the Wise Person..."). The composer's lines in {3} link previous themes: "No knowledge...no desires*" corresponds to "empty their minds...weaken their ambitions" in {2}. The "clever" ones are the *hsien*/"wise and worthy" of {1:1-2}, whom one should not put in positions where they can "do" anything, a connection to "not doing*" in {4}. As in 77[57], the last lines here link criticism of social improvement* programs to the recurrent theme of "not doing*."

---

1. See p. 59.
2. 1B/7,3.

80[65]

Those Excellent at doing Tao in ancient times— {1}
it was not to enlighten the people, but to keep them stupid.

The difficulty in governing the people— {2}
because of their knowledge.

Yes: {3}
By "Knowledge!" govern the state—
    a crime against the state.
By "Ignorance!" govern the state—
    a boon to the state.

Always: To understand these two lines, {4}
    is also to understand the Ideal Pattern.
Always: To understand the Ideal Pattern,
    is to have mysterious Te.

Mysterious Te is deep, far-reaching, {5}
in opposition to things—
only afterward comes the Great Harmony.

Some say, "Stop letting society run along the same old ruts. Take control. Learn how to think and plan, to steer the society along new and better paths. Teach your people to think and plan, to analyze everything in terms of ends and means. Make 'New Thinking' the motto of your government" {1–3}.

But thinkers are full of themselves and their plans, caring nothing for the goodness already present in the actual and present society. "Thinking" rulers ruin the society in their care. "Thinking" people upset the order of things. One should say rather, make "Not Thinking" the motto of your government {3}. Cultivate a not-thinking mind and try to infuse society with this not-thinking spirit. Yes, this will bring you into opposition with some strong tendencies taking root in society nowadays, but eventually you will restore the Great Harmony {5}.

Sayings {1}, {2}, and {3} are probably directed against programs such as that of the Mohists*,[1] who saw utilitarian rationality as a central instrument of progressive improvement*. Saying {1} is a normative* description of the policy of one who has Tao*. It poses a deliberately shocking and exaggerated image in which idealized ancient* rulers, far from encouraging the spread of rationality, had the policy of "keeping the people stupid." Saying {2} suggests that a rationalizing spirit will make people begin calculating their own self-interest and so make them uncooperative with their leaders. I think "Knowledge" in {3} is a motto describing a governing philosophy centered on utilitarian rationality, advocating both that governing officials calculate rational utility in deciding public policy and that the people be taught to think about their lives and tasks in the same fashion. For Laoists, rational calculation is the enemy of the *organic* social harmony they prize so highly (compare 79[3]:3, and comments on "Understanding*" and "Naming*"). Hence "Ignorance" is suggested as an exaggerated countermotto. Saying {5:1} celebrates the greatness of Laoist Te*.

The composer's comment in {4} presents {3} as an expression of the fundamental principle behind Laoist political wisdom. (This should not be pressed. Something similar is said of 36[42]:6:2.) To understand this principle—to see everything from this perspective—is to have (Laoist) Te. I take *yü wu fan*/"opposition to things" in {5:2–3} to refer to the way this Te, as the spirit guiding the ideal ruler, runs counter to the tendencies of people to develop in certain directions Laoists consider negative—here, the development toward increased rationality (compare 36[42]:2). "Only afterward" is it able to restore ideal Harmony. (*Shun*/harmony also means "submission." In paternalistic Chinese political thought, shared by Laoists, part of "natural*" social harmony is the submission of all to proper norms and authorities.[2])

---

1. See Graham 1989: 37–41.
2. See ibid.: 302–303.

81[37]

Tao invariably Does Nothing, and nothing remains not done.   {1}

If the princes and kings can watch over it   {2}
the thousands of things will change by themselves.
If they change, and become desirous and active,
I will restrain them with the Nameless One's Simplicity.
Restraining them with the Nameless One's Simplicity
    will cause them no disgrace.
Not being disgraced, they will be Still.

The world will order itself.   {3}

When self-assertion disrupts social contentment, something must be done. But strict law enforcement and strong repression makes people feel disgraced. Disgraced people are not at peace. The ideal ruler has cultivated in her own spirit the Simple Uncarved Block, which remains without names, without worded prescriptions. Such a person alone can restrain disruption gently and without making anyone feel humiliated. This brings about a real atmosphere of Stillness in the society {1–2}. Under the care of this person's Not-Doing spirit, the world will put itself in order {3}.

Sayings {1} and {2:1–2} celebrate the benefits* of ruling by Tao. Saying {1} pictures the Tao that animates the ideal government as identical with the spirit of "Not Doing*," and celebrates its wonderful effectiveness in ensuring social order. (It is based on the saying in 25[48]:2.) As in 77[57]:5, hua/change in {2:2} describes the utopian "conversion" of the society that results from ruling by Tao. Saying {3} counters the "doing*" attitude of self-important rulers, posing instead the image of a society whose order arises organically from within (when the ruler sets the proper tone).

The composer's comment in {2:3–7} uses {2:1–2} as a take-off* point. He reads hua/change now as something negative, leading to discordant "desire*" and "activity," which need to be restrained. (Tso/activity is a negative opposite to "Stillness" in 28[16]:2 too.) Such desire/activity poses a dilemma for Laoists: On the one hand, they are against ruling with a strong hand. On the other hand, they have a definite ideal of an organically harmonious society that the ruler ought to foster. This must mean sometimes taking firm action against disquieting movements in the society. The answer given here draws on the state of mind that is the focus of Laoist self-cultivation, here called *The Nameless One's Simplicity*. (*P'u*/Simplicity elsewhere is translated "Uncarved* Block.") Having cultivated this Simplicity, the ruler can act in a tactful and nonconfrontational way that restrains disruptive people without making them feel put down, which would stir resentment leading to further social disorder. (See further under "Hurt*.") His tactful treatment leads instead to a genuine Stillness* pervading the society. Like 72[64], this chapter helps to define what it means to engage in "Not Doing" government, under whose subtle influence the world will seem to order itself {3}.

This last chapter is a good climax to the earlier chapters in Section 7 (see comments concerning "climaxes" in 39[25]). In the traditional order, Chapter 37 is also the final chapter of the "first book" of the *Tao Te Ching* and the final chapter of the entire book in the newly found Ma-wang-tui version.

Additional Textual Notes

Included here are notes concerning (a) my choice of variants from the various Chinese manuscripts of the *Tao Te Ching* and (b) ways of construing the Chinese text that might be especially controversial.

Abbreviations and special terms used in these notes:

HSK = The Chinese text of the *Tao Te Ching* used in the commentary of Ho Shang Kung (as printed in Ho Shih-chi's *Ku pen tao te ching hsiao k'an*).

Lectio dificilior = "The more difficult reading." A principle of textual criticism I often have used in preferring MWT to WP, according to which the textual variant that is more difficult to make sense of, but still intelligible, is the one to be preferred. The rationale is that, over time, manuscript copyists are prone to introduce changes in the text to make it read more smoothly, thus the more difficult readings often are likely to be more original. This principle is especially appropriate to the *Tao Te Ching*, which frequently uses very colorful language, paradoxes, deliberately shocking images, and so forth.

MWT = The Chinese text of the *Tao Te Ching* as printed in two manuscripts from the second century B.C., recently discovered in a cave at Ma-wang-tui in China. I rely on the edition of this text printed in Henricks (1989). These are by far the oldest extant manuscripts, but they also clearly are corrupt in many places—many more than the Wang Pi text, I believe—and this counts against their replacing Wang Pi as the standard text.

WP = The Chinese text of the *Tao Te Ching* used in the commentary of Wang Pi, until recently accepted by all as the standard text. My translation is based on WP (as printed in Ho Shih-chi's *Ku pen tao te ching hsiao k'an*) except when there seems some positive reason for accepting the readings of MWT or HSK, in which case I always mention explicitly in these notes that I am doing so.

1[24]. "Ambitious" (lit. "has desires") is MWT both in {4} here and in 67[31]:2. This is the *lectio dificilior*, and it is doubtful that a mere copyist's error would be repeated twice. WP avoids the (seemingly un-Laoist) positive use of "desire" by changing to "has Tao."

2[9]. "Win the fame" in {2} is the *lectio dificilior* of HSK, omitted in WP and MWT.

3[67]. MWT's "I am great" in {1} is the *lectio dificilior*. WP avoids the seeming arrogance with "My Tao is great."

4[22]. "Shepherd of the World" in {4} is MWT. WP has "Pattern of the World."

18[13]. In {1:2} I borrow from Waley the understanding of *jo* as "your" rather than "like." My understanding of the line before this is new: I take *ch'ung-ju*/favor-disgrace as a phrase referring to the ups and downs of politics, being now in favor, now in disgrace (formally similar to phrases like *p'in-fu*/poor-rich, referring to financial circumstances generally). And (with Waley) I take *ching*/startle in a more general sense referring to a state of mental disturbance: "being upset" due to ups and downs of political fortune. I take *jo* in {1:1} as a quasi-copula, "is equivalent to," though perhaps it also could be taken to mean "your" (lit. "favor and disgrace [are] your upsetness"). My understanding of *ch'ung wei hsia* in {2} as "favor is degrading" also is new. I think it is meant to be a "shocking" opposite to the commonsense view that "favor raises one up" (*ch'ung wei shang*). A version of {4} is found in the *Chuang Tzu* (Watson 1968: 116), where however it is given a "Yangist" meaning opposite the one I suppose here (attribute no special importance to the world, take care of your self instead). In the *Chuang Tzu* there is a slight difference in the wording—a *yü* following *shen* that does not occur in WP: *i shen yü wei t'ien hsia*. The omission of *yü* in WP {4} produces the familiar construction *i X wei Y* "treat X as Y," which allows for my understanding of *i shen wei t'ien hsia* "treat yourself as [no more important than] the [rest of the] world." This interpretation makes the point of {4} accord with the point of {3}.

20[46]. {2:1} is a *lectio dificilior* found in HSK and MWT, omitted entirely in WP.

27[10]. *Wei tz'u*/"remain Feminine" in {1:10} is MWT. WP has *wu tz'u*/"not Feminine."

31[4]. Most translators punctuate {1} differently, yielding something like "Tao is empty but useful. It never [needs to be] filled." I follow Karlgren's basic understanding of this line, in which *yung chih*/"use it" is equivalent to *yung chih che*/"one who uses it," and *yung* refers to "using*" (practicing/internalizing) Tao, as in 46[35]:3.

36[42]. Most translators take *ch'ung ch'i* in {3} to mean "*blending* the *ch'i*'s"; that is, blending the *yin ch'i*/energy and the *yang ch'i*/energy. But (a) although the character for *ch'ung* here also can stand for a word meaning "blend," *ch'ung* always means "Empty" elsewhere in the *Tao Te Ching*. And (b) the idea of *balancing yin* and *yang*, central to later Taoism, is not found anywhere else in this book, which always advocates cultivating *yin* qualities as opposed to *yang* ones.

42[2]. I take *ch'eng*/complete in {2:4} to mean that the idea "difficult" is given its full content only by contrast with the idea "easy." I take the MWT reading *ying*/fill in {2:6} and interpret it similarly: The content of the idea "noble" is fully "filled out" only when one sees it in contrast with the idea "lowly." The concluding particle *heng*/always at the end of {2} is the MWT reading. With MWT I omit "produces but doesn't possess," which WP places at the beginning of {5}.

43[1]. "Source *of the thousands of things*" in {2:1} is MWT, which has this same phrase in both lines of this saying. WP has "source *of Heaven and Earth*" in {2:1}. I think MWT rightly makes the *name Mother* the entire point of the contrast between the two lines. I also adopt the MWT reading of {3}, and Henricks's basic understanding of it. I believe that "what is sought" here is conceptual clarity. WP makes a very similar point with different words: Where MWT has the phrase *so chiao*/ "what is sought," WP has the single word *chiao*, meaning here probably "boundary," "outer edge"—that is, the "outer surface" of things as opposed to their "hidden essences." Line {4:1} reads literally "these two, merged." I take "these two" as a reference to the partial *subject* of the preceding two-line *saying*, "not desiring." See the further explanation in 37[14]:2.

55[66]. I translate *chiang*/river as "Yang-Tze" because *chiang* is the name associated with the great southern river, the *Yang-tze chiang*. The great river in the north, the *Huang Ho* or "Yellow

River," is not called *chiang* but *ho*. This is one piece of evidence Erkes (1935) cites for the southern origin of the *Tao Te Ching*.

56[61]. Most translators take the phrase *hsia liu* (lit. "low flowing") in {1} as a river image, translating it "flows downward," or "low-lying river," and so on. But *liu* is used in the *Mencius* (7B/37,11) to refer to conduct following *"current* customs" in a negative sense (as opposed to the principled conduct of the superior man). Hence the advice in the *Doctrine of the Mean* (10:5) to be *"ho*/harmonious but not *liu"* must mean something like "agreeable, but not wishy-washy." The phrase *hsia liu* itself occurs twice in the *Analects* (17:24:1 and 19:20), where it clearly describes someone of very low social status. The term clearly has negative connotations, either of weakness ("floating" or "drifting") or excessively "common" ("current"), as opposed to aristocratic/principled moral conduct. In MWT (adopted here) the line about *hsia liu* is followed immediately by the phrase "woman for the world." It seems that anyone familiar with these resonances of *hsia liu* would naturally see here the image of a prostitute, which probably is why the WP text makes "woman of the world" the third line of this saying rather than the second. But *chiao* "unite with" in the remaining line of the saying is regularly used in the *Analects* of friendship and intimacy. Thus this word, too, helps reinforce the prostitute image.

60[49]. WP transposes MWT's *heng wu hsin*/"constantly no mind" to *wu heng hsin*/"no constant mind." I accept MWT as the more "shocking" *lectio dificilior.* Some think that Te in {2} makes no sense in its usual meaning and want to take the character as standing for another word *te,* "to get, obtain." This is unnecessary: As in 27[10]:2, this saying describes how the Te* cultivated by Laoists typically expresses itself in conduct. Line {4:1–2} is omitted in WP, but contained in MWT and many other texts.

65[51]. "Talents" in {1} is MWT, WP has "abilities." *Events* translates *wu*/things—I think *wu* has a very general meaning in the *Tao Te Ching* and *"events* form them" makes most sense here. See further under "Things*," p. 553.

67[31]. "Mourning" in {7:2} is the MWT reading, WP has "ill fortune." WP may retain the original wording of the oral saying, MWT's "mourning" being a change by the composer to connect this saying to {7:5} and {8}.

68[69]. "The enemy is nothing" (*wu ti*) in {3} is the MWT reading. WP has a phrase similar in meaning, *ching ti*, "make light of the enemy." MWT here has the *lectio dificilior*, which still makes sense if one regards it as a motto.

69[30]. WP adds another line to {3}, not found in MWT: "In the aftermath of a great war, surely there will be a bad year." I omit this because it sounds like a rationalizing explanation of the more "superstitious*" sounding thorns-and-brambles saying.

70[60]. My tentative understanding of 3:4–5 depends on taking the MWT reading, "the Wise person does not hurt *them* [i.e., the ghosts]." WP has "not hurt *jen*/people."

76[80]. I follow Karlgren's understanding of the somewhat difficult construction in {2:1–2}. Others take it to mean "[Enough] weapons for dozens and hundreds of men." (*Ch'i*/talent also can mean "utensil, weapon.")

80[65]. In {3:4} WP has "not by knowledge." I take here the MWT reading "by not-knowing" (translated here as "Ignorance!") because this fits better with the idea of "Knowledge/ Ignorance" as mottos, applying both to the ruler and his subjects. WP also has a different *chih* in {2} and {3} that could be translated as (negative) "cleverness." This seems an attempt to tone down deliberately "shocking" language that is part of Laoist style. In {4} the first *heng*/always and the second *chih*/understand are in MWT, not in WP. In {5} "in opposition to things" follows Karlgren's understanding, which seems to me the most natural reading of *yü wu fan*. Others avoid this seemingly un-Taoist notion by translating, "It *fan*/returns *yü*/together-with *wu*/things."

81[37]. In {2:6} WP has "not desiring" instead of MWT's "not disgraced." I think the latter is the *lectio dificilior* here. The idea is connected to the theme of "not hurting" the people (see further under "Hurting*" p. 540. In {3} "order" translates MWT's *cheng*/norm:make-correct. WP has *ting*/settle: arrange.

Topical Glossary

Below are brief discussions of some topics that recur frequently in the *Tao Te Ching* and/or in the commentary. The topics are listed alphabetically under keywords marked with an asterisk in the commentary. (All forms of a word are listed under one heading: e.g. references to "desiring*," "desirable*," and "desire-less*" will all be found under "*Desire*.") These keywords are primarily a reference device—many are chosen merely because of the ease with which they could be worked into the commentary. This means that often keywords cannot themselves be used as an accurate clue to Laoist thought. Primary attention needs to be paid to the discussion following each word. (For example, the discussion under *Self-promotion** makes it clear that Laoists were not against seeking promotions. The discussion under *Metaphorical** is not an essay on Laoist use of metaphor.)

Some topics listed here are discussed in fuller fashion in Part Three. In these cases I give a summary of the main points in this Glossary, and give page references to fuller discussions elsewhere.

*Agitation**.   The target of one group of polemic aphorisms* is the human attraction to exciting things and stimulating activities, which Laoists criticize on the grounds that they agitate the mind. Among "agitating" things are included the stimulating life of the aristocracy (colorful clothes, fine foods and music, horse racing and hunting [21[12]:1]), luxurious living (22[50]:1-2, 51[75]:1-2), excited conversation (16[5]:3, 14[23]:1-2, 30[56]:1-2), and the pressures of one's job (29[52]:4). Desire* and desirable things are also mentally agitating. We tend to regard our lives as dull when nothing especially exciting or desirable "stands out" against our ordinary existence. But when something that stands out stimulates us, this causes our being to strain to align itself around this, losing the organic* order it has when all the parts are allowed to align themselves naturally with each other in a harmony arising from within. Our being can stand this only so long, and this is why prolonged stimulation eventually reduces the sensitivity of our senses (21[12]:1), causes internal agitation (21[12]:1:4, 23[26]), makes us vulnerable to disease (22[50]:1-2), wears us out (29[52]:4), and is bound to be short-lived (14[23]:1-2,

69[30]:5). In contrast, Laoists cultivate an extraordinary internal Stillness* that deepens and enhances the organic harmony toward which our being tends when left to itself. This gives us an inexhaustible source of energy (16[5]:2, 32[6]:4), an internal Steadiness*, a lasting* way of being as opposed to constant ups-and-downs, and preserves whole a capacity for deep satisfaction (21[12]:2). One who cultivates this Stillness and Harmony* on a deep level can engage in intense activity without becoming agitated or wearing herself out (33[55]:2:6–7). See further discussion p. 167, 170. Passages on this topic are 5[45]:3, 14[23]:1,2, 16[5]:2,3, 21[12]:2–3, 22[50]:2, 23[26]:1–3, 29[52]:4, 32[6]:4, 33[55]:5 (= 69[30]:5). Section 2 of the translation groups together chapters that center on mental excitement/desire/agitation, and the opposite ideal of Stillness* and contentment. These are the chapters in which Laoist thought comes closest to that attributed to Yang* Chu, and also to the emphasis on physiological self-cultivation in some later forms of Taoism (see comments under 22[50]). See also *Desire**.

Ancient*. Contemporary Chinese frequently invoked the image of idealized kings and their perfectly wise advisers who ruled in a legendary ancient Golden Age. To attribute a particular policy to these ancient worthies was a conventional way of putting forth this policy as an ideal, often with no appeal to any historical evidence that the ancient sages actually practiced it. See further discussion p. 173, and the analysis of a similar Mohist statement p. 30–32. Relevant passages are 4[22]:7, 6[15]:1, 11[38]:4, 12[18]:1, 37[14]:5, 38[21]:3, 48[62]:6, 57[68]:2, 80[65]:1.

Aphoristic*. A word I use to describe the meaning-structure of the proverb-like polemic aphorisms in the *Tao Te Ching*. Aphorisms are not rules or principles to be applied literally and consistently in all contexts, but are "corrective," "compensatory" wisdom, appropriate in limited contexts, counterbalancing some tendency in the opposite direction. Chapter 6 discusses the semantic structure of aphorisms, and Chapter 7 shows how this analysis applies to the aphorisms in the *Tao Te Ching*. The "polemic" thrust of these aphorisms describes one kind of thrust that Laoist sayings have, the other two kinds being instructional* and celebratory*.

Appearances*. The target of one group of polemic aphorisms* is the tendency to admire most, and cultivate in oneself, the appearances of good qualities that will impress others, qualities like uprightness (4[22]:2, 5[45]:2), competence, (5[45]:2), knowledge (8[81]:1), eloquence (8[81]:1, 5[45]:2, 30[56]:1), and Te (11[38]:1, 44[41]:3). These qualities would have been especially attractive to *shih** anxious to further their careers by making a good impression, as well as among rulers who wanted to impress* their people. Some of these sayings hold up ideals that would be commonly admired, but are not very strikingly impressive, as for example sincere speech in contrast to eloquent speech (8[81]:1). Others are more extreme, holding up for admiration qualities that would conventionally be regarded as positively bad or undesirable, (e.g., "compromised" [4[22]:2], "disgraceful" [17[28]:1]). Social admiration tends to make certain personal qualities stand out, and we then experience them as especially desirable and solid*, over against other qualities that are cast into the shade as Empty*, "Nothing*," even "disgraceful." But seeing things this way and "working*" to develop impressive qualities and repress disgraceful ones, ruins the organic* harmony, the goodness including the whole of each person's unique being, toward which it tends when this external influence does not interfere. Such working, typically motivated by self-promotion*, "cuts up the Uncarved* Block" (17[28]:2). Laoist self-cultivation aims at developing and enhancing this organic and holistic goodness, less impressive externally but more genuinely satisfying to the possessor ("useful" 5[45]:1, 11[38]:7, 15[11]:2). This means counterbalancing our tendency to emphasize socially desirable qualities, by deliberate attempts to develop and integrate the "shadow" side of ourselves (Jung), the qualities of our being we ignore or repress because in the eyes of conventional society they seem worthless or "bad." These ideas account for much of the paradoxical character of Laoist thought, in contrast to Confucians*, who tended to see their ideals as more continuous with conventional standards. Relevant passages are 3[67]:1, 4[22]:2, 5[45]:1–2, 7[8]:2, 8[81]:1, 11[38]:1, 14[23]:4, 17[28]:1, 30[56]:1, 44[41]:3, 48[62]:3. Section 1 of the translation groups together chapters that criticize admiration of impressive appearances, and propose Laoist ideals that contrast with this. See also *Self-Promotion**, and the further discussion of the relation of these ideas to organic harmony p. 164–66, 170.

*Benefits**. A large group of celebratory* sayings celebrate the wonderful powers or benefits that result from cultivating Tao and conducting government and personal life accordingly. The benefits described usually seem to be based on relatively realistic experiences, but the descriptions extrapolate from this to highly exaggerated and utopian images. These sayings are "celebratory*"; that is, they assume a primary audience who already experienced Tao as something wonderful, and the exaggerated images in these sayings express this shared experience of Laoist *shih**. See the fuller discussion p. 236–43. Relevant passages are 3[67]:3–4, 14[23]:3, 16[5]:2, 22[50]:3, 25[48]:2–3, 26[59]:2–3, 29[52]:2:1–2, 31[4]:3, 32[6]:4, 33[55]:1, 37[14]:5, 38[21]:1 and 3, 43[1]:3, 46[35]:1,3, 47[43]:1, 48[62]:2 and 6, 49[27]:3, 52[77]:2, 56[61]:3, 61[54]:1,2, 63[32]:2, 70[60]:2,4, 72[64]:5, 75[78]:1, 77[57]:5, 81[37]:1.

*Celebratory**. A word I use to describe the intent or thrust of many Laoist sayings, in contrast to a "polemic" (see *Aphoristic**) or "instructional*" intent. Celebratory sayings do not give information, but rely on previous shared experience of the greatness of what is being celebrated. Most sayings involving the special recurring terms (see p. 191) have a primarily celebratory thrust, including (1) sayings employing a formula connected to the "conquest* cycle," like "Softness overcomes Hardness" (see p. 230–32), (2) sayings linking* one quality cultivated to another (see p. 232–33), (3) sayings describing marvelous powers or benefits* (see p. 236–43), (4) sayings about cosmic* norms (see p. 249–51), and (5) cosmogonic sayings describing world origins* (see p. 251–56).

*Ch'i**. *Ch'i* means literally "breath, air," but the word is often used in ancient China to refer to one's bodily energy as felt internally. (I do not think the *Tao Te Ching* invokes any developed Chinese *theories* about *ch'i*.) Hence "the mind controlling the *ch'i*" (33[55]:4) probably refers to attempts to directly control the quality of this felt energy by will power, and "Empty ch'i" (36[42]:3) refers to an "Empty*" quality of mind Laoists cultivate. *Ch'i* occurs in 27[10]:1, 33[55]:4, 36[42]:3. See further discussions of *ch'i* in the *Mencius*, p. 107 n. 11, and in the *Nei Yeh*. p. 184–85, 188, 191.

Chuang Tzu*. An anthology of writings, roughly contemporary[1] with the *Tao Te Ching*, stemming from like-minded groups that only later came to be grouped together and labeled "Taoist."[2] The *Chuang Tzu* is the principal source of our knowledge of early Taoist movements in addition to the *Tao Te Ching*. Passages from this book like those quoted and discussed p. 202–208 are helpful sources of information about the meaning of some of the special terms (Stillness*, Emptiness*, etc.) that occur in the *Tao Te Ching*. Other passages from the *Chuang Tzu* are quoted p. 58, 246.

*Clarity**. *Ming*/Clarity is one of the names for the quality of mind Laoists cultivate, probably referring to the mental clarity experienced when the mind is at rest. *Ming*/Clarity in this meaning occurs in 6[15]:3, 24[33]:1, 27[10]:1, 28[16]:3, 29[52]:5,6, 33[55]:3, 49[27]:3, 73[36]:1. See further discussion p. 211–12.

Composers*. The term I use for the Laoist teachers whom I believe composed the collages of oral sayings which constitute the eighty-one "chapters" of the *Tao Te Ching* (see p. 128, 310).

Confucianism*. The target of one group of polemic aphorisms* is the approach of other contemporary shih*-teachers with a Confucian bent. Confucius (551–479 B.C.) was one of the earliest and the most famous of the *shih**-teachers (see p. 55). Several later teachers, including Mencius* (see Chapters 4 and 5), claim to be following "the Tao of Confucius." At a later time, Confucianism and Taoism became the two principal rival movements in China (Buddhism being a third upon its arrival in the 1st century A.D.) Commentators generally agree that, in Laoist sayings, *jen*/Goodness, *i*/Morality, *li*/Etiquette, and *hsüeh*/Learning serve as code-words referring to the focus of self-cultivation for contemporary Confucian *shih*-schools (see *Mencius* 7A/21,4, quoted p. 77). "Goodness," which might also be translated "benevolence," "humaneness," or "empathy," often functions as a summary reference to the highest Confucian ideal. "Morality" means doing what is right according to a refined version of conventional norms, especially those regarding conduct proper to one's station in life. (I translate *i* as "Rightness" in Mencius passages quoted in Chapters 4, 5, and 8.) "Etiquette" is a very approximate translation of *li*: It refers to elaborate religious and court ceremonial, but Confucian ideals tended to picture refined social interaction as a kind of ceremonial as well.[3] "Learning" refers primarily to character-formation, and only secondarily to the study of traditional customs and exemplars that were to serve as a guide.[4] Polemic aphorisms against Confucian self-cultivation are related to Laoist thought against impressive appearances*, against self-promotion*, and against "working*." Laoist sayings against "naming*" probably have at least partly in mind the Confucian project of "rectifying names." Laoist criticisms caricature their Confucian rivals, and they should not be taken as accurate representations of Confucian thought. See 11[38]:3,4,5, 12[18]:1, 13[20]:1,2, 16[5]:1, 42[2]:1, 72[64]:7, 78[19]:1. I believe that 7[8]:2, 25[48]:1:1, and perhaps 13[20]:3:1, are Confucian sayings.

Connective*. I believe that composers of the chapter-collages have often altered or added to an oral saying, in order to connect it to other sayings included in the same chapter. See the fuller discussions p. 314–27. In my translation I print suspected connective additions or alterations in italics.

Conquest* cycle. Some ancient texts make reference to a kind of primitive physics/psychology in ancient China comparable to the "four elements" theory of ancient Greece. In the Chinese version there was an attempt at a hierarchical ordering of certain hypostatized* powers or energies, expressed by saying that the superior energy *sheng*/overcomes ("conquers") an inferior one. Graham (1989: 326) calls this the "cycle of conquests." Several Laoist sayings borrow the formula "*X sheng*/overcomes *Y*" to celebrate the superiority of the internal powers or energies they cultivate over their opposites, as in "Softness overcomes hardness" (75[78]:2). See further discussion p. 230–32. Formulas borrowed from this speculation occur in 5[45]:3, 56[61]:2, 73[36]:2, 75[78]:2, and perhaps 23[26]:1 and 47[43]:1.

Contending*. *Cheng*/contend means both "to strive, compete" and "to quarrel" (see 57[68]:2). It is a negative term in the *Tao Te Ching*, referring especially to competition with others for higher status and reputation, so this term is related to the Laoist polemic against self-promotion* and against admiring only impressive appearances*, and to the positive Laoist ideal of "being low*" (see 57[68]:1–2). "Not-contending" describes an attitude/state-of-mind that is the contrasting Laoist ideal. Relevant passages are 4[22]:6 (= 55[66]:4), 7[8]:1,3, 8[81]:4, 57[68]:2, 58[73]:5, 79[3]:1.

Content*. Resting "content" within oneself as opposed to reaching out for desirable* and exciting things is a Laoist goal mentioned in 19[44]:3, 20[46]:2,3, 24[33]:2.

Cosmic*. Some sayings celebrate the foundational importance of Tao in the life of the ideal Laoist by ascribing to it a foundational role in the cosmos, as in the cosmogonic origin* sayings (see fuller discussion p. 251–66, and relevant passages listed under *Origin**). Other "cosmic" sayings frequently use the formula *X wei t'ien hsia Y*, "*X* is the *Y* of the World" (as in "Stillness is the Norm of the World," 5[45]:4). This formula probably draws on the tradition of the Chou Emperor* as one of the pillars of the cosmic order (see 35[39]:1, and discussion p. 52 n. 4). See further discussion of this sayings-form p. 249–51. Relevant passages are 4[22]:4, 5[45]:4, 17[28]:1, 28[16]:5, 30[56]:5 (= 48[62]:7), 32[6]:2, 35[39]:1:13, 39[25]:4, 48[62]:1, 65[51]:2:2.

Desire*. The target of one group of polemic aphorisms* is reaching out for "desirable" things, especially for material goods and for fame (21[12]:1, 18[13]:1–3, 19[44]:1, 72[64]:7), and for things regarded as "improvements*" (20[46]:1, 43[1]:3, 76[80]).

These desires are not criticized primarily on moral grounds, that is, as something egotistical. Rather, desire causes mental agitation*, disturbing mental Stillness* and contentment, and because of this causes social disharmony. See 18[13]:1–3, 19[44]:1, 20[46]:1,2, 21[12]:1, 43[1]:3, 72[64]:7, 76[80], 79[3]:1,3, and comments under *Agitation**. *Yü*/desire is also a recurrent term with a somewhat specialized meaning in Laoist thought. *Yü* is a negative term in 20[46]:2, 79[3]:1, 81[37]:3, and *wu yü*/"not desiring" describes the opposite, ideal Laoist state of mind in 43[1]:3, 64[34]:4, 72[64]:7, 77[57]:5, 78[19]:2, 79[3]:1,3, and 81[37]:2. As with "not-working*," this should not be taken literally, as a ban on all desires. "Desire" is negative *when and insofar as* it interferes with Laoist goals. "Ambitious" (lit. *yu yü*/"having desires") is a positive term in 1[24]:4 (MWT version).

Doing*.   See *Working**.

Dwelling*.   Several sayings use spatial imagery to describe maintaining a certain frame of mind, as though there are several mental "spaces" where one can "dwell." For example, the saying "achieves successes but doesn't dwell in them" (42[2]:5 = 52[77]:3), seems to envision a kind of floating "I" which can choose whether to "dwell in" (identify with) external successes or not. Similarly, 11[38]:7 speaks of "residing in" truly substantial personal qualities rather than in "thin" external show. See 1[24]:4 (= 67[31]:2), 42[2]:3,5, 67[31]:7,8, (= 52[77]:3). Sayings in 24[33]:3 and 72[64]:7 also seem to envision a mental "place" one should return to or not leave. The *Nei Yeh* and the *Chuang Tzu* also use the metaphor of a "dwelling" to speak of certain internal mental spaces one discovers in meditation. On this basis I translate *men*/gate:dwelling as "[mental] abode" in 32[6]:2 and 43[1]:5. See further comments p. 203 n. 3.

Embrace*.   A verb (*pao*) describing self-cultivation. See *Use**.

Emperor*.   Traditional Chou-dynasty (1122–222 B.C.) thought conceived of the Emperor as someone representing in his person the symbolic Norm of the World. This tradition is reflected in the *Mencius* (see p. 76–77, 100) and the *Tao Te Ching* (35[39]:1 and 39[25]:4), showing that, on one level, Mencian and Laoist *shih* did not question this idea. On another level, however, both groups regarded the person well-advanced in self-cultivation as having the most valid spiritual claim to this symbolic normative "cosmic" role in Chinese culture. (See *Mencius* 3B/2,3 quoted p. 75.) This is the background for many phrases in Laoist sayings that implicitly evoke the spiritual role of Emperor as an image of the cultural leadership role one deserves who is accomplished in Laoist self-cultivation. The Emperor-image is evoked by phrases in 4[22]:4, 17[28]:1, 18[13]:4, 25[48]:3,4, 28[16]:5, 55[66]:1, 57[68]:2, 75[78]:4, 77[57]:1.

*Empty**.* One designation of the quality of mind Laoists cultivate in themselves, referring to its intangible character. *Hsü*/empty has the connotation "worthless," and this negative connotation of Emptiness is also important in the *Tao Te Ching*. It refers to the fact that we tend to experience qualities that are not socially admired—this includes the most important qualities for Laoists—as somehow lacking full reality. They feel like "nothing*," a word with similar meanings in the *Tao Te Ching*. See further discussion p. 210–11. Relevant passages are 4[22]:2, 5[45]:1, 16[5]:2, 28[16]:1, 31[4]:1, 36[42]:3, and "vacant Valley" in 6[15]:2. The opposite word, *ying*/fullness, connotes a solidly felt, substantial presence in the world (see 6[15]:2,4). Because the English word "full" does not have these connotations, I translate *ying* as "solid." "Solid" occurs in this meaning in 4[22]:2, 5[45]:1, 6[15]:4, 31[4]:1. See also *Appearances**.*

*Etiquette**.* See *Confucian**.*

*Excellent**.* *Shan*/good:excellent is used very frequently in the *Tao Te Ching* to refer to the ideal Laoist way of being. In several passages (49[27]:1, 8[81]:1, 69[30]:4) it seems to refer to a very high degree of Laoist "goodness." Three other passages (22[50]:3, 49[27]:1–3, 61[54]:1) attribute wonderful and quasi-magical effects to actions done "Excellently." See further discussion p. 226. Relevant passages are 6[15]:1, 7[8]:1,2, 8[81]:1, 22[50]:3, 49[27]:1–4, 55[66]:1, 58[73]:5, 61[54]:1, 69[30]:4.

*Femininity**.* One designation of the quality of mind Laoists cultivate, conveyed by the synonyms *p'in* and *tz'u*, occurring in 17[28]:1, 27[10]:1, 32[6]:1,2, and 56[61]:2. The parallel with "disgraceful" in 17[28]:1 makes it clear that this was conventionally considered a negative characteristic in the male- dominated society of ancient China. See further discussion p. 217–18.

*Forcing**.* *Ch'iang*/force is a negative term in 33[55]:4, 69[30]:1,4, and 36[42]:6 (translated "violent" in this last passage). *Ch'iang* also means "hard, strong," the opposite of Laoist "Softness*" in 73[36]:2, 74[76]:1,2,3,4, 75[78]:1,2. *Ch'iang*/strength is used in a positive sense in 24[33]:1, 29[52]:5, 6[15]:2 and 39[25]:2.

*Framing**.* Sometimes the composers*, instead of juxtaposing closely related sayings, will try to unify their chapter-collages by placing closely related sayings at the beginning and the end of a collage, or before and after other material, "framing" these intervening sayings. See further discussion p. 310–314. I list the relevant passages here in the order of their obviousness, noting catchwords where appropriate: 4[22]:1 and 7; 7[8]:1 and 3 (contend); 22[50]:2 and 4 (death spot); 23[26]:1 and 3 (agitated/root/master); 28[16]:1 and 3:1 (Stillness); 31[4]:2 and 4; 65[51]:1 and 3; 76[80]:2 and 4; 9[79]:1 and 4 (good); 11[38]:1–2 and 4 (Te); 29[52]:2 and 6 (turn back); 32[6]:1 and 3–4; 44[41]:1–2 and 4 (Tao); 48[62]:1 and 5-6 (Tao), 2 and 6-7 (treasure); 50[53]:2 and 6 (display/boast), 1–3 and 6 (Tao); 58[73]:1–3 and 6 (Heaven); 63[32]:1 and 3; 67[31]:1 and 4 (weapons), 3 and 7, 6 and 8; 72[64]:4–5 and 8 (not working); 79[3]:1 and 3 (wise/clever), 2 and 4 (govern); 80[65]:1–3 and 5; 6[15]:1 and 5 (beyond-understanding/concealed); 14[23]:1 and 4; 35[39]:1 and 3, 2 and 4; 43[1]:1 and 4 (names), 3 and 5 (hidden essences); 59[58]:1 and 4; 60[49]:1 and 3.

Get*. A verb (*te*) describing self-cultivation. See *Use**.

Good*. See *Confucian**.

Heaven*. In Chou-dynasty thought, *t'ien*/Heaven served as a general name for the highest divinity, sometimes pictured as a personal being and sometimes as an impersonal principle or force similar to our "Fate." Traditional religious beliefs like this play no central role in the thought of Laoists. At times some traditional ideas associated with Heaven are indirectly alluded to or invoked in the *Tao Te Ching*, but this is always for the sake of making some other point, not to teach some Laoist doctrines about Heaven. See further discussion p. 173–74. The phrase "Heaven's Tao/Way" is a conventional designation of "the right way," which Laoists sometimes use to describe the Laoist way (see p. 174). "Heaven's Way" occurs in 2[9]:2, 8[81]:4, 9[79]:4, 41[47]:1, 52[77]:1, 58[73]:5. Other occurrences of "Heaven" are 3[67]:4, 10[7]:1, 14[23]:2, 16[5]:1,2, 26[59]:1, 27[10]:1, 28[16]:5, 32[6]:2, 39[25]:1,4, 48[62]:5, 57[68]:2, 58[73]:3 and 6, 63[32]:2.

Harmony*. One description of the quality of mind Laoists cultivate. See further discussion p. 214. *Ho*/Harmony as an internal quality occurs in 30[56]:3 (= 31[4]:3), 33[55]:2,3, 36[42]:3. See also the reference to social *shun*/harmony:submission in 80[65]:5.

Hurt*. Laoists stress the way that an impressive* and strict* ruler is felt by the people as someone trying to put them to shame by comparison, and so is experienced as burdensome and "hurtful," sparking resentment. See p. 168. This theme is explicit in 46[35]:1, 55[66]:3, 59[58]:4, 81[37]:2, and implicit in 54[17]:1, 60[49]:3.

Hypostatize*. To hypostatize something is to speak of it as though it were an independent entity or force. Laoists hypostatized the quality of mind they cultivated, and this is responsible for sayings that speak of *Tao, The Mother*, and so on as independent entities or forces. On the present interpretation, hypostatization is part of the Laoist imaginal and linguistic style; there is no attempt in the *Tao Te Ching* to develop a system of doctrines about Tao as an independent entity. See further discussion p. 185.

Impressive*.   The target of one group of polemic aphorisms* is the tendency of rulers to project an impressive presence, inspiring awe in their people, as for example by speaking to them in a haughty manner (55[66]:2), or by insisting on recognition of their privileged status by imposing high taxes and setting aside royal lands where peasants cannot live (53[72]:2). But for Laoists, even the Confucian* ruler who strives to impress people with his high moral qualities (16[5]:1) is a ruler trying to emphasize the way that he personally stands out over against the "ordinary" and inferior masses. This polarization ruins the organic* harmony of society, and causes people to resent the ruler (54[17]:1) as burdensome and tiring (55[66]:3, 53[72]:2), hurting* them by making them feel inferior, someone engaging in personal and quarrelsome contention* for social status, provoking his subjects to contend/quarrel with him to defend their own sense of worth. He thus loses the respect and cooperation of the people, a central basis for social order. The ideal organic* social harmony envisioned by Laoists includes the central figure of the ruler as symbolic norm setting the tone for the society, on the model of the traditional Chou Emperor*. Organic harmony for them still depends on the allegiance and cooperation that the people "naturally*" and spontaneously accord to a true ruler. (See Graham's enlightening comments [1989: 299–311] on "hierarchic anarchism" in ancient China.) But for them the preeminent characteristic of a true ruler is that in his style of ruling he strives mightily not to stand out. In transactions with his subjects he adopts the manner of one lower in social standing than they (55[66]:1–2, 35[39]:2). He works hard and competently at administration, but keeps such a low profile that his work goes unnoticed and people think good order is coming about spontaneously (54[17]:3, 81[37]:3). He quietly nips bad social tendencies in the bud (72[64]:1–2), or defeats his opposition by indirect and non-confrontational tactics (73[36]:1), so he will not have to have dramatic personal confrontations. He has no principles that stand in opposition to the general character of his society (60[49]:1). What he stands for, and what he tries to foster and draw out, is just the ideal goodness incipiently inherent in the way social groups spontaneously tend to structure their relationships to each other (72[64]:8). This is the kind of goodness that radiates from his person and his style of governing, as extremely subtle but powerful Te*, setting a tone and producing a perfectly harmonious and prosperous society. (This Te* is not a substitute for effective administrative work, law enforcement, etc., but radiates from the style in which the ideal ruler carries out these routine tasks; see p. 101–02, 242.) Sayings directly targeting the "impressive" ruler are 35[39]:2, 36[42]:5, 46[35]:1, 53[72]:1, 54[17]:1,3, 55[66]:1,2,3, 59[58]:4:5. Section 5 of the translation groups together chapters that center on criticism of the impressive ruler, and/or that propose contrasting Laoist ideals. See also *Strict**, and *Hurt**, and further discussion p. 167–68.

*Improvements**. Some polemic aphorisms* are directed against programs proposed by other *shih*-schools designed to introduce what Laoists see as fundamental changes in the "natural*" social order. Such fundamental "improvements" include the use of ("Mohist*") utilitarian rationality in deciding government policy, and encouraging this kind of rationality among the people (79[3]:1-2, 80[65]:1-3). They include the program of "rectifying names*," "carving up" implicit organic* social norms into codified legal prescriptions (63[32]:3, 77[57]:3:1-2, and 4). They include deliberate attempts to provide incentives for ambitious people to educate themselves and improve their administrative- or work-skills, thereby improving public administration and also general living standards (79[3]:1-2, 78[19]:1:5-6, 77[57]:3:5-6). Even the Confucian program of trying to spread consciously conceived "virtues" among the people is looked upon by Laoists as an attempt to fundamentally alter and replace people's organic, "natural*" goodness (78[19]:1:1-4). In Laoist eyes, these programs are spreading to the society those very things they struggle against personally in themselves in their self-cultivation practice. They are bringing about a general populace full of disquieting desires* destructive of social harmony, conducting personal and public business under the guidance of rational-conceptual ("naming*") knowledge, and replacing their natural goodness with the artificial appearances* of virtue. Laoists explicitly acknowledge (80[65]:5, 36[42]:2) that people left to themselves will often want to proceed in this "improving" direction, destructive of the "natural" organic* harmony of society which the ("conservative") Laoist administrator/adviser wants so much to protect and foster. Sometimes he must therefore set himself "in opposition to things" (80[65]:5). Of course, this is also a dilemma for the Laoist administrator, who would like as much as possible to let the mind of the people be his mind (60[49]:1), and to avoid confrontation with the people. The basic Laoist solution: "I will restrain them with the Nameless One's Simplicity . . . caus[ing] them no disgrace . . . [then] they will be Still*" (81[37]:2). *P'u*/simplicity:Uncarved* Block is a name for the quality of mind the Laoist cultivates, which governs the style in which he rules and therefore the tone he sets for his society. These "improving" trends must be opposed, but the hope is that this can be done in a manner that the people will not feel as a humiliation, so that it will result in a Still* people, content with a simple life (76[80], 77[57]:5, 79[3]:2–3). "Not-working*" is also a common term used for a style of ruling which does not try to "work over" (or allow others to work over, 79[3]:3) the society by implementing "improvements," but tries to maintain its organic harmony (72[64]:8). Laoist thought on this subject is contained mainly in chapters in my Section 7, "Against disquieting 'improvements'." See further discussion p. 169. Relevant passages are 62[29]:1, 76[80]:2,3,4,5,6, 77[57]:3,4,5, 78[19]:1, 79[3]:1,2, 80[65]:1,2,3.

Infant. A frequently recurring metaphorical* image representing one aspect of the state of mind Laoists cultivate. See 13[20]:4, 17[28]:1, 27[10]:1, 33[55]:1,2, 74[76]:1.

Instruction. "Instructive" is one kind of thrust that Laoist sayings have, the other two major kinds being "polemic" (see *Aphoristic*) and "celebratory*." Besides those instructive sayings listed under *Meditation* and *Normative*, there is another small group of sayings that give instruction in Laoist self-cultivation, typically by using several favorite Laoist terms or phrases: See 28[16]:1,2, 29[52]:4, 71[63]:1, 72[64]:7, 78[19]:2:4–5.

Laoist. A term of convenience I use, following Graham (1990a: 118, 124) for the thought of the *Tao Te Ching* and the *shih*-school out of which I think it arose, to distinguish it from other ancient and later forms of Taoism. See p. 49.

Lasting. Some passages speak of "lasting" as one of the benefits* of Laoist self-cultivation. Such lasting is contrasted with the "exhausting" effects of agitated*, short-lived excitement. In contrast to this, Laoists experienced the Feminine*/Still*/Empty* state of mind as an inexhaustible source of energy (32[6]:4, 16[5]:2). See 10[7]:1, 14[23]:2, 19[44]:5, 24[33]:3, 26[59]:3,4, 28[16]:5:6, 32[6]:4, 33[55]:5 (= 69[30]:5), 61[54]:2, and *Agitation*. Sayings in 24[33]:3

and 32[6] suggest perhaps that some Laoists extrapolated from this experience to an expectation of surviving death (this became a major goal in some later Taoist movements).[5]

Learning*. See *Confucian**.

Life*. *Sheng*/life:living has a negative sense in 51[75]:1-2 and 22[50]:1-2, referring to the high living of the "life-loving" aristocracy, which wears them out. Attempts by others to "increase *sheng*/vitality" by direct meditation* techniques is also criticized in 33[55]:4. But "fostering *sheng*/life Excellently*" describes a positive Laoist goal in 22[50]:3. And 38[21]:2 and 33[55]:2 mention *ching*/"vital energy" as something Laoists cultivate; in 33[55]:2 this is exemplified in the vitality of a young infant*, an image of positive, Soft* "life" also in 74[76]1-2 (see the use of *ching* in the *Nei Yeh*, p. 186–87, and the *Chuang Tzu* p. 207, selections 6 and 7). See also Graham's discussion[6] of the close relation between the etymologically cognate *sheng*/life and *hsing*/"[human] nature," and the use of both words by Yangists* expressing their concern to "keep life/nature intact."

Link*. One genre of Laoist sayings celebrates the way that cultivating one quality of mind is linked to the achievement of other qualities as well. For example, "Experiencing Steadiness* is Clarity*" (28[16]:3:4). See the discussion p. 232–33. The relevant passages are 28[16]:3:4, 29[52]:5, 33[55]:3, 36[42]:3.

Low*. *Hsia*/"[being] low" is a term used frequently to describe one aspect of the Laoist ideal. It describes a deferential manner in dealing with others, as well as a more general willingness to accept being one whom others look down upon, the consequence sometimes of cultivating qualities and practicing a Tao* that is not impressive. But Laoists also hoped that people would actually feel the subtle greatness of the "lowness" they cultivated, and would want to make such a low person the leader he deserves to be. See 35[39]:2, 55[66]:1,2, 56[61]:1,2,3,4,5, 57[68]:2. (Lowness is implied also in 7[8]:1 and 63[32]:4.) *Hsia*/low is also used sometimes in its ordinary negative sense to designate something of inferior quality, translated "poorest" in 11[38]:1 and 44[41]:1. A related word is *hsiao*/small:insignificant, also used sometimes in its usual negative sense to refer to someone of "small" worth or significance (e.g., 3[67]:1:6), but also sometimes used paradoxically to characterize "great" Tao (e.g., 29[52]:5, 63[32]:1, 64[34]:4).

Meditation*. Two sayings, 27[10]:1 and 6[15]:3, are fairly clearly meditation instruction, and this is probably true of 28[16]:2 and 30[56]:2-3 also. The entire chapter-collages 28[16],

29[52] and 30[56] probably have this intention. Four other sayings (30[56]:4, 37[14]:3–4, 38[21]:2, and 46[35]:3) are descriptive of the experience of trying to mentally grasp the elusive quality of mind Laoists cultivated. See further discussion p. 191–99.

Mencius*. Mencius was a Confucian *shih**-teacher (c. 385–303 B.C.) known to us from a large book bearing his name. Passages from the *Mencius* are the central topic of discussions in Chapters 4 and 5. These passages provide information about the social position of Warring States' *shih*-teachers and the nature of *shih*-schools. Formal similarities between the structure of Mencius' thought and the structure of Laoist thought (p. 69, 120–22) are a partial basis for my interpretive approach to the *Tao Te Ching*, although Laoists are directly opposed to Mencius on many issues of substantive content (see *Confucian**).

Merging*. *T'ung/*"[the] Merging" is one name for the state of mind that Laoists cultivate, a unified state contrasted with mental agitation and characterized by a lack of ("desiring*") activity and of clearly differentiated concepts. See 30[56]:3 and 43[1]:4–5, and further discussion p. 213.

Metaphorical* Images. Some sayings use images—mostly nature images like the behavior of water—as metaphors illustrating some particular Laoist idea or combination of ideas. I argue on p. 172–73 that these sayings do not reflect any Laoist desire to "imitate nature" as is commonly claimed. Laoists select natural phenomena that provide apt metaphors for points they want to make. Relevant passages are 7[8]:1, 10[7]:1, 14[23]:2, 15[11]:1, 16[5]:2, 23[26]:2, 33[55]:1,2, 33[55]:5 (= 69[30]:5), 44[41]:3:5–8, 47[43]:1, 52[77]:1, 55[66]:1, 56[61]:1, 63[32]:4, 74[76]:1,3, 75[78]:1.

Mohists*. Followers of a *shih**-teacher, Mo Tzu (c. 480–390 B.C.). According to Graham (1989: 39–41) and Schwartz (1985: 136–72) Mohist political thought was based largely on utilitarian rationality, that is, analyzing situations in terms of conscious goals and calculating the means best suited to achieve these goals. Mohists were also among the few ancient Chinese who reflected systematically on questions of formal logic.[7] Mohist or Mohist-like thought is probably one of the targets of Laoist polemic aphorisms* against Improvements* and against Naming*.

Morality*. See *Confucian**.

Mother*. *Mu/*Mother is one hypostatization* of the quality of mind Laoists cultivate. This partly reflects the theme that this quality is envisioned as the origin* ("Mother") of the world. But since the origin-image conveys the idea of something "fundamental" (see p. 253–55), this "Mother" one cultivates internally is also called the "Mother of the State" (26[59]:3), that is, the foundation of Chinese culture. "Mother" is also related to the idea that the hypostatized quality cultivated is internally nourishing (13[20]:5) and Feminine*. See further discussion p. 218. Relevant passages are 13[20]:5, 26[59]:3, 29[52]:1–2, 39[25]:1, 43[1]:2.

Naming*. For Laoists, *ming*/naming is generally a negative term referring to the use of conscious concepts to try to understand the world. Laoists may have lumped several different groups together here: Some early Chinese "Sophists" who concerned themselves with logic were later labeled the "School of Names."[8] Some Mohists* were also concerned with logic, and they may be included here. "Legalist" thinkers,[9] who advocated written codification of customary law, are possibly the target of Laoist criticism of naming in 63[32]:3. Included, finally, is the program advocated by some Confucians* called "rectifying names"—attempts to fix social norms by carefully defining moral terms.[10] Such naming "cuts up the Uncarved* Block" (63[32]:3), that is, true normative goodness perceived through unconceptualized experience. (See the discussion p. 166, 214.) "Unconceptualized" here only refers to the absence of conscious and explicit concepts. It does not imply perception of "objective raw data," completely uninfluenced even in an implicit way by cultural influences and subjective concerns. Laoist experience was shaped by ancient Chinese culture, by the social position and concerns of Warring States *shih**, and by their own particular value-orientation (see *Organic**). Laoist opposition to explicitly conceptualized "naming" also partly explains why Laoists are so "inconsistent" in their use of words: Verbal consistency is only important to someone whose worldview is centered on a conceptualized doctrinal system. See p. 72 and comments on *shen*/self at 10[7], *sheng*/wisdom at 78[19], *yü*/desire* p. 537, *ch'iang*/strong:forcing (under *Forcing**, p. 539), *t'ien*/Heaven p. 174, *sheng*/life* p. 543, *hsia*/low* p. 543. *Ming*/name itself has a positive use in 43[1]:1, 41[47]:3, and 38[21]:3 (in the last passage Tao's "name" stands positively for its power). See also *Understanding**. Criticism of conceptual naming is related to criticism of self-assured knowledge of norms and of the laws that govern events (58[73]:1–3, 59[58]:2, 62[29]:3). Passages critical of "naming"—or presenting nameless-ness or wordless-ness as an ideal—are 42[2]:1–4, 43[1]:1 and 4, 47[43]:2, 63[32]:3, 77[57]:3:1–2 and 77[57]:4. "Nameless" as a characteristic of Laoist Tao occurs in

37[14]:3, 39[25]:2, 43[1]:1,2, 44[41]:4, 63[32]:1, 81[37]:2. It is relevant to this last usage that *ming*/name can also mean "fame, reputation" (e.g., 19[44]:1:1).

Natural*. Being "natural" is a modern ideal that bears some similarity to a central Laoist ideal. Modern thought on this topic, however, has been greatly shaped by the foundationalist concern to discover "nature as it exists in itself" apart from all human experience and culture. This concern is foreign to Laoist thought. See further discussions of "the natural" in the *Mencius* p. 95, 96, 115–17, and in the *Tao Te Ching* p. 165–66. I believe the concept of "organic* harmony" comes closer to the aspect of the Laoist ideal often called "naturalness." *Hsing*, a common word for [human] nature used in other ancient Chinese texts, does not occur in the *Tao Te Ching*; the only *term* occurring here that comes close to our word "natural" is *tzu-jan*, (lit. "self-like"), occurring at 14[23]:1, 54[17]:3, 72[64]:8, 65[51]:2, and 39[25]:4 (translated in the last passage "things as they are").

Nei* Yeh. *Nei Yeh*/"Inward Training" is the name of a text that is a valuable source of information about early self-cultivation and meditation practices in China. The *Nei Yeh* and the *Chuang Tzu* are the main sources of comparative material I rely on in discussing Laoist sayings related to self-cultivation. Selections from it are discussed in detail p. 181–94.

Normative* Description. Some instructional* sayings give a normative description of what one is like who embodies Laoist Tao or Te. The main thrust of such sayings is to specify what true Laoist Tao/Te consists in, by describing ways of being or acting expressive of these qualities. They function in effect as definitions of Laoist "ortho-praxy." See further discussion p. 233–35. Sayings in this genre are 6[15]:4, 9[79]:3, 20[46]:1, 31[4]:1, 34[40]:1, 37[14]:6, 60[49]:2, 64[34]:1, 69[30]:1, 80[65]:1.

Nothing*. One designation of the quality of mind Laoists cultivate. On the present interpretation, "Nothing" (*wu* or *wu yu*), and its contrast *yu*/being, need to be interpreted not philosophically, but experientially. Like the pair Empty*/solid, the pair *wu/yu* refers to things that *feel* intangible and tangible, respectively. "Nothing" refers to a quality of mind in 15[11]:1–2, 34[40]:2, and 47[43]:1. See further discussion p. 212.

Oneness*. One name for the hypostatized* quality of mind Laoists cultivate, occurring in 4[22]:4, 27[10]:1, 35[39]:1, 36[42]:1. In the *Tao Te Ching* 27[10] Oneness is associated with being internally "undivided." The *Chuang Tzu* selections 1, 6, and 7 (p.

203–208) show a similar association. *I* could also refer to the fact that Laoist values focus on one single state of mind that is all important.[11] See further discussion p. 213.

Oracle*. Some Laoist sayings seem to borrow an "oracle" formula found also in the *I Ching*, as for example 7[8]:3, "Do not contend, then [there will be] no fault." The chief implication of this observation for interpretation is that no specific importance should be given to the phrases "no fault,"[12] "no trouble," etc. in sayings using this formula. These phrases are merely conventional ways of designating something as "lucky," an action or event that will bring good fortune. Sayings using an oracle formula are 7[8]:3, 13[20]:1, 19[44]:3,4 (= 63[32]:3:4), 28[16]:6 (= 29[52]:3), 50[53]:2.

Organic*. The Laoist view of the world is remarkably unified (45[70]:1), but this unity is suggested and "performed" (p. 160) rather than explicitly spelled out. I argue p. 160–170 that the best way to describe this unity is to say that most Laoist wisdom is motivated by a concern for "organic harmony" as that kind of good that deserves highest priority. Organic harmony in a social group is exemplified in the case of a harmonious family, or of a group of friends or co-workers who have been together for a long time. In such cases the unity and harmony of the group is "organic," a spontaneous and integral part of the way members instinctively relate to each other. A concern for this kind of organic harmony is the underlying value-orientation motivating the Laoist attitude toward ruling. (See *Impressive**, *Strict**, *Forcing**, *Improvements**, Sections 5–7 of the translation and commentary, and further discussion p. 167–68.) One can also speak, by analogy, of an "organic harmony" existing within a person's being. This might be (A) an organic harmony characterizing a person's "personality": She has developed a kind of goodness arising from a unique, organic integration of all the good potentialities of her own being. This kind of organic harmony is the value that motivates the Laoist attitude toward personal character-formation and interactions with peers. (See *Appearances**, *Self-Promotion**, Section 1 of the translation and commentary, and further discussion p. 164–66.) Organic harmony might also characterize (B) a person's psycho-biological being: All the parts and forces of her psycho-biological make up are working harmoniously and healthily together. This kind of organic harmony is the value motivating the Laoist attitude toward mental/physical health. (See *Agitation**, *Desire**, *Stillness** and Section 2 of the translation and commentary, and further discussion p. 167.) Finally, organic harmony might characterize (C) our conscious awareness of the world, as a whole perceived by a participant concerned with and involved in the ongoing processes of the world; this kind of organic harmony is the value motivating the Laoist attitude toward attempts to understand the world. (See *Understanding**, *Naming**, the first four chapters in Section 4 of the translation, and further discussion p. 166–67) In all these cases, organic harmony tends to be a taken-for-granted "background environment," against which certain things stand out in as "fore-grounded" in our awareness. Laoists emphasize the way that attending to and developing this out-standing foreground causes us to neglect, and also damage, the taken-for-granted background environment, which is a necessary sustaining basis (a "Mother"*) for our personal and social life. Although it needs to arise from within, organic harmony does not always and necessarily come about of its own accord. The high level of organic harmony Laoists desire must be cultivated.

Origins*.   Some sayings celebrate* the cosmic importance of Tao by picturing it as a cosmic origin*. This genre, important but difficult for us moderns to understand, is discussed at length p. 251–66. Relevant passages are 29[52]:1, 31[4]:2, 32[6]:2, 34[40]:2, 35[39]:1, 36[42]:1, 39[25]:1, 43[1]:2, 65[51]:1,3.

Self-promotion.*   The target of a large group of polemic aphorisms* is the tendency of people to try to achieve recognition by direct and conscious, "boasting" efforts to impress others as someone who stands out above others. This must have been a common tendency among *shih** anxious to draw attention to themselves to further their careers. These sayings offer several closely related images to counter this tendency: There is first the negative image of the self-defeating show-off who turns other people off by his obvious self-promotion (e.g., 1[24]:2). And there are several contrasting positive images: the image of attractive self-effacement that wins admiration from others on this basis (e.g., 4[22]:5); the image of the competent and successful *shih* who does not treat his successes primarily as a means to enhance his own prestige (e.g., 42[2]:5); the image of the *shih* in office who works selflessly for the good of others in society rather than com-peting with others for higher status for himself (e.g., 7[8]:1, 8[81]:3); the image of the person, selfless and secure in himself, who can be generous to others even when they do not reciprocate (9[79]:3, 60[49]:2); and the image representing a hyperbolic extreme of the above, that of a person willing to accept the lowest position in society (7[8]:1), and "fall like a stone into oblivion" (35[39]:4). One must not turn the aphoristic* thought here into a literal rule against seeking promotions of any kind. Laoists wanted to influence their society from positions of highest leadership, and hence must have wanted ultimately to "get promoted" to high government posts. On the other hand, a utilitarian interpretation of Laoist thought here is probably also mistaken, the view that self-effacement is merely a tactic adopted to further egotistic ambition (see p. 151). Being self-effacing is part of a certain posture and "style" of relating to the world that Laoists value for its own sake. Their hope is that the true hidden worth of the good-but-self-effacing person will subtly shine through and win public admiration and influence. Sayings on this topic "sublimate" the desire of *shih* for reputation and influence, substituting the subtle ideal of attractive self-effacement for the crass ideal of aggressive self-assertion. See *Appearances**, and the further discussion of the relation of these ideas to organic harmony p. 166. Relevant passages are 1[24]:2, 2[9]:2, 3[67]:2, 4[22]:5,6 (= 55[66]:4), 6[15]:2, 7[8]:1,3, 9[79]:3, 10[7]:1,2,3, 18[13]:4, 27[10]:2, 35[39]:4, 42[2]:5, 50[53]:2, 52[77]:3, 53[72]:3, 62[29]:4), 64[34]:3,5 (= 71[63]:5), 65[51]:4, 69[30]:3.

Shift*.   Some passages reflect an experience in which a shift in one's state of mind causes a shift also in the world-as-perceived. See further discussion p. 246–48. Relevant passages are 28[16]:2, 30[56]:3 (= 31[4]:3), 42[2]:1.

Shih*.   The name Cho-yun Hsu uses (1965: 89) for a social class of idealistic men in ancient China who aspired to moral and political leadership through service as government administrators or advisers. Chapters 3, 4, and 5 discuss at length the position and ambitions of *shih*. I argue (p. 118–22, 197) that the *Tao Te Ching* had its origins in a Laoist* *shih*-school. The word *shih* occurs in 6[15]:1, 44[41]:1, and 57[68]:1 (in the last passage it means "soldier").

Softness/Weakness*.   *Jou*/Softness and *jo*/Weakness often occur together as descriptive terms referring to the quality of mind Laoists cultivate (the opposite of *ch'iang*/hard:strong:forcing). This quality is a kind of energy one can cultivate internally (27[10]:1, 74[76]:1). But this quality of mind also expresses itself in a certain "Soft," non-confrontational way of dealing with the world (73[36]:1-2). *Jo*/Weakness is not, of course, to be taken literally. It is a term with ordinarily negative connotations that refers paradoxically to a positive quality (which can also be described as an inner *ch'iang*/strength, 29[52]:5). See further discussion p.

216–17. Relevant passages are 27[10]:1, 29[52]:5, 33[55]:2, 34[40]:1, 47[43]:1, 73[36]:2, 74[76]:1,2,3,4, 75[78]:1,2. See also *Forcing**.

Solidity*. See *Empty**.

Steady*. *Heng*/Steadiness[13] is another descriptive name for the quality of mind Laoists cultivate. I believe that the Laoist use of the term is similar to that of Mencius*, who uses it (1A/7,20, p. 101) to describe the "steady" mind of a good *shih**, able to keep his integrity even in the face of strong pressures from difficult life situations. See further discussion p. 215. Relevant passages are 28[16]:3,4, 29[52]:7, and 33[55]:3. In 43[1]:1 and 17[28]:1, *heng* serves as an adjective describing "true" Tao/Te, on which one can always rely as an unchanging internal standard. In these latter two passages I translate "invariant."

Still*. *Ching*/Stillness is another descriptive term referring to the quality of mind Laoists cultivate. *Still* is contrasted with a "stirred up" mind in 6[15]:3, with excitement and "agitation" in 23[26]:1 and 5[45]:3, and with *tso*/activity in 28[16]:2–3 and 81[37]:2. See further discussion p. 210. *Ching*/Stillness occurs in 5[45]:3,4, 6[15]:3, 23[26]:1, 28[16]:1,3, 56[61]:2, 77[57]:5, 81[37]:2. *Ching* also means "pure."

Strict*. A target of some polemic aphorisms* is the ideal of the ruler as a model and enforcer of strict moral norms. Laoists dislike the confrontational, "hurting" stance such a ruler takes towards his people, and reject his underlying assumption that he has full and certain understanding* of the unchanging norms that ought to be enforced (58[73]:1–3, 59[58]:2, 62[29]:3). Some passages pose the counterimage of a ruler who actually does enforce high standards, but does so in a tactful and non-confrontational way that does not make the people feel hurt (e.g., 55[66]:3,3, and see *Hurt**. Chapter 58[73] makes it clear that literally not-enforcing laws is not the issue; a "Soft" style of law enforcement is the ideal.) Also relevant here is the counterimage suggested in 60[49]:1: The ruler who imposes standards that are just an idealized version of the organic* harmony already inherent in the society. And one should also consider the kind of understanding* Laoists take as their ideal: They reject the use of concepts that incline us to impose fixed standard categories on fluid and always-different situations. The direct experience on which they rely instead is more able to adapt itself to new and unique circumstances. These seem to be the positive ideals underlying several other, highly exaggerated counterimages: The ruler who simply "drifts" to and fro (64[34]:1), who is like a prostitute devoid of standards (56[61]:1), appears "dull and incompetent" (59[58]:1), and "keeps his mind muddled" (60[49]:3). See *Impressive**, and further discussion p. 168. Relevant passages are 56[61]:1, 58[73]:5, 59[58]:1,4, 60[49]:1,3,4, and 64[34]:1.

*Superstitious**. There are some situations that make people uneasy for not-quite-rational reasons: Things have been going too well too long, someone is getting much too rich much too easily, a pridefully self-assertive person is stepping all over other people with impunity so far, someone is introducing radical changes in a very stable traditional community, etc. The kind of uneasy expectation we have in such circumstances that something bad is going to happen for not-quite-accountable reasons—this is what I am calling a "quasi-superstitious" feeling. Such a feeling underlies many Laoist sayings, especially those against war and violence that are grouped together at the beginning of Section 6. Part of this feeling is due to Chinese ideas about the close connection between proper ruling and good order in the world of nature. (A passage from the *Mo Tzu*[14] describes some of the effects of a bad ruler: "Phantom women came out after dark . . . , a woman turned into a man, flesh rained down from heaven, brambles grew on the state roads." See further comments at 70[60].) "Quasi-superstitious" Laoist sayings are half-rationalized, in that (A) things said to bring misfortune are always things that are rejected on the basis of Laoist values expressed elsewhere. And (B) there is a continuity between the Laoist worldview and the general sense of things that underlies "superstitious" thinking: In both cases the underlying sense is that there is a certain "natural"* way the world runs, and things that appear strange, novel, or individually self-assertive against this background are felt to be vaguely "dangerous." Self-assertive people acting with hubris are putting themselves in a "precarious" situation. See 1[24]:4 (= 67[31]:2), 19[44]:2, 36[42]:6, 66[74]:2, 67[31]:1,2,6, 69[30]:2–3, 70[60]:2, 77[57]:3. See also *Oracle**.

*Take-off**. Sometimes the composer of a chapter seems to quote a saying not for its own sake, but simply to use as a take-off point for some other comment he wants to make. See 9[79]:1, 25[48]:1,1, 34[40]:2,1, 40[71]:1,1, 58[73]:1, 66[74]:1, 77[57]:1,1. In 29[52]:2 and 81[37]:2 the composer's comments reverse the point of a Laoist saying commented on. See p. 328–30.

*Tao**. Along with Te, Tao is the predominant term Laoists use to refer to the hypostatized* quality of mind they cultivate. Tao has a variety of meanings in the *Tao Te Ching*, due partly, I believe, to the fact that the meaning of the term had not yet been systematized. Sometimes Tao is being used in a way common to ancient Chinese generally, and sometimes it is used in a way more specific to Laoism. Its main uses in the *Tao Te Ching* can be summarized as follows:

1. Some sayings use phrases that assume that Tao means "the right Way" generally; their point is to assert that some aspect of Laoist teaching is this right Way.

2. Some sayings use phrases that already assume that Tao refers specifically to the Laoist Way.

3. Some sayings use phrases that assume that Tao refers to the *internal spirit* that expresses itself in the Laoist way of being or acting.

4. Some sayings picture Tao as a hypostatized power or elusive internal presence.

5. Some sayings picture Tao as a cosmic reality, the origin of the world. See the fuller discussion of each of these points p. 218–223.

I argue, against most other commentators (p. 175–78, 243–46, 263–66) that there are no consistently held cosmological or metaphysical doctrines about Tao in the *Tao Te Ching* that serve as the epistemological and logical foundation for the Laoist worldview. Tao occurs in 1[24]:3, 6[15]:4, 7[8]:1, 11[38]:4,6, 12[18]:1, 14[23]:3, 20[46]:1, 25[48]:1, 28[16]:5, 31[4]:1, 33[55]:5, 34[40]:1, 36[42]:1, 37[14]:5,6, 38[21]:1,2, 39[25]:2,4, 43[1]:1, 44[41]:1,2,4, 46[35]:2, 48[62]:1,5,6, 52[77]:2, 63[32]:1,4, 64[34]:1, 65[51]:1,2,3, 69[30]:1,5, 70[60]:2, 80[65]:1, 81[37]:1. I translate Tao as "Way," in 2[9]:2, 9[79]:4, 26[59]:4, 41[47]:1, 50[53]:1,3,6, 52[77]:1, and 58[73]:5. See also "Heaven's Way" under *Heaven**. Tao also occurs in many passages from other books quoted here, passages from the *Mencius* (p. 75, 81, 84, 86–87, 92–94), the *Nei Yeh* (p. 190–91), and the *Chuang Tzu* (p. 202, 205, 207).

*Te**. *Te* was a common word in ancient China, with a meaning similar to our "virtue." Like Tao, it was a generic concept, whose specific content depended on the nature of the speaker's moral or spiritual ideals. Laoists appropriated it as one of the main designations of their own ideal way of being, even though their ideals departed considerably from what other Chinese would have considered "virtuous." Te also referred to the influence or "charisma" a person has, a meaning that is evident in 26[59]:2 and 57[68]:2, and in the story of Ch'i Tzu quoted p. 554 under *This**. Te is sometimes hypostatized* in the *Tao Te Ching* as a quasi-independent internal energy or force that one "accumulates" internally through self-cultivation (26[59]:2), and that can be envisioned as a cosmic force, the origin* of the world (65[51]). Three passages (9[79], 60[49]:2, 71[63]:3) emphasize the association with Te as self-forgetting generosity, able to "be good to those who are not good." In 61[54]:2, Te refers to the good character or spirit of larger social units (family, village, state). See the discussion p. 223–26. Te occurs in 9[79]:3, 11[38]:1,2,4, 14[23]:3, 17[28]:1, 26[59]:2, 27[10]:2, 33[55]:1, 38[21]:1, 44[41]:3, 57[68]:2, 60[49]:2, 61[54]:2, 65[51]:1,2,3,4, 70[60]:4, 71[63]:3, 80[65]:4,5. Te occurs in Mencius passages quoted p. 81, 84, 97, in the *Nei Yeh* passage quoted p. 188–90 sections {3}, {4}, and {9}, and in the *Chuang Tzu* selections 3, 5, and 6 quoted on p. 205–07.

Teaching*. Some sayings reflect directly on what it is like to be a teacher in the Laoist school, both the difficulty of this because of the subtlety and unconventional nature of the "wordless" Tao one is trying to teach, and the supreme importance of what one has to offer the world. See 3[67]:1, 36[42]:6, 42[2]:3, 45[70], 46[35]:2, 47[43]:2, 48[62]:4,5, 49[27]:3,4,5, 75[78]:3,5. Chapters dealing mainly with this topic are grouped together as the last six chapters in Section 4 of my translation.

Things*   *Wu*/thing(s), and *wan wu*/"the thousands of things" are common phrases in the *Tao Te Ching*, with a meaning I believe close to the colloquial use of "things" in English, as in "don't let things get to you." *Wu* refers not only to individual objects, but to many other kinds of realities, as for example the reputation/influence of a king (36[42]:5), or problems that a teacher resolves (49[27]:3). Although sometimes the "thousands of things" are contrasted with "people" (e.g., 74[76]:1), very often it is clear that "things" or "thousands of things" refers primarily to people (36[42]:2, 80[65]:5, 81[37]:2). Compare Mencius' statement (7A/19,4), "[The rulers] correct themselves and *wu*/things are corrected" (Legge translates "others are corrected"). This usage probably reflects the fact that Laoist *shih** look on the world primarily from the perspective of the ruler/administrator: The world at large—consisting of lands, crops, people, political cohesion, social tendencies, etc.—constitutes a field of "things" which it is his job to manage well. *Wu*/thing can also mean "substance," as in 38[21]:2, where Tao is called a *wu*/thing, inside of which there is *wu*/"something substantial." Finally, in 1[24]:4 (= 67[31]:2) *wu*/things refers to normative reality as seen from the Laoist perspective, the reality that one's actions ought to accord with.

This*. I believe the Laoist saying "Leave 'that' aside, attend to 'this'" (11[38]:8 = 21[12]:3 = 53[72]:4), uses "this" and "that" in a special sense (not, as some think, to mean simply "the former/the latter"). The key to this saying's meaning is found in a passage where it is quoted in the *Huai Nan Tzu*, a passage reporting Confucius' comments on the case of a ruler with such strong Te* (invisible influence) that fishermen threw back small fish of a size below the limit he set even when no one was looking, merely because they knew that he wanted them to.

> How perfect is the Te of Ch'i Tzu. He causes men to act even in private as though there were going to be stern punishment for any infraction. How did Ch'i Tzu achieve this? Confucius said, "I have heard . . . it said, 'Sincerity in this is [equivalent to] enforcement in that'." So Lao Tzu said, "Leave 'that' aside, attend to 'this'."[15]

Huai Nan Tzu here takes "this" in both the Confucian and the Laoist sayings to refer to the cultivation of Te in one's own person, while "that" refers to attempts to affect others by external means (here, through punishment). This is confirmed by a variation of the above Confucian saying that appears in the *Great Learning* (6/2) which substitutes "inside/outside" for "this/that" ("Sincerity on the *chung*/inside [is equivalent to] enforcement on the *wai*/outside.") This meaning fits the context well in 11[38]:8 and 53[72]:4. I think the meaning is extended somewhat in 21[12]:3, where the parallel of "this/that" with "belly/eye" suggests that "that" refers to eye-catching things "out there" in the world, while "this" refers to something truly satisfying internally, or perhaps to the mind itself, in a state capable of quiet satisfaction.

Three other sayings using "this" which need comment are those using the formula, "How do I know . . . ? By this." in 38[21]:4, 61[54]:4 and 77[57]:2. My conjecture is that this formula is a favorite Laoist reply to questions from others demanding reasons or evidence supporting their opinions. The Laoist reply appeals simply to "this," meaning either the reality right in front of you, intuitively understood and evaluated in the right state of mind, or your mind itself, in a cultivated state able to understand* things rightly by intuition. The latter use of "this" occurs in a passage from the *Kuan*

Tzu quoted by Waley:[16] "What a man desires to know is that (i.e., the external world). But his means of knowing is this (i.e., himself). How can he know that? Only by the perfection of this."

Turn* back. This is one designation of the activity of self-cultivation. It evokes two key Laoist ideas: the idea of an original and superior, "natural*" state of mental Stillness* we ought to "turn back to," and the idea of an unfortunate human tendency to become mentally active and direct energy outward. In this context Laoist self-cultivation involves a "reversal" of this tendency, "turning back to the place all others have gone on from" (72[64]:7). See further discussion p. 227–28, and comments on "knowing to stop" at 63[32]. Relevant passages are 4[22]:7, 17[28]:1, 28[16]:2,3, 29[52]:2,6, 34[40]:1, 37[14]:3, 39[25]:3, 64[34]:4, 72[64]:7, 78[19]:1.

Uncarved*. *P'u*/"Uncarved Block" is one term referring to the quality of mind Laoists cultivate. *P'u* can also mean "Simplicity" (see 81[37]:2 and 77[57]:5), but it is used in two passages in the *Tao Te Ching* that evoke the full image of an uncarved block of wood on a carver's shelf. These passages imply an image of "natural*" human goodness before it is "carved" to produced socially determined good/bad qualities (17[28]:1-2), or before rulers attempt to define it by "naming*" it in definite legal rules (63[32]:3). See further discussion p. 214. Relevant passages are 6[15]:2, 17[28]:1,2, 63[32]:1, 77[57]:5, 78[19]:2, and 81[37]:2. See also *Appearances*.

Understanding*. Some polemic aphorisms* are directed against ideas of other *shih** about the right way to go about understanding the world. The targets of Laoist criticism here are primarily the emphasis others give to broad learning (8[81]:1:5-6, 41[47]:1-2), others' emphasis on conceptual "naming*" (42[2]:1,2, 63[32]:3), and the confidence of some, based on this, that they know the universal norms and laws governing every possible situation (62[29]:3, 58[73]:1-3, 59[58]:2). This kind of knowledge gives the knower a sense of being in possession of something special, something more clear and more valuable, "standing out" over against the unreflective perception of the world given in plain experience. But plain experience of the world has a valuable "holistic" character; in it the world is directly perceived as an organic* whole in which things are all interrelated and interpenetrate each other in subtle and complex ways. This holistic character of unreflective experience is destroyed when one tries to relate to the world primarily through the medium of deliberately learned ideas and of conceptual categories. In addition, since the reality of any given social situation can never be completely grasped by analytical thought, a ruler/administrator who acts on the basis of rational analysis runs the danger of neglecting some important facets of unique situations that the categories of his thought are inadequate to grasp. Laoist *shih** do not want to rely on plain *conventional* experience; situations have a mysterious, deep and subtle dimension (6[15]:1, 43[1]:3), which the conventional-minded cannot grasp. But neither do they want to "improve" on unreflective experience by developing rational/conceptual thought. Their view is that the personal transformation achieved in self-cultivation also causes a shift* in the world-as-perceived, deepening the organic wholeness found in ordinary unreflective experience. To perceive the world in this new, ideal state of mind is to see the truth about events. One image for this: There is a "non-desiring*" mental abode one can rest in, where all particulars are Merged* into an organic whole. This is the abode where the *miao*/"hidden essentials" of situations reside (43[1]:3,5). Another image: To get in touch with the quality of mind Laoists cultivate is also to get in touch with a deeper level of reality, the source/foundation of the true meaning of events. Once you get in touch with this foundation, you understand the events (29[52]:2:1–2, 37[14]:6, 38[21]:3. And see p. 253–55). In the absence of any other likely candidates for the "hidden essence" of situations that Laoists see, I think we ought to assume that this is identical with the view of various situations expressed by Laoist polemic aphorisms*. (See the use of *miao*/"hidden essence" to refer to a "secret" truth about how to view teacher-student relationships in 49[27]:5.) See the further discussion p. 166–67. Relevant passages are 4[22]:3, 6[15]:1, 8[81]:1:5–6, 29[52]:2:1–2, 30[56]:1, 37[14]:6, 38[21]:3,4, 40[71]:1, 41[47]:1,2,3, 42[2]:1,2,4, 43[1]:1–5, 58[73]:1–3, 59[58]:2, 61[54]:3, 62[29]:3, 75[78]:3. See also *Naming**, and comments on the formula "How do I know . . . by this?" under *This**. Chapters on this topic are grouped together as the first four chapters under Section 4 of the translation. "Knowledge" is a negative term in 12[18]:1, 27[10]:1, 78[19]:1, 79[3]:3, 80[65]:2,3, probably referring primarily to conceptual ("naming"*) knowledge others pride themselves on. *Chih*/know can also refer to direct experience of something, as in "*chih*/experiencing Steadiness" (28[16]:3).

   *Use**.   *Yung*/use is one of several words to describe the action of self-cultivation, internalizing and practicing certain internal qualities. See 17[28]:2, 31[4]:1, 32[6]:4, 34[40]:1, 46[35]:3. Other terms constituting a special vocabulary related to self-cultivation are (A) *shou*/"watch over" (16[5]:4, 17[28]:1, 28[16]:1, 29[52]:2 and 5, 63[32]:2, 81[37]:2); (B) *pao*/embrace (4[22]:4, 27[10]:1, 61[54]:1, 78[19]:2); (C) *te*/get (29[52]:2, 35[39]:1, 37[14]:1). See also *Turn* back*. These terms are further discussed p. 226–27.

Valley*. An image associated with the ideal Laoist state of mind in 6[15]:2, 17[28]:1, and 32[6]:1 (see comments on 32[6]).

Watch* Over. See *Use**.

Weakness*. See *Softness**.

Wise* Person. *Sheng jen*/"Wise Person" is a term often used in contemporary literature, to designate the very highest human ideal. (Mencius [2A/2,19] quotes Confucius as saying that being a *sheng jen* was beyond his capacity.) "Wise" does not capture the full meaning of *sheng*, which some translate "holy," or "saint." *Sheng jen* figures in the *Tao Te Ching* mainly in a standard formula that the composers use to introduce sayings.

Working*. *Wei*/working:doing is often used in the *Tao Te Ching* as a negative term. It describes an attitude rather than a literal lack of activity, the attitude of one who thinks of reality as inert raw material on which to impose his plans and make his mark. All the importance is given to his ideas and efforts, and none to the innate character of what he is working on. The contrasting Laoist ideal, *wu wei*/"not-working" should not then be taken literally. It sometimes (e.g., 27[10]:1) describes an internal, Still* state of mind. It also describes the attitude—opposite that of the "worker"—of one who aims to draw out the inherent goodness of what is given, and who is willing to subordinate himself to the demands of the material and the task with subtle attention and extreme care. See especially comments on 71[63] and 72[64]. *Wei*/working is used in this special sense in 11[38]:2–3, 25[48]:1–4, 27[10]:1, 41[47]:3, 42[2]:3, 47[43]:1,2, 51[75]:1,2, 62[29]:1,2, 71[63]:1, 72[64]:4,5,8, 77[57]:1,5, 79[3]:3,4, 81[37]:1. Some of these passages (42[2]:3, 25[48]:3, 77[57]:1 and 5, 71[63]:1) use not *wei* but a somewhat synonymous term, *shih*/serve:work, commonly used to refer to "service" in a government post. "Working" in a negative sense is used predominantly in chapters against progressive social "improvements"*, but there is also a tendency to apply this key term to other areas of life as well, like self-cultivation (11[38]:2,3), gaining knowledge (41[47]:3), and even "working" at luxurious living (51[75]:2). Note that *wei*/work is also sometimes used in a positive sense, to refer to administrative tasks the *shih** ought to undertake: See 8[81]:3,4, 27[10]:2 (= 52[77]:3, 65[51]:4), and 72[64]:2.

Yang* Chu. A shadowy figure who came to stand for an attitude probably common to many others in Warring States China: The rejection of government service in order to care for one's own personal well being and peace of mind.[17] The Laoist polemic against mental agitation*—contained mostly in Section 2 of my translation—has something in common with the "Yangist" concern for peace of mind. See further comments under *Life**. I believe 18[13]:1 is probably a Yangist saying, "reinterpreted," however, by the Laoist composer to fit with the Laoist acceptance of public service as an ideal.

Yin*. Some thinkers in ancient China were beginning to develop schemes for categorizing forces in the world. One of these schemes centered around the polar opposites, *yin* and *yang* (originally terms meaning "shady" and "sunny," respectively). Under *yin* were grouped such things as femininity, darkness, passivity, moisture. Under *yang* were grouped such things as masculinity, brightness, action, heat.[18] Some later Taoist groups advocated deliberately trying to balance *yin* and *yang*, but Laoist aphoristic* wisdom emphasizes cultivating *yin* qualities as opposed to *yang* ones (see comments on 17[28]). The terms *yin* and *yang* occur only once in the *Tao Te Ching*, 36[42]:2.

Notes

Notes to the Introduction

1. See Metzger's discussion (1977: 3–20) of the concept of political culture and its importance in the study of political thinkers. I read these pages in Metzger's study of medieval Neo-confucianism only after completing the present study. There is a great deal in his approach that resembles the approach I try to take here to the *Mencius* and the *Tao Te Ching*.

Notes to Part One: Introduction

1. The hermeneutic theory presented here is a continuation of work on these problems I began while doing work on other texts from other religious traditions. See LaFargue 1985, 1988a, 1988b.

Notes to Chapter One

1. A term coined by Karl Jaspers (1953: 1–21). See p. 284 n. 17.

2. Although this account accepts many basic ideas underlying H.-G. Gadamer's (1982) critical history of hermeneutics, it can better be regarded as a counter-narrative directed against Gadamer's version, and particularly against the sophisticated defense of a "scriptural" approach to interpretation that seems the ultimate motivating force behind his narrative, and more especially behind his influential ideas of the "fusion of horizons" (273), and of the "effective history" of texts (267, 305–10).

3. For recent historical accounts of traditional interpretation of the classics in China, see Van Zoeren (1991), and Henderson (1991).

4. Scripture interpretation has the same semantic structure as the Mohist statement about ancient kings analyzed on p. 30–32. Its "perceptual basis" (A) is some good insight stimulated by reading the text. The authority of the text serves as a "background assumption" (B), leading one to attribute a certain meaning to the text (C).

5. I am using "goodness" here in a sense defined more precisely in Chapter 11, p. 270–77.

6. For an account of two key figures in the beginnings of this movement, see Berlin's (1976) *Vico and Herder*. I take Wilhelm Dilthey to be the prime representative of this movement at its height. See especially Ermarth's excellent account (1981) of Dilthey's thought and its background. Dilthey is developing ideas proposed by Friedrich Schleiermacher (1958; first published 1801), who first developed the idea that empathically entering into the experiences that gave rise to religious beliefs is the key to understanding them.

7. This empathic reliving is the basis of *Verstehen*, that particular mode of understanding that distinguishes the human from the natural sciences. See Ermarth 1981: 241–321; Dallmayr and McCarthy 1977; Strasser 1985: 1–54; Taylor 1981.

8. Collingwood (1956: 86–126) gives a good survey of developments that led from this assumption of timeless truths to the modern sense of the diversity of cultures and of historical eras.

9. I am referring here to interpretations that consist mainly in showing how badly some canonical texts appear when seen from the perspective of some particular set of modern values. This seems simply the flip side of traditional scriptural interpretation, which only has a point so long as *someone* reveres the texts involved.

10. See Gadamer (1982); Ricoeur (1974, 1976, 1981); Derrida (1972, 1974, 1977.) I presented a critical review of Derrida's contribution to hermeneutics in LaFargue 1988a.

11. For example: "It is senseless to speak of a perfect knowledge of history, and for this reason it is not possible to speak of an object in itself towards which [interpretive] research is directed." (Gadamer 1982: 253.)

12. I use "experiential" here advisedly, rather than "rational," to indicate my agreement with Gadamer (1982: 241–45) in reject-

ing the habit of subjecting all truth claims to the judgment of Enlightenment rationality. "Experiential" also refers to the holistic *Erleben* of Dilthey and the phenomenologists, in contrast to the atomistic "sense perceptions" of British empiricism (see Ermarth 1978: 97, 365 n. 3). On my view, "the good," which is the basis for true authority, is an experiential category (see p. 274).

13. "Understanding means, primarily, to understand the content of what is being said, and only secondarily to . . . understand another's meaning. . . . Hence the first of all hermeneutic requirements . . . [is] being concerned with the same subject." (Gadamer 1982: 262.) I wholeheartedly agree with this emendation of Romantic hermeneutics with its focus on "the *mind* of the author." If I show someone a poem I like, I do not want them to understand my ideas or feelings about the poem; I want them to see *in the poem* what I see in it. The "many worlds" theory explained below (p. 17), however, implies that to "be concerned with the same subject" as a distant author, one must attempt to enter that author's particular world and vicariously take on his or her mode of concernful engagement (see p. 25) with that world. Gadamer tends ultimately to picture the true content of classical works as "timeless" truths existing beyond all contingent historical contexts, as when he says, "What is stated in the text must be detached from all contingent factors and grasped in its full ideality, in which alone it has validity." (356) Gadamer does not believe in multicultural pluralism. For *Sachkritik* in biblical scholarship see Robinson (1964: 19–39, esp. 31–34.)

14. Gadamer's rejection of the Enlightenment's *rationalist* critique of tradition seems to end up replacing this with simple blind faith that tradition, and "classic" texts, simply are authoritative (1982: 235–74). This is a prior assumption which ought to govern the way we interpret these texts. For an explanation and critique of this cultural conservatism in Gadamer, see Warnke (1987: 73–138.)

15. Implicit here is a thesis that the valid authority claims of classical texts have two distinct bases: valid ideas concerning the good which they represent, and the appropriateness of giving priority to this good in our present cultural context. See p. 294.

16. This proposal is similar to that of Hirsch, who in deliberate opposition to Gadamer (see Warnke, 1987:42–48) draws a distinction between what he calls the "meaning" that the author of

the text intended, and the "significance" this meaning might have for other people or later eras. Texts generally have only one "meaning," though their "significance" might vary from era to era (Hirsch 1967: 8). Although I adopt a distinction similar to Hirsch's, I agree with Gadamer against Hirsch in identifying "the meaning of the text" with the reality of which the text speaks, rather than ideas in the mind of the author. See p. 9 n. 13.

17. As a *conscious and deliberate* strategy, this tendency is usually associated with the Left today. I want to make it clear that my opposition to it does not stem from opposition to the general program of the Left, with which I am in sympathy. I think the cause of the Left would ultimately be better served by the interpretive scholarship I am proposing here.

18. This seems an inevitable result of the "fusion of horizons" which Gadamer recommends (1982: 267).

19. See Cardenal 1975, Macy 1985.

20. See W. C. Smith 1982: 41–56.

21. See Rosenau 1992: 25–41, LaFargue 1988a.

22. This term gained importance in modern continental philosophy through its use in Edmund Husserl's phenomenology. See Husserl (1970: 103–89, 379–83.) Calvin Schrag's *Experience and Being* develops this concept in a direction similar to the one advocated here, with special implications for cultural pluralism (1969: 279–82). I use the term *Lebenswelt* in this work to refer not only to the sociocultural world common to all people in a given area and era, but the world-as-experienced by any given individual, giving full weight to the particularities of individual experience.

23. See especially Burtt 1952.

24. Prosch 1971: 9–162 gives a good sketch of the way that the development of the physical sciences set the agenda for early modern philosophy.

25. See Bernstein 1983: 1–220; Rorty's (1982: xvi) description of the radical separation between ("upper division") Objective Truth, and ("lower division") opinion captures what is essential to foundationalism, as I use that term here. This division is common both to empiricists and to (Kantian) idealists.

26. The classic statement of this thesis is that of Hume, Sec-

tion IV Part 1 of his *Enquiry Concerning Human Understanding* (quoted in Burtt 1939: 598).

27. This is especially evident in Wittgenstein's *Lecture on Ethics* (1976; first delivered 1929). In this essay from the transition period in Wittgenstein's thought, he is operating with the assumption that the world of "natural facts" is the world described by physical science. On this assumption, the entire realm designated by phrases like, "the meaning of life," "what makes life worth living," "the right way of living," (641) can only be described as "supernatural" (643). For a more general historical account of the crisis in ethical thought that accompanied the development of physical sciences, see Adams 1967: 1–34; Hudson 1970: 65–86; MacIntyre 1966: 146–77; Abelson 1967: 104–17.

28. See Bauman 1987: 21–109, and p. 113–16 below.

29. See Ermarth (1981: 43–45), Korff (1966). See also the sociologist of religion Peter Berger (1969: 3–28) on the cultural world as something produced by the "externalization" of the human mind.

30. See Caplan 1978.

31. This subjectivization is also a prime target of Gadamer's hermeneutics. See especially Gadamer 1982: 39–108.

32. I am using "ontology" here in the logic-oriented sense in which Quine (1983) uses it, to mean a general field of inquiry, anyone's assumptions about the ultimate kinds or categories to which belong all possible realities. (I disagree with Quine's actual ontology, however; if I understand it correctly, it is a version of the kind of restrictive ontology I am criticizing here. See Magee 1982: 143–52.) Quine's use of the term is different from other uses such as that of Neville (1981: 80; 1991: 143–52), who takes *ontology* to refer to one's views about the ultimate reality (such as God, Brahman, or Heidegger's "Being") that is the *basis* for the being of things. Ontology in this latter sense seems inescapably foundationalist. MacIntyre (1967: 543) discusses briefly these two different senses that *ontology* has in modern philosophy.

33. See Rorty 1979, 1982, 1989, and the collection of essays in Baynes 1987.

34. This argument is presented in more detail in LaFargue (1992b). It borrows from Allison's (1983: 14–34) interpretation of

Kantian vs. Berkleyan idealism. Putnam (1987) argues a similar version of realism with respect to the *Lebenswelt*, which rests on a neo-Kantian "idealist" basis, as does the view put forth here.

35. Putnam's version of realism also implies a relativity of cultural "realities" (1987: 17–21).

36. The term *metaphysical* seems warranted here, since this view ultimately does seem to assume that we can get beyond the *Lebenswelt* to grasp some truth that *radically* revises the view of reality delivered in ordinary experience.

37. This seems to me a mistake toward which Richard Rorty (1989: xiii–137) tends.

38. This view is the implicit basis of E. D. Hirsch's hermeneutics (1967: 1–67).

39. I take this to be the meaning of Derrida's famous statment (1974: 158) that "there is nothing outside of text" (*il n'y a pas de hors-texte*). That is, the "real" world is not a fixed point of reference, but is just as variable as our speech and writing about it. See LaFargue 1988a: 346–47.

40. This is the main target in Hansen 1983.

41. See Graham 1985.

42. See Fingarette 1972: 37–56; Roth 1990.

43. See Ames and Hall 1987: 12–17.

Notes to Chapter Two

1. This implicit assumption behind most modern treatments of "ancient Chinese philosophy" is made explicit in Hansen 1983: 1–10, 23–29.

2. I use "thick" here in the sense Clifford Geertz (1973: 3–30) introduced in his very influential essay, "Thick Description: Toward an Interpretive Theory of Culture." Geertz (6) credits the notion to Gilbert Ryle.

3. The modern meaning of this concept has its origin in Kant's replacing of the traditional distinction between reality and ideas, with the distinction between reality-as-it-is (*noumena*), and

reality-as-it-appears (*phenomena*) (Solomon 1972: 20.) Solomon's book surveys the development of continental philosophy from its Kantian roots, showing among other things how the concept of *phenomenon* is adopted, with crucial changes, by Hegel (50–51) and by Husserl (155). For a survey of the development of Husserlian phenomenology see Spiegelberg (1976).

4. See especially Heidegger 1962: 78–148.

5. The term "semiotics" is usually credited to Ferdinand de Saussure (1986; see also Culler 1986, esp. 105–50). Umberto Eco's *Theory of Semiotics* (1979) sets forth the approach to semiotics that I think is most fruitful for hermeneutics.

6. See Saussure 1986: 15–17, 99–120.

7. Eco 1979: 73–83.

8. Such atomistic analysis is especially evident in Hume's famous discussions about personal identity (quoted in Perry 1975: 159–76), and is responsible for his dilemmas on this subject. Hume's dilemmas could be solved by regarding the self as a semiotically defined "cultural unit" (see n. 7), a view close to that of G. H. Mead (see Miller 1973: 46–65).

9. This is a major source of my disagreement with Rudolf Bultmann's Heideggerian hermeneutics (see Johnson: 1987: 129–57), to which otherwise I am much indebted. See especially the criticism of Heideggerian hermeneutics by Hans Jonas (1958: 320–21.)

10. The foundationalist and systematizing ambitions of early structuralism are described in Gardner (1974). The main factor preventing Jacques Derrida's (1972) critique of early structuralism from becoming fruitful for historical hermeneutics is the continuing self-contradictory attempts by Derridians to make "poststructuralism" the basis for a *particular* political and cultural stance. This can only be done if one exempts Derridian thought itself from the universal application of the method of "deconstruction."

11. The pragmatism I have in mind is the kind represented in Dewey's *Reconstruction in Philosophy* (1957) and *Experience and Nature* (19297). See also Thayer (1973).

12. See Dewey's own critique of utilitarianism, 1957: 180–83.

13. Watson 1963b: 22

14. See Austin (1962: 4–11), and the discussion in Levinson (1983: 226–37.)

15. See Bultmann 1934, 1963; Rhode 1968; McKnight 1969; and further discussion p. 126–30 and 309.

16. See Whorf 1956.

17. This I take to be the basic meaning of Derrida's (1974: 158) statement that "There is nothing outside of text."

18. See especially 3–6, 20–24, 113–30. Culler is in turn elaborating on Noam Chomsky's theory of competence.

19. This is the point of Gadamer's rehabilitation of "prejudices as conditions of understanding" (1982: 245). I agree that we ought not try to approach texts with a *blank* mind, but with some questions and existential concerns in mind. But Gadamer converts this into the principle that we must approach the text with *our own* questions and concerns.

20. For a fuller presentation and critical evaluation of Derrida's arguments see LaFargue 1988a.

21. See Rosenau 1992. This is also the thrust of some "reader-response criticism," see Freund 1987.

Notes to Part Two: Introduction

1. See p. 302 n. 11.

2. E.g., 5B/8,1, 7B/23,2.

3. See the passages from Hsu quoted below p. 54–56. Hsu uses the word *shih* as a term in his sociological analysis. Mencius often, but not always, uses the term in this narrow meaning (e.g., 1A/7,20, 3B/10,2, 7B/23,2. See p. 57.) But the word also had a broader meaning. For example, sometimes (e.g., *Mencius* 1A/7,14, *Tao Te Ching* 57[68]:1) it means simply "soldier." Creel (1970a: 331–34) discusses older meanings of the term.

4. By the Han historian Ssu-ma T'an (d. 110 B.C.). See Graham 1989: 171, who also points out that earlier sources list the *Tao Te Ching* and the *Chuang Tzu* separately.

5. *(Ibid.*: 170–71. See also Graham's introduction to the *Chuang Tzu* (1991a: 3–33). In general the *Chuang Tzu* seems to dif-

fer from the *Tao Te Ching* most in its inclination toward a light-hearted and liberating skepticism, often leading to a rejection of any public responsibility.

6. Graham 1990a: 118, 124. H. G. Creel also (1929: 47) once suggested the term *Laoism* to refer to ancient Taoism in general.

Notes to Chapter Three

1. See Creel 1970a; Wheatley 1971: 113–15.

2. The similarities and differences between medieval European and ancient Chinese feudalism are discussed in Creel 1970a: 317–87, and Wheatley 1971: 118–22.

3. Later tradition had it that the title *wang* ought to be reserved for the one Emperor; its use by feudal heads of state began only in the Spring and Autumn period and was a usurpation (see Eberhard, 1977: 32; Wheatley 1971: 116). Creel, however, argues (1970a: 215–16) that this exclusive use of the title was not really observed in the earliest Chou period. At most "the Chou probably tried to discourage others [besides the Chou Emperor] from using it." On the use of this title in the *Mencius*, see p. 96.

4. See especially Wheatley 1971: 428–51. Although Wheatley's study focuses on the role of the capital city as symbolic normative center in ancient China, much of what he has to say applies also to the Emperor reigning in this city. See especially 123, 429–31.

5. Sometimes in discussions I find it helpful to give Chinese words along with their English equivalents. In doing this I have adopted a modified version of a format now being used by some sinologists (see Hansen 1983a: 52 n. 1): The Chinese word is placed first, followed by a slash and then an English equivalent. Where it is helpful to give two or more English equivalents, these are separated by colons. For example, "*hsiao*/small:insignificant" includes first the Chinese word *hsiao*, then two English equivalents "small" and "insignificant," separated by a colon. Where an English phrase is being used to translate a Chinese word or phrase, I mark the boundaries of the English phrase by enclosing the whole phrase in quotation marks following the slash, as in *wu wei*/"not doing." The reader unfamiliar with Chinese will have to keep in mind that there are many homophones in Chinese, words

with the same sounds but different meanings. *Ching*, for example, can stand for a word meaning "Stillness," another meaning "vital energy," and still another meaning "classic text." The use of different characters in writing, and of different tones in speaking, helps differentiate these words, and this is what is lost with transliteration in the Latin alphabet.

6. See Hsu 1965: 5.

7. See *Ibid*.: 3, 7, 14, 20–22; Wheatley 1971: 112.

8. See Bodde 1981: 104.

9. See Hsu 1965: 3–5; Wheatley 1971: 114.

10. See Hsu 1965: 31–34, 52.

11. See *Ibid*.: 117; Wheatley (1971: 194) mentions a possible 1,773 dependent territories at an earlier period; he says there were still 170 states in existence in 700 B.C., and only thirteen states of any importance at the beginning of the fifth century.

12. See Hsu 1965: 38.

13. See Hsu 1988; Balazs 1964.

14. Thus *ch'i*/utensil:instument is a negative term referring to men of inferior status in the *Analects* (2/12) and in the *Tao Te Ching* (16[28]:2).

15. Watson 1968: 54. The *Chuang Tzu* makes fun of Hui's seriousness, but Hui's sentiments must have been common among *shih* who are the targets of the *Chuang Tzu's* ridicule.

16. Graham 1989: 33–34. The story will be found in Mei 1929: 257–59.

17. E.g., 5B/6,1–3, where Mencius is describing Etiquette rules designed for *shih* as the class that Hsu describes, who include watchmen and gatekeepers. It is a source of some difficulty to Mencius that his idealistic *shih* belong to this general class, so far as Etiquette is concerned, and yet in his mind they clearly deserve higher treatment and respect. See p. 81.

18. See Creel 1970a: 334–35.

19. For *hsien* see 5B/7,3 (the person described as *hsien* is identified as a *shih* in 5B/7,4). For *chün tzu* see 7A/20 and 21, 3B/4,4, 5B/6,5. For the Mohist use of *hsien* see Schwartz (1985: 156–62).

20. *"Shang*/promote *hsien"* is the title of a section in the *Mo Tzu* (ch. 18–20). See *Tao Te Ching* 79[3]:1:1. Mencius (6B/7,3) says that the policy of *tzun hsien*/"honoring *hsien"* was part of the covenant solemnly sworn to by a meeting of feudal lords in 650 B.C.

21. See Creel 1970a: 81–100.

22. See Creel 1970a: 71–80.

23. See *Ibid.*: 453 n. 34.

24. Karlgren 1950: 61. I have lightly revised Karlgren's translation in a few places.

25. E.g., 5B/9, 2B/5,1–5. In the latter passage Mencius criticizes a judge because he neglects to criticize his king. When people asked why he does not turn this criticism on himself, Mencius replies that he holds no official office and so is at liberty to criticize or not, as he sees fit.

26. See Hsu 1965: 90–91.

27. As Hsu points out elsewhere (1988: 178), the position of these teachers, and of *shih* generally, was enhanced by the fact that Warring States China consisted of several states comprising a relatively large territory and population *culturally* unified but politically lacking strong centralized control. The heads of various states competed with each other for the services of highly qualified *shih*, making it something of a "seller's market."

28. Weber 1968: 18–27.

29. Hsu 1965: 100–101.

30. On the various types of rationality in Weber, see Kalberg 1980, esp. 1155–56.

31. Weber 1963: 59.

32. See Hsu 1965: 107–39.

33. *Ibid.*: 92–106.

34. Weber 1963: 30.

Notes to Chapter Four

1. Hsiao (1979: 145 n. 4) gives Mencius' dates as 385–303 B.C. Several stories about Mencius in the book are datable to the last quarter of the fourth century (see Graham 1989: 112). I believe

that the book itself was probably compiled sometime after Mencius' death by Mencius' disciples. On the dating of the *Tao Te Ching*, see p. 301.

2. Bauman (1987: 21–109) gives an excellent overview of the social and political ambitions of early modern philosophers.

3. See the comparable phrases in the *Tao Te Ching* 5[45]:4 and 35[39]:1:13.

4. Translations from the *Mencius* here are my own, based on Legge's (1895), with help occasionally from the translations of Lau (1970) and Dobson (1963).

5. These four terms—especially the first three—are those that the *Tao Te Ching* (11[38], 12[18], 78[19]) seems to group together as names for the Confucian ideal that it criticizes. (See p. 535 under *Confucianism**.)

6. See *Mencius* 2B/3, 2B/10,3, 3A/4,1, 6B/14,4.

7. This is presumably what Shen Tao (c. 360–275 B.C.) means by saying that "The state has the *li* of high and low rank but not a *li* of men of worth and those without talent" (quoted in Schwartz 1985: 247).

8. He is called a *p'i*/commoner in 1B/16. Legge (1970: 15) says that his surname *Meng* connects him with a family who had once usurped power in Confucius' state of Lu, but who had fallen from power in the early fifth century.

9. That obeying an *order* to come is the real issue is made clear below (5B/7,3). And see the story following this immediately below.

10. I assume "presenting a gift" here is meant to differentiate a high-ranking *ch'en* from a low-ranking one. Although this is not explicitly stated, it seems to be the most plausible way to make sense of first referring to individuals as *ch'en*, and then saying that they "have not yet become *ch'en*." Legge solves the difficulty by saying that in its first two occurrences *ch'en* means only "subject." But why would someone be called "*subject* of marketplaces"?

11. Legend has it that Tsu-ssu was the grandson of Confucius and the teacher of Mencius (see Hsiao 1979: 144–45). But Legge (1895: 19) points out that this tradition is late and finds no support in the *Mencius* itself.

12. More specifically it is *jen*/Goodness, one of the key qualities he elsewhere (e.g., 4A/9,2–4 and 1A/7,18, see p. 98) puts forth as what will make a feudal ruler deserving of the status of Emperor of all China.

13. Compare *Mencius* 2A/4,2 "honor *te* and promote *shih.*"

14. Legge says that P'ang Kang is a pupil of Mencius, but he appears only here in the *Mencius*, and from the interchange in 3B/4,4 we would rather guess that he is a high government official of some kind.

15. See the *Yao tien* section of the *Shih Ching*, verse 12 (Karlgren 1950: 4).

16. See Hsu (1965: 107–16) on the relevant economic arrangements and changes in them during the Warring States period.

17. The meaning of many statements in this passage seems to depend on distinctions between the meanings of key terms that are no longer entirely clear. I am following Legge's interpretation, in which *t'o*/dependent and *tz'u*/bestowed are quasi-technical terms, each referring to a different status to which regular material support was attached. This seems to make the best sense of the passages as a whole.

18. Excerpts from a book associated with Shen-nung are found in the *Huai Nan Tzu*, also describing an egalitarian agrarian utopia in which rulers worked alongside peasants. See Graham 1989: 64–74.

19. Elsewhere in the *Mencius, sheng jen*/"Wise Person" serves as the name of an almost unreachable ideal: Though Mencius has a very high opinion of himself, he follows Confucius' example in not allowing his disciples to call him a *sheng jen* (2A/2,19–20; see also 7B/25).

20. Legge notes that Ch'u is excluded from "The Middle Kingdom," the name for main territory of the Chinese empire.

Notes to Chapter Five

1. Graham 1989: 125.

2. It is not entirely clear that Graham seriously intends this. Elsewhere (ibid. 250), discussing the supposed disagreement

between Mencius and Hsün Tzu on this issue, he implies that observable facts are not really the basis for Mencius' ideas: "It is far from easy to locate any issue of fact on which [Mencius and Hsün Tzu] disagree. . . . if one of them prefers to see education as nourishing a spontaneous tendency to good, the other as disciplining a spontaneous tendency to disorder, on what tests would one decide between them? As is arguably the case with Western disagreements over human nature, the issue seems to come down to different proportions of trust or distrust in human spontaneity, *with practical consequences for education.*" (emphasis added) This last sentence implies an interpretation of Mencius much closer to the pragmatic one I argue here.

3. E.g., 2A,2,7 (see p. 106,) 4A/12,1, 4B/28,4,5,6, 7A/4,1.

4. As in the *Tao Te Ching* (e.g., 60[49]:1), "the hundred clans" is a general term that can be used to refer to the society as a whole that the ruler is in charge of.

5. See *Mencius* 4A/9,2, "People turn to *jen* government just like water flows downward." Compare 1A/6,6, and *Tao Te Ching* 55[66]:1.

6. See Hsu 1965: 90–91.

7. Graham (1989: 114) attributes Mencius' connection of *jen* with practical concerns to pressure from his ("utilitarian") Mohist opponents, which deflect him from his usual ("deontological") position that "you do a thing because it is . . . right, not . . . on calculation of benefit and harm." But Mencius' practical concerns like this are fully explainable by the fact that he is the teacher of aspiring administrators.

8. 2A/2. Legge (1970: 185, footnote) goes so far as to say, "It is chiefly owing to what Mencius says in this chapter . . . that a place has been accorded to him among the sages of China." The passage is discussed in Schwartz (1985: 269–78), and Graham (1989: 126–27). The idea of "nourishing the *ch'i*" does not play a big part in the rest of the *Mencius*. Mencius may well be borrowing here from language and concepts more in use by others. But this does not detract from its value in illustrating for us some of the concepts and ways of speaking current in fourth- and third-century China.

9. *Hsiu shen.* See *Mencius* 7A/1,3; 7A/9,6; 7B/32,2. This last passage brings out the implied agricultural metaphor of *hsiu* by

comparing the "cultivation" of self to "weeding fields." *Hsiu* also has a more general meaning of "repair," as in "repair the walls of my house," *Mencius* 4B/31,1.

10. As in the *Tao Te Ching*, I render *shou* literally here because I think it is a technical term used of efforts to cultivate certain qualities in oneself. See the discussion of this term p. 226.

11. The root meaning of *ch'i* seems to be "breath," but it extends to internally felt energy and feelings generally. In many uses it is similar to the colloquial use of "energy" in English (as in "She is full of energy today"). (Roth [1991a: 603 n. 11] also thinks that the English word "energy" is probably our closest equivalent to the Chinese term *ch'i*.) Some in China were beginning to use *ch'i* as a more technical term in the context of speculation about the physical makeup of the world (see Schwartz 1985: 358, 360, 382; Graham 1989: 351–54), but I think this and other passages in the *Mencius* suggest that *ch'i* has not yet become for *Mencius* a theoretical concept in a system of doctrines about the world or about human psychology. It seems rather still an unsystematized concept of folk psychology (see Schwartz 1985: 181). The use of *ch'i* in the present passage gives a good indication of the range of its meanings. For example in 2A/2,10, Mencius says "Stumbling or rushing—this is *ch'i* [one is feeling]. The *ch'i* in turn agitates the mind"; this statement makes clear the experiential reference of *ch'i* to the inner turmoil a person feels when in a rush or falling down. When the *Mencius* says that we must nourish the *ch'i* but not try to force it (2A/2,9–10, 16), this seems to reflect the fact that human feelings and instinctive reactions have a life of their own that can be directed and gradually molded, but attempts to control them directly cause more inner turmoil. Those involved in introspective self-cultivation took over the term to refer to the special internal "energy" they cultivated, and here (2A/2,11–13) Mencius uses the term in a way similar to its use in the *Nei Yeh* (see p. 188), the *Chuang Tzu* (see p. 202), and the *Tao Te Ching* (27[10]:1, 36[42]:3, 33[55]:4). In other passages (7A/36,1) Mencius uses *ch'i* to speak of something external: He feels a change in the *ch'i*, what we might call a "change of atmosphere," when a person of noble rank approaches. When Mencius speaks in 6A/8,2 of the good influence of the "morning *ch'i*" and the "evening *ch'i*," he seems also to be speaking of what we would call the "atmosphere" around us. See also the phrase "greet men with good [or bad] *ch'i*" in the *Nei Yeh* (Rickett 1965: 164 J). Here *ch'i* seems close to the

English word "air" as in "an air of indifference." Roughly, one might say that, internally, *ch'i* is similar to the English word "feelings," but it extends also to more bodily, physiological sensations. Externally, it refers to the felt character of the surrounding "atmosphere" (peaceful, tense, etc.).

12. He appeals to the last sentence of 2A/2,10, where "*ch'i* . . . agitates the *hsin*/mind" is directly parallel to "*ch'i* . . . agitates the *chih*/will" in a previous sentence.

13. Compare the criticism of "the mind controlling the *ch'i*" in the *Tao Te Ching* 33[55]:4.

14. See the similar statement about *ching*, "vital energy" in the *Nei Yeh*, quoted p. 187.

15. See especially Bauman 1987: 36–37.

16. See *ibid.*: 68–80.

17. This in contrast to early modern philosophers, who tended to "project . . . onto the huge screen of the 'good society' what they knew best and were most satisfied with: their own mode of life." This resulted in the fact that often "group peculiarity disguised itself . . . as the attributes of the human species." (Bauman 1987: 36–37.)

18. Chapters 50[53], 51[75], 52[77], 53[72], 66[74].

19. Chapters 1[24]:2, 2[9]:2, 4[22]:5, 42[2]:5, 54[17]:3, 64[34]:3, 52[77]:3; compare *Mencius* 1B/14,3, 2A/1,3,13.

20. Chapters 21[12], 22[50], 50[53], 51[75].

21. Chapters 1[24], 2[9], 19[44].

22. Chapters 3[67]:2, 50[53]:5.

23. Chapters 7[8], 8[81]:1 and 4[22]:5–6.

24. Chapters 19[44]:5, 23[26], 24[33]:3, 26[59]:3, 28[16]:5–6, 29[52]:4,6–7, 32[6]:4; and see the discussion of *Steadiness* * p. 215.

25. See the discussion of these terms p. 216, 217, 222, 225, and see also 77[57]:5, 78[19]:1, 79[3]:1.

Notes to Part Three: Introduction

1. A survey of this discipline is given in Levinson (1983).

Notes to Chapter Six

1. Welch 1957: 28. Writing in 1957, Welch is presumably referring to Hitler, Mussolini, and Stalin.

2. Fung 1948: 97.

3. Kaltenmark (1969: 36) indeed explicitly characterizes the thought of the *Tao Te Ching* in this way.

4. I use the word *aphorism* as a technical term of convenience in this work to refer to the genre of speech that has the semantic structure defined in this chapter. In this I am departing from the common use of the term to refer to any pithy saying.

5. Culler 1975: 22–26.

6. Grice 1975: 41–58; see also the helpful discussion in Levinson 1983: 101–103.

7. Levinson 1983: 102.

8. Grice 1975: 45; Grice calls the assumption involved here the "Cooperative Principle": The assumption is that people in general are being "cooperative" in a given conversation, as opposed to making irrelevant or nonsensical remarks.

9. Austin 1962: 4–11; discussion in Levinson 1983: 226–37.

10. I use "good" here in a special sense defined further p. 270–77.

11. The generalized notion of conversion employed here is further explained p. 278–79.

Notes to Chapter Seven

1. E.g., Welch 1957: 7–17; Kaltenmark 1969: 30.

2. Creel (1970b: 5) tends to interpret the "purposive" Taoism of the *Tao Te Ching* as utilitarian advice: "Cultivate [poise and inner calm] as a means to power! Be without desire in order to gain the things that you desire. It is by not venturing to put himself forward that one is able to gain the first place." A utilitarian interpretation of Laoist sayings underlies the charge made by some Chinese authors that the *Tao Te Ching* advocates "scheming methods" (see Lau 1958: 359).

3. E.g., Hansen (1981: 238) emphasizes the categorization of colors implied in "five," and takes the point to be that "conventional categorization of sensible qualities constrains and restricts the range of our ordinary sense capacity." The last three parallel lines of this saying tell against this interpretation.

4. This translation is based on the use of these same terms in the *Mencius* (3B/1) to refer to moral compromise and moral integrity, respectively, and on the parallel saying in 5[45]:2.

5. This point is probably related to the Laoist idealization of the ruler who appears to adhere to no fixed moral standards (56[61]:1, 64[34]:1, 60[49]:1, 59[58]:1), in contrast to the "moralistic" Confucian ruler whom Laoists criticize.

6. For example 4[22]:2, 17[28]:1, 56[61]:1, 59[58]:1, 60[49]:1,3, 78[19]:1, 80[65]:1,3.

7. On the possibility of more than one teacher in the school, see comments on 49[27]:4. It may be significant here that several other teachers besides Confucius appear in the *Analects*; see especially the reference to the Tsang Tzu's pupils gathered around him on his deathbed in 8/3, and the collection of sayings by a variety of men in chapter 19. The social picture one would gather from evidence in the *Analects* is that of a number of highly respected members in a close-knit group, some with pupils gathered around them, with Confucius as the most highly respected of all.

8. The fact that a few students are mentioned numerous times in the *Mencius* probably indicates that they were more committed and long term members of Mencius' school. See the references to Kung-sun Ch'au, Kung-tu, and Wan Chang in Legge's (1895) Index of Proper Names in the *Mencius*

9. E.g., 13[20], 3[67]:1, 44[41]:1, 45[70], 46[35]:2. See also the passages characterizing what Laoists cultivate as *hsiao*/small:insignificant (63[32]:1, 64[34]:4, 29[52]:5), as "lowly" (35[39]:1–2), and as "left out" (14[23]:3).

10. Further examples of ironic self-caricature are: 4[22]:2 (*compromised, empty, old and spent*); 17[28]:1 (*disgraceful*); 60[49]:3 (*keeps his mind muddled*); 3[67]:1 (*not normal*); 13[20]:4; 46[35]:2 (*flat, no taste*); 78[19]:1 (*discard Wisdom*). Many translators reduce the shock value of these passages by finding positive English words, as when Feng and English (1972) translate *ju*/disgraceful as "humility" in 17[28]:1.

11. See the discussion of Schwartz p. 176–77. See also Creel 1970b: p. 2 n. 2 and 3, and p. 45.

12. See the quotations in Lau (1958: 349), showing that this "one-sidedness" of the *Tao Te Ching* was well recognized in ancient China.

13. See p. 172 n. 32.

14. See p. 176.

15. See p. 18 n. 36.

16. See for example the views of Schwartz, discussed p. 176. See also Lau 1958: 349.

17. On the idea of the good invoked here, and the use of analogy in understanding the good that attracts those of other cultures, see p. 270–77.

18. See the discussion of these two special terms p. 210 and 212.

19. Chapters 16[5]:2, 5[45]:1, 15[11]:2.

20. Discussed in Chapters 8, 9, and 11.

21. This seems implicitly recognized in 36[42]:2 and 80[65]:5.

22. See 4[22]:5, 3[67]:2, 46[35]:1, 26[59]:2, 25[48]:3–4, 77[57]:1.

23. See p. 531 under *Agitation**.

24. See, for example, 55[66]:1,3, 63[32]:1–2, 46[35]:1, 80[65]:5, and Graham's comments (1989: 299–311) on "hierarchic anarchism" in ancient China.

25. The performance of routine administrative and managerial tasks is assumed in 2[9]:2, 57[68]:1–2, 58[73]:5–6, 75[78]:4. The fact that, unlike the *Mencius*, the *Tao Te Ching* lacks detailed advice for administrators is probably due to the genre of this work and the fact that the material is intended as spiritual advice.

26. Chapters 58[73], 59[58], 60[49], 61[54]:3, 62[29].

27. Chapters 72[64]:1–2, 73[36]:1–2, 81[37]:2.

28. Chapters 66[74], 67[31], 68[69].

29. See Needham 1962: 100–20, 291–93, 335–39, 562–70. And

see the comments on Needham in Schwartz 1985: 194–95, 369–73. I first began to see the organic as a central value in the *Tao Te Ching* through reading Needham's work. I disagree with his interpretation on many other points, though. He is surely wrong in thinking that the *Tao Te Ching* represents an attack on the feudal order itself (see p. 120). He is also wrong in thinking that Laoists had a "scientific" interest in investigating nature's laws (see p. 172). Laoists valued personal and social organic harmony because they experienced its goodness, not because they intuitively anticipated some of the results of modern quantum mechanics.

30. Quoted in Needham 1962: 338–39.

31. Mencius, however, does show strong "conservationist" concern about things like overfishing and slaughtering livestock during breeding seasons; see 1A/3,3, 1A/7,24 (quoted p. 102).

32. See especially Needham 1962: 33–99. I am in general agreement here with the criticisms of Needham by Graham (1989: 204) and Schwartz (1985: 202–203). But for a more positive comment on Needham's idea of "organicism" see p. 169 n. 29.

33. See Needham 1962: 63–68.

Notes to Chapter Eight

1. The tendency to give a metaphysical interpretation to these sayings is especially evident in Schwartz 1985: 192–205; Kaltenmark 1969: 28–46; Fung 1952: 177–83.

2. 1989: 192–205.

3. *Ibid.*: 193, 196–97, 199, 442 n. 31.

4. See the quotation in Kaltenmark 1969: 31.

5. See, for example, Kaltenmark 1969: 28–46; Fung 1952: 177–83.

6. I am drawing here on my experience studying T'ai Chi with Mr. John Li of Boston's *Hwa Yu Institute* in 1974.

7. The *Kuan Tzu* is named after a famous statesman Kuan Chung (d. 645 B.C.), but is generally thought to be a miscellany of writings from the fourth to the second centuries. Four sections in this book (in chs. 36, 37, 38, 49) have to do with introspective

meditation practices. The *Nei Yeh* is chapter 49. It is introduced and translated in Rickett 1965: 151–68, and commented on in Graham 1989: 100, and Roth 1990 and 1991a. Graham (1989: 100) thinks that the *Nei Yeh* is the oldest of these sections, stemming perhaps from the fourth century B.C. and "possibly the oldest 'mystical' text in China . . . providing clear evidence that the meditation practiced privately and recommended to rulers as an arcanum of government descends directly from the trance of the professional shaman."

8. 1990, 1991a, 1991b: 89–92.

9. Translations of the *Nei Yeh* here are my own, from the text published in Ling Ju-hêng's *Kuan-tzu chi p'ing* (1970: 247–53), with help from the translations of Rickett (1965) and Roth (1990 and 1991a). Notes on the translation are given below (p. 187–91) where the opening passage of the *Nei Yeh* is translated in full.

10. Other passages in the *Nei Yeh* using the term *hsing*/Form suggest similar meanings, as for example: When one expands the *ch'i* then "the Form will be at rest." (Rickett 1965: 167 N). "The Form of the mind's *ch'i* is more illuminating than the sun and moon." (Rickett 1965: 164 J). See also Rickett 1965: 159 A, 160 A, 161 D and E, 166 M and N.

11. See the discussion of this term, p. 107, n. 11.

12. See Frege 1980: 56–78. Frege's famous illustration of this distinction (p. 57) involves the phrases "the morning star" and "the evening star." These two phrases "mean" something different, in the sense that their meaning content is different, even though the two phrases may sometimes refer to the same object (e.g., the planet Venus).

13. Compare the hypostatization of Wisdom in the biblical books of *Proverbs* (ch. 1, 8, and 9), *Sirach* (ch. 1 and 24) and *Wisdom of Solomon* (ch. 6–9).

14. Quoted in Graham 1989: 243.

15. Rickett 1965: 166 M.

16. Rickett 1965: 160 B.

17. The wording of this passage is somewhat ambiguous. "Gave birth" in the first line is *wei sheng*, which could also mean "is their life." I understand *wei* in the last line as an ellipsis for this

same *wei sheng*. Roth (1991a: 613) translates instead "[*ching*] *wei*/becomes the . . . stars."

18. 2A/2,13, quoted p. 111.

19. Roth translates *chih* as "[cannot be] stopped," but "Tao . . . *chih*" seems clearly to mean "Tao . . . stays" in the last line of the passage quoted here.

20. "Mind" is an emendation, see Rickett 1965: 158 n. 21. The text has "by sound."

21. Or "perfecting Te."

22. Roth (1991a: 614 n. 42) accepts an emendation of this line that makes it read "things to the last one will be grasped."

23. The text has *hsing*/punish here, but this is surely a mistake (or loan character) for *hsing*/Form, as commentators agree.

24. *Fan* serves as an introductory particle in the opening saying as well. *Heng*/always has a similar use in the *Tao Te Ching*, as an introductory (43[1]:3, 64[34]:4, 80[65]:4) or concluding (42[2]:2) particle. This is important in 43[1]:3, where commentators sometimes mistakenly emphasize this word.

25. Others emend this line, so it reads "How bright! as though existing on all sides" (Rickett). But both *chê* ("bend down, humble") and *ts'ê* ("awry, perverted, mean") have normally negative connotations. As is often the case in the *Tao Te Ching*, the text probably means to picture the object of self-cultivation here as something negative when looked at from a conventional point of view.

26. "It sometimes goes and sometimes comes, but no one is able to plan this." See Rickett 1965: 161 F.

27. *Ibid.*: 162 F.

28. Rickett 1965: 158–59 A. Chinese text in Ling 1970: 247–48.

29. By "meditation" I do not mean meditation *on* something, but rather practices aimed at transforming one's state of mind or the quality of one's conscious awareness. Many Zen Buddhist practices have this kind of aim, for example, as does Vipassana meditation in the Theravada Buddhist tradition (see Naranjo

1971: 75–89). Saso (1983) describes meditation practices of a modern Taiwanese Taoist group that appear to me very similar to those suggested in the *Tao Te Ching*.

30. A version of this passage is also found in the *Chuang Tzu* 62/23/34–5. (References in this format are to the *Chuang Tzu yin te*, the *Chuang Tzu* Concordance published in the Harvard-Yenching Institute Sinological Index Series, hereafter HYC).

31. Rickett 1965: 165 L.

32. *Mencius* 6A/9,3. The chess-player needs to "concentrate [the] mind and apply [the] will," *chuan hsin chih chih*.

33. See, for example, Eliade 1969: 85–90, 177–80.

34. Another *Nei Yeh* passage says, "*Ch'i* and Tao then life, life then thought, thought then knowledge, knowledge then stop." Compare 63[32]:3 of the *Tao Te Ching*, "Begin making decisions, there are names. Once there are names, one will know to stop." See also 19[44]:4.

35. *Kuei-shen* originally referred to lower and higher spirits, respectively, of Chinese folk religion. The *Nei Yeh* uses this term of the "spirit"—a certain kind or level of consciousness—in people. See Graham 1989: 100–101.

36. Rickett 1965: 164–65 K.

37. I omit one stanza here that I think is added by the composer of this chapter to the original oral saying (see p. 311).

38. See Girardot, 1974: 82–83 and n. 22.

39. This poem is the *Yüan Yu* which Hawkes (1985: 191) dates to 150–100 B.C. and attributes to the same group of Taoists who produced the *Huai Nan Tzu*. The translation here is from Maspero (1981: 415).

40. Some commentators bring in here the Chinese belief in two souls, a *p'o*, "bodily soul," and a *hun* or *ying*, "spiritual soul." See Chen 1989: 79.

41. A version of this saying occurs in the *Doctrine of the Mean* (16/2) also, where it is initially said to refer to *kuei-shen*/spirits, but then (16/5) reinterpreted to apply to sincerity, the main focus of self-cultivation in this text. The context here makes it clear that Laoists used the saying to refer to the quality of mind they cultivated.

42. I omit two lines at the beginning of this section that I think were added by the composer (see p. 321). The exclamation marks represent the exclamatory *hsi*, present also in sections {2}, {9}, and {11} of the *Nei Yeh* passage quoted p. 188, 190.

43. *Hsiang*/form:image:model refers to a normative pattern of conduct in the *Chuang Tzu* (HYC 34/13/28), and the context in 46[35]:1 indicates that this is its meaning there as well (I translate *hsiang* as "Image" in 46[35]:1 and 44[41]:3:9). I now think I was mistaken in assimilating *hsiang* in 38[21]:2 to the *Nei Yeh's hsing*/"[the mind's true] Form" in my earlier (1992) translation. Others translate *hsiang* as "images" here, a possible reference to images one sees in a mental trance or spirit journey (see p. 195). In this case the *wu* of the following line could refer to "things" seen in a trance.

Notes to Chapter Nine

1. See p. 49 n. 5.

2. *Chuang Tzu yin te*, the Harvard-Yenching Concordance to the *Chuang Tzu*.

3. Others usually translate *men* as "gate" in these passages. *Men* seems to mean "abode" rather than "gate" in a phrase found in the *Chuang Tzu*, "take Tao as your *men*" (HYC 90/33/3). *Shih* gathered around a teacher are sometimes called *men jen*/"house men," i.e., men of the master's house; see *Mencius* 3A/4,13, 7B/29,1; *Chuang Tzu* HYC 87/31/46.

4. Note that Chinese words lack inflection, so there is no phonetic or lexicographic difference between the adjective *jou*/Soft and the abstract noun *jou*/Softness. So there is more fluidity in Chinese between cases in which *jou* describes a state or quality of mind, and cases where it designates a hypostatized energy Softness.

5. The first number here derives from the sequence of the group of passages quoted p. 202–08. Numbers following this refer to chapters and lines in the text as given in the *Chuang Tzu yin te*, the Harvard Yenching Concordance to the *Chuang Tzu*.

6. See also Roth's comparison of the ideal of *ching*/Stillness in the *Chuang Tzu* and the *Huai Nan Tzu* (Roth 1991b: 103–106).

7. HYC 85/30/12; Watson 1968: 341.

8. Munro (1969: 162) notes that this same phrase is used in the *Li Chi*, to describe a social ideal, an ancient utopia in which all belonged to the same family and the weak and poor were well cared for. Mao Tse-tung used the term to refer to Communism.

9. This represents a change from my previous translation, where I translated it "The One [important] Thing," under the influence of a comparison with *Doctrine of the Mean* 20/8–18. This still seems to me a possible, only slightly less likely, rendering. In this case it would probably be connected with the "rationalizing" unification of the Laoist worldview, see p. 66, 160.

10. MWT has *heng* where WP has *ch'ang*. Henricks (1989: xv) says that WP has probably changed the original *heng* to avoid the taboo name of the Emperor Liu Heng (179–156 B.C.).

11. See p. 189 n. 24.

12. Hansen (1981: 236) also urges this pragmatic rather than theoretical interpretation of "the invariant Tao."

13. See Eno 1990: 190–97; DeBary (1991: 49) connects the continued use of this appellation with the "institutional weakness, highly dependent condition, and extreme insecurity" of Confucian scholars in the rough political waters of the Han period.

14. Watson 1968: 82.

15. For women in later Taoism, see Cleary 1989.

16. I find no evidence for the commonly held view that the Laoist worldview was based on physical nature as opposed to human culture; see p. 172.

17. Eberhard (1942: 2:91–95, 96–100) suggests that in ancient times there were some cultures in Southern China that gave more prominence to the role of women.

18. The use of Tao in the *Mencius* is illustrated in passages quoted on p. 75, 81, 84, 86, 87, 92, 93, 94, 105, 111.

19. The adverbial *pu*/not presumably gives Tao an adjectival meaning here.

20. Waley (*ad loc.*) notes that *tai*/support usually refers to financial backing. I supply "person," because of the context in

this chapter which opens by speaking of *shih* practicing the Tao taught to them in a *shih*-school.

21. p. 106, 107.

22. p. 188, 189.

23. See *shou hsing*/"watch over the Form," and *shou i*/"watch over the Oneness" in *Chuang Tzu* 7.(11/35–43).

24. This seems the most basic meaning of the word; *shou*/guard is used of gold and jewels in 2[9]:1. Mencius also uses it in a more general sense of "take care of," as when he contrasts *shou*/"taking care of" one's parents with neglecting them.

Notes to Chapter Ten

1. See Forke 1925: 235, 251–54, 286; Graham 1989: 325–27; Schwartz 1985: 356–62.

2. Forke, 1925: 235. The examples quoted are from the *Tso Chuan*.

3. Forke 1925: 235.

4. See Major 1991: 67–74; Graham 1991b: 278–79.

5. See Schwartz 1985: 356–62.

6. We can be fairly sure this is an oral saying that assumed an audience who recognized what "It" refers to, because the saying preceding this in 61[54]:1 gives no plausible antecedent for "it." Other possible examples of "anonymous" sayings are 32[6]:4, 63[32]:2, 81[37]:2, 38[21]:2:2–9, 37[14]:1–4, 46[35]:3, 30[56]:4. Several sayings in the *Nei Yeh* also leave their object anonymous (see p. 188–90, sections 4, 6, 9, and 11). Form-critically, sayings like this can be explained on the hypothesis that these sayings were originally used in oral conversation about self-cultivation, where all participants would have shared a common familiarity with the state of mind being cultivated.

7. See *Phaedo* 100c.

8. This analysis is partly a development of the "demythologizing" approach of the New Testament scholar Rudolf Bultmann (see Schmithals 1968: 249–72) and draws also on Paul Tillich's

ideas (1951: 3–15) about "ultimate concern" as the essential subject matter of mythological religious language.

9. Watson 1968: 122 (slightly altered); HYC 28/11/53–55.

10. See 55[66]:1, 63[32]:4; *Mencius* 4A/9,2, 6A/2,2.

11. *Mu*/shepherd is the MWT reading; compare the same term used of rulers in *Mencius* 1A/6,6. WP has *shih*/Pattern, the same term translated *Pattern* in 17[28]:1.

12. Graham 1989: 161, and footnote reference to p. 124 and 154.

13. See comments on the image of internal "abodes" p. 203.

14. This is the MWT text. In WP, "unnamed" Tao created Heaven and Earth, while the "named" Tao/Mother created the thousands of things.

15. Quoted from Jan 1980: 198. I have only made one change in Jan's translation—writing "get" in the last two lines where he writes "obtain"—in order to bring out the similarity in vocabulary to other passages using *te*/get, discussed above.

Notes to Chapter Eleven

1. See p. 12–21, 139–42, 238–49. I have presented some more theoretical foundations for this theory in LaFargue 1992b.

2. Sociologists like Max Weber and anthropologists like Clifford Geertz tend toward this approach. Ninian Smart (1973: 20–23, 38–73) gives this approach a theoretical grounding in the idea of a phenomenological "bracketing" of questions about truth claims. On the present view (see p. 16–17, 25), there is nothing to bracket: Reality *consists* of *phainomena*. With this proviso, Smart's approach to the interpretation of religions and worldviews (see Smart 1983) is in many respects similar to the one I try to practice here.

3. See, for example, Hick 1989, Huston Smith 1982, Krieger 1991, Neville 1991. This view is often associated with a particular interpretation of "mystical" experience—that is, that mystics in many different traditions have direct experience of this same transcendent reality, which they speak of, however, in the language of their own cultural traditions. I am in general agreement with Katz (1978; 1983) in disputing this interpretation. W. C. Smith (1981)

holds a different version of this view, not necessarily connected with mysticism: All religions teach partial aspects of the single truth, which we can learn to grasp more fully through interreligious dialogue.

4. E.g., Hick 1989: 237; Huston Smith 1982: 74.

5. As Langdon Gilkey puts it "[The single 'essence of religion' which this approach seeks] represents—try as it may to avoid it—a particular way of being religious. . . . Thus it has to *misinterpret* every other tradition in order to incorporate them into its own scheme of understanding. In the end, therefore, it represents the same religious colonialism that Christianity used to practice so effectively: the interpretation of an alien viewpoint in terms of one's own religious center and so an incorporation of that viewpoint into our own system of understanding" (quoted in Musser 1989: 35).

6. The theory of religions proposed here is can be applied to worldviews in general, religious and non-religious. Note also that I reject the subjectivism that is often assumed in the mention of "worldviews." There is no world-as-it-is apart from worldviews (see p. 16–17).

7. Hume 1948: 43 (*Treatise on Human Understanding* III, i. 1).

8. I am using "ontology" in the formal and logical sense used, for example, by Quine, not the substantive sense (referring to some particular view of "ultimate reality") in which it is more commonly used. See p. 16 n. 32.

9. Wittgenstein 1976: 641. The lecture was first delivered in 1929.

10. The pluralist theory of the good developed here has some affinities with some of the recent work of Charles Taylor (e.g., 1989a: 3–107; 1989b).

11. I would argue that, from a pragmatist point of view, such discrimination is a better interpretation of the purpose of Socratic discussion—better than the traditional one that it aims to discover the one uniquely true set of absolute moral standards.

12. Those familiar with modern Christian theology will recognize my debt in this section to certain "existentialist" elements in the theology of Karl Barth, Rudolf Bultmann, and Paul Tillich.

These elements are partly derived from Heidegger's (1962: 210–24, 312–48) emphasis on personal "authenticity" as a condition for knowing the truth, and ultimately from Kierkegaard's emphasis on the priority of personal commitment over objective truth (see Kiekegaard 1973: 190–258, and the discussion in Evans 1983: 68–72, 73–93, 115–35). Bernard Lonergan's ideas on conversion (1979: 52, 130–31, 237–44, 267–70) are a representative example of the fundamental place this notion plays in modern Catholic existentialist theology. For more general accounts of existentialist influences on modern Protestant and Jewish thought, see Borowitz (1966), Hordern (1968: 111–229), and Brown (1953). Gadamer's idea (1982: 102) that great art "rais[es] reality into its truth" implies something like this same notion of conversion. I would say that "truth" here *means* "reality as seen by a a person converted to something good." Making conversion explicitly dependent on something good overcomes the important objections to Gadamer raised by Warnke (1987: 70–72). Plato invokes the notion of conversion, a fundamental "turning around" of the soul toward the good, in his comments on the Parable of the Cave (*Republic* Bk. VII, 518c–d). The pluralist theory of the good explained p. 270–77 divorces the present generalized theory of conversion from the *specific* worldviews of Plato, Heidegger, existentialism, and modern Christian theologians.

13. See, for example, Feuerbach 1957; Berger 1969: 3–28.

14. This theory has a neo-Kantian basis: The fact that the reality we experience has a *dimension* of good/bad is an unavoidably necessary ("transcendental") aspect of human conscious experience. (Note Kant's important distinction [1966: 222–23] between "transcendental" and "transcendent.") But, contrary to Kant, there are no transcendentally necessary *specific* moral categories or principles.

15. E.g., Kant 1966: 222–23.

16. This was partly a response to relativism, a threat brought aboŭt by the serious attempt to understand other cultures on their own terms. See Gardiner 1981.

17. This very influential notion was first proposed by Karl Jaspers in the first chapter of his *Origin and Goal of History*. It has subsequently been developed by Arnold Toynbee (see Gargan: 1961; Toynbee 1934–61: Vol 6:321–26, Vol. 7:423–49, Vol. 10:491–95; and

1976: ch. 25); Eric Voegelin (1956–: Vol. 1:1–11, Vol. 2:1–23, Vol. 3:1–11 and 300–35; 1974: 116–24); Lewis Mumford 1956: 57–81; Robert Bellah 1970: 20–50; John Cobb Jr. 1979: 52–124. The entire issue of *Daedalus* Spring 1975 was devoted to this subject and includes an article by Benjamin Schwartz on ancient China.

18. Derrida 1972: 248–49. Derrida is criticizing here the earlier structuralism of Levi-Strauss; see Lentricchia 1980: 163–77.

19. Hall and Ames (1987: 13) describe this assymetry as the crucial element in the traditional Western notion of "transcendence," which they think is characteristic of Western as opposed to Confucian thinking.

20. Durkheim's strictly descriptive idea of "morality," and his sociological analysis of the social and psychological roots of morality (Durkheim 1972: 87–122), can serve as a rough definition of what I am calling here "conventional morality." What is truly "good for its own sake" (p. 273–74) is usually only one factor determining conventional morality. Note also that "good for its own sake" is merely contrasted with "instrumentally good"; it does not mean "good in all cultural contexts." On this distinction, see p. 21.

21. This is the way I would interpret Voegelin's description (1956–: 1:1–11) of axial age movements as movements from "compact" to "differentiated" awareness of norms. "Differentiated" means that what is truly good in itself tends to be differentiated from "conventional morality" and from status symbols and other ordinary signs of social success.

22. Plato's transcendent "Perfect Forms" of the virtues are a good example here: They are the result of isolating what is truly good in itself in ordinary virtue notions, and conceiving of this good in its most pure and ideal form. Plato's thought also brings out the essential *continuity* between ordinary (relatively mediocre) good and transcendent Good. I would argue that much of Plato makes better sense on the assumption that what is essential to the Forms is that they are "more good," rather than that they are more objective or more absolute (in a transcultural sense).

23. An argument could be made that this is the main purpose of the *Bhagavad Gita* in its original setting. The author knows of others whose developed meditation practice and Sankhya philosophy has led them to break completely from traditional religion

(7/15, 9/11–12) and from participation in social life organized around caste (5/1–5). He integrates meditation and Sankhya with these latter by identifying the popular god Krishna with the cosmic Atman/Brahman contacted through meditation, and by formulating the ideal of performing caste duties with complete detachment.

24. Chang (1990: 17–31) gives an excellent description of this moderate transcendence in early Confucianism. DeBary (1991) describes the way that this critically transcendent ("prophetic") aspect of Confucianism surfaced at various times in Chinese history. Metzger (1977) takes this theme as the main focus of his study of the Neoconfucianism of Chu Hsi (1130–1200) and Wang Yang-Ming (1472–1529).

25. This point is put in generalized form as part of a general theory of perception in Polanyi 1975: 38–39.

26. A similar theme is the main topic of Daniel Bell's *The Cultural Contradictions of Capitalism*.

27. Bellah (1985: 82, 334–36) calls this "expressive individualism."

28. The absence of *positive* proposals for an alternative ethos is one of the main topics of Bernstein's (1991) survey of leading modern thinkers.

29. Bauman details this tendency especially among early modern philosophers, who tended to "project . . . onto the huge screen of the 'good society' what they knew best and were most satisfied with: their own mode of life. . . . Group peculiarity disguised itself . . . as the attributes of the human species" (1987: 36–37). "A 'good society,' all specific differences notwithstanding, invariably possessed one feature: it was a society well geared to . . . the flourishing of the intellectual mode of life" (147). These remarks seem to apply very well, for example, to Jürgen Habermas' recent attempt to ground normative social theory in a model of an "ideal speech situation"—that is, a conversation uninfluenced by any other than purely rational conversation (see McCarthy 1981: 286–91, 305–17).

Notes to Chapter Twelve

1. Waley (1958: 121–28) points to the main kinds of evidence used in this dating when he says that "in grammar [the *Tao Te Ching*] is typical of 3rd century B.C. philosophers. In vocabulary

there are elements . . . that point to the latter part of the 3rd century. . . . it is a controversial work, and the opponents with which it deals did not exist until the 3rd century." Duyvendak (1954: 6–7) says similarly, "The ideas of the *Tao Te Ching* belong entirely to the intellectual sphere, which we find dominant in China about 300 B.C. . . . It is impossible for me to place the *Tao Te Ching*, as a coherent book . . . earlier than about 300 B.C." Graham (1989: 216) thinks that it appeared in its present form "about 250 B.C." and Victor Mair (1990a: 126) expresses a similar opinion. D. C. Lau (1982: 140) places the text a little earlier ("Some form of the Lao Tzu existed by the beginning of the third century B.C. at the latest" because "in [it] are to be found many ideas which were associated with a number of thinkers of the second half of the fourth and the first quarter of the third century B.C."). Schwartz (1985: 187) dates it to the middle to late 4th century ("after Confucius and Mo-tzu and probably before the historic Chuang-tzu and the various 'Taoists' of the Chi-hsia academy"), citing in his support (440 n. 2) Fung Yu Lan, Takeuchi Yoshio, and Lo Ken-tse. (He may be relying here, however, on the questionable traditional idea that Lao Tzu was the "founder" of Taoism, and that the *Chuang Tzu* represents a later development.) Maspero (1981: 431) dates it to "the beginning of the fourth century." Arguments in the present chapter support the view that the *Tao Te Ching* took shape over a period of time. On this reading, those who welded together the oral sayings into the eighty-one sayings-collages of the *Tao Te Ching* expressed no views substantially different from the sayings they drew on. Given the usual development of thought, this seems unlikely if they lived more than two generations after those who coined the sayings. This suggests two stages in its composition, one stage in which the individual sayings were coined and circulated in the Laoist school, and a later stage no more than a generation or two (40–80 years?) later, when these sayings came to be reflected on as a store of group wisdom, giving rise to the composition of the sayings-collages that are our present "chapters". I argue here also (p. 310) that these chapter-collages were originally coined for use within the school, and this probably implies that it took a few years at least before the book became known outside the school. Han Fei Tzu commented on many of these chapters, and he died in 233 B.C. (See Hsiao index, s.v. Han Fei.) If we take this as a *terminus ad quem*, this suggests that the sayings were coined around 300 B.C. at the latest, and the chapter-collages were composed around 250 B.C. at the latest. However, there seems no guarantee that these sections of the *Han Fei Tzu* were written by Han Fei Tzu himself, and this could move the *terminus ad quem* down to around 210 B.C., the latest date when the Ma Wang Tui manuscript A could have been written down (see Henricks 1989: xv).

2. Some early commentators commented on a text divided differently, into a different number of chapters (see Chan 1963: 75–76). The recently discovered Ma-wang-tui manuscripts contain no unambiguous indications of chapter divisions. Dots which may indicate divisions in the material only sometimes occur in places appropriate to the traditional eighty-one chapter arrangement. According to Henricks (1979: 49–51), dots occur at the beginnings of chapters (in the traditional numbering) 46, 51, 53, 57, 63, 64, 69, 73, 75, 76, and 80. Dots are clearly missing at the beginnings of chapters 47, 61, 65, 67, 68, 70, and 71, and occur in the middle of chapters 46, 51, 52, 72, and 81. The state of the MWT manuscripts makes it impossible to tell whether or not dots occurred at the beginnings of chapters 40–42, 48, 54–56, 58–60, 62, 66, 74, 78, and 81. It is relevant that some chapters in the MWT texts are "out of order" relative to the traditional Wang Pi text (24 comes between 21 and 22; 40 comes between 41 and 42; 80 and 81 come between 66 and 67), and that these chapters begin and end precisely at one of our chapter divisions. The MWT texts thus tend to confirm the divisions between some of the chapters involved. We have similar evidence from chapters 20 and 21 of the *Han Fei Tzu* that comment on various chapters of the *Tao Te Ching*, which deal with them in an order different from that of Wang Pi. The order in *Han Fei Tzu's* chapter 20 goes 38, 58, 59, 60, 46, 14, 1, 50, 67, 53, 54; in his chapter 21 it goes 46, 26, 36, 63, 64, 52, 71, 64, 67, 41, 33, 27. Finally, chapter 6 is quoted verbatim in the *Lieh Tzu* (see n. 21). Taken together, this evidence tends to confirm the boundaries 1/2, 5/6, 6/7, 13/14, 14/15, 21/22,* 23/24,* 24/25,* 25/26, 26/27, 27/28, 32/33, 33/34, 35/36, 36/37, 37/38,* 38/39, 39/40,* 40/41, 41/42, 45/46, 46/47, 49/50, 50/51, 51/52, 52/53, 54/55, 60/61, 62/63, 63/64, 64/65, 66/67,* 67/68, 70/71, 79/80* (asterisks indicate evidence from MWT). This provides textual evidence for almost half of the chapter boundaries, and it is noteworthy that none of this evidence goes against the traditional boundaries. Likewise, the traditional division into two books (chs. 1–37 and 38–81; see Chan 1963: 36) is supported by the fact that the MWT texts begin with chapters 38–81, then follow with chapters 1–37.

3. For example, chapters 10[7], 15[11], 17[28], 23[26], 47[43], 55[66], 74[76], 76[80], 79[3], 81[37].

4. For example, chapters 5[45], 14[23], 16[5], 30[56], 35[39], 36[42], 42[2], 52[77], 59[58], 60[49], 61[54], 62[29], 75[78].

5. The few attempts to find an order in the text seem to me somewhat arbitrary. It may be worth noting, however, that my attempt to rearrange the chapters in a more topical order has unintentionally produced some rough correspondences with the original arrangement of the book. My arrangement proceeds in general from the personal (Sections 1–3) to the political (Sections 4–7). All but three (54[17], 78[19], 79[3]) of the first twenty-eight chapters of the traditional "first book" of the *Tao Te Ching* (chs. 1–37) fall into my "personal" sections; the same is true of all but four (60[49], 65[51], 50[53], 61[54]) of the first nineteen chapters in the "second book" (chs. 38–81). The last nine chapters of the first book all fall in my "political" sections except for two (24[33], 46[35]); the same is true of all but four (26[59], 3[67], 9[79], 8[81]) of the last twenty-five chapters of the second book.

6. Discussed in Chan 1963: 35–59.

7. Quoted in *ibid.*: 36.

8. Hsiao's (1979) dating (see index, s.v. Ssu-ma T'an). The biography is attributed to Ssu-ma T'an, although it is contained in ch. 130 of the *Shih Chi*, written by his son, Ssu-ma Ch'ien (*ibid.*: 650).

9. The relevant excerpt from Ssu-ma Ch'ien is quoted in full in Chan 1963: 36–37.

10. Waley 1958: 108. Graham (1990a: 111–24) has attempted a reconstruction of the historical circumstances in which the *Tao Te Ching* first came to be attributed to Lao Tzu. One should consider also the possibility that the Laoist school attributed its wisdom to a legendary "Old Master" (the literal meaning of *lao tzu*) in the same way that Hsü Hsing attributed his wisdom to the legendary Shen-nung (see p. 91).

11. See, for example, Carus (1900), replying to an attack on the *Tao Te Ching*'s authenticity (and worth) by Herbert Giles in the *China Review* (1886: 231–80). Lionel Giles, writing a preface to his father's translation in 1904, expresses the underlying modern assumption about the centrality of authorship and authenticity

when he raises the question as to whether the *Tao Te Ching* is the actual work of Lao Tzu, or "a garbled and *unauthorized* compilation of his sayings" (Giles 1905: 10, emphasis added).

12. See the discussion of authorship in ancient China in Waley 1958: 101–106, and Lau 1982: 122–26.

13. Reports of a teacher writing a book—such as Mencius' report (3B/9,11) that Confucius wrote the *Spring and Autumn Annals*—come from a later generation and are often, as in this case, very doubtful.

14. See the list given in Legge 1893: 17.

15. E.g., the *Shu Ching*, the *I Ching*, the *Great Learning*, the *Doctrine of the Mean*.

16. E.g., the *Kuan Tzu*, and the book attributed to *Shen Neng* (see Graham 1989: 66).

17. See, for example, Watson's comments on the cases of the *Hsün Tzu*, the *Mo Tzu*, and the *Han Fei Tzu* (Watson 1962: 133, 154, 175; 1963a: 12; 1964: 13–14). It seems significant that modern scholars defending the "original authorship" of given passages in an ancient work very often rely on negative arguments ("There is no reason why this passage cannot have been written by . . . "). This implies a presumption in favor of traditional attribution, unless we have positive reason to doubt it. But since the traditional attributions of classic works are usually of late (Han dynasty) date, this presumption does not seem to rest on any very solid basis.

18. This is made fairly clear in the case of the *Analects* and the *Mencius* by the fact that these books present themselves as *reports* of the sayings and doings of these men ("Confucius [or Mencius] said/did . . . "), rather than straightforwardly as the teaching of the author.

19. Arthur Waley (1958: 104–5) may well be right when, in commenting on this question, he speaks of a "ritual of self-effacement" which pre-Han custom imposed on such writers. Waley describes the later Chinese preoccupation with authorship as the result of a failure to understand pre-Han customs:

It occurred . . . to the Chinese [after the Han] that some of these [ancient] books were not in point of fact by the ancient worthies [to whom they had been ascribed]. But already the conventions of primitive authorship, and the ritual of self-effacement that [pre-Han] custom imposed upon it, were completely forgotten, and to the medieval Chinese there appeared to be only two alternatives: either the book really was by the worthy, or else it was by a forger, and therefore must not be read. For forgery is wicked, and nothing useful can be learnt from the books of wicked men. . . . [This is why they clung so firmly to the traditional attributions of authorship. But] in 'fathering' their works upon the Ancients or in issuing them anonymously in such a form that the public would accept them as inspired by the Ancients, . . . [pre-Han] Chinese writers were in point of fact doing nothing disreputable, but merely conforming to the accepted ritual of authorship.

20. Henricks 1989: xvi n. 7.

21. See Graham 1990b: 18.

22. See, for example, Karlgren (1932: 25 n. 1), Waley (1958: 97), Lau (1963: 163–74), Kaltenmark (1969: 13–15), Creel (1970b: 6), Mair (1990a: 119–26, 1990b: 14–18). The only serious exception I am aware of in recent times in R. G. Wagner (1980: 37), who has tried to show the existence of an elaborate pattern in the book ("interlocking parallelism") that could only have come about through the careful work of a single author in complete control of the material (ibid.: 37). For a brief criticism of Wagner's approach, see note 35 below.

23. Groups substantively related to each other are listed in the Topical Glossary under the following topics: (1) Agitation* and Desire*; (2) Appearances*, Self promotion*, Confucianism*, Contending*; (3) Impressive*, Strict*, Hurt*, Low*, Working*, Improvements*, Forcing*; (4) Naming*, Understanding*, Teaching*.

24. See those listed under Self-promotion* p. 548.

25. 1[24]:4 = 67[31]:2; 4[22]:6 = 55[66]:4; 11[38]:8 = 21[12]:3 = 53[72]:4; 14[23]:4 = 54[17]:2; 19[44]:4 = 63[32]:3:4; 28[16]:6 = 29[52]:3; 30[56]:2 = 29[52]:4:1–2; 30[56]:3 = 31[4]:3; 30[56]:5 = 48[62]:7; 33[55]:5 = 69[30]:5; 58[73]:4:2 = 71[63]:7; 64[34]:5 = 71[63]:5; 62[29]:2 = 72[64]:4.

26. 1[24]:2 and 4[22]:5; 25[48]:2, 79[3]:4 and 81[37]:1;

25[48]:3 and 77[57]:1:3; 27[10]:2, 42[2]:5, 52[77]:3 and 65[51]:4; 35[39]:2:3–4 and 36[42]:4; 73[36]:2, 74[76]:2 and 75[78]:2 (see also 75[78]:1 and 47[43]:1); 75[78]:3 and 45[70]:1; 38[21]:4, 61[54]:4 and 77[57]:2.

27. This is one of Lau's arguments (1982: 136–39) for oral tradition in the *Tao Te Ching*.

28. For example, 4[22]:2, 17[28]:1, 56[61]:1, 59[58]:1, 60[49]:1,3, 78[19]:1, 80[65]:1,3.

29. This is the case with the meditation instructions in 27[10]:1, and with the genre of sayings describing attempts to grasp an elusive internal presence: 30[56]:4, 37[14]:3–4, 38[21]:2, 46[35]:3. See also 28[16]:2, 6.

30. For example, 4[22]:4, 15[11]:1–2, 16[5]:2, 17[28]:1, 26[59]:3, 31[4]:1, 32[6]:2, 33[55]:5, 34[40]:1, 35[39]:1, 36[42]:1, 39[25]:3, 46[35]:1, 47[43]:1.

31. "Many chapters fall into sections having, at times, little or no connection with one another. . . . If we do not bear this in mind and insist on treating the chapters as organic wholes we run the risk of distorting the meaning" (Lau 1982: 134–35).

32. Ma 1956.

33. Kimura 1959. I am relying on Kimura's English summary of his conclusions in this work, and for the fuller treatment of Kimura's views by Leon Hurvitz (1961) which includes a full English translation of Kimura's rendition of the *Tao Te Ching*. Note that one aspect of Kimura's thesis—that some parts of the *Tao Te Ching* date from Han times and later (Hurvitz 1961: 311)— has now been disproven by the discovery of the Ma-wang-tui manuscripts of the *Tao Te Ching*, which date from the first years of the Han.

34. "Proverbs of the people and of the patricians, maxims of the strategist and realist [and] individualist . . . ; above all sayings of the older Taoists which . . . were at that period accepted as spiritual truths. . . .—all these conflicting elements the author of the *Tao Te Ching* reproduces or adapts, subtly weaving them together into a pattern perfectly harmonious and consistent, yet capable of embracing or absorbing the most refractory elements." In this process, Waley says, the sayings the author used were reinterpreted, "using a method which is essentially that of poetry." Partly by

adaptations and alteration, partly by the simple juxtaposition of accepted sayings ("with no apparent intervention on the author's part"), the author suggests to the reader's mind meanings that go well beyond those of the original sayings themselves. In this way, Waley says, old sayings were used to create completely new meanings (Waley 1958: 96–98). Holmes Welch explicitly refers to Waley's view with approval (1957: 179–80). H. G. Creel (1970b: 6) expresses a very similar view, without reference to Waley. Max Kaltenmark (1969: 13–15) and Wing-tsit Chan (1963: 72–74) also emphasize the coherence of the work, though they attribute this primarily to the single person from whom they think the sayings came. (Both picture the book of sayings itself taking shape gradually over time.)

35. This is the main weakness of R. G. Wagner's argument that the *Tao Te Ching* was composed by an author using a particular stylistic pattern, "interlocking parallelism." Wagner does begin (1980: 21–26) by discussing three passages where this pattern is plausibly present. But even in these three cases he does not present any arguments that an author composed the passage with this pattern consciously in mind. The arrangement of the text could plausibly have come about in a number of other different ways (e.g., by similar sayings juxtaposed in 72[64]:4–5 and 45[70]:1–2; by a composer commenting on a saying in 49[27]:4–5). The remainder of Wagner's seven examples (*ibid.* 27–42) seem forced; he does not appeal to any evident signs in the text that the pattern is present, but simply shows the meaning that would result if one imposed this pattern on it. Wagner completely ignores the indications presented above that the *Tao Te Ching* is composed of originally independent sayings.

36. This is an approach that I worked out in trying to find a method for dealing with a puzzling early gnostic text, the *Acts of Thomas*. See LaFargue 1985: 1–10, 15–21, drawing on the work of Jonathan Culler (1975) and the discussion p. 36–38.

37. Many points made in the discussion of "Sayings used as take-off points for comments" (p. 328–330) imply that the composers of the chapters involved were using oral sayings to reflect and comment on. This is some evidence of the existence of this practice among Laoists.

38. Karlgren 1932 is a systematic study of the rhymes in the *Tao Te Ching*, reconstructed according to ancient phonetic values.

39. It is interesting that the manuscript tradition varies in a few places that possibly involve connective alterations. MWT has "water . . . is still," rather than "water . . . does not contend," in 7[8]:1. "Not contend" links 7[8]:1 to 7[8]:3. WP also has "contend" in 58[73]:5 where MWT does not. On the other hand, sometimes MWT has readings which may represent connective alterations: MWT has "much Learning" in 16[5]:3, where WP has "much talking." "Much [Confucian] Learning" is possibly a connection between 16[5]:3 and the Confucian Goodness mentioned in 16[5]:1. In 75[78]:2 MWT has "water" for WP's "Softness." "Water" links 75[78]:2 to 75[78]:1. In 81[37]:1 MWT has "no name" for WP's "no working," a connection to "nameless" in 81[37]:2. Some of these variations may be due to a copyist's carelessness. But they may also indicate that there was a stage at which the sayings-collages were memorized and passed on orally. In this stage it would have been easy for variations to arise, some people adding connective alterations and others eliminating them, reverting to the original wording of the oral sayings.

40. *Hsiang*/image:model probably refers to the fact that Tao, as an internal spirit, takes the place of other normative "models" one might take as a guide to conduct. See p. 198 n. 43.

41. In Karlgren's reconstruction, each of the seven lines 6[15]:2:3–9 contains an internal rhyme (the first word of each line rhymes with the last), except for the sixth. In addition, the first two lines have the same rhyme (abab), and the second two have the same rhyme, but different from the first two lines (cdcd). Following this we have three lines (not the expected two) with a third internal rhyme, but the second line lacks this internal rhyme. The total scheme is thus abab cdcd edfded.

42. Translating *ch'an* with Karlgren and Lau.

43. See p. 197 n. 41.

44. Chapters 3[67], 4[22], 6[15], 8[81], 10[7], 11[38], 13[20], 15[11], 19[44], 22[50], 23[26], 26[59], 29[52], 31[4], 36[42], 41[47], 46[35], 47[43], 48[62], 49[27], 50[53], 52[77], 57[68], 59[58], 60[49], 66[74], 67[31], 68[69], 72[64], 79[3].

45. *Great Learning* 6 (commentary). My translation and arrangement, after Legge. Several other chapters of this book show examples of framing.

46. It seems closer to the saying in 14[23]:2 about other short-lived natural phenomena, reflecting the Laoist idea that exciting activities are shortlived.

47. For example, the connection between 16[5]:1 and 2; between 14[23]:1–2 and 3; between 42[2]:1–4 and 5; between 48[62]:3 and the rest of 48[62]; between 52[77]:1 and 52[77]:2–3; between 43[1]:1–2 and 3–5; between 36[42]:1, 2, 3, 4–5, and 6.

Part Four: Notes to the Introduction to the Translation

1. The translation and commentary are identical with the translation and commentary in LaFargue 1992a, with the exception that (1) i/one is here translated "Oneness" rather than "The One Thing" in chapters 4[22], 27[10], and 35[39], (see p. 213, n. 9), and (2) hsiang/image:pattern is translated "Pattern" rather than "[the mind's true] Form" in 38[21] (see p. 198 n. 43). The Topical Glossary is abbreviated, and refers to sections in Parts Two and Three for fuller discussions.

2. Henricks' work appeared during the last stages of preparation for this book. His detailed discussions of the differences between these manuscripts and the traditional text made possible for the first time a close comparison and evaluation of these differences, for persons like myself who are not specialists in pre-standardized Chinese writing and lexicography. More work evaluating these differences certainly needs to be done. My own impression so far is that the earliness of Ma-wang-tui texts (c. 200 B.C.), is counterbalanced by the fact that they contain many more surely corrupt passages than the traditional Wang Pi text contains. See the introduction to textual notes.

3. The reader wishing to consult a very literal translation can consult the recent translation of Yi Wu (1989), or the older work of Paul Carus (1913), each of which gives the Chinese text and places English equivalents next to the Chinese characters.

4. Compare, for example, my comments on 50[53]:2 with those of Duyvendak.

Notes to the Topical Glossary

1. Graham (1989: 173) thinks that the various strata in this book date from between 320 and 202 B.C. For the dating of the Tao Te Ching, see p. 301 n. 1.

2. Graham (1989: 170–71) points out that the term "Taoist" (*tao chia*/"Tao school") first came into use during the Han period (after 206 B.C.)

3. See especially Fingarette and Eno on this.

4. Further discussion of these terms, see the references to them in the index of Graham (1989).

5. See Maspero 1981: 413–21 and 446–553; and Kohn *passim.*

6. 1989: 53–59; also Schwartz 1985: 175.

7. See Graham 1989: 137–70.

8. *Ibid.*: 75–95.

9. *Ibid.*: 267–92.

10. *Ibid.*:23–25, 261–67, 283–85; Hansen 1983a: 72–82.

11. I translated *i* as "The One Thing" in my earlier *Tao of the Tao Te Ching*, on this basis, drawing on a comparison with *Doctrine of the Mean* (20/8–18). I still think this is a possibility in some passages, but a more careful look at the *Chuang Tzu* parallels has convinced me that mental Oneness is probably the primary meaning.

12. Hexagram 22, line 4, "Great Symbol" commentary. Similar formulas are found in the Main Text, Hexagram 23, line 5, and Hexagram 39, line 2.

13. MWT has *heng* where WP has *ch'ang.* Henricks (1989: xv) says that WP has probably changed the original *heng* to avoid the taboo name of the Emperor Liu Heng (179–156 B.C.)

14. Watson 1963b: 57.

15. Quoted in Morgan 1969: 132–33. My translation.

16. 1958: 47; parenthetical remarks are Waley's. The quote is from a writing similar to the *Nei Yeh*, found in chapter 36 of the *Kuan Tzu.*

17. See Graham 1989: 53–64.

18. *Ibid.*: 330–40.

References

Abelson, Raziel (with Kai Nielsen). 1967. History of ethics. In *The encyclopedia of philosophy*. 4:81–117. New York: Macmillan.

Adams, E. M. 1967. *Ethical naturalism and the modern world-view.* Chapel Hill: University of North Carolina Press.

Allison, Henry E. 1983. *Kant's transcendental idealism: An interpretation and defense.* New Haven: Yale University Press.

Ames, Roger T., and David L. Hall. 1987. *Thinking through Confucius.* Albany: State University of New York Press.

Austin, J. L. 1962. *How to do things with words.* Oxford: Clarendon Press.

Balazs, Etienne. 1964. *Chinese civilization and bureaucracy: Variations on a theme.* Ed. and trans. H. M. Wright. New Haven: Yale University Press.

Bauman, Zigmunt. 1987. *Legislators and interpreters: On modernity, post-modernity, and intellectuals.* Ithaca, N.Y.: Cornell University Press.

Baynes, Kenneth, James Bohman, and Thomas McCarthy, eds. 1987. *After philosophy.* Cambridge: MIT Press.

Bell, Daniel. 1978. *The cultural contradictions of capitalism.* New York: Basic Books.

Bellah, Robert. 1970. Religious evolution. In *Beyond belief: Essays on religion in a post-traditional world.* Ed. Robert Bellah, 20–50. New York: Harper and Row.

———. 1985. *Habits of the heart: Indivdualism and commitment in American life.* Berkeley: University of California Press.

Berger, Peter. 1969. *The sacred canopy: Elements of a sociological theory of religion*. Garden City, N.Y.: Doubleday.

Berlin, Isaiah. 1976. *Vico and Herder: Two studies in the history of ideas*. New York: Viking.

Bernstein, Richard J. 1983. *Beyond objectivism and relativism: Science, hermeneutics, and praxis*. Philadelphia: University of Pennsylvania Press.

———. 1991. *The new constellation: The ethical-political horizons of modernity/postmodernity*. Cambridge: MIT Press.

Bodde, Derk. 1981. *Essays on Chinese civilization*. Ed. and intro. Charles LeBlank and Dorothy Borei. Princeton: Princeton University Press.

Borowitz, Eugene B. 1966. *A layman's guide to religious existentialism*. New York: Dell Publishing Company.

Brown, James. 1953. *Subject and object in modern theology*. New York: Macmillan.

Bultmann, Rudolf. 1963. *History of the synoptic tradition*. New York: Harper and Row.

Bultmann, Rudolf, and Karl Kundsin. 1934. *Form criticism: Two essays on New Testament research*. Trans. Frederick C. Grant. New York: Harper and Row.

Burtt, E. A. 1952. *The metaphysical foundations of modern science*. 2d ed. Atlantic Highlands, N.J.: Humanities Press.

Burtt, E. A., ed. 1939. *The English philosophers from Bacon to Mill*. New York: Random House.

Caplan, Arthur, ed. 1978. *The sociobiology debate*. New York: Harper and Row.

Cardenal, Ernesto. 1975–77. *El Evangelio en Solentiname*. Salamanca: Ediciones Sigueme.

Carus, Paul. 1900–1901. The authenticity of the Tao Teh King. *Monist* 11:574–601.

———. 1913. *The canon of reason and virtue—being Lao-tze's Tao teh king. Chinese and English*. Chicago: Open Court.

Ch'en, Ku-ying. 1981. *Lao Tzu: Text, notes, and comments*. Trans.

Rhett Y. W. Young and Roger T. Ames. Republic of China: Chinese Materials Center.

Ch'u, Ta-kao. 1973. *The Tao Te Ching*. New York: Samuel Weiser.

Chan, Wing-tsit. 1963. *The way of Lao Tzu (Tao te ching)*. Chicago: University of Chicago Press.

Chang, Hao. 1990. Some reflections on the problems of axial-age breakthrough in relation to classical Confucianism. In *Ideas across cultures: Essays on Chinese thought in honor of Benjamin I. Schwartz*. Ed. Paul A. Cohen and Merle Goldman, 17–31. Council on East Asian studies, Harvard University. Cambridge: Harvard University Press.

Chen, Ellen M., trans. 1988. *The Tao Te Ching: A new translation with commentary*. New York: Paragon.

Chuang Tzu Yin Te [A Concordance to the Chuang Tzu] 1956. Harvard-Yenching sinological index series supplement no. 20. Cambridge: Harvard University Press.

Cleary, Thomas, ed. and trans. 1989. *Immortal sisters: Secrets of Taoist women*. Boston: Shambala.

Cobb, John Jr. 1979. *The structure of Christian existence*. New York: Seabury.

Collingwood, R. G. 1956. *The idea of history*. New York: Oxford University Press.

Creel, Herrlee G. 1929. *Sinism: A study of the evolution of the Chinese worldview*. Chicago: Open Court.

———. 1970a. *The origins of statecraft in ancient China*. Vol. 1. Chicago: University of Chicago Press.

———. 1970b. *What is Taoism?* Chicago: University of Chicago Press.

Culler, Jonathan. 1975. *Structuralist poetics: Structuralism, linguistics, and the study of literature*. Ithaca, N.Y.: Cornell University Press.

———. 1986. *Ferdinand de Saussure*. 2nd ed. Ithaca, N.Y.: Cornell University Press.

Dallmayr, Fred and Thomas A. McCarthy, eds. 1977. *Understanding and Social Inquiry*. Notre Dame, Ind.: University of Notre Dame Press.

De Bary, Theodore. 1991. *The trouble with Confucianism*. Cambridge: Harvard University Press.

Derrida, Jacques. 1972. Structure, sign, and play in the human sciences. In *The structuralist controversy: The languages of criticism and the sciences of man*. Ed. J. L. Macksey and Eugene Donato. Baltimore: Johns Hopkins University Press.

———. 1974. *Of grammatology*. Baltimore: Johns Hopkins University Press.

———. 1977. Signature event context. *Glyph* 1:172–97.

Dewey, John. 1929. *Experience and nature*. The Paul Carus Lectures 1925. LaSalle, Ill.: Open Court.

———. 1957. *Reconstruction in philosophy*. Boston: Beacon Press.

Dobson, W. A. C. H., trans. 1963. *Mencius*. Toronto: University of Toronto Press.

Durkheim, Emile. 1972. *Emile Durkheim: Selected writings*. Ed. and introd. Anthony Giddens. Cambridge: Cambridge University Press.

Duyvendak, J. J. L. 1954. *The book of the way and its virtue*. London: J. Murray.

Eberhard, Wolfram. 1942. *Lokalkulturen im alten China*. Peking: Catholic University Press.

———. 1977. *A history of China*. 4th ed. Berkeley: University of California Press.

Eco, Umberto. 1979. *A theory of semiotics*. Bloomington, Ind.: Indiana University Press.

Eliade, Mircea. 1969. *Yoga: Immortality and freedom*. Trans. Willard Trask. 2d ed. Bollingen series 56. Princeton: Princeton University Press.

Elorduy, Carmelo, S.I. 1961. *La Gnosis Taoista del Tao Te Ching: Análisis y traducción*. Oña (Burgos) Spain: Facultad de Theologia S.I.

Eno, Robert. 1990. *The Confucian creation of heaven: Philosophy and the defense of ritual mastery*. Albany, N.Y.: State University of New York Press.

Erkes, Eduard. 1935. Arthur Waley's Laotse-Übersetzung. *Artibus Asiae* 5:288–307.

————, trans. 1950. *Ho-Shang-Kung's commentary on Lao-Tse.* Ascona, Switzerland: Artibus Asiae Publishers.

Ermarth, Michael. 1981. *Wilhelm Dilthey: The critique of historical reason.* Chicago: University of Chicago Press.

Evans, C. Stephen. 1983. *Kierkegaard's Fragments and Postscript: The religious philosophy of Johannes Climacus.* Atlantic Highlands, N.J.: Humanities Press International.

Feng, Gia-fu, and Jane English, trans. 1972. *Tao Te Ching.* New York: Random House.

Feuerbach, Ludwig. 1957. *The essence of Christianity.* Trans. M. Evans. New York.

Fingarette, Herbert. 1972. *Confucius: The secular as sacred.* New York: Harper and Row.

Forke, Alfred. 1925. *The cosmo-conception of the Chinese.* New York: Arno Press.

Frege, Gottlob. 1980. *Translations from the philosophical writings of Gottlob Frege.* Ed. Peter Geach and Max Black. 3d ed. Oxford: Basil Blackwell.

Freund, Elizabeth. 1987. *The return of the reader: Reader-response criticism.* New York: Methuen.

Fung, Yu-lan. 1948. *A short history of Chinese philosophy.* New York: Free Press.

————. 1952–53. *A history of Chinese philosophy.* 2d ed. Princeton: Princeton University Press.

Gadamer, Hans-Georg. 1982. *Truth and method.* New York: Crossroad.

Gardiner, Patrick. 1981. German philosophy and the rise of relativism. *Monist* 64:138–54.

Gardner, Howard. 1974. *The quest for mind: Piaget, Levi-Strauss, and the structuralist movement.* New York: Vintage.

Gargan, Edward T. 1961. *The intent of Toynbee's history: A cooperative proposal.* Chicago: Loyola University Press.

Geertz, Clifford. 1973. *The interpretation of cultures.* New York: Basic Books.

Giles, Herbert. 1905. *The sayings of Lao Tzu.* Introd. by Lionel Giles. London: John Murray.

Girardot, N. J. 1974. *Myth and meaning in early Taoism.* Berkeley: University of California Press.

Graham, A. C. 1985. *Reason and spontaneity.* London: Curzon Press.

———. 1989. *Disputers of the Tao: Philosophical argument in ancient China.* LaSalle, Ill: Open Court.

———. 1990a. *Studies in Chinese philosophy and philosophical literature.* Albany: State University of New York Press.

———, trans. 1990b. *The book of Lieh Tzu.* New York: Columbia University Press.

———. 1991a. *Chuang Tzu: The inner chapters.* London: Harper Collins.

———. 1991b. Reflections and Replies. In *Chinese texts and philosophical contexts: Essays dedicated to Angus Graham.* Ed. Henry Rosemont, Jr. 267–322. La Salle, Ill.: Open Court.

Grice, H. P. 1975. Logic and conversation. In *Syntax and semantics 3: Speech acts.* Ed. J. Cole and J. L. Morgan, 41–58. New York: Academic Press.

Hansen, Chad. 1981. Linguistic skepticism in the Lao Tzu. *Philosophy East and West* 31 (July): 231–46.

———. 1983. *Language and logic in ancient China.* Ann Arbor, Mich.: University of Michigan Press.

———. 1989. Language in the heart-mind. In *Understanding the Chinese mind.* Ed. Robert E. Allinson, 75–124. Oxford: Oxford University Press.

Hawkes, David, trans. 1985. *Songs of the South.* New York: Penguin.

Heidegger, Martin. 1962. *Being and time.* Trans. John Macquarrie and Edward Robinson. New York: Harper and Row.

Henderson, J. B. 1991. *Scripture, canon, and commentary.* Princeton: Princeton University Press.

Henricks, Robert G. 1979. Examining the Ma-wang-tui silk texts of the Lao-tzu: With Special note of their differences from the Wang Pi text. *T'oung Pao* 65(4–5): 166–99.

———. 1989. *Lao-Tzu Te-Tao Ching.* New York: Ballantine.

Hick, John. 1989. *An interpretation of religion: Human responses to the transcendent.* New Haven: Yale University Press.

Hirsch, E. D. 1967. *Validity in interpretation.* New Haven: Yale University Press.

Ho, Shih-chi. 1936. *Ku pen tao te ching hsiao k'an.* Beijing: National Peiping Academy.

Hordern, William E. 1968. *A layman's guide to Protestant theology.* 2nd ed. New York: Macmillan.

Hsiao, Kung-chuan. 1979. *A history of chinese political thought.* Vol. 1, *From the beginnings to the sixth century A.D.* Trans. F. W. Mote. Princeton library of Asian translations. Princeton: Princeton University Press.

Hsu, Cho-yun. 1965. *Ancient China in transition: An analysis of social mobility, 722–222 B.C.* Stanford: Stanford University Press.

———. 1988. The roles of the literati and of regionalism in the fall of the Han dynasty. In *The collapse of ancient states and civilizations.* Ed. Norman Yoffe and George L. Cowgill, 176–95. Tucson: University of Arizona Press.

Hudson, W. D. 1970. *Modern moral philosophy.* New York: Doubleday.

Hume, David. 1948. *Hume's moral and political theory.* Ed. and introd. Henry D. Aiken. New York: Hafner Publishing Co.

Hurvitz, Leon. 1961. A recent Japanese study of Lao-Tzu. *Monumenta Serica* 20:311–67.

Husserl, Edmund. 1970. *The crisis of the European sciences and transcendental phenomenology.* Trans. David Carr. Evanston Ill.: Northwestern University Press.

Jan, Yün-hua. 1980. Tao Yüan *Journal of Chinese Philosophy.* 7:3 (September), 195–204.

Jaspers, Karl. 1953. *The origin and goal of history.* New Haven: Yale University Press.

Johnson, Roger. 1987. *Rudolf Bultmann: Interpreting faith for the modern era.* London: Collins Publishers.

Jonas, Hans. 1958. *The Gnostic religion*. Boston: Beacon Press.

Julien, Stanislas. 1842. *La Livre de la Voie et de la Vertu*. Paris: L'Imprimiere Royale.

Kalberg, Stephen. 1980. Max Weber's types of rationality: Cornerstones for the analysis of rationalization processes in history. *American Journal of Sociology* 85(5): 1145–79.

Kaltenmark, Max. 1969. *Lao Tzu and Taoism*. Trans. Roger Greaves. Stanford: Stanford University Press.

Kant, Immanuel. 1966. *Critique of pure reason*. Trans. Max Müller. New York: Doubleday.

Karlgren, Berhhard. 1932. *On the poetical parts of Lao-tsi*. Göteberg: Elanders Boktryckeri Aktiebolag.

Karlgren, Bernhard, trans. 1950. The Book of Documents. *Bulletin of the Museum of Far Eastern Antiquities* 22.

———, trans. 1957. Notes on Lao Tze. *Bulletin of the Museum of Far Eastern Antiquities*.

Katz, Steven T. 1978. *Mysticism and philosophical analysis*. London: Sheldon Press.

Katz, Steven T., ed. 1983. *Mysticism and religious traditions*. Oxford: Oxford University Press.

Kierkegaard, Soren. 1973. *A Kierkegaard Anthology*. Ed. Robert Bretall. Princeton: Princeton University Press.

Kimura, Eichi. 1959. *Roshi no shin-kenkyu*. Tokyo: Sobunsha.

Kohn, Livia, ed. 1989. *Taoist meditation and longevity techniques*. In collaboration with Yoshinobu Sakade. Michigan monographs in Chinese studies. Ann Arbor: Center for Chinese Studies, University of Michigan Press.

Korff, H. A. 1966. Kant romanticized by Fichte. In *The romantic movement*. Ed. A. K. Thorlby, 107–12. London: Longmans, Green and Co.

Krieger, David J. 1991. *The new universalism: Foundations for a global theology*. Maryknoll, N.Y.: Orbis Books.

LaFargue, Michael. 1985. *Language and gnosis: Form and meaning in the Acts of Thomas*. Philadelphia: Fortress Press.

———. 1988a. Are texts determinate? Derrida, Barth, and the role of the biblical scholar. *Harvard Theological Review* 81(3): 341–57.

———. 1988b. Socio-historical research and the contextualization of biblical theology. Eds P. Borger, J. S. Frerichs, R. Horsley, and J. Neusner. In *The social world of formative Christianity and Judaism: Essays in honor of Howard Clark Kee*, 3–16. Philadelphia: Fortress Press.

———. 1992a. *The Tao of the Tao Te Ching*. Albany: State University of New York Press.

———. 1992b. Radically pluralist, thoroughly critical: A new theory of religions. *Journal of the American Academy of Religion* 60:4 (Winter), 693–716.

Lau, D. C. 1958. The treatment of opposites in Lao-tzu. *Bulletin of the Society of Oriental and African Studies* 21:344–60.

———, trans. 1970. *Mencius*. New York: Penguin.

———. trans. 1982. *Tao Te Ching*. Hong Kong: Chinese University Press.

Legge, James, trans. 1885. (Delhi: Motilal Banarsidass, 1964). *Li Ki* [Li Chi]. In *The sacred books of China: the texts of Confucianism*. Oxford: Oxford University Press.

———. 1891. (New York: Dover, 1962). *The texts of Taoism, part 1.* In *Sacred books of the East*. Vol. 39. Oxford: Oxford University Press.

———, trans. 1893. (New York: Dover, 1971). *Confucian Analects, The Great Learning, & The Doctrine of the Mean.* In *The Chinese classics*. Vol. 1. Oxford: Clarendon Press.

———, trans. 1895. (New York: Dover, 1970). *The works of Mencius.* In *The Chinese classics*. Vol. 2. Oxford: Clarendon Press.

Lentricchia, Frank. 1980. *After the new criticism*. Chicago: University of Chicago Press.

Levi-Strauss, Claude. 1967. *Structural anthropology*. Trans. Claire Jacobson and Brooke Grundfest Schoepf. Garden City, N.Y.: Anchor Books.

Levinson, Stephen C. 1983. *Pragmatics*. Cambridge: Cambridge University Press.

Lin, Paul J., trans. 1977. *A translation of Lao Tzu's Tao te ching and Wang Pi's commentary*. Michigan Papers in Chinese Studies. Ann Arbor: Center for Chinese Studies, University of Michigan Press.

Ling, Ju-hêng, comp. 1970. *Kuan-tzu chi p'ing*. Taipei: Chung Hua Shu Chü.

Lonergan, Bernard. 1979. *Method in theology*. New York: Seabury Press.

Ma, Hsü-lun. 1956. *Lao Tzu chiao-ku*. Peking: T'ai P'ing Book Co.

McCarthy, Thomas. 1981. *The critical theory of Jürgen Habermas*. Cambridge: MIT Press.

MacIntyre, Alasdair. 1966. *A short history of ethics*. New York: Macmillan.

————. 1967. Ontology. In *The encyclopedia of philosophy*. Ed. Paul Edwards 5:542–43. New York: Macmillan.

McKnight, Edgar V. 1969. *What is form criticism?* Philadelphia: Fortress Press.

Macy, Joanna. 1985. *Dharma and development: Religion as a resource in the Sarvodaya self-help movement*. West Hartford, Conn.: Kumarian Press.

Magee, Bryan. 1982. *Men of ideas: Some creators of contemporary philosophy*. Oxford: Oxford University Press.

Mair, Victor H., trans. 1990a. *Tao Te Ching*. New York: Bantam Books.

————, trans. 1990b.*[The file on the cosmic] Track [and individual] Dought[iness]: Introduction and notes for a translation of the Ma-wang-tui manuscripts of the Lao Tzu [Old Master]*. Sino-Platonic Papers. Philadelphia: Department of Oriental Studies, University of Pennsylvania.

Major, John S. 1991. Substance, process, phase: *Wuxing* in the *Huainanzi*. In *Chinese texts and philosophical contexts: Essays dedicated to Angus Graham*. Ed. Henry Rosemont, Jr. LaSalle, Ill.: Open Court.

Maspero, Henri. 1981. *Taoism and Chinese religion*. Trans. Frank A. Kierman, Jr. Amherst, Mass.: University of Massachusetts Press.

Mei, Y. P., trans. 1929. *The ethical and political works of Motse*. London: Arthur Probsthain.

Metzger, Thomas A. 1977. *Escape from predicament: Neo-confucianism and China's evolving political culture*. New York: Columbia University Press.

Miller, David L. 1973. *George Herbert Mead: Self, language, and the world*. Chicago: University of Chicago Press.

Morgan, Evan, trans. 1969. *Tao the Great Luminant: Essays from Huai Nan Tzu with introductory articles, notes, analyses*. New York: Paragon Book Reprint.

Mueller-Vollmer, Kurt, ed. 1988. *The hermeneutics reader*. New York: Continuum.

Mumford, Lewis. 1956. *The transformations of man*. New York: Harper and Row.

Munro, Donald J. 1969. *The concept of man in early China*. Stanford: Stanford University Press.

Musser, Donald W. and Joseph L. Price. 1988. *The whirlwind in culture: In honor of Langdon Gilkey*. Frontiers in theology. Bloomington, Ind.: Meyer Stone.

Naranjo, Claudio, and Robert E. Ornstein. 1971. *On the psychology of meditation*. New York: Viking Press.

Needham, Joseph. 1962. *Science and civilization in China*. Vol. 2, *History of scientific thought*. Cambridge: Cambridge University Press.

Neville, Robert Cummings. 1981. *Reconstruction of thinking*. Albany: State University of New York Press.

———. 1991. *Behind the masks of God: An essay toward comparative theology*. Albany: State University of New York Press.

Palmer, Richard E. 1969. *Hermeneutics: Interpretation theory in Schleiermacher, Dilthey, Heidegger and Gadamer*. Northwestern University Studies in Phenomenology and Existential Philosophy. Evanston, Ill.: Northwestern University Press.

Perry, John. 1975. *Personal identity*. Berkeley: University of California Press.

Polanyi, Michael, and Harry Prosch. 1975. *Meaning*. Chicago: University of Chicago Press.

Prosch, Harry. 1971. *The genesis of twentieth century philosophy: The evolution of thought from Copernicus to the present.* New York: Crowell.

Putnam, Hilary. 1987. *The many faces of realism.* LaSalle, Ill.: Open Court.

Quine, W. V. 1983. On what there is. In *Contemporary analytic and linguistic philosophies.* Ed. E. D. Klemke, 378–90. Buffalo. N.Y.: Prometheus Books.

Rast, W. E. 1972. *Tradition and history in the Old Testament.* Philadelphia: Fortress Press.

Rhode, J. 1968. *Rediscovering the teaching of the evangelists.* Philadelphia: Fortress Press.

Rickett, W. Allyn. 1965. *Kuan-tzu: A repository of early Chinese thought.* Hong Kong: Hong Kong University Press.

Ricoeur, Paul. 1974. *The conflict of interpretations: Essays in hermeneutics.* Ed. Don Ihde. Evanston, Ill.: Northwestern University Press.

———. 1976. *Interpretation theory: Discourse and the surplus of meaning.* Fort Worth: Texas Christian University Press.

———. 1981. *Hermeneutics and the Human Sciences.* Ed. and trans. John B. Thompson. Cambridge: Cambridge University Press.

Robinson, James M., and John B. Cobb, Jr., eds. 1964. *The new hermeneutic.* New frontiers in theology. New York: Harper and Row.

Rorty, Richard. 1979. *Philosophy and the mirror of nature.* Princeton: Princeton University Press.

———. 1982. *Consequences of pragmatism.* Minneapolis: University of Minnesota Press.

———. 1989. *Contingency, irony, and solidarity.* Cambridge: Cambridge University Press.

Rosenau, Pauline Marie. 1992. *Post-modernism and the social sciences: Insights, inroads, and intrusions.* Princeton: Princeton University Press.

Roth, Harold D. 1990. The early Taoist concept of *Shen:* A ghost in the machine? In *Sagehood and systematizing thought in Warring*

States and early Han China, 11–32. Brunswick, Maine: Bowdoin College Asian Studies Program.

———. 1991a. Psychology and self-cultivation in early Taoistic thought. *Harvard Journal of Asiatic Studies* 51 (December): 599–650.

———. 1991b. Who compiled the Chuang Tzu? In *Chinese texts and philosophical contexts: Essays dedicated to Angus C. Graham*, 77–128. LaSalle, Ill.: Open Court.

Rump, Ariane, trans. 1979. *Commentary on the Lao Tzu by Wang Pi.* In collaboration with Wing Tsit Chan. Monographs of the society for Asian and comparative philosophy, no. 6. Honolulu: University of Hawaii Press.

Saso, Michael. 1983. The Chuang-tzu nei-p'ien: A Taoist meditation. In *Experimental essays on Chuang-tzu.* Ed. Victor H. Mair, 140–57. Asian studies at Hawaii. Honolulu: University of Hawaii Press.

Saussure, Ferdinand de. 1986. *A course in general linguistics.* LaSalle, Ill.: Open Court.

Schleiermacher, Friedrich. 1958. *Lectures on religion: Speeches to its cultured despisers.* New York: Harper and Row.

Schmithals, Walter. 1968. *An introduction to the theology of Rudolf Bultmann.* London: SCM Press.

Schrag, Calvin O. 1969. *Experience and being.* Northwestern University studies in phenomenology and existential philosophy. Evanston, Ill.: Northwestern University Press.

Schwartz, Benjamin I. 1985. *The world of thought in ancient China.* Cambridge: Harvard University Press.

Smart, Ninian. 1973. *The science of religion and the sociology of knowledge: Some methodological questions.* Princeton: Princeton University Press.

———. 1983. *Worldviews: Crosscultural explorations of religious beliefs.* New York: Charles Scribner's Sons.

Smith, Huston. 1982. *Beyond the postmodern mind.* New York: Crossroad.

Smith, Wilfred Cantwell. 1981. *Towards a world theology.* Philadelphia: Westminster.

———. 1982. *Religious Diversity*. New York: Crossroad.

Solomon, Robert C. 1972. *From rationalism to existentialism*. New York: Humanities Press.

Spiegelberg, Herbert. 1976. *The phenomenological movement: A historical introduction*. 2 vols. The Hague: Martinus Nijhoff.

Strasser, Stephen. 1985. *Understanding and explanation*. Pittsburgh: Duquesne University Press.

Strauss, Victor von. 1959. *Lao-Tse Tao Te King*. Zurich: Manesse Verlag.

Stryk, Lucien, ed, 1969. *The world of the Buddha: A reader—From the three baskets to modern Zen*. New York: Doubleday.

Taylor, Charles. 1981. Understanding and explanation in the *Geisteswissenschaften*. In *Wittgenstein: To follow a rule*, Ed. S. Holtzman and C. Leich. London: Routledge and Kegan Paul.

———. 1989a. The diversity of goods. In *Anti-theory in ethics and moral conservatism*. Ed. Stanley G. Clarke, and Evan Simpson, 223–40. Albany: State University of New York Press.

———. 1989b. *Sources of the self*. Cambridge: Harvard University Press.

Thayer, H. S. 1973. *Meaning and action: A study of American pragmatism*. New York: Bobbs-Merrill.

Tillich, Paul. 1951. *Systematic theology*. Chicago: University of Chicago Press.

Toynbee, Arnold. 1934–61. *A study of history*. Oxford: Oxford University Press.

———. 1976. *Mankind and Mother Earth*. Oxford: Oxford University Press.

VanZoeren, S. 1991. *Poetry and personality: Reading, exegesis, and hermeneutics in traditional China*. Stanford: Stanford University Press.

Voegelin, Eric. 1956. *Israel and Revelation*. In *Order and history*. Baton Rouge: Louisiana State University Press.

———. 1957a. *Plato and Aristotle*. In *Order and history*. Baton Rouge: Louisiana State University Press.

————. 1957b. *The world of the polis*. In *Order and history*. Baton Rouge: Louisiana State University Press.

————. 1974. *The ecumenic age*. In *Order and history*. Baton Rouge: Louisiana State University Press.

Wagner, R. G. 1980. Interlocking parallel style: Laozi and Wang Bi. *Asiatische Studien* 34(1): 18–58.

Waley, Arthur. 1958. *The way and its power*. New York: Grove Press.

Warnke, Georgia. 1987. *Gadamer: Hermeneutics, tradition, and reason*. Stanford: Stanford University Press.

Watson, Burton. 1962. *Early Chinese literature*. New York: Columbia University Press.

————, trans. 1963a. *Hsün Tzu: Basic writings*. New York: Columbia University Press.

————, trans. 1963b. *Mo Tzu: Basic writings*. New York: Columbia University Press.

————, trans. 1964. *Han Fei Tzu: Basic writings*. New York: Columbia University Press.

————, trans. 1968. *Chuang Tzu*. New York: Columbia University Press.

Weber, Max. 1963. *The sociology of religion*. Boston: Beacon Press.

————. 1968. *Max Weber on charisma and institution building: Selected papers*. Ed and introd. S. N. Eisenstadt. Chicago: University of Chicago Press.

Welch, Holmes. 1957. *Taoism: The parting of the way*. Boston: Beacon Press.

Wheatley, Paul. 1971. *The pivot of the four quarters*. Chicago: Aldine Publishing Co.

Whorf, Benjamin L. 1956. *Language, thought, and reality*. Cambridge: MIT Press.

Wittgenstein, Ludwig. 1976. A lecture on ethics. In *The enduring questions*. Ed. Melvin Rader, 640–47. New York: Holt, Reinhardt, and Winston.

Wu, Yi. 1989. *The book of Lao Tzu (the Tao Te Ching)*. San Francisco: Great Learning Publishing Co.

Subject Index

Translation and Commentary are indexed in the topical glossary, not in this subject index. Abbreviations: TTC = *Tao Te Ching*, CT = *Chuang Tzu*, MNC = *Mencius*, NY = *Nei Yeh*.

Abode (mental "abode"): 203 n.3, 537; CT, 203, 217; NY, 203; TTC, 203, 213, 217, 256

Absolute. *See* Foundationalism

Agitation (excitement, stimulation, polemic against): 154, 159, 163, 167, 334, 531

Analects: 331; quoted, 210, 216

Ancient (ancient utopia): 173, 532; symbolic meaning of temporal priority, 235, 257, 263

Aphorisms: defined 133 n.4; general analysis, 35, 135–44; polemic aphorisms in TTC, 127–29, 133–34, 148–60, 164–69, 209, 233, 236, 239, 241–42, 248–49, 254, 292, 306, 532, 549, 556, 558. *See also* Oral tradition, Corrective, Attitude, Image, and topics listed under Target

Appearances (polemic against fine appearances): 152, 159, 161–66, 211, 532, 535, 536. *See also* Organic harmony, in a personality

Attitude (stance, posture, value-orientation, perspective): expressed in aphorisms, 137–38, 139–43, 154, 159–61; cultivated as state of mind, 254; expressed in conduct, 214, 217, 234. *See also* Speech act

Authority (of classical texts): 42–43; assumed in scriptural hermeneutics; 6, 9, 11–12; critical evaluation of, 8, 11, 43, 281–82

Author's intention, as "the meaning" of a text: 13, 19, 40–41. *See also* Meaning (of texts); Subjectivization of meaning

Axial period: and the world's "sacred scriptures," 5; and differentiation of the good, 286 n.21; and transcendence, 284

Axiological: 272. *See also* Good (the Good)

Bedeutung (reference, contrasted with *Sinn*/meaning): 184 n.12, 184–85, 209

Benefits (sayings describing marvelous benefits): 236–43, 533, 534; and utopian images, 293

Book writing: in ancient China, 35, 94, 119, 149, 303, 333; TTC compared to modern books, 126

Book of Documents (*Shih Ching*): 51, 211, 223; quoted 61–63

Buddhism: 5, 12, 167, 279

Celebratory sayings: 534; TTC, 128, 178, 211, 213, 214, 220, 232, 233, 242, 244, 532; CT 247; *Hsün Tzu* 186; NY 187

Ch'ang/steady. *See* Steady, and 215 n.10

"Chapters" of TTC: problems concerning their composition 301 n.2,

Corrective (aphorisms as corrective): 138–39, 153–54, 158, 532

Cosmic importance (of qualities cultivated): in TTC, 178, 210, 212, 214, 217–20, 222–23, 230, 243–66, 282, 293, 534, 536, 537, 548, 552–53; in CT, 205; in MNC, 111, 185–86, 244; NY, 185–87, 244; in *Hsün Tzu*, 186, 244

Cosmogonies. *See* Origin sayings

Desire, polemic against: 121, 151 n.2, 157, 159, 323, 531–32, 536–37, 541, 545, 547; in NY 182, 189; not desiring (an ideal in TTC), 210, 213–14, 216, 236, 252, 325, 544, 556

Doctrine of the Mean (*Chung Yung*): 193, 197 n.41, 213 n.9, 303 n.15, 330–31, 547 n.11

Embrace (*pao*, a verb describing self cultivation): 227; TTC, 213, 214, 557; CT, 207

Empathic understanding: as a goal of the present hermeneutics, 19, 40; of the good as perceived in other cultures, 277; and aphorisms, 136; of the attitude expressed in Laoist aphorisms, 154. *See also* Hermeneutics, Subjectivization of meaning

Emperor: 537–38; Chou Emperor as symbolic normative center, 52 n.4, 62, 96, 158, 210, 222, 223–24, 249, 262, 293, 540; ambition of feudal kings to become Emperor, 96, 100; "true Emperor" as a moral/spiritual ideal, 157, 169; *shih* aspire to spiritual role, 537, (TTC, 122, 157, 169, 210, 213, 243–44, 249–51; MNC, 75, 76, 78, 85). *See also* Moral adviser

Emptiness: TTC, 157, 165, 177, 191, 208, 210–11, 212, 214–16, 217, 221, 223, 234, 237, 257, 292, 533, 538, 542; CT, 202–206, 212–14, 222

Epistemological foundations (basis for valid knowledge): in modern philosophy, 14, 29; of aphoristic truth, 141–42, 154, 160; of conquest-cycle sayings, 232; of marvelous-benefit

sayings, 237–42; of cosmic sayings, 246; of religious belief, 267–69; of views about the good, 270–76; of worldviews 277–78; of Laoism, 175, 255, 292. *See also* Ideal semantic structure

Esoteric sayings: difficult aphorisms, 153, 306; sayings related to self-cultivation, 306; cosmic sayings, 223; sayings describing marvelous benefits, 242. *See also* Paradox

Ethnocentrism: pervasive in premodern societies, 13, 291; an obstacle to understanding religious diversity, 267–68, 291; corrected by the "many worlds" theory, 17, and a pluralist theory of the good, 271, 274–75. *See also* Pluralism

Etiquette (*li*/Etiquette:ritual:ceremony): 77, 78 n.7, 87, 535; Hsün Tzu's eulogy of, 186. *See also* Confucians

Evaluative context: 243; wellfoundedness of worldviews as, 270–71, 278. *See also* Good (the Good)

Exaggeration: and the intent of Laoist aphorisms, 153–56; in the description of marvelous benefits, 236, 240–42, 293

Excellent (*shan*/Excellent:good): 226, 538

Experiential complex. *See* Image

Expressive (conduct expresses state of mind): 114, 178, 190, 209, 210, 212, 214, 216, 217, 219, 225, 233–35, 239, 242, 263, 265, 293, 546, 550, 552; expressive view of politics: MNC, 96–97, 101–02, 242; TTC, 118, 121, 235, 242, 293

Fact/value problem: 15, 18, 21 n.41. *See also* Good (the Good)

Femininity: 157, 176–78, 192, 194–95, 210–18, 217, 223, 225, 236, 250, 256, 307, 538, 542, 545; how this state of mind expresses itself, 234

Force (*ch'iang*/force:hard:strong): 216–17, 334, 538, 545, 547, 550; forcing *ch'i* in MNC, 112, in NY, 188. *See also* Soft

305, 331, 544; aphorisms interpreted as natural laws, 133

Nei Yeh: 181–94, 196–97, 203, 214–15, 219–20, 222, 224, 227, 244, 247–48, 537, 546

Normative description (a sayings-genre): 233–35, 546. *See also* Expressive

Nothing (*wu*): TTC, 165, 212, 216, 217, 228, 258, 264, 327, 329–30, 334, 533, 546; CT, 206, 212

One (*i*/One:Oneness): TTC, 177–78, 191, 194, 196, 209–10, 212, 213–14, 216–17, 223, 225, 227, 250, 259–62, 264; CT, 202–04, 206–08, 213, 546–47; NY, 193, 248; *Tao Yüan*, 264

Ontology: 12–21, 271; defined 16 n.32; of the Good, 14–15, 17–18, 271–75; ontology implicit in ordinary experience, 16–17, 18, 20; relevance to hermeneutics, 19–20. *See also* Foundationalism; Good (the Good); "Many worlds" theory

Oracle formula: 547

Oral tradition: TTC, 35, 119, 126–30, 149, 196, 341; NY, 187, 189. *See also* Life setting

Organic harmony: 160–72, 222, 239, 260, 277, 282, 287, 292–93, 547–48; in a personality, 161–65, 170, 533; psychological and physiological, 167, 170, 531–32; in human understanding, 166–67, 171, 556; in a society, 166–69, 171, 240, 540; and the ideal ruler, 167–69, 540, 550; and societal improvements, 169, 541–42; and "naturalness," 546; its relevance today, 295–300. *See also* Natural

Origin sayings (cosmogonies): 178, 212, 214, 217–18, 243–49, 251–66, 328–29, 536, 545, 548, 553; perceptual basis for, 245–48; background assumptions behind origin imagery, 251–56; analysis of, 256–63; non-literal understanding of, 263–66, 282; celebratory thrust of, 261, 534; in NY, 186; in Tao Yüan, 227, 264–65

Paradox: 151–56, 161, 211, 216, 221, 306, 533, 543, 549. *See also* Esoteric

Pen/root. *See* Root

Phenomenologically concrete: 34, 179–80, 197, 209, 223; reference of terms in the NY, 184–85; Tao as phenomenologically concrete, 245, 265

Phenomenology: 8 n.12, 13 n.22, 275; as a basis for hermeneutics, 25, 26, 28–29, 33, 36, 268 n.2. *See also* Ontology

Philosophy (modern foundationalist/doctrinal philosophy): 14–18, 21, 69–73, 278, 283; compared with Mencian thought 73–74, 77, 82, 95–98, 103–04, 112–18; compared with aphoristic thought, 133–34, 136–37, 139, 142–43; compared with Laoist thought, 155–58, 160, 166–67, 172–74, 175–80, 209, 215, 232, 245–49, 251, 253–54, 263–66, 267; compared with NY thought, 182–84, 193

Philosophical (doctrinal) approach to interpretation: 23–24, 28–31, 47–48, 278; of TTC, 113, 118, 175–80, 196–98, 209, 215, 245, 248–49, 251, 253–55, 258, 264–66, 267; of MNC, 69–74, 95–96, 112–13, 117; of NY, 183–86, 193. *See also* Hermeneutics adopted here

Philosophical foundations for interpretive method: 24–33. *See also* Phenomenology; Pragmatism; Semiotics

Plato/Platonism: 21, 176, 241, 272, 278 n.12, 280, 286 n.22

Pluralism (pluralist theory of religions and the good): 7, 18–19, 141–42, 267–75, 280–81

Pragmatics: 130 n.1, 131; and the analysis of aphorisms, 134–35, 142. *See also* Form criticism; Hermeneutics adopted here

Pragmatism: 29 n.11, 290; and hermeneutics 29–33, 48, 130–31, 179–80. *See also* Ideal semantic structure

Proverb. *See* Aphorism

P'u. See Uncarved Block

Author Index

Index of Passages Discussed

The *Tao Te Ching* translation and commentary is only indexed here under the main chapter numbers.

List of Chapters in the Traditional Arrangement

Old Number	New Number	Page	Old Number	New Number	Page
[1]	43	p. 436	[29]	62	p. 476
[2]	42	p. 434	[30]	69	p. 492
[3]	79	p. 514	[31]	67	p. 488
[4]	31	p. 410	[32]	63	p. 478
[5]	16	p. 376	[33]	24	p. 396
[6]	32	p. 412	[34]	64	p. 480
[7]	10	p. 364	[35]	46	p. 442
[8]	7	p. 358	[36]	73	p. 500
[9]	2	p. 348	[37]	81	p. 518
[10]	27	p. 402	[38]	11	p. 366
[11]	15	p. 374	[39]	35	p. 418
[12]	21	p. 388	[40]	34	p. 416
[13]	18	p. 382	[41]	44	p. 438
[14]	37	p. 422	[42]	36	p. 420
[15]	6	p. 356	[43]	47	p. 444
[16]	28	p. 404	[44]	19	p. 384
[17]	54	p. 460	[45]	5	p. 354
[18]	12	p. 368	[46]	20	p. 386
[19]	78	p. 512	[47]	41	p. 432
[20]	13	p. 370	[48]	25	p. 398
[21]	38	p. 424	[49]	60	p. 472
[22]	4	p. 352	[50]	22	p. 390
[23]	14	p. 372	[51]	65	p. 482
[24]	1	p. 346	[52]	29	p. 406
[25]	39	p. 426	[53]	50	p. 452
[26]	23	p. 392	[54]	61	p. 474
[27]	49	p. 448	[55]	33	p. 414
[28]	17	p. 378	[56]	30	p. 408

Old Number	New Number	Page	Old Number	New Number	Page
[57]	77	p. 510	[70]	45	p. 440
[58]	59	p. 470	[71]	40	p. 430
[59]	26	p. 400	[72]	53	p. 458
[60]	70	p. 494	[73]	58	p. 468
[61]	56	p. 464	[74]	66	p. 486
[62]	48	p. 446	[75]	51	p. 454
[63]	71	p. 496	[76]	74	p. 502
[64]	72	p. 498	[77]	52	p. 456
[65]	80	p. 516	[78]	75	p. 504
[66]	55	p. 462	[79]	9	p. 362
[67]	3	p. 350	[80]	76	p. 508
[68]	57	p. 466	[81]	8	p. 360
[69]	68	p. 490			

Made in the USA
Monee, IL
19 July 2020